B
DULLES

RNF

Grose, Peter

  Gentleman spy

GENTLEMAN SPY

GENTLEMAN

SPY

The Life of

ALLEN DULLES

Peter Grose

A Richard Todd Book

HOUGHTON MIFFLIN COMPANY

Boston New York 1994

For information about permission to reproduce selections from
this book, write to Permissions, Houghton Mifflin Company,
215 Park Avenue South, New York, New York 10003.

Library of Congress Cataloging-in-Publication Data
Grose, Peter, date.
Gentleman spy : the life of Allen Dulles / Peter Grose.
p.   cm.
"A Richard Todd book."
ISBN 0-395-51607-2
1. Dulles, Allen Welsh, 1893–1969. 2. Spies — United States —
Biography. 3. United States. Central Intelligence Agency — Officials
and employees — Biography. 4. Intelligence service — United States —
History — 20th century.   I. Title.
E748.D865G76   1994
327.12'92 — dc20   94-22677
CIP

Printed in the United States of America

MP 10 9 8 7 6 5 4 3 2 1

Book design by Melodie Wertelet

FOR M.K.G.,

who I know will never stop caring

CONTENTS

List of Illustrations

Book One

OVERT

PROLOGUE

THE EMPEROR PASSES

NOT SINCE LOUIS XIV had Europe known a monarch who reigned as long. Having ascended in the revolutionary year of 1848, Franz Josef I was the revered All Highest over more than fifty million souls: Magyars, Germans, Serbs, Jews, Moldavians, Croats, Slovaks, Gypsies, Ruthenes, Romanians — the list went on and on. His Catholic Hapsburg Empire embraced the valley of the Danube and reached out far beyond, from the Alps almost to the Black Sea, from Cracow in the Galician north to the Adriatic Sea, pushing even to the Aegean. When His Imperial and Royal Majesty succumbed to mortality in the Vienna Hofburg at 2305 November 21, 1916, the empire felt a sense of shock but hardly surprise. That this was the end of an era required little imagination to grasp.

The obsequies would clearly be the event of the Vienna season. The empires of Europe were grinding against each other in war, but the United States of America, as the leading neutral power, led the diplomatic corps into the Church of Saint Stephen's for the solemn ceremony. Duly in attendance with his ambassador was the new third secretary of the American Embassy, Allen Welsh Dulles. Court protocol put everyone comfortably in place: Dulles was to appear at the imperial church, along with other juniors of the corps, at 1445 November 30 in mourning dress (with overcoat), to be escorted to his row directly behind the German dukes. This was the young diplomat's first assignment for the government of the United States.

The passing of Franz Josef betokened the political exhaustion of his realm, and the end of an eighty-six-year plod through a life marked by personal tragedy. His son, Crown Prince Rudolf, had died by his own hand in 1889 in the company of a mistress at the royal hunting lodge, Mayerling. Franz Josef's empress, Elizabeth, beautiful, high-spirited,

3

never capable of returning her husband's deep love, was stabbed to death by an anarchist in Geneva in 1898. The heir to the throne, Archduke Franz Ferdinand, was shot dead in June 1914 during a seventy-minute visit to Sarajevo, a dusty Bosnian town on the fringe of the empire.

The rigid propriety of the Hofburg could never still the gossip of worldly Vienna. When Third Secretary Dulles had arrived on post the previous July, the whispering of the salons still lingered over the mysterious suicide three years before of one Colonel Alfred Redl. A diligent officer who had risen from a humble birth to the highest ranks of the Imperial and Royal General Staff, Redl had inspired respect throughout the military and court establishment. But in the decade before the incident at Sarajevo led to the outbreak of war Redl, extravagant in the exercise of his inclinations, was leading a hidden life of undisciplined homosexuality. To support his playful blond lieutenant lover in the manner desired, he systematically sold the secrets of the Austro-Hungarian General Staff to Imperial Russia. So efficient was the court censorship, and so horrid the scandal, that even the emperor was not told of the treachery until Redl had honorably dispatched himself with a pistol.

Dulles, at age twenty-three, had never before encountered this sort of human frailty. Of the homosexuality he knew little and understood less. It was the betrayal of trust that brought his first shock. As the years passed, shock gave way to wonder at the impact one individual could make upon affairs of state, then to fascination that a fleeting moment of carelessness could reveal a decade of evil contrivance. Redl was finally exposed, a mature Allen Dulles reminded his protégés in the art of espionage, only when he went in person to the obscure post office where the Russians were sending his payments.

Deception as a way of life was strange to a young man reared in the manse of a Presbyterian minister. But over a long life in the chancelleries and war rooms of powerful nations, the reality grew upon him that the means for shaping the world's destiny might be manifest — or they might be covert.

— 1 —

IN PREP

JOHN WATSON FOSTER enjoyed a certain renown across the span of American diplomacy, as the only secretary of state to leave office with a clean desk. When this elegant international lawyer submitted his resignation to President Benjamin Harrison in February 1893, he was confident that all the pressing diplomatic problems of the American Republic had been resolved. Just the week before, weary of the endless maneuvers of the randy Queen Liliuokalani, Secretary Foster dealt with the problem in a forthright and gentlemanly manner: he decided simply to annex her Hawaiian Islands to the United States. Problems of a legal nature remained, of course, but these were matters Foster could arbitrate, at splendid fees, when he returned to the private practice of law. Indeed, his brief service as secretary of state was only a minor diversion from the career in international law upon which he had made his name in fin-de-siècle Washington.

At age fifty-six he found it pleasant to be back in private life, to be called General Foster again, for his Civil War retirement rank, rather than the banal Mr. Secretary. Dinner parties could again be arranged for his own satisfaction, without the need to invite official guests who could not measure up to his real friends in style and wit. Invitations to the grand three-story mansion at 1405 I Street had long been prized by the international set; Foster's retirement from the State Department brought no impertinent hint of a loss in social standing.

Six weeks later came the happy news that his elder daughter, Edith, married to a serious Presbyterian pastor in upstate New York, Allen Macy Dulles, had been successfully delivered of a boy, Foster's second grandson. Edith's first-born bore his own names, John Foster Dulles. To her second son went family names from her husband's side; the infant born on April 7, 1893, was baptized Allen Welsh Dulles.

Baby Allen was blessed with a nurturing family of the highest order. For all his distinction in the social and political ferment of the United States, General Foster was rare among important men in his loving fascination with the children around him. His only son and a daughter had died of childhood fevers. To Allen's mother and her surviving sister he gave all the advantages that money and social position could provide. On joyous horseback rides through Chapultepec Park, he shared their girl-hood years in the cosmopolitan diplomatic community of Porfirio Díaz's Mexico, where he served as minister and envoy. Then he moved his fam-ily to St. Petersburg, where he was minister plenipotentiary to Tsar Alex-ander II, of whom he remarked, "I have met no other sovereign with whom personal intercourse was so cordial and agreeable." Allen's mother recalled the exotic family life she enjoyed before her marriage, with evening troika rides up to the Finnish frontier, there to be entertained by gypsy dancers in the clear, crisp midnight. She never forgot the Sunday afternoon in March 1881, as she and her parents sat reading in the diplo-matic residence, when a maid burst into the room to report that the tsar liberator of Russian serfdom had been assassinated.

Interspersed with the official business of the day were grand tours of Europe. In the summer of 1881 Edith, then eighteen, noted in her diary that she had met "a Mr. Dunnis (?)" at Sunday dinner after church. "I was later to find that his name was Dulles. . . . I had no thought of men at that time and although 'Mr. Dulles' was very attentive all the summer, I never thought he was interested in me. He had graduated from Princeton Col-lege and Seminary, had studied theology in Leipzig and Goettingen, and had just returned from a trip to the Holy Land." When the Fosters re-turned to America, a message of welcome awaited Edith at the New York dock from "Mr. Dulles" at his first parish in Detroit. A suddenly alert fa-ther remarked, "What does that mean?" During the winter and spring of 1882 the twenty-eight-year-old pastor called upon the Fosters in Wash-ington; one evening, after taking her to a lecture by Henry Ward Beecher, Dulles gently asked Edith if someday she might be his wife. "As soon as 'Mr. Dulles' had left I began to question as to whether I really loved him or not, and we continued to address one another as Mr. and Miss." They walked on the beach at Asbury Park that summer; he intro-duced her to Wordsworth, and they compared their love of Browning.

The relationship was abruptly broken early in 1883, when President Chester Arthur implored General Foster to interrupt his Washington law practice once again to become the United States envoy to Spain. Edith wrote the dramatic news to Mr. Dulles and suggested that their correspondence would have to be discontinued. For the next year and a half the Fosters lived in the social whirl of the Spanish court; the king and his royal family were their friends, the youngest infanta became Edith's close companion. The crown prince of Germany, Wilhelm of Hohenzollern, paid a ceremonial visit, and the daughter of the American envoy was noticed.

When Foster completed his diplomatic duties and returned to spend the summer of 1885 in upstate New York, the persistent Mr. Dulles managed to be nearby. "Suddenly, as I stood on a stone in the midst of the stream, I realized that I loved him," Edith remembered. "We became engaged that afternoon, and from that day on for forty-four years there was never a doubt of our love for one another."

— * —

If the family of John Watson Foster savored life at the summit of Washington society at the turn of the twentieth century, the Dulles side of the family was ever mindful of the truer aristocracy of birth. The Irish family name had been Douglas before being softened in the course of the seventeenth century. It was Dulles on arrival in the New World in 1779, borne by a bounder from Limerick who had fled to Holland concealed in a large butter churn, enlisted in the Dutch East India Company, and managed to make his way to Bombay, where he assembled something of a fortune — his descendants chose not to inquire just how he did it. Arriving eventually in South Carolina, this Joseph Dulles helped defend Charleston in the siege of the Revolutionary War, then managed a good marriage to the heiress of a cotton plantation, with its attendant Negro slaves. He prospered in commerce. Their one surviving child, a "delicate boy," they sent away to Yale. In the remote north this frail offspring survived to the age of eighty and fathered eight hearty children, who in turn produced sons and grandsons, including the serious pastor Allen Macy Dulles, who sought betrothal to the daughter of General Foster.

The Dulles and Foster families were joined in January 1886 at festivities Washington society considered only appropriate for the daughter of General Foster — until disorder struck. During the bridal dinner on the eve of the wedding, Foster's butler answered a sudden knock at the door to find a policeman announcing that the house was on fire! "My father rushed to the top floor and confirmed the report," recorded the bride. "Imagine the scene which ensued." A couple of doors down I Street, a large reception was under way at the home of the chief justice of the United States. The sound of fire engines alerted the bachelor escorts of the company; they excused themselves to help the neighbors and, in a display of acuity, they burst into the Foster home asking, "Where are the wedding presents?" Silver, china, crystals, and linen were carried by sundry volunteers and servants of nearby houses to safety as water poured down from the hoses on the Fosters' roof. "I saw my wedding dress being carried through the street by a colored man! All my wedding garments were scattered from one end of the street to the other and my veil was burned."

With the dawn there was not the slightest question of altering the day's wedding plans. "A new tulle veil was purchased, my sister's brides-maid's dress, soaked and apparently ruined, was remodelled. Our wedding gifts were assembled gradually by the family and, wonderfully to relate, not one was missing — though a few, among which was a lovely carved ivory box given us by the Chinese Minister, were the worse for hasty handling." Among the wedding presents was a mahogany bedroom suite from the bridegroom's parishioners at the Trumbull Avenue Presbyterian Church in Detroit.

Though respectable and proper, the Detroit ministry was not the crown of Allen Macy Dulles's aspirations, and the word got about in Presbyterian circles. Eighteen months after the marriage, two visitors from upstate New York came to hear him preach. The young pastor accepted their return invitation a month later, and the visit went well. On October 2, 1887, Dulles preached for the last time in Detroit, and the very next Sunday he delivered his first sermon as pastor of the First Presbyterian Church of Watertown, New York.

— * —

Watertown, the seat of Jefferson County, is defined by the Black River, coursing down from the Adirondacks to Lake Ontario. In one very short space the river descends 112 feet; early American settlers scouting their new frontier in the Iroquois lands built water wheels to power their emerging industries. Eventually no less than fifty-five factories were operating in a town that never had more than 35,000 inhabitants. With industry came wealth; Watertown may have been provincial, but it was not the sticks. Five nationally chartered banks did business; theatrical troupes from New York City passed through on tour. One day, just a few years before the Reverend Dulles arrived, a bright young stockboy in Moore & Smith's General Store piled up some odds and ends on a trestle table near the front with a sign reading "Any Item 5 cents"; he sold the entire discarded inventory in a matter of hours. The local boy took his novel marketing technique to nearby Utica, opened a store of his own in 1879, and proudly hung the sign bearing his name, Frank W. Woolworth.

On Sunday mornings the best people of Watertown attended the First Presbyterian Church. Its new and scholarly pastor, Allen Macy

Dulles, moved his bride into the white-frame parsonage on Clinton Street, but as the date for the birth of their first child approached he prudently moved her to her parents' home in Washington. There, on February 25, 1888, in the middle of a blizzard, was born John Foster Dulles. After just fourteen months came the second child, a daughter named Margaret. Childbirth was not easy for Edith, and the young couple were advised that they could not risk any further pregnancies for some years to come. With no artificial means of protection yet available, they confronted the necessity of celibacy in their marriage. "It was hard on your father," Edith confided many years later to a grown daughter, who remembered the remark as the closest her mother ever came to discussing sex with her children.[1]

For the next three years Edith Foster and Allen Macy Dulles endured the physical and emotional anxieties of a celibate marriage, a forbearance Edith revealed only in a memoir for her grandchildren forty years later. Thus it was with a note of triumph that the loving couple announced in April 1893 the successful delivery of their third child, Allen.

Not that the birth was altogether joyous, for the child appeared with what lesser folk would have considered a horror: Allie, as he was called from boyhood, was born with a clubfoot. In the not too remote past an infant with a "cloven hoof" would have been destroyed lest the curse of the evident devil infect all around. By Allie's generation the deformity usually went unattended, leading to a lifelong limp and derision of character. Edith and Allen Macy Dulles would have none of that. They located a learned orthopedist capable of repairing the bent foot of a tiny baby, twisting it around so that once he started walking, the weight of the leg and body would be carried directly on the sole of the foot as it should be. The operation on the infant was so successful that few of Allen's vigorous tennis partners in maturity ever knew — indeed, could ever have imagined — the defect of his birth.

After Allie two more Dulles children were born without untoward incident: Eleanor in 1895 and Nataline in 1898. They were a remarkable family in that quiet region of upstate New York. Then as now, family homes can be defined either as places where young people gather for fun and activity or places where children sense they are not welcome. The Dulles home was the former, a magnet for the neighborhood. Though headed by an austere minister of the church, it was a place of fun. The rope swing on the big tree in the front yard was irresistible after school; even more exciting was the tree house in the upper branches. Over the years the family collected two ponies and a pony cart, several King Charles spaniels, and a black cat named Sir Tibby of the Glen.

Though normally withdrawn in his study, preparing sermons and reflecting, Pastor Dulles would emerge to instill the values of self-reliance: take hold of all around you, seize the moment and the chance. To the question, Can you do this? a child at first responds, I'll try. Don't *try*, thunders back the father, *do* it! Little Allie had his share of neighborhood brawls; pummeled by the local bully, he was heard to yell back, "You may get me down, but you can't make me give up!" The learned churchman had his children practice swallowing pellets of bread pressed into tight cubes, so that their throat muscles would be able to tolerate large pills when the need arose. The boys were supposed to carry a pocketknife and were always subject to their father's challenge. If they could produce the knife from their britches, they would get a penny; if they had left it behind, they would owe a penny.* Introduced by a Norwegian visitor to the sport called "skiing," then unknown in Watertown, the father fashioned some "skis" out of barrel staves and built a slide from the upstairs porch down into the yard and up over the back fence. The third floor of the house on Mullin Street (the family had outgrown the original parsonage, but their new colonial-style mansion was still within sight of the church) was a communal playroom. Here were played out great theatrical epics: *Idylls of the King* was a regular favorite, with each child choosing one knight to portray; for some reason, no one ever took the part of the virtuous Sir Galahad. Most memorable to Eleanor was *The Merchant of Venice*, with Foster playing Shylock.

On Sunday mornings Allie and the others would be properly scrubbed, handed their Bibles and a coin from their allowance for the collection, and would walk as a family to the church at the corner of Washington Street. The Dulles family pew was fourth from the front on the right aisle. Edith led the singing in a warm contralto. After church even the pastor's family had fun. First everyone would gather around the kitchen table to make ice cream. Conversation would start with the topic of the sermon but move rapidly into Bible guessing games in which oldest and youngest competed on equal terms. "We never felt any hypocrisy in the religious note introduced into our reading and games; it all seemed natural," Eleanor recalled late in her life. "Father left us alone, . . . he just assumed that we would come out all right."

The Dulleses tried the local public schools for their children, but found them wanting intellectually — and intellect was the quality that mattered most. For most of the elementary years, live-in governesses tutored each child individually. Father and Mother would read lessons, and the older children would coach the younger. Allie, fascinated with history

* To his last days, Secretary of State John Foster Dulles always completed the sharpening of the pencils on his desk with his own pocketknife.

above all else, taught his little sister Eleanor enough Greek and Roman history to allow her to pass a school exam without ever attending the class — for which she was always grateful, even when as adults she and Allen found themselves irritated with each other beyond their capacity to cope.

Down in Washington Grandfather Foster was envious of this idyllic family life with young people all around. He scouted about for a vacation site nearby, telling his friends he wanted an escape from the Washington heat, but those who knew better understood that he sought to indulge his two infatuations, fishing and grandchildren. He found just the place at a cove called Henderson Harbor, on the windy shore of Lake Ontario just eighteen miles from Watertown. As the Dulles family grew and spread out, it was the settlement at Henderson Harbor that defined their collective identity. Seventy years later Allen Dulles, a retired master of spies, could recite the details of his boyhood summers on the shore of Lake Ontario; the memories of childhood ring like a metaphor for the secretive business in his maturity.*

> We used to set out every morning in the summer, except Sundays. We'd fish from 8:30 to noon, then we'd go ashore, one of the many little islands. There was great competition. You'd pour out your fish and then the other fellow would pour out his fish, and you'd see who had the biggest fish and who had the most fish. . . .
>
> Bass fishing is quite an art; you can blunder very easily. . . . One of the problems was to choose the right bait. . . . You don't want to just haul the fish right in, it'll break from you. . . . You have to wait until the bass gets the hook in the mouth, and gets the hook at just the right angle. And then you hit him, but don't hit him too hard. . . . It's a disgrace if you let the fish swallow the bait, so you catch him way down on the insides — it's very unpleasant getting the hook out, and that's not the way to fish. . . .
>
> You guard with greatest secrecy the bearings which give you your position . . . you get a man who over the years knows where the fish are. You don't want to let a fish jump if you can help it, because he'll shake the hook out when he gets in the air. . . . You've got to bring him up and get him into the net. It requires a lot of patience.[2]

To Henderson Harbor came the members of the extended family. General Foster's younger daughter, Eleanor, frequently visited her sister

---

* Allen was so intrigued with this passage, which he recorded for an academic oral history a few years before his death, that he had it extracted for use in some future memoir, which was never written.

in Watertown and joined the social circle of the Mullin Street neighbors, which included an interesting couple, Mr. and Mrs. John Lansing and their bachelor son, Robert. The Lansings were Democrats, unusual for that part of New York, but quite nice nonetheless. Young Lansing courted Eleanor Foster, and in due course they married. The new son-in-law was a promising lawyer who fit comfortably into General Foster's footsteps, first in his law practice and eventually as secretary of state under President Woodrow Wilson.

Adored by the Dulles children as "Uncle Bert," Robert Lansing shared General Foster's obsession for pursuing small-mouth bass. The two international lawyers would regularly bring foreign visitors to Henderson Harbor, but the only serious business was fishing. They went out in what they called catboats, large dinghies with a single sail. "Only two fishermen in a boat, so there were two boats," Allen described the typical pattern. "There would be one member of the older generation, which was my grandfather and Mr. Lansing, and one of the younger generation, generally Foster and myself. . . . We'd talk a great deal during the lunch, discuss the wind, the weather, the habits of the fish. And then sometimes we'd get on international affairs."

The catboats on Lake Ontario at the turn of the twentieth century served two growing boys as a folk seminar on diplomacy, led by America's thirty-third secretary of state, John Watson Foster, and the man who would become the forty-third secretary of state, Robert Lansing. Of the two boys, the elder would have his turn as the fifty-third secretary of state and the most influential of all. To the younger boy would come the opportunity for a different kind of impact on world affairs, in a realm of clandestine activity wholly beyond the comprehension of the fishermen on those windy waters.

— * —

Sharing summers with his grandchildren was not enough for General Foster. He arranged to "borrow" each of the Dulles children in turn for the winter months in Washington, where their education could continue with tutors and governesses, but most of all with exposure to the sophisticated life of the Foster home, one of Washington's great salons in the era of McKinley and Theodore Roosevelt. Allie's turn to be borrowed came the first winter of the twentieth century. At this academy of international life, the seven-year-old boy would watch through a half-opened door as coaches of diplomats and high officials, attended by liveried servants, halted before the front entrance. Presiding over all was the tall, white-whiskered, ruddy-cheeked patrician, a fishing companion and, despite the difference in years, close personal friend.

From his earliest years Allie displayed an insatiable curiosity about the people around him, thanks to his parents and other adults in his life who instinctively understood the importance of taking care to respond to a child's questions: encouraged, a child will persist in learning; ignored or put down, he will withdraw into his private world. Allie never withdrew. He was ever alert as the grownups conversed about serious matters — the war with Spain, America's acquisition of a colonial empire, and, most of all in his first months in Washington, the Boer War. Allie had watched as his father sat in the Watertown study, taking careful notes of his reading and consequent thoughts. Accordingly, during this grand winter, when no one was noticing, the little boy took to jotting down his own notes of views he heard expressed, trying to compare what he heard on one occasion with what was said on the next and what he could make out in the newspapers. It was quite improper for even a precocious seven-year-old to enter into the conversations, but he set out nonetheless to register his views.

Two months short of his eighth birthday he wrote a book. He called it *The Boer War*, and through twenty-six pages of careful exposition he left a reader in no doubt of his position:

> It was not right for the british to come in and get the land because the Boers came first and they had the first right to the land. . . . But it looks now as if the Boers were being driven out of the land. It is not because there is not enough room on the earth for there is room for every body to be comfortable, but the reason is that every nation wants more land than each other even if they have'nt enough people to cover the space.

The territorial imperative thus elucidated, the author turned to the military strategies of economic imperialism.

> The British did not know at first that the Boers were going to be so hard to conquer or they would not have started the war but now they have started they think that they cant surrender to such a little country. . . . That shoes how unmanly and cowardly the British are, trying to conquer the Boers. . . . Some people think that the British rule is not very bad, but you have to do just what they say, and you cannot feel free to do what you want, like you could if they had their own rule. . . .
>
> England ought to be content if she owned the mines where gold is, but no, she wants to have the land to. She is all the time picking into little countries. . . . The Boers want peace but England has to have the gold and so she goes around fighting all the little countries, but she never dares to fight eather China or Russia. . . . The Boers are very industrious and are hard workers and are very fond of the Bible. . . . They love their

country especially and they ought to have it in spite of the wicked English who are trying to rob them of it. I hope that the Boers will win for the Boers are in the wright.*

General Foster was so proud of his winter ward that he sent the treatise out for typesetting (spelling errors and all); it was published in an edition of 700 copies and sold at 50 cents apiece to benefit the Boer Widows and Orphans Fund. Foster's Washington neighbor Edward Everett Hale, chaplain of the Senate and author of *The Man Without a Country*, warned, "You will never make a diplomat of him, if diplomats are to use the language of the old chancelleries."

— * —

The security of Allie's life began to fray as childhood turned to adolescence. Upon his return to Watertown he and his sisters sensed tension growing between the two sides of their happy family: the scholarly Dulles father feeling himself challenged by the worldly splendor of the Foster grandfather. Allen Macy Dulles was a proud man, struggling to reconcile his religious faith with the contradictory demands of modern life; the Fosters, decent and honorable as individuals, were nonetheless parvenus in the Dulles eyes. The further fact was that the Fosters were rich while the Dulleses were merely comfortable. As each Dulles child came up for "borrowing," the Watertown residence was rattled by scenes. Daughter Margaret remembered her shock at overhearing an angry discussion between her father and mother, ending with the Reverend Dulles stomping upstairs and throwing over his shoulder the ultimatum "I will not have your father educating my children!"

Then Allie's brother abandoned him to go to college. At sixteen, Foster was intellectually qualified for Princeton — never mind the social and emotional aspects of character development — and when he graduated in 1908, he was the highest-ranking student and valedictorian of his class. In the games of Watertown and Henderson Harbor, and now the mature life of the university, Foster was a role model difficult for a younger brother to follow.

Finally came the most unsettling event of all. Allen Macy Dulles was offered the academic chair of theism and apologetics at the supreme center of Presbyterian education, the Auburn Theological Seminary. The family was uprooted to a stately old town just seventy miles south of Wa-

* Five decades later, as Allen Dulles delighted in nurturing a colorful popular image, he arranged for a reprint edition of this slim volume for the amusement of his friends. At the same time he felt obliged to apologize to his many British colleagues: "If I knew then what I know now, I'd never have said some of those things."

tertown, but leagues away in the life of growing children. Allie entered his teenage years in a new environment without his brother's support, seeking new friends and burdened with his peers' suspicious awareness that he was the son of a Presbyterian minister.

Competitive environments provoke remarkable responses among children. Allie had coped with the powerful older brother and three sisters, a dominating grandfather and respected uncle, and parents who served their community. Intellectual prowess was not enough to attract attention in that setting, for it was only what was expected of him — and Foster had set a high standard. Allie found a different style of personality: from an early age he set out to make people like him. Affability, he discovered, was a most useful character trait. People will help you if they like you. You can get someone to do something if you can get him to *want* to do it. "It is easy to get along with almost anybody if you show ordinary friendliness," he wrote home a few years later as he set out on his own travels. As boy and man, Allen Dulles acquired all the personality tricks of charm and seduction. Across the diverse exploits of his public life, even those who disagreed with him could not help but like him. With his brother, Foster, it was often precisely the opposite.

Summers at Henderson Harbor now included house parties devoted to pleasures other than fishing. On the matter of girlfriends, as all else, Foster set the pattern. Allen and his family were jolted one afternoon when Foster and his Princeton friends invaded the house where the young ladies were staying. They extracted armfuls of lace-trimmed underclothes and triumphantly hung them on the trees like Christmas decorations.[3]

Allie needed all the charm of personality he could muster when he enrolled for the first time in a large public school. Auburn Academic High School offered structure enough for the growth of the mind, but Allie was not yet exposed to the sociology of small-town teenagers. Eleanor looked back upon the shock she and Allie encountered when they learned about a clique of girls who always went off together in a group after school. They went into town to an upstairs room over a store, where, it emerged, they smoked![4] Emotional turmoil was never considered a proper topic for family introspection, but by the time Allie was fifteen the Dulles parents sensed that he needed a fresh experience. "All things considered," wrote mother Edith, "we decided that it would be a good thing for the family to spend the winter in Paris." Thanks to General Foster's benevolence, they had that option. Relieved of the social anxieties of high school, Allie settled happily into the home of old family friends in Lausanne for the purpose of learning to speak French. For the rest of his life he regarded himself as fluent, and indeed his conversation in French was quite uninhibited. The only problem was that French-speaking interlocutors had some difficulty in figuring out whether Allen was speaking "French" or some patois that bore only an operational resemblance thereto.

On weekends the family climbed the Swiss Alps, and Allen was thrilled to discover that a peak he had ascended was a full five feet higher than the one Foster had scaled. The serious business of the year was his preparation to enter college. Armed with a veneer of continental sophistication, he took his entrance examinations in June, a special round held for Americans temporarily living in Europe, and was accepted by Princeton to the class of 1914.

— * —

Seventeen-year-old Allen Dulles arrived at Princeton in the fall of 1910, braced for further comparison with his formidable older brother. He chose to be different. Foster had devoted himself to academic pursuits; Allen had a splendid time.

In later years, reacting against the snobbery of Old Nassau, Allen asserted with pride that he had never "bickered" for one of the upper-class eating clubs that stratified the campus scene according to family and social status. His class yearbook, however, lists him on the rolls of Cap and Gown, founded in 1892 and vaguely allied with an influential campus religious organization, the Philadelphia Society, whose members were sometimes branded as "Christers." Whatever his formal affiliations, Allie's reputation among his peers was considerably less than decorous. The class of '14 orator singled out "our w. k. Allie Dulles" with a convoluted tale of a weekend in New York when he almost landed in jail for disorderly conduct. "Not a native of the big city," the orator explained, Allie insisted on seeing the sights after a smoker at the Princeton Club; the obliging sister of a classmate "showed him some, and he drank them all in." He also figured in a dormitory scandal; the local cleaning establishment reported finding, in trousers sent from the room Allen shared with a roommate, a pair of dice! "We might have suspected it of Allie Dulles," noted the class history, but investigation confirmed that on this occasion at least, the incriminating trousers belonged to the hapless roommate.[5]

Fastidious in the somber dress of the era, lanky, straight-standing at five foot eleven, Allie parted his jet-black hair just to the right of center. He sported a neat black mustache, an expression of rakish chic, but he also favored shoes with buttons — not at all the fashion of the era. Among his contemporaries were Princetonians who would be important in his later life, including James Forrestal, Ferdinand Eberstadt, and an aspiring young writer named F. Scott Fitzgerald. Allie shunned the social cliques.

He never went out for organized sports, but in his fun-loving life of ease he collected countless admirers, including (apparently without his awareness) young men smitten with schoolboy crushes.

Allen did not neglect his studies altogether—indeed, for all his effortless ways, he won academic distinction in each of his four years and was elected to Phi Beta Kappa. He graduated with high honors in philosophy and was awarded a five-hundred-dollar academic prize in ethics. His best scholarly effort was an essay on William James and the then-fashionable philosophy of pragmatism. Allen, after all, had been an unwitting pragmatist since childhood; what worked effectively, what was useful, was therefore worthwhile. The shortcomings in the philosophy that later generations perceived—that being useful is perhaps not the ultimate virtue, that it may belittle the full potential of a person or object—had not yet been grasped. Allen found pragmatism just right for defining his purpose in life.* His friend Hamilton Fish Armstrong recalled being astonished that Allen could so readily see "the other side" in passionate controversies, could calmly "dissociate the legal concepts involved" from the human realities.

The real focus of excitement for the Princeton class of '14 was the visionary president who welcomed them to the university, Woodrow Wilson, a former history professor. Two months into Allen's freshman year, Wilson was elected governor of New Jersey, and two years later president of the United States. One of Allen's contemporaries wrote:

> At last scholarship and learning were to be vindicated in the *melee* of actual political life. . . . The town was made lively by the presence of numerous newspaper men eager to collect gossip [about that] austere professor, trained in history and economics but possessed of the political sagacity of a practical campaigner coupled with the moral earnestness of a Presbyterian *dominie*. . . . He has the student body behind him solidly. He is a wonder. . . .
>
> We received the returns in Alexander Hall. . . . The meeting immediately broke up to form a parade. . . . We cheered for everybody and sang "Old Nassau" as I've seldom heard it sung. . . . Mrs. Wilson and the girls were busy receiving the people who came pouring in through the open front door. It was all so simple and informal. After Woodrow's speech he stood on the front step of the piazza and shook hands with the whole crowd, which immediately broke up quietly and went home.[6]

* Fully five decades after Princeton he was astonished—and not a little unsettled—to learn that Foster, five years ahead of him, had also written a treatise on pragmatism. Like his club membership, this was a college memory that he had allowed to lapse.

Allen was among several hundred Princeton undergraduates who made their way to Washington for the presidential inauguration on March 4, 1913. Homage to a Democrat — the first to be elected in twenty years and only the second president of his party since the Civil War — was an unusual experience for a youth of Allen's background. To the intellectuals of Watertown, Democrats seemed narrow sectarians; the Republicans were the global-minded internationalists. Wilson changed everything. "Men's lives hang in the balance; men's hopes call upon us to say what we will do," he said in his inauguration speech. The United States would now lead the Old World; America had both the moral superiority and the actual power to make it happen. It was all quite heady for a twenty-year-old.

At the Princeton commencement of 1914 an alumnus approached Allen with the offer of a year's stipend to teach at the Ewing Christian College of India, at Allahabad. Missionary work was in the Dulles family tradition, and foreign travel with a respectable purpose was enticing. The further fact on that commencement day was that Allie had no other prospects.

Thus, not four weeks later, a tall, dark-haired American youth sprawled on a deck chair on the S.S. *Olympic* from New York, lost in a popular novel, *Kim*, by the English writer Rudyard Kipling. Allen was fascinated.

> From time to time, God causes men to be born — and thou art one of them — who have a lust to go ahead at the risk of their lives and discover news. Today it may be of far-off things, tomorrow of some hidden mountain, and the next day of some nearby man who has done a foolishness against the State. . . . When he comes to the Great Game, he must go alone — alone and at the peril of his head. Then, if he spits, or sits down, or sneezes other than as the people do whom he watches, he may be slain.

Kipling's Kim, the Irish orphan boy reared as a Hindu in the bazaar of Lahore, remains one of the classic characters in the fiction of espionage. On his way to India, where the plucky Kim learned the art of the Great Game, Allen could hardly have been more vulnerable to a book's charm; its mystery and folk wisdom stayed with him for the rest of his life, long after the business of spying became more threatening than an artful game.*

Allen's first stopover on the way to the Orient was Paris. On his first day, June 28, 1914, he spent the morning with a Princeton friend sipping an apéritif at a café on the Boulevard St.-Michel, blending in with countless other students past and future. There was not the slightest reason

---

* Allen's copy of *Kim* was on his bedside table when he died in 1969.

why they would pay any notice to the French newsboys running by, proclaiming the assassination by a Serbian patriot of some archduke of Austria-Hungary.

As the armies of Europe mobilized, Allen boarded the train for Trieste, to connect with a freighter to India. Docking in Bombay late in July, he was received in pomp by an Indian friend of General Foster's, who entertained him with princely hospitality for two days before putting him on the train for the thousand-mile journey to Allahabad. As Allen trundled innocently across the countryside of India, the Great War began in Europe.

Teaching the boys of India's Anglicized Christian elite was not easy. They were "clever at asking very difficult questions," he wrote his father. But Allahabad offered diversion outside the classroom to an extent unimagined in upstate New York or Princeton. He found a good-sized cobra in his bathroom and a monkey under the dining room table, saw fakirs in the streets reclining on beds of nails and gymnasts swinging, heads downward, over a raging fire. He rode an elephant across the Ganges — "not very speedy," he wrote home. He visited the palaces of rajahs and the shrines of Buddhists. He managed to have an interview with the Hindu poet Rabindranath Tagore, who was all the rage at Princeton. Allen thought him "a regular Homer, . . . truly poetical in his appearance, with long curling gray hair and a flowing beard." As for the political tensions between the British Raj and rising Indian nationalism, Allen sided with the Indians, just as he had with the Boers. But he insisted, not for the last time, "there is probably a good deal of Truth on both sides."

After his term at Allahabad, he arrived in Singapore just as a Muslim regiment, stirred up by German agents, failed in an attempt to overthrow the English garrison. Then he found his way into revolutionary China. The Manchu rulers, friends of Grandfather Foster, had been overthrown by Sun Yat-sen's republic, but amid the internal strife and anarchy he visited pagodas and opium dens and made an excursion to the Great Wall. Allen found himself noticed by the diplomatic circuit and invited to a reception given by the minister of foreign affairs. "It is a great thing to have had illustrious relations," he wrote home. He paused to observe an "army of pretty little Japanese maids" at a country inn after passing through occupied Korea, then boarded a steamer to San Francisco. By the late summer of 1915 his *Wanderjahr* was over and he had checked back in with the family at Henderson Harbor.

— * —

Allen still had no idea what he wanted to do with his life. The scope of his choices was clouded by reappearing tensions between Dulles and Foster family values. Allen Macy Dulles had always assumed that his first-born son would follow him into the Presbyterian ministry, but once John Foster had seen the world through the eyes of his grandfather, a life of devotion and, incidentally, poverty simply would not do. The father's expectations thus passed to his second son, an even less likely candidate for the pulpit. For Allen, honorable procrastination presented itself in a return to Princeton for a year of postgraduate study of world affairs.

President Wilson and Uncle Bert — now Secretary of State Lansing — were struggling throughout 1915 to preserve America's neutrality in the Great European War while maintaining trade with all parties. At one of his first Princeton graduate seminars, Allen found himself sitting next to a young man who, it turned out, had been born on exactly the same day as he and into a similar family from upstate New York. This was Hamilton Fish Armstrong, and he became Allen's closest friend for the rest of their lives. Armstrong was restless and disturbed by the war news, far more than Allen, who preserved an intellectual detachment. The professors labored, Armstrong reminisced, "to give body and reality to international law, handicapped by the fact that the war in Europe was steadily making it more and more abstract."[7] What good were laws guaranteeing neutrality and free commerce when British warships and German U-boats were violating those laws every day? Armstrong remembered his astonishment at Allen's dispassion in the face of unpunished violations. No surprise, on this seminar's experience, that Allen drifted toward a career of unemotional calculations while Armstrong deployed the outrage of a journalist and commentator. "Ham" Armstrong became editor of the influential journal *Foreign Affairs*, which over decades to come would chronicle the public thought of John Foster and Allen Dulles and the diplomatic establishment they came to embody.

In his year of postgraduate study, Allen shed the undergraduate's affectation of careless ease. A half-hearted inquiry into job prospects in banking, encouraged by his brother, came to naught. Allen finally summoned the courage to inform his father that he had chosen a career in diplomacy. As anticipated, Allen Macy Dulles was not pleased. "The Diplomatic Service is no career," he declared in contempt, for the reality finally dawned that Grandfather Foster had won the contest for the education of his sons. Professor Dulles withdrew into the theological seminary. Remote from the concerns of his family, he published a series of thoughtful treatises to challenge narrow-minded orthodoxies within his church. Eventually he became the moderator of the Presbyterian Synod of New York.

One final diversion threated to derail Allen's budding ambitions. On a patriotic impulse he enlisted in the New Jersey National Guard at the same time he was taking the examination for the Diplomatic Service. He passed the exam with high marks and was assigned to the United States Embassy in Vienna. But his National Guard unit was ordered to the Rio Grande to combat a band of marauding Mexican irregulars led by Pancho Villa. Would it be Private Dulles or Third Secretary Dulles? "I left the decision to Uncle Sam," Allen related later. His local draft board judged a diplomatic appointment more compelling than the need for another private soldier in the Mexico campaign; "discharged from military duty" was duly stamped on his papers, and Allen Dulles entered the Diplomatic Service of the United States.*

Two years after first reading *Kim* on a deck chair, Allen crossed the Atlantic again, heading toward France just as the bloodiest battle in history was being fought a little east of Paris. He had no way of knowing that he was embarked upon a calling that would draw him into the heart of Kim's Great Game. The means that would come to his disposal, and the ends toward which he would deploy those means, were beyond anything that he could possibly have imagined.

---

* His course thus diverged from the career of another New Yorker who did go to the Mexican campaign, William J. Donovan, nicknamed "Wild Bill" for his exploits against Pancho Villa. Donovan and Dulles later were joined in the profession of intelligence, as master and pupil, then colleagues, then rivals for leadership of the Central Intelligence Agency.

— 2 —

WAR AND PEACE

THE HONORABLE Frederic Courtland Penfield, sixty-one, of East Haddam, Connecticut, ambassador plenipotentiary to the Imperial and Royal Court of Austria-Hungary, was delighted with the notice that a promising newcomer, Allen Welsh Dulles, would be assigned to his embassy. The work in stately Vienna was somewhat trying by 1916; the United States was holding itself aloof from the war, but the dismal news from the European battlefronts, and the court scandals after the suicide of that dreadful man Redl, were taking their toll on the Hapsburg capital. Representing a neutral country, the American Embassy found itself encumbered by the routine affairs of half a dozen belligerent governments whose own diplomatic missions had been closed after 1914; these extra duties strained the limited energies and competence of Penfield and his diplomatic staff. The new third secretary was said to be quite bright, well-read, and personable. Penfield noted him as a fellow Princetonian, not to mention the nephew of the secretary of state — all in all, a splendid man to have on board. "Assignment Dulles pleases me," Penfield cabled Washington.[1]

Penfield was not notably equipped for Great Power politics. He had started out as a reporter for the *Hartford Courant*, then took as his second wife one of the richest women in the United States. Thus qualified as a diplomat, his only flair showed in his reportage of Viennese life during wartime, a series of elegant dispatches filed at precise six-month intervals. "Cafés, hotels and theatres are always crowded and the Court Opera seems to go its way as if Austria-Hungary were not involved in the greatest conflict in history," he informed the State Department early in 1916. The operas were mainly Wagner; *Aida* was acceptable, however, because Maestro Verdi had died before the start of war —

22

no living Italian or French composer could properly be heard at the Hapsburg court.

Allen arrived at his first diplomatic post on July 7, 1916, secretary of embassy class five, the lowest rank of the professional service (he was promoted to class four one month later, which meant a raise in salary from $1,200 to $1,500 per annum). By this time Ambassador Penfield's mood had turned gloomy. One of the most pathetic sights in the cities of Austria, the ambassador informed Washington, was the horses that pulled the cabs and delivery wagons. "They are the offscouring and refuse of all horsedom — poor, thin, dispirited, emaciated wrecks of horses that can scarcely lift the weight of their own heads, which usually droop in close proximity to the ground as if looking for the grain they never get." Short tempers and rivalries were rife in the General Staff, not least as a lingering consequence of the Redl affair. Allen could not remain oblivious to the sordid gossip, but his own more mundane tasks were confined to that rite of passage known as consular work.

As ambassadors and higher-ranking officers moved through formal dinner parties and sensitive negotiations, their juniors had the tedious job of processing passport applications, scrutinizing visa qualifications, visiting the country's nationals in jail (not to be considerate but to ascertain that legal procedures were being employed and the State Department protected against congressional or public outcries), and making burial arrangements for American citizens who had died in the area. Within a month of his arrival, Allen was signing passport renewal applications. His signature was neat, legible, and still somewhat childlike: "Allen" and "Welsh" efficiently connected into one word with a series of loops, the D of the last name — as it would always remain — big and bold.

Settling in, Allen succumbed to what the venerable Talleyrand considered the supreme vice of diplomacy, an excess of zeal. In trying to sort out the transnational finances of the Reverend Francis Xavier Gnielinski of St. Louis, working at a parish in Austria, Allen sent the priest a copy of an explanatory telegram that had come from Washington. An embassy superior promptly chastised the novice third secretary: "Don't transmit copies of official documents to private persons." The correct procedure was to retype and paraphrase. When Allen then sheepishly asked the priest to return the offending document, it was brought to the embassy by hand and placed in an envelope at the reception desk. Allen's bureaucratic tormentor noticed that the envelope had the embassy seal; Allen was sharply censured for permitting an outsider to use official stationery.

Allen's consular jurisdiction embraced a situation which his generation of diplomats viewed with special distaste. Indeed, a chance of twentieth-century social history colored the exercise of consular duties in eastern Europe, where so many prominent diplomats learned their art; it gave rise to an insidious attitude that would tarnish the American diplomatic corps.

One of the consuls' most demanding duties was responding to the plight of citizens in distress, persons claiming American nationality and entitled to protections under international law. In the borderlands between the realms of the Russian tsar and the Austrian emperor lived quite a few such persons: men, women, and children in southern Poland, western Russia, Galicia, Ukraine, and other regions where competing powers clashed over the centuries. Few of these people had actually been to America, but through relatives they had possible claim to citizenship and, thus, to official attention. This population made polite diplomats uncomfortable; in their demeanor, they did not measure up to the standards of drawing-room society in the capitals. Quite frankly, to Americans from East Haddam or Henderson Harbor, they often seemed not very clean. Their villages were strange to American eyes; the occasional outsider might comprehend the language they spoke in a loud jabber, but without penetrating to their subtle meanings. Theirs was a close-knit traditional society pressed and oppressed between alien forces. They were the Jews of eastern Europe.

As long before as General Foster's posting to the Court of St. Petersburg in 1880, American diplomats recognized a certain lore about this problem. Foster was briefed, as he prepared for his Russian duties, "that I might have to go to the Foreign Office about once a month to get a poor American Jew out of trouble."[2]

The letters and memoirs of distinguished American diplomats of the century—Allen Dulles no exception—are dotted with remarks, depictions, slurs that seem grossly antisemitic, at least as they relate to those difficult charges in the consular districts. But the tragedy that later befell this population has tended to blur a contemporary distinction: most, though not all, of these antisemitic responses were driven not by religious or group bigotry, but by class: poor, unfamiliar folk versus nice, polite society. Diplomats who voiced that cheap snobbery displayed little of the same distaste for the rich, sophisticated Jews who had scaled the heights in their various capitals. Historians and philosophers have yet to assimilate the profound implications for the American diplomatic tradition of simple class distinctions among the Jews of twentieth-century Europe.

For the young third secretary in Vienna, the matter was not so portentous. Allen reacted with practical efficiency, and no small amount of human concern, to the cases that came into his jurisdiction. Unlike some of his colleagues, who shunned contacts with organized Jewry, Allen cooperated in full sympathy with international relief organizations. He pleaded with the United States Embassy in Berlin to do something about the German consul in Lemberg (now called by its Ukrainian name, Lviv) who persistently set up bureaucratic obstacles to American citizens seeking to leave Galicia. Getting no satisfaction, he wrote a formal five-page letter to Secretary of State Lansing (Uncle Bert), describing the harassment and its consequences. This was one of the rare instances in which Allen presumed upon his family relationship in pursuit of his official duties. It brought no recorded response.

All in all, Allen's three hundred days in the Vienna embassy were not particularly memorable. The funeral of Emperor Franz Josef and the case of Colonel Redl, with its human tensions and practice of espionage, were the only memories of the period that stayed with him. He perfected his tennis game; he made one good friend at the embassy, Frederic R. Dolbeare, eight years his senior, who would move in and out of his life to the end. He went to the Berlitz language school to learn German, becoming as "fluent" as he was in French. At the height of the damp Vienna winter he suffered a bout of rheumatism. Secretary Lansing had to telegraph the Reverend Dulles in Auburn to disregard a press report that Allen was suffering from "rheumatic fever"; it was "rheumatic feet" that had him convalescing in the ambassador's residence: "do not think there is cause for alarm."

As a junior professional, Allen spent hundreds of worried hours poring over the diplomatic codes in pursuit of what passed at the time for sophisticated cryptography. There was one basic code book, "which I have not seen for over forty years," he wrote late in life, "but to this day I can still remember that we had six or seven words for 'period.' One was PIVIR and another was NINUD.... The theory then was — and it was a naive one — that if we had six or seven words it would confuse the enemy as to where we began and ended our sentences."[3]

Imperial Germany declared unrestricted submarine warfare at the start of 1917, just the step that Wilson and Lansing had been trying to avert. The United States broke off relations with Berlin a month later but maintained the Vienna embassy a few weeks longer. At the end of March Penfield was recalled; it took him nine days to make the farewells demanded by protocol and get packed and ready for departure. In the meantime Woodrow Wilson delivered a momentous speech to Congress: "The world must be made safe for democracy. Its peace must be planted upon the tested foundations of political liberty." That very day, April 2, Penfield telegraphed Washington to request that young Dulles be authorized to accompany him as far as Paris: "I have no secretary and only an American can help me; will immediately return him to Vienna, my expense."

Events were moving too fast: Allen's main mission in the closing days of American neutrality was arranging the evacuation of Red Cross doctors and an American nurse. Congress declared war on Germany on April 6; all but a remnant of the American Embassy staff boarded the train for neutral Switzerland during the night of April 6–7.

— * —

If Allen retained few memories of his time in Vienna, a brief episode afterward stayed with him for the rest of his life and gave rise to one of his favorite stories told after dinner or to classes of new recruits in the game of intelligence. Discrepancies of time and circumstance crept into the countless retellings, but the significant main line remained.

The morning of his arrival in Bern on the evacuation train, Allen was retrieving his uprooted personal affairs at the United States Legation, when he was asked to take a telephone call. It was Easter Sunday, and no more senior officer at the legation was available. The caller, an unknown foreigner, was apparently one of those Russian émigré agitators who used neutral Switzerland as a base to pursue subversive designs upon their crumbling homeland — the tsar had abdicated, and the revolutionaries were maneuvering to go home and take over. Allen's twenty-fourth birthday had passed without ceremony the hectic day before, and now all he wanted was a game of tennis with the daughter of a Swiss family he had met in his school years. No, he told his importunate caller, he would not be available to meet that day with the Russian émigré faction, no matter how urgent their wish to contact a representative of the United States. If it's so important, Allen responded impatiently, I'll see them on Monday. But Monday, the unknown voice said, would be too late. And with that the conversation ended.

Building to his climax, Dulles told how the future director of the Central Intelligence Agency, strategist of the Cold War, muffed the chance to meet Vladimir Ilyich Lenin, leader of the Bolsheviks. That Monday Lenin and his motley band left Switzerland on a sealed train for Russia, for the Finland Station.* Everyone loved the story, Allen above all. His message to young CIA professionals was, never pass up an opportunity to meet people, always answer your telephone, keep your door open, be available. The incident later launched Allen upon a philosophy of intelligence, so contrary to the secretive practices of Old World espionage.[4]

---

* This close encounter became such a piquant episode in Allen's career that debunkers tried to assert that it never really happened. Lenin spent his years of exile in Zurich, not Bern; but the Leninist archives in Moscow showed that in fact he and his common-law wife, Nadezhda Krupskaya, went to the Swiss capital that weekend to complete a still-unrevealed matter of intrigue. Lenin did leave Switzerland on April 9, the skeptics noted, but Allen was not posted to Bern until April 23. True, but as we have seen, Allen was in Bern well before

Over the next days the future leader of America's clandestine service wandered about in total ignorance of one of the great covert operations of the century. The secret diplomatic circuits in Bern and Berlin were bursting with a scheme to neutralize the Russian war front. The Germans and the Bolsheviks had separate agendas and interests, but they converged on the desirability of transporting the subversive Lenin back to Russia as quickly and discreetly as possible. Lenin and his revolutionaries wanted nothing to do with Germany lest they be charged with collaborating with imperialism; the kaiser's government readily understood the problem and was ready to comply. On Easter Day the German Foreign Office accepted Lenin's conditions. Late that night, April 8, the German Legation in Bern signaled final departure plans for the next morning. The scheme called for the Bolshevik band to make no contact with German territory on their secret journey. The vehicle became immortalized as a sealed train, but actually it was only a locked second-class carriage that was rudely shunted about for the next four days at switching yards the length of Germany.

On Allen's mind was the practical matter of his own future. His posting to Vienna had ended without ceremony, and no one had given a thought to what the novice third secretary should do next. Ten days passed before word came from the State Department that he was appointed to the Bern legation staff as a political officer, now free of the dreary demands of consular work. Thus entitled to a sense of new beginning, and contemplating the prospect of important deeds ahead, Allen approached the registration desk at Bern's Bellevue Palace Hotel late in the day of April 23 to seek residential quarters.

Surely no place in Europe in 1917 preserved the air of tranquil elegance as did the Bellevue Palace. This was a truly Grand Hotel, neutral Switzerland at its most unreal. A few hundred miles to the west a million men lay locked in trench warfare; to the east another massive army pursued its last forlorn offensive before losing discipline to the Bolshevik revolution. In Washington Congress voted to seek two billion dollars from the public in Liberty Loans to show that America meant business about war. At the Bellevue Palace guests on the flower-bordered terrace looked out across the green Aare Valley to the snowy peaks of the

his official posting. On the crucial Sunday the Bolshevik leader had an open schedule — no speeches to deliver, no fraternal delegations to receive. He spent the day drafting a fifth "Letter from Afar" to his Petrograd faithful, which he never sent, for instead he appeared in person. It does not strain credibility to imagine that he would contrive an opportunity to compare notes with a representative of the United States government, which just two days before had declared war on Germany and might — or might not? — seek to make common cause with a regime in Moscow.

Jungfrau and the Bernese Oberland. From the enormous, high-ceilinged lobby to the private suites with Louis XV furnishings, everything whispered of *grand luxe* and earthly serenity.

To be sure, beneath the surface were tension and intrigue; this was where all the "secret" agents — some of them quite well known to each other — found it convenient to stay over. "Enemies bumped into one another in the elevator, found themselves at the same desk talking to the concierge, ate in the same dining room," recalled one of Allen's colleagues. "Frequently the enemies had been acquaintances or even friends in past years; now they looked through each other at meeting and did their best to pretend the other was non-existent."[5]

The Bellevue Palace way of life presented particular challenges. Winsome maids and flirtatious bellboys were poised to search any private rooms to which they might gain access, and any interesting personal papers they might uncover could be passed to some mysterious stranger for a reasonable stipend. Across the dining room were drawn clear, if invisible, lines of demarcation. Germans, Austro-Hungarians, Turks, and other Central Power belligerents sat on one side; tables for the Allies were at the other end. "In between was a kind of no-man's-land of neutrals," recalled Hugh R. Wilson of the American Legation. "There had sat the Americans until, after our breach of relations with Germany, the head-waiter had solemnly moved us into the Allied zone." What the stately arbiter had overlooked, however, was that the acoustics of the high arched ceiling produced a whispering-gallery effect — meaning that the quiet voices of the German Legation staff, in their secure zone, could be heard in clear detail on the far side of the dining room by the newly arrived Allen Dulles, "fluent" in his comprehension of German.

The United States Legation in the Hirschengraben was a modest establishment; a bell hanging from a string at the front door signaled the arrival of visitors. Nonetheless it was a much more professional operation than the formal embassy in Vienna; here Allen learned the trade of international politics and forged lifelong friendships.

The minister himself, a Georgia schoolboy friend of Woodrow Wilson's named Pleasant A. Stovall, was, to the junior officers, a nonentity. Allen wrote home to Grandfather Foster, committing a rare indiscretion to paper, "One fails to see a spark of genius." The real manager of the legation was the second-ranking officer, Hugh Wilson, who instilled a style of crisp efficiency that was only welcome after the progressive disarray of Vienna. Wilson was the very model of a modern major diplomat: independently wealthy, from Evanston, Illinois, educated at the Hill School and Yale, bored in his father's business, eager for social and intellectual stimulation. Ten years Allen's senior, Wilson was a no-

table exemplar of that founding generation of the professional Diplomatic Service that considered itself to be "a pretty good club."* Other
early clubmates included Dolbeare, who came to Bern from Vienna with
Allen, and Hugh Gibson, who paid periodic visits after serving at the
embassy in Brussels and who reveled in the fellowship of good conversation, fine wines, and important matters of state.

With this little band of comrades the twenty-four-year-old Dulles
started defining himself as an ambitious, industrious, serious (indeed, overly
serious) diplomat, given to caution in attitude and behavior. A flair for imagination might be risky to his career or to Uncle Bert or to his country at war.
"You know our Allen," Dolbeare reminisced with Hugh Wilson years later.
Discretion was his hallmark, even on matters of office gossip. When Wilson
asked about Penfield or others from Vienna, Dolbeare remembered, Allen
"became the soul of discretion and no information whatever was forthcoming." But Dolbeare had been part of the Vienna circle, and thus Allen could
gossip with him. "I asked him the same things, . . . he told me with his customary clarity and good judgment all the 'dope.' "[6]

Some of Allen's foppish affectations lingered on. In conversation with
his legation friends, he would assume the style of old Samuel Johnson,
much favored at Princeton in his time. One day Dolbeare looked in at Allen's office to propose a game of golf. "Sir," Allen replied with all the arch
pomposity of a Johnsonian, "are you of the opinion that when Dr. Kra-
marz and other Czech political personages are about to visit this capital for
a brief interval only, I would forego an opportunity of such magnitude for
a mere exhibition of physical prowess in pursuit of a small painted object?"

Allen was never a prig, as his Princeton classmates well appreciated.
The Old World diplomatic style — formal dress, fine wines, good food
intended to elicit good conversation — combined the reassurance that
one was performing useful work with occasion to enjoy oneself. The tennis court, rather than the golf course, was Allen's great outlet. But by
1917 even Switzerland was feeling the rigors of war: it was almost impossible to get fresh tennis balls. Allen's mention of this hardship in a letter
home induced his brother, Foster, seconded from his law practice to a
desk job in Washington, to arrange for a dozen fresh balls to be sent each
week in the diplomatic pouch.[†]

---

* Wilson's career effectively ended after a brief but controversial term as the last United
States ambassador to Nazi Germany, where he gained the reputation of being an apologist
for Hitler.
† This immeasurable bounty gave the Americans and their chosen friends a virtual monop-
oly of the fashionable courts at Dählhölzli, to the exclusion of diplomats from other nations who had enjoyed playing there in better days. Foster commended Allen: "I am glad
that you have been able to keep the Huns out of the Tennis Club."

Allen worked long hours. A political officer in a neutral outpost had the task of pursuing and analyzing dozens of minority factions within the countries at war to learn their political aims and potential interest to the United States. Hugh Wilson quickly turned Allen's diligence to good use.

> I called him into my office and told him that he was appointed expert of all the places I had listed. "Sir," said Allen, "how long have I to prepare myself?" I replied, "Say, a week or ten days. We have to get started; Washington is clamoring." "I shall report on the subject in ten days," said Allen, bowed, and departed. . . .
>   I did not lay eyes on him in the meantime, and he duly reported. He had spent the ten days in Geneva, Zurich and Basle, had become acquainted with the refugee representatives of the South Slavs, of the Czechs, with the Bulgarian Legation, with Hungarian malcontents. In a word, he had come as near to accomplishing the fantastic assignment which I had given him in the ten days allotted as a human being could. Certainly from that moment on he was never at a loss as to the means of ascertaining any piece of information.[7]

Allen started filing dispatches about internal conditions in Germany and Austria-Hungary, gleaned from such sources as "an Austrian of intelligence and education, whom I believe to be well informed" or an informant "personally very friendly to the United States, where he has a brother residing, and . . . opposed to any close alliance between Austria-Hungary and Germany." He contrived regular conversations with a "naval officer in close association with the ruling house of Germany."* Thus the journeyman diplomat became familiar with the first problem of gathering intelligence. "It is almost impossible to stop for any length of time in Switzerland without coming into contact with questionable characters," Allen wrote home. "Berne is just full of agents and representatives of all nationalities. . . . It becomes quite an art to pick out the reliable and safe persons with whom one can deal and then to properly weight and judge what they give you."
Allen's dispatches went to Washington over the signature of the min-

---

* This source was a captain assigned to German naval headquarters who happened to be married to the daughter of the American consul general in Zurich. The captain paid regular weekend visits to his wife, who stayed with her father at the consulate, and the long conversations were not limited to family chitchat. This contact provoked years of intrigue and controversy: see *The Final Memoranda of Major General Ralph H. Van Deman*, ed. Ralph E. Weber (Wilmington, Del.: SR Books, 1988); and Robert Murphy, *Diplomat among Warriors* (New York: Pyramid Books, 1965), p. 18.

ister, as was customary in diplomatic missions. After several months came a remarkable response: "The Department [of State] finds these dispatches of the highest value, and considers that they show not only careful labor in preparation but also exceptional intelligence in the drawing of conclusions." Only after receiving that extraordinary commendation did Minister Stovall identify the principal author as Robert Lansing's nephew.

Soon Allen tired of merely collecting and assessing information. There must be more to the Great Game than this.

— * —

Kipling's *Kim* had become a sophisticated classic, but the popular fare of the day was served up by racy writers like E. Phillips Oppenheim. For all his seriousness on the job, Allen delighted from the start in catering to the public imagination about his work. "Oppenheim with all his gumshoe work has nothing on us," Allen wrote an American friend, "and we can beat the best of his diplomatic detective stories from real life." Even the staid Hugh Wilson got caught up in the adventurous mood of the Bellevue Palace. "Up to this time in my life I had never encountered a spy outside of the pages of a thriller," Wilson recalled. "Suddenly I found myself in a society where spies and spying was one of the principal subjects of conversation."

"Spy" is a loose word, seldom used among practitioners as the game of intelligence became more professional. Novelist Somerset Maugham provided a realistic account of the Great Game in Switzerland during World War I.*

> He saw his spies at stated intervals and paid them their wages; when he could get hold of a new one he engaged him, gave him his instructions and sent him off to Germany; he waited for the information that came through and dispatched it; he went into France once a week to confer with his colleague over the frontier and to receive his orders from London; he visited the market-place on market-day to get any message the old butter-woman had brought him from the other side of the lake. . . . This work he was doing was evidently necessary, but it could not be called anything but monotonous."[8]

* Maugham used his literary status as cover for assignments from the British Secret Service at just the time and place that Allen was learning to play the game. He later published a collection of autobiographical stories titled *Ashenden*. Though dismissed by Maugham's coterie as a slight and minor work, to intelligence buffs *Ashenden* is one of the best accounts in print of the typical life of what is now called a case officer running his agents.

To Allen the work was never monotonous. As a diplomatic political officer, he worked on a subtle basis with a type of person whom contemporaries and historians alike have difficulty defining. They are not real agents or "spies"—indeed, the implication would be offensive to them — but they are hardly disinterested bystanders. For want of a better word, they are called go-betweens, less than mediators, more than fixers. They are simply individuals who happen to have access to different parties and are willing to make their access available. A go-between who serves as a specific connection between two persons who do not wish to be in direct contact is called a cut-out. Their motives may be altruistic, even idealistic, or they may be crude; they may wish to bring about world peace or improve the sale of their next book, save lives or gain new clients for their law practice.

Open and curious, Allen began meeting go-betweens everywhere he went, first in Vienna and then in Bern. The most prominent, though his work as a go-between was conducted in great secrecy, was Julius Meinl, the Viennese coffee and tea magnate whose chain of shops across the empire gave his name resonance in Austria similar to that of Watertown's F. W. Woolworth in the United States. Allen found an avuncular friend in a noted expatriate biologist, Henry Haviland Field, descendant of New England Quakers, who had a wide range of intellectual associates across Europe. The young diplomat frequently called at the large house in Zurich where Field lived with his British wife and four children, one of them an alert and sensitive adolescent boy named Noel. Allen and Noel Field would meet again in another war.

Minister Stovall heartily disapproved of his diplomatic staff having contacts with unsavory persons who were probably from "the enemy," and Allen felt his emerging style cramped in the high visibility of the Bellevue Palace. Leaving Wilson to the elegance of it all, he moved into a small apartment of his own where, he wrote his brother Foster, he could better "entertain all the strange characters whom one can hardly meet in the hotel or a restaurant." Through this circle of new friends Allen devised his first foray into the realm that came to be called covert action; not content with merely analyzing the flow of political events, he set out to try shaping the course of those events for the national interest.

Allen's first covert action was a fiasco. It started at Field's home in Zurich and the equally congenial residence in Geneva of George D. Herron, another American academic, a friend of President Wilson's. Both of these academics drew visitors from the Central Powers — Germans, Austrians, and Hungarians — who maintained the fiction that they, like their "old American friends," were mere private citizens with no official status. The protestations were necessary, for early in 1918 several of these cut-outs came to Switzerland on an extremely sensitive mission: Emperor Karl of Austria, the recent successor to Franz Josef, wanted to make a separate peace with the United States. "The pot of political intrigue really begins to bubble," Allen wrote Uncle Bert in mid-February.

Allen arranged a meeting between Herron and Julius Meinl, who then asked that a responsible American receive an important visitor from Vienna. In the game of go-betweens, cut-outs serve for other cut-outs, layer upon layer. Allen remembered the name of the important Austrian from the guest lists at General Foster's home before the war: Heinrich Lammasch, scholar of international law, boyhood tutor to Emperor Karl, a leading Viennese liberal who was opposed to the strong pro-German influence upon the Hapsburg Empire. A "casual" meeting between Herron and Lammasch was set up for February 2 at a secluded chateau outside Bern, owned by a self-exiled German industrialist.

Allen and Hugh Wilson were naive in imagining that their emerging scheme could be kept secret from all the diverse intelligence corps of Bern, allies and enemies alike, and their efforts at security were primitive. Herron was to arrive at the chateau in a car with drawn blinds, but the vehicle was clearly registered to the United States Legation, two armed American army officers flanked the professor in the back seat, and the driver was a moonlighting British sergeant. In short, everyone who cared knew about Allen's first covert operation before it even began. German agents sent word of the Herron-Lammasch encounter to Berlin, and the kaiser threatened Austria with outright invasion if young Emperor Karl persisted in his independent diplomacy. Another interested party, the well-connected agitators for an independent state of Czechoslovakia, protested to President Wilson about any deal that might deprive them of their national self-determination. The notion of a separate peace between the United States and Austria-Hungary was stillborn.

Allen went back to the legation dejected but wiser in the methods of secret diplomacy. The more worldly Hugh Wilson rationalized the abortive Herron-Lammasch exchanges: "I was often reproached . . . for having 'selected' two such men, and non-official men, to do work of such a delicate and confidential character," he wrote. "The answer was easy: they were there. . . . In war you don't 'select' your tools, you make use of what lies at hand." Allen would have occasion to use the same tools, cut-outs upon cut-outs, two decades later under the same cover of Swiss neutrality. The next time he would be more successful but criticized even more for the moral ambiguities of secret bargaining between forces at war.

What must have hurt Allen most of all about the Herron-Lammasch operation was a letter from Foster a couple of months later. The news of the debacle was all over Washington, and the older brother had no hesitation in including a patronizing gibe: "Didn't the Austrians perhaps pull your leg a little?"

— * —

Allen's career prospered in his fourteen months in Bern, and he gained skill in collecting and assessing political intelligence. At age twenty-five he was promoted to second secretary, disproving his father's injunction against diplomacy as a career. Henderson Harbor and Auburn were now a generation away, his roots but no longer his life. Occasionally Princeton friends would write reminiscences of their undergraduate days, reminders of the life of ease Allen had once known. Puzzling, and not a little unsettling, was one letter he received in Bern from Allen G. Shenstone, a young American soldier embarking for war. "I can't tell you how much I have missed you. You know very well, of course, that I never had any real friends at college except you. I don't suppose I ever shall have many, and it makes me feel often that it might be the best that could happen to me if I were knocked out." Allen kept the letter but left no indication of a reply; later he said he had no memory of what was apparently a schoolboy crush.* A milestone was passed in November 1917, when Allen received a telegram informing him that his grandfather, John Watson Foster, had died in Washington. Allen telegraphed the family that "his life will always be example and inspiration for me."

Even Foster was beginning to show a modest respect for his younger brother's experiences. "Write me again sometime," he wrote Allen at the beginning of 1918. "Your views are valuable and I can utilize them to advantage." But the first-born never shrank from expounding his own views. "The way things are going, I do not see any prospect of a military victory over Germany." Allen's reply is revealing, not only of his habits of cautious expression and his grasp of German politics, but of the cerebral relationship between two brothers even in personal exchanges. "While I agree with you that the situation is not one for undue optimism, we must not underestimate the difficulties of the Germans and overestimate our own," Allen lectured Foster. "The great thing now for the political leaders in America and the Entente is not to make any statement which will drive the two classes in Germany together, and to accentuate the split between the Liberals and the Pan-Germans."

Personal feelings were apparently not proper subjects for family cor-

---

* Shenstone survived combat in France and became a distinguished professor of physics at Princeton, retiring in 1962. Their friendship did not endure into maturity, and Shenstone remarked with sadness that he had found his old college friend becoming "rather pontifical."

respondence, even between brothers; the intimacy of the Dulles family extended only to matters of the mind, not the emotions. But Allen, no longer a fun-loving youth, was still deeply imbued with the idealism of Woodrow Wilson's Princeton, and this emotion, at least, he could properly convey. He wrote his parents in September of 1918:

> If the crushing German military defeat that seems possible now is realized, we will have the task of restraining the Imperialist ambitions of our Allies, especially the British and Italians, and we must keep all our moral strength and balanced judgment for that occasion. Otherwise we will not see the just arrangement of the world that America can bring about and that alone can secure peace for the future. . . . We have the greatest obligation and opportunity that a nation ever had. . . . We are called to put the world in order again.

The Bern legation scored a coup in intelligence collection early in November. As the world waited for word of Germany's readiness to surrender, Dolbeare, lunching alone at the Bellevue Palace, was summoned to the telephone. On the line was a contact at the Swiss Telegraph Agency who had access to all the messages coursing across Europe. Abandoning his lunch, Dolbeare rushed over to the cable office to be shown a message sent from Berlin to Vienna, indicating that Germany was about to ask for an armistice. "I dashed to find the Minister, . . . lunching at the French Embassy," Dolbeare years later reminded Hugh Wilson, who happened to be at the same luncheon. "I told the butler I must see the Minister. He protested that everyone was at table. I said 'Never mind that,' so he whispered a word and you came out. You took the message to Mr. Stovall and he read it aloud. That was the end of the luncheon party."

On the day of armistice, November 11, neutral Switzerland would not celebrate officially. For the moment of triumph Allen planned to drive across the French frontier to be with the troops. He invited a newcomer to the legation, Christian Herter, a tall Bostonian, thoroughly eligible for the club, to join him. Herter came over to Allen's hideaway apartment, and they had just started downstairs when suddenly Allen keeled over. All Europe was in the throes of an epidemic of influenza, which eventually took the lives of twenty million people, twice the number killed in the Great War. The grippe, as they called it, hit Allen on Armistice Day. A frightened Herter carried his new friend back upstairs to bed and stayed with him through the celebrations.

Four decades later Herter became the fourth of Allen Dulles's intimates to be named secretary of state, at a time when Allen was serving his country in a more secretive post. But on the day of armistice, an indul-

gent Herter only listened as Allen held forth feverishly about Wilson's aspirations for putting the world in order again. If those principles were to
fail, Allen ranted, the old balance-of-power era would return — and that
would mean another war in a generation or two.

— * —

By the closing months of 1918 it was difficult to recall that Woodrow
Wilson had once been an inquiring scholar. After six years as president of
the United States, Wilson no longer felt the need to acquire information
before forming his opinions. Allen and his clubmates in the Bern legation, however, were not alone in perceiving the need for accurate, sensitive, current data about the various forces that would compete in the
postwar world.

America's entry into the Great War in 1917 had brought to the forefront a halting effort to collect reliable "intelligence" about those forces.
Ironically, it was Secretary of State John Watson Foster who had set the
process in motion, without realizing the effect it would have on his descendants. During his short term in office in 1892, he had introduced the
system of assigning military attachés to embassies and legations to gather
information for Washington about foreign countries. He sent uniformed
officers to London, Paris, Vienna, Berlin, and St. Petersburg to "examine
the military libraries, bookstores and publishers' lists in order to give
early notice of any new or important publications or inventions or im-
provements in arms." A Military Intelligence Division was established in
Washington, manned by one army officer and one army clerk.

By 1917 the intelligence force had more than doubled — to three officers and two clerks. As the first American divisions were preparing to
embark for combat in France, the army chief of staff assumed that the
United States could be assured of intelligence simply by telling the
British and French armies, "Here, we are now ready for service; we would
be pleased if you hand over to us all the necessary information concerning the enemy which your intelligence services have obtained."[9]

The major in charge of the Military Intelligence Division, however,
was not a man to be dissuaded from a pursuit he considered important.
Ralph H. Van Deman, a Harvard graduate from Delaware, Ohio, set out
to build a unique intelligence service for the United States. By the 1918
armistice his division had grown to 282 officers, 29 enlisted men, and 948
civilians. With a vigor that became obsessive, Van Deman saw intelligence as a matter of investigation, not of analysis; his was not the gift of
subtlety. Early in 1918 he sought reports from his military agents about
"the principal Teuton tricks, so as to avoid them." He asked the right
questions, without necessarily understanding the reasons for obtaining

the answers: he requested reports of German divisions just transferred from the eastern front "and probably undermined with Bolshevikism, . . . the location of Saxon regiments probably with a big percentage of socialists; locations of Bavarians, jealous of Prussians; of Czechoslovaks, likely to desert."

Allen first encountered Van Deman in the summer of 1918, when this tenacious army officer was attempting to join his division to the parallel services of the British and French allies. They met as colleagues in intelligence, yet from the start it was clear they were coming at it from opposite directions: Allen the earnest, politically sensitive diplomat, Van Deman the jaded cop. Allen was interested in political intelligence, clues of the intentions and capabilities of diverse foreign forces; Van Deman looked for security leaks wherever he could find them, and then some. Allen's fellow diplomats were snobbish in their scorn for the likes of Van Deman, but even when Van Deman started poking into the dubious backgrounds of some of Allen's best sources, the diplomat and the cop maintained a mutually respectful relationship — until three decades later, when their divergent paths met in confrontation.

In believing that the collection of intelligence was a responsible function — indeed a duty — of government, they were lonely voices within the American contingent in Europe, preparing to remake the world order. Minister Stovall could never quite appreciate the importance of what his political officers were doing. "The doors of the Legation were plastered with ethnological and geographical charts," he wrote with no small measure of scorn. "It took the entire time of a special force to listen to [the émigrés'] tales of woe and to prepare them for those whom they might concern." Military attachés in the embassies would report the drawing-room gossip they could pick up from their comrades, generally majors and colonels of foreign armies, but the Bern intelligence operation was unique in its sensitivity to political interests. Even Foster at his Washington desk job shared with his brother his frustration that "there is no cohesion in our military operations, nor are they based on adequate intelligence, the importance of which is nowhere recognized."

Allen was devising a novel plan, and he made bold to present it in a personal letter to Uncle Bert — undaunted by the secretary of state's notable neglect of his suggestions thus far. Why not assemble a group of scholars to study "the problems of nationalities and to determine where justice lies in the various claims of the European races and nations?" Allen wrote. He could not have known how grimly his innocent suggestion would be received. To his credit, Lansing had already realized that the ideas his president was expounding for the future world order were not based on adequate knowledge. The previous August, in fact, the secretary had instructed one of his up-and-coming diplomats, Joseph C. Grew, to prepare memoranda about conditions in Europe for use at a future peace conference. Grew pondered the request and concluded that it would be a "seemingly colossal task" without a competent researcher; otherwise he might have to spend a *full week* of his vacation doing the job.

Fortunately or not — it is debated — the president put the professional diplomats out of the intelligence business; independently of his secretary of state, and surely without knowledge of Allen's modest proposal, Wilson assigned to the academic community the task of assembling proposals for the postwar settlement, under the coordination of his trusted aide, Colonel Edward M. House. The result was the Inquiry, a secret commission to collect, organize, and present for political consumption everything that needed to be known about Europe after the Great War.

The greatest academic names of the current and next generations were brought to the Inquiry, among them Frederick Jackson Turner of Harvard and William E. Dodd of Chicago, Samuel Eliot Morison to look into Slavic eastern Europe, the young and promising Charles Seymour of Yale to study the remnants of the Hapsburg Austro-Hungarian Empire. House named geographer Isaiah Bowman as director; as secretary, and thus central recruiter and organizer, came the brilliant Walter Lippmann, just twenty-eight, a Harvard-educated journalist already established as a profound and adventurous philosopher of public policy.

Lippmann, Bowman, and their staff plunged into the job with the special arrogance of the intellectual unleashed on public affairs. "We are skimming the cream of the younger and more imaginative scholars," wrote Lippmann. "What we are on the lookout for is genius — sheer, startling genius, and nothing else will do." The secretary of state and others of the diplomatic establishment looked on in dismay and suspicion.

Through the winter of 1917–18 the scholars of the Inquiry produced nearly two thousand separate reports of particular problems that they assumed would arise in writing the final peace treaty, complete with bibliographies, maps, charts, and sundry data. The lasting impact of the reports was not their substance — most were quite forgettable — but rather their style. Specialists in any field always try to set their own agendas of questions that can be answered with ease. Lippmann and his staff invariably put specific, pointed questions to their "genius" specialists, demanding answers that were difficult to contemplate. The discipline of the Inquiry produced a blunt style of analysis, quite different from the airy and imprecise diplomatic reporting customary at the time.

Lippmann, ever restless, quickly tired of the Inquiry's sterile isolation and jumped at an offer to examine conditions on the ground in Europe as an army intelligence officer. From a base in Paris he sought out American

officials who might help him. Van Deman was an early contact, and the
dour soldier was sympathetic to Lippmann's ideas for distributing propaganda among the newly liberated peoples of central Europe. Lippmann
also wanted to organize political intelligence to bring up-to-date reports
to the attention of policymakers, but that was not Van Deman's concern.
The newly uniformed man from the Inquiry found a much more congenial colleague in Hugh Gibson, who was roving around the capitals
of liberated Europe. Lippmann and the military intelligence officers
"pussyfooted carefully to see whether they would be treading on my
toes," Gibson recalled, "but I whooped with joy at the prospect of having
somebody to play with."[10] No time elapsed before Lippmann's sharp eyes
noticed the reports of Allen Dulles and his colleagues in Bern on the collapse of the Central Powers; these dispatches stood out for the clarity and
insight that the Inquiry was always seeking. "In Bern, a group of the very
best young men in the diplomatic service did contrive to act as a source
of information."[11] Lippmann resolved to keep his eye on Dulles.

With the end of the war in sight, though before the front lines had
gone quiet, Colonel House himself sailed for Europe, under destroyer escort, as President Wilson's advance man in organizing the peace settlement. His first meetings in Paris with Lippmann and other Americans
persuaded House that the collection of current intelligence was an urgent priority; if the conventional diplomats had little interest in pursuing
it, the task certainly could not be left to the scholars of his beloved Inquiry, who were far from the scene. House's telegram, "Secret for the
President and Secretary of State," on November 8, three days before the
armistice, marked the end of the innocence shown by the army chief of
staff the year before and opened a new era in American intelligence.

> We are getting a mass of misinformation respecting present conditions
> in Austria, Bohemia and the Ukraine, practically all of which is being
> provided by the English, French and Italians. We have no American
> sources of information. The reports received are . . . colored by the self
> interest of the persons furnishing them. I regard it as exceedingly impor-
> tant that we send at once to these countries agents who will be in a posi-
> tion to furnish us with accurate and unbiased information. . . . This mat-
> ter I believe is most urgent.[12]

The problem was simple for House to state, but the presidential adviser's musings posed more problems than he had envisaged. In 1918 the
United States government had no "agents." Van Deman's military intelligence officers were not up to the job of political analysis; the diplomats,
who were, spurned clandestine intelligence work as unseemly. And, once
the right individuals were found to serve as agents, should they travel and

interview as government officials or under some innocuous cover? What
level of personal risk would be acceptable and necessary for the tasks of
gathering intelligence?

An answer readily presented itself, at least to Colonel House's satisfaction. Crossing with his cable was the signal from Washington that the
day before, November 7, Wilson had named Herbert Hoover, a strong-
willed mining engineer from Iowa, to direct postwar relief and rehabilitation efforts in the ravaged societies of central Europe. Then forty-four
years old, Hoover had built a spectacular reputation for getting difficult
jobs done during his wartime relief service in Belgium. House cornered
Hoover, passing through Paris, and learned of his plan to send relief
teams across central Europe. House conceived the idea, though he did
not yet share it with Hoover, of insinuating intelligence agents, complete
with code clerks, stenographers, and interpreters, into these relief teams.
It was an ingenious idea, novel for the time, and fraught with sensitive aspects that would raise practical, ethical, and bureaucratic hackles. Sensing the delicacy of his proposal, House cabled his idea "Secret for the
President," unlike the telegram four days before, which had gone to
Lansing as well.

President Wilson was not concerned with gathering information; despite House's caution he referred the message to Lansing, who approved
the plan "in principle" but showed no sensitivity to the obvious problems: was it wrong or dangerous to use humanitarian relief teams for ul-
terior state motives? Could qualified agents be found quickly, with the
political sophistication to make their reports worthwhile? Hoover was a
personage of stature, no mere civil servant. House's political antennae
were not unique in sensing Hoover's prospects in American politics,
though it was not yet clear whether the Iowa engineer was a Republican
or a Democrat. Would such an executive permit his humanitarian teams
to perform unrelated clandestine functions? Here, at the very start of
America's twentieth-century intelligence organization, was a dilemma
that would endure.

House was no novice in the art of devious persuasion. He started the
softening-up process with Hoover's protégé and intimate from their wartime work together in Belgium, the ubiquitous Hugh Gibson. House gave
Gibson a full briefing on the scheme at a meeting on November 18, slyly
and without the slightest authorization dangling before the ambitious
diplomat the possibility of a ministerial post in Vienna to coordinate incoming intelligence reports. Then House broadened the circle to line up
support. Van Deman and his military intelligence colleagues agreed to
provide a list of 250 officers who knew the languages of eastern Europe.
Lippmann would vet the candidates for their suitability to the task of col-

lecting political intelligence. Military officers, they concluded, need not be the only ones under consideration as agents. First on a list of civilian candidates experienced in political analysis was Allen Dulles of Bern.

Lansing flatly rejected the outrageous notion of employing professional diplomats for questionable intelligence purposes, and certainly not his own nephew — who thereby lost the opening for what seemed a choice assignment in the process of making the peace.

The opinion that counted, however, was Hoover's. Gingerly, Gibson did House's bidding and took a tentative sounding with his mentor. Hoover's reaction came in no uncertain terms.* He took violent objection to House's proposal and ordered a distressed Gibson to pull out of it. House, however, had prepared a fallback position. He had at hand the concurrence "in principle" of the State Department, including the secretary himself, and even President Wilson had given vague approval to whatever House had in mind. At a face-to-face meeting with House in Paris on November 27, Hoover saw the inevitability of the outcome; all that remained in his power was to insist on working conditions that would preserve the appearance of integrity in his nonpolitical mission. Most notable was his demand that all communications from the intelligence attachés be transmitted *en clair*, in plain English, not coded like diplomatic messages. This simple procedure, Hoover argued, would reassure any suspicious governments or other authorities who might wonder if the relief teams were up to nefarious activities.

Thus protected from awkward exposure, Hoover reluctantly accepted House's plan. The United States relief program in Europe after the war would serve as cover for the collection of intelligence.†

— * —

"The whole management of foreign relations has an uncoordinated, amateur touch," complained Wilson's ambassador to London, Walter Hines Page. The diplomacy of the republic often seemed a casual affair, at least to outsiders if not to the self-conscious club of professionals who imag-

---

* The participants in these days of discussion were reticent about committing their conversations with Hoover to paper, and thus the record is unclear about which of the controversial aspects of the plan brought the sharpest response.

† Two years later, as he planned a relief mission to Russia, Hoover reverted to his insistence that the agents keep "entirely aloof not only from action but even from discussion of political and social questions." Hoover's own memoirs and prolific writings late in his public career are strangely silent or evasive about the intelligence function of his relief missions. Gibson, even in his private diaries, took care not to portray his chief in a role that could be criticized. Van Deman, typically, is the one who minced no words, and the opening of the Van Deman papers in 1988 finally made possible this reconstruction of the episode.

ined themselves following in an elegant tradition. In retirement Allen was delighted to find in his Uncle Bert's private papers a puerile little memorandum that Wilson had typed out early in 1915 about preserving secrecy during a negotiation: "One person to draft all dispatches. . . . *No flimsies* of such dispatches." The president shared this tactic with his then secretary of state, William Jennings Bryan, who circulated the president's memo among his diplomatic staff and, after five days of consideration, pronounced the suggestions "entirely feasible."*

As late as the week before the armistice, United States policymakers had not bothered to think about where the peace conference should be held. Prodded by House, Wilson gave the matter a few moments' thought and opted for Lausanne. But by then Switzerland looked less and less secure. Lenin's departure eighteen months before had not silenced the Swiss revolutionary workers' movement, and a wave of protests and police countermeasures disturbed the neutral calm. "On second thought," Wilson penned, "it occurs to me that Versailles may be the best place for the peace conference, where friendly influences and authorities are in control, rather than Switzerland which is saturated with every poisonous element and open to every hostile influence in Europe."[13] Thus Lenin's unwitting legacy was that Versailles, and not Lausanne, was the site of the diplomatic act that set the scene for the second, and greater, global conflict of the twentieth century.

One immediate problem for all the delegations was to secure hotel rooms and office space in Paris. On Armistice Day, when House discovered that the British had stolen a march by snapping up the Majestic and Astoria hotels, he sought urgent authority to requisition for the American staff the Crillon on the Place de la Concorde, with accommodations for about one hundred persons, and a smaller adjoining building. An army lieutenant, once manager of New York's Hotel Vanderbilt, was seconded to manage the Crillon. Enlisted men were trucked in from the quieted battlefront to man the elevators, make the beds, and drive the brown and gray army Cadillacs that became a fixture on the streets of the French capital.

Paris may have been preferable to Switzerland on security grounds, but from the start high priority was assigned to the task of protecting the American delegation from penetration by Old World intelligence forces. Van Deman was the man for the job. He was given two sergeants, a mes-

* The Xerox generations might need the explanation that "flimsies" was the term for the thin copies produced by carbon paper. Forty years later Allen found this absurd Wilson-Bryan exchange in his uncle's papers; delighting that the architect of "open covenants, openly arrived at" should have been so concerned with confidentiality, he reproduced the memos in his retirement memoir, *The Craft of Intelligence*.

senger, and an office at 4 Place de la Concorde, the building adjoining the Crillon. Five days after assuming his functions, Van Deman discovered what he considered a most unfortunate feature about the office space that House had arranged so efficiently: the building was connected at the back, on the Rue Royale, to the restaurant Maxim's, long fabled for the romantic trysts within its *cabinets particuliers* on the upper floors. "Due to the reputation of Maxim's Restaurant it had been placed off bounds for all American armed forces personnel in Paris," Van Deman reported.

He was shocked, therefore, to discover early in December "that a trap door existed leading from one of the offices at 4 Place de la Concorde down to the second floor above the restaurant, giving access to it." So close was this proximity that a sophisticated member of the British delegation, Harold Nicolson, concluded — with no small degree of envy — that the American staff was using those private rooms of romance as quarters. Nor had all of the rooms, Nicolson suspected, been removed from their original service to the clients of Maxim's. Van Deman promptly ordered a padlock to bar the offending trap door, and he placed the keys "in the charge of a sergeant reported to be entirely reliable." Inevitably the young man's reliability was strained to the breaking point — along with the padlock — and a distressed Van Deman reported two weeks later that the locked door was again open, and traffic between the American delegation and Maxim's private rooms was proceeding unimpeded.[14]

From their separate postings, Allen and Foster Dulles were maneuvering to snag a prized assignment to Paris: Allen recovering from the grippe at the legation in Switzerland, Foster enmeshed in the Washington military bureaucracy. Uncle Bert should have been helpful in this matter, but Secretary Lansing was by now too far out of Wilson's inner circle to have much influence — and in any case, he had not shown any interest in promoting the careers of his eager nephews. Allen was in the stronger position, a seasoned analyst already versed in the political tasks before the Paris Peace Conference. Thanks to the favorable notice taken by bureaucratic insiders, early in December the younger Dulles received the summons coveted by all of his clubmates and, indeed, by every American diplomat in Europe: assignment to the American Commission to Negotiate Peace.* Hugh Wilson was generous in acknowledging the reversal of roles between mentor and protégé. "Do your utmost to get us

---

* It took Foster a month longer to get to Paris from Washington. He sailed on December 21 as a statistician for the American delegation and promptly became embroiled in a turf war with the economists of the Inquiry. Foster wasted no time in seeking Uncle Bert's help in shoring up his position, but support from Lansing was of little avail, and Foster had to fight his way to a position of authority at the conference on his own — which he did successfully.

planted on the Paris end," Wilson wrote, "and even if we had to clean the front door for the Mission it would be worth being there. . . . I hope you have a bully time, as I know you will."

— * —

Paris in 1918, for a junior diplomat like Allen, meant engagement in American foreign policy at the highest level. No longer would he have to employ Johnsonian pomposities to secure his status or fear taking steps that might be considered imaginative. He wasted no time in making contacts — with Van Deman, for one, though the cop was too busy with the problems of Maxim's to have much interest in the rarefied circles of policymaking. Allen was junior enough to ignore the tensions developing between House and Lansing, and he managed to make himself useful to members of both camps. One who spotted his talents early on was pleased with his success. "It has been a great pleasure to have Dulles here," wrote Lippmann.

President Wilson crossed the Atlantic by ship and arrived in Paris on December 14, "a day long to remember," Allen rejoiced in his retirement writings.

> No foreigner ever received on the soil of another country an acclaim comparable to that of Woodrow Wilson's on that December day in Paris. . . . [He] came as the man whose ideals had helped mightily to break down the resistance of the enemy. . . . He was the prophet of the self-determination of peoples, the author of the Fourteen Points which was proclaimed to be, but was not, the charter for the peace, the peace of reconciliation which never was realized.

Another young American on the delegation staff, Adolf A. Berle, wrote that night:

> Place de la Concorde was solidly packed with thousands upon thousands. . . . A lane was cut from the Pont Alexandre III, and edged with blue soldiers in double line — there were mobs everywhere. . . . At half past ten the guns saluted, and a little time later the Republican guards galloped down the lane, and then came a couple of automobiles; and then open carriages, Wilson, Poincaré, Mrs. Wilson, Bliss, Pichon, Castelnau, Jusserand, Pershing, etc. — amid cheers. Then the blue lines folded inward and the lane was lost in a seething mass.[15]

Also lost in the seething mass, to his enduring annoyance, was Allen Dulles. For days he had been working on protocol arrangements with the French Foreign Ministry. At six in the morning of December 14 he dutifully posted himself at the Bois de Boulogne railway station for the presi-

dent's arrival from Brest. Unfortunately his planning ended too soon; he
sent the presidential party off on its triumphal route through Paris but
neglected to arrange his own passage back to the Crillon for the official
arrival. His friends managed better: Lippmann watched from the balcony
outside his office; Ray Stannard Baker, Wilson's press secretary, mingled
with the crowds on the Champs-Elysées. Allen was nowhere. "I was
caught in a fearful mob of people," he wrote home to Auburn; they surrounded his car, wildly pushing and shoving in the hopes of seeing Wilson himself.

The ultimate annoyance of that December day came with the unannounced arrival at the Crillon of his sister Eleanor. Fresh from Bryn
Mawr, she had snagged a slot on a war relief mission and had spent the last
months serving a civilian population just behind the front lines. Allen well
knew that Foster was maneuvering to get to Paris; to his prickly and determined sister he had given no thought, certainly never imagining that she
would turn up there first. The purpose of her unheralded visit was solely
to have a hot bath in her brother's posh billet, and then she was gone.

The days in Paris were exhilarating. The policymakers of the victorious powers were finally joined with their men in the field. From Whitehall came Harold Nicolson, Arnold Toynbee, and John Maynard Keynes;
from the Inquiry, Lippmann and Harvard professor Samuel Eliot Morison, who supposed that his temporary diplomatic status required him to
wear striped pants and a cutaway coat. Over the next six months Allen
found himself mingling with French socialists Anatole France and Léon
Blum; Eduard Beneš and Tomaš G. Masaryk of the emerging Czechoslovakia; Ignace Paderewski, the reincarnation of Chopin from Poland;
Jan Christiaan Smuts from South Africa, T. E. Lawrence from Arabia;
Chaim Weizmann of the new Zionist movement; Ho Chi Minh from Indochina; and a Persian aristocrat turned radical named Mohammad
Mossadegh. All and sundry were determined to press their particular
causes upon the makers of the new world. Those who could gain admit-
tance gathered for tea each day at 4:30 at the ministry on the Quai d'Or-
say, as in an Oxford common room, where conversation could range
widely without the slightest commitment to action.

Once his protocol duties were accomplished, Allen's actual job was
undefined. Much of his time, he reported, was engaged in arranging office furniture for the new arrivals. As the secretary of state's nephew, he
was assigned a desk in Lansing's office suite. Hugh Gibson, ever the iconoclast, recorded:

[Lansing] is established in a huge corner room at the Crillon surrounded
by palms and statuary and an air of Olympian calm. He has a waiting

room about ten acres in extent and two or three youths whose main function is to gaze out onto the Place de la Concorde and entertain the waiting visitors. One of them is [Alexander] Kirk who has been at The Hague
and has been assigned down here. Another is Allen Dulles who came up
here from Switzerland a few weeks ago and has been held for work in
connection with the Peace Mission. They have not got into things yet
and probably will not until their business is more organized than it has
been thus far.[16]

A less cheerful portrait came from a technical expert to the American
delegation, a Wisconsin geology professor who was not accustomed to
the effete airs of the diplomatic establishment. To him those young men
gazing out of the secretary's windows were mere "pulchritudinous
youths" who somehow seemed to set the official tone of American foreign relations.[17]

Pending more orderly working arrangements, Allen helped his
friends get established at the Peace Conference. Foster arrived, and the
brothers shared a suite at the Crillon. A Princeton classmate, James
Bruce, who had sat with him on the Boulevard St.-Michel in 1914, was at
loose ends in the army; Allen managed to get him assigned to President
Wilson's personal bodyguard. When James's younger brother, David K.
E. Bruce, turned up, Allen pointed him to an assignment as junior
courier to the Peace Commission. For another Princeton classmate in
uniform, William M. Whitney, the best Allen could do was arrange an introduction to the president. Reverting to the breeziness of the campus,
Whitney asked, "Well, what are you doing over here, Mr. Wilson?" The
president, just embarking on the last, greatest political and diplomatic
experience of his life, replied in the sudden candor due a man from Old
Nassau, "I'm really not sure that I know."[18]

Allen, however, was not yet secure enough for self-deprecation. At
hand was his main chance; he was on the verge of encountering the force
that would organize the rest of his life.

— 3 —

BANQUO'S GHOST

RELAXED ON HIS OCEAN CROSSING in December 1918, Woodrow Wilson mused about the new force of Bolshevism taking hold in Russia. It is such "a curious policy," he remarked to his staff, its excesses a poison loose upon the civilized world, yet a force to be comprehended in sympathy. The president called it "a protest against the way in which the world had worked"; he said the "susceptibility of the people of Europe to the poison of Bolshevism was that their governments had been run for the wrong purposes." Wilson had welcomed the first phase of revolution, in February 1917, when Lenin's Menshevik rivals forced the overthrow of the tsarist autocracy; with that act, Wilson declared, "the great, generous Russian people [were] added in all their naive majesty and might" to the forces fighting for freedom and justice.[1]

Within his administration, however, were some who did not share the president's academic detachment. Throughout 1918 his advisers were deeply divided about how the United States should react to the revolution in Russia. Secretary Lansing was in the forefront of those raising the alarm. In August 1917, before the Bolshevik coup, Lansing predicted that Russia would have to pass through a "Jacobin" terror before a Napoleon could finally emerge to establish political liberties. He warned that the Russian terror would "far surpass in brutality and destruction of life and property the Terror of the French Revolution." Perhaps, but Colonel House, Wilson's most intimate foreign policy adviser and a more crafty political strategist, broke ranks with the secretary of state and advised that public criticism of the Bolsheviks "should be suppressed," for it would only "throw Russia into the lap of Germany." House dominated the preparation of Wilson's Fourteen Points program for the postwar settlement, delivered on January 8, 1918, and managed to keep the

47

American hand outstretched to Russia, even under the new revolutionary leadership.

Wilson was most receptive to the anti-Bolshevik arguments when they came not from conservative voices like Lansing's but from the American left. He was impressed by a memorandum he received in February 1918 from William English Walling, an American socialist and labor organizer, who warned in blunt terms of Bolshevik excesses. Wilson sent the memo to Lansing for comment, and the secretary jumped at the all too rare opening to the president's attention. "[Walling's memo] is really a remarkable analysis of the dangerous elements which are coming to the surface," Lansing replied, using the moment to press his anti-Bolshevik position.[2]

Allen, in Bern, found himself torn between the factions competing for the president's mind. Had things gone differently the year before, of course, he could have spoken with authority, as a man who had actually met this man Lenin in the course of his duties. That gaffe was too recent and too awkward to be talked about just yet. Hugh Wilson held forth with distaste about the Bolshevik representatives sent to neutral Switzerland; he found them uncouth — they employed "guttersnipe phraseology" — and he was delighted that the diplomatic corps chose to snub the impolite new Soviet mission. Allen made bold to differ, arguing that it was a tactical mistake to ostracize the Russian revolutionaries. "While we have a good right to have a righteous horror of the Bolsheviks," he wrote Foster in August, foreshadowing House's line, "it is no use telling them what we think of them and thereby throw them entirely into the camp of the Germans."

Allen wrote Uncle Bert to dampen what he imagined to be excessive fears in Washington, not realizing that Lansing was among those most given to excess on the subject. The spread of Bolshevism outside Russia was not inevitable, Allen argued: "It is quite generally realized that revolution means general and immediate starvation for great masses of the people." The secretary of state would not be soothed, certainly not by a young nephew who seemed to be presuming upon his limited experience; by October Lansing was becoming downright rabid on the subject of Bolshevism, "the most hideous and monstrous thing that the human mind has ever conceived. It appeals to the basest passions and finds its adherents among the criminal, the depraved, and the mental unfit."[3]

If in approaching the Paris Peace Conference the president was of two minds about the specter of revolution from the east, the military intelligence branch of the United States Army was on high alert from the start. On November 13, just two days after the armistice, Van Deman reported to Washington that across Switzerland, Italy, Holland, and elsewhere, "the Bolshevik elements and those associated with them are beginning their propaganda. . . . The first thing to be done is to ascertain how far this propaganda has permeated our troops. . . . Every possible effort should be made to get our troops home and demobilize just as rapidly as possible." Van Deman had no doubt of what the Bolsheviks were about: "a world-wide social and political revolution. In other words, the fulfillment of the dream of the Internationalists. If they are able to carry out their plans, we all know what will happen."[4]

At the very first meeting of the Peace Conference, Sunday afternoon, January 12, President Wilson interrupted the proceedings to raise the problem of Bolshevism, a "much vaster problem" than any on the conference agenda, he said. Though he personally doubted that this complex threat "could be checked by arms," the Allies should find some "course of action for checking Bolshevism as a social and political danger." Expressing agreement were David Lloyd George of Britain, confidently, and Georges Clemenceau of France, warily.*

Attempts to measure the impact of Bolshevism upon the Paris Peace Conference have stirred flights of imagery in the prose of diplomacy. Herbert Hoover called Russia "the Banquo's ghost sitting at every Council table." Thorstein Veblen, the liberal American economist, wrote that the effort to contain Bolshevism "was not written into the Text of the Treaty [but] may rather be said to have been the parchment upon which that text was written." Such contemporary assessments sounded odd to those who came after the Treaty of Versailles. After all, the text said nothing about Russia or Bolshevism. Eloquent chroniclers like Nicolson and Keynes led future generations to judge the Peace Conference on what it decided for the future of Germany, not of Russia. But in the mood of January 1919 when the conference began, the picture was quite clear. Ray Stannard Baker, faithful scribe of the Wilson legacy, wrote, "Paris cannot be understood without Moscow. Without ever being represented at Paris at all, the Bolsheviki and Bolshevism were powerful elements at every turn. Russia played a more vital part at Paris than Prussia!"[5] As final testimony to that academic exercise called the Inquiry, it is necessary to note that as the Peace Conference began, there existed not a single report, not a single recommendation, not a single study about the potential impact of Bolshevism upon the world.

Allen had returned to Bern for Christmas to close his flat and say his mellow farewells to the diplomatic clubmates upon his new assignment

---

* Looking back, George Kennan saw a class basis for opinions about Bolshevism. "Allied social circles," including, of course, the State Department and Secretary Lansing, were much more anti-Bolshevik than elected politicians like Wilson and Lloyd George.

to Paris. These were men senior to him who had nurtured his professional skills and who now watched in envy at his entrée to the realm of high policy. Wilson, Dolbeare, Herter, Gibson, and the others had laid on a Christmas dinner at an old Bern townhouse — but the Swiss butler intervened to warn that the floor might give way and propel the whole crowd into the river. So for old times' sake, Allen and the club took their Christmas dinner at the Bellevue Palace.

After a holiday pause Allen went back to work, paying farewell visits to the disparate persons who had helped establish his expertise. From those conversations came forebodings that settled his earlier ambivalence about Bolshevism. His final report from Bern was dispatched on December 30:

> During the past few days I have had occasion in Berne to talk with a number of Lithuanians, Poles, Hungarians and Austrians. Their own internal, political and economic difficulties appear to be forced into the background as a result of their dread of the Bolshevik invasion. In pleading for immediate military assistance, two leading Lithuanians stated that the present feeble but anti-Bolshevik Government in Lithuania and the Pilsudski Government in Poland were the last line of defense between a Germany that was tending more and more toward Bolshevism and the forces of Lenine in Russia.
>
> Polish and Lithuanian informants in Switzerland agree that the Allies should not be deterred from a military expedition because of the fear that it would require hundreds of thousands of men. All they ask is a small army as a nucleus for their own forces. They affirm that the growth of the Bolshevist power is due to the fact that they have never met a serious military defeat.[6]

Allen thus confirmed in his own mind that Bolshevism represented a transnational threat to the established order. Gone were his earlier musings about the social grievances that made Bolshevism so attractive to the masses of eastern Europe. And he argued that the means to confront Bolshevism need not be massive, just a small nucleus of armed professionals to bolster indigenous democratic forces. Allen Dulles had begun his Cold War.

— * —

On the second day of 1919 Allen reported to his new boss at the Paris Peace Conference, Charles Seymour, a thirty-four-year-old historian from Yale. No longer could the pulchritudinous youths be content with gazing out upon the Place de la Concorde; the task of remaking the world was about to begin. "At least I have a desk and some paper to work with," Allen wrote Herter. Seymour, though knowledgeable about the English Constitution, found himself responsible for assessing obscure political movements in Germany and Austria-Hungary; he was desperate for an assistant who knew what cryptic messages from faraway places were all about. Seymour was one of those sheltered gentlemen of New England who sought, and always found, the best qualities in members of their own class — and who of course knew no others. Thus young Dulles, Princeton '14, the secretary of state's nephew and all that, was "absolutely first-class, just as nice as he can be, young, very willing to work in any capacity." Seymour was far too confident to ignore his limitations, and he gave his assistant plenty of room. "Dulles is working out very well," he wrote his wife at home. "He knows all about political intelligence and I know little."[7] Allen, in turn, seemed perfectly prepared to accept Seymour's lack of expertise — after all, his first role models had been Penfield and Stovall. "I do not want to get the reputation of being a disturbing element," he wrote Hugh Wilson.*

With his proven amiability, Allen fared considerably better in getting established at the Peace Conference than his brother Foster, who arrived thinking he could take over all the economic planning of postwar Europe. The brothers had a reunion dinner at a fashionable restaurant, where Allen tried to convey the realities of bureaucratic politics, but to little avail. Foster went on agitating among competing factions of specialists to the point that President Wilson himself had to step in to check his evident power plays. Allen's style proscribed ever being caught in such maneuvering. Quietly and without calling attention to it, he enlarged the scope of the duties Seymour gave him, displaying his analytical skills to an ever broader constituency of delegates. His uncle, however, was not impressed. Uncle Bert and Aunt Eleanor invited Allen to dinner one night with Hugh Gibson and others of the diplomatic club, but the evening was tedious. Lansing held forth with a pomposity swollen to the same degree that his influence had contracted, and Allen matched him. Lansing noted in his diary that his nephew gave him "a lot of advice on how to run things [but] his judgment was not very sound."

Allen remained under Seymour's tutelage less than one month, for his expertise was summoned to the higher task of coordinating the intelligence reports that were coming in from all sources. As his replacement, Allen furthered club loyalty by proposing Chris Herter, who, Allen knew, had the background to get on with Seymour. The scholar of the English

---

* Wilson and the other diplomats languishing in the provinces (that is, away from Paris) hungered for scraps of information from their more fortunate colleagues, and Allen was loyal to his old friends, sending a letter every few days with the latest gossip.

Constitution promptly pronounced young Herter "just as nice as they make them."

In supervising all the American observers roaming around central Europe — the agents in Hoover's relief teams were slow in getting started, and other ad hoc sources had to be improvised — Allen learned important lessons about managing intelligence networks. He found that field agents far from headquarters were full of insights into their own region but longed for a sense of what was happening back home. Allen took care to send informative advisories as well as to ask the pointed questions pioneered the year before by Lippmann and the Inquiry. "Is there evidence of Russian propaganda?" he asked his agents. "Are there active revolutionary groups of importance? Are revolutionary outbreaks likely to occur? If so, will they succeed?"

> It has been difficult in some instances in the reports already received to make out whether you are merely exposing the position which is presented to you, or whether you are actually in sympathy with that position. It would be most helpful if you will clearly distinguish between what is told to you and your valuation or criticism of it. . . . Wherever possible, make definite and precise recommendations of lines of policy which it would be desirable for America and the Entente to follow.[8]

Terse instruction, specific questions: many could not be answered with certitude, of course, but the effort was often enlightening to uninformed policymakers, who needed all the help they could get. The contrast with the mushy and poignant appeals from the State Department for "political information" — whatever that might be — could not have been more striking. Across the committee rooms of Paris, Old World delegations were taken aback at how much better informed the newly arrived Americans were about current realities across central Europe. "Their knowledge was greater than mine," wrote Harold Nicolson; "their power was infinitely more impressive, their scope was wider."[9] At the start of a new international era, when few guideposts directed procedures for the new statecraft, the Allen Dulles style of intelligence reporting was taking shape.

Over four days in February Allen helped brief one of the pulchritudinous youths, William C. Bullitt, about a mission to Moscow to ascertain Lenin's real objectives. Van Deman was skeptical about the mission. "Many loyal Americans have been badly fooled by the propaganda put out by the Russian-Bolshevik set-up," he wrote, citing Bullitt as a prime example. Allen, characteristically, was more willing to give a colleague the benefit of the doubt. In the event "Billy" Bullitt, headstrong and ambitious, exceeded his authority, and upon his return from meetings with

Lenin and other leading Bolsheviks found that no one in Paris — not even Allen — would listen to him. Years later Allen looked back in sorrow upon another near miss for useful contact with the Bolsheviks. "Here the first chance — if in fact it was a chance — to start talking with the Communist leaders was lost."

— * —

When the Dulles brothers lunched together on Saturday, March 22, Allen informed Foster that "the bubble has broken in Budapest," citing urgent telegrams flowing in with reports of a rebellion in Hungary. The revolution was spilling across the borders of Russia.

The defeat of 1918 had brought unceasing ferment to Hungary, a backward portion of a dying empire suddenly cast out on its own. Socialists and revolutionaries of all stripes clashed daily with unrepenting monarchists and reactionaries, each with loyalists inside the country and mentors in outside capitals east and west. Hugh Gibson had made a quick reporting trip to Budapest in January, and he repeated to Allen the remark of Count Michael Károlyi, the liberal politician who maintained a tenuous grip on state power after the fall of the Hapsburgs: "Why do you go on pretending that you are fighting for the rights of small peoples?" Károlyi asked the American envoy. "Why not . . . say frankly, 'We have won and shall now do with you exactly as we please?' Hungary would then know definitely where she stood."[10]

By March the manipulations of the victorious external forces lit the fuse under Károlyi's government. A French military agent conveyed garbled news that the Peace Conference was deciding to establish a neutral zone in Transylvania, the Alsace-Lorraine of eastern Europe, constantly disputed between Hungary and Romania. Hungarians, seething in their national identity crisis, concluded that their homeland was being dismembered. The weary Károlyi gave up, and into power was swept a thirty-two-year-old soldier named Béla Kun, who as a prisoner of war in Russia had well learned the rhetoric of Bolshevism. Kun proclaimed a Soviet Hungary and denounced "Wilson's deceitful and perfidious peace program."

The assessments flooding across Allen's intelligence desk were contradicotry. Some saw the long-feared international revolution and urged military intervention. "The Bolshevik leaders in Bohemia, in Germany-Austria, and in Hungary have close connections, and a unified movement is being attempted," wired the intelligence agent attached to Hoover's team in Prague. "It is, therefore, essential to use a strong hand to show the people that the Allies will not tolerate anarchy." From his desk in Paris Seymour recommended that Romanian and Czechoslovakian troops be unleashed to march on Budapest: "The more the movement spreads, the greater the danger that it will really get hold of Germany. . . . I believe that a small Allied force holding Budapest could control the situation, for that is the center from which everything radiates."[11] Others, however, saw indigenous sources of revolution. A member of Allen's analytical staff stressed that land reform and inept government had led to the explosion. The most authoritative voice was that of Captain Nicholas Roosevelt, an intelligence agent in Budapest who lived through the first thirty-six hours of the Kun regime and rushed back to Paris to report. He found the revolution in Hungary "primarily nationalistic in character. The Hungarians . . . have made use of Bolshevism as a last desperate resort." Roosevelt's civilian colleague (and Allen's old Princeton professor), Philip Marshall Brown, remained in Budapest and counseled calm. "I venture to state that I believe it possible to prevent Hungary from becoming completely Bolshevist by prudent action," he informed the delegation in Paris.[12]

Soviet Hungary in 1919 was Allen's first experience of revolution. Though diligent in assembling the incoming intelligence reports, he did not shrink from appending his own views of a policy response. Not for him any academic handwringing about root causes or iffy reactions; the Monday morning after the Budapest coup he was ready with a full-scale plan for military intervention to crush the revolution. Entitled "The Present Situation in Hungary: Action Recommended by A. W. Dulles," the paper went straight to President Wilson.[13] It outlined a three-point program to isolate Hungary from neighboring countries, restore "control" over Budapest, and, a point that raised diplomatic eyebrows, prevent "repetition of the mistakes" that allowed the coup to happen. Czech and Romanian troops should be unleashed across the Carpathian Mountains; gunboats should be sent to Budapest and food supplies as well, as long as orderly distribution could be arranged. As for those diplomatic "mistakes," Allen was blunt in suggesting that France should no longer be allowed to make mischief to preserve her own power position in eastern Europe.

One of Allen's proposed measures was implemented: a twenty-five-car train of Hoover's food supplies was allowed to pass through an Allied blockade. As for the rest, Allen was growing accustomed to rejection. "There is not a flicker of a hope of having American troops sent into Hungary, or anywhere else in Central Europe at the present time," he wrote Hugh Wilson.

The call for military intervention against Soviet Hungary divided friends and allies as March turned to April. French officials, deep in their eastern intrigues, were all for Allied military action; Allen opposed the

French designs but argued, as he had earlier for Lithuania and Poland, that a modest military intervention would restore and sustain democratic government. Nicolson, though he had become Allen's best friend among the British diplomats, argued firmly that whatever else might be done, "we cannot attack Bolshevism by force." It was, ironically, the American military representative on the Peace Commission, General Tasker H. Bliss, who made the most articulate arguments against the kinds of military intervention that Allen and others were contemplating: "Any nation which takes upon itself expenditures for military operations intended to check the universal revolutionary tendency in Europe, will be assuming a burden that will last for indefinite years. If we are once committed to it, in any degree, it will be difficult to withdraw. . . . I cannot convince myself that it is wise, from any point of view, for the United States to engage in the work of combatting these new forces of revolution."[14]

President Wilson never recorded his personal reaction to the Bolshevik coup in Hungary. He spoke with airy eloquence in the conference plenary sessions, echoing General Bliss: "To try and stop a revolutionary movement with field armies is like using a broom to stop a vast flood." He also confessed to feelings of guilt for Károlyi's downfall; the fateful discussion about Transylvania had taken place in his absence.

Allen chafed under the immobility of the statesmen in Paris. "If the present defiance of Hungary is left unchallenged, the last credit of the Paris Conference will have vanished and any peace treaties which may be made here will be discredited before they are seen. Now is the opportunity before the peace to reestablish the prestige of the peacemakers. The world needs a declaration from President Wilson to restore its confidence in his principles." House found it difficult to focus the president's mind — on the Kun coup, on the proposals from Lenin brought back by Bullitt, on anything connected with Bolshevism. Wilson's "one-track mind was against taking up this [Russian] question at present," House complained to his diary. Not quite so. Wilson had not finished with Bolshevism; it was rather that he did not want to discuss it with House or any other advisers whose differing views he knew quite well already. On March 26, the very day he rebuffed House's attempt to get a hearing, Wilson turned to another source for an opinion, to the freewheeling Herbert Hoover, who was deeply involved in the realities of both central Europe and the Peace Conference but independent of the diplomatic establishment.

Allen lunched that day at the Crillon with Gibson, who was excited about a new and unconventional perspective on Bolshevism jelling in Hoover's mind. Two days after Wilson asked his views, Hoover submitted a remarkable memorandum, the last thoughtful statement about Bolshevism to appear in the records of the American peace delegation, the finale in the ailing president's attempt to comprehend and cope with the threat of revolution from the east. In his diary Gibson cut through the verbiage of a formal memorandum to convey the essence of Hoover's thinking.

> [Hoover] has come home with some new thoughts on the Bolshevist question and is embodying them in a memorandum for the President. He begins with the statement that there have been grievous injustices to the lowest classes in all the countries that have been affected.... If we were to send an army of occupation into Hungary, it would in effect be for the purpose of forcing the peasantry back into their old position and consolidating the rich landowners in their old privileges.... Our soldiers would soon find out the true state of affairs and we should soon have great discontent at home at our doing the work of other countries. Further it would entail an occupation of the Lord knows how many years and would cost a great many lives.
>
> The constructive part of the idea is this. [Hoover] says that each side [in the Russian civil war] is now frightened to death of the other and that if we know how to avail of the opportunity we can perhaps get something done. He proposes to send a neutral who could command the confidence of both sides to Petrograd to talk to the Bolcheviki, tell them that he thinks he might secure from the Entente a contract to supply Russia with food supplies if the Bolcheviki would undertake to refrain from military aggression or foreign propaganda. That at least would tend to keep the trouble localized and if food could be got in to them it might in time stir the orderly classes to take some steps to straighten matters out.[15]

To the president, Hoover concluded with a ringing peroration, in effect the outline of a proposed presidential address comparable to the Fourteen Points.

> I feel strongly the time has arrived for you again to reassert your spiritual leadership of democracy in the world as opposed to tyrannies of all kinds. Could you not take an early opportunity to analyze, as only you can, Bolshevism from its political, economic, humane and its criminal points of view, and, while yielding its aspirations, sympathetically to show its utter foolishness as a basis of economic development; show its true social ends; rap our own reactionaries for their destruction of social betterment and thereby their stimulation of Bolshevism; point, however, to the steady progress of real democracy in these roads of social betterment.[16]

The economic power of American capitalism was thus invoked at this early stage as the most devastating weapon to confront Soviet communism, wherever in the world it might spread.

Hoover's specific proposal of using food supply as a political lever caused turmoil among the diplomats at the Crillon, was denounced as insulting by Bolshevik apologists like Bullitt, and was ultimately rejected by Moscow. More significant is that as late as the spring of 1919 an American capitalist like Herbert Hoover could argue for sympathetic consideration of the Bolsheviks — not for the way their revolution was working out, but for the conditions of social injustice that brought it about; further, could argue that the United States should not succumb to the forces of reaction and social oppression but rather accept the Bolsheviks' grievances and attempt to turn their practices and tactics in a direction more conducive to real democracy. The last serious appeal for an accommodation with Bolshevism that Woodrow Wilson ever received came not from the liberal idealists or Democrats in his faithful entourage but from the millionaire Republican engineer who would stand for future generations as the symbol of stolid, conservative reaction in the United States.

The story of Bolshevik Hungary petered out over the months of summer. Nicolson regaled Allen with the comic-opera aspects of a mission to Budapest in April by the formidable General Jan Smuts of South Africa, representing the powers of Paris, about as unlikely a personage as could be imagined to deal with a bewildered Hungarian soldier-turned-Bolshevik. Béla Kun was finally overthrown on August 1, as a reactionary Romanian army closed in on his capital, only to be replaced by a monarchist regime under the Hapsburg Archduke Josef. To the Peace Conference a Bolshevik Hungary seemed bad enough, but a return of the Hapsburgs was totally unacceptable.

Filing reports faithfully throughout the Hungarian turmoil was the military intelligence officer of the Hoover mission in Budapest, Captain Thomas T. C. Gregory, who would achieve a modest immortality in the annals of American diplomacy. Hoover's insistence that the intelligence agents on his relief teams report *en clair*, without suspicious diplomatic codes, had produced an outpouring of American ingenuity in phrases and descriptions that only another American would understand. "Slang that had been dead for fifty years came to life," Hoover wrote late in life, by that time rather proud of his intelligence men. "Slang of armies, baseball, football, colleges, stock markets and service clubs spread over the wires." Gregory proved without peer in the exercise. The Peace Conference ordered the American officer to inform Archduke Josef that his government would never gain recognition and must step down immediately in favor of a more representative social democratic coalition. Persuasive in his mission, Gregory transmitted the following message to Paris, faithfully *en clair*. "Archie on the carpet 7 P.M. Went through the hoop at 7:05."* Thus the official communications of the United States government reported the final downfall of the House of Hapsburg.

— * —

Bolshevism was the nightmare to the men of Versailles, but morning brought the practical tasks of designing a new Europe upon the wreckage of the Central Powers and of fashioning a League of Nations that would make future wars unnecessary. Allen and Foster were settled into the Crillon: Foster's preoccupation was the package of reparations that would draw a defeated but ever industrious Germany back into the world economy; Allen's responsibility, once his estimable intelligence system was up and running, was defining the borders of the successor states in the former German and Austro-Hungarian Empires.

He and Seymour were assigned the problem of Czechoslovakia, which was declared an independent state after the collapse of the Hapsburgs, embodying all that was promising and problematic in the Wilsonian dream. The patterns of history, ethnic division, strategic concern, and economic viability were all invoked to define the new Czechoslovakia. But Allen's enduring legacy in the Versailles peace settlement was the status of three million ethnic Germans in what came to be called the Sudetenland of Bohemia. His decisions led to a *casus belli* two decades later.

The Sudeten Germans were an industrious and proud population, holding themselves comfortably aloof from the Slavic working class all around. From the Middle Ages on, entrepreneurs had spread into the Sudeten hills from Saxony and Bavaria; over five centuries these Germans lived as a privileged elite in a backwater of the Hapsburg domains. The Czech nationalists who descended on Paris in 1919 regarded them as intruders upon their homeland. Their presence was not a political threat, for the Germans of the Sudetenland had not developed a strong political consciousness, but rather an economic distraction, for the founders of modern Czechoslovakia counted upon the Sudeten riches to

* "I had this code message translated into more formal language and sent to Prime Minister Clemenceau," Hoover related. The Old Tiger, "having been a reporter on a New York newspaper, needed no translation, but seized the original as a 'memento' of the war." Months later, as Hoover left Paris, he paid a courtesy farewell on Clemenceau, who pulled out a drawer in his desk and produced the original telegram, saying 'I keep it close by, for that episode was one of the few flashes of humor that came into our attempts to make over the world'" (Hoover, *Memoirs*, pp. 307, 404, 482).

endow the less developed Slovakian region. Even before the armistice the British Foreign Office had warned its American counterparts that with regard to this German population of Bohemia, "we shall be confronted with a very difficult problem."[17]

From his experience in Vienna and Bern, Allen was assumed to know more about the arcane ethnic problems of central Europe than the others at the Crillon, so it seemed only appropriate for him to be the American representative on the Czechoslovakia commission. His French and British counterparts were Jules Cambon and Harold Nicolson. Cambon considered Allen and Seymour the "two babies" of the conference; Nicolson hit it off with Allen from their first lunch together and noted that "it seemed to us that the drafting of peace would be a brisk, amicable and hugely righteous affair."

The cause of Czech nationalism had acquired a resonance in the United States out of all proportion to the population and space involved. As far back as 1889 a young Princeton history professor, Thomas Woodrow Wilson, had written, "No lapse of time, no defeat of hopes, seems sufficient to reconcile the Czechs of Bohemia to incorporation with Austria." "Everything about the Czechs appealed to Wilson," George Kennan wrote years later. "He liked little peoples, and disliked big ones. He liked Slavs, and disliked Germans.... To Wilson, the Czechs were innocent and idealistic, and in every way eligible to be patronized."[18]

By the time of the Peace Conference, therefore, the Czechs were far ahead of the Hungarians, Serbs, Romanians, Ruthenians, and other minorities of the fallen empire in gaining American sympathies. Tomáš Masaryk, the liberal philosophy professor who was proclaimed Czechoslovakia's first president, stood out from the nondescript leaders of lesser European minorities, an urbane European intellectual of bearded dignity. President Wilson could converse with him as a fellow professor; his Czechoslovak declaration of independence was deliberately fashioned upon the American experience. By the armistice Masaryk already had in his pocket a ten-million-dollar loan from the United States. Nicolson's superior on the British delegation, an Australian diplomat with limited knowledge of central Europe, was invariably ready to let "our friends the Czechs have what they want."

In Masaryk and Eduard Beneš, the protégé who became his foreign minister and eventual successor as president, the Czechoslovak independence movement was blessed with two sophisticated and persuasive champions, skilled at making their case most compelling to the outside world. Within the ranks of the Allied delegations, partisans of Czechoslovak independence had found good placements for furthering their cause.* Beneš went to work in Paris right after the armistice; he was worldly wise enough to ignore the considerations of protocol that other diplomats took in such earnest. To anyone at any level who might be helpful, he would turn on charm, intellect, or idealism as appropriate. Seymour was a pushover: Beneš, he wrote, "is a delightful little chap, just as friendly and as moderate as one could wish." Nor was Allen immune to flattering approaches. Beneš dispatched the provisional prime minister, who had met Allen the year before in Bern. "The other night, the Prime Minister of Czechoslovakia called for me in his motor-car," Allen wrote his mother, "and took me out to a tête-à-tête at Foyots, all because he wanted a little more of the Silesian coal mines."

The victors of World War I would almost have had to go back to war, Allen wrote later, if they had tried to take away the independence of Czechoslovakia.[19] At the start of the Peace Conference Seymour could innocently assure President Wilson that "the establishment of a Czechoslovak state is now a fait accompli. Its governmental machinery has been organized, and it only remains to fix the conditions of its existence and of its frontiers." Only. The state was an artificial construct from the start in its cavalier disregard for the fact that Czechs and Slovaks were quite different peoples and that neither populace had elected Masaryk and Beneš as their leaders.

The frontiers Seymour and Dulles set out to draw could follow various lines, none of which made sense all around. Allen later described the shape they finally settled on as "a banana lying across the face of Europe."[20] Ethnic and linguistic distinctions were an obvious measure, but often these intertwined from one farmyard to the next. Topography was a natural guide to defensible frontiers, but in some places long historical associations defied the natural barriers. Economic linkages were considered essential to the viability of the emerging states. Within the frontiers claimed by Czechoslovakia were some of the richest coal mines of the Hapsburg Empire, upon which Vienna, Budapest, and other non-Czech centers depended. The new nation embraced so many minority groups — Hungarians, Ruthenians, and, above all, Germans — that fully one-third of the population claimed by the new state turned out to be neither Czech nor Slovak.

At one solemn meeting, as Allen's working commission attempted to

---

* In this effort, accompanied by effective "penetration" of the American policymaking machinery to gain sympathy, the Czechoslovak campaign had a notable analogue some years later in the Zionist campaign after World War II to gain United States support for a Jewish state in Palestine. Chaim Weizmann played a role comparable to that of Masaryk and Beneš, and Zionist sympathizers like David Niles and Ben Cohen were strategically placed within the administration of Harry S. Truman.

explain the options to the four heads of government in Paris, Nicolson found Lloyd George making suspiciously fast work of the exercise. Only gradually did it dawn on the young British diplomat that his prime minister believed he was looking at the lines and colors of an ethnic map, when it actually was topographic — relief lines defining mountains and valleys, not fault lines of language or nationality.

Though Allen later found it convenient to forget it, his intelligence teams confirmed the restiveness of the Sudeten Germans; they predicted that newly empowered troops from Prague would enter age-old German villages and summarily order that the signs on storefronts be written in Czech. Most notable was a dispatch on January 12, 1919, from Archibald Cary Coolidge of Harvard, sent from Paris as a special fact-finding emissary. Analyzing in scholarly detail the conflicting claims to the Bohemian rim, Coolidge concluded:

> The great argument on which the Germans of Austria and Bohemia rest their case is, as they are never tired of repeating, the principle of self-determination. To tear away some three millions of Germans from their fellows and to unite them against their wills to a Czechish population of barely double their numbers would not only be a most flagrant violation of the principles which the Allies and especially the United States have proclaimed as their own, . . . but would utterly destroy any hope of a lasting peace.*

This argument was persuasive, at least among the Americans, in the first weeks of the Peace Conference. Seymour's early papers simply assumed that northwestern Bohemia should be incorporated into Germany. "The small line . . . separating Germany from Bohemia . . . has been very easily fixed up," the constitutional historian from Yale wrote home. Allen concurred. If Germans of the former Hapsburg domains want to join Germany, he wrote Hugh Wilson, "nothing should be done to stop" them. That letter was written on January 29, and on that same day the Peace Conference felt the full impact of the contrary Czech case: Foreign Minister Beneš was formally presented to the assembled powers.

Eloquent and sincere, wreathing himself in Wilsonian idealism, he pledged his people "to adopt the European and human point of view, and base their claims on the very principles the Conference was assembled to establish" — such a welcome contrast to the other petty nationals parad-

---

* This dispatch is perhaps the most articulate — and prescient — statement to reach the Peace Conference of the Sudeten German case, which would later be trumpeted by Hitler and conceded by Britain and France in appeasement at Munich in 1938. It was also one of the early intelligence reports that provoked Dulles's instructions to Coolidge to "clearly distinguish between what is told you and your valuation and criticism."

ing so presumptuously through Paris. Beneš drew variously upon the claims of history, nationality, security, and economic viability to argue his case, smoothly choosing among these criteria the one in each claim that happened to justify the broadest possible expanse for his new state. In an injured tone Beneš dismissed the pretensions of the Sudeten Germans. Their numbers had been exaggerated by simple mendacity. The borders of Bohemia had been recognized from time immemorial. The presence of any Germans at all within these hallowed lines was "the result of centuries of infiltration and colonisation"; all the Czechs wanted was "restoration of the land taken from them."

Allen, Seymour, and Nicolson, sitting behind their principals, were enthralled. "He displayed a moderation of tone, an appreciation of the needs of the presumptive minorities, a recognition of the responsibilities of the Czechoslovak state towards these minorities, that promised well," Seymour wrote. "His reasoning that the economic resources of the new state deserves especial protection was cogent." Nicolson gushed even further: Beneš sought "to maintain in Paris the moral prestige which the Czechs had won during the war. I say, '*Parfaitement, Excellence.*' Altogether an intelligent, young, plausible little man with broad views."

Beneš spoke for three hours: spellbinding and compelling, but three hours. When he finished, Clemenceau abruptly closed the meeting with the injunction, "Now we had better have a cup of tea." As they walked out of the chamber, a delegate of one of the yet unheard nationalities wearily remarked to Seymour, "The fact that our case is of the greatest importance does not prevent the big men from going to sleep, and the fact that they go to sleep will not prevent them from judging."

About the Sudeten Germans there was no further real discussion as the commission on Czechoslovakia continued to draw lines on the maps. Reversing his earlier views, Allen warned the commission on March 14 of "great danger" in separating the Sudeten territories from the new Czechoslovakia. Some two decades later, when the Sudetenland became the token to appease Adolf Hitler, Allen and Seymour compared notes about their fateful decisions in Paris.* Allen expressed amazement that the demoralized Germany of 1919 had not even tried to annex the Sudetenland, in such contrast to the audacity of Hitler. "Apparently it did not occur to the Germans at that time that they could ask for any territory which had not been German before the war," he wrote. Seymour replied, in convenient forgetting, "the Sudetens themselves gave no indication of a desire to be incorporated in Germany."

---

* The two peacemakers had gone their separate ways, Seymour having become president of Yale, Allen a prosperous Wall Street lawyer.

The night of April 3 Wilson fell ill. The formal decision about the problematic frontier came the next day in a manner that revealed the Paris Peace Conference at its most capricious. Lansing had previously made a feint at asserting Wilsonian self-determination, though everyone knew that even his own delegates had abandoned the principle as far as the Sudeten Germans were concerned. The French delegates, ever mindful of continental strategy, argued that the Sudeten hills would be more effective than any League of Nations in protecting young Czechoslovakia from invasion by a future expansionist Germany. House, rather than Lansing, took the American seat at the plenary session that day; unlike Lansing, House had paid little attention to this bothersome German-Czech issue and wanted only to move on to serious matters of world peace.

House arrived six minutes early for the meeting and by chance so did Clemenceau. They chatted informally. By the time Lloyd George and Vittorio Orlando of Italy appeared, the United States and France had agreed that only the historic border of Bohemia made sense, with the Sudeten Germans inside Czechoslovakia. "It was so much simpler and less full of possibilities for trouble," House explained in his diary. There was no discussion. The Paris Peace Conference made its decision, which would stand until the leaders of Britain, France, and Nazi Germany met in September 1938 in Munich.

— * —

Allen's work at the Peace Conference droned on through the summer and fall, the pulchritude of youth fading before the calluses and wrinkles of power politics. "Notwithstanding all the pious utterances of European statesmen," Allen wrote to his father, "the policy of most of these governments over here is just as devious as it was a hundred years ago." The League of Nations, he complained, was being perverted into just another Holy Alliance, and Paris was turning into a replay of the Congress of Vienna. Instead of Wilsonian open diplomacy, decisions were being made in camera, on whim, and without due process. Lansing, smarting under House's preeminence, doodled intricate caricatures as he sat through endless sessions of palaver.* When even the doodling paled, the secretary of state spent much of his time wandering around Paris looking for antique Dutch silver for the old Washington home of John Watson Foster, which had passed to him.

* As he finished each drawing he would drop it on the floor. Seymour retrieved them as souvenirs and got Allen to have his uncle affix his signature. Lloyd George became equally intrigued. "I say, could I have one of those," he asked Lansing at one point; "they're awfully good." Lansing gave him the current sketch, which the prime minister folded carefully and put in his pocket with gratitude.

Even in Paris the pleasures of the diplomatic club were decorous; Allen and "Charlie" Seymour (as he had become by now) would sneak away from the Crillon for afternoon games of golf. In the evenings Foster and others would gather for bridge and amuse themselves with the erudite wit of the well-bred. Hugh Gibson noted the doggerel making the rounds of the American delegation:

ODE TO COLONEL HOUSE

Wholly unquotable
Always ungoatable
Secretly notable
Silence's spouse.

Darkly inscrutable
Quite irrefutable
Nobly immutable
Edward M. House.

On May 7 the printed draft of the peace treaty was to be presented to the German government; up to this point the vanquished had played no role whatever in the deliberation of the victors. "We have no special reason to be overproud of the treaty," Allen wrote, but "it affords the only existing basis on which the world in general can now get back to work. The future will show where its weak points are and where it must be changed." The formal signing ceremony convened June 28 in the Hall of Mirrors at Versailles; Allen and Foster were among the throng observing. "The German delegate couldn't stand up, he was so affected with emotion," Allen recalled. "Everybody attributed it to insolence. Poor fellow, he wasn't insolent that day, he was just plain frightened and he couldn't stand on his legs. I was sitting there not more than thirty, forty feet from him; the fellow couldn't get up, under the weight of the treaty."[21]

On Bastille Day of 1919 Foster and Allen Dulles finally ventured out into Paris. They roamed Montmartre, they explored the bistros. The two boys from the parsonage at Watertown joined young people the world over in taking their ease and did not return to the Crillon until four in the morning. Foster left Paris soon thereafter.* His work on postwar eco-

---

* Impressed with Foster's work at the Peace Conference, one of Wilson's top economic advisers arranged to have him offered a partnership at a leading New York law firm at three times his prewar salary. Dulles was careful to let this word out, and Sullivan and Cromwell, from which he had taken leave, got the message. At age thirty-two, Foster Dulles became a full-fledged partner of the firm.

nomic planning completed; the partners at his law firm were eagerly awaiting his return to scout out the new European business that would surely emerge. Allen was left to his own devices in the rapidly emptying Crillon. From afar, and in uncomprehending dismay, he observed the United States Senate tear apart the work of the Peace Conference. "What a mess the Senate is making out of the Treaty," Allen wrote home. "In view of the present state of the world, it is rather a serious responsibility to take, to hold up the instrument that more than anything else can contribute to the restoration of order."

With the senior diplomats gone, their juniors assumed ever greater responsibility for the lingering problems of a Europe reborn. Once again Allen found himself concerned with the stateless Jewish population. Circulating clandestinely through the diplomatic offices of Paris was a mysterious tract called *The Protocols of the Elders of Zion*, purporting to expose a Jewish plot to rule the world, and some serious people took the matter seriously. Allen argued before conference committees against the view that the Jews deserved national rights just like other ethnic minorities. "If we endeavor to set [the Jews] up as a privileged community," he asserted, "they will be subject to oppression on the part of the people who are not ready for so radical a change."

"The Conference has gone down hill pretty rapidly," Allen wrote a friend in October, "and nothing indicates this more clearly than the fact that it is almost impossible to rally a foursome for golf, and absolutely impossible to get four for bridge. . . . The charm has left the piazza, especially on a cold October morning when it is even too chilly for morning exercise on the cold stones." In a more serious vein he summed up his mood in a letter to the president of Princeton, John Hibben.

> The past year at the Peace Conference has been for me one of thrilling interest and opportunity. I have had a rare chance to get a glimpse into world politics and to play a small part on some of the minor committees of the Conference. . . . A year ago Europe was just waiting for us to lead them, and now we seem to be the ones that are dragging behind. . . . I hope to get back to the United States in the spring as I have been away almost four years, and a four years at that which has brought so many changes that I sometimes wonder whether I appreciate what is taking place in the United States.

Allen was homesick. Auburn and Henderson Harbor seemed an eon away, the nurturing home irrelevant to the concerns of maturity. Only with Foster, sharing the heady days and nights of Paris, was family intimacy maintained. Compounding the malaise of loneliness was a justified concern about his professional future. Many a young diplomat from many a land had been spoiled by the Paris Peace Conference — the attention lavished, the aspirations that seemed so clearly within grasp. As the year turned toward autumn and winter, Paris was no longer the center of action, and Allen scanned the world in vain for a diplomatic posting that might prove as challenging.

For the second time in his early career, the answer to professional uncertainty came out of the blue. On his Princeton graduation day, it was the unexpected offer of a teaching fellowship in India, allowing him to delay a career choice for which he was not yet ready. In late 1919 came Washington's decision to open official relations with the new Weimar Republic of Germany. Allen was still too junior, of course, to be entrusted with such a sensitive posting, but the more seasoned envoy named to head the new mission was Ellis Dresel, one of Allen's colleagues in Bern. Dresel, a lifelong bachelor from Boston, had assumed the role of paterfamilias to the younger clubmates; for his new posting he promptly asked for Allen as his deputy and Dolbeare as well, in a nostalgic reassembly of the old fellowship; Gibson had been named ambassador to Warsaw, but soon Hugh Wilson joined the others in Dresel's mission. Berlin, to Allen, was the one diplomatic post that, for action and high-level attention, might match the excitement of the Peace Conference.

The United States had no policy toward defeated Germany. Foster had been in the forefront of those in Paris who argued for lenient treatment of the kaiser's democratic successors, particularly the German industrialists, who could be brought so usefully into the emerging world economy. No one was as pleased with Allen's new assignment as his older brother, whose New York law practice represented syndicates of Wall Street bankers eager to invest in central Europe. Foster wasted no time in asking the new American mission to Germany to keep him apprised of investment opportunities. Allen, more sensitive than his brother to potential conflicts of interest, replied with cold formality.

> Ellis has shown me your telegram and letter to him regarding possible American investments in Germany. This will certainly be one of the questions that we will try to look into carefully when we get into Germany. As regards replying, I think you will understand that it will be difficult to submit the result of our investigation to any one group of businessmen in the United States such as might be represented by your firm. I should think the best way would be for you to keep in close touch with the Department of State and the Foreign Trade Advisors, who will probably get any information we may send on this point.

Foster persisted, patiently informing his younger brother that he had major deals in the offing and was not merely asking Allen's diplomatic co-

BANQUO'S GHOST

operation. "I may try to get you to help me, provided you felt that you could resign from the service, and I personally see no reason why you could not properly do so. . . . I will call you. . . . Think over this possibility." This was a heavy fraternal message, proposing a change of career from diplomacy to investment banking, and Allen was not ready to contemplate anything of uncertain propriety. "I feel rather strongly that it would be inappropriate to step out of government service *in a foreign country* and immediately take up private business there. In any case, therefore, I should desire to return to the United States before taking any final action." The idea hung in suspension.

— * —

Allen and Ellis Dresel boarded the train from Paris in the middle of January. Berlin at the start of 1920 was not yet in the throes of the elegant decadence celebrated a decade later by Christopher Isherwood and his boys, or Vicki Baum in her Grand Hotel; of the old imperial elegance none was left, and the seediness of democracy had not yet blossomed into abandon. Unemployed men walked the streets aimlessly; shabby women waited in bread lines. Reactionary military gangs, smarting under their defeat in war, swaggered through the nearby countryside on foraging missions, propagating the sophistry that they had been "stabbed in the back" by politicians. Radical leftists, some Bolshevik, some not, were agitating to spark a revolution. The social democratic Weimar government seemed vulnerable to a putsch from either extreme at any moment.

Gray rain clouds hung over the dilapidated stone buildings of a dirty, depressed, half-starved city as Dresel and Dulles arrived in the old Prussian capital to reinstate the American presence. They found the once imposing edifice of the prewar American Embassy at 7 Wilhelmplatz all of a piece with its surroundings. The plaster on the ceilings was flaking, heavy rains had not been kind to the tile roofs, and the diplomatic dining rooms were dotted with tin pans to catch the drips from above.

Under the leaking roof Dresel and Allen divided the social and political circles to be cultivated. Dresel, who had served in Berlin before the war, sought out the Weimar elites, the business and merchant classes. "They consider the financial condition of Germany almost beyond redemption and are afraid of losing all they have," he reported. He was puzzled when leftist demonstrators cheered the representative of the United States as he was driven by in his open gray army Cadillac, and concluded, "We are still more trusted in Germany than any other nation."[22] He left personal contact with these ungainly revolutionaries to his younger and more pliable deputy.

In the later Cold War years Allen would regale young CIA associates with tales of sitting cross-legged on the floor at communist cell meetings, which he found mundane and banal, in working-class sections of Berlin.* More impressive to his mind were the independent socialists, "the most mentally honest of the lot." Two young politicians of this faction became Allen's particular guides through Weimar Germany, Rudolf Hilferding and Rudolf Breitscheid, both destined in the years ahead to play tragic Hamlets in the German democracy.

Another new friend of this period had a different and more direct impact on Allen's later life. Gerhart von Schulze-Gaevernitz was a respected backbencher in the Weimar coalition. An eminent professor of economics at Freiburg, he was intimately connected in the financial and industrial circles of both Britain and Germany; even during the war he had risked outspoken criticism of the kaiser's foreign policies. In his world vision he was a protégé of Cecil Rhodes: Germany, Britain, and the United States, destined to global economic leadership, needed to find a basis for political cooperation so as to "preserve the dominance of Western European civilization." The wisdom of aging intellectuals seemed to appeal to Allen. He spent hours discussing the world of ideas and politics with the old professor, just as he had with Henry Haviland Field in Bern. Von Schulze-Gaevernitz too had a son whom he thought Allen might find congenial, but young Gero was off at university preparing for a career in international banking, so they did not meet at this time.

Shortly after Allen arrived in Berlin the Allies presented their first list of "war criminals" to be handed over for trial. The demand included nearly nine hundred people who had held public positions during the war, including von Hindenburg and three other field marshals, dozens of generals, admirals, chancellors, and ministers — even the crown prince and two royal brothers, charged, in a dethroning indignity, with petty larceny.† Allen worried about the effect that demands for vengeance would have within Germany; but he alone knew that the clause on war criminals in the Versailles Treaty had been drafted in Paris many months before by his own brother. That family happenstance could be kept quiet,

---

* The story went around the CIA in the 1960s that Allen had even met Rosa Luxemburg, by then a fabled heroine to radicals and feminists of all stripes. Unlike the Lenin story, there is no possibility of truth in this tidbit. Luxemburg was dead a full year before Allen set foot in Berlin, and it is doubtful that Allen claimed to have met her. A number of his associates in the intelligence business liked to embellish stories for after-dinner consumption as much as their boss did, with an obvious multiplier effect of exaggeration.

† When the humiliating list was handed over in Paris, the German representative took one look at the personages named and refused to accept the note. The French government had to arrange a special messenger to carry it to Berlin.

but another family development the same week put Allen in an awkward position: Lansing, obviously estranged from the ailing President Wilson, finally resigned as secretary of state. Allen's professional standing owed nothing to any special protection from Uncle Bert, but the gossip of the diplomatic corps swirled around him, and Dresel sensitively bundled his deputy off on a motor tour to Leipzig and Munich, where he could study local conditions and avoid embarrassment.

Allen spent only three months at his Berlin post, but in that time occurred the most momentous upheaval in the young Weimar Republic: the long-feared outbreak of revolutionary violence, but from the right, not the left.

On March 12, 1920, a Friday, two motley divisions of armed German troops, called the Freikorps, marched on the capital. Although the bulk of the German army had been disbanded, the Allies had allowed these units to remain in Lithuania to guard against a Bolshevik takeover of the Baltic states. Their officers joined with a reactionary politician named Wolfgang Kapp to challenge the socialist Weimar coalition.* Frightened cabinet ministers fled the capital, and on Saturday the Kapp forces seized the empty government buildings. The swaggering militarists seemed to have taken power; on their helmets was their private good-luck symbol, a bent-armed cross called the swastika.

That weekend Allen was on his way to Warsaw to see Hugh Gibson, but he quickly doubled back. "It was lucky that I took the Sunday night train from Danzig instead of waiting over a day," he wrote in apology to Gibson, "as otherwise I would not have been in time to see the revolution." The Danzig train was one of the last to reach Berlin before the socialist labor unions, more courageous than their political leaders, called a massive general strike, which paralyzed the country. Writing to Gibson, Allen at first made light of the situation.

> [Kapp] had absolutely no support, except 5,000 odd troops largely from the old "Iron Division" of the Baltic. . . . It will turn out to be a costly experience for Germany, but should at least show the democratic elements their strength. [President] Ebert and his cohorts hardly played the "Horatius at the Bridge" in the affair and their undignified flight to Stuttgart will not add to their prestige, but if they can find some new men to strengthen their cabinet and get back to Berlin before the Extreme Left is able to organize, I do not look for real trouble. . . . If you want a tame revolution instead of the opera, you may have to come soon.

---

* Another obscure politician of the day, agitating in Bavaria, tried unsuccessfully to fly to Berlin in time to exploit the uprising. This was Adolf Hitler.

But the Kapp putsch turned out to be not so tame after all, and Allen experienced for himself the violence of postwar Europe that he had previously analyzed only from afar. He started keeping a detailed day-by-day diary. Upon returning to Berlin on Monday morning, he found his embassy office facing barbed wire, cement bollards, and machine gun emplacements across the Wilhelmplatz. Trying to size up the situation with Dresel and Dolbeare, he worried that the social democrats "were actually allowing themselves to be fooled into negotiations with the Kapp gang. . . . If they did, I had no more use for them," he harrumphed. On Tuesday an impasse developed between the putschists and the crippling general strike. Factories, stores, and schools were closed; there were no street-cars, buses, water, electricity, or gas. By the end of Wednesday it was obvious that with the mobilization of the left-wing militants the Kapp putsch would go no further. "As a matter of fact the most interesting, if not the most critical, days were yet to come"; Allen saw for himself the raucous passions of antisemitism under the badge of the swastika. Preparing to evacuate their positions in the capital, he wrote,

> the Kapp forces indulged in some anti-Jewish demonstrations right before our windows. Thanks to posters and corner discussions the soldiers had worked themselves up to a high pitch of indignation against the Jews which they indulged by seizing the Jews they could lay their hands on and torturing them. I saw one in the Wilhelmplatz bleeding profusely taken by the soldiers into a dark court from where he did not reappear. . . . About noon the Kapp troops began to assemble in the Wilhelmstrasse with red, white and black banners flying, music and all the martial show possible. It was almost four o'clock before they started to leave and instead of going out the "back way" as they should have, they paraded down the Unter den Linden out through the Brandenburger Tor. . . . [They] shot into the crowd, killing and wounding a good many people.

The next day was not much better. Allen and a U.S. Army colonel

> took our automobile and started for the Wilhelmplatz, had just turned the corner of the Linden when some very heavy shooting took place just behind us in the Pariser Platz. In the Platz was a large Pantzer wagon manned by Sicherheitswehr and surrounded by a very large crowd of curious people. Suddenly the crew of the Pantzer wagon espied an automobile with some suspicious looking officers in it. As the auto did not stop in reply to the challenge the pantzer wagon fired and cleaned up the whole lot. It was a sight to see the crowd run. In two seconds the whole square was entirely vacant and the only people in sight were four men carrying a body across towards the Adlon under a white flag rigged with

handkerchiefs. It is remarkable on how little provocation there was shooting in Berlin during these days.

Emotion was never prominent in Allen's view of the world. He spent that Saturday arranging for the evacuation of Americans in his charge. Sunday morning he was awakened by heavy shooting, no longer from the reactionary militarists but from the radical left. An official of the foreign office warned the American diplomats of the possibility "that a Soviet government would be proclaimed in a section of Berlin in the course of the day." Allen immediately saw the ploy: the Germans were "trying to overexaggerate the difficulties of the situation" in the hope of gaining American sympathies. He went out to look for himself.

> The first thing I did on Monday morning was to take a ride in the auto around the working men's part of town. Around the post office we ran into very complicated wire entanglements which, in this direction, were apparently the outer defenses of the government troops. . . . It was impossible for them to hold all points against communists and looters. I saw many Communist posters and was told of quarters of the town where notices were posted up giving the recruiting places of the Red Army.

Almost overlooked in Allen's experience of a revolution was the fact that his brother Foster happened to be traveling through Germany during the week of the Kapp putsch in pursuit of investment opportunities for Sullivan and Cromwell's clients. The brothers had spent a few preoccupied days together before the marauding troops marched upon the capital, but their interests were sharply divergent. At the height of the tension, Foster went off to meet a young economist who was full of ideas to attract American financial support for the German future. His name was Dr. Hjalmar Schacht, and from that encounter grew a relationship between American investors and German industry that endured well into the 1930s, when Schacht was no longer quite so attractive to Foster's American clients.*

Foster worried that the Kapp putsch and the general strike would alarm American clients seeking secure investment opportunities. "Is there nothing that you can do," Foster wrote Allen, "either through the State Department or through the newspapermen to give a more truthful picture of the situation?" Allen saw through his brother's ploys as clearly as he did those of the Germans. He replied with no sympathy for investment opportunities won or lost and expressed confidence that the reports of unrest in Germany *were* giving a "truthful picture of the situation."

---

* Schacht was tried and acquitted of war crimes at Nuremberg after World War II.

More than ever before, the Dulles brothers' career interests were at odds. Foster's big deals were proving too precarious to allow him to renew his offer of giving his younger brother a piece of the business, and indeed Allen was not very taken with what Foster was doing. Though he was becoming intrigued by the international network of high finance through his long evenings with von Schulze-Gaevernitz, Allen was not impressed with the way his brother seemed to go around grubbing for deals. After Berlin they went their separate ways, each content in his chosen calling, at least for the time being.

Allen had been promised a home leave before the Berlin assignment came up, and Dresel understood that his deputy had the right to a break after the intensity of those March days. Allen turned twenty-seven on April 7, and three days later he formally applied for the two months' vacation in the United States that was due him. He crossed the Atlantic in mid-May, laden down with three heavy boxes of books and papers accumulated in his four years of European diplomacy. When he arrived at 67 South Street in Auburn, New York, at the beginning of June, social opportunities came up that were considerably more enticing than any he had previously known.

— 4 —

FINDING HIMSELF

THE INVITATIONS POURED IN that spring of 1920. Allen, hometown boy who had gone off to Princeton and then the world, was socially adept, affable — and, it was noted, thoroughly eligible. Should the conversation turn serious, Allen had quite a few stories to tell, of the Peace Conference, of Berlin in revolution, of the promise and tragedy of Woodrow Wilson. But usually the company was not serious, and in a relaxed setting, the earnest airs of the striving diplomat fell away to reveal the fun-loving undergraduate. On one of his first weekends home, Allen went to a house party at the Thousand Islands, a fashionable resort near Watertown. Among the Princeton men and socially acceptable young ladies, sons and daughters of old New York families, Allen was introduced to a Miss Todd. Clover Todd had actually seen Allen from afar once before. During the war she had served soldiers blinded in combat at an American officers' club in France. Among the "pulchritudinous youths" of the Peace Conference she had noticed this one, but had been told by a cousin that Allen Dulles was serious and pompous, not worth meeting. At the Thousand Islands house party, Clover decided her informant had been quite wrong — or at least Allen was now different from the man she had seen at the Crillon. That weekend he seemed handsome and witty, capable of an easy charm that beguiled all around him. As for Allen, he quite simply and on the spot fell in love with Clover Todd — the work-absorbed bachelor smitten as never before.

Allen returned from the house party, head whirling in infatuation, and announced to his parents that he had met the girl he wanted to marry. Wary at how such a meeting had occurred and whom he might have encountered in the years abroad, Edith Foster Dulles asked sharply, "Is she a Presbyterian?" By chance she was, and there was no further discussion. Allen proposed marriage to Clover one week after he met her.

Martha Clover Todd, a year or so younger than Allen, had wispy dark blond hair, brown-flecked green eyes, and a soft voice that was called, even by those who were not smitten in her presence, ethereal. If she appeared waiflike, a frail flower of the Victorian drawing room, she turned out to be vigorous and robust, an adventurous woman who loved the outdoors, riding, camping, and canoeing through the backwoods. She showed her venturesome nature early. Once, on vacation from boarding school in Farmington, Connecticut, she was invited to an evening with a New York society matron who wished to show social conscience by entertaining "some poor convicts" just paroled from Sing Sing penitentiary. The awkwardness of the evening was thoroughly predictable — until Clover called for some cards and challenged the earthy ex-cons to a game of poker. During the Great War she volunteered for duty in France, first as a canteen girl for the YWCA in Grenoble and Monte Carlo, then at the Paris officers' club. On a day off she dressed in rags and strolled the streets of Paris as a *mendicante*, just to feel for herself the experience of begging for bread.

"Clover" was an old Todd family name; a cousin, Admiral Richardson Clover, had served with the Office of Naval Intelligence during the Spanish-American War. Her father was the imperious Henry Todd, professor of romance languages at Columbia University, versed in Latin, Greek, and Sanskrit. His first reaction on hearing of his daughter's suitor was to consult the university library card catalogue to see if the young man had any scholarly achievements to his name. Coming upon the entry "Dulles, Allen W., *The Boer War*," acquired by the library some years before, he did not bother to read the small print: "The author of this pamphlet is eight years old." Dr. Todd declared himself satisfied with his daughter's intended — though, as the family retold the story in later years, it did occur to him when he noted the date of publication that this Dulles might be "a bit old" for Clover.[1]

The couple met as often as proper chaperons could be arranged over the next few weeks, but looming uncomfortably was the end of Allen's home leave. The bachelor fellowship of the Wilhelmplatz having lost its allure, Allen asked Dresel for a bit more time off: "A number of things have come up which slightly alter matters on my end. . . . It is just possible that for family and personal reasons it might be rather difficult for me to leave this country immediately on the expiration of my leave." But Dresel, determined to have his deputy and clubmate back, bombarded the State Department with pleas for Allen's return. To Allen himself he cabled, "Your presence is indispensable." Allen could not bring himself to admit what his "personal reasons" were, so he turned to Hugh Gibson for a discreet intervention. Dresel's pleadings notwithstanding, Allen was transferred temporarily to Washington duty just two days before the end of his home leave. The State Department blandly informed the head of the Berlin mission that "in view Dulles' knowledge general situation Central Europe his temporary detail to Department most desirable. . . . This detail agreeable to Dulles for personal reasons."[2]

In her personal correspondence, Clover confessed to a maiden's apprehensions about this meteor who had so suddenly come into her life. Her previous infatuations had been older, unapproachable gentlemen of spiritual bent—Henry James, for instance, to whom she had once been introduced: "so handsome, so nineteenth-century, . . . conveying something spiritual [which] enveloped him like a veil, . . . already living with a part of himself in that forward place, to which we all are going, and was looking on our world from that distance and vantage point." To Clover, Allen seemed like a character in a Henry James novel, "a gentleman, a bachelor in the prime of life, handsome and bold and pleasant, offhand and gay and kind." The lingering question, not yet ripe for answer, was whether Allen might be one of those Jamesian young men who hid, under his silk waistcoat, a soul of papier-mâché.

The engagement of Allen W. Dulles and Martha C. Todd was formally announced on August 3, 1920, and they were married two and a half months later at Woodlands, the imposing Baltimore estate of Clover's grandmother. Foster was Allen's best man. The marriage endured until Allen's death — almost fifty years. It was not, on the surface, a happy match. For long periods Allen and Clover lived fundamentally separate lives. From their three children came seasons of sorrow as well as pleasure. Several times they contemplated divorce. The years of intense, job-driven bachelorhood had set Allen on a self-centered course that a mere marriage ceremony, even a romantic infatuation, could not change. Clover was hardly the first woman he had known, and later he very much enjoyed the company of vibrant and powerful women. Clover, for her part, sought a life companion who could communicate, as Allen never could, on an emotional level. But when it came right down to it, the couple could not separate. Life with each other always remained preferable to life without each other. One of the few friends who was close to both remarked, "Allen and Clover weren't exactly made for each other. But they were both such extraordinarily unusual people that neither one could have found a *perfect* mate." When a curious nephew inquired many years later, Clover offered a matter-of-fact explanation: "I married Allen because he was attractive, and doing interesting things."

That autumn of 1920, Washington was not a happy place for partisans of Woodrow Wilson, certainly not for a nephew of the fallen Secretary Lansing. "I was too desperate and dangerous a character to keep" on State Department duty, Allen wrote Gibson. "The chief preoccupation of the Department appears to be to get me as far from Washington as possible." His one remaining mentor, Undersecretary of State Norman Davis, who had come to respect the abilities of both Dulles brothers at the Peace Conference, persuaded Allen that a new foreign post would be his best prospect at this juncture, however inconvenient for a new bride.

Allen turned down the first offer, the embassy in Bucharest, knowing from the reports of his intelligence teams that the Romanian capital was "a degenerate city," no place for the well-bred Clover. He was given only one alternative. Allen had experienced the collapse of two Old World empires, those of Austria-Hungary and Germany. The day before their marriage he announced to his bride that they would be moving together to the diplomatic life of another imperial capital in transition, the Byzantine and Ottoman city of Constantinople.

— * —

Constantinople in 1920 was a capital city without a country, a diplomatic crossroads without markers to any destinations among the ruins of the Ottoman Empire. Allen's area of responsibilities included once again the protection of American citizens — largely missionaries and oil men working in the Near East — but also the defense of United States interests against the imperial ambitions of Britain and France across the domains of the sultan.

Allen and Clover arrived on the Orient Express at two o'clock in the morning of December 12; despite the hour, waiting to greet them was Ferdinand Lamot Belin, their new diplomatic colleague at the American High Commission.* The Belins took Allen and Clover into their own home, one of the finest European houses in Constantinople, with a broad panorama upon the Bosporus, which divides Europe from Asia Minor, from the harbor of the Golden Horn far out to the Sea of Marmara, filled with the warships of a dozen nations. "On Sunday afternoon, their house becomes quite a 'salon' for the diplomatic and local society," Allen wrote his mother. "The latter consists largely of Levantines, Greeks, Americans, Jews, etc., who consider themselves quite superior to the Turks but who, with a few striking exceptions, are quite impossible."

It took Allen and Clover nearly a month to find their own first home,

---

* Technically Allen's new post was not an embassy. Since the Peace Conference had placed the former Ottoman domain under the direct rule of the victorious Allies, the mission was headed by a military high commissioner rather than an ambassador.

"a little frame ramshackle," Allen wrote, that stood alone amid vast blocks of dilapidated, burned-out buildings left from the war. "On the outside it has the appearance of a wooden hovel with all the peculiarities of local Turkish architecture — a second story with a perilous overhang and a general rambling appearance." The saving grace was a magnificent view over the Bosporus (not, of course, as grand a view as the Belins') and a small garden overgrown with wild vines of wisteria climbing up to the third story. "As for rooms we have seven or eight, depending on what you honor with that name. In any case there is plenty of space for the two of us and for the servants. Of the latter we now have three, a Greek chef (male) and two maids, one Russian, the other a Pole. Both have seen better times."

Indeed, all around them had seen better times. Constantinople had become the eastern entrepôt for the ruins of old Russia, with tens of thousands of refugees from the Bolshevik revolution and from the civil war raging in the newly independent states of the Caucasus to the north, Georgia and Armenia. Bearded Cossack generals and penniless noblemen spent their days selling violets and shoelaces from trays slung around their necks, their nights trying to sleep in the old city's cobblestoned alleys. The sole landmark of the shabby neighborhood where Allen and Clover settled was the Pera Palace Hotel with its discolored Moorish floor tiles and scrawny palm trees in copper pots, a favorite haunt of the Russian émigrés.*

The month before Allen and Clover arrived, the refugee population was swollen with the arrival of the defeated Cossack army of Baron General Peter Nikolayevich Wrangel, one of the last of the White armies to hold out against the Bolshevik advances. The revolutionary poet Mayakovsky later glorified Wrangel and his swashbuckling Cossack cavalrymen, but by the time they had evacuated the Crimea and arrived at Gallipoli, they were a starving and typhoid-stricken mass of punctured dreams, held together only by the charisma of their defeated general. "The suffering of these poor people is quite pitiful," Allen wrote Gibson. "Meanwhile, Clover and I find that we are expected to go to champagne dinner every night." Such contrasts of lifestyles became a major irritant. After their first month, Allen wrote home to Auburn: "On the whole, Constantinople is rather gay to suit us. People seem to have the mania of balls and often, to excuse their gaiety, they involve charity as the excuse. The other night we went to a great Jew charity ball, next week the Armenians do the same, then the various navies here have their balls, not to

---

* The Pera Palace also became a favorite site in popular espionage tales like Eric Ambler's *A Coffin for Dimitrios* and Ian Fleming's *From Russia with Love*.

mention the armies. We dodge as many balls as we can, but are lucky if we get off with less than two a week."

At first Clover coped; then, ever the adventurous soul, she came to thrive on the new experiences. Setting off on her own, laden with blankets and food parcels, she would pay regular visits to the Red Cross canteens on the docks, sometimes in the company of Olga Wrangel, the general's wife. They brought solace to the refugee camps on Gallipoli — clothing, cigarettes, and Russian magazines.[3] These expeditions caused no small alarm at the High Commission; the ranking officers pleaded with the new diplomatic secretary's wife to enlist a chauffeur-driven official car for her errands of mercy — precisely the display that Clover Todd Dulles did not want.

Belin ushered Allen in to his first meeting with the high commissioner, Rear Admiral Mark L. Bristol, a cagey old salt who launched into a shotgun briefing about the status of the former Ottoman lands stretching from the Balkans to Palestine and beyond. The briefing, Allen admitted, left him "entirely bewildered," but the point was clear: the Near East, Bristol said, was like "a mass of jelly — if you touch any part of it, the whole mass quivers." Allen settled into his responsibilities as Bristol's principal deputy on all diplomatic matters.

His first crisis came on February 25, 1921, when the advancing Bolsheviks occupied the Georgian capital of Tiflis (Tblisi). Once again the headstrong diplomat, Allen chafed at the outside powers' impotence to defend Georgia's independence, bestowed in the hubris of self-determination at the Peace Conference. He complained to Gibson, "Tiflis, their capital, is, they say, a very delightful city . . . on the road between Persia and the Black Sea and therefore a great place for antiquities and rugs which the Bolos have now probably seized or burned. When is it all going to end?"

"Constantinople is entirely isolated from direct contact with Soviet Russia," Allen cabled Washington after the fall of Tiflis, "as no ships have arrived from Bolshevik ports for days, and contact through Georgia and Armenia is now broken." Then he reported a singular discovery, that wireless radio communications between Moscow and Bolshevik outposts could be intercepted by shortwave receivers on Admiral Bristol's flagship in the sea of Marmara.[4] Allen was quick to exploit this novel intelligence source, and over the next months he supplied Washington with detailed information about the Bolsheviks in Russia and the Caucasus, including their designs on the capitals of Europe and even South America. This was an innovative means of intelligence collection, astonishing (and not a little unsettling) to conventional styles of diplomatic reporting.

Allen's haul was impressive. Between the shortwave traffic and General Wrangel's own intelligence nets, he pieced together a long Bolshevik report sent secretly to the Kremlin about how the world could be prepared for revolution. On July 2 he transmitted to Washington the text of a speech delivered at a Moscow party meeting. He pulled off the air a dispatch from a Bolshevik agent in the Western Hemisphere, reporting in glowing tones the "possibility of arousing a Communist movement in South America."*

Before long the task of monitoring the wireless traffic required two full-time translators, whom Allen hired from among the White Russians at the Pera Palace. By the autumn Allen's information flow was causing concern in Washington, not because of the content or even the means by which it was obtained, but rather because of the two translators, who were quite a drain on the budget, about $1,500 per annum. When Admiral Bristol could no longer support the expense from his War Department budget, he petitioned the State Department. The reply was negative. Thus ended Allen's first unique source of intelligence from Soviet Russia.

— * —

"There is one thing about Constantinople that is worth your while to remember," a seasoned diplomat advised a novice journalist: "If you only stay here long enough you will meet many men who matter, and you may find the key to many strange secrets." Receiving this advice, no longer a novice by the time Allen came to know him, was Philip Graves, the Constantinople correspondent of *The Times* of London. The two young men sought each other out amid the endless social whirl for they had a common interest in book collecting — for which pursuit Constantinople was a paradise with the arrival of erudite but penniless Russian intellectuals. "Hardly a day passes without a number of refugees turning up at this High Commission with a stack of old books for sale," Allen wrote.[5]

One spring day in 1921 a prominent member of the Russian émigré community approached Graves with a puzzling book. The Russian had

* "Of all the South American states the highest is Argentina and the situation there is the most advantageous for our work, as the economic position of this Republic is of great interest to capitalistic Europe," reported a Comrade Abramson. "Uruguay and Paraguay have no political meaning of their own and will be seized by any movement that will take place in Argentina. Work is also possible in Chile, but my idea is that to strike a real blow at European capitalism we must see to the victory of the Argentine proletariat. . . . There are in Argentina a great lot of Russians and Ukrainians, but they are mostly busy with field work and are not interested in town life. In quite a special position are the English; they do no work as they receive pecuniary aid from their consular agents, but rove from one settlement to another, robbing and cheating."

purchased it several months before as part of a collection from a former officer of the tsar's political police, the Okhrana. Browsing through his new acquisitions, this learned Russian had noticed something strange about one volume in French; its contents reminded him of the mysterious antisemitic tract *The Protocols of the Elders of Zion*, which purported to show how leading Jews of the world were staking out a plan to seize power from secular governments for their own profit. The title page had been torn out of the French book; there was no evidence of the author or date of publication. But as the Russian intellectual compared the texts, Graves told Allen, he confirmed that the tattered French book and *The Protocols* tracked closely. If the French publication could be shown to predate *The Protocols*, the antisemitic tract would be exposed as plagiary.

Allen understood immediately what Graves was telling him; clandestine copies of *The Protocols* had circulated at the Peace Conference in 1919. What remained unknown to the diplomats in Paris was the provenance of this explosive document, who the ominous conspirators were, and when the alleged plot had been — or would be — launched. A year before Graves and Allen talked, *The Times* had taken the specter of a world Jewish conspiracy seriously enough to ask, "Have we been struggling these tragic years to blow up and extirpate the secret organization of German world dominion only to find beneath it another, more dangerous because more secret? Have we ... escaped a 'Pax Germanica' only to fall into a 'Pax Judaica'?"

Graves knew that any information about the mysterious *Protocols* would be of intense interest to his editors in London and beyond. The little French book unearthed by chance in Constantinople depicted a philosophical dialogue about world domination, but it contained no reference whatever to Jews. If this text was in fact older, as internal evidence suggested, a purposeful and artful editor easily could have converted vague dialogues from another historical era into a text showing a secret pattern of Jewish conspiracy in the present day.

With Allen's encouragement Graves sent the French book to London, asking his editors to analyze the discovery. In the British Museum a copy of the French volume was found with date of publication intact. It was 1856, long before *The Protocols* was supposed to have been written. The antisemitic tract was exposed as a plagiarism from an innocuous earlier tract; the notorious "evidence" of a Jewish plot to dominate the world was a fake. *The Times* made amends for its ungrounded suspicions the year before by publishing three successive columns by its Constantinople correspondent in August 1921, reporting the drama of his discovery and its analysis. At the conclusion of Graves's series the newspaper solemnly withdrew its warnings about a sinister "Pax Judaica." "The fact of the plagiarism has now been conclusively established," declared *The Times*, "and the legend may be allowed to pass into oblivion."

Allen was not so confident that the matter would disappear; the deep-seated antisemitic impulses that made people inclined to believe such a fanciful document as *The Protocols* would not be assuaged merely by newspaper articles.* With Graves's help, he prepared his own dispatch to the State Department, asking that the United States government join in denouncing the antisemitic myth. Allen informed Washington of two points that Graves had omitted from his reports to *The Times*. First, the anonymous Russian gentleman who originally spotted the evidence had a particular motive for approaching the great British newspaper: not himself a Jew, though long troubled by the antisemitism of tsarist politics, he believed the disclosure would carry more conviction if it emerged from an impeccable "Christian" source. Had it come out as a result of investigations then under way by Jewish organizations, it might have been dismissed as self-serving. Second, as a poignant footnote to the whole saga, the Russian refused to accept any payment beyond the trivial purchase of a secondhand book, even after the importance of his discovery became known. Learning of the refugee's poverty, *The Times* attempted to compensate him properly; he was finally prevailed upon to accept a "loan" of several hundred pounds, and the newspaper never asked for repayment.

How to persuade Washington to act on what he suspected the diplomatic establishment would consider an irrelevant parochial matter? Allen first called attention to *The Times*'s published articles. The American Embassy in London weighed in by dispatching to the State Department a specially reprinted collection of the Graves articles, more impressive than cuttings from a newspaper. Allen then supplied his additional information and asked the department to consult the Library of Congress, where the original French volume might be found, and perhaps other evidence. If all this were made public by the United States government, it would add weight to the disclosures of a British newspaper.

Allen's main dispatch reached Washington on September 22, and the London reprint arrived two weeks later. Both made the rounds of the relevant divisions—Near Eastern Affairs, Western European Affairs, Russian Affairs, and finally the office of the undersecretary of state. The newspaper articles were promptly filed; Allen's request that the State Department help in denouncing an antisemitic fraud languished in the various offices for no less than seven months. When that dispatch, too, was

* Even though it has been exposed as a fraud, *The Protocols* strikes such resonance that more than half a century after these events the discredited manuscript still circulates in numerous editions across the Arab world.

finally sent to the files, on May 23, 1922, there was no notation that any-one in the Department of State had seen fit to take any action on the matter.

— * —

Newlyweds learn that starting a life together is not easy. For Allen and Clover the adjustment to everyday sharing was particularly difficult, for the only time the infatuated bride and groom had spent in each other's company had been an atypical interlude of vacation. Clover had never known her new husband while he was at work; Allen simply assumed that a wife would find her own devices for fitting into the professional circles that were his life. Single-minded and thorough on the job, Allen was not a drone — he thoroughly enjoyed what he was doing. He apparently saw no reason why his new marital status should inhibit collegial friendships with other women, such as Betty Carp, the clever secretary at the High Commission. Their friendship was so intimate that he found no discomfort in confiding to her his ambition to be secretary of state someday, a topic that would not be proper to discuss in casual circles.* Another encounter during Allen's Constantinople years, with an American missionary named Fanny Billings, developed into one of those platonic crushes, like young Shenstone's, that Allen never seemed to reciprocate or even notice.

A problem in the newlyweds' daily life was the never-ending round of social commitments imposed by Allen's position and the expectations of the diplomatic community. Clover and even Allen came to find these frivolous demands oppressive. But the social obligations also revealed a practical difficulty that the young couple did not need at this early stage in their shared life. Unlike Belin and other clubmates of the professional service, Allen could not afford to live at this high a standard, and the Department of State would not consider providing a special entertainment allowance. Whenever Allen began wondering whether the diplomatic life was quite right for him, his brother Foster, rich and successful on Wall Street, was always at hand to fuel his doubts.

Such frustrations, however, paled before the personal differences separating Allen and Clover. Had they known each other better before marrying, they could have explored their opposing character traits and made some accommodations; instead, the discoveries came as a surprise to both. Allen was ever the extrovert, but as a gentleman of the era he avoided personal intimacy in conversation and relationships. Clover was

* Betty Carp, who was an invaluable part of successive American diplomatic missions to Turkey, maintained a lifelong correspondence with both Allen and Clover.

an introvert, charming and sociable but driven by the inner life. Her needs were intensely emotional, even spiritual; the impact of Henry James remained strong. Her closest confidant was not her unfeeling husband but an older Episcopalian cleric named Elwood Worcester of Emmanuel Church, Boston, with whom she carried on an intense correspondence for many years. The young bride and this kind churchman shared their innermost thoughts without regard for conventional propriety. Allen and Clover related to the world around them in totally different ways. Clover, with her airy sensitivity and insouciance, found lasting meaning in every casual encounter; Allen's personality was intellectual at base, leavened by a successfully cultivated charm to serve only the purposes of the moment.

On Allen's twenty-eighth birthday he took his bride on an outing to Prinkipo Island in the Sea of Marmara.* They rode donkeys up a steep mountain to the old Monastery of St. George. Clover recorded the contrasts in the setting: "We had our lunch set out on a tiny table behind some sheltering rocks, where we sat contentedly for hours in the sun watching the sea way below us — and the maneuvers of our destroyers at target practice." The two visited remote British Army outposts at Gallipoli, he on official inspections, she for the sheer pleasure of the scene. Decades later, savoring her memories in a diary written for her children, she described being lifted onto a horse by a joyful young subaltern for a ride to the promontory and the view over the bay. "I felt for myself all that Conrad has conveyed in his strange tales, all that is weird and nostalgic about Asia to Europeans cast onto its vast uncomprehended spaces. In that atmosphere they — the Anglo-Saxons at least — take on the immaterial quality of ghosts, lacking substance or reality." As this experience mounted, Allen went into a round of military briefings by the commanding officers at the site.

Allen cared for Clover, of that there is no doubt, for all the contrasts in their emotional responses. Embarking on a quick official trip to Paris that first September, with the boat still in the harbor, he sat down to write to his new wife of emotions he could not convey comfortably in person. "This is our first real separation. It may be a good thing for us both to realize how hard it is to be apart, but, like taking medicine, it is not pleasant." He added to the letter each day as he crossed the Mediterranean. "I have been thinking about our future. . . . I hope this trip may help to clear things up a little. . . . I miss you more and more, but the trip may do some

* Allen remembered the island as the unlikely site early in the Peace Conference for an equally unlikely meeting between the Allies and representatives of that man Lenin — one of Woodrow Wilson's abortive ventures to learn about the "curious policy" of Bolshevism.

good. You may be surprised to find how much better I am going to be-
have when I get back.... There will be no one about nagging you to go
to stupid parties or such like."

In November 1921, two months after his return to the wisteria-
covered cottage in Constantinople, Allen and Clover conceived their first
child. At first, the pregnancy did not interfere unduly with Clover's charity activities, and for one of the rare occasions in their life together, Allen
expressed pride in his wife. He wrote the family in Auburn:

> Clover is still as busy as ever with her Russian work, and gets a great
> deal of human satisfaction out of it.... The gratitude of some of the
> people she has helped is quite touching.... We are planning to give a
> Russian Christmas on their Christmas, which comes on January 7....
> We are inviting as many of our Russian friends as our little house
> will hold, including the Wrangels.... General Wrangel recently deco-
> rated Clover for her refugee work. It was a silver medal with a St. Anne
> ribbon.

As her pregnancy advanced, Allen determined that Clover should
proceed to someplace where the medical facilities were more reliable
than those in Constantinople. The couple left for Athens, Allen on a
brief leave, Clover for a medical checkup. On the day of their departure,
without the slightest warning, a telegram arrived at the High Commission naming First Secretary Allen Dulles to be head of the Near Eastern
Division of the Department of State. The hostile political environment
of Washington the year before had changed. Not only was Allen being
rewarded professionally, the personal tensions of the young couple were,
at one stroke, eased. Clover's pregnancy had turned difficult, and she was
burdened with anxiety upon the news that her older brother had committed suicide.

Allen resolved to close up the cottage in Constantinople by himself,
letting Clover continue on to Athens to rest. Clover's sister came over
from America to help him pack up the little household. On March 18, after farewell dinners and a festive lunch at the Circle d'Orient, Constantinople's finest restaurant, given by Admiral Bristol, Allen boarded the
S.S. *Celio*, bound for Athens, his wife and unborn child — and Washington. It was the end of his diplomatic career overseas.

— * —

One week after his twenty-ninth birthday in 1922, Allen reported for
duty. The Division of Near Eastern Affairs in the Department of State
kept watch on United States policies in a five-million-square-mile area
stretching from Romania to Afghanistan and, in the south, deep into

Africa. The head of this division had just five diplomatic officers under his command.

Much that crossed his desk seemed obscure. There was the matter of some rifles bought in the United States by Ras Tafari, the autocratic regent of Ethiopia, for his palace guard.[6] The British, who claimed responsibility (along with Fascist Italy) for preserving Ethiopia's security, protested the start of an arms race. Allen poured soothing remarks upon the complaints over the ensuing weeks, and the consignment of properly purchased rifles went through. The episode had unanticipated long-term implications. Ras Tafari grew to a prominence far beyond the hills of Ethiopia, under the title and name Emperor Haile Selassie I; from the first rifle purchase he grew to be kindly disposed toward the United States, particularly thirteen years later, when he discovered the true worth of those supposed guarantees from Britain and Italy. Allen Dulles acquired a reputation, thoroughly undeserved, of expertise in matters of arms and munitions. He was named the American delegate to a League of Nations conference on the international arms traffic.

Lamot Belin, who had left Constantinople for Washington several months earlier, urged Allen and Clover to buy a house near his own in Georgetown; the only problem was that Belin could afford it and Allen could not. Instead the young couple moved into a modest red-brick row house not far from Rock Creek Park and the Washington zoo. For the last month of her pregnancy, Clover went to her parents' home in Newport, Rhode Island; there, in August 1922, was born their first child, a daughter named Clover Todd, who became known as Toddy.

Allen visited his wife and infant daughter in Newport early in September, but in Washington he found himself as restless with domestic life as he had been in Constantinople. As always when he and Clover were apart, he pledged to mend his ways. When you and our daughter return, he wrote, "you will find me a little less 'beast' than usual," using Clover's Victorian term for an inattentive husband. Allen began to seek out his brother in New York somewhat more regularly; they started what became a lifelong obsession with chess, which they played with an intensity and single-mindedness that shut out the entire world around them. After one such game Foster persuaded his younger brother that even if he was determined to remain in the diplomatic service, it would be worthwhile to have a law degree.

Allen took his brother's advice and signed up for night classes at George Washington University Law School. After his day's work at the State Department he would go off to class, then typically rush home to dress for a diplomatic reception or dinner party. By now he almost seemed to enjoy the social whirl — or at least preferred it to an evening at home with his wife and baby. Clover learned to lay out his dress clothes for a quick change; she even accompanied her husband sometimes if she was able to arrange for a baby sitter. Then, late into the night, the exhausted young mother would be asked to drill her obsessive husband in his law texts. Later, when Allen added early morning classes to his law school schedule, the couple had even less time together. Clover took Toddy back to Newport for the summer of 1923; she was again pregnant, and the Washington heat was stifling — at least she blamed the heat for her eagerness to get away. Allen promised to visit regularly, but inevitably he did not.

Allen assured his wife that he was "working like a dog," and indeed he was. But he was also, in effect, reconstituting some of the bachelor camaraderie he recalled so fondly from Bern, Paris, and Berlin. Old friends from foreign posts would turn up and resume the bachelor friendships with Allen as if there had been no interruption. Rather than confronting an empty kitchen at the end of a long day at the office, Allen took his meals at the Metropolitan Club. After a game of golf he might stay for dinner at Hugh Wilson's or Chris Herter's and then sleep over in the guest room. On weekends he would go the country homes of his rich friends, the Belins or David Bruce, and the conversation and brandy flowed nonstop.

Allen did not lose all sensitivity to his shortcomings as a husband. "I am a stiff, unmanicured thing and I give you very little satisfaction," he wrote Clover in Newport. "You must try to make me over," he pleaded. There were no marriage counselors in those days, at least in their circles, but Allen went so far as to suggest that Clover seek advice from friends about "how to live with a queer duck like me." On went the correspondence, but vacation times together seldom materialized. Their second daughter, Joan, was born just three days after Christmas of 1923.

Allen long remembered the night of Thursday, August 2, 1923, and he used it as a favorite after-dinner anecdote for decades to come.[7] After completing his day's business, he took off with Hugh Wilson for a quick golf game and dinner. As he walked home he heard a newsboy shouting the headline that President Harding had died suddenly in San Francisco. Allen rushed back to the department in case there was anything to be done and found the duty officer in despair because Secretary of State Charles Evans Hughes had apparently retired for the night and was not answering his telephone. And no one could find a telephone number to reach Vice President Calvin Coolidge, on vacation in Vermont. Hughes, finally aroused, located Coolidge and advised him to take the presidential oath of office without delay. Allen copied down the prescribed text from an almanac on the shelf and read it over the telephone to Coolidge's father, a local justice of the peace, to start the swearing in of the next president of the United States. As Allen told it, the constitutional formalities completed, Coolidge asked, "What do I do now?" Hughes suggested that he might wish to return to Washington. Coolidge replied that he already had an upper berth reserved out of Boston the following Tuesday; would that be soon enough? No, said the secretary of state, and reassured Coolidge that it would be appropriate to engage a special train for the journey to the White House.

A large part of the work of the Near Eastern Division involved the competition among the Great Powers over the unexplored oil reserves of the Middle East. Allen had learned something about the oil industry in Constantinople. Oil men could go to all sorts of strange places on prospecting missions without having to explain their presence or establish their credentials. Their curiosity was not considered suspicious; they saw and heard things that other travelers might not notice. And oil men of that era loved to talk. Scarcely a week had passed at the High Commission without Allen sitting down with a visiting manager from Standard Oil or Shell or Socony to discuss the latest monarchist coup in Persia, anti-Jewish riots in Palestine, civil war in Arabia, British maneuvers in Iraq. Next to missionaries, Allen discovered, there were no better sources of international gossip than the oil men.

In July of 1924 he was bold (or careless) enough to spell out in an official State Department communication his interest in using the search for oil as a cover for gathering intelligence. The director of the Near Eastern Division proposed assigning a Vice Consul Fuller to Baghdad, with which the United States did not have diplomatic relations, to keep an eye on oil-drilling activities. "There are other reasons for having Fuller in Baghdad," Allen went on. "There is important work to be done there, particularly of a political character. . . . We have not been receiving as full information on political and economic affairs in Iraq as I should like to have."*

— * —

Two promotions came with remarkable rapidity; Allen was making close to $8,000 per year, a figure that only made his brother Foster laugh. He was the father of two daughters, and his wife was packing to take them away again for a long summer. "How can a man follow the way of the Great Game," wailed Kipling's young Kim, "when he is so always pestered

* Interestingly enough, this memorandum was found not in the State Department archives under the substantive categories where it would belong but rather in Allen's personnel file — as if he, or someone else, had thought better about having it so easily accessible to subsequent scrutiny.

by women!" Allen spent the summer of 1925 at a diplomatic conference in Switzerland, continuing the flow of apologetic letters to Clover.

By late in that year it was clear that he would have to go to a foreign post again to retain his rank as a professional diplomat. The assignment offered was counselor of embassy at Peking, rich with Foster family memories but remote from Allen's own experience. He stalled off the appointment while he completed his law degree at George Washington University. Sullivan and Cromwell promptly offered him a job. This time Allen was tempted, but he still held back. "I can't decide whether it would be wise for me to come into an office where you have made such a mark," Allen wrote Foster in fraternal sincerity. The offer was held open, awaiting Allen's convenience.

Allen took Clover with him for the 1926 session of the diplomatic conference on the world arms trade in Geneva. She went off on bicycle rides as Allen slogged through the working sessions; every once in a while they would go on a walk or a climb together. They spent a fortnight in Britain, visiting one of Allen's naval disarmament colleagues in Rye, then going on to Scotland, where Allen played golf. They were apart even as they were together — the pattern for the rest of their life. On the train back from Edinburgh to London, Allen was absorbed in a biography of Thomas Jefferson; Clover, in *The Memoirs of the Countess Potocka*.

For the first time in four years, Allen could contemplate a summer vacation, and now his attention returned to Henderson Harbor. Both Allen and Foster had grown to look down on the old family retreat as quaint and simple, not up to the intellectual and social standing that the two brothers had achieved. Foster's wife, Janet, in particular, found the relatives at Henderson Harbor boring beyond belief. But that August it was just what Allen and Clover needed.

Uncle Bert, now quite forgotten in Allen's world, was there. Lansing still knew something of diplomacy and foreign policy, and he told Allen not to go to Peking. "That problem will not be solved in your lifetime." Foster's offer of a lucrative career in New York loomed larger. "I am having a hell of a time," Allen wrote Hugh Gibson, uttering an oath rarely heard in the Dulles family. Gibson, ever jocular, tried to cajole Allen out of his funk. "I am alarmed, perturbed and concerned. . . . How do you expect to be secretary of state if you just become a prominent money-owner? Please tell Clover to use her influence with you and make sure you don't do anything I would regret."

Allen Dulles resigned from the Foreign Service on September 22, 1926, after ten years and three months in the career. His formal letter to Secretary of State Frank Kellogg shunned the usual hypocrisies; Allen said he had decided to resign because he could no longer afford to be a professional diplomat. "The financial burden involved in the acceptance of the higher positions in the Diplomatic Service is such that outside resources are increasingly necessary," he stated. He noted the impossibility for one "who is not able materially to supplement his salary from his private resources to follow a diplomatic career." To Gibson the next day, Allen wrote, "I feel rather like the man Victor Hugo describes, who had fallen from an ocean liner and watched it disappear in the distance." Secretary Kellogg replied hoping "that some day you will feel that you may return, either in the State Department or abroad, to the service in which men of your character and ability are much needed."

The formalities were followed by two interesting reactions from within the State Department. By chance, Allen's old clubmate from the Bern Legation, Hugh Wilson, was that season charged with keeping the press informed about American foreign policy. He saw an opportunity to help a friend and the Foreign Service at the same time. Allen may not yet have been a headline figure, but as newsmen were quickly told, he was the grandson of John Watson Foster and the nephew of Robert Lansing, secretaries of state both, and clearly an up-and-coming figure in American diplomacy. His financial status was worth pondering, for the sake of the diplomatic profession. *The New York Times* thus decided to report Allen's resignation on its front page with an accompanying editorial the next day. "A [Benjamin] Franklin could live in modest chambers and wear the plainest of clothes while representing an infant republic," declared the *Times* editorial page, "but the world — like the American people — demands today that the United States be less niggardly toward its officials abroad."*

The bookkeepers of the State Department failed to get the message. Allen had sent a polite cable of regret to the minister in Peking. A few days later the department accounting office sent around copies of Allen's courtesy telegram with the notation, "Who pays for this?" No less than three senior officers of the Department of State had to vouch for the telegram as a proper official expense. That proved insufficient. Happening to pass through Washington at that moment was Allen's first friend in the Diplomatic Service, Fred Dolbeare, from the embassy in Vienna. This carefree soul, driven by loyalty to his friends, saw the insulting inquiry, pulled out his own checkbook, and, without saying anything to Allen or anyone else, took it upon himself to pay the cost of Allen's farewell telegram to the Foreign Service.

* Allen thus arrived on page one of *The New York Times* long before the ultimately more prominent John Foster Dulles achieved that distinction.

— 5 —

MAN OF AFFAIRS

TO CALL THE SULLIVAN AND CROMWELL of the 1920s a law firm is to miss the point. The partnership of lawyers at 49 Wall Street constituted a strategic nexus of international finance, the operating core of a web of relationships that constituted power, carefully crafted to accrue and endure across sovereign borders. Whether in railroads, chemicals, nitrates from Chile, or sugar from Cuba, the mammoth trusts and cartels found their way to profits — with more than a little help from their friends the lawyers. In those years mere governments had not yet learned to demand disclosure of significant financial information, investors did not expect audits or independent scrutiny of their holdings, and a wink and a nod from an influential person could be worth a million. The men at Sullivan and Cromwell were such influential persons. The firm did offer legal associates to draft contracts, preserve estates, and argue in courtrooms, but this was not the profession of law as practiced by Foster and Allen Dulles. Their Sullivan and Cromwell sought nothing less than to shape the affairs of all the world for the benefit and well-being of the select, their clients.

William Nelson Cromwell was just thirty-three years old when the venerable Algernon Sydney Sullivan died in 1887. As protégé and mentor they had started a dynamic law practice, marked by boldness and innovation in areas where conventional lawyers feared to tread. National prominence came with the project of a canal across the Central American isthmus connecting the Atlantic and Pacific Oceans. Cromwell's clients sponsored a route through Panama; powerful forces in Congress had their eyes and interests on an alternative Nicaraguan route.

Cromwell developed a most unlawyerly technique of public relations, a propaganda blitz to promote his clients' interests, followed by lobbying, intrigue, and an engineered "revolution" in Panama, all under Cromwell's guidance. "He can dig deeper and do big things more quietly than almost anyone downtown," said a 1908 gossip columnist. "His eyes are a brilliant light blue, as clear as a baby's and as innocent looking as a girl's." Cromwell charged very big fees for very big services. After the fight for the Panama Canal was won, the Bar Association decided that the good name of the profession required a formal definition of legal ethics. Amid one of the firm's many controversial deals, Theodore Roosevelt warned his successor, William Howard Taft, to keep his distance from Cromwell: "I can never be sure that some day he will not be working for a big fee in connection with this very matter, while you and I are entirely ignorant of what he is doing." Frustrated in his ambitions for an appointment in Taft's administration, and with legal battles closing in on him, Cromwell decided simply to leave the country.

To this firm in 1911 came John Foster Dulles, young and untested, hired frankly as a personal favor to his grandfather, John Watson Foster, a personal acquaintance of both Sullivan and Cromwell. The new legal clerk showed merit. While on leave to work at the Peace Conference, Foster paid court to the founding partner, Cromwell, in Paris, who continued to dominate his firm from luxurious exile on the Avenue Foch. Shortly after returning home Foster was accepted as a full partner.

Europe after the Versailles Treaty confronted the world of capital with bewildering prospects for investment. While Wall Street competitors busied themselves with the Florida land boom, Sullivan and Cromwell were eyeing the need for reconstruction financing in defeated Germany. Foster jumped at the chance to scout investment opportunities, but the unseemly Kapp putsch and all that bothersome uproar shattered the prospects he had dangled before his partners. Allen, the professional diplomat, with all his scruples and not yet comprehending the opportunities for profit on the outside, had been notably unhelpful. Foster returned to New York empty-handed. Cromwell reassured his protégé with his philosophy of the long look in practicing law. "This kind of work is the most effective and far reaching in the future (as well as the present) of S&C. It is only a matter of time when you will be called to take a more active part in these great questions."

Four years later, in 1924, Germany's shrewd industrialists argued that they could not even begin to meet the Allies' reparations demands until their own war-shattered infrastructure was rebuilt. They needed seed capital. An international committee headed by a prominent American banker, Charles G. Dawes, with John Foster Dulles as special counsel, came up with the convenient idea of linking reparations payments to the rebuilding of German productive facilities — using millions of dollars of foreign capital on loan.

Who better to put up the money for this reconstruction than Sullivan and Cromwell's clients? Over the next seven years the firm managed loans to German interests totaling over a billion dollars, which was more than half of what the Dawes Plan envisaged from all sources. German municipalities, utilities, and private enterprises saw across the ocean an overflowing cornucopia of capital — with high interest rates, to be sure, but suddenly available and with few questions asked. Foster's banking clients would underwrite the loans, float a bond issue, and pass the risk on to a gullible public — after deducting a generous commission for themselves. These were the junk bonds of the day. One son of the mighty Stinnes industrial family paid a visit to America late in the 1920s to figure out this sudden eagerness to invest. On the New York stage he found an operetta about old Heidelberg, Sigmund Romberg's *The Student Prince*, and there was his answer. "This sentimental German play was successfully used by Wall Street as propaganda for the sale of the Heidelberg bonds," Edmund Hugo Stinnes wrote; he stood in wonder of the Americans' "hardest business sense coupled with a childlike mentality."[1]

Even as the legal business thrived, Sullivan and Cromwell went through a series of crises and deaths within the partnership, such that at thirty-eight Foster Dulles was in line for the top management responsibilities of a large and famous Wall Street law firm. One of his first acts of management, in September 1926, was to offer a job to his thirty-three-year-old brother, just graduated from law school and not yet a member of any bar but growing weary of genteel parsimony.

Upon his resignation from the Foreign Service, Allen moved his family to the intimidating noise of New York. He then took a symbolic step that signaled his own insecurity and his determination to succeed in his new undertaking: he shaved off the little mustache raised ages ago at Princeton. Now, he judged, the clean-shaven look would better equip him for corporate life, might even make him look more like his successful brother. He braced himself for the years of "primer work . . . before I will be of any use in the law." Indeed, two years passed before he even gained admission to the bar, and it would be fifteen years before he spoke a word in a courtroom.

Sullivan and Cromwell expected very particular services from Allen Dulles, late of the Department of State. Foster was promoting the firm's ability to serve special clients; it claimed "unusual and diversified means of obtaining information." The claim was never elucidated, nor was that expected by clients to whom discretion meant everything. No matter that Allen did not understand the complexities of a foreign bond prospectus; he did understand the policymaking process of governments, and he knew how to extract and insert information as the process flowed toward deci-

sion. And for all his apostasy in becoming a "money-owner," Allen contrived to preserve his credentials in the diplomatic club, "as if I had not
been contaminated," he wrote an old colleague. "I want to keep as good a
reputation as I can, notwithstanding the taint of my environment."

The State Department lured him back to official status after only five
months, naming him legal adviser with the American delegation to one
of the endless naval disarmament conferences in Geneva. Some thought
world peace was at stake in these tedious exercises; others knew that lucrative industrial and shipbuilding contracts were threatened. Was Allen's role as an official participant consistent with his obligations as a
Wall Street lawyer? Probably not at a normal law firm, but Sullivan and
Cromwell had the longer view. Who knew what returns might come
from having one of their number present at a solemn diplomatic conference? "Possibly I shouldn't have done it," Allen wrote Gibson. "You remember what happened to Lot's wife."

Hardly a novice at diplomatic conferences, Allen nonetheless had new
experiences in store at the 1927 naval disarmament sessions. It was not
that his own status, hovering between public and private service, was difficult. He understood the problems of disarmament, of rivalries between
Great Powers and conflicting economic interests, as well as anyone of
those days. Nor was there ever a suggestion that he should serve the clients
of Sullivan and Cromwell under cover of his government position — that
he would have found quite unacceptable. What puzzled him was the attitudes and activities of other private Americans at the conference.

In June and July of 1927 strange things began happening in Geneva:
unexpected arguments kept arising between American and British admirals about tonnage ratios for future ship construction. There was no reason for this dispute, Allen argued; why should the navies of Britain and
the United States regard each other as potential menaces? The whole
mood of the conference was troublesome. Why, after the formal negotiating sessions, did delegates gather at cocktail parties, talk with journalists, and then act much more hostile than when they were negotiating
in plenary session? Who were all those people hanging on at the conference and stirring up trouble? The meetings ended in failure; no
limits whatever were placed on the shipbuilding industries of the Great
Powers. After everyone had returned home, the history of the Geneva
Naval Disarmament Conference of 1927 survived only in one of Allen's
favorite stories about himself.[2]

"I was in my office when the telephone rang," Allen would begin.
"The telephone operator, who by the tone of her voice was obviously surprised, said that Mr. Paul D. Cravath wanted to talk to me." Puzzling indeed, for Paul D. Cravath was illustrious among Wall Street lawyers, "a

man of venerable size, shape and age." Allen replied that Mr. Cravath surely meant to speak to his brother, Foster Dulles, upstairs. Mr. Cravath expressed irritation, declaring that he knew whom he was calling and that furthermore he wished to come over to speak with Mr. *Allen* Dulles face to face. Allen, rattled, muttered that he would be honored to call at Mr. Cravath's office, but the senior lawyer made clear that he would pay the call himself, and within the hour.

This put Allen in a logistical dilemma, for as a lowly associate he shared a cramped office with six other lawyers and could hardly receive visitors of any standing, let alone the leader of the Wall Street bar. He ran upstairs to beg the loan of an absent partner's empty paneled suite.

> I hastily took a few of my own papers up to his office and sat at his big desk, and waited for Mr. Paul Drennan Cravath. With the great courtesy and dignity that he always showed, Mr. Cravath said, "Mr. Dulles, I would like to retain you on an important matter . . . concerning the Naval Disarmament Conference."

Allen protested mildly but sensed that some of the mysteries of that strange assemblage were about to be revealed. Cravath asked if Allen recalled a man who claimed to be a freelance journalist, "Big Bill" Shearer. Indeed Allen did, a boisterous, backslapping Irish-American who gave lavish parties for the admirals, was always full of detailed nautical information of a technical sort, and inevitably stirred up trouble between the Americans and the British. Cravath, in growing discomfort, explained that one of his clients, Bethlehem Steel Corporation, which had an interest in shipbuilding, had retained Shearer to "observe" the conference for Bethlehem — not, Cravath insisted, to interfere in any way, just to report back.

Allen began getting, as he always put it, "hot under the collar." He bluntly confirmed what Cravath had feared but hoped was not true, that this Shearer "had been about as effective a man as there was in blowing up the conference." Cravath got to the point. "In that case, Mr. Dulles, I would like to retain you to go down to see the secretary of state and explain to him the very unfortunate situation in which we are placed." Shearer was about to go public in denouncing diplomacy, and his connection to Bethlehem Steel would then become known. If only to contain the damage, Secretary Kellogg could at least be warned in advance by a trusted voice.

Allen made a quick decision. Without consulting Foster or anyone else who might try to dissuade him from his scruples, he refused Mr. Cravath's retainer. But he agreed, as an official participant at the conference, to report the unexpected circumstances to Kellogg. "I never saw a man so mad in my life," Allen recalled. Kellogg saw the potential headlines around the world: AMERICAN DELEGATION ARRANGES, THROUGH BETHLEHEM STEEL, TO WRECK CONFERENCE. "I went back and reported to Mr. Cravath. . . . He said it was about what he had expected." The flap did come out in the press, and Bethlehem Steel and the war-profiteering industrialists suffered the inevitable treatment in a congressional investigation. "Shearer suggested that I was a modern Benedict Arnoldette," Allen joked. "The shipbuilders were made monkeys of."

Allen had played his role in forewarning the secretary of state and thus softening the blow, for which service the Cravath law firm remained deeply grateful. Mr. Cravath's proffered retainer was trivial compared to the reputation for access and confidence that Allen tidily confirmed — for Sullivan and Cromwell and for himself.

— * —

It was a heady beginning to the practice of law, but the private life was slow in catching up. Allen and Clover established themselves with Toddy and Joan, aged four and three, in an apartment at Fifth Avenue and 102nd Street, comfortable and overlooking Central Park, but not quite elegant (Foster lived eleven socially important blocks to the south). Clover had children to put in school and a home to make for her work-preoccupied husband. Allen and Foster shared the concerns of the firm, but neither their personal nor their professional lives proceeded in tandem; the brothers' social interests — and more acutely, those of the sisters-in-law — scarcely coincided. Though loyal to and respectful of each other, they had separate circles of friends, and their personalities were starkly different.

Allen, now free of diplomatic airs, was informal, cheerful, and always on the move; his wealthy brother was severe, intellectual to a fault. Colleagues remembered that Allen's blue eyes could be just as penetrating as his brother's, but they also appeared to convey an intense personal interest. A European banker recorded the impressions of his first visit to the partners' suite:

What a difference between them! John Foster looked like a clergyman, . . . vivid and somewhat nervous. Allen . . . quiet, relaxed, but at the same time hard-working. . . . Allen relied on his brains, and John Foster on his faith. . . . I formed the impression that John Foster conceived an idea and had it carried out by his experts, while Allen worked on an idea given to him by others. . . . Allen was certainly more broadminded than his brother, and that is why his contacts with people were so much easier. I think Allen was loved by the men who worked with him, while John Foster was respected.[3]

Allen's legal work consisted largely of dealing with the State Department on the necessary formalities for the firm's foreign lending business, to Bolivia, Chile, Denmark, Sicily. Years later the muckraking columnist Drew Pearson would say that Allen simply took the train to Washington "to play a few games of golf with his former chief" and come back with loan approvals in his pocket. Allen did play golf, with Gibson, Wilson, and the other clubmates, but obviously "the Washington end," as Wall Street called it, involved more than that, and Allen understood just how much more.

By early 1928 he took the important step of engaging a client of his own: one Arthur Bunker, the younger son of a New York Social Register family, an adventurous electrical engineer with an entrepreneurial spirit.* The way things happened in those days — through friends, chance, and the house of Morgan — Bunker found himself in control of the Carib Syndicate, commanding lucrative oil concessions in Colombia and Venezuela. He needed a good lawyer who was independent of all his family's interests.

The first problem, involving diplomatic technicalities, Allen was able to sort out with the State Department in short order. The real challenge lay in asserting the Carib Syndicate's rights against the domineering power of the Royal Dutch Shell group, personal fiefdom of that legendary baron in the empire of international oil, Sir Henri August Wilhelm Deterding. Allen did not yet know men like Deterding, and his knowledge of international oil, which he had begun to pick up in Constantinople, was political in nature, not commercial. But Allen had learned the subtle art of negotiating with people face to face, and that is what he had to do in May 1928 at the Royal Dutch Shell headquarters in London.

Deterding, who came on as a cheerful, white-haired gentleman, took over the meeting in a quick, high-pitched voice, announcing what he expected to happen. Allen let him talk, then quietly declared that what Deterding expected would *not* happen, that his client was prepared to bring suit and would do whatever was necessary to protect rights that unquestionably were his. A standoff and verbal sparring; suddenly, to Allen's unexpressed amazement, Sir Henri Deterding backed down. Bunker and the syndicate had won their point, and lawyer had done well by client.

Allen was ambivalent about his change of career; though engaged in diplomacy almost as much as before, he was no longer truly a diplomat.

* Arthur Bunker had to be entrepreneurial, for his older brother, Ellsworth, was in firm control of the family's Cuban sugar refineries. At an advanced age Ellsworth Bunker became one of America's most distinguished diplomats, as ambassador to Italy, Argentina, India, and Vietnam. Allen tried in 1953 to recruit him for a top post in the CIA, but the elder Bunker preferred his independence.

His personal interest was public service, as he understood it from all he had heard at Henderson Harbor and Princeton. Was service to clients on Wall Street truly public service? In these early years, at least, Allen and his colleagues at the firm were rigorous in shunning conflicts of interest. Even Foster allowed Allen to operate in the circles he knew best, as his own man.

At the same time, Allen savored the pleasures of making money for his family. And, far from being branded as an apostate by the diplomatic club, he found himself blazing a trail for others — just as the editors of *The New York Times* had feared when they lamented his resignation. Hugh Wilson was tempted by an offer from an American bank, but he had family wealth and the money was no lure. Similarly, Hugh Gibson held back, hoping for high office under Herbert Hoover (in the end, nothing worthy was forthcoming). But at least three other members of the club, including Fred Dolbeare, followed Allen into the financial world in the late 1920s. "The work is bully," Dolbeare wrote Wilson after a few days in banking. "To study balance sheets is just as amusing as 'contract' [bridge]. . . . I am seeing the inside of investment 'stunts.' . . . I don't dare have any opinions yet but give me a little more time and I'll tell you how to earn more than five percent, and it's fun."

Hoover's nomination as the Republican candidate for president in June 1928 prodded Allen's ambivalence, and he planted the seed with Gibson that he might want to help out on the political campaign. Uncle Bert died that October, and though Allen had spent little time with Lansing in his uncle's declining years, the onetime secretary of state was always a reminder of Allen's ambition to hold that office himself someday.

Allen built up his public stature as an authority on international affairs in an era of populist isolationism. Between legal and pro bono diplomatic chores, he worked the lecture circuit, addressing audiences as diverse as the League of Women Voters and the Royal Institute of International Affairs in London. He even ventured into radio discussions, offering conversational charm and incomparable expertise about the arcane details of disarmament, making them almost interesting to an apathetic public.

Allen found his most enduring public role through his old Princeton friend Hamilton Fish Armstrong. The two had not seen much of each other in their first years out of graduate school, but the friendship picked up mightily as Allen settled into New York. Armstrong had always been more intrigued by the studying and writing of international relations than by the practice of it. After Versailles, as isolationism settled upon America, he linked up with an exclusive little club of bankers, lawyers, and academics infected by the Inquiry, eager to keep alive the collegiality and serious pursuit of international affairs that Colonel

House had started five years before. They founded what became known as the Council on Foreign Relations, part research center, part influence on government, and throughout a club of cultivated gentlemen (women were admitted to membership only the year after Allen's death) who comfortably smoked cigars and pondered matters of state over their glasses of port. For Allen the council offered in noisy New York the civilized fellowship he had known in Bern and Paris a decade earlier. He became a council mainstay and eventually its president.

From the start the council published a serious quarterly journal called *Foreign Affairs*. Archibald Cary Coolidge, the Harvard professor who had served in Allen's intelligence networks in central Europe during the Peace Conference, was named the journal's first editor. To manage the publication Coolidge picked Armstrong, who was happy to have a job that kept him in touch with the men of international politics. The eager protégé took charge, and upon Coolidge's death in 1928, Ham Armstrong assumed the editorship of *Foreign Affairs*, a post of ever-increasing authority that he held for the next forty-five years.

Allen was just the sort of author that Armstrong sought to encourage: knowledgeable and authoritative on topics that few understood, yet independent-minded and not inhibited from speaking out by any official responsibilities. Allen's first article, "Some Misconceptions about Disarmament," appeared in April 1927; in a second, "The Threat of Anglo-American Naval Rivalry," which led Armstrong's January 1929 issue, Allen seized upon an Anglo-French naval treaty to make his confession of disenchantment with the whole effort at Great Power disarmament: "Nothing is so calculated to whet the appetite of the public as an international agreement of which the existence is known and the text withheld. Now that the text of this agreement has been published the element in it which is surprising is its futility."

"Personally I consider it a very dull article," he wrote one of the clubmates in affected modesty, "but the press here seems to have taken a fancy to it." Particular praise came from Allen's old mentor Walter Lippmann, who was gaining influence as a syndicated columnist. Lippmann was another mainstay of the early *Foreign Affairs*, a pioneer council member from 1922 and a close social friend of Armstrong's.*

Withal it was a good life those first years in New York as Allen and Clover tried to make their contrasting personalities complementary un-

---

* Lippmann was suddenly lost to *Foreign Affairs* when his friendship with Armstrong's wife intensified; their elopement in 1937 was an unpleasant establishment scandal. Allen, caught between loyalties to two old friends and their wives, remained, as ever, on more or less amiable terms with all concerned.

der easier conditions than they had known in Constantinople or Washington. Toddy and Joan were growing up as vibrant young girls, imbued by their mother with culture and wonder. In March 1929 Allen and Clover conceived a third child. The young family reached out to new friends and began to accustom themselves to the high living style that they finally could afford.

High living was the norm during the first ten months of 1929, whether one could afford it or not. After Hoover was elected president, William Nelson Cromwell wrote from Paris that the new administration would serve the American people better than "any nation in the realm of civilization." The "common man," to whom Hoover so appealed at first, found license to participate in a prosperity that had been the preserve of the upper class. With the same gullibility Wall Street had exhibited in succumbing to Old Heidelberg schmaltz, America's Main Street sent family savings to massive investment trusts, confident in the expectation of extravagant returns.

Allen, still a bit green in the ways of money, was on the fringes of the frenzy. As always, he carefully watched his brother, who was emerging as one of the most creative architects of the 1929 investment pyramids. An important client held a 40 percent interest in an investment trust called the Shenandoah Corporation. Foster joined the Shenandoah board of directors and became a major investor. At its August 1929 peak, Foster's Shenandoah stock was valued at $36 per share; four months later it had collapsed to $8—and later the price dropped to 50 cents. Following his brother's example, Allen invested where his insider knowledge led him, in Arthur Bunker's Carib Syndicate. In the five days of the Wall Street crash the value of his shares dropped 80 percent.

October 1929 was the beginning of a national and, eventually, global depression. Small investors across America were wiped out. Even on Wall Street there was hardship. "Many very rich men," Paul D. Cravath observed, "are now only moderately rich." Allen maintained his jauntiness about the collapse. He wrote a friend in Europe:

I had been in Wall Street just long enough to get the fever, and as a result I am a poorer, and I think a little wiser, individual than a month ago. . . . I have reached the philosophical frame of mind where I believe that it will do the country a lot of good, as a considerable section of the population had reached the conclusion that it wasn't necessary to work to make money. However it would be more considerate if those who decided to stop living would use Brooklyn Bridge rather than these tall buildings. These days it is rather safer to walk in the middle of the street, or it would be if the taxis didn't pick you off.

But Allen's commitment to the life of New York and to the roles of husband and father were never more than nominal. During fifteen years as a Wall Street lawyer, he went on eleven extended missions abroad, some of many months' duration (and rarely could Clover come along); seven times he represented the United States at international conferences. After barely three years in the legal profession, and as Wall Street was still reeling from the crash, Allen was accepted into the partnership of Sullivan and Cromwell. His financial future, to the extent that he sought it, was assured. At the start of 1930 was born his only son, the second Allen Macy Dulles. Nine days later Allen boarded the luxury liner *Bremen* with Foster to spend a full year in the Sullivan and Cromwell Paris office. He left instructions for Clover and the children to join him there when "the baby" reached the age of three months.

— * —

A year in Paris for a prosperous young American family. Allen had taken his crash course in diplomacy there in 1919, and Paris in 1930 would introduce him to the world of high finance. In his first, bachelor months, Allen lived with Cromwell in his "swell suite" on the Avenue Foch, sumptuous chambers complete with a sunken marble bath. Foster had long since lost patience with the garrulous and tipsy old expatriate, whom he had courted a decade earlier but now no longer needed. Allen, however, was "really fond" of Cromwell and justified his freeloading by writing home that "it really gives him pleasure to have me around."

In mid-November Allen received word that his father had died in Auburn at the age of seventy-six. He seemed strangely unmoved at the loss. Through all his adventures in diplomacy and finance, ties to a once strong family had grown frail. Two of his sisters had married and settled into quiet lives not far from their childhood home; Eleanor, his third sister, was pursuing an academic career as an economist. With none of them did Allen find much identity, nothing to compare with the fellowships forged in the diplomatic club and related endeavors. Allen seldom found the time to visit Henderson Harbor and did not seem to regret it. The quaint and pleasure-loving Cromwell may have given Allen more paternal warmth than he had ever received from his introverted father, who always regarded his first-born son as the rightful bearer of family standing. As the relatives noted sadly over the years, Allen was too absorbed in his business in Paris even to return home for his father's memorial service.

Clover and the three children arrived in Paris in May; Allen had rented a wing of an old mansion on the Left Bank, 11 Rue Masseran, townhouse of the Comte Etienne de Beaumont, patron of the arts, of

Picasso in particular. This would be the family home for the year; Cromwell's flat continued to provide bachelor digs when itinerant clubmates like Fred Dolbeare passed through. Together, the two homes were Allen's window upon Paris of 1930, and he lived it to the hilt: a playground of monarchs reigning and deposed, where Morgans and Vanderbilts, maharajahs from India and stars from Hollywood, old wealth and new, sought perpetual gaiety in reckless expenditure, escape from the spreading depression back in America. Far from feeling revulsion at the gaudy display, Allen reveled in the luxury that other people's money could buy. Nannies were readily available for the children; Allen would often take Clover or other companions to a kitschy Montmartre bistro, the Scheherazade, a favorite haunt for Russian noblefolk, displaced but more prosperous than those the newlyweds had known in Constantinople. The waiters were bedecked in the uniforms of Circassian warriors; the dance floor, dark and smoke-filled, was made up like a festival tent from the Caucasus, a single spotlight upon a lone gypsy fiddler playing mournful Cossack love songs. (Four years later, when Allen revisited the Scheherazade, he wrote to Clover, "The bearded proprietor had not forgotten me and asked of your health, etc.") On weekends the family would motor up to Le Touquet on the coast, where Allen would even try his hand at fly-fishing.

As a partner of Sullivan and Cromwell, Allen was plunged into a realm where sovereign frontiers were transparent and the trappings of democracies seldom were allowed to penetrate. Like beguiled readers of Eric Ambler or Graham Greene, Allen discovered that only a thin line divided respectable high finance from a shadowy underworld. Among the economic consequences of the peace, as John Maynard Keynes had defined them, were complex challenges to the international capital markets that Sullivan and Cromwell had so exploited. A decade after the collapse of a strong imperial order, central Europe was fragmented into struggling new states, each clinging in nationalistic zeal to jerry-built financial structures and artificial trade barriers. On top of all was the web of reparations and debts, an unfathomable set of long- and short-term obligations, official and private banking loans, that bound disparate nations together in finance, even as their governments practiced rugged individualism in politics.

Tending this delicate machinery was an elite club of central bankers who met privately in the Swiss safe haven of Basel, far more discreet than Geneva, where the noisy League of Nations exchanged rhetoric. The club members at Basel discussed gold flow, currency exchange, and interest rates — topics that may have been analyzed with academic purity in *Foreign Affairs* but that Allen could now see in action. He never bothered to understand the technical aspects of financial maneuverings, but under the influence of Foster and the firm he grew sensitive to the elite's goal of transnational power to generate prosperity for the world and, of course, themselves.*

Allen's primary entrée to the realm came through the house of J. Henry Schröder, a venerable banking firm dating from the Napoleonic era (the Schröders regularly noted the origin as one year *before* that of the more flamboyant Rothschild empire). The German founder, Baron von Schröder, had emigrated to the emerging financial capital of London, prospered, and acquired local respectability — becoming not quite a lord like the Rothschilds, but at least a baronet. For the rest of the nineteenth century the bank was headed by a dynasty of German-born von Schröders transplanted to England. The London Schröders and the German cousins, running their own bank in Hamburg, had cooperated on ventures in eastern Europe and Latin America until the events of 1914 brought untoward interruption.

Once the Great War was over the bankers found something even better than business as usual. With defeated Germany's need for investment capital, it seemed only natural for the British Schröders to reestablish "normal" relations with the Fatherland, and they founded a New York subsidiary to work with Sullivan and Cromwell to attract American venture capital. The J. Henry Schroder concern (the umlaut was dropped for the New York business) became one of Allen's biggest clients. This was where Allen managed to plant Fred Dolbeare, who assured Hugh Wilson and the others that "the NY end of the old contingent, Allen and Foster Dulles, . . . seem to think I have joined up with a good outfit."

During his fourteen months in Europe, Allen came of age as a lawyer for international business. He was proving to his brother that he was not inept in the arts of commerce, and he was proving to himself that it might be possible to serve the cause of security among nations and make money at the same time. He returned to Wall Street in March 1931, leaving Clover and the children to spend their summer holiday in Switzerland.

The America to which Allen returned was a nation dazed by financial panic. Thousands of banks had closed, five million Americans were out of work, and for those hanging on to jobs, wages had plunged to bare subsistence. For all the optimism of the moneyed classes, worse was yet to come. In May the Austrian Creditanstalt bank failed; the bankers' club of Basel watched impotently as their world economic order collapsed like a

---

* Allen's sister Eleanor was one of the early chroniclers of this framework, called the Bank for International Settlements, but there is no record that brother and sister spent much time talking about it.

house of embossed paper, forcing the nations of Europe into downtrodden step with the American depression. A score of near-bankrupt governments defaulted on the loans that Sullivan and Cromwell and the rest of Wall Street had so eagerly flogged, and Main Street was left clutching certificates of savings once valued at over a billion dollars, now worthless.

Early in 1932 the global financial community was shaken further by the sudden bankruptcy and suicide of the Swedish "match king," Ivar Kreuger, owner of 250 factories on five continents, producing virtually every match struck in the world. After his death were revealed dossiers of forged documents, fictitious accounts, and falsified ledgers that added up to one of the most spectacular swindles the world had yet known. As a multinational legion of attorneys, bankers, and bankruptcy trustees fought over the remaining Kreuger assets, Foster and his longtime financial associate, George Murnane, backpedaled furiously to demonstrate that although they may have profited from the Kreuger business, the misdeeds had been those of others.

In Europe on another diplomatic mission at the height of the Kreuger crisis, Allen received an urgent request from Foster to pull out of the diplomacy of disarmament and become the full-time European representative of the American companies embroiled in the Kreuger bankruptcy. Allen did not hesitate long before delivering his brother an extraordinary rebuff. In a blunt telegram he declined to "dabble" in the Kreuger matters. "Political developments and my close association [with] Geneva work render it difficult for me to move around Europe freely without arousing misapprehension that [I am] secretly involved [in] other negotiations."* Allen was busy making his name in respectable diplomacy, working toward his goal of becoming secretary of state. Public connection with a financial scandal would hardly be useful.

— * —

Allen and Clover attempted a new beginning upon their return from Paris. Though the preoccupied husband was ever ready to continue renting apartments, by now several notches up from what their budget had permitted before, he was also content to let his wife go off in search of a house of their own. She eventually found a classic New York townhouse, a four-story brownstone at 239 East Sixty-first Street. Not spacious, it nonetheless had a lovely dining room that opened onto a little garden

* In his discretion Allen was wiser than his senior, Norman Davis, who did accept missions involving the Kreuger bankruptcy while still representing the United States at the Disarmament Conference. Just as Allen had warned, the critical press (in this case the Hearst newspapers) lambasted Davis for working for government and private business interests at the same time.

with sheltered flower beds. The top two floors were bedrooms, including one for live-in domestic help. Best of all, it was in one of the few city blocks still lined by trees that the fumes of traffic had not destroyed. The Upper East Side neighborhood was not yet as elegant as it would become, but the people of the block were genteel. Down the street lived author John Gunther, fashion designer Elsa Schiaparelli, and even actress Tallulah Bankhead.

One unattractive feature of the neighborhood actually was especially convenient for Allen. The old elevated trains still rumbled the length of Third Avenue, making it noisy, dirty, and forbidding to pedestrians below. But the El station at the end of their block provided the fastest and most convenient access to Wall Street. One car in the middle of each express train was sternly reserved for gentlemen in chesterfield overcoats. As he made his daily commute, Allen would often meet Foster, who boarded the train two stops before, on the middle car. Unemployment and poverty blighted the rest of the land in these years, but hardship was scarcely visible from East Sixty-first Street.

For Toddy and Joan life in New York was blissful. They learned adventure and grace from their wonderful mother, who was as capable of catching a snake in the garden as of telling the neighborhood children all about the Italian Renaissance painting they had seen at the Metropolitan Museum of Art, a short bus ride away. Clover could serve an elegant tea in front of the fireplace, with gleaming silver and delicious savories, and just as readily pitch a tent in the woods on a camping, canoeing, or riding weekend. When she occasionally joined Allen on one of his foreign junkets, the girls missed her terribly. Passing time in Geneva while Allen was at meetings, she immersed herself in a book of Greek philosophy and wrote her thoughts to Toddy and Joan at home. Their disappointment on tearing open the letter was palpable. "Dear Mother," the girls, then ten and eleven, replied. "Please don't write any more about Socrates. We just want to hear some *news!*"

Clover sent both girls to an informal boarding school on the north shore of Long Island, between Cold Spring Harbor and Huntington, at the home of Archibald Roosevelt (son of Theodore). There the Dulles girls and the three Roosevelt daughters sat on the floor of an old-style farmhouse, drank tea, and recited poetry. The curriculum centered on romantic verse. On Saturdays, if the Dulles girls were not summoned home for a family adventure, Mr. Roosevelt would take them walking, sometimes with his son and his nephew, Archie and Kim, who themselves would grow up to play the Great Game.

Something, of course, was missing from this idyllic picture. Toddy and Joan knew their father as a dashing figure; they adored him when they saw him, most predictably when he returned from some long mission. On those occasions Allen might trundle up the stairs to read to them from *The Three Musketeers* at bedtime. On occasion he would affect what the girls called his "party manner," between elegant dinners and tennis at the country club. And sometimes on weekends they would all go for a drive in the family Stutz — with the girls and even baby Allen in the rumble seat. But in the family's daily routine, Father was the preoccupied figure behind his newspaper at the breakfast table and after dinner in the overstuffed chair in front of the fire.

For all his sense of fun with adults, Allen never developed the joyous talent of communicating with the very young, even his children. From afar he worried about them in an absent-minded way. "I hope we can do something to make this a good year for Toddy," he wrote Clover from Europe. "It is so terribly important that she should get all the self-assurance that she needs." Maybe the children were not being exposed to "as much of life as they should at their age — they are too much hot-house products." Young Allen, in particular, did not fit his father's idea of what a growing boy should be. He needed to be "toughened up."

Young Allen Macy Dulles was a brilliant, high-strung, solitary boy. He had an almost pretty face, with long curly brown hair and blue eyes, but he was slight and unathletic. His schoolmates at the Buckley School on East Seventy-third Street called him a "smart aleck." He was clearly struggling to get his father's attention; his favorite pastime became chess, which he had seen Allen and Foster play with such concentration many an evening. As a ten-year-old, he tried hard to read and understand international affairs in obvious — and forlorn — hopes of opening a conversation with his uncommunicative father. One summer Allen took his son along when he went off with Foster to sail down the St. Lawrence River. Such father-son activities were all too rare; more typically it would be Clover, skipping a neighborhood cocktail party, who would take young Allen off to the target range to share her skill with a Winchester .22, or drop a string weighted with chewing gum into the subway grill on the sidewalk in hope of snagging a penny.

Allen's competitive nature showed up on the tennis court, and his game was much too fierce to be enjoyed with his children. Sometimes, however, his tennis season was interrupted by an attack of gout, a chronic ailment of stress and intense living that Allen suffered throughout his life. The disease had nothing to do with his long-overlooked clubfoot, for Foster suffered from gout as well. The difference between the two brothers was that Foster never neglected to take the preventive pills, while Allen too often forgot.

For all their efforts, the 1930s did not go well for Allen and Clover.

The children remembered no scenes of anger or tension between their parents; indeed, there was not much of anything between the two when they were together, and Allen's guilt-ridden correspondence when they were apart belied their emotional distance. "I feel the need of finding more things to bring us together — I don't mean physically, but mentally," he wrote Clover during one long overseas trip. "I am thinking of you and trying, after all these years of thoughtlessness, to see if I can't find some way to make our life more satisfactory."

Throughout his career Allen's most notable talent was his sensitivity to the persons working with him; perhaps this trait excluded that same sensitivity to those nearest to him in his private life. His personal letters during these years reveal no consideration for how Clover would receive his news. After acknowledging his "thoughtlessness," he went on to tell her all about the merry social life of the international set, including a night on the town in Paris with "an attractive (but not beautiful) Irish-French female whom I took to Scheherazade where we stayed until the early hours as usual, somewhat to the annoyance of her husband, I learned.... Her name is 'Gregoire.'" Another letter from London: "Lunched with an English girl, ... rather good-looking.... Danced and drank champagne until quite late." Back in Paris: "Dolbeare and I had a quiet little lunch at the Ritz.... That evening Helen Armstrong and I went out on the town (Ham being off in Berlin) to Café du Paris and Scheherazade. She is a most pleasant companion." From shipboard he described a Mrs. Powell, "your only rival ... a sense of humor, ... a sensible soul, also by no means ugly.... We have been most decorous in our behavior."

Any sense of tact left him in describing to Clover a dinner party for sixteen guests, "including some very attractive ladies, including also a charming widow about whom I may tell more anon, but if I don't I shall when I get back — for as you know, with all my vices, I still have the virtue of honesty (but as I read this over it sounds more ominous than intended)." The party, he informed Clover, was "quite a success, even though I didn't sit next to that widow."

These jolly accounts of her husband's evenings with other women arrived as Clover was attempting to manage a household with three children in rainy New York, and were not welcomed. When she told him so, he replied, "I can sympathize with what you are going through in trying to settle the house in a downpour," not altogether getting the point and then only making matters worse. "I don't feel I deserve as good a wife as I have, as I am rather too fond of the company of other ladies." At one point Allen discussed the tensions in his marriage with the wife of a diplomatic colleague, Norman Davis, whom Clover scarcely knew. "Mrs.

Davis and I had a heart-to-heart talk about you and me. Her thesis was that you wanted more of life than you were getting with me now and while she didn't blame me especially she seemed to feel that I had better be on the lookout to give you more. Think it over. What shall I do? I think Mrs. Davis is probably right." That, however, was the end of his concern.

Soon Allen's self-indulgence spilled over into his life in New York. His first serious extramarital affair started on the tennis courts at Cold Spring Harbor Beach Club. He was not the only member who noticed a White Russian émigré in her mid-thirties, a tall, Nordic blonde with bright eyes and a ready laugh. She was a spirited tennis player, and her chronically ill husband was never in attendance. Their affair crackled with all the magnetic force that was so lacking in Allen's marriage.* In front of Clover and the children he would talk openly in glowing terms about his "tennis partner."

Clover's friends began to question how long she could stand for this. But her friendship with Allen, for friendship was what defined the marriage, was an anchor of stability for a sensitive woman consumed with internal conflicts of her own. Clover's letters to Dr. Worcester reveal a deep guilt about her comfortable upper-class life, resulting in a compulsion to strike up conversations with street beggars and men in the bread lines. With her husband off on diplomatic missions and her children settled in private schools, Clover would try to help the world—and herself—in her own way. From her Upper East Side townhouse she paid regular visits to prisons and became indefatigable in promoting the cause of penal reform.

Then Allen would come home, and with him the sense of fun. When he went away again, well, he and the fun would eventually return.

— * —

In 1932, the last year of the Hoover administration, Allen's ambition was well served by his aloofness from Republican politics. In the Harding and Coolidge administrations the Republicans had seemed secure as the party of the presidency. But the Hooverism so welcomed by the likes of Gibson and Cromwell was not working out. The pain may not have reached East Sixty-first Street or the regulars hanging out at the Scheherazades of the world, but for the United States as a whole, the bold Republican era was over—and would be for longer than anyone could then imagine.

* The lady, now in her nineties, is direct and outspoken but not interested in discussing her fling with Allen six decades ago.

Though he defined himself as a Republican, Allen had started out in public service inspired by Democrat Woodrow Wilson, and as a diplomat and international public servant he was perfectly ready — indeed, eager — to serve a Democratic president. Franklin D. Roosevelt was moving toward the White House, and Allen was on the closest professional terms with the Democrat Norman Davis, who had stuck by him in the post-Lansing purges of the State Department. Even Hoover had to admit that Davis was skilled in patience and persistence; he was a man who "could continue talking long after everyone else got tired." Now this expert in the arcane realm of disarmament negotiations seemed a good bet to be Roosevelt's secretary of state, and Allen was his trusted partner on negotiating missions.

After the year in Paris Allen tried to concentrate on the business of Sullivan and Cromwell, but he agreed to join Davis for the climactic Geneva Disarmament Conference, which was to begin early in 1932. Although disarmament was not exactly the Great Game of Allen's aspirations, in the foreign policy of isolationist America it was the only game in town. The conference on disarmament was spurred by the emergence of a restive Germany out to defy the limitations on arms mandated at Versailles. Germany was in fact rearming, secretly and ominously. At the same time Italy's dictator, Benito Mussolini, was presenting fascism as a new form of political and social organization. The nervous democracies were floundering in search of leadership. "Since the days of Wilson at the Paris Peace Conference," declared one European political newsletter, "no American statesman has been awaited with so much eagerness and expectancy as Norman Davis."[4]

Returning to public service would mean, of course, that Allen would have to take leave from his law practice. Though Sullivan and Cromwell never seemed to mind having its own man in high government circles, Allen's letters to his brother were almost sycophantic in his eagerness to please. He was not yet really close to Hoover's secretary of state, Henry L. Stimson, he wrote Foster, "however he asked me to his table from time to time" on the ocean crossing. And Allen assured his partners at Sullivan and Cromwell that he was quick to "let it be known quietly that I am a lawyer and not a diplomat"— always available if his services might be useful. Davis would be no small private client himself (he was a millionaire from the Cuban sugar business), and Allen assured Foster he had "told [Davis] that if anything comes up in connection with his financial work where I could be of use, to let me know." "Feel about two years out of date on modern disarmament styles," Allen cabled Gibson, "but am starting work with Norman Davis as tutor." Months later, after trips back and forth to Geneva, he wrote his old clubmate, "As usual I have no business to be going, but also as usual I am. As usual, this is the last time."

Nothing turned out to be as usual that winter of 1932–33. A Democrat elected to the White House promised a "New Deal" for Americans. Allen's gout became so severe that he could hardly walk. "I was distressed to find AD on crutches," Gibson wrote Hugh Wilson as Allen and Davis sailed home for Christmas. "He was suffering a good deal of pain and looked pretty badly when we put him on the boat train."

In Germany the National Socialist Party, nicknamed the Nazis, emerged from the radical fringe of discontent to gain a commanding 330 seats out of 647 in the Reichstag, and shortly thereafter the charismatic Nazi leader, Adolf Hitler, assumed dictatorial powers over Germany. In his rhetoric he was audacious enough to challenge the whole Versailles settlement, among other alleged atrocities, but Weimar Social Democrats like Breitscheid, Allen's friend in Berlin, applauded the New Order — believing that under the weight of political responsibility the inexperienced Hitler would only ruin himself.*

After Roosevelt's victory in November 1932, Allen made his rounds among the New Deal upstarts and confessed his amazement at "the extent of the movement to break with the policies, and the individuals who have been responsible for the policies, of the last twelve years." Central to his frustration was that Davis was not, after all, appointed secretary of state. "I have no doubt that Norman's work for the past administration was one of the controlling reasons influencing FDR against appointing him," Allen complained. In fact, Davis's problem was quite different: a conviction for fraud in a Cuban business venture over three decades before; Davis always claimed it was a mere technicality, but it was sufficiently embarrassing to keep him from a cabinet appointment.

Allen, who did not judge the peccadilloes of wealthy businessmen as all that important, saw the situation differently. "I am not at all sure that the country at large wants any very vital change in our foreign policy toward Europe," he wrote a friend, "but the people in Washington will probably wish to make it look as though the policy were being changed, and it is easier to do this with new people than by using those who have been closely identified with the past." Two days after Roosevelt's inauguration, New Dealer Herbert Feis expressed astonishment that Davis was still drafting diplomatic instructions as if no change had occurred. Drew

---

* Breitscheid and his Social Democratic colleague Rudolf Hilferding, both of whom were Allen's friends in the early Weimar Republic, were arrested in southern France in 1941 and delivered up to the Gestapo by the Vichy collaborationist government. Hilferding committed suicide in his Paris cell; Breitscheid died in Buchenwald.

Pearson, the angry columnist of the left, weighed in with personal denunciations of Allen himself, calling him an "operator for the bankers." Raymond Moley, keeper of the New Deal Brains Trust faith, complained that FDR was about to let "an outspoken internationalist" like Allen return to the disarmament conference.

The new secretary of state, Cordell Hull, was more appreciative of the disarmament experts. Davis, accompanied by Allen, was invited to the White House shortly after the inauguration for a presidential massage. "We sat on the back verandah, looking out over the garden to the Washington Monument and discussed all manner of things," Allen wrote Clover. "It was almost informal and the president put on no airs. We all did our share of the talking." Davis and Allen sailed back to Europe on the eighteenth of FDR's Hundred Days. On March 23, 1933, Adolf Hitler became the führer of Germany.

— * —

For disparate individuals yet unknown to Allen or his circle, the spring of 1933 was a life-defining juncture:

- A manager of large mining and banking concerns in the old Silesian city of Breslau, one Eduard Schulte, was flattered to be invited to the Berlin residence of Hitler's lieutenant Hermann Göring on February 20, with industrialists much grander, richer, and more prominent than he. Hitler himself addressed the group, telling how he would save the Fatherland from the decay brought on by the squabbling politicians of Weimar. Schulte was one of the few who were not convinced, though years would pass before he was able to do anything about it.
- A small German advertising agency went under, one of many bankruptcies that led their petit bourgeois proprietors to admire Hitler despite his workingman's socialist veneer. This particular bankrupt, Karl Wolff, was an army veteran who began a meteoric rise in the Nazis' elite SS unit. At a critical moment twelve years later, he and Allen would cross paths uneasily.
- That spring a bumptious apparatchik from Ukraine was being noticed in the Kremlin. He had the task of constructing a glorious subway system for the Soviet capital, and, though he had already risen to the post of second secretary of Moscow's Communist Party, Nikita S. Khrushchev thought nothing of donning overalls and supervising the men working deep under the city streets.
- Around this time (he never pinned down the date exactly) a six- or seven-year-old Cuban boy in the south coastal town of Santiago threw a tantrum to force his godparents to let him leave his foster home and

go to boarding school. Fidel Castro called the incident "my first rebellion," and it worked so well that others followed.

· A seemingly diffident English student, finishing his degree at Cambridge, was approached that spring by a Soviet intelligence officer with
a secret long-term proposition. Angry at the British ruling classes, the
quiet rebel agreed to live a life of deception, starting off as a student
agitator in Vienna, where he fell in love with a lithesome Austrian
communist woman. Some years later, in 1951, one of their circle, a
young Zionist with a prodigious ability to remember names and faces
— his name was Teddy Kollek — recalled the romance and their marriage when he chanced upon that same Englishman lingering just
outside Allen Dulles's office in one of the more secret corridors of
intelligence. What is that guy doing here? Kollek asked his host, the
head of American counterespionage.[5] With a shrug, James J. Angleton dismissed Kollek's casual reminiscence of the communist past of
Kim Philby.

— * —

"I haven't felt so rested for months," Allen wrote Clover from aboard the
S.S. *Manhattan* late in March 1933. "My foot seems to be quite all right."
He even suggested that Clover join him, a charming idea that only a busy
mother would recognize as thoroughly impractical.

Allen and Norman Davis went through a string of consultations outside the official conference framework with French premier Edouard
Daladier and foreign minister Joseph Paul-Boncour, British prime minister Ramsay MacDonald, and the emerging Tory diplomat Anthony
Eden. The curious European press speculated about the "mystery mission" of the two American diplomats. Foster and others at the firm saw
possibilities. Could Allen manage to be photographed at these high-level
meetings to call attention to Sullivan and Cromwell? This sort of thing
went against Davis's and Allen's inclinations. He reported back to Foster
that though he had managed to fit in meetings with Schröder partners
and other clients during his visits to London, the "publicity angle is not
going much better than before."

In their talks the two Americans pressed Washington's simplistic no-
tions of disarmament. Let everyone maintain defensive weapons but cut
back sharply the stockpiles of offensive weapons. The British declared
their tank force entirely defensive. The French explained that their submarines served simply to defend their shores. Countries without a significant air force insisted that bombers were offensive weapons, but the
United States replied that they simply misunderstood aerial strategy.
One European statesman told a parable: "The animals met to disarm.

The lion looked the bull straight in the eye and said, 'Let us abolish horns.' The bull looked at the eagle and suggested abolishing talons. The eagle, eyeing the lion, recommended the abolition of teeth. 'Yes,' said the bear, 'let us abolish everything and then just have one universal hug.'"

The new political forces on the rise confounded measurement. Mussolini and his fascists were worrisome enough, but Hitler in Berlin was beginning to look like considerably more than a junior partner in dictatorship. "The Hitler party is so strong," Allen wrote home, "it is questionable whether they can be induced to enter into any coalition German government, and it is doubtful whether the other parties would let them take over."

As Allen and Davis left 10 Downing Street on March 31, they were handed distressing news about "attacks on Jews in Germany." Clearly something ominous was building in Europe, and the government of the United States needed more information about it. On April 7, 1933, his fortieth birthday, Allen Dulles boarded the train with Davis for Berlin to meet and talk it out with this man Adolf Hitler.

— * —

The encounter that ensued is one that, amazingly enough, Allen never chose to talk about in later years, either in after-dinner conversations or in more serious office discussions.* It came upon foundations well laid.

Allen had met Mussolini the previous November. The Italian dictator was full of charm and good feelings about disarmament, but his questions suggested a different preoccupation. A League of Nations commission had just a month before denounced the Japanese occupation of Manchuria; Davis and Allen noted that on the side table of Il Duce's Palazzo Venezia office was a large atlas open to the maps of Japan and China. What would the League do about one member state invading another, Mussolini wondered. Three years later, when Italy invaded Ethiopia, the two diplomats understood better what had been on Mussolini's mind. At the time Davis sent Washington a glowing report of the meeting: "It will prove well worth while as regards securing a friendly attitude on both naval and Far Eastern matters on Italy's part." Allen said only that he had found Mussolini to be "quite a fellow."

The discussions of fascism in 1933 that made an impact on Allen took

* Richard Helms, who became one of Allen's successors as head of the CIA in the 1970s, was astonished to learn, during the writing of this biography, that his longtime boss had actually met Hitler. He could offer no explanation why Allen, who never missed an opportunity to tell a good story, kept silent on this one. Allen mentioned the meeting in passing during a radio interview in 1966, but no one picked up the hint as worth pursuing.

place, not in offices of state, but in the bucolic setting of the Bucking-hamshire seat of Lord Astor and his American-born wife, Nancy. "You couldn't imagine a more lovely place than Cliveden, high above the wind-ing Thames," Allen wrote Clover. "Vast lawns, lovely trees and hedges and vistas. . . . It is a typical English weekend we're having and on a large scale. . . . Political and international discussion takes up the time from 5 to 7 and again after dinner."

The so-called Cliveden set became a symbol of the British flirtation with fascism, leading to the policy of appeasement at Munich. This was somewhat unfair to the house and to the Astors, for their grand weekends included politicians and other influential people of many political views. One whom Allen met there, the author Rebecca West, was ever scorn-ful of charges that Britain's ruling class was betraying their country. "Treachery is alert and quick-witted and expectant of gain," West wrote after a Cliveden weekend, "whereas the mood of our governors was drowsy and hallucinated." Allen loved it. "Have had another delightful weekend with the Astors — the more I see of this place the more en-chanted I am with it." One weekend he motored over to nearby Che-quers, country home of England's prime ministers, to see Ramsay Mac-Donald. Another day he was invited to Baron Schröder's home for lunch, to inspect a world-famous collection of orchids. "Here was another lovely English country place, but none of them, not even Chequers, can compare with Cliveden for sheer beauty of setting." Driving back to the Astors' home, Allen "got lost on the way in an English mist, but finally arrived in time for the late tea."

Not only at Cliveden was Europe's emerging fascism perceived through a drowsy mist. Allen and Davis prepared themselves as best they could about what to expect from a general conversation with Hitler. Da-ladier advised them that the führer had little "idea of either what he was doing or what he wanted to do, . . . and seemed to be considerably lost as head of the government instead of head of an opposition." Indeed, Da-ladier had received an intelligence report just two days before that Hitler was worried about foreign reaction to his sanctions against the Jews of Germany and was considering a compensatory gesture.*

Hitler had been chancellor since January 30; less than a month later a suspicious fire destroyed the Reichstag building in Berlin, and the ensu-ing parliamentary chaos resulted in the Gleichshaltung, an official act

---

* If that was what French intelligence was picking up, Hamilton Fish Armstrong learned otherwise. After meeting with Hitler two weeks later, Armstrong noted that "he did not ask me a single question or by any remark or reference reveal that he was in the least concerned by what the world thought of him or of the position in which he had placed his country."

passing all legal authority to the führer. That was on March 23, two weeks before Allen and Davis arrived. Daladier had been right about one thing: the new führer did not have a detailed foreign policy in readiness. The day the two American diplomats reached Berlin, Hitler was briefed at a cabinet meeting on the international scene. "We must for tactical reasons primarily strive for disarmament of the other nations," the meeting concluded. Foreign attitudes toward the New Order came in for some discussion; the Nazis were frankly unsure of where they stood. "The lack of interest of the United States in European conditions will probably not change under Roosevelt's presidency. . . . We cannot count on active support from Washington for our political demands and wishes."[6]

Hitler's office in the old Chancellery on the Wilhelmstrasse was just across from the American Embassy of Allen's 1920 memories. At four o'clock on the afternoon of April 8, he and Davis were escorted into the presence by Ernst ("Putzi") Hanfstaengl, the German-American who served Hitler in the early years as translator, court jester, and shill to perplexed Americans.* Hitler was given in those days to quoting Machiavelli's advice that one must either destroy or conciliate an enemy. Accordingly he took the initiative from the start of the meeting.

Explaining Germany's plight under the Versailles settlement, Hitler asked Davis and Allen how Americans would have felt after the Civil War if the North had made the southern states sign a treaty keeping them in indefinite subjugation. Not a shrewd beginning, for Davis, a gentleman of the South, jumped to reply. "Without fear of exaggeration," he informed Hitler, "the way the North treated the South after the Civil War was far worse than anything France had done to Germany." The North had even gone so far as to install former slaves as judges! Hitler caught the racial innuendo immediately — black judges! — and conceded he had chosen a bad example. What about America's gentle treatment of Spain after that turn-of-the-century war? "One of the reasons why the terms of the peace were made easy for Spain," Davis explained, as Allen took careful notes, "was because the United States had no fear whatever of Spain. Such was not the case as regards the relations between France and Germany."

Such sparring would go nowhere. When Hitler launched into his standard denunciation of the Versailles war guilt clause, neither man

---

* Putzi had gone to Harvard; his mother was a Sedgwick from Boston. A pathetic figure, he had fallen out of favor with Hitler by the time World War II started. He escaped to Canada and ended his days helping American psychological warfare teams interpret Nazi propaganda.

chose to reply; how could Hitler have known that Allen's brother and
Davis were among those who had written the offending text fourteen
years before? Davis was provoked to go just a bit beyond his State Department instructions to raise reports of recent German "excesses,"
which "had been very disturbing to public opinion abroad . . . and shaken
international confidence in Germany." Hitler, knowing these men to be
deeply involved in international finance, played his own card back: the
world should be careful about making it difficult for his government "adequately to protect the millions of foreign capital that are invested in
Germany."[7]

On and on, over fixed positions, the German leader and the American
envoys got a sense of each other, but it was not a fruitful or informative
encounter. On their return to Paris Davis and Allen briefed Daladier over
dessert and coffee. Davis reported finding Hitler "not being very sure of
his ground on many subjects, apparently relying largely upon forensic
ability to produce an impression." Both Americans foresaw "a future rift
within the party between Hitler and Goering." Davis later pressed his in-
dulgent view that Hitler found it to be in Germany's interest to limit armaments "and that in point of fact he is less militaristic than Neurath,
von Papen and others." Allen wrote Foster to discount an alarmist view
about the new German regime that had been conveyed by a mutual
friend. "I think conditions are not quite as bad as he would indicate."

Hitler went from the meeting to a mass rally at the Berlin Sports-
palast, where he gave one of his most bombastic speeches. The world
would soon become accustomed to the shouted response *Sieg Heil!* Long
afterward the führer dismissed Norman Davis as a "petty profiteer"
and took no notice whatever of Allen, the modest note taker, whose central preoccupation a decade later would be the effort to deal with Hitler
once and for all — through assassination.

But that spring of 1933 Allen seemed to be in the mood of Cliveden — if not hallucinatory, certainly drowsy, which may be why he was so
reticent later about his encounter with Hitler. In a letter to Clover he
wrote that his talk with the führer had been "long and interesting," but he
complained, "I am getting somewhat tired of this trip and want to get
back as soon as I can."* Respected friends of Allen's saw into Hitler at that
early date much more clearly than he did. Over Easter dinner in Paris a
week after his quick visit to Berlin, Allen gave a lackluster briefing to

* Allen's ennui contrasts sharply with the vivid impression Hitler made upon Richard
Helms. As a young reporter for United Press, Helms managed a widely published interview
with the führer in 1936 — making it even more puzzling that Allen and Helms never reminisced about their separate meetings with Hitler.

Ham Armstrong, himself on his way to see the chancellor and scout out articles for *Foreign Affairs*. Through Armstrong's subsequent accounts Allen saw how wrong he had been in relegating Hitler to the category of just another normal, if somewhat irritable, head of state. Armstrong saw the same storm troopers in jackboots who had greeted Allen in Berlin, the policemen giving the *Heil Hitler!* salute, the propaganda blaring from loudspeakers on the street corners. With none of Allen's complacency, he wrote of the Nazi leader:

> A few words at the start of a sentence about some indignity inflicted on Germany would suddenly carry [Hitler's] voice up to the breaking point, his eyes flashed and a wisp of hair fell down over his left eye.... The rocket went up with a whiz, then there was a splutter, he smoothed his hair and went on again comparatively calmly.
>
> A people has disappeared.... Almost every German whose name the world knew as a leader in government, business, science or the arts in the Republic of the past fourteen years was gone.... The waves were swiftly cutting the sand beneath them, and day by day, one by one, the last specimens of another age, another folk, were toppling over into the Nazi sea.[8]

Allen and Davis had simply gone through the motions of traditional diplomatic intercourse, and the memory was apparently one that Allen did not wish to retain. A short time later, meeting Nazi propaganda minister Joseph Goebbels, Allen differed with colleagues who denounced the Nazis' aims and methods. He found himself "rather impressed with [Goebbels's] sincerity and frankness." Davis, returning from the meeting with Hitler to the ever civilized Adlon Hotel at the corner of Unter den Linden, was startled to find the world "Juden" coarsely scrawled on the door of his room.[9] Such a display of discourtesy was deemed offensive, and the embarrassed hotel management offered deep apologies to the American diplomats.

Allen Welsh Dulles in 1922 at twenty-nine, aspiring to a career in diplomacy with ambitions to become secretary of state in the footsteps of his uncle and grandfather. He had already served as a junior diplomat in Vienna and Bern during World War I, in Paris during the Peace Conference, and in Berlin at the launching of the Weimar Republic.

Allen, circa 1897, the "published" author of a schoolboy's treatise on the Boer War, written during a semester at his grandfather's home in Washington.

The family of John Watson Foster. Standing, left to right, are General Foster's grandchildren: Nataline, Allen, Eleanor, Foster, and Foster's wife, Janet. Seated, left to right, are Allen Macy Dulles, Edith Foster Dulles (Allen's parents), John Watson Foster and his wife, Mary Parke Foster, and two unidentified adults and children. Seated in front are Margaret Dulles Edwards (Allen's sister) and her son Robert Lansing Edwards.

The Dulles brothers at play at Henderson Harbor, circa 1910. Left to right: John Foster, then an undergraduate at Princeton, Allen, and an unidentified friend.
(Allen Dulles Papers, Princeton University Library)

Clover Todd as a debutante in Baltimore. This formal portrait was taken for the season before Allen first saw his future wife. They met at a house party in Thousand Islands, New York, in 1920, and he proposed marriage within the month.

Allen and Clover
in Scotland, 1926.
*(Allen Dulles Papers,
Princeton University Library)*

The three Dulles children, Allen, Toddy, and Joan, with their
nurses and dog, at Henderson Harbor.

Above left: Mary Bancroft, Allen's OSS research assistant and mistress, in Bern, 1943. Mary was a student of Carl Gustav Jung, and she became a lifelong friend of Clover's; their love for the same man was more a bond than an obstacle.

Above right: Wally Toscanini, Countess Castelbarco, in 1948. Allen first noticed the daughter of Maestro Arturo Toscanini in wartime Switzerland, where she was a valuable contact with the antifascist Italian resistance. "If ever a woman could be called a lady while having an affair with a married man," said Allen's daughter Toddy, "Wally was that lady."

Clover and son Allen Macy Dulles, circa 1937. "He was a beautiful, winning child, big blue eyes, curly hair; people would stop on the street and stare at him," his older sister Joan said. "I honestly don't know why my father never appreciated him."

Above: The American disarmament delegation arrives in Berlin in April 1933 to meet with the new chancellor, Adolf Hitler. Chief negotiator Norman Davis is at center; Allen, his aide, is at left, carrying a briefcase. *(Allen Dulles Papers, Princeton University Library)*

Below: An example of the vast haul of Nazi documents smuggled out of Berlin by Allen's best German agent, Fritz Kolbe ("George Wood"). In his office, two doors from Foreign Minister von Ribbentrop's, Kolbe would photograph the papers that crossed his desk and pass them through clandestine cut-outs to Allen in Bern.

Above left: William J. ("Wild Bill") Donovan returning from England in 1940. Founder of the World War II Office of Strategic Services, Donovan gave Allen his start as a professional intelligence officer and later became his rival for leadership of the CIA. *(UPI/Bettmann)*

Above right: An early promoter of covert action against the communists, George Kennan is interviewed on his arrival in Frankfurt in 1952. His offhand remarks resulted in his expulsion as United States ambassador to the Soviet Union. *(Associated Press)*

Walter Bedell Smith, director of central intelligence from 1950 to 1953, easily enticed Allen away from his New York law practice into the CIA, then fought with him about launching covert actions to defeat communism.

Joan, Toddy, Clover, and Allen Macy Dulles at Lloyd Neck, Long Island, in the late 1940s.

— 6 —

ON THE WAY TO WAR

OVER THE YEARS the word "internationalist" has meant different things to different people. To the father of American military intelligence, Colonel Ralph Van Deman, as the waves of Bolshevism pounded against the Paris Peace Conference, the word was a synonym for the revolutionaries who sought to engulf the world. To the founders of the Council on Foreign Relations, taking up where the Wilsonian peacemakers left off, it became a badge of honor against the "isolationist" general public. With the Wall Street crash of 1929, "internationalist" became the populist epithet for the bankers and lawyers alleged to have duped Main Street America.

In the thinking of the early New Deal, therefore, the word was again pejorative. Internationalists in 1932 were profit-chasing tools of the bankers, greedy plutocrats whose only concept of the national interest was their own profit line. It was the bankers and their international connections that had dragged the United States into the Great War, according to the dogma, and by the 1930s these same financial forces were trying to engage the United States in "foreign" problems just to protect the loans they had made so irresponsibly and for such profit in the 1920s. By contrast "isolationist" was not the badge of craven mindset that it would later become among FDR's more liberal Brains Trusters. Economic nationalists like Raymond Moley and Rexford Tugwell found that the imperatives of national planning at the depths of a deep depression simply left no room for international economic cooperation.

Allen never had a problem accepting the label "internationalist." To him it had no negative connotation, nor did it seem wrong to assert that public officials were serving the interests of international commerce and finance. Ever since his Constantinople days, seeing the imperial tradition of trade following the flag, Allen held to his own concept of the contrary American tradition: trade, generally speaking, *was* the flag. American national and business interests were parallel and complementary. He may have felt that his roles as a lawyer for private clients and as an official representative of the United States government occasionally conflicted, but only on technical, operational matters, never on fundamental purpose. Allen and his circle saw no conflict between American economic interests and Wilsonian political ideals of freedom and democracy; on the contrary, the ideals were sure to follow the trailblazing businessmen.

Without being deliberately spelled out, this philosophy allowed Allen to reconcile his lifelong dedication to the Wilsonian ideal with the Republicanism of his family and background. It was a merger of two traditions that in the later twentieth century were usually considered to be in opposition. For Allen the merger was so internalized that he simply could not comprehend critics who found fault with government and business operating in tandem. In the implementation of his philosophy over decades to come, in lands as far afield as Iran and Guatemala, Allen never felt obliged to explain or justify why American business and American government (or at least the one sensitive branch for which he was responsible) were working in such intimacy. How could anyone be so churlish — or malevolent — as to question the self-evident?

That said, the notable feature in the evolution of Allen's political thought in the troubled 1930s, as the world drifted toward war, was his rejection of the internationalist dogma on a central point: the sanctity of financial relationships among nations. Important though this network of obligations might be for stability and well-being, it was not for Allen the full measure of the American national interest. On that issue he seemed at times almost sympathetic to the suspicious populists of the New Deal. He found himself uncomfortably embarked upon six years of open dissent with his brother Foster for the first time in their public careers. Their differences started over those controversial foreign loans for which Sullivan and Cromwell was both cheerleader and beneficiary, but gradually built into opposition on the fundamental foreign policy question of the day: should the United States intervene or stay aloof as the fascist challenge mounted to threaten democratic Europe?

The first signs of fraternal dissent came with Allen's refusal to help in the Kreuger cleanup. Foster did not press the matter with his brother, and Allen sailed for home in October 1933 rather than remain in Europe as a business representative. As had become the pattern, Allen was judged newsworthy by the pack of reporters wandering the decks of incoming liners for interviews with arriving passengers. His measured views on disarmament and international affairs attracted more journalistic interest than anything offered by his fellow passengers on the S.S. *Europa:* Fritz Kreisler and Serge Rachmaninoff of the concert hall, Katherine Cornell and Basil Rathbone of the stage, all of whom worked much harder than Allen at maintaining their celebrity.

Back at the firm Allen found the perspective of his law partners, including his brother, on the depression in Europe quite different from his own. At the beginning of 1932 Germany had officially vowed that it would make no further reparations payments; then, as the financial collapse escalated, more and more of the 1920s loans turned bad.

For years to come, Foster argued the importance to the nation's economic health of large and sustained private lending to foreigners.* Allen and Norman Davis considered that approach wrong-headed; already there had been significant "over-lending." As Davis wrote to a friend in the spring of 1932, "While last year the idea became prevalent here that Europe was suffering more from a lack of proper credit facilities than from tariffs, the countries which are now having the most trouble financially are those which have had *too much credit.*" Allen's dissent came to a head his second year back.

His position at Sullivan and Cromwell was somewhat special. He was a full partner, of course, and had gained the appreciation, even respect, of his peers for his perseverance and the smooth sophistication with which he managed his influential connections. Allen carried his share of the legal drone work as diligently as he had tackled consular duty in his previous career, and his natural personal magnetism won him the affections of class after class of young associates, men whom Foster seldom seemed to notice. But he never was in the inner circle of the Wall Street legal community. Foster was the senior partner and in charge — of that there was never any doubt. Allen's income, comfortable though it became, was only half of Foster's, at most. Even when the Dulles brothers shared an office, everyone knew which was beholden. But if it ever occurred to Allen to bolt from Foster's stable and join a firm where he could be more independent, there is no evidence of it.

For all their continuing loyalty to each other, the Dulles brothers remained in different leagues professionally and socially. They and their families enjoyed summer vacations together, though both found it harder to tolerate the old-fashioned family gatherings at Henderson Harbor with the sisters and families who seemed provincial and tedious to high-powered Wall Street lawyers.

---

* Decades later George Murnane, Foster's financial partner, still argued that if the United States had been more generous with the Brüning government of Weimar Germany before 1932, Hitler's advent might have been avoided.

What really set Allen apart from the others at Sullivan and Cromwell was that he was well known to the press and to foreign leaders. Because he was just such a public figure, the partners asked him to address the firm's annual dinner for 1935, at the clubby Down Town Association next door to Sullivan and Cromwell. Allen could have delivered one of his usual speeches on disarmament, collective security, morality among nations, or the like. Instead, he presumed to talk from notes about the business of the law firm. He reviewed the heady period from 1924 to 1931 and the $1.15 billion in foreign securities that the firm had managed. The fact that many of these were now in default, he reassured his associates, "was no reflection on legal work involved." The problem, rather, was the lack of any "safeguard against economic conditions such as during the last few years." Sailing perilously close to criticism of his partners (including his brother), he suggested that the firm may have "permitted debt to pile up too fast and too high, [taking] bad moral risk."

That was a heavy statement, and Allen hastened to explain: "Bonds of [a] foreign borrower are only payable out of excess revenues of debtors after meeting his internal costs of administration and political exigencies." The consequences of default, therefore, are "moral and not legal . . . as the obligator is without effective remedy." Delivering a body blow to all claims of financial prudence, he laid bare the fallacy upon which the firm's business has been based, declaring that the "foreign bond, except in being a promise to pay [a] certain amount of money, has few of the attributes of a bond," that is, of a conservative, prudent vehicle for investment by the unwary Americans of Main Street.[1] For all the mellowness and bonhomie of the occasion, Allen's message was unsettling to his partners, his brother, and the younger associates seeking role models for their own careers. But it was not his only act of guarded insubordination.

— * —

During the heyday of Sullivan and Cromwell's business in Germany, before the loans started going sour, the firm maintained legal representation in Berlin with the venerable firm of Albert and Westrick. Dr. Heinrich F. Albert, the senior partner and Sullivan and Cromwell's corresponding counsel, was sixty-five years old in 1930, a powerfully built Junker with straight, parallel saber scars lining the side of his face. A man to be reckoned with, he could have been a force in sustaining the fragile democracy of Weimar — had he chosen to do so. He was well connected and respected in the business circles that counted. Indeed, so appropriate was he for Sullivan and Cromwell's purposes that no one in the Wall Street office found it worthwhile to recall Dr. Albert's previous, disastrous encounter with the United States.

In 1915, early in the Great War, as America held itself neutral but sympathetic to Britain and France, the kaiser's strategists had the idea of sending Albert to New York, ostensibly as a commercial attaché but in reality as an agent provocateur — to spread sabotage and foment disruptive strikes in American factories suspected of supplying munitions to the Allies. The clumsy conspiracy came to light in New York in July of that year when an undercover policeman lifted Albert's briefcase on the Sixth Avenue El and found sheafs of incriminating documents that led to more than $27 million squirreled away for covert actions. Albert was promptly declared *persona non grata;* President Wilson described him as "the directing and more dangerous mind in all these unhappy intrigues."[2]

But that was long ago. Cromwell's law firm never let the peccadilloes of yesterday inhibit the good business of today and tomorrow. Such was the capacity for denial that Allen himself could remark upon "the hostile and criminal acts of German agents in the United States" without acknowledging that his firm's German partner was among those committing such acts. It was the Sullivan and Cromwell style to seek out and cultivate persons of influence and effectiveness, however irregular their credentials, and in 1930 Berlin Albert was just their man.

Allen may have been drowsy when he met Hitler in 1933, but he had regained his customary alertness when he went back to Berlin two years later and felt a growing "sinister impression" of the city he had known in younger years. Albert and his junior partner, Gerhardt Westrick, welcomed their New York partner in the grand old Prussian manner. At lunch Allen agreed to play golf the following morning at the course near Westrick's country home. By his arrangement, a car arrived after lunch on Sunday to take him to the home, out beyond Potsdam, of another business associate, a banker who could not comfortably be entertained by the likes of Albert and Westrick. This was Paul Kempner, a Jewish banker of means, sophistication, and confidence — until, as he told Allen late into that Sunday evening, the Nazis' antisemitic mob actions had begun. The indignities, hardships, and humiliations were endless for even the richest German Jews.* Allen found during his visit that even Sullivan and Cromwell clients were affected. The Warburgs, the leading Jewish financial family of Germany, had lost so much of their operations under the Aryan laws that they could no longer afford to retain the high-powered American firm.

---

* Allen was later instrumental in helping Kempner escape from Germany and establish himself in the United States. Along with Henry Maxwell Andrews, Allen and Clover functioned as the New York end of an informal "Scarlet Pimpernel" network to aid well-heeled German Jews, bankers and lawyers with whom they had done business.

Upon his return, Allen took steps even more unsettling to orthodoxy than the speech he was about to deliver to the annual dinner. Lining up several of the junior partners who regarded him with great loyalty and enlisting as well the support of two Jewish senior partners, Allen called a special meeting of the partnership to recommend that Sullivan and Cromwell close down its Berlin office and phase out its relations with the likes of Albert and Westrick.

It was an awkward personal situation, not least because at that very time Dr. Albert's son, Christian, was working as a friendly intern in the Wall Street office. Foster resisted the "rebellion," arguing that Sullivan and Cromwell still had good and profitable business to conduct in Germany. Allen and his co-conspirators retorted that Nazi discriminatory legal procedures made it impossible to practice legitimate law in such a regime, and furthermore they found it "morally objectionable" to maintain a presence under such conditions. Many years later Allen reminisced that Foster was taken aback at this insurrection, bewildered at the whole argument, until finally he "capitulated" with an anger and emotion evident to all around the conference table.*

Until this confrontation Sullivan and Cromwell had been content to perceive the economy, industrial base, and fascist adventures of Nazi Germany as the peculiarities of one set of difficult clients. After the "rebellion" the firm's record could withstand the scrutiny of the post–World War II years. But from 1935 up to the moment of war six years later the two Dulles brothers were pulled, by habit and conviction, in opposite directions on the fundamental responsibilities and ultimate purpose of United States foreign policy.

— * —

Ham Armstrong wasted no time in engaging Allen in the affairs of the Council on Foreign Relations. A regular contributor to *Foreign Affairs*, Allen had been named to the council's board of directors in 1927, a fresh

---

* The details of this partnership "revolt" have spawned conflicting mythologies in the Dulles record, from the convenience of hindsight. In 1949 Foster, his memory clouded by postwar recriminations, claimed that "as soon as Hitler came into power in Germany, my firm, as a matter of considered policy, refused to transact any business with Germany, and the few German clients we did have we immediately dropped." Equally untenable, however, is the version attributed to Allen himself that Foster "burst into tears" before his partners, an unlikely occurrence for Foster Dulles under any circumstances. Foster's successor as managing partner, Arthur Dean, who was present at the meeting, firmly denied that there had been any revolt or, certainly, any tears. Part of the confusion arises from the fact that Allen's colorful details are available only through the recollections of later CIA colleagues, who were as good at embellishing stories as Allen himself.

presence among the investment bankers, corporate executives, and lawyers who had founded the organization. Allen was adamant in preserving the objective, nonpartisan cast of the council. "It is a workshop, not a propaganda agency," he would tell impatient critics. As his ties to the diplomatic club gradually lapsed with the development of his legal career, the council, just a few blocks from his home, offered another center of masculine fellowship. His colleague Norman Davis became the council's president in 1936.

Allen also found the council to be a useful forum for flattering distinguished foreign clients. He would invite them to speak and, over dinner afterward, develop friendly relationships that could be turned to business advantage. It was unseemly, then as now, to stress this self-serving aspect of the council's utility, though Allen would find delicate ways of pointing it out when he solicited contributions to the council's endowment. And when diverse clients of Sullivan and Cromwell could be included appropriately in council functions, the entrée to the American "establishment" did the firm and Allen no harm.

After returning from his meeting with Hitler and the ineffectual Geneva Disarmament Conference in late 1933, Allen arranged for the council to convene a high-level private study group to ponder the question of how the United States might preserve its neutrality in the event of a war in Europe. The formulation of the question was a sop to the isolationism still prevailing in America, even though the course of discussion would show that Allen had his own agenda to impose upon the council's deliberations. Leading the study group through 1934 and 1935 was former Secretary of State Henry Stimson; Norman Davis participated, along with two members of Congress, the chairman of the board of United States Steel, the presidents of International General Electric and General Motors Export, and a senior partner of the house of Morgan.

Neutrality was a vision of foreign policy that fit the American mood of letting the Europeans deal with their own problems. The group at the council proceeded to define the policy in legalistic, operational terms: the right to trade freely with belligerents, the right of Americans to travel unimpeded, and such. Some argued that it had been an overly rigid stand on principles of international law that drew the United States into war in 1917. How could such a mistake, if mistake it was, be avoided in a hypothetical future conflict?

One possibility worked over in the study group was total "nonintercourse" with any belligerent, or, as Allen sarcastically described it, "batten down the hatches and wait until the storm has blown over." His reply to that straw man was that at a minimum American business could lose many markets from self-quarantine. Then came the pettifogging idea that

Americans who wished to trade with belligerents or travel in war zones should simply be put on notice that they would do so at their own risk.

Allen seized the occasion to propose another alternative, which he cautiously called "benevolent neutrality." If one country bent on conquest threatened another, and the major powers took collective economic action to isolate the warmonger, the United States could forsake "disinterested impartiality" and deny arms and dollars to the aggressor. This stance would be no mere altruistic gesture, Allen argued, but would serve America's enlightened self-interest in preventing a global war. Fine, but was this really neutrality? And did it really serve American national interests? It all smacked of internationalism.

Allen developed the arguments of the council study group in delivering the keynote address to a seminar in London organized in June 1935 by Armstrong and Arnold Toynbee, the latter representing the council's British counterpart, the Royal Institute of International Affairs. Allen's worries about an imminent breakdown in the world order established at Versailles were not supported by the business-as-usual mood he found on his business trips to Europe, he confessed. "I admit that the nearer one gets to Europe from America, the less one is impressed with any danger of an early war. . . . At the same time one must recognize that the forces at work may eventually lead to war, and that the counteracting forces for the organization of peace have not kept peace."

Thus Allen was cautiously diverging from Foster's orthodoxy. Foster was not at all concerned that forces were leading toward war, or that peace — at least for the United States — was endangered. About the same time as Allen was speaking in London, Foster submitted an article to the *Atlantic Monthly* arguing that the emerging dictators might have a legitimate grievance, and it would be foolish to resist making changes in the status quo that might avert another war. The language was guarded, but its underlying message came through clearly to at least one seasoned reader, Cromwell in Paris. He wrote Foster, his onetime protégé, with scarcely contained anger: "You will be the first to recognize the inevitable application of this principle by nations for revision of territorial expansion and treaty provisions — as in the cases of Germany, Japan, Italy, Hungary, Austria, etc. Doubtless your article will be quoted in support of such national claims."[3]

On October 3, 1935, Mussolini invaded Ethiopia, and the hypothetical questions moved a few notches toward reality. Allen and Armstrong worked over the records of the council's study group deliberations to produce a book, published early in 1936. (For all his other writings and speeches, it was Allen's first book since *The Boer War*, several ages back.) Entitled *Can We Be Neutral?* this essay laid out the internationalist case for American responsibility in the affairs of a broader world. *The New York Times* called the book "a lawyer's brief into which emotion intrudes only when they hint at their conception of the 'ultimate' American interest in the current [Ethiopian] war."

Here was the hidden agenda that Allen took into the council's study group and which he was now ready to unveil in public, well knowing that it would not find favor among many of those intellectually and personally closest to him. "In many circles it was considered almost improper to speak of war as a possibility," Dulles and Armstrong wrote. "The only sure way for the United States to escape entanglement in foreign wars is for there to be no wars."[4] As simple as that — the internationalist, collective-security agenda under the guise of merely preserving America's comforting neutrality. Thus they reached their ringing conclusion: "No nation can reach the position of a world power as we have done without becoming entangled in almost every quarter of the globe in one way or another. We are inextricably and inevitably tied to world affairs. We should not delude ourselves that, like Perseus of mythology, we can put on neutrality as a helmet and render ourselves invisible and immune to a world in conflict around us." If some thought of classical heroes, much of the American intelligentsia responded more like long-necked African birds. Allen and Armstrong quoted with delight a senator wryly asking if the import of ostrich feathers might possibly be outlawed as contraband.

Foster started work on a contrary book of his own, to be published as *War, Peace and Change*. Without confronting his younger brother directly, he made clear his conviction that too much of America was sinking into war hysteria. As he saw it, Europe was acting out the struggle "between the dynamic and the static — the urge to acquire and the desire to retain." Foster's sympathy to Germany's plight after Versailles was only fueled by the eagerness of Sullivan and Cromwell's European correspondents to maintain a stance of business as usual. As Hitler reoccupied the Rhineland in March 1936, the firm's Paris representative, Max Shoop, wrote Foster that the "French people would not plunge into a war to prevent or avenge the German government asserting its full sovereign rights within its own territorial borders."

To an American friend critical of his seeming nonchalance about the threat to European democracy, Foster protested that he disagreed with much of what Hitler was doing but could not be unimpressed with "one who from humble beginnings, and despite the handicap of alien nationality, has attained the unquestioned leadership of a great nation." He added that Mussolini presented "more serious threats to the general peace than any act of Hitler."[5] "Only hysteria entertains the idea that Germany, Italy, or Japan contemplates war upon us," he told a New York audience.

As Foster's friend Thomas E. Dewey, the interesting new governor of New York, recalled about their many conversations during these years, Foster believed "Hitler was a passing phenomenon . . . reflecting a basic economic problem. . . . His thesis was that the fat and happy should gracefully yield to avoid war."[6]

Thus the issue was joined across the intellectual establishments of Britain and America: to appease the dictators or resist them? Allen found himself uncomfortably isolated from his brother, from the civilized folk he had met at Cliveden, and even from his old diplomatic clubmate Hugh Wilson, soon to be named ambassador to Germany. Wilson argued that in confronting the dictators, "the only way which shows any hope is to give them an occasional glimpse of green pastures and try to whet their appetites to come with us to graze." After presenting his credentials to Hitler in March 1938, Wilson wrote President Roosevelt in the language of Foster rather than Allen: "It was a moment of great interest to me to meet a man who had pulled his people from moral and economic despair into the state of pride and evident prosperity they now enjoyed."

Of Allen's close friends, only Ham Armstrong and Norman Davis fully shared his internationalist views. Allen was discouraged. He advised Davis against delivering a strong warning about the threat of war in Europe in June 1938, saying the country was "unprepared," and too alarming an analysis might backfire or at least have "unforeseeable implications." In his own public statements Allen characteristically kept his voice low and his analysis gentle. "I am not sure, for all that, that we can stay out of war," he would tell audiences across the country. "I don't know whether we will want to stay out."[7] Clearly, he himself would not want to stay out, but he despaired of bringing the public along.

Public disagreements did not intrude upon the brothers' private relations during these years. Later, of course, historical retrospect was so uncompromising in deciding the merits of their opposing viewpoints that it was awkward for both of them — as for countless other American and British intellectuals of the generation — to recall this season of ambivalence toward fascism.

Foster and Allen were, after all, practicing law together. Allen was now in his late forties, Foster in his early fifties. Foster had reached the pinnacle of the legal profession; Allen was still cultivating his stature in the world of public affairs, hoping that would propel him to high government office. Both men now moved in elite circles on either side of the Atlantic, Allen with sophisticated ease and charm, Foster with effort and a gaucheness that never quite disappeared, even years later when he emerged as the towering diplomat of his age. Both men took pleasure in relaxation, Allen with casual acquaintances, Foster only among family.

Both enjoyed laughter, but Allen could laugh in public while Foster maintained for the outside world an air of solemnity. They both appreciated good food and wine, Foster in a studied way, Allen without effort. But throughout, the brothers' mutual loyalty was never shaken. If either was ever jealous or disappointed with the other, such normal but unworthy sentiments between brothers were not revealed to those closest to them.

Sometime in the late 1930s came a subtle shift in their roles. Foster had always been content to let Allen be the front man in public service — it was Allen, after all, who wanted to become secretary of state. But gradually Foster began showing interest in a public role. Perhaps the impetus was his friendship with Governor Dewey, who showed growing potential for the presidency, and the wider world of political power that this friendship presented. Foster was never as active in the Council on Foreign Relations as Allen, though he had been a member since 1922. With the publication of *War, Peace and Change*, Foster seemed attracted by the notion that public service might be worthy of his ambitions after all.

— * —

It was Allen who first ran for political office. The idea came up as something of a fluke in August 1938.

Allen had just returned from a business trip to the few remaining central European clients. Vienna, he found, five months after Hitler's Anschluss, had lost all trace of the post-Hapsburg abandon. Trolley cars were decorated with swastikas, Gestapo thugs were tracking down Jews and other threats to the Nazi future. In Berlin, which seemed more sinister every time he visited, he caught up with Ambassador Hugh Wilson, who was still inclined, to Allen's sorrow, to tolerate Hitler's methods. Some of Allen's old German friends were confessing alarm at what their führer might do next. Prussian aristocrats, of whom Allen had been skeptical in quieter days, were now cautiously questioning their earlier support for the Nazi alternative to Weimar. Allen began to sense the emergence of something that could one day be called "Germany's underground." In London he dined with Rebecca West and her husband, Henry Maxwell Andrews, who had reluctantly decided to leave his pleasant post with the British Schröders. So had Fred Dolbeare; fed up with the banking world and still enjoying bachelorhood, he had accepted a post as diplomatic adviser to the king of faraway Siam. The old European friendships were wearing thin.

"I got the impression," Allen told the swarming newsmen on his return, "that the intelligent Germans had allowed politics to slip out of their hands. As a result they lost their liberties. Democracy works only if the so-called intelligent people make it work. You can't sit back and let democracy run itself."

Within days of his return to East Sixty-first Street, in a way that he least expected it, Allen had to deliver on that conviction. Republican leaders in Manhattan's East Side congressional district put the proposition: the Democrats of the district were split between Roosevelt's foes and supporters, and the Republicans calculated they could reap the advantage if they could field a new, vigorous candidate of bipartisan appeal. Running for political office was nowhere in his family tradition, but Allen's competitive spirit was aroused.* On August 20, just four weeks before a primary in which the conservative Democratic incumbent had cross-filed to run in both parties, Allen announced his candidacy for the Sixteenth Congressional District.

The New York Times promptly endorsed this man of "high character, proved abilities, his fresh and liberal outlook." Allen called at GOP clubs and neighborhood groups; he spoke on the radio to all who would listen. He tipped his hat to conservatives, denouncing "state socialism," paid lip service to "elementary thrift in government, . . . restoration of private enterprise, . . . curbing that ever-increasing Washington bureaucracy." But he was merciless against those "die-hard Republicans who do not realize that the world has changed in the last fifty years." As for the New Deal, the Republican Wall Street lawyer declared without hesitation: "Reform came and it was long overdue, hence hasty, often ill-conceived; but with all that I would not undo a single one of the real social reform measures of the past six years." Under constant provocation, Allen refused to vilify Roosevelt. He understood better than almost anyone in his audiences the international crisis mounting in Europe, but he refused to make politics with it — even when his doughty opponent charged that while *he* was in Congress, "doing the best I could to serve my country," Dulles was in Europe at one of those conferences, "selling out my country to England."

Ham Armstrong, who lived down in Greenwich Village and so could not vote for him, worried that his friend might be swayed by the isolationist views of his affluent neighbors; Allen replied jauntily, "I don't plan to let my temporary incursion into politics turn me from acting in the normal and natural way." From far away in time and space came encouragement; Betty Carp, who was still in Constantinople, reminded him that "you told me once long ago that you would be someday secretary of state — I have a hunch that day is not too far off."

The campaign brought an unimagined personal bonus for those

---

* "Uncle Bert" Lansing had haughtily declined an incipient movement to have him run for president in the disarray of the Democratic Party after Wilson's collapse.

around him. For four blissful weeks the entire Allen Dulles family was together, working as a unit and rejoicing in the sharing of a common endeavor. Clover managed her own desk at the Belmont Plaza campaign headquarters and would pinch-hit for her husband when the afternoon tea circuit became too tedious. Toddy, Joan, and even eight-year-old Allen stood on street corners handing out leaflets at rush hour, reported to headquarters after school to stuff envelopes, then unabashedly led the applause as their candidate strode into the evening's rally. Such a combined effort had never happened in this family — and never would again.

Election day, September 21, was cold and rainy. Allen and Clover voted early, said they had enjoyed the campaign, and then went home. The conservative Democratic incumbent narrowly lost in his own party but picked up 2,495 Republican votes to Allen's 1,701. In maturity's paraphrase of his childhood taunt, the defeated candidate announced, "I admit the mathematical indications, but I do not concede anything." Allen never again ran for elective office.

With his newfound prosperity, Allen had managed to build what he called "a modest abode" in one of the poshest summer preserves of the Wall Street crowd, Lloyd Neck, on Long Island near Cold Spring Harbor. Foster had long since planted his family in a mansion nearby; other neighbors were the Roosevelts, including young Archie and Kim, and Allen and Clover's glamorous new friends, Charles and Anne Lindbergh. Another new couple, the Charles Wrightsmans, Clover thought unpleasantly *nouveau*, but Allen enjoyed their high style of living. Henry Andrews and Rebecca West came for a weekend, and Allen invited Ham and Helen Armstrong along. Those last prewar summers at Lloyd Neck were a never-ending house party, with riding and sailing lessons for the children at nearby Oyster Bay.* Allen's gout was a continual problem, but he refused to let it get him down. Arriving on the 4:50 train after a day on Wall Street, he would plunge into vigorous tennis with the athletic Princeton undergraduate employed for the summer as companion and mentor to young Allen. Everything seemed idyllic, though as one of the Princeton youths noted, "Mr. and Mrs. Dulles were always convivial and charming with their friends, but they never seemed to spend any time alone together."[8]

Confronting the competing roles of wife and mother, Clover chose the latter, pouring her energies and enthusiasms into nurturing a rich family life of culture and fun for the children. The husband was not alto-

---

* The sailing instructor was a young man named Robert Amory, who, like Archie and Kim Roosevelt, would join with Allen in the Great Game years later.

gether pleased; Allen saw how his sister-in-law, Janet, had made the other choice, devoting her life to Foster's needs. Looking back on an otherwise happy childhood, Joan, for one, believed that her father was by nature incapable of taking family seriously against all the competing interests. He was constantly off on business trips, including, one of those springtimes, a Western Hemisphere junket with investment banker Roger Cortesi, a world-class sophisticate who enjoyed the good life. Allen deluged Clover with merry letters, by now without guilt, but also without tactless mention of any women companions. "I wear my Palm Beach suit," he wrote in rakish pleasure. "Roger and I had breakfast looking out at the sea and the tropical gardens of the palace and a few minutes after we were flying off again." Flying over the coast of Brazil, he gave his wife all the atmosphere of Dutch Surinam but insisted, "I have read a good bit, mostly light stuff, detective stories." After a week in Buenos Aires: "Roger Cortesi is a most congenial companion and we get on admirably both in work and play. . . . Today after lunching with the Spruille Bradens, Roger and I took a taxi drive through the park out to the race course and polo field."

Such pleasurable interludes came less and less frequently as the storm gathered in Europe. After the Munich accord of September 1938 Allen invited Anthony Eden to speak to the Council on Foreign Relations. This up-and-coming Tory had no use for the prevailing appeasement psychology of Prime Minister Chamberlain, and Allen cheered him on, hoping to sway the complacent intellectuals of America.

For political tensions complicated their friendship with the Lindberghs, for instance, their Long Island neighbors. Clover found them "very pleasant social companions." Anne, the daughter of Dwight Morrow, onetime American ambassador to Mexico, published a volume of poetry in 1938, and Clover found her sensitivity enthralling. Allen loved talking about the Lindberghs' flying exploits; during one session of reminiscence, Anne remarked quietly, "Those were the days when we had nothing to fear except death." It was when the conversation veered into politics that Allen became nervous. Lindbergh admired Hitler more outspokenly than Foster ever would. He was defeatist about the prospects of the democracies' confronting the dictatorships. "Anne and I had supper at the home of Mr. and Mrs. Allen Dulles on the Cold Spring Harbor shore," Lindbergh noted in his diary. "Dulles was interesting to talk to, and we have somewhat similar views in a number of instances."[9] Perhaps, but not a very big number.

The American intellectual community was fundamentally divided between those who saw the national interest in remaining aloof from the war tensions in Europe and those who feared that America had to fight dictatorship in order for democracy to survive. Allen and Armstrong were often lonely voices in arguing the latter. In a sequel volume called *Can America Stay Neutral?* they tried to place their polemic for collective security within the mood of 1939, even going so far as to quote Charles Lindbergh approvingly as saying, "We should never enter a war unless it is absolutely essential to the future welfare of our nation." The war threatening in Europe was just that to Allen's mind, and he invoked the devices of patriotism to argue it.

> Since the beginning of the present European conflict the American public have been advised to keep their emotions under control. . . . To recommend coolness is not to recommend indifference. . . . A cause to which we incline emotionally is not for that reason wrong any more than it is for that reason right. . . . The country should be slow to anger and should judge the acts of foreign governments in the light of our own national interests. This does not mean that Americans count the preservation of liberty here and the survival of human liberties in other countries as of only trifling importance in a world largely given over to *Machtpolitik*. It would be a stupid foreign leader indeed who thought so.[10]

Foster was starting from different premises. "These dynamic peoples" — referring to the Germans, Italians, and Japanese — were "determined to mold their states into a form which would permit them to take their destiny into their own hands and to attain that enlarged status which, under a liberal and peaceful form of government, had been denied them."* Such a view made Allen despair, "as long as some nations feel that they can only reach their objectives by force."

Armstrong arranged a lecture tour for Allen to spread the gospel of benevolent engagement. Clover went along this time, and the couple enjoyed a winter holiday together at Boulder (later Hoover) Dam. Vacation over, Clover decided to stay on in California, sending Allen back to New York to handle the children in his absent-minded way. He spent little time on East Sixty-first Street; often he passed the evening at the Council on Foreign Relations, on the lecture platform, or arguing at a dinner party with Republican friends.

After a heralded debate at the New York Economics Club, chaired by the man who would challenge Roosevelt for the presidency in 1940, Wendell Willkie, Foster was publicly labeled an isolationist, a term he hastened to qualify in a letter to Senator William E. Borah of Idaho. "If the world is bound into a cycle of recurrent violence, then I should like to see the US avoid involvement. I fear this is the situation in Europe today.

* The statement was used against Foster by liberal columnist Drew Pearson in 1944.

However, I am 'isolationist' only in this sense." However, he admitted that "my thinking has been somewhat philosophical and abstract rather than in terms of the concrete problem of what our country should do at the present time." For his part, Allen argued before the Women's National Republican Club in April 1939 that the United States had to build its military defenses against the possibility of Nazi outposts in the Western Hemisphere and must make its position in the Caribbean "absolutely invulnerable."

As late as the spring of 1939 Foster told cheering audiences that the dispatch of "a huge American army to Europe at the cost of one to two million lives" would be worse than the defeat of the Allies. A German victory in such a war would be "deplorable" but not necessarily "catastrophic." Hugh Wilson seemed even to take comfort in Nazi aggressiveness. "If a spirit should develop in Europe which would permit a cessation of hostilities in the West to allow Germany to take care of the Russian encroachment, I, for one, should enthusiastically applaud and believe sincerely that the ends of civilization would be furthered thereby."

On August 23, 1939, Nazi Germany and Soviet Russia signed a nonaggression pact, proving that the opportunism of national governments could surmount all ideology. One week later, when Germany invaded Poland, Europe — but not yet the world — was plunged into the second great war of the century.

Sullivan and Cromwell found itself in a difficult situation. Foster had called on the remaining European contacts the previous July, but he told the estranged Dr. Albert that he saw no reason to visit Berlin unless the firm's German counsel saw "any particular advantage" in such a visit. Tensions within the firm were high. A junior partner, Rogers Lamont, had enlisted in the British Army to show that he, for one, could no longer stay neutral.* "Is it true that Lamont has gone as volunteer to England in order to fight us?" asked an incredulous Dr. Albert of Foster. "I have not grown old without an understanding for the most unbelievable actions of men but I am sorry because I liked him and I am afraid he would not have done that if he would not hate Germany very much notwithstanding the good friends he has got here."[11]

Dissent at the highest ranks of the firm reached the breaking point in the autumn. On October 25, 1939, a senior partner, Eustace Seligman, addressed a remarkable memorandum to the managing partner, John Foster Dulles.

---

* Lamont, killed in action during the retreat to Dunkirk on May 27, 1940, was said to be the first American officer to die in World War II. He was Sullivan and Cromwell's only casualty in two world wars.

I regret very much to find myself for the first time in our long years of association, in fundamental disagreement with you. . . . Your position now is that the Allies' position is in no respect morally superior to Germany's, and in fact you go further by implication and apparently take the view that Germany's position is morally superior to that of the Allies. . . . I agree entirely with your fundamental position in regard to peaceful change, [but] I can see nothing in it which furnishes any logical basis for the position you have now come to. I think it is unfortunate from your own point of view that you are taking this position publicly.[12]

Strong words of tight-lipped anger between solemn colleagues. The Dulles brothers continued to share an office, but their mood was anxious, with the world and each other. "They had heated debates, and there were tensions about it," recalled Foster's son Avery, "because they were both writing letters to *The New York Times* and were often confused when something Allie said was attributed to Foster, or vice versa."

Early on the evening of June 14, 1940, sixteen-year-old Joan Dulles wandered down the stairs of the townhouse to find her father sitting in the armchair by the fireplace as usual, preoccupied as usual, face buried in the newspaper as usual. But something made her look at him more carefully: her father was quietly weeping into his newspaper. The news on the radio was that Nazi soldiers had occupied Paris; France had fallen.[13] It was the only time, as child or adult, that she ever saw her father lost to his emotions.

— * —

During that same June a public lobbying group was founded to argue for "nonintervention" in the conflicts of Europe, calling itself the America First Committee. With the glamorous Lindbergh on the platform, the group drew in the brightest of the young Ivy League generation, including some, like Kingman Brewster, Jr., and Richard Bissell, who would later change their minds with a vengeance. Janet Dulles donated fifty dollars to the committee. Sullivan and Cromwell did the legal work of incorporation on a pro bono basis.

A month later Allen and a few other stalwarts of the Council on Foreign Relations, meeting for dinner at the Century Association in midtown Manhattan, decided to form a pressure group of their own to mobilize national sentiment in opposition to the isolationism of America First. To the dismay of the Century's board of governors, committed in the bylaws to avoid any form of publicity, the pro-intervention lobby came to be called the Century Group.

The divergence between the Dulles brothers was becoming publicly awkward. As long as it could pass without much notice, Allen's intellectual insubordination to the head of both family and firm could pass without response. But once it became a matter of discussion, all the traditions of their upbringing and heritage allowed Foster to pull rank. In August 1940 Allen was supporting an effort organized by an ambitious Washington attorney named Dean Acheson to publish an appeal advocating the transfer of fifty old destroyers to Britain, at that point the supreme act of American intervention. But as the appeal was being prepared for submission to *The New York Times*, Allen withdrew his name; Foster had persuaded him that the publicity would be detrimental to Sullivan and Cromwell's various clients. "I am glad your letter was published," Allen wrote Acheson later. "I still regret that circumstances prevented me from adding my name to the document." Acheson never forgot that Allen Dulles had caved.[14]

Who should arrive in America just then but Sullivan and Cromwell's former partner in Berlin, Gerhardt Westrick, seeking the support of American friends for Germany's grievances in Europe. Renting a lavish estate in Westchester County, Westrick set about to build a Cliveden of the New World, inviting for bucolic weekends all the New York legal and banking friends he could locate. His impertinence had quick consequence: Westrick lacked the charm of the Astors, and when he impatiently told a fib on his application for a driver's license, the system started working against him, followed quickly by the New York press. Responding to the furor, Foster delivered remarks that were used against him for years to come: "I don't believe he has done anything wrong. I knew him in the old days and I had a high regard for his integrity." Allen, however, flatly refused to see his former colleague.[15] By the end of August Westrick's clumsiness had exceeded even that of his mentor Dr. Albert's twenty-five years before, and he was forced to leave the United States.

By September Foster was putting pressure on Allen to reconcile their public positions. Once President Roosevelt agreed on September 3 to transfer the destroyers to Britain in return for ninety-nine-year leases on British bases in the Western Hemisphere, a chastened Allen argued that the Century Group had served its purpose and should be disbanded. His view did not prevail, and the national debate went on. Isolationists like the voluble Senator Gerald Nye of North Dakota assailed the Century Group as a "conspiracy to involve America in the war." Clover, on furious impulse, walked down Sixty-first Street to the nearest Red Cross station to give blood for the British war effort. Anne Lindbergh wrote her sadly that "what one wants so terribly today is not to be agreed with, or even to be understood, but a kind of mutual belief in the integrity of intent."

By the winter of 1940–41 the best that Sullivan and Cromwell could do for its European clients was to shelter their assets from war, preserving and concentrating property in neutral or otherwise secure hands. Foster joined his Long Island neighbor and faithful financial partner, George Murnane, in assuming proprietorship of the Robert Bosch electrical industries of Stuttgart, making it look as though this venerable German family firm had passed to American control (in retrospect, a ludicrous supposition). Allen's closest collaborator in similar, if less audacious, endeavors was the banker Paul Kempner, who had safely emigrated from Germany to the United States and was working through the Wallenbergs' Bank of Sweden and the Mendelssohn Bank of Amsterdam to conceal the ownership of vulnerable Jewish properties.

The ethics and politics of financial maneuvering during that winter became a matter of partisan debate after World War II was over. Perhaps, as Foster and Allen would justify it, Sullivan and Cromwell and others were simply working to keep industrial assets out of Nazi hands. Their subterfuges, however, involved faking titles of ownership and management, claiming neutral rather than German control. To critics of the Wall Street mentality, it looked as though American capitalists were conniving with their German counterparts to circumvent their respective governments; the "integrity of international capital" was taking priority over the "national interest." Others, however, including Allen, regarded the preservation of capital in "friendly" hands as a perfectly straightforward and honorable purpose.

That winter Allen Dulles argued his first case in a court of law. Under the circumstances it was something of an anticlimax. He represented not a company but the Belgian government, newly in exile from Nazi occupation, which claimed possession of four oil tankers that the Gulf Oil Company's Belgian subsidiary had hastily transferred from Antwerp registry to Port Arthur, Texas. If the government in exile could confirm the title, the tankers could join the fifty destroyers for Britain's war effort. Jurisdiction fell to the federal district court in Beaumont, Texas.

Allen's case was sheer political expediency. "Belgium is at war; the life, the very existence of Belgium is at stake," he argued before the judge, a man well versed in matters of title and contract but not concerned with naval strategy. "Belgium is still fighting, day by day, cooperating with the government of Great Britain against Germany. We are here on behalf of the government of Belgium to help carry out that war effort. Great Britain needs ships, needs these ships." At a pause in the trial he wrote home to Clover like a schoolboy emerging from his first debate class: "I have had a major share, by my own choice, in the presentation of the arguments and the examination of witnesses. . . . It has been a very interesting experience and somewhat exciting for a beginner at trial law."

Beginner indeed; Allen was a loser. His rhetoric might have swayed a low-level diplomatic conference, but it was totally devoid of the compelling legal arguments necessary in court. The Beaumont judge had no problem in deciding in favor of the company, and Allen lost his first courtroom case. As the situation evolved, however, Roosevelt's Lend-Lease program, passed on March 11, 1941, provided a far more effective system of material support for Britain than Allen's four oil tankers.

— * —

"Times are so tense," Anne Lindbergh wrote Clover early in the spring of 1941. "It is a relief to feel one can talk across a gulf of difference in beliefs." The spiritual and philosophical interests of the two women may have transcended world conflicts, but between the husbands the differences became unbridgeable. Lindbergh was working full-time for America First; it remained to Allen to declare himself publicly, to throw off the caution that had been pressed upon him by his brother and the firm. The occasion presented was an invitation to address a Republican fundraiser in New York in May. Allen spent the evening before organizing structured and logical arguments about the issues over which he had anguished so long. What emerged he called his War Speech, and he carefully filed away the fragmentary scribbled notes made that night as a milestone in his thinking, his public move from objective detachment to passionate engagement in the conflict between nations.

When the European war began in October 1939, Allen began, he had hoped it could be settled within the Wilsonian formula of a "peace without victory." Then, after the fall of France, he had favored "aid short of war" to embattled Britain. If now he was ready to go further, to join in the battle itself, it was because (he told himself and his audience) he had carefully considered the aims of American foreign policy. The nation's first concern should be defense against foreign enemies. We had "no right to go off on a moral crusade" abroad, he noted. But "to rid the world of bandits"—that was no quixotic cause but necessary protection against international lawlessness.

Morality and power were thus joined in Allen's scheme. The United States had entered the Great War for the sake of *realpolitik*, "to preserve some friends in the world" and, ultimately, to "save democracy," for America could not survive on a planet dominated by "military autocracy ... any more than the present world can remain half-Nazi and half-free." To those who claimed that the war of twenty years before had been fought in vain, Allen replied that the disillusionment after Versailles, the failure of just and permanent peacemaking devices, was "no excuse for an ostrich policy" in 1941. It was not President Wilson's idealism but rather two decades of "isolationist folly" that had led America to abandon its responsibility for world leadership. It was the foolish "abuse of victory" by former allies that "pushed Germany into Nazism" and brought on the present conflict. Allen had come a long way since those anodine and futile talks on disarmament in the European chancelleries.

Where, then, is America's first line of defense, he asked the Republican leaders in his War Speech. Isolationists like Lindbergh said unequivocally "at our shores." Others, like former President Hoover, may have believed that one could support Britain without committing to war. Allen broke from all the temporizing; calling his belief the "Realist/Idealist" school of thought, he blurted out that we must "stop them before they have the power to come to our shores," stop them at the "Azores — Dakar — Singapore."

"America [has] never realized its strength since the days when [we] wiped out [the] Barbary pirates," Allen's notes claimed, building up to his peroration. It was simply "vain" to think of any "clear and happy destiny for us alone, *after* an Axis victory." Hostile forces would then dominate every strategic point of Europe and Asia, every global trade route beyond our hemisphere. Even if Fortress America could hold out against these foes, we would become "an armed camp for fifty years." It was fantasy to imagine that our English cousins, even with our material support, could hold out alone against Hitler. Therefore, Allen put it to the Republican leadership, "the world is waiting to know what America will do!"

When he delivered his War Speech in May 1941, Allen's position as a public figure was no longer hedged and he could no longer show restraint, whatever Foster and the Lindberghs might wish of him. His voice carried some weight, but the schism within the American intelligentsia would not be healed by words alone.

As it happened, that same month Allen chanced upon an opening for tangible action against fascism, not in public debate but as a creative lawyer. Acting in behalf of both national and client interests, he found the occasion to chase the swastika out of the skies of the Western Hemisphere. During the 1930s the national airlines of South America had fallen under the influence of German management. The Council on Foreign Relations was one of the first to call attention to the danger of aircraft operated by potentially hostile forces flying within easy reach of the Panama Canal. An expansive new figure in the State Department, Nelson Rockefeller, used his responsibility for commercial relations with Latin America to weigh in with the government's concern. Bolivia was a prime target: Lloyd Aereo Boliviano (LAB) operated under tight control from Berlin and, by fortuitous circumstance, was also grossly mismanaged. Rockefeller was friendly with both Dulles brothers, and when one of the businesses they represented, the Pan American–Grace (Panagra) airline, expressed interest in operating any routes that could be taken over from German influences, it seemed only natural to expect a government subsidy. The interests of corporate business and democratic America were parallel, as — Allen would say — any reasonable man could see. He set off for La Paz in June 1941 to see what could be done.

Bolivia was embroiled in its own politics. Picking up hints of the American design, Germany's diplomats warned Berlin that "the handing over of our airlines to the interests of Wall Street is treason to our country." But not to worry; the Bolivian air force commander, a pudgy soldier draped in gold braid and dark glasses, would soon take over the government. Then, the German diplomatic dispatch went on, "with one sole ideal and one sole supreme leader, we will save the future of South America."

Arriving at the Sucre Palace Hotel in La Paz, 13,000 feet above sea level, Allen gasped for oxygen and embarked on a three-point strategy: first, to see the pro-German coup averted; second, to engineer the ouster of the German aviation managers in favor of reliable Americans from Panagra; and finally, to get out of the country without being detected as an instrument of either the United Sates government or Wall Street. The pattern was one that Allen would come to know quite well in the years ahead; this first time he succeeded.

The Bolivian government preempted the rebellious air force commander, ousted the German airline managers, and welcomed the Panagra "liberators" (and the modern new aircraft that the American government so generously provided). Allen was safely home before the deed was done, and in the afterglow he informed Rockefeller that "I was not sure that they would ever have the nerve to put it over." As an "added frill," he reported, the Bolivians even expelled the manipulative German diplomats.

That summer of 1941 was an unreal moment for Americans, whether or not they concerned themselves with the war in Europe. The Dulles children's tutor and companion for the summer was Philip Moore, Princeton class of '42, who delighted in amusing teenage Toddy and Joan, and in teaching tennis and sailing to young Allen. Nor did he mind helping to release some of Mr. Dulles's own tensions with an hour or so of hard-hit tennis balls. In August Clover, the children, and Philip Moore went up to Henderson Harbor for a real vacation; listening to the radio and studying an old map of eastern Europe, they followed the course of Hitler's advance into Russia.

Allen stayed in New York. His longtime "tennis partner" was nearby in Syosset, but that was not his only reason for remaining behind. He be-

gan devising a scheme for playing an effective role in the war effort, but it
was an idea he did not want to talk about, even with family and friends.

— * —

At the Republican Convention in 1940, Allen had spent time with a fellow New York delegate and attorney named William J. Donovan. Wall
Street lawyers of those days often had outside interests—Donovan's was
in the military reserve, as Allen's was in diplomatic missions. Ten years
Allen's senior, Donovan had fought Pancho Villa in 1916 in the Mexican
campaign that Allen had missed by joining the Diplomatic Service. All the
years that Allen was overseas, Donovan was gaining stature in Republican
politics, but when Hoover became president in 1929, Donovan was notably
absent from the list of cabinet appointments. He set up a law practice on
Wall Street. Allen played tennis with Donovan occasionally; they would
meet at the Century, the Council on Foreign Relations, or the Down Town
Association. Neither had reason to know much about the other's interest
and (in Allen's case) experience in intelligence. When he returned from
Bolivia at the end of June 1941, Allen heard talk that President Roosevelt
was about to appoint Donovan to a vaguely defined mission for war preparedness, with a half-million dollars in unvouchered funds at his disposal.

During two decades of isolationism, the government's facilities for
collecting and analyzing information about other countries' governments and armies had languished. "Intelligence" as such had been
handed back to the military services, which had their own narrow fields
of interest. For all the efforts of Allen and others to make the State Department's Foreign Service into an effective source of political intelligence, the diplomats had long since reverted to form, chatting up foreign
ministers and other ambassadors and imagining that this would tell them
everything worth knowing. Donovan's new group was supposed to mobilize intelligence resources across the government and assemble data for
policymakers. The enabling order was so vague as to authorize almost
nothing—and countenance almost anything—a rather nice kind of executive order, as Allen would come to appreciate.

Foster, eager to establish himself in public service, volunteered to
work with Donovan, to set up a group of consultants in New York who
could advise the government about "various phases of the international
situation." Wary of Foster's business interests and vaguely isolationist
views, Donovan was cool to the approach, but he recruited Hugh Wilson,
who had been recalled home from Berlin, for analytical work in Washington. As Allen watched, not only Wilson joined Donovan but also his
friends David Bruce, Lamot Belin of Constantinople memory, and, of all

people, the debonair Fred Dolbeare, for whom the court of faraway Siam had become too boring for words. Columnist Drew Pearson called Donovan's team "one of the fanciest groups of dilletante diplomats, Wall Street bankers, and amateur detectives ever seen in Washington." Allen held aloof, waiting for a proper role to play — should the United States ever become involved in the European war.

December 6, 1941, was a day to live in gaiety for the family of Clover and Allen Dulles. Their younger daughter, Joan, just short of her eighteenth birthday, was presented to New York society along with her friend Gregor Armstrong, Ham's daughter. Clover had worked for months preparing for the debutante ball at Hampshire House on Central Park South, lining up suitable escorts, making the agonizing decisions for the invitation list and then the dance cards; it was the biggest moment in a young society maiden's life. Allen and Clover danced the night out, Joan recalled, and even young Allen seemed to have a schoolboy's merry time.

Sunday morning, December 7, Joan took the train back north to Cambridge, where she was enrolled as a freshman at Radcliffe. In the afterglow of the party, Allen and Clover puttered through the morning at home; he worked at tidying up his papers from the long-ago Peace Conference. Over the radio after lunch came news: Japanese bombers had attacked the American naval base at Pearl Harbor in Hawaii. The United States was at war. In one stroke, Allen's conflict with his brother, his partners, his friends, was over. America First and isolationism evaporated overnight; Foster and the Lindberghs had nothing more to say. Allen's internationalism was now public policy. The attack on Pearl Harbor "startled us like some gigantic, dissonant fireball in the night of our false security," wrote David Bruce. "We felt betrayed, and indeed we were. We were betrayed by the complete failure of our intelligence agencies." At last the scheme that Allen had kept to himself was on the verge of serious notice.

Foster, managing partner of Sullivan and Cromwell, took a dim view of lawyers who failed in their duty to business-as-usual. Worse, some even succumbed to the impulse of enlisting in the armed forces. Just two days after the Pearl Harbor attack, Foster issued an internal memorandum stating that members of the firm should not assume they could, "at the termination of their government service, ... resume their relationship with us where they left off."* If that was a threat, it failed; four partners and thirty-five associates out of Sullivan and Cromwell's sixty-six lawyers enlisted and fought in World War II.

Life changed for all New York. With patronizing indulgence Allen

---

* Another partner was seen rushing to gather up all copies of this extraordinary memo before it could be passed to outside persons and embarrass Foster and the firm.

watched Clover set out from her Sixty-first Street command post as district air raid warden for their corner of Manhattan's Upper East Side. She carried a huge, well-taped screwdriver, her badge of office, which was supposed to be useful for disconnecting dangerous electrical wires.

Allen was planning to return to South America early in February to confront the Italian-dominated airline of Brazil just as he had done so effectively against the Nazis of Bolivia, when a fateful call came from David Bruce. Donovan was seeking, for a task he could not yet disclose, a man of "absolute discretion, sobriety, devotion to duty, languages and wide experience." Bruce knew such a man.

Allen had grown accustomed to both the income of a Wall Street lawyer and the public stature of a spokesman on world affairs. The proposition Donovan put to him through Bruce offered neither — just a routine government salary and a commitment to a secret life until the job was done. With scarcely a pause, Allen accepted.

In the ensuing days, subtle and mysterious changes came over Allen's working habits. He promptly canceled the Brazil trip — someone else would have to deal with the Italian fascist airline — and by February, without calling attention to it, he had quietly tidied up his pending legal work. He went on working from his office at Sullivan and Cromwell, though none of the other partners could see what he was doing, and he said nothing to family and friends. More peculiar, he took a lease on some other office space, on the thirty-sixth floor of the International Building at Rockefeller Center, for purposes about which he was reticent. The adjoining suite, if anyone had presumed to notice, was the office of William Stephenson, a Britisher known in some circles by the code name Intrepid; insiders knew that he was already established as Donovan's mentor in the tradecraft of intelligence. Allen's name was not listed in the telephone and building directories.[16]

As others joined him in the new offices, they tried to pass themselves off as a group of financial consultants, until the need for ever more office space left Allen's group second in size only to the Rockefeller family as tenants at 630 Fifth Avenue. The assorted businessmen, bankers, lawyers, and intellectuals whom Allen gathered around him finally had to admit to their friends that they were doing "government work for the war effort." Theirs was a "research unit," they said, and they stressed the "dull, statistical" nature of their work, a thoroughly unlikely story to anyone who knew Allen and his disinterest in balancing his checkbook.

During that spring and summer of 1942, Allen moved through the city's social circles with his customary ease but without evident purpose. He would be spotted over lunch at the Century with a diplomat from Vichy France who was suspected of collaborationist inclinations. In black tie he would attend stag dinners at the Waldorf Towers with diverse guests from unfamiliar parts of Europe, not at all the types of persons with whom Sullivan and Cromwell would do business. Lunches at the Century and dinners at the Waldorf were nothing unusual for Allen, of course, and that part of his mysterious new life could pass without undue notice. But he was also seen with labor union leaders from the New York garment district — even some former communists! He was noted spending an extraordinary amount of time with a motley assortment of foreign immigrants. To be sure, during the 1940 presidential campaign Allen had worked with the Republican National Committee's Naturalized Citizens Division, developing contacts with Russian, Polish, and Czechoslovak émigrés to encourage them to vote Republican. But there was no apparent reason to maintain those contacts in a nonelection season.

Allen could hardly sustain the pretext that he was continuing to practice law as usual, but he gave family and friends no explanation for his unusual activities. He retained his credentials as a Republican Party worker, keeping the post of treasurer of the party's New York County organization and dining periodically with Governor Dewey and the like; his name even appeared on a list of possible candidates for governor of New York.[17] In August the party, having no way of knowing what he was really doing, elected him a delegate to the state convention.

Allen's cover could not go on indefinitely, nor could Donovan's in Washington. Succumbing to bureaucratic pressures, Roosevelt split the Donovan mission into two parts: a propaganda bureau called the Office of War Information (OWI) and another, more titillating, agency with an undisclosed name whose initials the gossip mills promptly translated as "Oh So Secret!" Allen still admitted nothing of his own role, but a week after being elected as a convention delegate, he resigned his Republican Party positions, pleading the "time that I am spending on my government job." The first public notice of Allen's secret mission in all these months was an obscure announcement published September 17, 1942, in *The New York Times* from the Republican Committee of New York County: Allen Dulles was being replaced as the committee's treasurer because of his "war work with the government Office of Strategic Services."

Whatever he had been doing in New York, that part of the job was done. Now, in common with so many other American men in time of war, he would have to go overseas, to remain for the duration. Six weeks later, with no idea what her preoccupied husband was going to be doing, Clover drove Allen to La Guardia Airport for the first leg of a journey to neutral Switzerland. Allen's life as a Wall Street lawyer and articulate advocate of national purpose was over. He was entering in earnest upon a secret career in intelligence.

Book Two

COVERT

PROLOGUE

Behind the Pretense

ALLEN'S DOUBLE LIFE those first months after Pearl Harbor had specific purpose, of course. The mysterious émigrés he was cultivating in New York were potential assets for an intelligence network to penetrate Nazi Germany. So were the American union leaders, who had contact with fraternal labor movements in occupied Europe. Indeed, any individuals or groups with natural pretexts or opportunities to be in touch with lands under Nazi occupation were judged useful. Having organized the immigrant communities of New York to vote Republican in 1940, Allen regrouped these same contacts for a nonpartisan effort two years later.

The telephone call from David Bruce at the beginning of 1942 started Allen on the task of building a national intelligence service. His first assignment was to devise a system for collecting foreign intelligence from the cosmopolitan business, financial, and scholarly communities of New York and to recruit agents for eventual foreign service. Only a little imagination was involved in scouting out potential sources: insurance underwriters or the executives of an American railroad locomotive company, for instance, who were happy to provide technical data on the transport systems of their clients, the governments of Algeria and Morocco — invaluable data to strategists planning an invasion of North Africa.

Even before Allen came on board, Donovan's aides had set up an oral history office in New York to debrief persons who had intimate personal knowledge of Europe's cities and countrysides — details like the verge at a crossroads or the number of smokestacks visible on a factory. Sophisticated intelligence analysis could convert visual trivia into strategic information. The Port of New York immigration authorities gave Allen the identities of passengers coming from Europe. Armed with ample unvouchered funds, he could subsidize newly arrived refugees, "enemy aliens," in exchange for their happily surrendered dog-eared road maps, worn clothing, ration and identity cards from Nazi-occupied territory — mundane items of rare value for future American agents infiltrating behind enemy lines. The OSS New York office ended up buying some 1,000 men's suits of French and German manufacture, 600 overcoats (convincingly weathered), 500 hats and caps, 1,400 shirts, 450 pairs of shoes, 450 pieces of underwear, plus uncounted pajamas, neckties, and socks.[1]

OSS New York opened a special maritime union office at 42 Broadway to interview arriving sailors about what they had seen in European ports. The foreign seamen had to check in at this office for their shore passes, so the interviews could be casual and discreet. Through such means American naval strategists assembled accurate and detailed information about the port installations of Genoa, Marseilles, Naples, and Gdynia.

Without understanding what was happening, even Allen's family was drawn into the effort. Among the émigrés arriving in New York was the newly exiled King Peter II of Yugoslavia. The Council on Foreign Relations asked him to speak. When Ham Armstrong learned that His Majesty was just nineteen years old, he proposed an informal weekend on Long Island with Allen and Clover — and, most particularly, with their attractive daughters, just home from college. The king had little to tell Allen; the girls had a lovely time, but it ended without a hint of royal romance. "Peter was too shy; I was too shy," Toddy conceded long afterward. "Nothing happened."[2]

Eventually the OSS New York office occupied space on four floors of Rockefeller Center's International Building (space previously occupied and precipitously vacated by the government of Japan), with eight ancillary offices scattered across Manhattan, Brooklyn, and nearby New Jersey. Allen's task of assembling sources of information was not the only work going on in the New York office. Next to his "statistical research" offices was the innocuous-sounding Mohawk Trading Corporation. This office placed orders for sniper rifles, silencers, explosives, booby traps, knockout drops, poison pills, and any other exotic items they could conjure up for action in the field. Allen became intrigued with this side of the Great Game (unfamiliar to him up to that time), and he savored figuring out ways in which he could be uniquely helpful in what they called "direct action" — while naturally maintaining the cover of a New York gentleman going home every night to a townhouse on Sixty-first Street.

That luncheon at the Century with the Vichy French diplomat, for example: a normal activity for Allen, and social conversation might produce something of value. But his real mission was to keep the diplomat safely occupied away from his office while an OSS undercover agent huddled in the furnace room of the French mission building, photographing the contents of the diplomatic pouch.

The OSS flirted with the politics of the German émigré communities, attempting to organize recently arrived refugees into an anti-Nazi front. Its head was to be Heinrich Brüning, last of the non-Nazi Weimar chancellors and a favorite of the Wall Street financial community. To broaden the group's base of support, the OSS proposed to join him in coalition with a left-wing psychologist who had attracted Eleanor Roosevelt's notice and a former Weimar cabinet minister named Gottfried Treviranus to represent the Prussian ultranationalists. Balancing of that naive sort revealed the low level of political sophistication of the early OSS.

Allen had more success with a project to identify persons within Germany who might someday come forward in opposition to Hitler. He had sensed incipient dissent behind the facade of Nazi loyalty during his last visit to Berlin in 1938, but now he had the resources to assemble a research staff, starting with the encyclopedic biographical files of a German diplomat who had defected, Baron Wolfgang zu Putlitz, the sort of man one might encounter at a stag dinner in the Waldorf Towers.

In this effort, however, Allen grew frustrated that he had to keep all his activities secret. People who might have information of value did not know how or where to come forward. Even government officials who might have been useful held back out of ignorance that such an effort was under way. George Kennan, a rising Foreign Service officer serving in the Berlin embassy when the war broke out, had spent long hours with Count Helmut von Moltke and others of his circle and realized that he had found the start of an anti-Nazi underground. "I hugged the secret to myself," Kennan wrote Allen years later, "because I knew of no organization which I felt could be relied upon to make really discreet and constructive use of it."

— 7 —

NETWORKING

IN THE JARGON of intelligence tradecraft, the "crown jewels" are the agents: the individuals, groups, and (more recently) technical devices that secretly provide information of value. Agents, broadly defined, are the essence of secret intelligence, but they cannot function in isolation. Whether human or technological, they must be connected to a head-quarters, case officer, or handler, who picks up what they have gathered and issues instructions or guidance about what next is required. Skill in "running agents" is the art of espionage. This is no simple one-to-one re-lationship. "Usually there are numerous go-betweens or cut-outs who serve as messengers between the head agent and his subordinates," Allen explained about the craft of intelligence. "A major purpose of the cut-outs is to preserve the security of the network."

The network is the system that makes it all work, covertly connecting the various sources, distilling fragmentary information, converting raw data into a form that policymakers will find meaningful. The subtle, deli-cate, often intuitive process of constructing a network against Nazi Ger-many was the secret mission that Allen undertook at the start of 1942.

His task began at the OSS New York office, home to what one of their number called "the enthusiastic amateurs." But evident early on was that Allen would not be happy staying at home while colleagues around him were going off to war. By early summer Donovan suggested that Allen might go to the London office as David Bruce's deputy. Allen demurred courteously, saying he preferred "a less glamorous post" — leaving un-stated that he would not relish serving in a bureaucracy almost as large as the New York office and as deputy to someone he considered his junior.

The OSS was preparing to open a base in neutral Switzerland; the State Department had even (reluctantly) agreed that this listening post could operate under the official cover of the United States Embassy in Bern. Donovan hired an experienced facilitator from the NBC shortwave news desk, Gerald Mayer, to go to Switzerland in May as advance man.[1] To head the new operation, the planning called for "some person of assured diplomatic ability, who could mingle freely in intellectual and business spheres in Switzerland, who had previous contacts in European political circles, and a specific and superior background for the cover he would use." Allen recognized that he was a good match, and he coyly proposed to Donovan that instead of London, he be sent to a post where "my past experience would serve me in good stead." The OSS promptly assigned him to the outpost where he had first learned about intelligence in 1917.

If the assignment seemed obvious for a man of Allen's experience, the means of getting there, through other neutral countries in time of war, was quite another matter. There were no direct air links to Switzerland; Allen's itinerary called for a flight from New York to Bermuda, then across the Atlantic via the Azores to Lisbon, a connecting plane to Barcelona, and a train across Vichy France to the Swiss border. Portugal and France promptly stamped their visas on Allen's new diplomatic passport, noting his title as special assistant to the ambassador at Bern. The Spanish consul in New York, however, friendly with Axis circles rather than the Allies, was less responsive, and even less so after the announcement by the Republican Party that Allen's war assignment was to the still highly secret OSS. Only at the end of October did the Spanish visa finally come through.

Allen was one of the few who understood that this delay had more significance than mere annoyance. The Allies were planning to invade North Africa early in November, an escalation of war likely to provoke the Nazi occupiers of northern France to move south and suppress the official neutrality of the Vichy regime. If the new OSS man in Switzerland wanted to pass through Vichy France, as his itinerary prescribed, he had better do so before November 8. That was D-day for Operation Torch, the Anglo-American landings in Casablanca and Algiers.

The first leg of his commercial flight from La Guardia to Bermuda aboard a six-engine Pan American Clipper "Flying Boat" took six hours. There, during refueling, a new passenger joined the flight: Allen's English friend Arnold Toynbee, a stimulating conversationalist in less pressured days. At the next refueling stop, in the Azores, the aircraft was held up because of bad weather, a delay that stretched into the next day. Under normal conditions, Allen would scarcely have minded hiking the hills, playing golf, and musing over the nature of history with Toynbee. But Allen knew that every hour of delay endangered his chances of getting to his post. "For reasons I could not explain to [Toynbee], I was unable to face our delay as philosophically as he did," Allen recalled. "He was accustomed to thinking in terms of centuries and millennia. I was worrying about hours and minutes."

And the delays only got worse. When the plane finally took off, the passengers could not help but notice that it was flying a longer, meandering course to Lisbon; Allen alone understood that the detour was to avoid flying directly over the armada of Allied ships moving toward Casablanca. He finally arrived in Lisbon late on November 5, spent the night at the Hotel Aviz (which refused guests from the Axis countries), caught a plane on to Madrid and Barcelona, then boarded a dreary local train that crawled along the Spanish Mediterranean coast. At Port Bou, the last station in Spain, the train was held up into the morning of November 8 for a long passport check.

> I had lunch in the station with a Swiss . . . acquaintance I had struck up on the train. . . . While we were eating, another Swiss passenger ran up to our table somewhat breathlessly and told us the exciting news: the Americans and British had landed in North Africa! I tried to appear surprised and unconcerned — I was not surprised but I was deeply concerned.
>
> The question for me was only whether the Nazis had begun to move into southern France. . . . I had about an hour to decide whether to stay on safe ground in neutral Spain or to move across the border and take the train which would bring me, I hoped, to Geneva the next day. I excused myself from my Swiss friend, saying that I wanted to take a little walk in the fresh air. . . . It was one of the toughest decisions I ever had to make, but I have never believed in turning back where there is any chance of going forward.

Allen remained on the train as it crossed into France, to be greeted by loud celebration in the border town of Cerbère. "The news of the landing in Africa had electrified the French. When the townspeople heard that an American had arrived, they seemed to feel I was the advance guard, that American troops were on the next boat, and that the defeat of the Nazis was just around the corner." Allen had a bottle of cognac in his one suitcase, "and as Cerbère was under strict rationing, it was the only liquor available in the town." Only at nightfall, after a stopover mellow for the town but tense for Allen, did the train resume the journey across southern France to Annemasse, the border point across from Geneva.

> I hardly slept. I had a feeling that when we reached Annemasse we would find that the Nazi forces had already moved in. . . . I was glad, at least,

that I had had the foresight not to bring any classified papers with me —
nothing compromising could be found on my person.... As we approached the Swiss frontier, stopping at small towns on the way, I
alighted from the train each time and stayed on the platform until just
before it pulled out, thinking by this to avoid any German controls in advance of the border.

Allen knew that Gestapo agents would be supervising French passport
controls at the Swiss border. "As I walked up to the desk where the
French gendarmes were sitting, I had no difficulty picking out the
Gestapo man who was standing behind them." Inevitably the Nazi agent
paid special attention to Allen's diplomatic passport.

Next ensued a little charade of the sort that colors the fortunes of nations. After a brief consultation between the Gestapo man and the gen-
darmerie chief, the French officer informed Allen that top authorities in
Vichy had to be consulted before an American citizen could cross into
Switzerland. Allen took the gendarme aside and delivered an impassioned speech in French — anyone knowing Allen's "gift" for languages
shudders at the thought of it. "Evoking the shades of Lafayette and Per-
shing, I impressed upon him the importance of letting me pass." Allen
pulled out his wallet, stuffed with Swiss thousand-franc notes; "to his
credit, he declined my offer and said only that he would consult his superior officer."

As noon approached, the train for Geneva started steaming up. The
gendarme tried to placate the American gentleman, assuring him that
they were still telephoning Vichy. Allen considered slipping out of the
railroad station and taking to the countryside to slip across the Swiss
border illegally. Precisely at noon the lunch break began for the first shift
of passport control officers, including the Gestapo man. Once the German officer was safely off to the nearby pub where he took lunch every
day, the French gendarme was on his own. He returned to the American
gentleman, handed back his passport, and confided, "Now you see that
our *collaboration* is only symbolic. *Allez passer.*" Not twenty minutes later
Allen stepped off the train in Geneva. "I was the last American for a year
and a half to cross legally into Switzerland."

— * —

For all the maddening delay in departure and transit, Allen's uprooting
had come with relative abruptness. He had left the comfortable support
system of a gentleman's life in New York, his office, his clubs, his familiar colleagues. He had also left his wife, his children, his brother, his
"tennis partner." There had been little time to plan what he would do

once he arrived on station. Yet when such an official arrives in a new
city, even if embarked on a one-man mission that cannot be planned out
ahead of time, he is hardly without resources. People were expecting
him, though they could not be sure exactly when he would arrive; some
of them he knew and some he did not. And he had a one-million-dollar
letter of credit to a Swiss bank, with immediate and unquestioned access.

Stepping off the local train that brought him to Bern from Geneva,
carrying one bulging suitcase, Allen reported to the American Embassy
on the Dufourstrasse, across the river from the Bellevue Palace Hotel.
Gerry Mayer, the OSS advance man, had been anxiously awaiting him.
Mayer put his new boss up for the night in embassy quarters, and the
next day they performed a solemn ritual of bureaucracy, the arrival
message to headquarters. In its enthusiasm for the clandestine the OSS
had devised a system of code numbers — utterly transparent to anyone
serious about deciphering — to replace names in communications that
might be overheard. Donovan himself was 109; Allen Dulles was 110
(Allen's bureaucratic rivals in later years were pointed in observing that
the sequence was determined, not by hierarchy of power but by the
alphabet). From the little code room of the American Embassy in Bern
went the triumphant message to OSS Washington: "110 has arrived."

Then Allen paid a call on one contact of discretion and independence — Kurt Grimm, Sullivan and Cromwell's man in Austria, who had
fled to Switzerland ahead of the Nazis to continue the firm's international representations, such as they were. Making it clear to this portly,
agreeable friend that he was not in the business of law anymore, Allen
nonetheless asked his cooperation on a personal matter of some urgency.
Grimm promptly introduced Allen to a Swiss tailor, for the special assistant to the ambassador had arrived with only one crumpled suit.

Bern had changed little since Allen had been stationed there in 1917.
The capital of Switzerland remained a placid little town that justified its
reputation for preserving calm and decorum whatever the surrounding
distractions. The Bellevue Palace, crowded as always with "secret"
agents of every description, sat just as grandly atop the steep cliffs dropping down to the Aare River; the arcaded Herrengasse and Münster-
gasse of the nearby medieval quarter were unchanged. The pattern of
life was orderly and dependable, unaffected by the grim reality that this
neutral land was now completely encircled by the armies of the Axis
powers.

Allen faced the matter of a place to live. Neither the Bellevue nor the
Dufourstrasse, heart of Bern's gracious embassy quarter, offered the appropriate style. He supposed he would be meeting with all sorts of peo-

ple, just as he had in New York, and it might be hard for some of them to explain what they were doing near the American Embassy. Allen preferred a busier neighborhood, where strollers might have innocent reason to linger. Above all, his quarters must allow several means of discreet access. Strolling around medieval Bern, he quickly found what he needed: a ground-floor flat just off the Casinoplatz, where shoppers and strollers would have no problem explaining themselves to any surveillance and where the wartime blackout required that streetlights be turned off every night at ten, providing cover of darkness to trysts of all kinds. Herrengasse 23 was a fine old Swiss burgher's mansion dating from 1690 but rebuilt with a grand facade, mansard roof, and five chimneys. The house had been divided into four apartments; the available ground-floor flat had a precious back door opening into a patchwork of grape arbors and vegetable gardens, which lined the hill down to the river — providing comfortable entry and exit to anyone who did not want to be spotted from the street.

Starting from nothing, how does one build an intelligence network to penetrate an enemy nation? If one believed what Allen called "storybook stuff," the spymaster would immediately dispatch teams of trained agents into the heart of enemy territory, with papers expertly forged, cover stories neatly arranged, and reliable means of communications and exit to safety. That, Allen well understood, was thoroughly unrealistic in his circumstances. He determined that 110's network would consist of agents already in place, persons living under their own covers and with their own access to useful information, who were desirous, for whatever reason, of cooperating with an inquiring American. This tactic was practical but, as it turned out, controversial, for among those agents would surely be enemy aliens, perhaps even Nazis, with whom Allen would have to transact business and, within limits, trust.

Around those agents, once they were located, 110 would have to spin a network, a means of access and safe contact, ideally a set of innocuous circumstances that would justify one person's engagement with another person without arousing suspicion. Shared ideologies and political views are a traditional basis on which contacts thrive within or among nations, but in war or revolution such contacts are probably subversive and thus, for the spymaster seeking the inconspicuous, self-defeating. The best contacts in espionage come through harmless affinities: stamp collectors, musicians, and athletes, for example, do not need to explain why they maintain contact with people otherwise unknown to them.

From his advance work, Mayer had picked up hints of an underground transnational group with most powerful potential, a network of upperclass homosexual men — Germans, Englishmen, Americans, Swiss, and

Greeks — who met even as their governments moved into war.* Information passed through this network with awesome speed and accuracy, it was said. Such were the social inhibitions of the era, however, that Mayer judged that given his upbringing and station, 110 could not cope with this rather special affinity group, however tempting the prospects for espionage. He decided to let Allen find other means of entrée into the Nazi regime.

Allen assumed that the members he would build into his networks would be self-motivated, perhaps by some grievance, personal or political, or just venal, seeking money or a good life in placid Switzerland. What they would be called upon to do — consorting with the enemy — would be regarded in society as illegal, so the cover for their actions would be as important as the circumstances that brought them into the net. Allen's task was threefold: to identify the right people, establish secure contact with them, and then devise the cover to make it all look like a legitimate relationship.

One fundamental point 110 insisted upon from his first days in Bern: Herrengasse 23 was no secret; it was an address where information could be volunteered, to be assessed and transmitted to powerful people in the Allied camp, yet where the confidentiality of the sources could be reliably preserved. Allen was not at all dismayed when the local press began hinting that he was not just a modest assistant in the legation but a confidential and well-connected "personal representative of President Roosevelt." As an envious British colleague observed, Allen "was like a man with a big bell, who rang it to attract attention, saying 'I've got plenty of money and I'm willing to buy information.'" Allen did not much care for the "big bell" idea; he preferred the subtle image of flypaper, but the point was the same. "Too much secrecy can be self-defeating," he wrote, "just as too much talking can be dangerous."[2]

In a delicious irony, Gestapo headquarters in Berlin seems to have been the last place to believe the sound of Allen's big bell. Though well aware of his presence in Switzerland from the first, the Nazi chieftains evidently could not imagine that an enemy agent with political designs would present himself so blatantly. Until late in the war Berlin believed

---

* Mayer had picked up clues that might help explain the puzzling flight of Rudolf Hess, Hitler's deputy führer, to the Scottish estate of the duke of Hamilton in May 1941. In the Berlin of the 1930s a special elite social set included, on the fringes, both Hess and Hamilton (then known as the marquess of Clydesdale). Such leisure-time diversions, for all their motivating power, are seldom described in writing. Yet fragmentary evidence is accumulating to suggest that an undercover British intelligence operation, shrewd and personally targeted, may have lured Hess out of Nazi Germany by promising him renewed contact with Hamilton.

that Dulles, coming straight from Wall Street, was on a mission of economic espionage against the Nazi industrial war effort.

In Bern Allen once again changed the affectations of his personality. As an apprentice diplomat he had found Johnsonian pomposity useful for conveying his serious intent; that manner then faded into the affable dignity of a Wall Street lawyer. He had allowed the little mustache to return once he became confident that resembling his successful brother was no longer necessary. Now in Bern he took the next step and dropped all the sartorial composure of the legal profession. With the help of his new Swiss tailor he became tweedy in sports jacket and gray flannel trousers, "a tall, burly, sporting type," in the observation of one foreign agent trying to size him up, "healthy looking, with good teeth and a fresh, simple open-hearted manner." Against the Swiss winter he wore a tired raincoat, pockets overflowing with carelessly folded newspapers, and a fedora perched at a precarious angle on the back of his head. Deep in thought, he might not even remove hat or coat when he entered a room.

This was the persona that would stay with Allen for the rest of his career. But accompanying the casual appearance and absent-minded manner was a natural aura of integrity that never left him. "If faced with any serious negotiators, [Dulles] would never do anything underhand," reported one of the first undercover Germans to look him over. The old charm and bonhomie in his style — and his calculations — increased by several notches. Allen could conjure up, said a respectful American colleague, "just the right key to appear *sympathique* to any character who might be of use."

One of those who came forward in response to the big bell, a German Jewish journalist named Robert Baum-Jungk, was eager to confide the anti-Nazi activities he had engaged in since his teens and to relate at passionate length just why. Allen gave the intense young man his full attention, or so it seemed. That was one of Allen's tricks, to radiate concern convincingly while maneuvering the conversation to his own interests. Baum-Jungk was startled to find an American intelligence officer capable of laughing so easily and loudly, so unlike the "sinister and eerie" personalities he had met in secret services before. When he did not want to answer a question, Baum-Jungk reported, Dulles would give a "mischievous wink of the eye, instead of putting on a forbidding mask." He had a "marvellous, low-key way of speaking." Like other young men before him, Baum-Jungk was infatuated with Allen: "I loved him right away." In no time 110 calculated how Baum-Jungk could be put to use.

Allen received visitors in a wood-paneled study with dark red draperies framing windows looking down to the Aare. He took care to have a fire burning in the fireplace, mindful, he later wrote, of "the subtle influence in a wood fire which makes people feel at ease and less inhibited in their conversation." Of course there would be con men, émigré fanatics, adventurers, and double agents among his callers — Allen was no novice in the art of assessing people — but maybe there would be one genuine "walk-in," someone with access to political or military information that he was ready to share.

Among old friends Allen located the elegant and cosmopolitan Royall Tyler, whom he had first known as an army intelligence officer at the Peace Conference. Tyler, independently wealthy and married to a woman of the Italian aristocracy, had chosen to settle into the rarefied universe of European high finance during America's isolationist decades. Allen found him at work in banking and monetary affairs at the League of Nations in Geneva, dabbling in art and archaeology and savoring the cultured repose of a Renaissance man. Traveling with Tyler, wrote David Bruce, "is like taking a witty, urbane, human Baedeker as a courier."[3] A sophisticate like Tyler was no stranger to the role of cut-out, especially in the spy-infested air of neutral Switzerland. Solicitously, Tyler thought to put Allen in touch with Prince Max-Egon von Hohenlohe, a landed gadfly of Mittel-Europa who made it his business to move in circles of power across all boundaries.

Prince Max, forty-six years old in 1943, came from an illustrious family that had given the empires of Europe statesmen, field marshals, and ambassadors over centuries past. He himself possessed vast ancestral estates in the borderland between Germany and Bohemia; he was, in fact, one of those Sudeten Germans whom Allen and Charles Seymour had treated in such cavalier fashion during the Paris Peace Conference.[4] Long since established as a citizen of neutral and secure Liechtenstein, married to a Mexican marquesa of wealth equal to his own, a social favorite on the French Riviera and resident of Spain, Hohenlohe maintained (he asserted) some thirty residences in Europe and Latin America. At one of them, in the Sudetenland, he had entertained a political envoy of British prime minister Neville Chamberlain and the Sudeten Nazi leader, Konrad Henlein, in the summer of 1938, helping to pave the way for the Munich conference of appeasement.

Of all the persons who walked in on 110 in those early months in Bern, probably none gave him so little current value and so much later grief as Prince Max. Hohenlohe was an agent of Heinrich Himmler, no. 144/7957 in the files of Nazi intelligence. He had been part of the Nazi network in 1940 that tried to manipulate and ultimately kidnap Britain's duke of Windsor from exile in Spain and Portugal. He was on a governing board of the Skoda munitions works, and he and his family were thick with the Nazi leadership even as they moved freely in the circles of neutral and Allied statesmen. Hohenlohe was not a man who could be ignored.

Was he the "walk-in" Allen was looking for, a wedge into the Nazi power structure? One weakness in Allen's Bern operation was that he was isolated from other information resources; had he not been so cut off, Allen could have learned of Hohenlohe's reputation among Americans in other capitals: "a very dangerous person," according to one embassy report, "as he gives a convincing appearance of being neutral and is always engaged in some obscure peace-making activities, counting very frequently on the assistance of religious organizations and noble families in Europe." The United States ambassador to Switzerland, Leland Harrison, had been running into Hohenlohe for years; his talk was always of fuzzy "peace efforts" by private Americans and Germans or political intrigues within the Nazi leadership—hardly one to inspire confidence. American diplomats in Madrid regarded him as "totally unscrupulous, . . . endeavoring to ingratiate himself with the democracies in order to protect his considerable fortune. . . . [He] can send to Germany false reports of the results of such contacts, . . . does not hesitate to lie in the most flagrant manner."[5]

None of this was known to Allen when Hohenlohe finally came to the Herrengasse flat in February 1943. He gave the arranged code name, "Paul," and was duly escorted into the study to meet an American with the code name "Mr. Bull." Ever anxious to put strangers at ease, Allen set the mood by fiddling with the wood fire, then assumed a manner of astonishing frankness and charming indiscretion to suggest intimacy. Allen even gave Hohenlohe to believe that they had actually met before—in Vienna, wasn't it, twenty-five years ago, or perhaps Berlin or New York in the twenties?

Hohenlohe informed Berlin that "Roosevelt's special emissary . . . the most influential White House man in Europe" had begun by saying he was "sick of listening to bankrupt politicians, émigrés and prejudiced Jews." The postwar settlement must not repeat the unjust errors of Versailles (that much Allen may well have said), driving nations like Germany once again into "hysterical adventurism." Prussian militarism must be cut out, but perhaps Germany could keep Austria and maintain a "protective shield against Bolshevism" across Poland, Czechoslovakia, and Hungary. On and on Hohenlohe went, embroidering his dispatch to please his Nazi masters. He proudly reported his own interjection against the Jews, in which he told Allen his fear that the United States was "planning to return them to power in Germany." Allen replied, according to Hohenlohe, "making clear his own antisemitic sympathies," with a hint that the United States planned to settle displaced Jews in Africa.

Though Allen saw Hohenlohe several times during those first months, he was not impressed with this particular walk-in, nor with the line of communication into the heart of the Reich that he claimed to represent. Occasionally 110 would convey snippets of information to Washington obtained from "an informed and wealthy Liechtenstein national." But when Swiss intelligence officers with whom Hohenlohe had also been hobnobbing suggested to Allen that he make direct contact with Hohenlohe's superiors in Berlin, Allen dismissed the offer, remarking that "every high Nazi officer can be bought." Whatever the reservations of old-time intelligence professionals about 110's unorthodox style, none could deny the shrewdness of his intuition about the diverse and unusual people he would meet.*

— * —

Fortunately for 110, not all the walk-ins of those first months had Hohenlohe's reputation for duplicity. To his flypaper came persons from another affinity group with compelling occasion to operate across frontiers, a community in which Allen was well established: the realm of international finance. Lawyers, bankers, venture capitalists of a dozen countries knew each other and knew how to communicate with all necessary discretion, regardless of their politics. Switzerland was a traditional entrepôt for financiers as well as spies, and the two professions could work well together. Once the obvious precautions were in place, agents of American intelligence could actually meet and deal with German nationals even as their countries were at war.

One of the most significant, and ultimately tragic, figures who crossed Allen's path was Eduard Schulte. Just over fifty when Allen met him, Schulte was managing director of the giant Giesche mining industries astride the German-Polish border in Upper Silesia (the Polish assets of the German company had been sold after World War I to an American consortium led by financier W. Averell Harriman and the Anaconda Copper interests, to be called the Silesian-American Corporation). Schulte was never as well known as Krupp or Stinnes or the

* To Allen's embarrassment in his later career, the Hohenlohe saga did not end with the conversations of February and March 1943, of which, unfortunately, there is no full American record. After World War II, among the Nazi archives captured by the Russians were Hohenlohe's spurious dispatches from Bern; triumphant Moscow propagandists published them with face-value commentary in 1960, when Allen was the notorious director of America's CIA. The opportunity was irresistible for the Kremlin — not only was America's top intelligence boss and rabid anticommunist given to antisemitism, he had been demonstrably plotting with German militarists against the Soviet Union as early as 1943, "on direct instructions" from the White House!

other major German industrialists invited to Göring's home in 1933 to meet Hitler, but in his own circle he had equal stature and authority.

Schulte always disdained politics as an unnecessary distraction, but his scorn for the Nazis he met that day grew into contempt. By his nature he was not inclined to political conspiracy; he was a loner in his activism (this, as it turned out, was his undoing). He never joined the Nazi Party, though as a captain of German industry he appeared at the clubs and in social circles frequented by leading Nazis, military and civilian. The atmosphere where Schulte lived and worked in Breslau (now Polish Wrocław) was much more relaxed than Berlin, and one could talk of matters that never would be raised in the capital. Indeed, on social occasions Schulte was outspoken in his criticism of Nazi power, and well-meaning friends advised him to show more prudence.*

Proud, vain, and rich, Schulte never regarded himself as an "agent" of Allen or anyone else. He always operated on his own initiative, as what players of the Great Game call a wild card, not on assignment or payroll. Allied intelligence services did not get his information directly; he always protected himself with several layers of cut-outs, Swiss financial contacts or old Polish friends. Schulte had a streak of the German romantic in him, and he considered it an act of patriotic virtue to alert the outside world to the madness of the Nazi regime. This hard-driving entrepreneur was ingenious enough to devise means to get the word out. His business often took him to Zurich, where the Giesche complex sustained a prosperous zinc trade even during wartime; there he had a loyal mistress, a young Jewish milliner named Doris. Anyone observing the movements of Managing Director Dr. Schulte in the early years of World War II would find everything properly explained: he worked alone, his cover was perfect.

Schulte informed a Swiss banking contact in August 1939 that Hitler had set September 1 as the date to attack Poland; the word went straight from the bank to a French intelligence source, thence to Paris and Lon-

---

* Records of Schulte are scattered through Dulles's papers and in the OSS files, but with scant indication of his importance or of what he actually did for Allied intelligence. His name was carefully deleted in one declassified document but was overlooked by the security reviewers a few lines later. It is hardly surprising, considering his pride and position, that certain of his actions are treated with virtually inscrutable discretion even in classified documents. It was only in 1986 that two scholars of the period, Walter Laqueur and Richard Breitman, managed to overcome the reticence of Schulte's surviving family and the obscurities of the official archives to piece together the dramatic story of his career. Their book, *Breaking the Silence*, finally resolved decades of frustrating inquiry into the identity and personality of a "mysterious messenger" of the Holocaust; many were the false leads and erroneous guesses, including some by Laqueur and Breitman themselves in earlier writings.

don. In April 1941 Schulte arrived in Zurich with word that a Nazi attack on the Soviet Union was imminent, despite their nonaggression pact; from his Upper Silesian borderland Schulte was easily able to pick up the signs of a vast mobilization. In the event, the attack was postponed at the last minute and came only on June 22.

On July 17, 1942, Heinrich Himmler paid a surprise visit to an obscure and rundown little town in Schulte's vicinity, Auschwitz. The chieftain of the Nazi SS seldom spent time away from his headquarters of power; among those in nearby Breslau Schulte was not alone in being puzzled that Himmler was actually staying overnight in this unlikely backwater town and remaining into a second day. On that July 17 a train arrived in Auschwitz carrying 449 Jews from Holland; Himmler watched the first mass death by gassing. Then he went to a festive party at a villa in the forest of Kattowitz, a villa owned, as it happened, by the company of which Schulte was chief executive officer.

Schulte was too independent of the Nazi hierarchy to be among the honored guests at a social function for a high party official. But friends and business associates were there. Over the next eleven days Schulte learned enough to conclude with certainty that Himmler's mysterious mission was to inspect the implementation of a fateful decision: that when Hitler promised the "elimination" of European Jewry, as he often did in his bombastic speeches, he did not mean their dispersal or resettlement abroad; he meant, literally, their elimination. And the process was beginning a few kilometers from Schulte's headquarters.

The managing director of Giesche suddenly found compelling reason to make another quick business trip to Switzerland. Schulte's latest information was not of mere military significance; he assigned to it the highest political and moral importance. A plan under way to kill by mass gassings the millions of Jews of Europe? This was information to be absorbed at the highest political levels, by Churchill and Roosevelt. Schulte did not expect his usual contacts in Switzerland to have such access.

Arriving in Zurich on July 29, 1942, he first telephoned Doris at her dress shop — aside from any personal motivation, the call served as cover in case anyone was watching him. Schulte told his mistress that he would arrive at her apartment a little later than usual that night. Then he arranged to meet a private banker with whom the Giesche firm did business, one Isidor Koppelmann, whose relevance at this point was that, rare in the banking circles of Basel, he was Jewish. Koppelmann heard Schulte's news in silence, then thought of a contact to get the report into credible political channels. Through yet another cut-out the news reached Gerhart M. Riegner, a young lawyer representing the World Jewish Congress in Geneva. It was Riegner who ultimately transmitted Schulte's information, along with his own attempts at corroboration, to London and Washington.*

When Allen arrived in Bern three months after these events, cut-outs like Koppelmann were among the first to hit the flypaper. They might meet Allen casually at the Bellevue Palace bar, the Restaurant du Théâtre off the Casinoplatz, or some other public place; more often, at least in Koppelmann's case, contact consisted of hushed exchanges in the darkened streets around the Herrengasse after lights out. The few operatives who knew of Schulte's earlier momentous errands never told Allen the details; in the Great Game, then as now, it was not only bad form but downright dangerous to link any one person with any one piece of intelligence.† Koppelmann and others, however, cited Schulte as a man whom Allen should get to know.

They met, free of cut-outs, in May 1943 in the Herrengasse study. As so often, early in their conversation Allen realized that he had actually encountered Schulte some fifteen years before, in a Sullivan and Cromwell conference room where the business of Anaconda, one of the firm's clients, was under discussion. It also became clear that both men had met Hitler at about the same time: Schulte at the home of Hermann Göring, Allen at his ill-remembered interview of April 1933.

Even though no formal working relationship developed, Schulte became no. 643 in OSS records (the alphabetical ordering had long since given way to date of contact in the crude numbering system). Allen was unusually impressed by his visitor — not so much as a source of current intelligence but as an economist and businessman who could embody the "good Germany" that would surely emerge after the Nazi scourge was routed. He asked Schulte to prepare a plan for German recovery after the war. In 150 turgid Germanic pages of the comprehensive memorandum that ensued, Schulte argued for the promotion of German agriculture to make the economy less dependent on industrial exports. Urban dwellers, he argued, should be encouraged to leave the crowded cities and live on

---

* The details of this first solid report of the Nazi Holocaust, and the sluggish response of the American State Department, have been told before, including in my own 1983 book, *Israel in the Mind of America*, but without identifying the German informant by name. Cooperative in every other way during my research, Dr. Riegner always firmly refused to name the man who brought the news out, saying he had given his word that he would not do so. Even after Laqueur and Breitman finally published the story of Eduard Schulte in 1986, Riegner went through the motions of refusing to confirm anything — though in a cheerful interview in my New York office in 1989, he seemed almost relieved to acknowledge that the mystery had at last been solved.
† Even after the war, when Allen was asked the identity of the mysterious messenger of the Holocaust, he replied that he did not know.

independent farms. Small craft shops should be subsidized to preserve a middle class independent of big business.*

It was a careless security breach within Allen's own network that led to Schulte's exposure. OSS Bern had messaged Washington of a contact between 643 and a non-American agent, 497. OSS communications were secure, but 497 had carelessly mentioned Schulte by name in a message to London that was intercepted by the Gestapo. OSS Bern learned of the breach in time to get a cryptic telephone message to Schulte, who was in the midst of a business meeting, that critical negotiations required his presence in Switzerland immediately. Without even returning home to pack a suitcase, Schulte left the Third Reich on December 2, 1943, never to return.

— * —

Bern established Allen's standing as a spymaster. In his first Swiss posting in 1917, it had been research, analysis, and influence on policy that made his name. This time, for thirty months of World War II, it was sheer espionage — the dark exchanges in hushed streets, seemingly casual encounters with strangers just in from Romania or Hungary or with commercial travelers from Stuttgart or Marseilles, a quick train trip to Geneva for tea with a university professor who had just received an interesting letter from a former student in Berlin. Allen was in action, and the memories of his Wall Street law practice evaporated without the slightest regrets. To be sure, a wife was holding on at home; two daughters and a son were growing up without their father — but this was war, and Allen was content in the belief shared by so many at the time, that a man's job was at the front.

"The front"? Herrengasse 23 was not exactly the trenches; it was a comfortable gentleman's residence presided over by a French-Swiss butler whom Allen was assured had served only in the best of homes. The patriotic duty of a spymaster consisted of befriending headwaiters at the Restaurant du Théâtre, a few minutes from home, which was equipped with a discreet back door for quick or undetected exits. Allen looked up old bachelor friends and quickly found new companions among the political networks of neutral Switzerland. Then, to finish settling in and make his contentment complete, he took a mistress.

Mary Bancroft was thirty-eight years old (to his forty-nine) when they

* It is tempting to find here the germ of the American Morgenthau Plan for the "pastoralization" of post-Nazi Germany; Schulte, however, rejected drastic deindustrialization, and it is unlikely that the planners around Treasury Secretary Henry J. Morgenthau had any knowledge of Schulte's lengthy memorandum to Dulles.

met, barely a month after his arrival. Mary was no Swiss fräulein; she was a former debutante from Boston, reared on Beacon Hill by her step-grand-father, C. W. Barron, publisher of *The Wall Street Journal*. A hearty product of the roaring twenties, Mary had been married twice and collected numerous lovers. She was a handsome woman of the world, purposeful and profoundly intelligent. She had lived in Switzerland since 1934 with her school-age daughter, Mary Jane, and her second husband, an accountant named Jean Rufenacht, who was constantly on the road with business clients. Never one to accept boredom, Mary spent her days writing a novel, then entered upon serious study of the bold and challenging Swiss psychologist Carl Gustav Jung, eventually becoming what show business friends would call a "groupie" of the great man, who enjoyed her company. Until meeting Jung, she reminisced, "I had never regarded men more than ten years older than myself as sex objects" (actually, her second husband was fourteen years older, but Jung was twice that).[6]

In his advance work Gerry Mayer had scouted the small community of American residents for talents that could be useful to the new OSS office. Mary was an immediate asset, with her literary style and curiosity, her ease in French and German, and her natural sophistication in a man's world. Mayer put her to work analyzing the German press, even bringing her Jungian insights to the speeches of Hitler, Göring, and Goebbels. At last she could escape the tedium of a boring marriage; pounding out political analyses day and night on a beat-up old typewriter, cigarette rakishly dangling from her lips, she felt purpose and excitement coming back into her life. By the time Allen appeared on the scene, Mary was in harness, restless, randy, and ready.

Over a drink one day early in December at Zurich's Baur au Lac Hotel, Mayer introduced Mary to a man in tweeds and gray flannels, with a "ruddy complexion, a small, graying mustache, and keen blue eyes behind rimless spectacles," the new special assistant to the American minister to Switzerland. When Rufenacht heard that evening of his wife's new acquaintance, he scoffed, "Everyone knows Dulles is the head of your intelligence service," and urged her to go to work for him — it would help his business to have such good connections.

Allen invited her to dinner at the Herrengasse apartment a few days later, and over the customary small talk of travels and families, he remarked that he was having trouble finding the right kind of household linen for the flat — would she, by chance, know of anyone who might want to "rent" him some extra sheets, towels, and such? A perfect Allen Dulles ploy of courtship: working toward a practical end while setting an intimate tone with a woman he did not yet know well. Mary naturally jumped to the bait and offered to "rent" him some extra linen from the

Rufenacht country chalet, closed down for the duration of the war. Thus an occasion for another meeting, this time in Mary's apartment, for him to collect the goods. They sparred and teased. Mary showed herself the clever coquette by taking hold of his briefcase and spinning the little wheels of the combination lock. She shrewdly guessed the number code to be 23961, his New York address (which she had looked up), and Allen pretended to be devastated at a breach in official security.

That evening, after dinner in Zurich's old quarter, they went for a walk along the lake and talked about Mary's work; I've read your "stuff," Allen said inelegantly, and now he wanted these political memoranda and reports to come directly to him instead of to Mayer. Sitting on a park bench, Mary recalled, the OSS chief lit his pipe and uttered a cryptic remark, which contained, if one reflects a bit, the essence of the style he was devising as a spymaster who also knew how to enjoy life. "We can let the work cover the romance, and the romance cover the work." Never mind that neither work nor romance had yet been consummated between them; Allen was leaping ahead to the tasks and pleasures in store.

At Christmas Allen went off to Italian Switzerland with Kurt Grimm. Rufenacht, Mary, and Mary Jane took their Christmas holiday in St. Moritz. At the hotel on their arrival was a huge arrangement of yellow chrysanthemums with Allen's card. Rufenacht went off on a year-end business trip, and a letter for Mary arrived from Allen. Just returned to Bern, he told her of the rain and his dismal golf games, the sort of news he used to write to Hugh Gibson. But for Mary there were gentle undertones:

> In the afternoons, I visited various acquaintances in the environs which even the weather couldn't spoil. The lake is surrounded by villas tucked away in the hills, full of refugees and lonely souls who have found temporary soulmates or maybe only more corporeal companions. . . . My plans are nonexistent. I shall probably be right here for weeks with an occasional visit to the suburbs, including Zurich. . . . I am keeping away from the social life — and trying to do a little work and some thinking. There should be plenty of ways to contribute to winning the war. Give me some ideas. Let me know your plans if ever you leave your mountain retreat.

The letter was signed, "As ever, A.W.D."[7]

Mary's new friendship intrigued Dr. Jung as much as it did her husband. The eminent psychologist was deep into realms of abstract consciousness and metaphysics, but he was no stranger to power politics, and there was much about Allen to fascinate him as a case study. "Your friend Dulles is quite a tough nut, isn't he? I'm glad you've got his ear." That stopped the ever blunt Mary; why, she asked, should Jung be so glad? "He said that men like Allen, very ambitious and holding positions of power, needed to listen to what women were saying in order to exercise their best judgment and not go off the deep end. Not that they necessarily had to follow anything the women said, but they needed to listen to it and take it into consideration when they made their decisions." Jung had expressed such a view more formally a few years before: "Woman . . . always has been a source of information about things for which a man has no eyes. She can be his inspiration; her intuitive capacity, often superior to man's, can give him timely warning, and her feeling, always directed towards the personal, can show him ways which his own less personally accented feeling would never have discovered."[8]

Jung would find in Allen a remarkable blend of gender traits: on the job an unexpected intuitive capacity, an ability to play ever so subtly on the personal feelings of those working with him — Jung's notion of woman. Away from his work he acted the Jungian man, having no eyes for things of which a woman is clearly conscious. Dr. Jung had told Mary it would not be easy to get such a man's ear. But it was easy for Mary, under the mutual covers of work and romance.

The work part developed into a strict routine. Every morning precisely at 9:20, Allen in Bern would telephone Mary in Zurich to say what memos and reports he wanted from her that day. They would talk in American slang, using informal code words that only they could understand, just to complicate the life of anyone listening to their calls. She was to meet this journalist or that salesman to extract whatever information might be of use. Mary could parlay her infectious curiosity and independence into the most interesting situations, and her reports to Allen were timely and businesslike — interspersed, however, with remarks conveying somewhat more intimacy than normal in a bureaucratic memo. Ahead of schedule on a report, Mary interrupted her work to say, "I think I am justified in giving myself the pleasure of writing you."[9]

The romance part also evolved into a fixed routine. Once a week Mary would take the train to Bern, check in at the Hotel Schweizerhof just across from the station (more commercial and efficient than the Bellevue Palace), and taxi over to the Herrengasse for drinks. Allen would debrief her on her latest assessments and they would argue the substance: "Hitler's got his facts all wrong," Allen, the Jungian man, would huff, provoking Mary, the Jungian woman, to "attempt to 'enlighten' my new boss about the Nazi theory of propaganda, how it had nothing to do with presenting facts accurately but solely with an appeal to the emotions of the German people."

Then they would have dinner, and the professional atmosphere would start to soften. Actually a circumstance of communications justified the

routine to this point: Donovan, back in Washington, had impressed upon
110 that it was futile to collect information "unless you can quickly and
accurately get it to the user." He arranged for an official radio-telephone
call to Herrengasse late each night, no small technological feat in those
days. Over dinner Allen and Mary would assemble the data for the
nightly report. She would monitor the calls, and when Allen hung up,
they would rehash what he had said. Would Washington understand his
cryptic references on an unsecure line? That when he casually talked
about finding something of interest to a "stamp collector" he meant the
information should go straight to President Roosevelt? All the other nuances that he could not spell out? The review might take some minutes
and raise suggestions for Allen's follow-up report the next night.

When they were talked out, Allen and Mary would go to bed together.
"I was impressed by how we were never disturbed," Mary recalled. "No
phone calls. No visitors. He might not have been a good administrator,
but he obviously knew how to protect his privacy." When they had finished, Allen would sink into a weary sleep, and Mary would make her way
through the blacked-out streets to her single room at the Schweizerhof,
prepared to board the Zurich train first thing in the morning.

Mary and Allen surely had happy times in the unreal, isolated mood
of wartime Switzerland, where the rest of the world was only dimly perceived through insecure telephone lines and the encirclement of hostile
armies. Their relationship was always discreet. Allen's American colleagues came to assume that they were having an affair — "She was constantly coming to Bern and he was constantly going to Zurich," said one
of the later members of the OSS team in Switzerland. But so carefully did
they manage the affair that no one knew for sure.[10] One night they were,
in fact, interrupted by the doorbell at a tender moment. "Allen put his
left hand over my mouth and, reaching for a pad and pencil on the night
table at the head of the bed, he scrawled DON'T MOVE, DON'T MAKE A
SOUND." The ringing persisted, the couple lay motionless; on the fourth
ring, accompanied by pounding on the door, Allen wrote a further comment: PERSISTENT BASTARD, ISN'T HE? After many more minutes had
passed and the unwelcome visitor had apparently given up, the worldly
Mary delighted Allen by asking sweetly, "How do you know it was a
'he'?"*

Mary brought to Allen a human earthiness that had gone unaddressed

* Long after the war, at an OSS reunion, one member of the Bern team confided his puz-
zlement to Mary over why Allen would not answer the bell one night. He knew Allen was at
home, but he would not answer the door. "Not even when you pounded on it!" Mary
blurted out. "Oh, my God, so it was you, was it? Congratulations!"

in his upbringing. Amid an intense discussion of Paragraph 175 of Nazi Germany's criminal code, the clause that made homosexuality a criminal offense, Allen suddenly asked his mistress, "What do those people actually do?" After some stuttering, Mary said, "Do you want me to tell you?" He replied nervously, "If you know." Mary quickly devised clinical phrases to make it palatable to a sheltered Presbyterian gentleman, concluding, " 'Those people' do different things just like everyone else." Allen, red in the face, laughed hesitantly, snorted, and declared, "I'm glad to know. I've always wondered."

The dark side of Allen's character also showed in his relations with Mary. Free of social conventions, he grew careless on matters of correct behavior and of honesty in relationships, both at work and at ease. There began appearing the self-involved man for whom selfish gratification took precedence. Mary vividly remembered a peak moment of passion, after which the romance started to go downhill. One day Allen rushed unannounced into her Zurich apartment, hat perched back on his head, raincoat pockets stuffed with newspapers. He knew that his mistress's husband was traveling and that Mary Jane was at school. "Quick!" he said. "I've got a very tricky meeting coming up. I want to clear my head." Not even a moment to move into the bedroom. "We settled in on the living room couch," Mary recalled. "In scarcely more time than it takes to tell the story, he was on his way again, pausing in the doorway only long enough to say, 'Thanks. That's just what I needed.' " Calming down in the next hour or so, Mary resolved that no matter how urgent Allen's forthcoming meetings, she would not again cooperate in "clearing his head."*

In the months to come, once Allen's first flings of wartime abandon were spent, 110 would find other useful ways to engage Mary Bancroft's abundant talents.

— * —

Allen's first months of network building were an impressive achievement by any measure. He had twenty-five years of professional connections and experience to draw upon, and he left no potentially useful contact untouched. Thanks to the international reach of Sullivan and Cromwell, important nodes in the network were in place by his third day on post.

Kurt Grimm was regularly in touch with other émigrés from Nazi Austria, and from that connection there grew a flourishing network of

* In 1983, as Mary was writing of this episode, she tactfully approached Allen's daughters to ask if they would mind her candid portrayals of intimacies with their late father. Their mother had also died by this time. Both Toddy and Joan, mature women who loved their father more than they really knew him, told Mary Bancroft to write what she wanted to, the way she wanted to write it.

agents within the Austrian resistance. Allen located another Sullivan and Cromwell associate from the prewar Paris office, Max Shoop, who had settled for the duration in St. Moritz. Shoop had been an apologist for appeasement, a sympathizer of the Vichy regime until a lawyer's life in occupied France became unworkable. Closer personally and politically to Foster, Shoop had nonetheless enjoyed festive Left Bank dinners with Allen in the Sullivan and Cromwell days of another decade, and their reunion in Switzerland bore immediate fruit. Shoop was in close touch with Vichy colleagues who were perfectly ready to turn against the Germans as soon as given the chance; notable among these was the French military attaché in Bern, an old intelligence hand who had kept his private network of agents intact to report on German military movements in France, Italy, and the Balkans.

Within the French resistance was also the Gaullist underground, reporting to a headquarters in London and deeply suspicious of all Vichy collaborators. But Sullivan and Cromwell family connections again brought down barriers. Working with Shoop in Paris in the 1930s had been an idealist ex-communist lawyer named Philippe Monod, now a Gaullist partisan in the resistance around Lyons but still loyal to his old circles in law and business. Shoop became an intermediary between Monod and Allen, and OSS Bern was able to penetrate the Gaullist faction as well.

This left only the powerful communists of the resistance to cover, and on this front the Sullivan and Cromwell network could not help. Allen, however, had other resources. Through the OSS wires he learned by chance of a young American refugee worker in Marseilles who had barely escaped the Nazi occupation, arriving in Switzerland on one of the last trains, as Allen had. He was Noel Field, the sensitive teenager Allen had met during World War I at the Zurich home of his father, Professor Henry Haviland Field.

Young Field, after graduating from Harvard, had joined the American diplomatic service about the time Allen resigned, worked as a junior aide to Norman Davis and Hugh Wilson, and knew many of Allen's friends. But he had other State Department friends, too, including the promising Alger Hiss. For Field had become a dedicated communist, part of a Washington cell, and had been identified as such in congressional testimony as early as 1938.[11] Allen did not know all the political interests of his old mentor's son when they met for the first time as adults, nor at that time would he have cared. For Allen's purposes, Noel Field, by then thirty-nine and resigned from the Foreign Service, presented opportunities for access to escapees from occupied France and to underground cells of the resistance working to obstruct the Nazi war effort. The fact that these particular resistance cells were under orders from Moscow rather than London or Washington was immaterial in those days of the wartime alliance.

Noel Field was not the only reminder of Allen's long and rich professional roots. One of Professor Field's protégés, William Rappard, had settled in Geneva and become a revered fixture at the university and in the international community. Mentor to a new generation of rebels, romantics, and intellectuals, he was for Allen another point of access to interesting people.

One final crown jewel, an institution rather than a lone agent, came to Allen early in his Bern mission. Royall Tyler had done him no favor by presenting Prince Max von Hohenlohe to him. But as a League of Nations financial officer, Tyler more than made up for it in his easy and regular exchanges with German, Japanese, and other financial bureaucrats meeting at the Bank for International Settlements of Basel. The BIS, an accounting instrumentality founded in 1930 to arrange payment of German reparations, was caught between the belligerent governments as they declared war. The central bankers hurriedly sought to insulate their mechanical capital transactions from the war effort of either side. "During the fighting, these matters are kept rather quiet," noted a postwar economist, "out of deference to people who are being shot or bombed and who might become confused if the subject were raised." The bankers' devices were not entirely successful, for Nazi-looted gold trickled into well-laundered accounts in Switzerland. Once these transactions were noted, the Basel countinghouse became established in the popular mind, an officer of the New York Federal Reserve wryly remarked, as a club "where representatives of Allied high finance gather around a table with their opposite numbers from Germany in order to participate in fat dividend distributions while our boys are dying at the front."[12]

Chief executive officer of the BIS throughout the war was an American, Thomas H. McKittrick, who was well known to the Wall Street community, the Down Town Association, and such. He was about as nonpolitical a technician as the times could have conjured up: just before D-day in 1944 he said of his international bank, "We keep the machine ticking because when the armistice comes, the formerly hostile powers will need an efficient instrument such as the BIS." *

---

* Two months after this remark, the monetary and financial conference at Bretton Woods formally recommended "the liquidation of the Bank for International Settlements at the earliest possible moment." But when the war victors came to the point of organizing postwar finance, the Bretton Woods resolution was forgotten; half a century after World War II, the BIS still thrives, an efficient, respected instrument of international finance, just as McKittrick anticipated.

Upon Tyler's introduction, McKittrick and Allen fell into as much of an association as their respective positions would permit, and through McKittrick Allen had comfortable access to the thinking of central bankers on both sides of the conflict. Another BIS contact already known to Allen from Paris in 1930 was the convivial Swedish economist Per Jacobsson, who seemed to have the particular confidence of the Japanese financial community. As international civil servants, men like Jacobsson, McKittrick, and Tyler could travel freely in and out of Nazi-occupied territory as well as within Germany itself even at the height of war. With their readiness to tell Allen what they saw and heard behind enemy lines, these financiers were as good as gold in the spymaster's cache.

Allen maintained amiable social contacts. He fit warmly into the Zurich home of publisher Emil Oprecht, director of Europe-Verlag and literary mentor to the intelligentsia of central Europe. The Oprecht home was almost a crown jewel in its own right, an ongoing literary salon where 110 could hear the sentiments of intellectuals from a dozen countries. And it was a home for him as well; Frau Oprecht was ever solicitous about Allen's gout, always pressing her special medicines upon him. Accepting a dinner invitation, Allen graciously praised her twice-a-day pills "and can now report that I am entirely recovered, as I shall demonstrate to you on Friday evening."

The outpouring of old-boy acquaintances in Allen's first weeks was heady, securing a spymaster's access to the mood of the Nazi periphery. The harder part lay ahead: how to penetrate the power centers of the Third Reich itself?

— 8 —

INTO THE REICH

LETTERS OF INTRODUCTION are a means of separating a gentleman of sophisticated background from a pushy parvenu. Depending on the subtlety and tone of the invariably courteous phrases, such letters can open — or close — doors. If the newcomer lives up to his expected role in a correct and pleasant manner, further welcome, status, and mutual benefit are forthcoming. Allen knew the routine. From OSS colleagues in Washington came names of potential contacts in his new post; the gentlemanly and affable Allen turned such leads into friends who became useful.

One name triggered memories of mellow evenings in 1920 Berlin with the worldly, Cecil Rhodes–like economist and liberal legislator Gerhart von Schulze-Gaevernitz, from whom Allen had drawn so much insight into the fatal flaws of the Weimar Republic. Here was an introduction to the professor's son Gero, now resident in Switzerland, who had been away studying for an investment banking career while Allen was in Berlin. How the circles of the elite and the like-minded strive to close, across frontiers, oceans, and the passage of time. Allen and Gero met for the first time late in November 1942, just ten days after Allen arrived in Bern, closing the circle drawn two decades before by an elderly father eager that his son and his new intellectual protégé should become friends. Friends they became. Through Gero, Allen gained entrée into a Germany that the old man would not have dared contemplate, a Fatherland dominated by forces the liberals of Weimar could not believe would actually come to power.

Gaevernitz at forty was, in the image of a later generation, a jet setter, glamorous scion of the royalty of capitalism. Blessed with the durable good looks of a champion skier and the wealth of a mother who belonged to the family of financier Otto Kahn, he was ever debonair and ever a bachelor, of wide experience. The Wall Street boom of the mid-1920s had drawn him to New York; through his mother it was easy for him to take American citizenship, and he plunged into speculations in Brazilian coffee plantations and Honduran gold mines. Educated as a European, secure as an American, Gero moved freely between continents and cultures. Felix Gilbert, a distinguished German-born historian who served the OSS for a time, remembered an attractive brother-sister couple he met at a costume ball in Berlin in the 1920s. He did not notice the brother until much later, but "I immediately fell in love with Miss von Schulze-Gaevernitz and asked her the next day whether she would be willing to marry me." She declined on the spot.[1] Instead she married a son of the German industrial baron Hugo Stinnes — the one member of that powerful dynasty who refused to support the emerging Nazi New Order. Gero's brother-in-law broke with his family as the Nazis took over and withdrew to luxurious exile in Switzerland, to a villa compound on the shore of Lake Maggiore. These were the sorts of people Allen met that first Christmas when he wrote Mary Bancroft about the "refugees and lonely souls who have found temporary soul mates."

Gaevernitz poured his heart out to "President Roosevelt's special representative." He told Allen that the land of his revered late father was courting "folly and disaster," that he himself had been trying since 1940 to entice his German and British friends into discussions about ending their conflict. He had approached relatives of his mother in the moneyed Anglo-American Jewish community and of his sister in the moneyed German exile community — to see if war could be averted or ended. No one seemed willing to take this playboy of the capitalist world seriously.

Playboy or not, he knew of clandestine groups of officers and civilians who were seeking to overthrow Hitler while saving something of German nationhood. As an American citizen he had sought out the American military attaché in Bern as soon as war broke out. The good General Barnwell Legge, an officer and gentleman of the old school, was not comfortable coping with delicate information of this nature. Gaevernitz, who continued to move back and forth between Switzerland and Germany, happened to be in Berlin on December 7, 1941; a friend tipped him off, before anyone else knew, that this was not the moment for an American citizen to be in Germany. Gero rushed back to Switzerland, carrying an advance text of Hitler's speech declaring war on the United States. Even this General Legge could not accept in comfort. When Allen arrived many months later, the military attaché was relieved to commend this "thoroughly well intentioned" person to Allen's care.

Gaevernitz became the latest in the line of impressionable souls who fell "in love" with Allen, unfulfilled as he was in ambitions and goals and uncommitted in personal relationships. On his side, 110 was delighted to put Gero to good use. Once their acquaintance took hold, they spent endless hours together ruminating about people and politics. Which Germans could be approached? How? Why? For what end? These were just the insights Allen needed as he settled into his mission. Gaevernitz was happy finally to be taken seriously; Allen was relieved to have a sophisticated bachelor companion, as in the old days. They would meet daily to exchange notes; frequently Gero would stay the night at Herrengasse 23.

Mary Bancroft was more aware than anyone of this working friendship as it developed. She found Gaevernitz "extremely handsome" — she was hardly alone in that — but she, unlike the others, understood the true nature of his relationship with Allen. She took particular delight in a report from Hungarian intelligence, one of the many secret services keeping an eye on the OSS chief, alleging that Gaevernitz was bisexual. Since he and Allen spent so many days and nights together, the Hungarian spies concluded that they had become lovers. Mary knew that Allen was indeed "sleeping with one of his associates," as the enemy report declared; the Hungarians had just picked the wrong associate — and the wrong gender — for their titillation.

Gaevernitz was "476" on the OSS rolls, but unlike most of the other numbered sources he became a full-time executive officer. He served as Allen's eyes and ears, frequently interviewing German and other sources with whom Allen did not want to be seen or had no time to meet. "Dulles was primarily interested in obtaining a general impression of the character and trustworthiness of the person he had before him," Gaevernitz explained. "He usually left it to me to maintain the contact in a manner which would be most useful." At first Allen, wanting to give Gaevernitz some kind of official cover, took to calling him an attaché for the Office of Economic Warfare. This could pass muster in Switzerland but not in Washington.* The State Department desk officers knew nothing of Allen's networks, of course, and they were disturbed to discover that the

---

*From an anti-Nazi refugee settled into Wall Street, the State Department received a complaint that this "attaché" was directly linked to Nazi business interests, specifically to one Werner von Clemm, who was at that time under American indictment for trying to import diamonds looted by the Germans in Holland and Belgium. Gaevernitz had indeed had dealings with dubious people in pursuit of his business deals, and he knew von Clemm had relatives in Hitler's foreign and economics ministries. Such business contacts were cover for the high-level connections that made him so useful to Allen and the OSS.

Office of Economic Warfare in Washington had never heard of their "attaché" in Switzerland. Only when word came that Gaevernitz's work in Bern was "of a very confidential nature" did the State Department reluctantly drop the investigation.

Unable to provide him with official cover, Allen let Gero von Schulze-Gaevernitz move around as a private citizen engaging in his diverse business interests and acting for clients in America and Europe. Indeed, as United States Treasury investigators were to find out after the war, Gaevernitz managed to pick up no small amount of commission income during the time he was 476. Allen was not naive. He understood the risks of engaging in transactions that developed under a cover of one kind or another. Everyone in Allen's world had his vulnerabilities. Challenges were raised about the bona fides of an ambiguous American like Royall Tyler once it became known in Washington that Allen was using him. In his official position at the League of Nations, Tyler enjoyed most unusual access to financial interests in Nazi-occupied countries. That is precisely what made him so useful, but it could easily seem suspicious to people unfamiliar with the cryptodiplomacy of the Great Game. As far as Allen was concerned, Gaevernitz was personable and attractive, rich and well connected where it counted, uncommitted and loose otherwise. And he was dedicated to working for 110.

Allen never seemed to appreciate that people might question his use of international financiers for purposes of national policy. To him the network of capital was a powerful and accessible affinity group upon which a sound intelligence network could be built. He had no sympathy for those outside his circle who challenged the identity of interest between democratic government and business, who resented the fact that the world's financial communities were promoting their own interests at the same time they served their governments.

As the American intelligence chief in Switzerland, Allen's assignment was, in blunt terms, to consort with the enemy. That subtle undertaking left everyone he knew open to recriminations, and in the fullness of time the recriminations came. Gaevernitz, Noel Field, Eduard Schulte — all served Allen's interests at a time and then came upon trouble in years ahead. For himself, Allen accepted the consequences of his dealings without hesitation; the seemingly open and affable nature concealed a growing toughness of character, an instinct for pragmatic calculation about every relationship. Mary Bancroft wrote: "'Useful' was a word that was constantly on his lips. He judged everyone and everything by the yardstick of its usefulness in the war effort, even going so far as to wonder why one of the men at the legation was getting married — he didn't consider the girl he was marrying 'useful.'"[2] It was Mary who first recorded, from her special vantage point, that Allen's beguiling laugh, a Santa Claus–like ho ho ho, often had a mirthless quality to it, particularly when used in conversation to avoid a more meaningful response.

— * —

For nine days in January 1943, President Roosevelt and Prime Minister Churchill met at Casablanca, in French Morocco, to chart their war plans. They agreed upon a joint strategic invasion of the European continent but not on when or where it should start. They argued over rival claimants for the postwar leadership of France — Churchill supporting the upstart Charles De Gaulle, Roosevelt unconvinced. Allen's OSS reports in the weeks before had carefully assessed all factions of the French resistance, but the anti-Gaullists in Washington found ample material in his dispatches to press upon Roosevelt the merits of the conventional French claimants surviving from the Third Republic. As for Germany and the Axis powers, the leaders of the United States and Britain decided that their alliance would accept nothing less than "unconditional surrender": no separate agreements, no deals with one cabal of anti-Nazis over another, no political terms that would allow one German faction, democratic or otherwise, to take over the wreckage of Hitler's Third Reich.

Allen judged the policy of unconditional surrender to be sound psychological warfare when it was first announced. Only later did he see that it was, rather, "an ideal gift" to Nazi propaganda, a declaration of Allied war aims that offered the German people no alternative to humiliation, even for those who dared to defy Hitler. As his networks widened and deepened to embrace such persons, he found himself "tongue-tied by the fear that any explanation of what unconditional surrender meant might be construed by the Germans as a promise some future Hitler could say had been broken." Allen had experienced firsthand the emotive power of the "stab-in-the-back" legend after the Versailles Treaty.

The subnetwork that Gaevernitz was assembling for Allen reacted swiftly to the Casablanca meeting. First to appear was Adam von Trott zu Solz, an idealistic Rhodes scholar who had built his Oxford friendships into an international fellowship for Anglo-Teuton harmony. A career German diplomat, Trott used his official travels to try persuading the outside world that an anti-Nazi Germany still existed underground.[3] He had met Donovan (they "got on very well together," he said) and also Allen's Sixty-first Street neighbor and friend in the Council on Foreign Relations, Whitney Shepardson. Somehow Allen never met Trott zu Solz.

But through the academic network, Professor Rappard in Geneva quickly put Trott in touch with Gaevernitz, who passed on Trott's warning that the Casablanca declaration gave the anti-Nazi underground nothing to offer the German people — not even those conspiring to overthrow Hitler.

— * —

In spite of the totalitarian apparatus of the Third Reich, pockets of resistance to Hitler had formed early in the decade of Nazi power. Allen and George Kennan, separately, had sensed this movement. Some of the opposition was principled or ideological — on both left and right — and some resulted from sheer opportunism, especially in 1943, as those privy to the real military news (as opposed to what Goebbels put out for mass consumption) could see that the war was going badly. Within the church and intellectual circles singular individuals like the charismatic Pastor Martin Niemöller quietly sought to attract the attention of outside powers and build political interest in a democratic post-Hitler Germany. Eduard Schulte happened to be a loner; others, like Adam von Trott or Helmut von Moltke, nervously maintained contact with like-minded individuals sprinkled through the middle ranks of the German power structure.

The Abwehr, Germany's military intelligence corps under Rear Admiral Wilhelm Canaris and his chief of staff, Colonel Hans Oster, was a more formidable presence. This was no common room of intellectuals; it was an apparatus, clear and disciplined, with access to Hitler and the top Nazi leadership, and it was capable of concealing activities under legitimate claims of secrecy. Canaris had silently turned against Hitler even before the war started, but he maneuvered within the coarse intrigues of the Nazi leadership not only to retain his sensitive position but also to pack his intelligence apparatus with officers and men who shared his fatalistic views. Fully ten percent of German military intelligence operatives, Allen estimated after the war, were consciously anti-Hitler.[4]

In that number was a singular personage, Hans Bernd Gisevius. A civilian from a long line of Prussian civil servants, Gisevius was an old-fashioned German nationalist, a reactionary, and a snob who regarded Hitler and his Nazi cronies as scum. Though trained as a lawyer, his civil service career led him into police work and criminal investigation for the Ministry of the Interior, seemingly nonpolitical posts that offered him unparalleled exposure to the criminality of the Gestapo and other Nazi security organs. In the tentative way of a conspirator seeking new connections, he sniffed out other anti-Nazis in other government agencies, including the Abwehr, where he contrived to maintain a professional liaison.

At the outbreak of the war Canaris took Gisevius into his apparatus and dispatched him to Switzerland as an Abwehr agent under diplomatic cover. If nothing is ever simple and straightforward in the Great Game, Gisevius's position in Zurich was one of the more complex, for in fact he was working under three layers of cover. Formally he was an innocuous vice consul in the German Consulate General. Under that guise his function was to serve German military intelligence in a neutral listening post. Finally was the job that Canaris had sent him to perform: to make and maintain contact with the Allies on behalf of the German resistance in the midst of war.

Gisevius was just the sort of man Allen had been sent to Bern to cultivate — if he could do it safely. In the first weeks 110's antennae started picking up clues about this ambiguous German. From the stiff-backed height of six foot four (within the OSS he came to be called "Tiny"), squinting through thick spectacles, this arrogant Prussian would ever look down upon his fellow men, of whom he was never found very fond. "There was a good deal of sparring on both sides before I met Gisevius," Allen recalled. He was a German diplomat, at least formally; Allen was an American diplomat of a sort. "Our countries were at war. A meeting between us was hardly according to the protocol." Here "private citizen" Gaevernitz could step in, arrange to meet Gisevius, and return to Allen with an assessment. Impressed with Gaevernitz's opinion, Allen pursued his own inquiries, setting out to learn all he could "as to the character of the man I was to meet, and I assumed he did likewise."

Indeed, Gisevius was alert to Dulles. Early on, British intelligence officers and General Legge of the American Embassy had turned the vice consul away, suspecting entrapment, double agentry, or just another dubious Hohenlohe type. Allen was sympathetic to Gisevius's plight even before meeting him. "An indiscretion would not only have been fatal to him, as he was then traveling back and forth between Zurich and Berlin, but might have endangered the conspirators in Germany."

Late in January 1943 Gaevernitz finally brought the problematic German to the Herrengasse by carefully brokered appointment and under cover of the Swiss blackout. Then the congenial welcome, the fussing with the wood fire — but this time even Allen could not conjure up a prior meeting between two utterly contrasted players in the Great Game. Gisevius tested for clues of the OSS man's access to the top Allied leadership, Allen pumped his guest for gossip and information about intrigues in the Nazi high command — tidbits that started flowing back to Washington from "a key agent with close connections to high German political circles." They met again a week or so later, and the German agent volunteered a step of disclosure that every intelligence professional recognizes as fateful. Allen remembered the moment vividly: "He took his little black notebook out of his pocket and pieced together the general contents of a considerable number of telegrams which had been sent from Berne to Washington. He had just returned from Berlin and by chance his friends in the Abwehr had learned that the German deciphering services had succeeded in breaking one of the American codes."[5] This was the so-called "Burns" (Allen) to "Victor" (Donovan) communications channel that Allen used for general political commentary. Evidently it had been compromised.

"The incident of the broken code actually brought Gisevius and me closer together," Allen wrote. "It was strong evidence of his sincerity." And aside from confirming some degree of good faith, the vice consul's disclosure presented an opportunity that the true intelligence professional knew how to exploit. Allen would never again send any sensitive messages in the "Burns" to "Victor" code, but if he abruptly stopped using the channel the Germans would realize that the Americans knew the code was broken. Thus "Burns" to "Victor" became a channel for messages that Allen was ready to let Nazi intelligence see.

As their relationship developed, Gisevius proved his good faith more than once as he alerted Allen to breaches of security, the most valuable tool of counterespionage. One day at his office in the German consulate, after dining the night before at the Herrengasse, Gisevius was startled to receive an agent's report that a tall, heavy, German-speaking man with the initials "H.B.G." embossed on his hatband, had slipped into the OSS apartment through the back door and spent over an hour with the chief. Only a member of 110's household could have provided such information; the German-Swiss cook was apparently a German agent. Gisevius had no problem explaining away the report to his superiors; clandestine meetings with enemy intelligence personnel were surely a proper Abwehr function. But for Allen, enemy penetration of his own household was disastrous, and he promptly fired the cook. Gisevius was able to amuse his new American contact with ongoing reports that continued to flow in from this woman, gossipy tidbits she had obviously made up on the assumption that her German case officer would not know she had lost her inside position.

Through Gisevius, Allen wrote, "I began to get acquainted with the secrets of the German underground." Gisevius was no less impressed. "Dulles was the first intelligence officer who had the courage to extend his activities to the political aspects of the war." He was embittered by the lack of welcome granted him by the British and other Americans who, Gisevius said, "stuck to the old fashioned scheme in which the 'enemy' was considered solely as an object of espionage" — never as an opening for "political advantage."[6] The two intelligence professionals set out to use each other. Allen saw to it that Gisevius "became convinced that I used every precaution in handling his reports," and over time Allen repeatedly defended his new source against all the natural suspicions that he was a Nazi plant, a double agent in particular and a double-dealer in general. For his part Gisevius found in Allen just the contact Canaris and Oster of the subversive Abwehr had been seeking for years past. "His bureau on the Herrengasse in Berne grew in time into a virtual center of the European Resistance. Not only Germans, but Austrians, Hungarians, Italians, Rumanians and Finns, not to mention the citizens of occupied countries, met there. Everyone breathed easier; at last a man had been found with whom it was possible to discuss the contradictory complex of problems emerging from Hitler's war."

— * —

From the start of Allen's service in Switzerland, OSS Washington was skeptical about the intelligence issuing from this new listening post. His integrity and judgment were respected, but more than a few in Washington had a bureaucratic interest in questioning the networks he was assembling.

The military intelligence operation left by Colonel Van Deman after World War I had fallen into neglect during the interwar decades, but it had not disappeared altogether. When Donovan and the brash civilians of the OSS stormed onto the scene, officers in uniform saw their turf threatened. Their suspicions were only fanned by their more experienced British counterparts, with whom American military intelligence maintained close liaison and who were turning up no such detailed information. Allen ignored the skepticism, and as he got into his stride he flooded Washington with rumors and gossip picked up on the run, from "a Berlin source which our agent considers reliable," "a man of wide experience in European political life," or, occasionally more cautiously, "a source considered of the highest political interest, but whose credibility has not been definitely established." The intelligence from such sources was diffuse.

"The new Nazi policy is to kill Jews on the spot rather than to deport them to Poland for extermination there," Allen wired in March 1943.*

---

* Allen's report went on: "High officers of the SS reportedly have decided that Berlin shall be liberated of all Jews by mid-March. Accordingly, 15,000 Berlin Jews were arrested between January 26 and March 2. All closed trucks were requisitioned; several hundred children died; several hundred adults were shot. Extension of these methods to other parts of Germany in the near future is expected" (Map Room files, OSS reports, box 72, Mar. 10, 1943, Roosevelt Library).

This message, probably based on word from Schulte, went straight to President Roosevelt. So also did Allen's intelligence a month later that "whole streets in Germany are now reported to be plastered at night with signs reading 'Down With Hitler' and 'Stop the War.'" That item must have come from international civil servants who could travel behind enemy lines.

The State Department showed some nervousness that what purported to be intelligence contacts might turn into political approaches from German factions seeking to chip away at the policy of unconditional surrender. Donovan was ordered to remind his men in the neutral listening posts that any approach by an enemy national had to be reported immediately to the State Department. The upstaged military intelligence officers were even more outraged at Allen's rich pickings. On April 29, 1943, Donovan sent Allen a grim advisory:

> It has been requested of us to inform you that "All news from Bern these days is being discounted 100% by the War Department." It is suggested that Switzerland is an ideal location for plants, tendentious intelligence and peace feelers, but no details are given. As our duty requires, we have passed on the above information. However, we restate our satisfaction that you are the one through whom our Swiss reports come, and we believe in your ability to distinguish good intelligence from bad with utmost confidence.[7]

An operative as experienced in the ways of Washington bureaucracy as Allen could detect the green-eyed devil behind that advisory — though to be fair, retrospective examination of 110's early Bern dispatches showed the injudicious enthusiasm of a new man on the scene. Some of his intelligence turned out starkly wrong: on the eve of a massive Nazi attack on the eastern front in August 1943, Allen reported that Hitler would not attempt any "large-scale offensive against Russia."*

The complexities in the daily life of an American spymaster were logistical as well as substantive. Allen found the efficiency of the Swiss train service a mixed blessing. A 6 A.M. train from Bern could get him to a clandestine meeting with a cut-out at the French, German, or Italian border, a civilized luncheon with Tyler in Geneva, or a less gentlemanly encounter with a guerrilla leader in sleepy Lugano, and still he could be home for dinner with Mary by nightfall, in time to draft a hurried dispatch for Washington. Workdays of sixteen hours were commonplace, seven days a week.

---

* Allen conceded after the war that he had also erred in minimizing the effect of Allied bombings of German population centers.

Allen had arrived in Bern with no staff, and as his diverse networks began to flourish, no American professionals could be sent in through the surrounding enemy territory to provide staff support. The handful of Foreign Service officers at the embassy had neither time nor reason to make themselves available for OSS missions, and other Allied intelligence bureaus were suspicious of a rank amateur newly arrived from America who insisted on such untraditional methods of operation. He would be likely, as the local head of Britain's MI-6 complained, "to run riot over Switzerland, fouling up the whole intelligence field."

Allen turned for help to the small band of American residents and those who had been stranded in Switzerland at the outbreak of war. Over time he managed to meet and recruit just about every American citizen in the country for appropriate OSS assignments: the Standard Oil executive who could collect intelligence about the enemy's petroleum supplies, the National City Bank representative who quietly carried out the foreign currency transfers necessary for paying agents. An unexpected source of skilled American personnel appeared in the form of army air force fliers whose planes had been shot down in bombing raids but who managed to limp into neutral airspace instead of being taken as prisoners of war. Crash-landing in Switzerland, they were interned as belligerent combatants, but Allen arranged with the skittish Swiss authorities for the fliers to be quietly available to him for staff work as long as they did not openly violate Swiss neutrality.*

Relations with the Swiss authorities were in fact one of Allen's most bothersome distractions. An important obligation of neutrality is the stricture against espionage by any belligerents in the jurisdiction. Like all other foreign "diplomats" bent on intelligence, Allen had to watch his step with the Swiss — and should he get careless, the officious hosts were there to watch it for him. Early in his residence, he became aware of steady, and clumsy, surveillance by plainclothesmen hanging around Herrengasse. Stepping out one morning in a sportive mood, as he told it, he spotted "an obvious flatfoot" idling in an arcade across the way; Allen sauntered over, suddenly turned on the man, and demanded, "Are you a German?" The policeman, caught unawares, blurted back, "No, sir, Swiss!" and produced his police badge to prove it. This time Allen's Santa Claus laugh had the mirth of triumph.

Allen could not resist another little test. Assuming that the Swiss police were tapping his telephone lines, he arranged for an anti-Nazi Hungarian émigré in his employ to telephone a fellow Hungarian from his Bern study and chat in their own language, which he guessed the Swiss

* Among these airmen was Bruce Sundlun, who later became governor of Rhode Island.

would not understand. Scarcely had they started their contrived and innocent conversation when the telephone line went dead. Without unseemly scolding, the Swiss authorities made clear their intolerance of attempts to evade their neutrality.

From then on, Allen took precautions — including what seemed a most insensitive lecture to a messenger of the French resistance who had sneaked through the woods of the frontier to give his report. Sitting before the wood fire at the Herrengasse, Allen had the temerity to demand that the agent, having just risked his life in an illicit crossing, should shine his shoes! The point, of course, was that mud-caked footwear would be a sure tip to the observant and fastidious Swiss that the visitor had been treading ground far from the safe city streets.

With such concerns on his mind, and as the first exhilarating months of bachelor freedom and patriotic adventure succumbed to routine, Allen began growing impatient with the demands of the difficult people around him. Mary Bancroft, for all the pleasure of her nocturnal visits, did prattle on in her hearty way about theories of human behavior collected from that psychologist friend of hers. "I wish you'd stop this nonsense," Allen blurted one night. "I don't want to go down in history as a footnote to a case of Jung's."[8] And the overbearing Gisevius, though valuable in conveying the innermost intrigues of the Nazi leadership, was becoming annoying in his demands for attention. He was the "type of man who makes enemies," Allen wrote long afterward, "and . . . rather enjoys it."

A shrewd manipulator of men (and women), Allen hit upon a useful solution: he introduced his two needy associates with a pretext for keeping them busy together. One night late in May 1943 Mary Bancroft found Allen preoccupied after their dinner, lost in thoughts that were obviously not of the lovemaking to come. Suddenly he pulled the pipe from his mouth and fixed her with a stern stare. "Contrary to general opinion, I think you can keep your mouth shut," he said. He told her what he wanted her to do. A certain German officer would call upon her; she was not to ask his real name. He would offer her a ponderous book-length manuscript about Nazi criminalities and ask her help in translating it for publication immediately after the war. This, Allen explained, would be just the excuse for a relationship. "I want you to report to me everything he says to you — *everything*. With you working on his book, he may be off his guard and say things to you that contradict the story he is telling me. That's what I want to find out."

Thus the spymaster arranged a method of checking on his important new source and provided alternative diversions for two people whose demands were becoming tiresome. Mary inevitably found a new sex object in Gisevius, this "giant of a man, fair-haired, blue-eyed, with a healthy tan, . . . so engaging, his smile so beguiling," and the dour Gisevius turned on the charm for the adoring editor who was going to make his tedious book into a powerful message. Why not let work and romance proceed hand in hand, just as Allen always liked to arrange it?*

OSS Bern still needed better operational penetration of the Third Reich, and Gisevius, though he had knowledge of the Nazi system, was not a steady source of current military or political intelligence; based in Zurich, he had only incidental access to the routine paper flow of decision-making in Hitler's high command. Furthermore, in his arrogance and self-importance, he refused to engage in what he considered "mere espionage." Yet at the height of the war, with armies clashing and battles raging all around, "mere espionage" was exactly what the Allied governments most needed.

— * —

Nothing sours an intelligence operation more surely than a case officer who imposes his ego upon his networks, who takes it personally whenever the veracity of his information is questioned or some chancy maneuver goes wrong. In his first year on the job in Bern, Allen was impervious to this occupational hazard, but his British counterparts had a long lead on him.

A prime example of the flawed case officer was Colonel Claude Dansey of the British secret service. A veteran security officer from the Peace Conference — he and his American counterpart, Colonel Van Deman, got on well together — the stiff-backed Dansey was a master of the bureaucratic infighting that went on in the various unmarked office blocks of Whitehall long before America's OSS learned the business. Dansey was less perspicacious, however, in the art of building effective intelligence networks. Shortly after the outbreak of the war the Nazis captured two men whom Dansey considered his best agents as they set out on a clumsy attempt to contact the German underground at the Dutch border.[†9] With both his network and his pride badly burned, Dansey mandated that his agents in Switzerland and elsewhere give little quarter to any walk-ins who claimed to represent anti-Nazi Germans.

Thus, when a certain unknown German functionary appeared at the

* As it happened, Mary's hopes for romance with Gisevius were short-lived. His ardor quickly cooled before the political tasks ahead, and the manuscript ended up with other translators before finally being published in the United States in 1947 under the title *To the Bitter End.*

† One of the two was quite possibly a double agent from the start.

British Embassy in Bern on August 17, 1943, the military attaché played according to Dansey's rules and received him with unveiled contempt. The nervous bureaucrat tried to explain that he was a confirmed opponent of Nazi power and was ready and able to supply a steady flow of sensitive Foreign Office documents to the Allies. "I don't believe you," the English officer responded, "and if you are telling the truth, you are a cad." The attaché, Colonel Cartwright, encountered Allen at a social occasion that evening and remarked airily, "He'll undoubtedly turn up at your shop in due course."

The next morning a somber gentleman of indeterminate nationality, a cut-out, appeared at the American Embassy on the Dufourstrasse asking for Gerald Mayer, the only American name he knew. Mayer had long since moved away from Allen's OSS operations, but he reluctantly agreed to receive the visitor, who pulled an envelope from an inside pocket, opened it, and placed three typewritten sheets on Mayer's desk, summaries of recent top-secret diplomatic cables to Berlin. "There is more from the same source," the unwanted caller informed Mayer. "I am merely acting as an emissary for a friend who works in the Foreign Office. This man is here now in Bern. He has much more information he wishes to give you."[10]

Mayer asked the visitor to wait in the anteroom and rushed upstairs to Allen's office. He did not have Gaevernitz's experience in dealing with cut-outs, but these documents seemed to establish their own credibility. Mayer well recalled the immediate reaction of the spymaster. Three possibilities, Allen replied: an attempt to break American codes, assuming that the legation would immediately transmit the texts to Washington over a circuit that could be monitored and then compared with the originals; a provocation that would allow the Swiss to expel American "diplomats" caught in the act of unlawful espionage; or "just the glimmer of a chance that this man is on the square." No prisoner to Dansey's rules, Allen promptly agreed to meet the unknown German, incognito, at Mayer's apartment in the Bern embassy district late that night after their usual round of diplomatic dinners.

Two visitors, the cut-out and the still nameless functionary, were with Mayer in his bachelor apartment when Allen walked in a few minutes after midnight and was introduced as "Mr. Douglas," Mayer's assistant. The four men sparred nervously in German as Mayer mixed highballs. On the coffee table was a thick bundle of papers stamped with swastikas and other official seals. As the small talk grew strained, Allen started on business without his usual amiability: How do we know that you are not an agent provocateur? If I were, replied the German with equal brusque-ness, why would I have brought you 186 documents instead of just 2 or 3? A logical, if not definitive, retort, which led to more repartee.

The German described his modest background in the civil service, his hatred of both Bolshevism and Nazism, which spurred him to do anything he could to bring the war to an early end. Allen pressed him on these motives. The German insisted that he wanted no money or other payoff, only that he, and friends whom he would name, be well treated after the war. Allen had heard that dangerous request before and refused to make any promises that might appear to undermine the policy of unconditional surrender or set up a new stab-in-the-back legend. The German nonetheless agreed to arrange another courier mission to Bern in about two months, giving the Americans ample time to check the quality of the materials provided.

They talked until 3 A.M. Allen and Mayer stayed up the rest of the night, poring over the sheaf of secret German Foreign Office papers: memos of conversations with Foreign Minister Joachim von Ribbentrop, the location of a rendezvous for German and Japanese submarines, a German one-time cipher pad, details of a spy network in Portuguese Mozambique that was monitoring Allied shipping — a treasure trove of current intelligence, the supply of "mere espionage" that Allen had been seeking. As the German prepared to leave Mayer's apartment, Allen was impressed enough to drop the pretense and suggest they meet next time at his real operating center, Herrengasse 23, after curfew, using the garden entrance. On an impulse he assigned the German functionary the code name "George Wood."

Over the next twenty months, up to V-E Day 1945, "George Wood" — his real name was Fritz Kolbe — would make five trips to Bern bearing courier packets, and in between he smuggled out urgent materials with other couriers. In all, Kolbe provided some 1,600 secret documents from the center of the Nazi Foreign Office, including military and technological intelligence. So efficient did the traffic become that on one occasion Allen had the text of a document prepared in Berlin just four days before. For extra security he was assigned two OSS code numbers, 674 and 805, used interchangeably. Kolbe became "undoubtedly one of the best secret agents any intelligence service has ever had," Allen wrote. And an official OSS report to the Joint Chiefs of Staff recorded, as the war ended, that even "usually skeptical and conservative British intelligence officials rated this contact as the prize intelligence source of the war."[*]

Fritz Kolbe belongs in a novel about a powerful secret agent lurking

---

[*] Dansey had retired by the time of this judgment.

under the guise of an utterly insignificant drone, Superman known as Clark Kent. A plodding bureaucrat, he conveyed to his peers and superiors no particular ambition, imagination, or other notable ability beyond diligence at routine paperwork and competence in doing what he was told. He was forty-three years old when Allen met him, the son of a saddlemaker who managed by concentration and determination to be accepted, after years of night school, into the roster of staff diplomats. After twenty years in the professional service he had risen no higher than personal assistant to an officer of ambassadorial rank. Beneath the drab surface, however, were some clues to a flair within. He was an avid fan of all sports, and he worked out regularly. He had married twice, and while his second wife lived out the war in South Africa, he found mutual attraction with women as modest of demeanor as he was himself. At the time he was making contact with Allen, he was in love with a nurse in Berlin named Gerda.

Among the anti-Nazi Germans, Kolbe and Schulte were alike in some respects: never members of the Nazi Party, loners, inclined to direct action rather than talky conspiracies, reckless enough to blurt out incorrect sentiments on social occasions — Kolbe once publicly called Mussolini a pig, and he refused to recant when challenged by a superior. The difference between them was that Schulte could get away with indiscretions because he was so nonpolitical and important in his district, while Kolbe was too insignificant even within his own bureaucracy to attract hostile attention.

The man to whom Kolbe was personal assistant was an ardent Nazi, Karl Ritter, a tough-minded diplomat in charge of Foreign Office liaison with the military high command. Kolbe's job was to arrive in the office before anyone else, sift the reports from the various military and diplomatic centers — over a hundred of them on some days — and decide which needed to be put before Ritter and, ultimately, Ribbentrop. Preparing summaries of cables was his daily work; he had long hours alone to do the job in his office, just two doors away from Ribbentrop's own office. At first he copied key documents manually; apologizing for typos and misspellings, Kolbe explained, "I write these lines in wild haste, scanning the material with one eye and typing it with the other hand." He had, as Allen put it, "the kind of access which is the intelligence officer's dream."

Access was the first step, but then the materials had to be passed into a network. Switzerland was a natural place for clandestine contact, and for a year Kolbe had asked, without success, for the privilege of a skiing holiday. Finally he approached a friend from his hiking club, one Fräulein von Heimerdinger, who happened to work in the office that dispatched diplomatic couriers, and put an unexpected proposition: could she arrange for him to be the officer to carry the next pouch to Switzerland? She agreed on the spot. That is how Kolbe found his way to Mayer and Allen.

The deceptive bureaucrat managed another courier mission just six weeks after their first meeting. He passed through Swiss customs on October 7 bearing a twelve-by-eighteen-inch manila envelope secured by two red diplomatic seals, addressed to the German Legation in Bern. But the envelope he delivered measured only ten by fifteen inches and was not quite as thick as before; it was in fact an inner envelope, also officially sealed, that reached the legation, after Kolbe had removed the remainder of the contents for his own purpose. With amusement he told Allen of the grief that had come to him after the August trip. The Foreign Office security branch had summoned him to explain his absence from his hotel during that night in Bern — obviously they had been maintaining surveillance on their new courier. Kolbe was perfectly prepared: not only did he concede that his appetites led him to seek feminine company when he had the chance, he proceeded to present a medical certificate that he had reported to a doctor the next morning for a blood test and a preventive prophylactic. The dull and colorless Kolbe, it seemed, could summon imagination as well as courage.

On his third visit, in the second week of December, Kolbe brought telegrams sent to Berlin by the Nazi ambassador in Turkey, Franz von Papen, telling of a special source within the British Embassy that promised a rich trove of espionage. "I shall designate this source 'Cicero,' " von Papen cabled. "Request that questions about him be sent eyes only to the ambassador." As Allen recounted the story, "I immediately passed word of this to my British colleagues, and a couple of British security inspectors immediately went over to the British Embassy in Ankara and changed the safes and their combinations, thus putting Cicero out of business. . . . Our rifling of the German Foreign Office safes in Berlin through an agent reporting to the Americans in Switzerland, put an end to the rifling of the British Ambassador's safe by a German agent in Turkey."*

In March 1944 OSS Washington found a sudden need to deepen the information flow on Japanese political and military developments. Allen never knew when Kolbe could manage to reappear in Bern, but he and

---

* Allen's cheery sentence in *The Secret Surrender* telescopes a tense intelligence drama. Colonel Dansey was not inclined to accept a tip of this delicacy from an American — and on the evidence of an agent rebuffed by his own men. British officials tried to claim that Cicero was in fact their double agent.

Mayer hit upon the idea of sending an open postcard from a name in Zurich. "Dear Friend. Perhaps you remember my little son. His birthday is coming soon and I wanted to get him some of those clever Japanese toys with which the shops here used to be full, but I can find none. I wonder if there might be some left in Berlin?" When Kolbe arrived a couple of weeks later over the Easter holiday, he carried extensive microfilmed reports on the order of battle of the Japanese Imperial Fleet, along with political and economic developments from German agents in Tokyo. Allen cabled Washington on April 11 that "Wood" had brought in "more than two hundred highly valuable Easter eggs." (Washington replied, "What a bunny!")

The sheer bulk of Kolbe's material caused Allen problems. It was too much to transmit to Washington by cable, and there was always the nagging fear that radio transmission of known documents might allow German counterespionage to break the American codes. Using the downed American airmen as code clerks for the essentials, Allen fell back on his own summaries, succumbing in the process to flights of rhetorical extravagance most unfamiliar to the American diplomatic practice he had left behind. He knew what Gisevius was telling him, what Mary Bancroft was telling him that Gisevius was telling her, and the actual evidence in the George Wood dispatches. That April of 1944 he sent the OSS a remarkable report on the looming death throes of the Third Reich:

> Sincerely regret that you cannot at this time see Wood's material as it stands, without condensation and abridgment. In some 400 pages, dealing with the internal maneuverings of German diplomatic policy for the past two months, a picture of imminent doom and final downfall is presented.
>
> Into a tormented General Headquarters and a half-dead Foreign Office stream the lamentations of a score of diplomatic posts. It is a scene wherein haggard Secret Service and diplomatic agents are doing their best to cope with the defeatism and desertion of flatly defiant satellites and allies and recalcitrant neutrals. The period of secret service under Canaris and diplomacy under the champagne salesman [Ribbentrop] is drawing to an end. Already Canaris has disappeared from the picture, and a conference was hurriedly convoked in Berlin at which efforts were made to mend the gaping holes left in the Abwehr. Unable now to fall back on his favorite means of avoiding disconcerting crises by retiring to his bed, Ribbentrop has beat a retreat. . . .
>
> Bomb shelters are being permanently used for code work. Once messages have been deciphered, a frantic search begins to locate the particu-

lar service or minister to which each cable must be forwarded; and, when a reply is called for, another search is necessary to deliver this to the right place.

The final death-bed contortions of a putrified Nazi diplomacy are pictured in these telegrams. The reader is carried from one extreme of emotion to the other as he examines these messages and sees the cruelty exhibited by the Germans in their final swan-song of brutality toward the peoples so irrevocably and pitifully enmeshed by the Gestapo.

The undiplomatic zeal of this particular telegram raised some eyebrows among Allen's fellows in Washington, and he was politely asked if he wanted to tone it down a bit before it was circulated: 110 refused to change a word.[11]

— ∗ —

As always, Allen's superiors had the task of determining the authenticity of the Wood materials. Skepticism still reigned in Washington, and no less than four challenges to the various Bern networks came during the winter of 1943–44, including a particularly distressing cable on January 25 from his old friend Whitney Shepardson, pressed into war work at OSS headquarters.

> We think it is essential that you be informed at once that almost the entire material [of a recent telegram] disagrees with reports we have received originating from other sources, and parts of it were months old. . . . Information from other neutral lands indicates . . . that the order has been given [by enemy intelligence] to go all out against our intelligence activities. The possibility appears to correspond with the sudden degeneration of your information, which is now given a lower rating than any other source. This seems to indicate a need for using the greatest care in checking all your sources.

Intelligence analysis requires a constant vigilance against plants, deceptions, and fabrications, and Shepardson's advisory was neither meanspirited nor inappropriate given the war of wits being waged on all sides. The Wood materials in particular had to be considered suspect from the start; they were too good, too timely and sensitive, the motivations of the agent too murky. Thus, before pronouncing his own judgment on the source, Allen had risked sending Washington a few of the first pages given him by Kolbe with the request to apply all possible tests of validity. Included among those tests would be the opinion of Claude Dansey in London.

Still smarting from his own intelligence failures and the presumption of the OSS amateur in Switzerland, which he considered his personal fiefdom, Dansey scarcely bothered to read the texts from Allen. They were "obviously a plant, and Dulles had fallen for it like a ton of bricks," a Dansey underling reported. At that, given the parallel instincts of the Americans in the War Department, the George Wood file might have ended — had it not been for the molish curiosity and ambition of a young man in Dansey's office, one H. A. R. (Kim) Philby. "I was very anxious to get a certain job that would soon become available," Philby recalls. "I therefore decided to study the Dulles material on its merits" — as Dansey, his superior, had not. Philby passed the sample of Allen's Wood documents to Commander Alexander Denniston of the Royal Navy, whom he knew to be expert in the German diplomatic cable traffic. "Two days later, Denniston telephoned me in a state of some excitement. He told me that three of my telegrams exactly matched intercepted telegrams which they had already deciphered, and that the others were proving of the utmost value to his cryptographers in their breakdown of the German diplomatic code. Could I get him some more?" Philby pursued his own bureaucratic games with Dansey, who eventually reversed his impulsive dismissal of Allen's source; British intelligence decided to confirm Wood's veracity.*

The advisory from London was received in Washington by Lamot Belin, Allen's old friend from Constantinople, ever eager to believe the best about an old clubmate. "Both the material and the source have stood the test," Belin informed Donovan, "and are thought to be of great value." Donovan went to the further pains of submitting the Wood documents to a panel of the highest military intelligence specialists. Their interim report, submitted some six weeks after Kolbe first appeared in Bern, was both conclusive and cautious. The material was authentic, but "the Germans may be employing the technique of disclosing genuine information not particularly harmful to them in order to instill, and later to take advantage of, a false sense of confidence."

Allen knew nothing of Philby or the outcome of the investigation he

---

* In his memoirs, written after he finally defected to Moscow in 1963, Philby would have history believe that his gratuitous intervention in the George Wood affair was simply a ploy to gain professional advancement in the British secret service. On the basis of what is now known about this extraordinary double agent's single-minded devotion to the Soviet cause over the decades, it is logical to assume that he also wanted the Wood channel to flourish for the benefit of Soviet intelligence as well as the Western Allies,. It would be helpful for the ever suspicious Stalin to know the information Roosevelt and Churchill were getting from inside Germany, and without their knowing that he knew it. The Wood documents would also help Moscow confirm and fill out German intelligence coming in from other sources not available to the West.

had requested in Washington. But after meeting Kolbe twice again, he cabled Donovan on December 29, 1943, "I now firmly believe in the good faith of Wood and I am ready to stake my reputation on the fact that these documents are genuine." Donovan had enough in hand to take the plunge. On January 10, 1944, he sent the Wood file to President Roosevelt. His covering memo was uncharacteristically measured for the enthusiastic OSS, but it was powerful in its portent:

> We have secured through secret intelligence channels a series of what purport to be authentic reports, transmitted by various German diplomatic, consular, military and intelligence sources to their headquarters. The source and material are being checked as to probable authenticity both here and in London. We shall submit later a considered opinion on this point. It is possible that contact with this source furnishes the first important penetration into a responsible German agency.

Hesitantly but with increasing confidence, OSS and military officers began using the materials from 674 and 805 in their tactical planning, even as the authenticity checks continued.[12] Belin cabled Allen on April 20, 1944, "The increasingly significant character of the data impresses us particularly, and at the same time we notice that it becomes proportionately more damaging to [German] interests." Yet could this still be a confidence-building technique before deceptive information was thrown in? Allen replied in a friendly but firm manner six days later: "I am aware of the risk of becoming so impressed with one's sources that one steps into traps. . . . From the beginning I have tried to take a critical examination of the . . . information with this in mind."

As for motives, Allen told his friend at headquarters that Wood seemed "naive," lacking "any of the characteristics which would make him competent to work a double-crossing scheme." In hours of interrogation he had said nothing to "create a doubt as to his genuineness. . . . To date the only factor creating concern has been indications that Wood has occasionally been reckless. . . . With illegal plotters this is quite normal behavior."

Sometimes only the course of events can confirm the authenticity of secret intelligence. In May 1944 military intelligence officers pointed to one Wood dispatch as a possible deception inserted into the flow of otherwise genuine information: a citation of German military orders to destroy Rome's industrial and utility installations and the bridges over the River Tiber should the Allies try to storm the Imperial City. Might the Americans thus hesitate to attack Rome, leaving the German defenders free to be deployed elsewhere? Such suspicions were definitively put to rest a month later, after the fall of Rome in June, when Allied occupiers

did indeed find the destruction orders, countermanded only at the last
minute.

Eventually even the most skeptical intelligence analysts came to accept Kolbe's unparalleled contributions to the Allied war effort. Though
the full benefits were slow in coming, it had taken Allen just nine months
to achieve the goal of his mission to Switzerland, penetration of the Nazi
high command to learn the secret deliberations of the Third Reich at
war. Creative espionage, however, need not rest with collecting intelligence. Networks can be employed also to alter the course of events, to
provoke direct action toward a desired end.

— 9 —

THE END

A GERMAN ARMY LIEUTENANT, unknown to Allen, attempted to murder Adolf Hitler on March 13, 1943. The would-be assassin, Fabian von Schlabrendorff, thirty-six years old, was a Wiesbaden lawyer in civilian life. Schlabrendorff and several fellow officers in the Abwehr had worked secretly for months to craft a bomb, using explosives and a British detonator recovered intact after an air raid. The lieutenant managed to place the lethal packet on the airplane taking Hitler that day to his East Prussian command post. He set the fuse, left the plane, and waited for the news which never came. The homemade bomb failed to explode and was never detected. With cool cunning, Schlabrendorff boarded the plane after its return and removed the incriminating dud.

If intelligence about secret operations is never easy to come by, information about a plan that aborts is almost beyond reach. But just as Schulte picked up gossip of secret operations in the vicinity of Auschwitz, Gisevius and his anti-Nazi contacts learned that something serious was afoot around the führer's headquarters. Word of the failed attempt reached the Abwehr man in Bern in nuances and innuendos, was passed to Allen, and finally appeared on Roosevelt's White House desk three weeks later in greatly attenuated form: "[Hitler's] prestige is shaken among important members of the Nazi party," was all that Allen dared to report, "and talk of his elimination is not rare."

Schlabrendorff's bomb was one of more than half a dozen attempts by the German military to assassinate their führer. He and his fellow plotters tried again a week later, on March 21, as Hitler was scheduled to visit an exhibition at Berlin's Unter den Linden museum. This time the führer moved through so fast that there was no time to set the fuse. Subsequently plans were set — and aborted by cruel circumstance — in September, November, and December 1943 and in January 1944, when a handsome twenty-one-year-old officer named von Kleist volunteered to model a new army uniform for the führer's admiration; with a concealed grenade he was ready to blow himself up alongside Hitler.* An air raid intervened and the "model" never had another chance.[1]

The seasoned operatives of British intelligence had had years to build up a line into the German military opposition and were far ahead of Allen in depth of contact. Schlabrendorff himself, a descendant of Queen Victoria's devoted confidant and physician, Baron Christian von Stockmar, was well known to the British establishment and an occasional visitor to London before the war. But Dansey's jaded approach prevailed in the circles of war policymaking, and Whitehall chose to ignore the various hints and reports of anti-Hitler intrigues that mounted during the second half of 1943. Allen, whether naive or prescient, took these matters more seriously, though initially he had only one solid source, the difficult Gisevius.

At the end of January 1944 Allen sent the OSS by his most secret code the first of a series of detailed dispatches about the German opposition group, to which he assigned the code name "the Breakers."† The American spymaster was fully aware that he was parting from his British colleagues in his assessment, and there is even a hint that he suspected security breaches or other professional dangers inside the British intelligence system — not a popular attitude to take at that time. "For a number of reasons," he informed Washington, "I have not talked with the British about the Breakers' situation at this particular time, and pending further developments I recommend that you also refrain from doing so on the basis of information in my messages."

As Allen was preparing his first dispatch about the Breakers, British intelligence solemnly reported finding "no evidence that any faction exists within the Army or within the Party, or still less among the people as a whole, which is likely to overthrow the present regime within the foreseeable future." A month later London's intelligence chiefs repeated that "direct revolutionary action is highly improbable. . . . There is no subversive organization."

Not so. Allen was at that same time reporting with considerable accuracy on the political complexion of the loosely organized German opposition groups, "composed of various intellectuals from certain military

---

* Von Kleist was the son of a prominent anti-Nazi conservative; the father was eventually executed, but his son survived.

† Allen's prosaic code name survives only in the American records; history records what became the July 20 movement as the conspiracy of the Valkyrie, the Wagnerian label the plotters used for themselves.

and government circles." They were prepared to take "drastic action" to get rid of Hitler, 110 reported, and establish a new government before a total military defeat. Allen took pains to reassure Washington that he was not describing a rebirth of German militarism. "These groups are made up of well-educated and liberal individuals . . . they do not have rightist tendencies and are confident that in the future the government will have to be really leftist."

He alluded only vaguely to his sources, who were Gisevius and his junior partner in the Abwehr's Swiss outpost, Edward von Waetjen. In his cable Allen called them "a line to Breakers which we think can be used now for staying in close touch with events. Since any slight break would be disastrous, no constructive purpose would be served by cabling particulars." He also asked Washington to pursue, with greatest discretion, the role of an Abwehr man with the surname John operating in Spain and Portugal, who was trying to establish British and American contacts. OSS Washington was impressed with the sensitivity of what Allen was trying to convey; they sent one copy of the message to the State Department for policy guidance, then withheld all other copies from circulation.

Allen followed up with information about the alleged plot leaders, naming Abwehr general Oster and Carl Gördeler, former mayor of Leipzig. In a dispatch that Donovan sent directly to President Roosevelt on February 15, he reported the tensions building within army and Gestapo circles and suspicions "that the SS may arrange for an incident, such as the discovery of a plot against Hitler, as an excuse to proclaim martial law under SS administration, . . . calculated to forestall any future attempt by the Army to institute martial law under its own auspices."

Early in April Gisevius and Waetjen brought to Allen a direct message from Gördeler and Colonel-General Ludwig Beck, prewar chief of the German General Staff, who was emerging as the military head of the conspiracy. Allen assigned them the code names "Lester" and "Tucky," respectively, and on April 7 he informed Washington: "The opposition group led by Tucky and Lester say that at this critical point they are now willing and prepared to try to start action to oust the Nazis and eliminate the Fuehrer. Theirs is the only group able to profit by a personal approach to Hitler and other Nazi chiefs, and with enough arms at hand to accomplish their ends."

Thus arguing their credentials, the Breakers asked a quid pro quo: advance assurance from the Western powers that they would enter into direct negotiations with a post-Nazi successor government, a capitulation that would leave the German army free to pursue the war on the Soviet front. Allen reported: "The principal motive for their action is the ardent desire to prevent Central Europe from coming ideologically and factually under the control of Russia. They are convinced that in such event Christian culture and democracy and all that goes with it would disappear in Europe and that the present dictatorship of the Nazis would be exchanged for a new dictatorship."

The Gördeler-Beck message put Allen in a dangerous position, for it amounted to yet another attempt to evade the policy of unconditional surrender and gain favorable terms from the Western allies. Indeed, throughout these tense months Allen was being pressured by his German contacts to help them open political contacts with the West that would exclude the Russians. Allen may have sympathized with their point of view, but his official position in Switzerland imposed a more pressing inhibition.

Allen was an intelligence officer, not a diplomat; he was not empowered to speak for or negotiate on behalf of the United States government. A diplomat, under policy discipline from the State Department, could not even have listened to the Gördeler-Beck proposals, for that would appear to be the beginning of a negotiation — and policy said the surrender must be unconditional. As an intelligence officer, however, Allen could listen to anything and everything — for its informational or operational value — as long as he never claimed to be speaking for the government of the United States. The distinction between the two functions is not a subtle one, but its proper definition had plagued Allen and his more traditional colleagues in diplomatic intelligence since the early days of World War I. Inside his own government channels, of course, Allen operated with all the confidence of a diplomat and did not shrink from offering policy assessments of his own intelligence. In his view, for instance, Gördeler and Beck seemed caught in "the old predicament of capitulating to the East or to the West: the Germans can never perceive the third alternative of capitulating to both at the same moment."

In looking back at the whole record for accurate intelligence about the progress of an anti-Nazi plot, one finds that Allen's little network was superb; it can stand as a case study for the lesson that a few perfectly placed agents are preferable to a legion of informants of doubtful credibility. Through Gisevius and Waetjen he had a secure line to the military leaders of the Breakers. Then Adam von Trott of the Foreign Office paid a final visit to Switzerland that April and reported through Gaevernitz on the civilian side of the plot. Throughout this time Kolbe was bringing out documents of state about the collapsing war effort.* Armed with

---

* Kolbe was aware of the opposition coalescing in the Foreign Office and military hierarchy, but he was skeptical that they would be able to pull anything off. He preferred to continue undermining the Nazi regime in his own expeditious way, though once he suggested to Allen that to protect his own position after the war was lost he should establish some

sources such as these, 110's confidence showed through. By the middle of May the circles of official Washington having access to Allen's reports had widened, and the weight of his factual evidence gave the reports ever greater credibility.

Only in London did skepticism survive: toward the end of March British intelligence chiefs had noted some "slight evidence" that there might be an opposition movement within Germany, but in April and as late as June 3, the official British assessment was that there was no organization behind the opposition sentiments. By this time, of course, Allen had sent Washington the names of the key plotters, their political inclinations and aspirations, and even a precise military plan for ending the war on the western front and permitting American and British forces to occupy Germany before the Russians could arrive.

By June Gisevius, for one, had begun to lose confidence in his co-conspirators' courage and ability to act against Hitler when the moment was squarely in front of them. And through his contacts with Allen (and Mary Bancroft), even this heavy-handed Prussian came to realize that the notion of separating the Western powers from their Soviet ally would not fly. This discouraging conclusion he and Waetjen communicated to their friends in Berlin.

June 6, 1944, was D-day, the long-awaited landing of Allied forces at Normandy, bringing a ground war onto the Nazi-controlled European continent. The military pressure that the Breakers conspirators had anticipated arrived, and at the same time came the word from their Swiss informants that hopes of a separate peace and a non-Russian future for central Europe were not to be. June was the month that the "alternative of capitulating to both at the same moment" finally sank in; over these weeks the nervous case officers in Switzerland — German and American alike — heard nothing from the Breakers.

— * —

During the weeks of silence, Allen busied himself with the other strands of his diversified networks. He encouraged the self-exiled Eduard Schulte to write his massive memorandum about the polity of postwar Germany. Fritz Kolbe arrived for his fifth visit, and the interned American airmen had another rich cache of documents to encipher and transmit to Washington. On June 22 a British reporter brought Allen a description of con-

---

connection with the plotters. At one point, in fact, Kolbe happened to miss a clandestine meeting of the July 20 plotters where, foolishly, a list was made of those in attendance; the incriminating list subsequently fell into Gestapo hands. Allen pleaded with him that he might lose his access and consequent usefulness to the Allied war effort.

ditions inside the Auschwitz camp from two former inmates who had escaped into Slovakia. "He was profoundly shocked, . . . disconcerted, . . . said 'One has to do something immediately.'"[2]

Finally, amid everything else in those weeks of June, Allen found a new personal interest. He met her through his coverage of the resistance movement in northern Italy, which was gaining support as the American army advanced on Rome. Countess Wally Castelbarco, recently arrived in the security of Switzerland away from both her troubled land and her difficult husband, was a key cut-out with these partisans. She was the forty-three-year-old daughter of Maestro Arturo Toscanini, who then dominated the musical life of New York even as he sought to aid the antifascists of his native Italy by sending his daughter whatever funds were needed. From her Pension Florissant in Ouchy-Lausanne, the countess had ways of contacting the partisans, and Allen's OSS operation had ways of transferring money across currencies without anyone knowing.[3] A true angel of the underground, Wally Toscanini Castelbarco also was a gracious, passionate lady. Once again Allen saw an opportunity for doing useful work and pursuing pleasant romance, with each covering for the other. But his moves of courtship were constantly interrupted, for the present.

Early in July, Abwehr courier Captain Theodor Strünk arrived in Switzerland bearing full details of the plan for Colonel Claus Schenk von Stauffenberg of the General Staff to assassinate Hitler in the days immediately to come. Strünk's dangerous intelligence could not be sent to Washington by any of the available means. The evening of July 5, in his nightly radio-telephone link, Allen sought only to alert his government of something important about to happen within the ranks of the Nazi high command. Using all the cryptic jargon he had developed with Mary's help, he casually concluded his routine press review with a little tidbit about a "mysterious Himmler stamp" and his researches among "Swiss stamp collections." Donovan got the meaning, even without the substance, and rushed the apparent tipoff directly to Roosevelt. Six days later, on July 11, Stauffenberg flew to Hitler's headquarters at Berchtesgaden with a bomb hidden in his briefcase. When he discovered that Himmler and Göring would not be attending the scheduled conference, he held back. On July 16, when he was again prepared, Hitler, Himmler, and Göring all failed to show up.

But Allen was emboldened to send another dispatch to Washington by his most secure code. On July 12 he alerted Donovan of "possibility that a dramatic event may take place up north. . . . Ruthless repression is, of course, a possibility, even a probability." And he added a bland informative note that Gisevius was determined to return to Berlin to be on hand for the event. "I was afraid it might be the last time I would see him," Allen said later.

Mary Bancroft had a casual telephone call from her literary collaborator (as he was called). Gisevius told her he would be going away for a few days, but not to worry, "Homer" would bring over the pages of manuscript they had been reworking. Homer, she quickly understood, was Waetjen, so named because while he was working under cover in Switzerland he was spending his leisure time translating the *Odyssey* from the original Greek. Three days later, thinking little about anything important, Mary took her daughter off to their summer vacation home in Ascona.

Each day from July 12 to the twentieth, while waiting for the event, Allen fed Washington with his assessments of the possibilities looming, treading water before the Breakers. "I am not making any forecasts regarding the prospects of success for the Breakers program," he stated on July 13. Subsequently: "The next few weeks will be our last chance to demonstrate the determination of the Germans themselves to rid Germany of Hitler and his gang and establish a decent regime."

At 4 P.M. on July 20 Allen was relaxing in the embassy on the shaded Dufourstrasse with an interesting young Englishwoman, Elizabeth Wiskemann, who later described the encounter: "After we had talked a few things over, his telephone rang. He answered it very briefly, as if accepting a piece of news he had rather expected. He put back the receiver and said to me 'There has been an attack on Hitler's life at his headquarters.' I was not surprised either, but rather excited. We neither of us knew whether it had succeeded."

Mary was scrambling eggs for her daughter in their Ascona chalet when the announcement came on the radio. For the next hours she turned the radio dial to learn details. After supper she ventured into the village to call Allen on a public telephone. "I don't know anything more than you do," the American spymaster said quickly, to reassure all those who would surely be listening. "You might drop in on our friend up on the hill," he added, which Mary properly understood to be Homer, also vacationing nearby. Then Allen asked her how the weather was, and that was that.

— * —

The frantic, familiar voice of the führer on the radio close to midnight told the world that the July 20 putsch had failed. Beyond that, the helpless case officers in their Swiss idyll could learn nothing in time to do anything useful. The Gestapo purge swung into action; thousands were arrested within hours, General Beck shot himself, and Stauffenberg was executed by a ten-man firing squad just minutes after Hitler's radio address.

On his radio-telephone link to Washington the next night, Allen confined himself to general military gossip, perhaps expecting that marked silence on the major development would itself be a signal of his anxieties.[4] Instead a cable arrived from the lower reaches of OSS headquarters, requesting information about some reported putsch in Germany — another of those inane messages that diplomats and foreign correspondents receive from desk clerks who think they are showing initiative by raising the obvious. Allen and Gaevernitz sat the night out in the Herrengasse study waiting for some word from someone, speculating about Trott, Strünk, Gisevius, and the other Breakers they had come to know and trust. One of their émigré contacts who wandered in later recalled, "I never saw them so completely downtrodden."

Despite the conviction of a later radical generation that an American spymaster like Allen Dulles could pull the strings on all the political puppets of the world, no serious case can be made that Allen masterminded, or even made substantive contribution to, the putsch of July 20. To the contrary, German oppositionists like Trott and Stauffenberg himself despaired at how little outside support they could muster, bent as the Allies were on an undefined but adamant policy of unconditional surrender. Over the weeks following, Allen and his network were able to piece together details of what had happened to the Breakers, and these dispatches were duly submitted to Roosevelt. With relief they learned through layers of cut-outs that Gisevius had escaped the first Gestapo dragnet; on instinct he had set out to flee Berlin during the night but had returned to fade into the populace of the capital while the Gestapo screened everyone attempting to leave. Gaevernitz set out to have false identity documents fashioned and smuggled into Gisevius's hands.

British intelligence had problems of a different sort with the events of July 20. Caught by their jaded refusal to acknowledge the existence of an anti-Hitler movement, Colonel Dansey's men in Stockholm had gone through the motions of receiving the desperate Adam von Trott toward the end of June, just as they had in Bern earlier, but Whitehall's official estimate on July 6 was that "these people . . . won't act without our backing, which, if given, might gravely embarrass us later." As late as July 14 the British intelligence chiefs doggedly concluded that any action against Hitler was unlikely. Four days later, apparently under prodding from Washington, a suspicious 10 Downing Street asked the intelligence service to review the evidence for that conclusion one more time.

The official history of British intelligence in World War II acknowledges this sorry record.* But it generously goes on to note the detailed

---

* Yet so awkward was the record that the entire narrative of the July 20 conspiracy was relegated to Appendix 22 of the official history.

reports that Allen had been sending Washington, in embarrassing contrast to their own misjudgments. A fortnight after the assassination attempt the British Embassy in Washington quietly informed the State Department that advance word had indeed come to London, from an unnamed German informant, of a plot to overthrow Hitler. The story "bore every resemblance to similar stories which have been produced at intervals since 1938 and it was accordingly discounted as probably of little importance." But with the announcements of July 20 the British had to blandly admit their error. "It would therefore appear that this German and the information provided through him are in fact serious," the British note acknowledged, without bothering to comment further.

Allen's information about the philosophy and goals of the July 20 plot was not as impressive as his tactical and operational reports. He knew that the conspiracy aimed to kill Hitler and bring down the Nazi regime, and that is all he cared to know. Only later, after all was over, could Allen and his various contacts pause to figure out who the Germans of the underground really were. They were puzzled to learn that Stauffenberg himself, for example, was far more tolerant of Soviet Russia than were the conservative German nationalists; the quip at the time was that he sought to replace "national socialism" with "national bolshevism."[5] Adam von Trott, upon the collapse of his fantasy to build the loyalties of Rhodes scholars and Oxford common rooms into congenial Anglo-Teutonic harmony, likewise flirted with the alternative of a deal with Russia.

The personalities were diverse, from Count von Moltke's easy aristocratic security to Gisevius's tight bourgeois concern for propriety. "One of the underground's strangest characters was Albrecht Haushofer," Allen wrote in a postwar memoir. Strange indeed, from Allen's perspective, for the son of Watertown had finally discovered that special affinity group of upper-class homosexuals that his worldly aides had been reluctant to describe for him. Haushofer, son of a famous geographer, was a Germanic Oscar Wilde, "fat, whimsical, sentimental, romantic and unquestionably brilliant," in Allen's description. "He was also the bosom friend of Rudolf Hess," and after Hess's bizarre flight to Scotland, Haushofer had difficulty staying off Hitler's black list. He was arrested after July 20 and, in another eerie parallel to Wilde, composed morbid poetry from his jail cell in Berlin. Looking at the fate of the German intelligentsia under Nazi rule, Allen cited Haushofer's ballad from the Lehrterstrasse jail:

> Early I saw the misery's whole course —
> I spoke my warning, but not harsh enough nor clear!
> How guilty I have been I now know here . . .

Haushofer was murdered by the SS in April 1945, a few days before the liberation of Berlin.

For all the variety of philosophies and lifestyles revealed in the diaries and letters of the passionate German underground, the only Nazi crime that did not seem to generate their outrage was the extermination of the Jews. None of the conspirators seems actually to have defended the policy of antisemitism, to be sure, but its implementation did not rank high among the concerns of this circle.

For help in understanding the collapse of July 20, Mary Bancroft turned to Jung. When Allen first entrusted her with the secret of Gisevius and the existence of a plot, she had gone to her distinguished therapist, and Jung had offered support. Of course she could keep the secrets that her friend Allen was bestowing upon her; indeed, it was a peak moment for her emotional growth. "Only after you have had to keep a secret can you learn the true outlines of self," Jung said.

Mary arranged for Gisevius to have sessions with Jung. Long after July 20 but as the war still raged, Jung confided to Mary his impressions of Gisevius and everything he could learn about the conspiracy. He found it fascinating that the dour German was projecting his own psychology upon Stauffenberg, the man who actually set out to do the deed. Mary recorded Jung's words in her diary: "'It is probably just as well that the *putsch* failed.' He hopes the Americans understand that what Gisevius and Stauffenberg were really fighting for was the same thing that Hitler had, namely 'pure power.' Jung saw the Nazis and the conspirators of July 20 as two of a kind, 'a couple of lions fighting over a hunk of raw meat.'"[6]

Both before and after the collapse of the conspiracy, Allen had the problem of settling on his own course of action. "Unconditional surrender" was for him a straitjacket: "I do not understand what our policy is," he had cabled OSS Washington a full year after the Casablanca conference, "and what offers, if any, we could give to the resistance movement." Allen the intelligence officer was struggling with Allen the diplomat, and neither ever got a meaningful reply.

In March 1943 Allen had cabled his view that unconditional surrender would signify "total catastrophe for the country and for the individual German. We ourselves have done nothing to offer them a more hopeful meaning for this expression; we have never, for example, indicated that it refers only to military and party leaders." Particularly troubling to an intelligence officer dealing directly with the German resistance was the fact that Stalin was not at Casablanca. "Unconditional surrender" was Roosevelt's phrase, reluctantly accepted by the Old World in the person of Churchill; it was never in Moscow's lexicon. Indeed, six months after the

Casablanca meeting, the Kremlin's war command announced formation of the National Committee to Free Germany, a political action movement headed by captured German officers and prisoners of war in a thinly disguised effort to impose communist war aims upon the defeated Reich.

The Free Germany movement represented a threat to the "maintenance of Western democracy in central Europe," Allen cabled on September 24, 1943. A month later he sent two long dispatches, both of which went directly to Roosevelt, warning that the United States was "losing credit among the masses of European peoples. . . . Reports suggest that Russia understands the psychology of the 'masses' and is gaining strength among them in an extraordinary way; the inevitable revolution after the break in Germany will find the 'masses' turning to Russia instead of to the US unless something concrete is evidenced in US propaganda to show understanding of what the people really desire." A full year later, his assessment was plaintive. "Moscow has been the only source of hope for the Germans."* Allen's frustration was shared, particularly after the invasion of Normandy, by General Dwight D. Eisenhower and the American military command confronting the task of occupying Nazi-held lands and taking German prisoners. What political future could they hold out, in contrast to the detailed and sugar-coated programs of Moscow's Committee to Free Germany?

The men in the field could not have known that they were confronting the jaunty certitude of the one man whose views mattered, Franklin D. Roosevelt. "Frankly, I do not like the idea of conversation to define the term 'unconditional surrender,'" Roosevelt wrote Secretary of State Cordell Hull in January 1944. Let the German people be told simply "what I said in my Christmas Eve speech — in effect, that we have no thought of destroying the German people and that we want them to live through the generations like other European peoples on condition, of course, that they get rid of their present philosophy of conquest. I forget my exact words, but you can have them looked up."

As the pressures from Allen and others in the field kept mounting, an exasperated Roosevelt lectured his Joint Chiefs of Staff:

> A somewhat long study and personal experience in and out of Germany leads me to believe that German philosophy cannot be changed by decree, law or military order. . . . I am not willing at this time to say that we do not intend to destroy the German nation. . . . I think that the simplest way of approaching this whole matter is to stick to what I have already

---

* An emerging rival in secret intelligence, William J. Casey, noted that "Dulles kept talking into the wind — but he kept talking."

said — that the Allies have no intention of destroying German people, . . . [but rather are] determined to administer a total defeat to Germany as a whole.

Cavalier guidance such as that gave Allen no flexibility in discussions with the men of the German resistance — until that resistance, and those men, were no more.

— * —

The failure of the Breakers on July 20, 1944, demolished the ill-starred German underground that Allen and others, such as George Kennan, had detected — without useful effect — years before. More immediately it decimated the network Allen had stitched together into the power centers of the Third Reich. Captain Strünk, courier of the final plot, was promptly caught and executed. Waetjen's Swiss cover was exposed, but he remained safely at his family's home and spent the rest of his long and contented life in Switzerland translating Homer. Otto John, one of the Breakers' contacts with the Allies whom Allen had not met, boarded an airplane to safety in Spain; he reemerged years later to play a puzzling role in the postwar politics of the German Federal Republic. The unnoticed Kolbe, reluctantly aloof from the conspiracy, continued to go about his routine business in the Foreign Ministry, but he could not risk another trip to Bern until April 1945, by which time everything in Berlin was falling apart anyway.

Gisevius ultimately escaped the Gestapo after spending six months as a fugitive in and around Berlin. He somehow received the fake identity papers Gaevernitz had fashioned for him, and in January 1945, without advance notice, he turned up in Bern. The first signal that he was safe came when Mary picked up her telephone and heard the familiar bombastic greeting of her "literary collaborator."

The end of the Breakers' plot was the political turning point in Allen's OSS mission to Switzerland, but as far as his personal life was concerned, the real break in his Swiss idyll came five weeks later. The Allied invasion force was sweeping the Nazi occupiers out of northern France; De Gaulle entered Paris amid a frenzy of liberation on August 25. Four days later, toward nightfall, American army units advancing from the south reached Annemasse, the French border post from which Allen had talked his way into Switzerland a seeming lifetime before. The haven in which he had built his expertise as a spymaster was opened. Colonel Edward Glavin of the OSS contacted 110 in Bern, and Allen crossed into France the night of August 29–30 to a safe house, his first venture out of Switzerland in twenty months. Only in the morning did an American security guard discover a Nazi time bomb ticking away in the basement.

The opening of Switzerland to the Allies transformed Allen's OSS mission. New staff help could arrive; the interned airmen could be released; the accumulated George Wood documentation and Gisevius's and Schulte's manuscripts could finally be dispatched by direct and secure military communications. OSS headquarters determined to retrieve their man in Bern, by now somewhat legendary in the burgeoning organization, for personal consultations about all the information he had been sending through code and indirection during those twenty months.

It was almost as hard to get 110 out of Switzerland as it had been to get him in. David Bruce complained from London about the "bothersome mess arising out of the failure to bring Allen Dulles out of Switzerland by plane, a matter in which so many OSS people are now involved, as well as British personalities, that it is almost hopelessly tangled."[7]

Pushing hardest for access to Allen was Donovan himself. The OSS director, newly promoted to major general, had landed at St.-Tropez with the joint French-American Mediterranean invasion force on August 15, making personal contact with the various OSS networks within the French resistance. As Donovan headed north in hopes of meeting up with 110, Allen was moving with one of his resistance agents toward the airport at Lyons, where he hoped to catch a plane. Instead he found Donovan in person, accompanied by a young aide from the London office, Lieutenant William J. Casey, to whom Allen, to his later regret, paid scant attention.[8] The men exchanged their first briefings in a Maquis safe house, but it took even the head of the OSS a few days to commandeer a plane that could fly them out of the battle zone.

Donovan and Allen finally reached London on September 8. At precisely 6:43 that evening, as the two men were settling into a civilized dinner at a London restaurant, "everything shook with a tremendous bang." The first of the German V-2 guided missiles landed in the nearby suburbs of Chiswick and Epping. "Liberated" from neutral Switzerland, Allen found himself closer to the war than ever.

Donovan wanted Allen to go straight back to Washington with him to explain his various penetration efforts and networks among the resistance groups and to provide more detailed briefings to OSS analysts. Allen jumped at the occasion. Only incidentally did it dawn on the self-involved spymaster that returning to the United States would permit him a reunion with his wife and children.

— ✳ —

Clover's picture had been prominently displayed on the mantelpiece of the Herrengasse study. On her very first visit Mary Bancroft, ever alert to clues about her men, spotted the classic portrait in the silver frame — the wavy hair, the high cheekbones. Allen was gentleman enough to let his new lady friend know that he was a married man. "That's my wife," he said in response to Mary's inquiring glance. "She's an angel." As she came to know Allen better, after they had become lovers, Mary was sensitive enough to conclude that, for all his randiness and impatience for ego gratification, Allen somehow depended on Clover; he loved her in a way that did not contradict his need for the stimulation of other women. "She's an angel," he repeated that first evening, and with wonder added, "She's always doing things for other people."

And so she was, during those two years as a war widow in New York. It was not only Allen who had left the family home: Toddy was off at Bennington, Joan at Radcliffe. Young Allen had survived a year of "toughening up" at a ranch school near Tucson and was safely ensconced at a more conventional boarding school, Phillips Exeter Academy in New Hampshire. Clover was alone on Sixty-first Street.

She looked back upon those years as a long overdue passage in life, a moment for developing her own identity without the domineering presence of a husband and the demands of growing children. Friends looked after her, and she was always good company. She and the wife of Allen's great friend in Switzerland, Thomas McKittrick, would compare notes about their husbands at war, without having the slightest idea of what the men were actually doing. Special joy came regularly from Allen's friend Fred Dolbeare, ever loyal and ever alone, now working for the OSS and happy to join in noncommittal friendship with Allen's wife. From friends like this Clover picked up gossip and innuendos about the work her husband was doing, the intensity of life in Switzerland under siege.

And there was her brother-in-law. Foster proceeded daily to his Wall Street office whatever the war news, and he earnestly tried to care for Allen's wife. He regarded Clover as somewhat naive and helpless until he discovered, to his astonishment, what she had set out to do on her own.

Clover became, as the popular song of the day called women like her, Rosie the Riveter. Every weekday morning at dawn she would board the subway train to Brooklyn to a job supervising a platoon of young women painting luminescent radium dial markings on the control panels of army air force planes. It was the typical substitution of women in the industrial work force when men were not available. But Clover was no simpering substitute. After a few weeks on the job she saw that her bosses were discriminating against the black workers. One of the few men left in the plant, observing this lady's outraged protests to management, commended Clover Dulles: "You're probably the toughest son-of-a-bitch in the place!"[9]

Clover turned fifty in 1944, and on the eve of that birthday, finding herself alone at home, she wrote a diary note to herself and to Allen. The usual crowd of friends had taken her to dinner. "I returned to the fire, to the brandy in the bottom of the glass, and to my favorite Strauss waltzes. I felt very sad to be spending my second birthday with you away, Allen. I opened my birthday presents, . . . I was not sleepy and the thought of bed was unbearable."

Suddenly she thought of someone else, and her self-pity vanished: the young man who had been washing the windows of the townhouses on the block when he fell from the ladder. Neighbors had told her that he was taken to the public hospital on Welfare Island (now called Roosevelt Island) with broken ribs and head wounds. With not a moment's delay, she found her way onto the last ferry, talked her way in, and spent the entire night at the bedside of a stranger. "He was restless," Clover wrote in her diary. "I got up a dozen times to take his hands from his head wound, and to keep him covered. Through six hours, I did not let my mind wander from him." She was the only passenger on the 6 A.M. ferry back to Manhattan. "It was bitter cold, the trolley was not running, and I took refuge in a corner restaurant with steaming windows." Reaching home about eight, she fell into bed and slept. A few hours later a knock on the door signaled the delivery of a dozen roses for her fiftieth birthday, from Allen.

World War II wives grew accustomed to hearing nothing from their husbands at "the front," but Allen was more distant than most because of the sensitive nature of his work. "I am missing Dad badly these days," Clover wrote Joan. "For a year my morale was good; now I am slumping. But I have no reason to complain in view of what goes on for other people." Then in September she learned, and wrote the three children, "Dad is coming home."

Allen's three weeks in the United States that September of 1944 were jarring to him, a return to real life and a break from the fulfilling life he had created for himself in isolated Switzerland.

His record on the Breakers, versus the default of British intelligence, added inestimably to his stature among the Anglophile intelligence establishment, and as the George Wood documents began to be absorbed the Dulles reports from Switzerland gained new authority. As for family life in New York, the diaries are strangely silent about how long he actually spent at home. Clover's concerns paled beside the vibrant political engagement of women like Mary Bancroft and his new friend, Wally Toscanini Castelbarco.

Unexpectedly this brief furlough confronted Allen with the transformation in American attitudes toward the world, as reflected in the changed public stature of his much-esteemed older brother. From the narrow focus of a man concerned only about the business of Wall Street law, Foster had built his friendship with Tom Dewey into a new identity. That September Dewey was the Republican challenger to President Roosevelt. At his side was "internationalist" foreign policy adviser John Foster Dulles, dedicated to a bipartisan postwar foreign policy that would resurrect the Wilsonian vision of American leadership through international cooperation. Forgotten were the isolationist concerns of 1940. The metamorphosis triggered mixed sentiments in a younger brother: satisfaction that Foster had finally come around to the internationalist position that Allen had argued so intensely, and family pride that Foster was seen as a potential secretary of state in a Dewey administration. Yet who could overlook the fact that Foster's success in this new identity preempted the ambition that Allen had entertained for himself?

Allen, it seems, could not wait to get back to Switzerland. He wanted no part of the 1944 election campaign, and with the war still raging in Europe and the Pacific he could not see himself returning to the gentlemanly life of New York. How long will you be gone this time? asked Clover, trying to sound matter-of-fact. Perhaps until Christmas, Allen replied, but how could he make promises when the war was still to be won and important work had to be done to secure the peace? Then Clover came up with what Allen must surely have considered the most unappealing idea of all: could she perhaps join him in Bern? Out of the question, Allen replied. War-battered Europe was no place for a Manhattan lady; the life of a spymaster was, of necessity, a bachelor's existence, at "the front."

Clover, Joan, and Toddy waved Allen off on a Dixie Clipper for the return flight to Europe early in October, this departure as well timed as his last crossing. Two years before he had beaten the Nazi occupation of southern France by hours; this time he managed to get out of the United States just one day before the name of Dulles became a campaign issue. The Democrats opened their foreign policy attack with charges that Governor Dewey's top adviser was a Wall Street manipulator who had developed "intimate relationships [with] banking circles ... that made Hitler's rise to power possible." In the 1944 campaign surfaced the first negative stories about the Dulles relationships with the Schroder Bank and other corporate interests in the 1930s, leading to charges, suitably embroidered and embellished, that would be leveled against the brothers for decades. At this point Foster was the primary target. Allen was safely en route back to his secret life in Switzerland.

— * —

Allen had been away only a month, but the Bern to which he returned was a different place from the spy capital he had made his own. The Swiss frontiers were open: operations officers, code clerks, secretaries, experts, and staff came flooding in from Washington and other OSS stations, eager to organize the networks Allen had assembled from Berlin to Bologna. They were sent in to help, but inevitably they made more work. Allen's loner operation became a bureaucracy in the Dufourstrasse, and Allen suffered accordingly.

"Much of the sparkle and charm went out of Allen's personality as I had known it," wrote Mary. " I never again saw the Allen Dulles I had watched operating with such consummate skill when he was cut off from all outside influence and just acting on his own. . . . It was rather like the way an exuberant young person behaves when his parents suddenly show up." On reflection Mary decided her image was wrong; it was not his parents, who no longer played the slightest role in Allen's self-esteem. It was his brother who brought on Allen's suppression of his own personality (as her Jungian analysis would put it) when he returned to Europe. "Allen has a very strong family feeling and a genuine devotion to Foster, but there was something subservient in his attitude that infuriated me. His relationship to Foster was the one sore point between us — the one subject that, after one knockdown, drag-out fight, I never mentioned again."

Surely other factors produced Allen's mood change, not least being the recent reminders of his wife's obvious eagerness for companionship. When he had been cut off from contact, it had been easy to put such responsibilities out of mind. Now he could correspond normally with Clover and, just as during his European travels in the 1930s, he did so regularly. But this time his letters reflected no joy and certainly no talk of dining and dancing with attractive ladies. "The rain and wind is beating around the Herrengasse," he wrote Clover one night a month after his return, "but my little library is snug and warm, and I spend most of my time in it when I am not in the office — as I have become a hermit as far as going out to parties is concerned. . . . There is too much to do."

Seldom before had Allen complained of overwork, but the newly bureaucratized Bern, station made the kinds of demands that he least comprehended or liked: procedures, routines, personnel. He even had to acquire a Swiss driver's license, which involved the indignity of a road test. Codebooks and secure telephone devices would never become second nature to Allen; he bypassed the careful OSS registry of code numbers and pseudonyms, forging ahead with his own codes and neglecting to inform headquarters about them. The ensuing bureaucratic confusion added to Washington's perennial doubts about the authenticity of incoming intelligence. "What does this mean?" Donovan would scrawl on a cryptic cable from Bern, or "Who is he?" at some crucial citation of a source. Between Allen's habits and the newly arrived code clerks, cables got misnumbered, replies were requested for the wrong queries.[10]

"I am somewhat oppressed by the work," he wrote Clover. "There is vastly more to do than when the frontiers were closed.... Meanwhile, they are flooding me with cables from all directions and asking generally that we do the impossible."

Why, suddenly, such impossible demands? It was more than the unwelcome bureaucracy in his own offices; the entire OSS had exploded into a sprawling, undisciplined machine: 10,000 American employees and as many foreign collaborators deployed across the world. Some 60,000 coded messages were flowing into Washington headquarters each month by 1944, to be evaluated by a corps of academic specialists distinguished enough to staff a great university. When motivated and talented people are brought together, they find things to do that generate even more to be done.

Contrary to expectations, the war on the western front was going badly that autumn of 1944; France had fallen, but the defenses of Germany proper had not collapsed. The American invasion force was stalled inside German territory west of the Rhine. Thus pressure bore down upon Allen from a more specific factor, a subtle change in the OSS mission after the Normandy invasion. Instead of the long-range strategic intelligence function he had originally envisaged, Donovan found himself pushed into tactical and battle-support missions.[11] The tension between these contrasting functions would recur again and again in the history of American intelligence. The former was especially political in character, and in this Allen excelled; on the latter, military intelligence, the realm of Donovan's current interests, Allen could summon up neither interest nor perspicacity.

A yearlong OSS campaign to penetrate occupied France had succeeded brilliantly before the invasion, with dozens of agents parachuted behind the lines to make contact with carefully nurtured resistance networks. With these missions having worked so well, reasoned an enthusiastic Donovan, why not expand the operation and attempt direct penetration of the German countryside as well? This strategic concept reopened an old dispute over intelligence sources and methods. Allen had settled this problem for himself before setting off for Switzerland, but now it was posed anew.

Allen's position had been, and remained, that the best intelligence would come from "indigenous" sources, people already in place who had the motivation, the opportunity, and the courage to report out. The alternative — smuggling in, by parachute or cargo truck, credible (one hoped) outsiders who could observe and report out—was the sort of thing Allen ridiculed as "story-book stuff." Hints began emerging that Donovan no longer agreed.

Early signs of trouble came in that first meeting at the Lyons airport in September, when Donovan casually raised the idea of dropping teams of agents into Germany. During their next days together, Allen was able to smother the idea with discussions of other matters, including the explosive potential of a surviving German underground that could take action against the führer. Allen spoke on the matter with "intensity and unshakable conviction," noted Lieutenant Casey, the young aide at Donovan's side. Unbeknownst to 110, that young, round-faced lieutenant was quietly but systematically stirring up the director's propensities for direct action of a less subtle sort.

William J. Casey was thirty-one years old at the time, trained as a lawyer but successful from early on as a risk-taking venture capital financier.* Assigned to establish a European secretariat for the itinerant Donovan, he enlarged his mandate and set up something more interesting than a secretariat. Barely a week after they had landed in southern France, before meeting with Allen, Casey composed the first of a series of memoranda to Donovan arguing for penetration missions into central Europe. In September he drew up the outlines for "An OSS Program Against Germany"; by mid-October the Casey plan called for "immediate penetration of a fighting Germany." Just before Christmas 1944 Donovan gave Casey a mandate and carte blanche "to get us into Germany."

Allen, struggling to find his stride in a transformed Bern, was only dimly aware of this counterproposal. He never had the occasion to argue the strategy directly with Casey, nor would such a confrontation have been seemly; the fabled 110 had barely met the young man. Allen argued his own strategy impersonally through the autumn at weekly meetings just across the French border with American army liaison teams. For once in this period Allen and the British intelligence officers were of one mind, and it was the men of Whitehall who took the lead, unsuccessfully, in dissuading Donovan from his enterprise.

The British argued a fundamental difference between dropping agents into occupied territory and into a homeland—in this case the difference between France and Germany. In the former a parachuted newcomer could anticipate some kind of welcome, an underground of sympathizers

---

* As director of central intelligence under President Ronald Reagan, Casey succeeded in rejuvenating an agency demoralized by successive freewheeling excesses, including the Watergate scandal. But he then involved the service in manipulations of Iran hostages and Nicaraguan Contra fighters, which put the CIA back in as sorry a state as he had found it.

prepared to give him cover. Such would not be the case in a homeland.*
The distinctions on the practical level were endless: a clever and able-
bodied young man could talk his way into any French village and fade
comfortably into the human landscape as he prepared to carry out his assigned mission. The same young man arriving in a German *dorf,* even if
claiming to be an enslaved foreign worker moving to a new post, would
promptly be drafted into the German armed forces, like everyone else his
age. This left the pool of potential penetration agents limited to those
who were too old or too young for the draft; Allen found little merit in
the strategy of parachuting small boys or old men into hostile settings.

Allen's final argument against the enthusiastic Casey/Donovan strategy was that once this undercover penetration agent was in place, how
would he get his information out to where it could be used? This was a
point Donovan had impressed upon 110 two years before, leading to the
strained radio-telephone conversations from Allen and Mary in the Herrengasse. A stranger arriving in the Bavarian countryside with a backpack
full of electronic equipment would not go unnoticed by a population accustomed to life under the Gestapo. Such calculations were the reason
that Allen had deliberately set out to discover and build "agents in place."
Whether a Schulte or a Gisevius or a "George Wood," Allen's agents
were not the sort to be sent into the Third Reich by parachute.

Nonetheless, by the autumn of 1944 Allen's principal network into
the Reich had collapsed. The dramatic alternative presented by an inventive man of action like Casey had its appeal, and, too far from headquarters to know the exact state of bureaucratic play, Allen had to follow orders as best he could.

He was confident that attempts to penetrate southern Germany from
Switzerland stood no chance of success. The efficient Swiss border
patrols would permit no such movements — in distinct contrast with the
situation within France and along the Rhine. Of the handful of Swiss-
based agents that OSS Bern managed to assemble at the south German
frontier in response to Casey's program, none managed to test the
Gestapo's vigilance, for not a single one got through the counterespionage guards on the Swiss side of the border. And Bern's experience was
not unique. Of the twenty-one teams of American agents successfully
parachuted into Germany carrying radio transmitters, only one established communication. The record was slightly better for the teams sent
into occupied Austria, but even there the Gestapo captured the agents,

* This theoretical point would recur in the 1950s, when Allen presided over attempts to
"penetrate" the Iron Curtain and his CIA found significant differences between operations
in the eastern European satellite countries and in the Soviet Union itself.

seized the transmitters, and sent back phony messages that deceived the OSS into thinking they were receiving legitimate agent reports.[12]

Whatever the human drama and heroism involved in these efforts, their military impact was minimal. General Eisenhower's directives to his intelligence staff assigned no priority whatsoever to deep penetration efforts. Secret intelligence missions were to take no risks, enter upon no long gambles, "save in exceptional circumstances with the express permission of this headquarters."

Allen managed to hold himself largely aloof from the frenetic planning in Casey's secret intelligence division, but Gaevernitz, his imaginative aide, hit upon an alternative that might turn Donovan's enthusiasm to particular political advantage. He proposed a plan to have captured German officers accompany Allied armies advancing into Germany, to guide and advise on sites and personnel to be targeted or won over — a sort of conservative response to the Soviet-sponsored Free Germany Movement, which was doing the same thing on the eastern front. This might lessen the need for information from agents dropped in by parachute, Gaevernitz argued. He did not add that it could also serve the political interests of the conservative German officer class, which he supported. Allen was skeptical but let his trusted aide proceed. After weeks of consideration at Eisenhower's headquarters and in Washington, Gaevernitz's proposal was rejected entirely. "The Western Allies did not propose using German militarists to defeat German militarism," as Allen summed up his dejected assistant's scheme.

Equivalent proposals inevitably came from other political interests. Noel Field was following Moscow's orders in promoting a front organization directly equivalent to the Free Germany Movement, to be called the Comité de l'Allemagne Libre Pour l'Ouest (CALPO). Field came to Allen with the idea of an OSS-CALPO alliance: CALPO would produce the able-bodied agents, the OSS would drop them into Germany. The advantages to Moscow were obvious — communist-chosen agents entering Germany from the west under American military auspices. As always, Allen received all comers, puffing on his pipe and listening. As a gesture to his old ties to the Field family, 110 sent the young Quaker idealist to present his plan, just as Gaevernitz had done, at OSS headquarters in Paris. There a twenty-seven-year-old political analyst, army corporal Arthur Schlesinger, Jr., listened to Field's impassioned presentation, judged it totally unworkable, and ended the matter.

— * —

In spite of the demands upon him, Allen could not stir up any interest in collecting military intelligence. Not a single map was to be found in Allen's Dufourstrasse office or Herrengasse home in late 1944, none of the paraphernalia of a normal wartime intelligence headquarters. Instead, 110 was acting his chosen role of a gentleman engaged in spying, managing his own personal networks — and about them, the less explained to headquarters the better. The scuttlebutt of railway engineers and Rhine bargemen continued to flow into Allen's nets, and he passed on his particular brand of intelligence. At one point Allen eagerly debriefed, of all people, Mary Bancroft's husband, the traveling accountant, upon his return from a train ride past the Romanian oil refineries of Ploeşti after an Allied bombing raid. What damage did he see? How many smokestacks were still standing? The husband of the spymaster's mistress had no qualms about telling whatever he knew.

Through his social network Allen became friendly with a Swiss physicist who had long been friends with Germany's top atomic research scientists; even during the war these professionals met at academic conferences to compare research results. The Swiss physicist promptly became "Flute" in Allen's code scheme, and in December 1944 he provided the OSS with important information about Germany's atomic bomb program.[13] From Austrian sources, with Kurt Grimm as cut-out, Allen learned of a German industrial plant at a site on the Baltic called Peenemünde, and also of German research into something called heavy water, a dispatch to which Washington promptly assigned top secret classification, though Allen did not understand why. He sent the OSS rough drawings of guided and ballistic missiles that had all the sophistication of a child's sketch of an airplane, but they led to a careful study of the differences between the V-1 "pilotless aircraft" and the V-2 rockets.

To Allen's frustration, one of his most exotic networks had crumbled even before the Breakers' plot of July 20 — through a security lapse in the OSS itself. The unlikely cut-out was a beautiful Greek-born concert pianist, Barbara Issikides, who, after an all-Chopin program in Zurich would drive to Grimm's flat at the Hotel Bellerive au Lac to convey the latest information from Vienna. Her intelligence came from a priest named Heinrich Maier and a Viennese industrialist, Franz Josef Messner. By late 1943 this anti-Nazi circle was concerned that their hard-earned information was not actually getting through to the Allies; to be certain, and against Allen's warning when he learned of it, they passed reports similar to what they were conveying to Grimm (and then to Allen) to a contact at OSS Istanbul. The OSS station in Turkey, however, had been penetrated by the Gestapo, and in March 1944 Maier, Messner, and Issikides were arrested in Vienna. Thus 110 found himself bereft of his best networks into both Germany and Austria, even as the Casey/Donovan duo was pressing for direct penetration.

Late one autumn evening, shortly after Allen's return to Bern, Gaevernitz brought a stranger to the doorstep of Herrengasse 23, an unshaven, hungry, and exhausted Viennese, only a few months out of his teens. The youth had crossed the mountain passes from Austria, sometimes crawling on his hands and knees, seldom sleeping or eating, to contact the Allies on behalf of an underground net of politicians and military officers.

"It's good to meet an old Viennese," Allen welcomed the young man. "I lived there for two years." The Austrian, Fritz Molden, proceeded to pour out his story. He was the son of a Viennese editor, his mother a noted poet, both of them active in underground networks. He himself had been conscripted into the German forces, had escaped to join the Italian resistance, and, under death sentence from the Gestapo, had fled to Switzerland. He had first contacted British intelligence, which, typically, turned him away. Next he had tried another name he had heard, von Schulze-Gaevernitz. Molden poured out a stream of organizational data about the resistance, as well as detailed descriptions of Nazi positions and defenses, all of which he had committed to memory rather than risk being captured with incriminating notes.[14]

The fire in the book-lined library was warm and welcoming, and a distraught young man, encountering Allen Dulles at a moment of vulnerability, succumbed to his charm. Molden later described that meeting: "My first impression ... was that of a rather delicate, but wiry, grey-haired gentleman with a large flat face, short moustache, and high forehead.... Through thin nickel-framed glasses, clear blue eyes looked at me in a friendly, interested and encouraging manner.... I had a warm feeling in my heart. This was a man in whom one could have real trust."* Through Molden, Allen was able to build an effective new network into the Austrian resistance.

But it was the Italian partisans who gave Allen the greatest satisfaction and adventure that winter of 1944–45. The situation north of the Po River was chaotic; Mussolini's fascist regime had crumbled, but the northern part of the country, not yet conquered by the advancing Allies, was controlled by the Nazi SS. Allen's favorite line of access to the underground nets of northern Italy was Countess Wally Castelbarco, now finally available to his full attentions without annoying interruptions.

Years before, at the vulnerable age of seventeen, Wally Toscanini had fallen in love with Count Emanuele Castelbarco, who was nearly twice her age and already married, with two children. For seven years she sus-

* Unlike the other young men whom Allen unwittingly collected, Molden succeeded in establishing a serious relationship — not with Allen but with his younger daughter, Joan. A few years after this meeting, quite independent of Allen, Molden met the attractive Joan Dulles; to her father's astonishment when he learned of it, they fell in love and married.

tained a secret romance with him, until finally the count filed for a divorce. His spurned former wife then went to Maestro Toscanini to inform him that his daughter had ruined her marriage. When Toscanini confronted Wally, she related, "Glasses, dishes and everything else he could put his hands on went flying. He said terrible things to me and he hit me." But Wally defied her father's ire and announced that she intended to marry Castelbarco. Toscanini's rage reached the ultimate: "He is blond and an aristocrat! Who ever heard of marrying a blond man? Who ever heard of an aristocrat being worth anything?"[15]

By the time Allen met Wally, her father's forebodings had proved true. The countess was a lonely lady trying to help her Italian friends from the nervous safety of Switzerland.[16] The financial networks of the OSS provided early cover for a romance, as Toscanini (finally reconciled with his daughter) sent funds from New York for Wally to distribute to her friends in the antifascist underground.* At one point in April 1944 the maestro advised Wally, in a message relayed through the OSS, that an American named Noel Field of the Unitarian Service Committee might be helpful in organizing underground relief. Field was one of 110's main cut-outs with the French resistance, of course, but as he relayed her father's message, Allen told Wally not to pursue him right then, since Field was away from Geneva "on account of illness."† These early exchanges, surviving in the files of OSS Bern, were warm but correct, between "Mr. Dulles" and "Countess Castelbarco," using the polite *vous* form in French. As their contact grew more personal, the stilted correspondence ceased and the financial dealings were transferred to other OSS personnel.

For all his Presbyterian propriety, Allen found real affinity with the lusty and undisciplined Italians in his networks, and this was reciprocated. In the lore of the Italian partisans Allen was affectionately codenamed "Arturo," the embodiment of Allied wealth and power who could magically produce lire by the millions and make American aircraft appear over their valley on moonlit nights to drop guns and ammunition. Sometimes the Italians' enthusiasm caused problems. One of the best OSS op-

* At the start there was some confusion about the purpose of these funds. The first OSS cables on the matter in December 1943 report that Toscanini was willing to send his daughter 15,000 Swiss francs every month (the huge sum of $3,500), but wondered why she was living so extravagantly at her Swiss pension. It emerged that a telegraph clerk had mistakenly added a zero to Wally's requested budget of 1,500 Swiss francs. As her "needs" increased, she explained to her again indulgent father that she was supporting Italian political refugees, "including Jews and musicians."
† Since this was just two months before the Allied landing in Normandy, and Field was mobilizing the French communists for the Allied effort, Allen may simply have been sparing his cut-out an unnecessary distraction.

eratives was an intemperate doctor code-named "Como." When Swiss police discovered that he was smuggling an arms cache into Italy in a full railroad car, Como impetuously hijacked the entire train and crashed through the frontier at high speed into the safety of partisan-held territory. But in the confusion he left behind his mistress, who was promptly taken into Swiss custody as hostage until the train was returned. No novice at the ruses of the underground, that young woman tied three bed sheets together, nimbly climbed from an upper-story window in the detention house, and escaped to join her lover. Allen had to impose restraints upon the Italians, telling them there would be no more infractions upon the Swiss frontier unless it was a matter of life or death.

One Italian source, code-named "Black," caused the OSS particular difficulty when in the fall of 1944 he started supplying, through channels of the Italian underground, a stream of reports that seemed to originate from the Vatican. Black's early dispatches were in illegible longhand; Allen managed to smuggle him a typewriter which, 110 reported to Washington, "he is trying to learn to use."* From Black came evidence that German diplomats in Rome, including some who were tenuously linked to the July 20 conspiracy, were winning the sympathies of Pope Pius XII. "Although very humble, [the pope] is very prone to be offended by people who do not approach him the right way," Black reported, "and to have a deep affection for people who do."[17]

Allen was ever on the alert for persons of intellect and political stature among the underground antifascists, potential leaders who might offer a democratic alternative to the hard-driving communist resistance when the time came to install postwar governments. Schulte was one such among his German contacts, but more successful was Allen's encouragement of Ferruccio Parri, a tall, silver-haired moderate socialist and early opponent of Mussolini's fascism, who served as a sort of Scarlet Pimpernel for the Italian underground, arranging the escape of some of the most prominent antifascists in the early years of Mussolini's power. Parri had been arrested twice, but when influential friends managed his liberation in 1933 he lived through the rest of the fascist years

* As this source continued, the code name "Vessel" replaced "Black." The source's authenticity remained a matter of bitter controversy decades after the war. At the start of James J. Angleton's stormy career in counterespionage, he argued that Vessel was a fake, though why he felt so strongly on the matter was never clear. The Vatican had its own reasons for promoting Angleton's skepticism, for church officials were uncomfortable at being seen as a source of military intelligence. Others in the OSS secret intelligence branch, however, insisted that Vessel was a genuine source of sound intelligence. Considering the diverse controversies that marred Angleton's later career, the Black-Vessel episode that started him off deserves reexamination.

under the respectable cover of research director for Societa Edison, the electric utility of northern Italy, a corporate giant that Allen knew well from his Wall Street financial network.[18]

Allen had already nurtured his contacts with the utility company to provide cover for OSS missions in northern Italy. Singling out Parri as a particular asset,[110] gave this lean intellectual the code name "Maurizio" and arranged for him to cross through Switzerland and France in the fall of 1944 to meet with the American occupation headquarters in southern Italy, in preparation for a leading role with partisan forces at the enemy's rear when the invasion force moved northward. Parri was "considerably heartened" by pledges of OSS support in the future, but the Gestapo discovered his clandestine travels and promptly arrested him on his return to his Milan flat in December. Once again Allen had lost a key asset, and for the moment his sense of helplessness festered.

— * —

The most bizarre of Allen's Italian operations in the final year of World War II became a celebrated case of a secret document that was bound to stir distrust and confusion among the enemy — if only the Allies could lay their hands on it and display it to an incredulous world.

Mussolini's longtime foreign minister, Count Galeazzo Ciano, was a rakish, free-minded soul who had shown the pluck to marry Il Duce's daughter. He had shared in the most secret conversations between Hitler and his father-in-law over the years and, Allied intelligence learned, he had kept a detailed diary.

Il Duce grew wary of his foreign minister's personal and political peccadilloes and, son-in-law or no, he fired Ciano in February 1943. The fallen count's life was threatened; his oft-wronged wife, Edda, fled her father's clutches the following winter with the aid of one Lieutenant Emilio Pucci, an elegant and ambitious young artisan who would never let the hardships of fugitive life inhibit his burning quest for romance. As surety for the noble name, and potential income for her remaining years, Edda Ciano brought her husband's diary notebooks with her. When the police checks and roadblocks became more intense, Pucci acted the gentleman and made his new lover pregnant to all appearances: the countess strapped the five notebooks to her hips in a deceptive manner, and Pucci hastily designed an ample but clinging shift to convey a condition that no one would be churlish enough to challenge.* At the Swiss frontier the

---

* After the war Pucci's name and artistry gained worldwide renown in fashion circles for just the kind of clinging dress that he had created for Edda Mussolini Ciano, who later had to deny formally that she had secretly married Emilio Pucci.

border guards were courteous toward a lady in a delicate state, and Edda Ciano made good her escape from Italy just three days before her husband was executed.[19]

Allen had picked up rumors of Countess Ciano's arrival in Switzerland, but there seemed no immediate reason to track her down. Only upon his return from the United States in October did he receive word through the State Department that Mussolini's daughter had in her possession a potentially explosive document.* The imperious widow refused to deal with anyone but a top official, so on January 7, 1945, Allen motored to Monthey, in the Valais, where the woman was confined to a sanitarium under the watchful eyes of the Swiss security police. There he spent a charming afternoon persuading her to make her late husband's diaries available for the information of the United States government. But she refused to part with the originals; they would have to be copied.

The staff reinforcements sent to help 110 finally proved their usefulness. Among the early arrivals was a thirty-four-year-old paratrooper, Captain Tracy Barnes, blond and athletic, hailing from Groton, Yale, and Harvard Law. He had twice jumped behind enemy lines in France; on leave in England he made parachute jumps at an RAF base for sport. No parachuting would be involved in getting into Edda Ciano's sanitarium, but good measures of charm and ingenuity — Barnes was possessed of both — would be essential in keeping the countess from changing her mind as she saw her future meal tickets slipping from her personal grasp.

The next day, carefully passing Swiss surveillance, Barnes and another OSS man went to the sanitarium with cameras and lights concealed in their satchels. The Swiss guards were not troubled by one handsome male visitor to Edda Ciano's room, but two at the same time were somewhat more worrisome; nevertheless, they looked the other way. Copying manuscript pages on film clandestinely was a precarious undertaking; when first plugged in, the photographic lights blew a fuse, making the cover of a social visit even more dubious. Eventually, working hidden in the closet and under the bed, Barnes and his colleague managed to make hasty photographs of 1,200 notebook pages in one day.[20]

No one knew what the diaries contained, of course, but Allen was able to report to Washington on January 11 that he had copies of authentic texts in Italian, covering the activities of Mussolini's foreign minister

---

* The State Department, in directing the ambassador to Switzerland, Leland Harrison, to try obtaining this document, suggested that he might ask assistance from the OSS. Considering the mood of suspicion between the diplomatic service and Donovan's men, this suggestion was evidence of Washington's continuing regard for Allen and the good relations he had maintained with Harrison, notable especially in light of the deep feuding in other capitals between the official American representatives and the undisciplined intelligence operatives.

from January 1, 1939, through February 8, 1943. A minor mystery emerged as Allen and his colleagues studied the filmed copies. On many pages were noticed capital letter initials in bold pencil; when Barnes went back to ask Edda about them, as Allen reported, "The Countess examined these rather carefully but said, and I believe truthfully, that she knew no explanation for them." Perhaps she did not; Allen later relished the story that careful study of the diary pages evinced a clear correspondence between these initials and those of Count Ciano's various lady friends, apparently noted down on the days of their visits.[21] Whatever else they conveyed, the initials were strong evidence for the diligence of the diarist and the genuineness of the document.

The Ciano diaries revealed a sordid side of the Axis dictatorships, duplicity in relations between Berlin and Rome, and with the war still raging Allen leapt upon them as a potent weapon of psychological warfare. But how could the diaries be most usefully published? In that era the State Department, and certainly the OSS, did not have well-greased machinery for leaking sensitive information to the press. One of Allen's most helpful contacts over the months in Bern was Paul Ghali, correspondent of the *Chicago Daily News*, who was already apprised of the Ciano story, despite Swiss attempts to keep it suppressed. Allen allowed Ghali access to the diary texts, but his newspaper had to negotiate the publication rights with Countess Ciano, and the negotiations were tedious. By June, when excerpts of the diaries were published in Chicago and in other syndicated newspapers, the war in Europe had ended, though it ground on in the Pacific. The immediate psychological warfare benefits that Allen had envisaged were by then superfluous, but in shaping the history of the fascist era the Ciano diaries became a basic text.

In rare restraint from trumpeting its achievements far and wide, the OSS leadership found the episode of the diaries' acquisition so audacious that the intelligence organization avoided claiming any credit whatsoever.[22] But the germ was planted in Allen's arsenal of psychological war weaponry: the acquisition of a secret, embarrassing document at the height of conflict would again become his preoccupation a decade later when the opportunity arose to acquire and publish a secret speech delivered by another hostile dictator.

Allen was swept up in other concerns those early months of 1945. The fugitive Gisevius finally escaped from Germany and told Allen and Mary Bancroft the full story, as he knew it, of the failed July 20 putsch. Roosevelt, Churchill, and Stalin were about to meet at the Crimean resort of Yalta to discuss the shape of the postwar world. And to 110 from the SS command in northern Italy came an unexpected and provocative proposition.

— 10 —

COLD SUNRISE

UPON ALLEN'S RETURN TO EUROPE Clover's life resumed its busy loneliness of luncheons and dinners at the Sulgrave or the Cosmopolitan Club with friends or, more accurately, people to spend time with. At one such she learned that the aging Mrs. Harold Pratt was about to give her splendid townhouse, on the corner of Park Avenue and Sixty-eighth Street, to the Council on Foreign Relations. There would be the libraries and common rooms where Allen would spend so many evening hours in years to come. Clover took pleasure in learning of the benefaction before Allen. And, given her inner resources, Clover was not a woman to be bored.

At one point Fred Dolbeare and some of the other New York–based OSS men told her that two Australian officers were arriving on an official but clandestine visit. Could she possibly put them up at her townhouse to avoid the hassle and public record of a hotel? She could indeed, for Clover longed to help, to serve. After their days of government business the startled Australians would return to the guest rooms of a New York family home to find the bedclothes turned back and their pajamas neatly laid out, not by chambermaids but by the lady of the house, back home after her own projects.

The break in routine that Clover had been seeking came at the turn of 1945. From Washington friends she learned that the newly activated United States Embassy in liberated Paris had ordered ten American automobiles, and the State Department was seeking volunteers to drive the cars up from Lisbon, the port of debarkation. Clover hesitated not a moment; she wanted to be useful, she enjoyed driving and was a good driver, and she wanted to be closer to Allen in Switzerland — whether invited or not. Foster, when he learned about it, tried without a chance of success to dissuade her from her mission. The motley assemblage of cars and volunteers sailed on a Portuguese freighter from Philadelphia at the end of January.

The crossing was not the pleasant shipboard life that Clover had known in less stressful years.[1] The cabin she shared with three other women was "cold as a refrigerator." Her "bed" was a shelf hanging from chains on the wall. The seas were rough, and there was still danger of German submarines. Clover's main complaint, recorded in her journal, was that most of the other passengers were from "an austere band of Mennonites who fled whenever anyone played a little music to dance by." A Portuguese naval officer paid her some attention, and she was worldly enough to see through that ploy right away. As she primly recorded her reaction: "My father had often explained the maneuvering of young blades in making love to older matrons, in part-payment for being allowed by the matrons to gain access to maidens." One of Clover's cabin mates was a most attractive American girl, to whom she neither aided nor inhibited the officer's ardent access.

The vessel finally docked at Lisbon, and the automobiles with their complement of thirteen intrepid drivers set off in convoy through neutral Portugal, the Basque country of Spain, and across the Pyrenees into southern France. The party spent one night guarded by a French resistance fighter in a small hotel in Bordeaux. American officers reluctantly parted with what gasoline they could spare, but Clover was skeptical: "It will be exciting to see how far it takes us." As it happened, it took them all the way to Paris, where they arrived exhausted after a full week of hazardous driving.

The embassy's administrative officer happily accepted the fleet of cars, but had neither provision nor care for the drivers. "We sat like mourners on a bench in the lowest depths of the chancery." Hoping that Allen would be on one of his periodic consultations in Paris, Clover had wired ahead to him, but the embassy underlings disclaimed any knowledge of such a person. "Probably Allen is sitting comfortably upstairs with the ambassador," she fumed, and jumped up from the mourners' bench with the imperious demand to see the ambassador immediately. Ultimately only the ambassador's secretary could pacify this persistent lady with the aristocratic air; he confided in hushed tones, "Good thing you came up — the ambassador and I are the only ones here who know that your husband is in Paris." In fact, 110 had received the message that his wife was arriving and had left instructions for her to check into an obscure little hotel and wait until he could break loose from his secret and sensitive strategy meetings. For nearly three full days Clover waited without a single word from Allen.

The Allied armies were closing like a vise upon Nazi Germany; Allen was struggling to make the best of the secret penetration missions, which he still distrusted. Strange hints were pouring in from pro-Nazi sources in Switzerland that some "compromise peace" might still be possible, and 110 needed responsible orders. One could conjure up a degree of sympathy for the harassed executive pressed by "impossible demands" from his superiors and maneuvering through bureaucratic minefields of war and peace, upon the sudden arrival of an uninvited wife.

Nothing, however, can excuse Allen's behavior when, late on Clover's third day in Paris, he finally acknowledged her arrival. Materializing as if from thin air at her hotel room, without warning, he declared that he could spare her ten minutes. He instructed her to meet him at *his* hotel at five the next morning to begin the motor trip to Switzerland. Then, without pausing for a moment of gentle preparation, he brusquely informed his wife that her aged mother had died while Clover was on the high seas. With that announcement he walked out of the hotel room.[2]

Clover spent the night alone in a state of shock. All the next day she sat in the back of an army staff car in silence, unnoticed, as Allen and an OSS aide discussed the technical details of forging German passports and like matters of intelligence tradecraft. As they approached the Swiss border at nightfall, they passed within twenty miles of a large Nazi garrison making a last desperate stand against the Allied offensive. A French resistance fighter frantically flagged the car down, demanding that the driver douse the headlights lest they draw enemy fire. They reached Switzerland in total blackness. It was after midnight when Clover finally set foot in Herrengasse 23.

The circumstances could not possibly have made the next days a pleasant reunion for either Clover or Allen. In a journal to Joan, Clover put a cheery face on her welcome, raving about the "most attractive old villa," the antique furniture and wall hangings, the wallpaper in her bedroom, "a quaint buff with tiny red flowers," which she chose to believe Allen had arranged especially for her arrival. But it took her no time to understand that she had presumed upon a closed world: that of men at war.

She was made to feel like an uncouth trespasser in an exclusive club. The French-Swiss couple who had been managing Allen's bachelor household took immediate umbrage at the arrival of a wife who might interfere with their routine. Strange men would arrive at all hours of day and night, often sleeping over without being introduced or paying her any attention, and Allen made no effort to enlighten her about any aspect of his shadowy existence. "Tell the gentleman on the second floor," he barked as he rushed out the front door, "not to shoot if a strange fellow comes in tonight." One day when Allen allowed her to stroll with him through the medieval streets of Bern, two strangers approached. Allen gave a furtive signal of recognition and walked away with one of the men, leaving Clover to make small talk with the anonymous other for what seemed like an eternity. Allen returned with not a word of explanation, expecting her to resume their promenade as if nothing had happened.

Many days Allen would be away on his mysterious missions, and Clover wrote of feeling "bereft of companionship." Yet, afraid of missing out on matters of moment, she was reluctant to sally forth on touristic expeditions. Only when Allen came down with gout did he spare her a few moments of conversation, using her offers of tenderness for his own comfort — only heightening a wife's loneliness "when he would recover, to find myself again ignorant of the very stirring events taking place."

Clover soon discovered that not all of Allen's intimates were men; ever since his affair with the "tennis partner," she had grown resigned to sharing her husband with other women. Always insensitive to her feelings, Allen conveyed no awkwardness in introducing his wife to Mary Bancroft; once again he found it useful to introduce to each other two persons whom he felt were making demands on him. Bereft of companionship, Clover accepted Mary's friendship with eyes wide open. The second or third time they were alone together, Mary recalled, Clover said to her, "I want you to know I can see how much you and Allen care for each other — and I approve." The subject of their shared intimacy with the same man never was raised again throughout the friendship Clover maintained with her husband's wartime mistress for the rest of their lives.

As Clover recognized her mistake in intruding upon Allen's working life, she wrote to their children about their absentee father. "It would not be possible for you to imagine how engrossed he is in his work, and how he neither thinks, speaks or asks of anything else. There is no doubt he is different from most, but I do believe that he does everything that he does, not only because he likes it, but as a way of showing his affection for us." The ever optimistic Clover said she believed her husband to be "paying us the compliment of believing that what we want is for him to do something worthwhile in the world." That was the face she presented to her children; to Mary she confided a growing sense of despair about this glamorous man she had married, who had so changed since the fun-loving days of their courtship. "If I could only make out what Allen's *goal* is, what he wants from life, I might find it easier to understand all this sound and fury."[3]

— * —

"We knew they were there," recalled one of Allen's OSS aides. "We knew they were operating in Bern. But who they were, or where they stayed, we never could be sure." "They" were the networks and agents of the Soviet Union in Switzerland. Unlike all the other "secret" agents, who consorted openly at the Bellevue or maneuvered through the diplomatic reception circuit, the agents of the Kremlin were never seen. "They," it eventually emerged, operated out of Lucerne, where a Bohemian intellectual named Rudolf Rössler, under cover of a Catholic publishing firm, managed a highly effective network of agents, code-named "Lucy," within the Nazi high command.[4] There is no evidence that Allen knew of Rössler's existence or his cover before the Swiss police made the first arrests to break up the ring in March 1943; Rössler himself was finally arrested in May 1944.*

Intelligence cooperation, such as it was, between the Western Allies and their Soviet partners proceeded at a higher level than that of the cutouts of Bern. General Donovan had personally visited Moscow late in 1943, meeting with Foreign Minister Vyacheslav Molotov on Christmas Day to propose a systematic exchange of military information between the OSS and the Soviet intelligence agency, then called the NKVD. In this proposal Donovan was exceeding his mandate from Washington, and by early February 1944 his rival in intelligence, J. Edgar Hoover of the FBI, weighed in with a firm denunciation of any plan to allow the Russian secret service access to any American intelligence. Though the American ambassador in Moscow, W. Averell Harriman, supported Donovan's plan, the opposition from Hoover (and the conservative public opinion that Hoover could mobilize) proved too much for Roosevelt, and the high-level exchange was scuttled before it could begin.

The leaders of the anti-Nazi coalition met at Yalta from February 4 to 11, 1945, designing a plan for the postwar settlement that seemed to many analysts a worthy perpetuation of the wartime alliance. Praise for the Yalta agreement came from, among others, Allen's brother — to his subsequent embarrassment. John Foster Dulles, who had approached the war opposed to the internationalism that Allen espoused, unabashedly reversed himself. Yalta, he declared, opened a "new era," as the United States "abandoned a form of aloofness which it has been practicing for many years and the Soviet Union permitted joint action on matters that it had the power to settle for itself."[5]

---

* Such are the complex interconnections among intelligence networks: one of Lucy's initial recruiters had been a German-born woman named Ruth Kuczynski, living in Oxford through the war, who had first been spotted by the Soviet agent Richard Sorge in Shanghai in the 1930s. Her brother, Jürgen Kuczynski, equally sympathetic to the Soviet cause, was the air force officer charged with screening agents for Casey's deep penetration raids into Germany. A Soviet intelligence officer later wrote that Moscow believed the Lucy network to have been penetrated by the British and thus did not give high credence to the intelligence received from that source: see Pavel Sudoplatov et al., *Special Tasks* (Boston: Little, Brown, 1994), pp. 142–43.

Allen himself, consumed by matters closer to hand, was not impressed with the Yalta plan. Then, not two weeks after Stalin, Churchill, and Roosevelt went home to their capitals came an approach to 110 in Bern that threatened to blow the wartime alliance wide open. Before long Allen found himself straddling the lines between military strategist, intelligence officer, and diplomat to an extent he had not experienced before. Though he was unaware through most of the episode of all the high politics involved, Allen's maneuvering through a thicket of competing interests and personalities came to be perceived by many historians as the first battle of the Cold War.

— * —

The episode became known to history as Operation Sunrise. It was triggered by a discreet visit from an Italian baron and his friend, a teacher at a fashionable Swiss boys' school, and it reached its climax some two months later with the unconditional surrender of a million Nazi troops in Italy.

Allen remembered February 25, 1945, as a cold and sunless Sunday. Leaving Clover to her own devices, he and Gaevernitz had driven across the French border for their weekly meeting with the intelligence staff of the American Sixth Army. The problem of the week was the disappearance near the German front lines of an American army truck carrying a safe full of secret documents. The tedium Allen found in matters of such inconsequence was broken by an urgent message from Bern that Major Max Waibel of Swiss intelligence needed to see the two OSS men in Lucerne as soon as possible that night. Assuring their military colleagues that they were hot on the trail of the missing safe, Allen and Gaevernitz drove back into Switzerland and caught the first train to Lucerne.*

Waibel, the officer assigned to maintain liaison with American intelligence, was Allen's closest confidant in the Swiss security apparatus. The three men enjoyed a dinner of fresh trout at a small restaurant near Lake Lucerne, as Waibel told of two visitors who had just called on him, a garrulous Italian baron named Parilli who dabbled in business and industry and his unlikely partner, a pedantic Polish-born Swiss schoolmaster, Max Husmann. They were asking for the good offices of the Swiss in opening a channel for peace talks with the German command on the Italian front.

By now the war was going badly for the Third Reich. Waibel and Allen both knew that Himmler, for one, was showering the Western Allies with peace feelers of dubious validity, dangling what he apparently thought would be the irresistible offer of turning his SS fighting divisions

---

* The safe was soon recovered intact, half submerged in an Alsatian stream. The unknown hijacker wanted only the truck and never bothered looking inside the sensitive cargo.

against the communists on the eastern front. Waibel nonetheless sensed something unusual about this particular approach, taking it seriously enough to suggest that the OSS office might want to give the unlikely cut-outs a hearing.

To keep Waibel happy, 110 sent Gaevernitz to meet the two visitors later that evening at the Hotel Schweizerhof in Lucerne. Next day Gaevernitz reported back on a pleasant but rambling conversation, sprinkled with the dropped names of a strange collection of German personalities and their vague aspirations. Gaevernitz thought it best to dismiss the baron and the schoolmaster courteously, saying that any meaningful talks leading toward a surrender would have to be conducted by recognizable military or SS representatives.

To Allen's surprise there appeared at the Swiss-Italian border five days later two SS officers from the command defending northern Italy against the American and British armies advancing slowly from the south. Waibel put the two officers into a safe house in Lugano to await an American contact. Gaevernitz had gone off on a skiing holiday, and Allen was not ready to intervene personally. He dispatched another OSS aide, Paul Blum, who would be passing through Italian Switzerland anyway, to look in upon the two mysterious Germans and figure out who they represented and what they were really about.

With any clandestine approach, an obvious first step is to test the authority of the cut-out. A technique that became frequent later in Allen's career was to require that some innocuous but precise phrase be included in a public statement from the other side, just to establish that a direct line existed from cut-out to responsible authority. For the sort of field contact before them, however, Allen equipped Blum with a less public but far more useful test of authority in case Blum thought the matter worth pursuing.

Still rankling Allen was the capture the previous December of Ferruccio Parri, the anticommunist partisan leader on whom the OSS had pinned such hopes for building a postwar Italian government. If these two SS officers in Lugano expected United States representatives to consider them seriously, let them show their authority and good will by delivering Parri to Switzerland and, for good measure, Major Antonio Usmiani, coordinator of one of 110's intelligence networks in northern Italy. Blum gave the two SS officers little time or courtesy — their meeting lasted only twenty minutes — but he conveyed Allen's message, passing over a piece of paper with the names of the two Italians. Aware that freeing a political prisoner of Parri's importance would be a tall order for any SS underling, Allen, like Gaevernitz, assumed that the approach would now dry up.

On March 8, just eleven days after the first contact, an excited Waibel called Gaevernitz at Davos (he was afraid of surveillance on Allen's office telephone) to convey astonishing news. "Parri and Usmiani are here," he said, delivered by a young SS officer at the Swiss border post of Chiasso without comment or explanation. And there was more: the commandant of the Italian theater, General Karl Wolff, a personage second only to Himmler in the SS hierarchy, was himself crossing secretly into Switzerland from his command headquarters in Italy and inviting a representative of the United States to contact him.

Allen suddenly started taking the approach seriously, but to be sure of his grounds he rushed to the sanitarium where Waibel had hastily arranged to house Parri and Usmiani. Still somewhat dazed, the two liberated prisoners had no idea what was happening to them, having assumed when removed from their cells in Milan's San Vittori jail that morning that they were about to be shot. Allen shared a tearful embrace with his partisan friends and persuaded them to lie low in secrecy while he explored the greater political forces at work in their release. Then 110 set about deciding how to make himself known to the second-ranking officer of Hitler's SS.

Both at the time and looking back there was something strange about this particular Nazi network of odd individuals. Allen had come to recognize all types of undercover approaches and had learned also to be wary of hidden motivations. Just in the previous few months Austrian general Glaise von Horstenau had signaled readiness to deal in the Balkans, and the archbishop of Milan had sent minions to start discussions to prevent northern Italy from being destroyed in a war to the finish. To these approaches 110 did not feel authorized to respond.

Once the authority of the first cut-out has been proved, the next test is the quality of the agents and the measure of coherence that binds them into a useful apparatus. Are the nodes of the network policymakers or clerks? Both can be useful — witness the role of the clerk Fritz Kolbe, for example. It is crucial to understand why the members of a network are collaborating with each other, what holds them together, and how secure or reliable their affinity is. Could they withstand torture, blackmail, or bribery? Finally, and centrally, can the network deliver?

With the liberation of Parri, this network had clearly delivered, and the unexpected arrival of General Wolff added formidable credence. Who were these people, and why had they come together (beneath their pious protestations of wanting to end a ruinous war)?

It had started with Baron Luigi Parilli. Allen checked with OSS members from his old Wall Street network about this resourceful industrialist and discovered that for fifteen years before the war Parilli had been the competent sales representative in Italy of an American appliance company. At their first meeting Gaevernitz had pressed Parilli for some clues to his standing, his relationship with the German command in Italy. After some hesitation the baron confided that he had fallen into a close friendship with a handsome young SS captain, Guido Zimmer. When the SS suddenly transferred Zimmer to Milan, Parilli found a business pretext to go with his young friend. Allen sized up Zimmer, when they finally met, as "somewhat of an aesthete and an intellectual," and among the interests he shared with Parilli was a concern to protect the art treasures of northern Italy.

Encouraged by the baron, Zimmer had made bold to present himself to a superior in the SS, Colonel Eugen Dollmann. Zimmer had guessed from the demeanor of this senior officer that a friendly approach from a pleasant young man might be sympathetically received. As they became acquainted, the forty-four-year-old Dollmann acknowledged that he had also met Zimmer's friend Parilli twice before, on what he called social occasions. Dollmann shared Zimmer's passion for Italian art and his sense of futility about the German war effort; he agreed to raise the possibility of a timely surrender with his superior, General Wolff. Meanwhile Parilli was pursuing a Swiss friend, the schoolmaster, to post the necessary financial guarantees to obtain Swiss entry visas for use if a peace probe got under way.

This was how Operation Sunrise had started, and the loyalties within the little network, brought together by aesthetic interests and personal friendships, gradually became explicable. It was the young Captain Zimmer who drove Parri and Usmiani to the Swiss border from captivity in Italy. Zimmer and Dollmann were the two SS officers who traveled to Switzerland together; when Wolff decided to come to Switzerland himself, he brought Dollmann and Zimmer back with him. Parilli and Husmann, the schoolmaster, hovered around to help with arrangements and introductions.

Allen wrote long afterward, "To us in early 1945, Wolff, . . . Dollmann and their subordinates were only names, principals in a chain of command. In our minds all of them shared the black reputation of the SS. We saw them to a great extent through the eyes of our friends in the Italian resistance, who feared them and hated them and had frequently suffered at their hands."[6]

Allen had the immediate problem of deciding whether to meet Karl Wolff and, if so, how. Gaevernitz, abandoning the ski slopes, had caught the first train from Davos and managed to position himself at the designated time at the suburban Zurich train station where Wolff would secretly disembark on March 8. Independently Allen proceeded to his

Zurich base, an apartment on the ground floor of a bleak building facing the Lake of Zurich. Husmann met him there and proposed that to ensure secrecy, Allen should call upon Wolff at the Swiss safe house. Allen refused. Though he could envisage the headlines if news of the meeting leaked, ENVOY OF ROOSEVELT RECEIVES HIGH SS OFFICER, Allen insisted that Wolff should come to his apartment in Zurich, and alone.

Allen busied himself laying and lighting the fire as he awaited the SS general's arrival. Gaevernitz answered the knock on the door. "I remained in the library," Allen wrote. "Gaevernitz led him in. . . . We nodded and took seats around the fire."

Wolff had sent ahead a curious dossier of papers, including photographs of himself in the German popular press, a résumé, and a list of references, as if he were applying for a job. Allen learned that the SS commander had started out as an advertising salesman in Berlin; after his agency failed in the depression of Weimar days he drifted into the Nazi Party in 1930, rising quickly into the ranks of the SS to become personal adjutant to Himmler in 1933.

Wolff apparently led an exotic social life in those prewar years, trading on the personal charm that had kept him going during the depression years and then gained him access to circles frequented by Rudolf Hess.* Even the straitlaced Himmler came to call him by the affectionate nickname "Wolffchen." His career track became that of a staff officer rather than a commander of troops or police officer; Allen later called him, not without some admiration, "a kind of diplomat or political advisor to the SS leaders. He had unobtrusively slipped into very high places as a man who could manage other men by dint of his personal qualities and an ability to deal with people."† At the start of the war he became the chief liaison officer between Hitler's various command posts, Ribbentrop's foreign ministry, and Himmler's SS headquarters.

As his status rose, he tired of the wife who had borne him four children and proposed to marry another woman. This provoked a crisis within the SS hierarchy, where concern for bourgeois propriety was a fetish, however hypocritical. Himmler's personal permission was necessary for any SS officer to get divorced; in Wolff's case Himmler refused. Wolff, however, had access to Hitler and no compunctions about using it. The führer approved his divorce. The overruled Himmler felt humiliated

---

* Hess was the first name on the list of references sent over to Allen that night, even though the long-disgraced deputy führer was being held as a British prisoner of war. Second on his list was Pope Pius XII, who had received Wolff at the Vatican before Rome fell to the Americans.

† Among his privileges was authority to draw funds from the special "S" account to which Baron von Schröder and other industrialists paid their contributions to the Nazi Party.

and summarily banished his high-living aide to Italy, where he would have command over a million men but would be far from Berlin.

Far from feeling exiled, Wolff actually seemed to relish life in Italy, away from the rigid social conventions of the Nazi capital. In seeking a social life beyond the structured confines of the SS, he relied on introductions by the urbane Dollmann, scion of a family that had served the royal courts of both Bavaria and Austria, a scholar of Renaissance art who had fled the Third Reich's Teutonic discipline long before the war, to settle in Italy. Dollmann had been unwittingly propelled into Nazi prominence in 1937 when, guiding a troop of Italian youths, he suddenly had to act as interpreter for Hitler when the führer's personal interpreter fell ill. Both Hitler and Himmler were impressed by him; Dollmann became Himmler's personal diplomat-agent in Rome and assumed a high SS position without ever going through the ranks. His German comrades, including Wolff, playfully called this unlikely SS officer "Eugenio" for his adopted Italian manners; while fully enjoying the privileges of his authority, he seldom wore the SS uniform for fear of offending his artistic friends. "Dollmann hardly filled the bill as a blond Germanic hero," Allen recalled. "He had long black hair, combed straight back and curling a little over his ears, and almost effeminate gestures."

Dollmann, Zimmer, and their special circle of intellectual officers were drawn to Wolff's personal staff. They were the heart of the Sunrise conspiracy, and the Americans were under no illusions about motives or values in their private lives. As Allen and Gaevernitz prepared to meet General Wolff, 110 noted, "We were more interested in his power than in his morals. We did not expect to find this SS General a Sunday School teacher."

The first meeting with Wolff lasted about an hour. Though not exactly cordial, it was businesslike. In fact, all through his Sunrise contacts Allen suppressed his customary amiability — so much so that Dollmann, otherwise sensitive to the foibles of his fellow men, never saw through the officious mask. "He always struck me as a leather-faced Puritan archangel who had fled from the European sink of iniquity on the *Mayflower* and now returned to scourge the sinners of the old world," Dollmann later wrote of Allen. "He was incorruptible and totally humorless."

Allen asked the SS commandant to state his position, and Wolff did most of the talking thereafter. Allen and Gaevernitz recorded their impressions shortly after the meeting. "Wolff gave the impression of a man of energy.... He wasted no words and did not attempt to bargain for himself. He said he had committed no crimes and was willing to stand on his record. He did not dispute either the hopelessness of the German military position nor the fact that the German armies must surrender unconditionally. He said he was completely won over to the need for immediate action."

Allen returned to Bern late that night, but Gaevernitz stayed on for a further meeting the next morning, March 9. This time Wolff brought Dollmann with him. They worked out a procedure for arranging a complex surrender involving a number of chains of command on both sides. Wolff was treading a delicate line, for with all his own determination to surrender as promptly and neatly as possible, he had to persuade others above him not to get in his way. Both Allen and Gaevernitz had pressed him hard on one point: Wolff insisted that he was acting on his own, that neither Himmler nor Hitler knew of the SS commander's initiative.

— * —

A ranking member of American intelligence had met face to face with a ranking member of the Hitler regime while millions of soldiers advanced, retreated, and killed each other. No special perspicacity was required to understand the damage of disclosure should the fact of the meeting become known. Yet as intelligence professionals long before Allen had learned too well, the tightest operational security cannot anticipate the coincidences of daily life. "What makes intelligence officers despair," Allen once wrote, "is the unexpected and usually silly accident that threatens to spoil everything, after the most careful preparations have been made."

Who should happen to be strolling by the suburban Zurich train station the evening of March 8, when Gaevernitz greeted SS general Wolff, but Mary Bancroft, one person who was alert enough to recognize the various Nazi personalities pictured in the popular press. "Gero did not see me, for I had quickly stepped into a small shop near the station so I could take a closer look at the men accompanying him," Mary wrote. "Later I told Allen about seeing Gero, adding 'I may be crazy, but I could swear that one of the men with him was SS General Karl Wolff.'" Allen retorted, "You must be crazy," laughing his disingenuous ho ho ho. "What would an SS general be doing in Zurich? And why were you hanging around the Bahnhof Enge instead of doing something useful?"[7]

To Mary, Allen could dissemble. When it came to his first substantive report to Washington on the contact with Wolff, Allen had to walk a delicate line, one thoroughly familiar to intelligence operatives over the ages. A responsible intelligence officer in the field must keep his home office informed. But "he may overdo it," as Allen wrote in a candid mood years later. "If, for example, he tells too much or asks too often for instructions, he is likely to get some he doesn't relish, and, what is worse, he may well find headquarters trying to take over the whole conduct of the operation."

Control over contact with this peculiar SS network was not something Allen wished to relinquish to a far distant headquarters. "An intelligence officer should be free to talk to the devil himself if he could gain any useful knowledge for the conduct or the termination of the war," he wrote. Yet aide-mémoires of conversations with the devil have no easy passage through bureaucracy. If he told too much, Allen reasoned, "too many people would have to be brought into the act at too early a stage." Furthermore, "I had no desire to stir up exaggerated hopes in Washington that we were about to engineer a German surrender, or to create the impression that we were engaged in any kind of high-level negotiations requiring policy decisions."

If this was the balancing act required of Allen in March 1945, it must be said that he failed on all counts. His first reports on the Wolff meeting indeed brought too many people into the act; they provoked the exaggerated hopes that he sought to avoid; and they allowed a suspicious ally, the Soviet Union, to believe that the United States had opened a channel to the Nazi high command for high-level policy negotiations.

Allen's reports went both to Washington and to the Allied military command in southern Italy; British field marshal Sir Harold Alexander was directing the Allied armies moving up from the south, while the supreme Allied commander, Dwight Eisenhower, was preparing to cross the Rhine and enter Germany from the west. On receiving Allen's first report Alexander quickly dispatched two of his top staff officers to Switzerland to — as he perceived it — receive the surrender of the Nazi Italian front. Allen's reports failed to make clear that Wolff was acting alone and might not be able to carry the German army's high command with him.

Developments on the diplomatic level were almost as precipitous. Just the day before Allen's meeting with Wolff came a chance occurrence of combat that set Soviet suspicions flaring: on March 7 Eisenhower's frontline units found the bridge across the Rhine at Remagen structurally intact after all the others had been destroyed by the retreating Germans. The astonished American Ninth Armored Division poured across the Remagen bridge to establish an unplanned foothold on the Rhine's right bank. Suspicious Moscow saw clear collusion here between capitalist militarists of Germany and the United States: leaving the bridge intact must have been a ruse to allow the Western Allies to occupy the German heartland before the advancing Russian troops could move in from the east. Then they heard reports from Switzerland of actual conversations between the intelligence man Dulles and the second-in-command of the SS. Washington and London hastily agreed that Moscow should be officially informed of the Wolff approach immediately, lest a garbled account filter through from hostile intelligence services. Foreign Minister Molotov replied promptly to American ambassador Harriman that the Soviet government "does not object to the proposed conversations," as long as two, possibly three, Soviet generals join the talks along with the British and American officers.

Allen and Gaevernitz, meanwhile, were driving back and forth between Bern and Lucerne, where Baron Parilli was relaying messages from the faithful Zimmer and the network they had assembled. "This was the first time I had met Parilli face to face," Allen wrote. "He was bundled in a large handsome overcoat with a fur collar (it was bitter cold outside) which made him look twice his size, as I discovered when he removed the coat." From Zimmer and Parilli they learned that Wolff was having his own problems: Himmler had got word of the meeting with Dulles and sent Wolff "peremptory instructions" to break off contact.

"We haven't caught the fish yet," Allen muttered in despair as he and Gaevernitz drove back to Bern in the bleak cold of a Swiss midnight on March 12. The drive was not easy; all the direction signs had been removed early in the war against the threat of German invasion. Everything was snow-covered, and although the Americans knew the landmarks in daylight, Allen remembered steering on this drive "by the stars." Arriving at the Bern embassy at 4 A.M., 110 sent off a cautionary report.

Awakened a few hours later, he learned that Alexander's "armistice" team was already on its way; two staff generals, American and British, escorted by a substantial corps of retainers from the OSS and their respective armies would arrive at Lyons that very day, expecting to proceed to Switzerland. Allen, appalled at the enthusiasm his reports had generated, signaled that the team should remain in France. Commanders have not the slightest idea of the security and logistical problems that their ranks endure. It would be hard enough to smuggle two generals in uniform through the neutral Swiss border guards; supporting staff would be out of the question.

To Allen's immense relief when he finally met the "armistice" delegates at Annemasse on March 14, Major General Lyman L. Lemnitzer of the U.S. Army and Major General Terence S. Airey of Britain turned out to be calm and sophisticated gentlemen. Apprised of the tenuousness of the situation, they readily shed their extravagant retinues, but having come this far, they allowed as how they might as well proceed into Switzerland by themselves under Allen's guidance and await whatever would happen. They even accepted a hastily contrived ruse for passing the border controls incognito. Allen enticed two American sergeants, radio operators at Annemasse, into parting temporarily with their dog tags. Generals Lemnitzer and Airey memorized serial numbers and brief biographical data against possible interrogation at the frontier. The distinctively British General Airey won special recognition within the little spy net for successfully presenting himself to the border patrols as a New York Irishman, Sergeant McNeely.

Back in Bern Clover Dulles was keeping up a good front. "Life here is very attractive," she wrote her daughter, "especially when the sun is out. Then I bask on our balcony-terrace and take walks in the quaint little streets. . . . Dad generally is having conferences until two in the morning, and the house is always full of people, coming and going." That night, March 15, the two strangers who checked in to the second-floor bedrooms wondered if they were about to accept the surrender of the Nazi armies in Italy.

Lemnitzer immediately took in hand the problem of slipping a Russian officer into Switzerland for any proposed talks. The Soviet Union had no diplomatic relations with Switzerland; there could be no official cover, and the loan of a New York sergeant's dog tag would stretch credulity too far on all sides. "I have now had an opportunity to observe the security measures required in getting Airey and me into Bern," he radioed Alexander. "Our position is considerably underground since we are [by now] in civilian clothes and are using assumed names. The introduction of a Russian officer must obviously be even more underground." Allen added his caution: any hint that a Soviet officer had been introduced secretly into Switzerland would cause a major sensation.

For that day it was only the security and logistical complications that troubled Allen about possible Soviet participation in Operation Sunrise, a point of no small significance in light of later accusations as the history of the Cold War entered its revisionist phase. The Bern reports on March 15 even went so far as to suggest alternative devices for getting a Russian representative to the scene if it was absolutely necessary.

Unbeknownst to 110 and his team, however, President Roosevelt and Prime Minister Churchill were themselves focusing on the process unfolding in Bern, developing second thoughts about Molotov's deceptively mild request for Soviet inclusion. Why should Soviet officers be involved in a surrender in an Anglo-American theater of war? Would Stalin invite British and American officers to participate in armistice talks on the eastern front? The same day that "Sergeant Nicholson" and "Sergeant McNeely" crossed into Switzerland, instructions flashed from Washington to Moscow that "the Berne meeting is only for the purpose of establishing contact," that authorized German representatives would be flown to

Alexander's headquarters in liberated Italy for the actual surrender discussions, at which Russian representatives would be welcomed. But not in Switzerland.

Just twenty-four hours later came a stern reply from Molotov declaring it "utterly unexpected and incomprehensible [that the] United States refuses to the Soviet Representatives the right to participate in the negotiations in Bern." Speaking for Stalin, he demanded that the contact be broken off.

In transmitting this message by the most secret radio channel available to him, Ambassador Harriman saw a fundamental turning point in relations among the Allies. Ever since the Yalta conference, Harriman cabled, "the Soviet leaders have come to believe that they can force their will on us on any issue." Some could date the beginning of the Cold War to this exchange of March 16–17, 1945.

Nothing of all this was known in the Herrengasse, of course. When the household awoke the morning of March 16, the immediate problem was to sustain the cover by which two dignified foreign civilians had arrived in Bern as Allen's personal guests. Any number of undercover security services were watching the elegant old mansion overlooking the Aare, and its various transients were well advised to have an excuse for being there.

As it happened, Terence Airey was a dog lover, and Switzerland was home to a special breed of dachshund that he had long fancied. The British gentleman was more than happy to while away the hours contacting kennels as he awaited surrender of a million Nazi soldiers. The official report to Donovan explained: "The security angles of this abnormal 'operation' were carefully considered, and it was decided that no one would suspect that an eminent British general on an important secret mission would go shopping for a dachshund, and that this was in fact an excellent security measure. Thereafter, 'Fritzel' accompanied us wherever we, or rather General Airey, went." But Mary Bancroft, aware that something was going on but not knowing exactly what, warned Allen that "something had to be done about the small dog . . . which the sharp-eyed Swiss had spotted waiting forlornly outside the most unlikely places."*

On March 17 word came through Baron Parilli that Wolff would return to Switzerland in two days' time to present a concrete plan for accomplishing the surrender. Zurich was obviously too public a place for this second meeting, so Gaevernitz offered the Stinnes family's isolated

---

* Not privy to Operation Sunrise, Mary had it a little wrong; she thought that the British gentleman had actually brought his dog with him to Switzerland. There are, in fact, limits to the devotion of British dog fanciers.

lakeside estate in Ascona, where both Wolff and the American officers could slip in and out unnoticed. This time Allen took Clover with him as natural cover (she knew full well that her husband was not in a holiday mood), and by separate train went Generals Lemnitzer and Airey (and Fritzel), along with a crew of OSS radio technicians.

Once again the Americans' heavy electrical equipment proved to be too much for the circuits of the Swiss countryside, and the Stinnes villa was plunged into darkness the minute the radio gear was plugged in. Once that was repaired, Clover led the party in taping black paper over the windows, drawing a fine distinction of security, "not for the purpose of pretending we were not there, but so as not to draw attention to ourselves."

At the appointed meeting time on March 19, Lemnitzer and Airey withdrew to a second Stinnes villa on the hill to let Allen start the discussion at lakeside. Clover was ordered to leave the house and take a rowboat out for a leisurely morning on Lake Maggiore. Once again Wolff was invited to meet Allen and Gaevernitz alone, leaving the aides accompanying him (including Zimmer, now promoted to major) to wait outside in the garden. The three men talked for two hours, with Allen posing questions and Wolff replying.

Wolff readily conceded that the war was lost, that there would be no point in continuing, but he still had Hitler adamantly refusing to concede anything, plus dozens of military and civilian toadies around the führer who prevented any individual initiatives. "It is easy to start a war," Allen remarked, "but difficult to stop one." Wolff reiterated his determination to prevent the wholesale destruction of northern Italy, art treasures and industrial plant alike, but in describing the motley forces technically under his command, it was clear that he faced formidable problems of making his authority stick, of getting out the proper orders and ensuring that they would be obeyed. Gaevernitz wrestled with the technicalities: "To make a fighting army put down its arms is in many respects as painstaking a task as to mobilize it. Most important of all is to fix the precise hour when hostilities are to cease, and to see to it that orders reach the front line units in time and are carried out. Nothing would be worse than to have one side stop fighting while the other continued."[8] Wolff pleaded for time to get his arrangements in place and, above all, to persuade his army counterparts to cooperate in the surrender plan.

The meeting broke for lunch. Clover remembered being "peremptorily summoned" from the lake to whip up a picnic for Wolff and his aides, while Allen and Gaevernitz strode up the hill to brief the two Allied generals in the other villa and decide whether they should meet the SS commander. Wolff obviously did not have the authority to open the "armistice talks" that Field Marshal Alexander had expected, but Allen wanted to allow Lemnitzer and Airey the option of interrogating the SS general in person. Up to this moment Sunrise had been nothing but a civilian intelligence probe, disavowable and without policy standing; once the British and American generals entered, it would become a dialogue between opposing armies, with pitfalls of misunderstanding and betrayal. To keep the meeting as low-key as possible, Allen proposed to introduce Lemnitzer and Airey simply as unnamed "military advisers."

Strange human responses crop up when opposing forces meet. Leaving the lunch table that day, the burning issue was whether the Allied generals should shake hands with a German officer. Each of the Americans in Operation Sunrise had found his own solution. Paul Blum, the first OSS official to meet the SS officers two weeks before, had determined that despite his hatred of Nazis, he would not refuse his hand to anyone who wanted to meet him. Allen avoided the issue by busily stoking the fire when General Wolff first walked in. As they prepared for the afternoon encounter on March 19, General Airey abruptly announced that he would not shake hands with an SS general. Ever inventive, Gaevernitz proposed the following: Allen and Wolff would enter the meeting room from the terrace, the two incognito generals from the kitchen door opposite. The room was small, dominated by a heavy octagonal table in the center, so the two parties would find themselves too far apart to permit handshakes. Gaevernitz's stratagem, alas, failed to take account of the heartiness of Wolff, the former advertising salesman. No sooner had the generic introductions been accomplished, Allen related, "when Wolff stepped briskly around the table, squeezing his large body through the narrow gap between the table and the wall." He grasped Airey's hand, and the British general found himself incapable of refusing a reflex response.

That hurdle crossed, Lemnitzer led the meeting in explaining to Wolff in tough military language that the only topic open for discussion was the unconditional surrender of all German forces on the southern front. When those in effective authority were ready to execute such a surrender, they should dispatch at least two fully authorized officers to a designated site in Switzerland, to be flown from there to Alexander's headquarters in southern Italy to confirm the myriad of technical details and sign the required documents. Wolff nodded his understanding of what had to be done and pledged his determination to do it.

Five frustrating weeks would pass before the SS commander could deliver on his pledge. By then, however, Sunrise had moved to High Noon, a confrontation between political powers with stakes far more dangerous than furtive handshakes and imperfectly coordinated field orders. Over the next three weeks President Roosevelt and Marshal Stalin set out to stare each other down through a remarkable correspondence.

— * —

Foreign Minister Molotov's exchanges in Moscow with Ambassador Harriman were getting steadily ruder. Though Roosevelt's health had been failing after his return from the Crimea, the sixty-three-year-old president was kept informed of Allen's temporizing reports, and he concurred with Churchill that the "Bern incident" needed high-level airing in the so-called spirit of Yalta. "An open break between Russia and her Anglo-Saxon allies would be the only miracle that would prevent the speedy collapse of the German armies," noted the head of Roosevelt's military staff, Admiral William D. Leahy.

A carefully crafted letter went to Stalin on March 24 over President Roosevelt's signature, describing as blandly as possible the meandering course of the Bern exchanges up to that point. Stalin waited four days, then scorned Roosevelt's explanations. Tempers flared for another round. On April 3 Stalin told Roosevelt, "It may be assumed that you have not been fully informed." This letter was delivered to the White House by the Russian embassy and dispatched to Warm Springs, Georgia, where the secretly ailing president was hoping to regain his strength. Leahy and other White House aides prepared a response for Roosevelt's signature the next day, declaring, "I cannot avoid a feeling of bitter resentment toward your informers, whoever they are, for such vile misrepresentations of my actions or those of my trusted subordinates."

Watching these extraordinary exchanges from the wings, Churchill egged Roosevelt on. If the Russians "are ever convinced that we are afraid of them and can be bullied into submission," Churchill cabled, "then indeed I should despair of our future relations with them and much else." Stalin's next letter was cast in the injured tones of a partner wronged — "as near as they can get to an apology," Churchill noted. From his Warm Springs rest home on the morning of April 12, Roosevelt signed an equally conciliatory reply. A few hours later the president complained of a bad headache, lost consciousness, and died.

The shattering news from Warm Springs reached Bern just as Allen and Gaevernitz were setting off for Paris for a climactic round of high-level briefings with General Donovan. Allen had passed his fifty-second birthday the previous weekend with Clover and his OSS staff. There was not much to celebrate. Lemnitzer and Airey had returned to Alexander's headquarters (taking Fritzel along) a few days before; nearly three weeks had passed without any substantial word from General Wolff. Momentous military decisions were being made about where the Western Allies should direct their next advances, and Sunrise looked more and more like a mirage. Periodically the hapless Parilli and Zimmer would turn up in Switzerland, singly or together, pleading for more time to put the elusive surrender procedures in place.

The death of the commander in chief cast a heavy pall over the company of hardened professionals as they convened at the Ritz Hotel in Paris the next morning, but the business of war and peace had to go on. Donovan had summoned Lieutenant Casey from his London base for a briefing on the covert action missions parachuting into Germany ahead of the invading armies, missions that Allen still doggedly refused to support. The briefing turned to the Sunrise contacts and the problems they were raising with the Russians. Here Allen learned for the first time about Roosevelt's correspondence with Stalin. Casey recalled that "Dulles fidgeted in his chair, alternately outraged and embarrassed by the reaction his activities had triggered. Bluntly put, all hell had broken loose."[9] Eisenhower's chief of staff, General Walter Bedell Smith, had called his OSS liaison men on the carpet. Donovan had been summoned to the White House to give assurance that his OSS was not pursuing an independent diplomacy, but after hearing Allen's full report, Donovan authorized the Bern team to continue stringing along the Sunrise contacts.

Emerging lost in thought from an intense day in the Ritz conference room, Allen was suddenly approached by a stranger in the darkened hotel corridor, mildly asking where he "might find 110." Allen absent-mindedly started to reply, "You're talking to him — I'm 110," when it dawned on him that the stranger was simply looking for room 110, down the hallway.

Back in Bern, Allen found Zimmer waiting with an urgent personal message from Wolff — not an announcement of the long-awaited surrender program but a message of condolence "on the occasion of the passing of the President with whom you were so close." The myth of Allen's intimacy, as "Personal Representative of President Roosevelt," never died across warring Europe.

— * —

Aside from the obvious desirability of a military surrender, a further strategic consideration gave special importance to the Sunrise contact, the hypothesis that the Nazis, even when expelled from Berlin, would seek to establish a last-ditch "redoubt" in southern Germany.[10]

Hints that Hitler's General Staff was planning for such an eventuality had started reaching Allen's networks in September 1944, and the reports were routinely fed into the OSS intelligence mill. They fit neatly into some of the other rather fantastic stories being peddled out of Germany about formation of "Werewolf" guerrilla cadres designed to keep the Nazi flame alive in a last-ditch campaign of resistance. The Nazis' own intelligence networks soon became aware of the American speculation, and Goebbels, ever on the alert for effective propaganda themes, seized upon the tactic of inflating stories about a formidable Alpine resistance — not in a defeatism that would only upset his führer but as a ploy to give the Western Allies pause in their drive for Germany's total defeat. Leaked stories began cropping up about "impregnable positions, massive supplies carefully hidden in bombproof caves, underground factories and . . . elite units of troops to man the whole bastion."

Thus when General Wolff had first come to Switzerland early in March, Allen saw in him a special strategic asset: his command lay astride the Allies' southern access route to an Alpine fortress. In his earliest reports to Washington Allen argued that Wolff's approach could be exploited to "reduce the effectiveness of enemy plans for the German *reduit*" (using the Swiss word). By mid-March, as the Sunrise discussions proceeded, 110 became even more expansive: a deal with Wolff "may present a unique opportunity to shorten the war, permit occupation of northern Italy, possibly penetrate Austria under most favorable conditions, and possibly wreck German plans for establishment of a *maquis*" (this time he chose the French model).

Doubts persisted over whether the redoubt was anything more than a psychological ploy. Allen asked Wolff about it at their meeting on March 19, and the supposed linchpin of the strategy denounced the redoubt concept as "madness." At supreme Allied headquarters, however, the military planners wanted to take no chances. In the middle of April Eisenhower diverted his land armada of four million men away from their drive toward Berlin and Prague, turning them southward to overrun Bavaria and the land of the redoubt. His chief of staff, Bedell Smith, unwittingly revealed the confused perceptions of the strategists in those days by telling British and American newsmen on April 21 that headquarters did not know much about this redoubt, but "we are beginning to think it will be a lot more than we will expect."

Thus a Nazi ploy of disinformation backfired. The perpetrators of the redoubt myth could only watch helplessly as what they most feared took place.* The Russians, not the Western Allies, occupied Berlin and

---

* Perhaps Soviet archives of the Stalin era will reveal the extent to which Moscow consciously exploited the redoubt myth to steer Western strategy toward Soviet goals; one can easily hypothesize Soviet disinformation piled atop Nazi disinformation to confound Western intelligence assessment. Titillating evidence comes in the fact that Noel Field and fellow-traveling colleagues were flooding OSS channels with memos inflating the potential dangers of the redoubt.

other centers of eastern Europe that would have been within Eisenhower's reach had his attention not been diverted. After the war Nazi field marshal Kesselring termed the redoubt "a playful fantasy." Allen himself maintained in later years that he certainly studied the flow of redoubt reports that passed across his desk but never took them very seriously. But Casey blamed the OSS itself for faulty intelligence analysis.

> The OSS ... played a key role in the redoubt myth. ... We were unable to explode it and we should have, easily. We had a dozen teams in the redoubt area and none of them reported anything justifying belief that enough military strength could be generated in that pastoral, undeveloped country to resist five million Allied troops for more than a few weeks. ... So fragmentary reports of construction and SS troops in the redoubt area and Goebbels' deception and propaganda were blown up and sensationalized in the Allied press to create a myth that changed the shape of the postwar world. America had failed to develop the kind of multidisciplined organization able to coordinate and evaluate all kinds of intelligence.[11]

Not much common ground existed between Allen Dulles and William Casey in the closing months of World War II, but one position on which they could agree was the need for a broader, more comprehensive, and more professional intelligence service for the United States, even in time of peace.

— ∗ —

Sunrise turned to sunset those next April days, as Allen saw his promising operation fade into the twilight of insignificance. The armies were closing in upon Germany from east, west, and south; American forces reached the Elbe on April 11, the Russians fought their way into Berlin, and American and British forces swept into northern Italy. By the time Wolff finally returned to Switzerland with surrender arrangements in hand, the führer was preparing his suicide.

The armistice documents for the southern front were finally signed at Alexander's headquarters at 2 P.M. on April 29—in the presence of a Russian officer, as Roosevelt had promised—to take effect on May 2. Just what Gaevernitz had feared happened: the German surrender orders got through, the American responding orders did not. Leading the advance in the Dolomites, the American Eighty-eighth Infantry Division first heard of the Sunrise capitulation in a signal from across the front line, from the German First Paratroop Division. Suspecting a ruse and lacking confirmation through their own field communications, the American infantrymen fought on for twelve hours, and the German paratroopers fought back, with dozens of casualties on both sides after the hour of surrender.

On Sunday, May 6, Allen, hobbling on a crutch because of gout, was summoned across the French border to Rheims to witness the final act of Nazi capitulation on all fronts, a signing ceremony in the red school-house that served as General Eisenhower's forward headquarters. Last-minute protocol matters and special pleadings from the German emis-sary, General Alfred Jodl, delayed the proceedings for half an hour; then, as Allen watched, Jodl and two aides were escorted into the schoolroom, now hot and stuffy with the klieg lights of the press pool. The Nazi gen-eral bowed stiffly before taking his seat at the doughnut-shaped confer-ence table across from General Bedell Smith, representing the supreme commander. Brief technical exchanges were translated between English and German, and Jodl signed three copies of the Act of Military Surren-der at 0241, to take effect at 2301 hours that night.

Eisenhower, waiting in a second-floor office nearby, was in no mood for ceremony, and Allen limped out wordlessly to return immediately to Bern for the delayed announcement of V-E Day. Implementation of the surrender was ragged. It was dawn of May 11 before all the battlefields in Europe went quiet.

— * —

In the glow of victory and for two decades to come, Allen savored every detail of his sixty-five days in Operation Sunrise. So, for that matter, did Donovan and the OSS as the congratulatory cables swamped the intelli-gence communications systems. Driven by personal and professional motives alike, the men of intelligence sought some share of the glory be-ing heaped upon Eisenhower and the Allied armies after V-E Day. The meager results of Lieutenant Casey's penetration missions into Germany could hardly be made credible to celebrating civilians, but for public rela-tions an OSS undercover surrender operation was irresistible. Donovan and Allen managed to leak the story as soon as they could safely do so. In September 1945, not three weeks after the final surrenders of World War II, a dramatic account of Operation Sunrise appeared in the pages of *The Saturday Evening Post*.[12] Two decades later, retired as the chief of United States intelligence, Allen pulled out the official report he and Gaevernitz had written in the first weeks after V-E Day and expanded it into a full-length book, *The Secret Surrender*.

No one can doubt that Operation Sunrise involved plenty of colorful episodes to entice a public eager for adventure stories of war: Gaever-nitz's panic on forgetting the assumed names of the German armistice envoys being smuggled through Switzerland to get the surrender orders to the troops in northern Italy; the modest OSS radio operator, code-named "Little Willy," whom Wolff accepted into his headquarters even as the war was raging, to transmit messages between generals across the lines. Later came revisionist historians who found in Sunrise the first elements of distrust and deception between the United States and the Soviet Union to explain the origins of the Cold War.

One of Allen's own staff reluctantly called *The Secret Surrender* a "fraudulent" book—not the story as told but the dubious significance of the operation as a chapter in the closing of World War II or, for that matter, as the start of the Cold War. Real questions remain about Wolff's motives—and those of Dollmann and Zimmer—in stringing Allen along during those five final weeks. Were they simply trying, once they saw that the Nazi defeat was inevitable, to prepare an honorable record to ensure their own postwar rehabilitation?

Those who were part of Sunrise, including Allen, were actually saddened by news of the champagne party in the Dolomites on Sunday, May 13, five days after V-E Day. It was Karl Wolff's forty-fifth birthday; the royal palace at Bolzano was the SS commander's last headquarters. "The guests stood on the lawn of the palace, glasses in hand, as though this delightful sort of social occasion could go on forever," Allen related. "While they stood there, a loud rumbling was heard on the cobblestones of Bolzano. Shortly a convoy of two-and-a-half-ton trucks, belonging to the 38th Division of the American Fifth Army, lined up around the Palace." Wolff, Dollmann, Zimmer, and the other assembled figures of the Nazi SS in Italy were loaded onto the trucks and taken to a prisoner-of-war cage.

A fair judgment on Sunrise is that when it started late in February, the proposal for a surrender of the Nazi Italian front seemed a worthwhile opportunity to shorten the war and protect both the Renaissance art treasures and Italy's modern industrial treasures. At that time, no one knew that the European war was only three months from its conclusion. By mid-April, however, when even Wolff saw the disintegration of Nazi Germany as inevitable, what had started as a daring initiative for surrender had deteriorated into a mere technical arrangement between military staffs.

It was that April day in Paris, at the OSS briefings, that Allen first learned of the broader strategic significance of his foray into German surrender talks, as Donovan told him of the acrimonious Roosevelt-Stalin correspondence. He wrote long afterward: "As I thought over the Soviet attitude, I began to see what was probably troubling the Soviet leaders. If we were successful in getting a quick German surrender, Allied troops would be the first to occupy Trieste, the key to the Adriatic. If we failed, . . . then communist forces, either Soviet troops coming across

Hungary or Tito's followers reaching up out of Yugoslavia ... would be in Trieste or possibly west of there before we arrived."[13] At stake in Sunrise, as Allen finally came to perceive it, was where the future Iron Curtain would be drawn across the heart of Europe.

— * —

Granting the tendency of OSS veterans to trumpet their achievements (and conveniently forget their gaffes), the official record of Allen's Bern operation is nonetheless impressive. An accounting in a classified history written before the end of the war helps convey what a working network of intelligence sources in wartime actually looked like. "From a comparatively humble beginning, through cut-outs and subterfuge, means which we at this time [October 1944] can only guess," wrote the OSS historian, Allen managed to collect and report information from this array of sources:

- Anti-Nazi undergrounds: French, Italian, Polish, Austrian, Yugoslav, and German; pro-Allied groups of Bulgaria, Greece, Hungary, Belgium, Holland, and Czechoslovakia
- Pro-Allied sympathizers and double agents within the intelligence networks of the enemy
- "Old-time" politicians of various European nations
- Labor groups, both national and international
- Religious groups in many countries, particularly Germany
- Scientists and professors of various European nations
- Refugees and relief committees
- Diplomats and other official representatives of foreign governments in Switzerland.[14]

These are the filaments in the network Allen spun during his thirty months in Switzerland. Then, for overall impact, the OSS historian measured Bern alongside Istanbul and Stockholm, the other neutral points of access to the enemy. The Istanbul and Stockholm bases operated with more than fifty intelligence officers each. Stockholm recorded some successes, according to the British secret service; Istanbul, by contrast, "resulted in almost complete failure." It was Bern, according to the same British assessment, that came up with "the best intelligence source of the war" (George Wood). And Bern, under Allen, never had more than a dozen Americans on staff.

Allen's experiences in the spy capital of World War II defined his character and style for the rest of his life. The tasks of intelligence drew upon the best aspects of his skill as a diplomat and his training as a lawyer but liberated him from the routine tedium of those callings. He worked best as an intuitive loner; the minute he was surrounded by bureaucracy, he lost interest and stumbled. He was doing "something worthwhile in the world," but he did not have to explain himself to others at every turn. Duplicity was not actually a virtue, to his way of thinking, but it certainly could be useful, and if it was necessary for a worthwhile purpose, so be it.

"When in the course of his wartime work he had seemingly to violate any of the generally accepted ethical or moral values," Mary Bancroft wrote, "Allen knew precisely what he was doing and took responsibility for it." Allen, it seems safe to say, came to enjoy a life of intrigue and deception, both gross and petty. The boy from the Watertown manse had become a man capable of amiable encounter with the enemy and the devil; he learned to deal comfortably in perfectly bad faith, without ever violating a personal sense of moral rectitude and decency.

A nonchalant double standard infected his personal dealings as well. Clover was not the only woman he deceived. Allen described one such deception in his Bern memoir, which could be relegated to the petty or at least to *raison d'état*, but the person affected was Wally Toscanini Castelbarco, to whom he had become deeply attached. In the closing days of the war the partisan leader Ferruccio Parri was straining to be allowed to return to his antifascist cadres in Italy. His delivery to Allen's care as a good-will token by the Sunrise conspirators remained a tightly held secret; as far as the outside world knew, Parri was still languishing in a Nazi jail. One day Wally called upon Allen at his Bern office to plead for an OSS effort to rescue Parri. At that moment Allen knew, but the distraught Wally could not, that Parri was actually free, indeed, sitting in the next room. "It was hard for me to keep a straight face as I assured my eloquent and persuasive visitor that I was doing everything I could to save her friend," Allen wrote later. "I had quite a time of it explaining my deception." But he did it and reminisced about it without any sign of shame.

Allen never permitted Clover to share in his life of espionage, though she had come to Bern to be close to him. Their relationship these months was tempestuous; they had terrible fights, Mary recalled, "which Allen invariably won by the simple device of clamping an iron curtain down between them." At a vulnerable moment Clover wrote many years later in the diary that she left for her children, "My husband doesn't converse with me, not that he doesn't talk to me about his *business*, but that he doesn't talk about *anything*. . . . It took me a long time to realize that when he talks it is only for the purpose of obtaining something. . . . He talks easily with men who can give him some information, and puts himself out with women whom he doesn't know to tell all sorts of interesting things. He has either to be making someone admire him, or to be receiving some information worth his while; otherwise he gives one the impression that he doesn't talk because the person isn't worth talking to."

Clover was nonetheless there for Allen when he needed her as cover for secret encounters or the occasional personal discomfort. At the height of the Sunrise contacts, as Allen anxiously waited in Lucerne for word from General Wolff, he was seized by the most searing gout pains he had endured since the disarmament confrontations in the late 1930s. Without explanation, he summoned Clover from Bern. An OSS chauffeur drove her at breakneck speed through one sleepy Swiss village after another to her husband's bedside. There a suspicious Swiss doctor was persuaded that an injection of morphine would not be improper. Allen recovered the composure to resume his secret life, and Clover was driven back to her vigil in the Herrengasse.

— * —

Having found his métier, Allen was in no hurry to stop pursuing it after the surrender, though a pull from the opposite direction came once again. Foster, in San Francisco as an American adviser to the conference establishing the United Nations, reached his younger brother by telephone. "Come back to the firm," Foster pleaded for the dozenth time. "We'll clean up together. An awful lot of things are opening up. We'll clean up!"[15] Though Allen could never share his brother's excitement in the law, it was nice to know that he had a reserved berth on a first-class express.

Allen chose to stay at his post. The war in the Pacific was yet to be won against Japan, and the wreckage of Nazi Germany required a strong American hand of occupation. Allen saw to it that his services were in demand for both tasks.

Leaving Clover in Mary's loving care, he made a quick trip back to Washington in June to confer with Donovan about his immediate future, now that his Swiss networks were superfluous. Both at a stopover in London and at OSS headquarters, 110 was not at all displeased to find himself something of a star. Churchill received him personally, and the chief of British intelligence — all grievances from the Dansey era buried — hailed Allen as the "Kohinoor," crown jewel of the Allied secret services. His colleagues in Washington had long since accepted his coup with the George Wood documents, and Operation Sunrise gave him status as a local hero.

In the midst of his meetings with Donovan came word that his protégé, Parri, had been elected democratic Italy's first prime minister. In Parri, Allen assured his chief, "We will have an honest and true friend; . . . he naturally feels a deep sense of personal gratitude to me." Allen's visible pride may have strained Donovan's patience, as the equally proud founder of the OSS sensed a potential rival for future leadership of an intelligence service. Donovan called Allen "an artist of intelligence," adding the muted reservation that perhaps his organizational skills for running a large bureaucracy left something to be desired. The upshot of a few days of meetings in Washington was that Allen should remain in Europe, not as head of all OSS operations on the continent, as he had allowed himself to anticipate, but as head of the intelligence mission in occupied Germany.[16]

Returning to Bern, Allen found his little OSS company dispersing. His favorite colleague, the dashing Tracy Barnes, was the first to "demob," accepting a berth in a New England law firm and what he (wrongly) supposed was the end of his career in intelligence. Then, with Gaevernitz and Gisevius as his guides, the former 110 left for a first reconnaissance of the dismembered Third Reich on July 4, while Clover remained at the Herrengasse flat.

Scarcely had the trio set out by car through France than there came one of those unanticipated calls that made the life of an intelligence man so enticing. Allen's attentions were diverted momentarily back to the other theater where the war against fascism still raged, in the Pacific. An old friend from the community of international financiers, Swedish economist Per Jacobsson, had called at the OSS Bern office with a proposition just received from two Japanese representatives at the Bank for International Settlements. It amounted to the question of whether, within the formula of "unconditional surrender," Japan could retain its national symbol, the emperor.[17] Allen, learning of the approach while on the road, expressed skepticism, but after sleeping on it, he ordered Gaevernitz back to Bern to meet Jacobsson.

Gaevernitz tested Jacobsson and temporized, just as he had with the first Sunrise conspirators. Jacobsson, no stranger to the ways of secret contacts and go-betweens, finally asked coyly, "Have you never done or said anything without authorization?" Gaevernitz responded with the Sunrise tactic of asking that the Japanese contacts arrange for the release of ten high-ranking Allied prisoners of war. These contacts were not capable of responding as quickly as Wolff's men had in Italy; Jacobsson himself, however, had credibility with Allen from their long years in international finance together, as well as OSS dealings during the war. Allen received Gaevernitz's report at his new base in Wiesbaden and ordered his Bern staff to have Jacobsson driven there on July 14 to discuss the whole approach in person.

Travel for civilians was never easy in those early postwar days, and among the OSS travel documents hastily prepared for Jacobsson was a translation of his first name, Per, into French, which came back into English as "Reverend Father," giving the well-meaning economist pause.* Then, crossing into the debris of Germany's countryside, Jacobsson found himself waiting with a group of American GIs, who eyed the tall, burly Swede up and down until one finally made bold to say, "Another traveling Congressman, I presume!"

For eight hours into a hot July night Allen grilled his old friend about Japanese intentions, the feasibility of an early surrender before the Soviet Union declared war on Japan, and the possible longer-term implications of that action. Neither knew, of course, that two days later, on July 16, a powerful new explosive device would be successfully ignited at a secret test site in Alamogordo, New Mexico.

The new president, Harry Truman, was about to arrive in Potsdam, outside Berlin, for the first postwar meeting of the Allied Big Three. Allen put in a call to an old friend from the Council on Foreign Relations, Assistant Secretary of War John J. McCloy, who promptly arranged for Allen to fly to Potsdam to brief his boss, Henry L. Stimson, if not Truman personally, on this ambivalent Japanese approach. As Allen later discovered, the whole question of arranging a Japanese surrender, including the treatment to be accorded the emperor, was high on the Potsdam conference agenda.

It was July 20, 1945, one year to the day after the abortive bomb plot against Hitler, when an Army C-47 courier transport flew Allen into the destruction and debris of the city he had known as Berlin. The seventy-seven-year-old Stimson, for whom Allen had worked in his earlier life as a diplomat, gave a polite hearing to the story of Jacobsson's contacts, muttered something to the effect that the approach "fitted in with other intelligence he had received," but otherwise gave no instructions or encouragement to take back to Jacobsson. Allen left Potsdam just an hour later.

On August 6 the atomic bomb tested in New Mexico was dropped on the Japanese port city of Hiroshima. Years later Allen allowed himself the inevitable second thoughts about an intelligence operation that never came to fruition. On the American side he knew that full information of the approach to Jacobsson reached "authoritative quarters in a timely and, I believe, effective manner." But then he considered what had befallen Japan. "One wonders whether, if the Japanese negotiators had

---

* As he told his daughters years later, he decided to go through with the deception: "If I did have to baptize, marry and bury someone, I suppose I'd better go through with it — it can always be put right later."

come a little earlier and had been more clearly authorized to speak for their government, that explosion would have taken place."[18]

— * —

Germany after V-E Day was a shattered and sorry land, where little blond children competed for the teasings and chewing gum of friendly GIs, while their parents foraged for food and shelter amid the rubble left from relentless bombardment. Beyond that, the central purpose of daily life for Germans was the systematic obliteration of any association honest citizens might once have had with the now despised Nazis. Allen swung into action to try rehabilitating the "Good Germans" who had secretly served Allied intelligence during the war.

Eduard Schulte, the mysterious messenger of the Holocaust, presented the toughest challenge. Allen arranged for Schulte to return to Germany from Switzerland immediately after V-E Day to be available to the American occupation authorities as they attempted to rebuild a native German democracy. He was clearly a potential government minister for finance or industry. But it was not to be.

Anyone who secretly assists enemies of the country in which he goes about his daily life is bound to have ambiguities compounded on his record. Schulte had received a Nazi decoration in 1941.* Such eminence was troublesome to those in the American occupation charged with the "denazification" of Germany, unschooled as they were in the subtleties of resistance to a totalitarian regime. And then from Washington the Justice Department pursued hostile investigations into the ambiguous international status of the Silesian-American Corporation and Schulte's role in Giesche's foreign business.

Viewed from the German perspective, Schulte had committed — not to mince words — treason; quite a few Germans, including those professing hostility to the Nazis, were disturbed by that harsh reality. (The enduring power of such sentiments was one of the reasons that Schulte's contribution to the Allied war effort went so long unacknowledged.) Nor could Schulte justify himself, as did so many others, by showing his activism against Hitler — in the plots against Hitler's life, for instance — for all his deeds were secret and solitary.

Allen intervened repeatedly in his behalf, though he could not afford to be specific in recounting Schulte's deeds. "I was personally familiar with Dr. Schulte's activities and attitude," Allen wrote the denazification office in September 1945, "and can testify to the fact that he was pro-

---

* Actually, at the moment he received the award, he was on a visit to Switzerland providing information to the Allies.

foundly anti-Nazi and was exerting himself in every respect to bring about the downfall of the Nazi regime." That was as far as Allen felt he could go about 643's wartime activities, and it was not far enough. The American military government declined Schulte's services at any level.

Thus life for Eduard Schulte after the war was one of unrelieved frustration, personal and professional. When an old leg injury acted up in moments of tension, Allen managed to pass him a supply of penicillin, a rare commodity at the time. Schulte resigned himself to living in exile in Switzerland. His wife, Clara, had joined him from the comfort of their Breslau home, but she sank into depression on learning of the death of their elder son in a Russian POW camp. And when she learned about her husband's mistress, Doris, the marriage survived only in form. Upon Clara's death in 1955 Schulte quietly married Doris. Rejected by the emerging Federal Republic of Germany, hounded by American financial investigators, unknown to all the curious scholars and survivors of the Holocaust, Schulte died in Zurich in January 1966, aged seventy-five.*

Almost five years later, in December 1970, a West German court took up certain benefits claims of Doris Schulte and Eduard's surviving son, Ruprecht, who was making a happy new life with his family in southern California. Court investigators looked carefully into the records available to them. Schulte had played no role in the known conspiracies against the Nazi regime; his flight from Germany in 1943, the court ruled, was "not a political escape but the act of an agent who wanted to escape punishment and arrest." By passing information to the Allies, Schulte had committed a crime "punishable according to the law of every country." He was judged, in effect, a traitor, and no one of legal standing was left to take his part.

— * —

Kipling saw to it that his Kim understood the ambiguities of the Great Game from boyhood. Allen was well into middle age before the Game's inherent unfairness became real to him.

Contrasting with Schulte's uneasy fate was the postwar reputation of Hans Bernd Gisevius. This stiff mole of the Abwehr served his times and

* Dr. Riegner of the World Jewish Congress managed to meet his "mysterious messenger" face to face just once, as the war was ending, he recounted in interviews in 1980 and 1989. The Jewish official was eager to discuss the crucial episode in the discovery of the Holocaust in which they had both played their roles, but Riegner sensed that Schulte did not want to talk about anything he had done during the war. With the professional discretion of the intelligence business, the two men never discussed their previous indirect encounter. Riegner sent Doris Schulte a condolence message upon her husband's death.

history as a unique chronicler of the sordid Third Reich. Both in his reports to Allen and in his stormy testimony at the postwar Nuremberg trials of Nazi war criminals, he is the primary source for many of the stories of early Nazi corruption — capricious arrests and tortures by the Gestapo, Göring's and Himmler's kinky power plays with each other and everyone else. At Nuremberg the American prosecutor, Robert H. Jackson, called him "the representative of the German democratic forces," a wildly excessive claim, for Gisevius was neither a political force nor a democrat. Like Schulte, Gisevius was always outspoken in his personal contempt for Nazi pretensions; but unlike Schulte, his scorn rose not from any devotion to democratic society but from self-righteous snobbery against the coarse Nazi parvenus.

Gisevius helped Allen locate and assist the few survivors of the Breakers conspiracy. A Stauffenberg cousin, an obscure Luftwaffe sergeant, turned up in a British POW camp, overlooked in Hitler's sweep of vengeance against the families of those who had tried to kill him. Allen located Freya von Moltke, widow of Helmut, and assured her a steady supply of U.S. Army rations as she wrote her memoir of Moltke's resistance activities and his Silesian homestead under Russian and Polish occupation.[19]

In the first days after V-E Day Gaevernitz came upon Fabian von Schlabrendorff, architect of the failed assassination attempt of 1943, at an Allied detention camp on the island of Capri. Schlabrendorff had been arrested after the July 20 plot, though he had played no serious part in that conspiracy. He had been tortured and had gone on trial before the notorious "People's Court" judge Roland Freisler on February 3, 1945. As he stood handcuffed in the dock, an American bombing raid began, the heaviest daylight attack ever launched on Berlin. The court building suffered a direct hit; a heavy beam crashed from the ceiling onto the head of the presiding judge, crushing his skull and killing him on the spot. Schlabrendorff remembered seeing the docket of his own case in the dead judge's hand. The trial, perforce adjourned, was never resumed.[20]

In a throwback to his earlier life, Allen took pity on seventy-four-year-old Heinrich Albert, the prewar corresponding counsel of Sullivan and Cromwell in Berlin. Having narrowly escaped execution by the Gestapo, Albert was in broken health after years in solitary confinement, and Allen managed to have him named to a sinecure position of responsibility for captured properties.

Allen found Fritz Kolbe continuing his modest existence in Berlin — his "treachery" as George Wood never discovered by the Nazis. His career as a secret agent was over, of course, but even the ordinary life that followed served up its dangers. An American corporal driving Kolbe to a job interview at OSS headquarters smashed into a truck, fracturing his passenger's skull and breaking his jaw, three ribs, and his right ankle. Kolbe spent the first five weeks of victory against Nazi tyranny in traction at an American army hospital.

Kolbe never expected much from life, and he did not complain when nothing much came to him. As Europe and America settled into the postwar era, OSS veterans managed to set him up in the United States with $10,000 in capital and a few business contacts. "It was a honeymoon for Gerda and me," he reminisced. "New York is a wonderful place; America is so big and so abundant."[21] Within days the naive functionary lost all the money to a New York con man; he and Gerda decided they preferred the quiet life of their native Germany, with its soccer games and familiar surroundings. His death, like his life, was unreported.

The devoted network of Sunrise conspirators survived relatively well. Baron Parilli wasted no time after the surrender in making himself known to American military intelligence, and he maneuvered to keep the personal relationships of the network intact. His devotion to Zimmer endured all the tests; the young SS officer, after being easily cleared of war crimes charges, emigrated to Argentina, where his faithful baron set him up in business.

"Eugenio" Dollmann managed to escape from an American internment camp at Rimini, but unlike some harder-line SS veterans who fled to South America, he headed back to Milan, where longtime friends in church offices helped in his rehabilitation. He spent a luxurious few months in Rome under the protection and care of American intelligence operative James Angleton, who was working also with Parilli to build a new network for the United States against communist Russia. Ever unconnected and urbane in his personal life, Dollmann eventually returned to his old family home in Munich to pursue his artistic and historical interests and settle into the comfortable life of a worldly, cynical gentleman scholar.

General Wolff's postwar career was more troubled. Held for four years as a witness and potential defendant at the Nuremberg war crimes trials, he sank into depression and paranoia and had to be confined to a mental hospital. In 1949, largely on testimonials from Allen and Gaevernitz, he was acquitted of war crimes, but in 1962 the West German government resumed prosecution of officers implicated in the Holocaust. Documentary evidence came to light showing Wolff to be more knowledgeable about the death camps than he had let on, and a West German court sentenced him to fifteen years' confinement. He was released in the mid-1970s, established a comfortable retirement life in Munich, and appeared from time to time on television as the highest-ranking SS officer alive to tell a new generation about World War II.

— * —

One afternoon late in the summer of 1945, Allen drove through the Soviet-occupied sector of East Berlin to the Wilhelmplatz, his home in the early 1920s and the site of the old German Chancellery, where he had met with Hitler in 1933. Ignored by the Cossacks and Mongolians of the Red Army guarding the ruined premises of Hitler's last stronghold, Allen climbed through the wreckage of the Voss Strasse and came upon the notorious bunker where the führer had taken his life. The underground rooms were virtually untouched months after the deed. Allen stared at the small sofa on which Hitler had killed his mistress moments before his own suicide; the fabric was still marked by dark stains of dried blood. With scarcely a moment's pause to reflect on what he was seeing, the spymaster scooped up every piece of paper, every document he could find scattered through the bunker, for dispatch back to Washington and the analysts of intelligence and history.

Over the summer and into the fall Allen shuttled between his new base in Wiesbaden and the Herrengasse in Bern, where Clover awaited his periodic visits. Mary Bancroft had proved to be Clover's solace during these lonely times, stimulating her fascination with analytical psychology and the work of Dr. Jung. Allen had overcome his annoyance with Jung's clinical interests in the closing months of the war, and exchanged letters with the great doctor on the best use of psychological techniques for turning the German collective mind away from Nazism and toward a democratic future. Now, in Allen's absence, Clover was spending much of her time in Zurich, embarking upon a course of Jungian analysis that she would continue long after leaving Switzerland.

For Allen everything was tentative and uncertain. Hordes of new colleagues, military and OSS, swarmed over Germany and passed through Allen's Wiesbaden base on diverse missions. From France Allen's old friend and agent, Noel Field, turned up on mysterious errands that looked more and more like the biddings of Moscow. Even his sister Eleanor, who seemed to have a knack for showing up in Allen's life when least expected, arrived in Wiesbaden on an inspection tour; she was an economist working with the occupation administration in Austria. In one of those odd tangents of crossing lives, Allen laid on a lunch for his sister and Fritz Kolbe.

Two young Americans with whom Allen became particularly close during these weeks were just starting out on the life of intelligence that the three would share for the coming two decades: Navy Lieutenant Richard Helms, a thirty-two-year-old journalist who had been seconded to OSS service, and a former Wall Street lawyer named Frank Wisner, whose OSS team had been booted out of Romania by the occupying Soviets.

Donovan's wartime intelligence organization was crumbling in the uncharted territories of the postwar era. The year before, Donovan had proposed to President Roosevelt a plan to transform the OSS into a peacetime intelligence organization for the American republic, newly emerging as a world power. The dynamic Donovan had never gained the full confidence of official Washington, and a correspondent for the isolationist *Chicago Tribune* broke the story of Donovan's plan to an American public unaccustomed to such grandiose aspirations.*

President Truman was even less inclined than his predecessor toward anything like an "American Gestapo," and excesses within the OSS began coming to light with the easing of wartime secrecy. Field was not the only operative within the organization to be shown up as red-sympathizing, but hostile stories came out about corruption and personal venality as well; low-level OSS officers, it seemed, were running black-market rings in Germany, where anything could go. Just as with the peccadilloes of his financial friends in the 1930s, Allen regarded such charges as a terrible nuisance, the rotten apples inevitable in any barrel. Learning of one blatant case, that of an OSS major arrested in Berlin at the luxurious villa he had made his own (along with the wife of a missing German banker, a liveried butler, and a chess set made of platinum), Allen grumbled to aides demanding prosecution, "No evidence. You can't condemn a man without evidence."[22]

On September 20, 1945, President Truman abruptly abolished the Office of Strategic Services, forfeiting for the United States a coordinated intelligence capacity for peacetime. OSS bases in a dozen capitals of Europe, Africa, and the Middle East were closed down. While British intelligence was at work recruiting agents and networks in Germany for future clandestine services, Allen was ordered to make no "formal postwar commitments." Helms and Wisner were two of Allen's men who decided to hang on in military intelligence, but their boss saw no future for himself in government.

* A generation of CIA professionals was convinced that the damaging leak had come from the FBI and Donovan's longtime rival, J. Edgar Hoover. When a CIA historian finally got the *Tribune* correspondent, Walter Trohan, to admit his source, however, the heirs to the Donovan tradition were dismayed to be told that it was Roosevelt's press secretary, Steve Early, who had leaked the ambitious intelligence plan, saying, "FDR wanted the story out": see Thomas F. Troy, *Donovan and the CIA* (Frederick, Md.: University Publications of America, 1981), p. vi.

Late in October Allen picked up his wife in Switzerland, and they began the trip home together. Stopping for a brief holiday in Rome, they met Angleton, who, like Helms and Wisner, had decided to stay on in military counterintelligence. Both Allen and Clover found Angleton immensely attractive and pleasant company; their friendship — personal and professional — endured for the rest of their lives.

Harry Truman's Washington was not hospitable to a personage of Allen's stature in clandestine service, especially the prominent brother of the even more prominent Republican foreign policy adviser. After a few weeks of searching around the bureaucracy, Allen wrote Gaevernitz, who was resuming his prewar business ventures in Germany, that he found "the sands were too shifting to offer any firm foundation, or assurance of ability to do constructive, useful work." On December 7, 1945, Allen Dulles resigned from government service for the second time in his career. After the first time, in 1926, it was sixteen years before he returned to a public career. This time, not four years would pass before Allen was back in the Great Game.

— 11 —

ATTORNEY IN WAITING

BACK HOME ON SIXTY-FIRST STREET and in his old Sullivan and Cromwell office, Allen remarked what an appalling thing it was, after heading a spy network, to pretend interest in corporate indentures. To only one aspect of his resumed peacetime career was he attracted: the money to be made. John Foster Dulles, the enterprising senior partner, was said to be taking in upward of $300,000 each year, while lesser lights of the firm, like Allen, could claim at least half that. Though desiring the high lifestyle of his brother and partners, Allen was bored beyond endurance at what they had to do to earn it.

As he reviewed the briefs prepared by the firm's young associates, Allen carried on nostalgic correspondence with wartime comrades, including Field Marshal Alexander, elevated to the House of Lords as a viscount, and General Lemnitzer, back in Washington on his way to the Joint Chiefs of Staff. "I must admit that these days I find it hard to concentrate on my profession of the law," he wrote. "Most of my time is spent reliving those exciting days when the war was slowly dying."

At fifty-two Allen found it necessary to trade the role of man-in-action for the pose of the benevolent, pipe-smoking uncle holding forth in a richly carpeted office, walls lined with books. Visitors gained access by the partners' elevator after passing portraits of famous Sullivan and Cromwell clients. His office was appropriately smaller than Foster's, but visitors found a far more amiable welcome. Chatting and listening for two hours at a time, as if he had nothing else to do (and perhaps, by choice, he didn't), Allen had lost none of his seductive charm. Legal colleagues knew that both Dulles brothers were cold and calculating on the job, but as one associate, Louis Auchincloss, compared them, "Allen knew exactly the impression he was making on a visitor; Foster didn't care."[1]

Future great names of America's intelligence service were among the reverent callers to Allen's suite: Kermit "Kim" Roosevelt, grandson of Theodore, collecting stories for an official history of the OSS;[2] Tracy Barnes, reliving the days with Countess Ciano; Richard Helms, bringing news of Germany. Frank Wisner reported that he had angrily abandoned intelligence when his army superiors in the German occupation regime refused him the petty cash to buy bicycles for the agents he was running in the Russian zone of Germany. Per Jacobsson and Royall Tyler passed through New York; Jacobsson had been named managing director of the International Monetary Fund, and Tyler was to be head of the Paris office of the World Bank.

Old friends like these would complement the dinner parties on Sixty-first Street or join the gentlemen's lunches on Wall Street. After one such, the investment banker Prescott Bush remembered Allen fondly: "He entertained us beautifully, as only he could. We thought afterwards how much fun it was to get on the 'inside' of things. And yet, when he was gone, we discovered that he had really told us nothing, but nothing." Allen's social skills served him well for years to come.

The revelations of Operation Sunrise had established his stature for the public at large, where previously he had been a shadowy figure. Isolated voices were heard to regret that all the talent mobilized in war seemed to be drifting away from government into private life. Walter Lippmann, at the height of his influence as a syndicated columnist, wrote: "They are being allowed to leave Washington because their specific war jobs are more or less finished. Yet at this moment there is the job of making peace, a job for which their experience in the war has been an excellent preparation. It is the height of folly not to use them."*

Allen could only welcome the sentiments of his old friend from the Peace Conference, but they were clearly alien to Harry Truman's Washington, where demobilization was the more popular cause. And for one with the suspiciously Republican name of Dulles, the most that the Truman administration was willing to offer Allen in 1946 was a short-term mission to China to negotiate an aviation treaty. Allen was sorely tempted; "a first-hand knowledge of postwar China would be of real value," he wrote Foster, then on his own diplomatic mission in Europe. The senior partner vetoed the idea, replying that one brother absent on government business was quite enough.†

---

* Allen clipped this column and filed it with his papers of December 1945.
† China, and Asia in general, was thus remote from Allen's awareness of public policy during the controversies of the communist takeover in the late 1940s. His was an era when it was still appropriate for an informed American to be "Eurocentric."

Shortly after his return to New York at the end of 1945, Allen was elected president of the Council on Foreign Relations. The remodeled Harold Pratt house became the base for his intellectual operations in addressing the issues of the day. Foreign statesmen, prominent Americans, and less prominent persons of substance and influence would gather for discussion evenings in the book-lined studies at Park Avenue and Sixty-eighth Street. Ham Armstrong and Allen would confer endlessly across Armstrong's heavy oak desk about editorial decisions for *Foreign Affairs*. At the council's study groups, Armstrong could identify potential authors and persuade them to put their remarks on the record. In those years the council was a school for statesmen, not only a think tank for ideas; its exclusive membership offered a reservoir of talent for future government postings.

The Dulles brothers were well known to at least a select public in those first postwar years, but in different ways. Publicly and privately they spent much time together, not just in the office but in discussion circles around the city where great issues were pondered and digested for the speeches and interviews given to the public. Foster was the chief foreign policy adviser to Thomas E. Dewey, the Republican challenger for the presidency in 1944 and expected to run against Harry Truman in 1948. Given Truman's still modest stature, Dewey would surely win the election and, just as surely, Foster would be his secretary of state. As the leading Republican voice on foreign policy, therefore, Foster was included by the Truman administration on delegations to international conferences, a gesture to bipartisanship.

No one seemed to think of Allen as a potential secretary of state. His stature was less that of a public figure than an influence within the establishment. As president of the Council on Foreign Relations and with an imposing roster of foreign connections, he was a force to be reckoned with as the consummate insider, party affiliation aside.

From the start Allen used the council to promote his ideas about the "Good Germans," inviting speakers and directing discussions of a new, less punitive German policy. He well understood that his background with international legal and financial interests would make his views questionable. "Both you and I are somewhat suspect," he wrote a colleague, "as allegedly representing 'predatory' interests but, if we could get some people who reflected the views of labor and possibly the churches to join with us, we might be in a better position to get our views over."

Tilting precariously at the public mood in his speeches and correspondence, Allen criticized the belief that rooting out Nazis took priority over efforts to rebuild the German economy. He argued that the Good Germans, courageous men who had tried to resist Nazi bigotry, however

ineffectively, should be encouraged, and could become the future leaders
of a democratic nation. "If we are ever to rescue anything out of the
semi-chaos in what was once Germany, it is useful to counteract the fairly
deep-seated impression in this country that in this whole area there had
been nothing but gangsters and SS men. . . . There was a very considerable group of men who risked and, for the most part, lost their lives, and
while I do not sympathize with all the political views or motives which activated them, still their story deserves to be told."[3]

Gero von Schulze-Gaevernitz joined in the campaign for the Good
Germans. Secure in his American citizenship, Gaevernitz had stayed in
Switzerland, working to rehabilitate the German political contacts he had
brought to the OSS during the war, to say nothing of old business associates who might be worthy partners in obtaining lucrative contracts from
the American occupation. He compiled a card file of German personages
who should, and those who should not, be consulted by the occupation
authorities. On one hand, Gaevernitz wrote Allen, Americans "consider
all Germans, whether Nazis or anti-Nazis, guilty." The Germans, by contrast, considered any of their countrymen who had been willing to work
with the Allies as traitors. He warned of a "new wave of nationalism" in
Germany and pressed the view that "unless we are prepared to give the
fullest support to the truly democratic forces in Germany the country will
sooner or later come again under the control of totalitarian elements, en-
tailing disastrous consequences for the whole of Europe." Gaevernitz was
also upset at the American "failure to encourage the resumption of German export trade"; it was scarcely coincidental that the cause of the Good
Germans and business interests could be pursued at the same time.

The indomitable Gisevius, Allen's best source on the July 20 conspiracy, deserved—and fully expected—careful handling. Allen arranged
for him to meet the American prosecutor at the war criminal trials at
Nuremberg, Supreme Court Justice Robert Jackson, in the comfort of
the Rosenhof, above Salzburg, to prepare Gisevius's explosive testimony
against the Nazi leaders and thereby establish the credentials of another
Good German.[4]

As an exception to conspiracy theories about an axis between Wall
Street and German industry, Allen's roster of Good Germans included
socialists.* "We should not be disturbed at, in fact, we should welcome, a
liberal and leftist-oriented Germany," Allen declared, defying his Republican Party's orthodoxy. "Socialists in Europe have not been great trav-

* Eugen Gastenmaier and Kurt Schumacher, leading figures in the postwar Social Democratic Party, came in for Allen's special attentions.

ellers and we have had relatively little opportunity of getting in contact with them," he explained. "As a result, we are inclined to start out with a totally false approach toward the socialists of Europe." They were really nothing more than Democrats, he suggested.

To make sure he did not lose his audience with views too unfashionable, Allen prefaced all his attentions to the Good Germans with fervent denunciations of the fallen Nazis. Berlin, scene of his own youthful experience and now destroyed, was his chosen symbol. "Berlin, like Carthage, has represented the spirit of destructive conquest," he wrote in *Collier's* magazine. "It has lost its right to be the capital of the Germany of the future." For all his personal memories of the Wilhelmplatz, Allen proposed that the half-mile circle around Hitler's Chancellery should be forever left in its bombed-out condition of rubble and destruction, "as a perpetual memorial to the Nazis and to Prussia."*

On September 6, 1946, Secretary of State James F. Byrnes delivered a major speech in Stuttgart, signaling the reversal of priorities: the drive for rapid and wholesale denazification — a quixotic enterprise at best — would give way to cooperative engagement to build a new democratic Germany.† Allen cheered the Truman administration's new attitude when business friends complained of the continuing dismantling of Germany's industrial plants. Allen replied, "This is a foolish procedure and I hope we are beginning to realize it."

Out of Allen's campaign for the Good Germans came what stands decades later as the best of his six books, *Germany's Underground*, published in March 1947. For the impact of the message as well as for its author's ego, Allen dared to hope for a bestseller. Through terse narrative and colorful detail known only to those within intelligence, Allen told of the men (not many women in his book) of the anti-Nazi resistance, stories that the American public had heard only vaguely before. Allen was uncharacteristically modest about his own role concerning the conspira-

* Though it was none of Allen's doing, to be sure, something of that design came about. Most of the Nazi landmarks fell into the Soviet sector of East Berlin and along the no man's land where communist East Germany eventually built a forbidding wall to separate the two halves of the city. The site of the Chancellery and Foreign Ministry, the Wilhelmplatz remained in rubble and vacant lots for four decades of the Cold War, dotted only by new gray blocks of Soviet-style construction. The Wilhelmplatz no longer exists as such, though at its location now stands the dreary East Berlin U-Bahn station of Mohrenstrasse.
† Forty years after the speech, Horst Teltschik, foreign policy adviser to the West German chancellor, Helmut Kohl, declared that the Stuttgart speech "finally put paid to American plans for a Punic peace for Germany" (*Deutsches Allgemeines Sonntagsblatte*, reprinted in *German Tribune* 1244, Sept. 21, 1986).

tors of July 20, unlike the self-congratulatory accounts of Operation Sunrise that he encouraged and later wrote himself. *Germany's Underground* conveyed a message of tolerance and appreciation for the Germans who survived the Nazi aberration. "It is the first factual publication since the end of World War II which has the courage to point out that there are good Germans," wrote one of his OSS colleagues after receiving a complimentary copy from the author.

The book was a flop. The American public was obviously not interested in reliving the intrigues of the war or learning about Germans who did not fit their ugly stereotype. Three short months after publication Allen complained to his publisher that no copies of *Germany's Underground* were to be had, even in New York. "Our salesmen have been all over the city trying to sell it," his editor at Macmillan replied. "We just can't make the booksellers buy the book. . . . I am afraid we are going to have a substantial overstock."

— * —

Allen dedicated *Germany's Underground* to Clover: "To C.T.D., for her unfailing help and encouragement." Clover replied with the gentle barb of a woman patronized: "Accept dedication with pride, if you mean beds I made, dinners I cooked, midnight excursions I undertook." Her response came in a transatlantic cablegram, for by the turn of 1947 Allen and Clover Dulles were living apart. It was not a formal separation, nor was there any talk of divorce. It was simply that after their first postwar year together, Clover saw herself shut out of her husband's interests in the law and public affairs just as she had been in Bern. Her consuming interest was the psychology of Dr. Jung, a realm different from anything Allen knew. Accordingly, in January 1947 she returned to Switzerland — *her* Switzerland, this time — to resume her study of Jungian psychology. Allen took off on a bachelor vacation in the Caribbean even before Clover left.

Between Allen and Clover was a wall of interests not shared and Allen's inability to communicate, except on the most superficial level. But there was also something else in those first months back in New York: Wally Castelbarco happened to be stopping over in the city. Barely a month after V-E Day, Allen had intervened through official channels to speed the visa process for the glamorous daughter of Maestro Arturo Toscanini to rejoin her father in America. Such diplomatic courtesy was fully deserved, given Wally's wartime services to the Italian resistance and the OSS. But when Allen himself returned, he was delighted to find Countess Castelbarco in New York and not at all reluctant to resume the relationship they had enjoyed in Switzerland. This phase of their relationship lasted less than six months. The countess soon determined to return to Milan to escape the smothering affections of an overbearing and temperamental father. But her stay was long enough for Clover to see that Allen was having an affair with Wally, and so did their older daughter.

Toddy, by then twenty-four, had graduated from Bennington, and though she was living a high-spirited New York life, she was uncomfortable that her father could carry on in this way. Toddy loved her mother and her father too (little as she knew him); she also admired Wally Castelbarco. "Of course, I did not approve of what they were doing," she confided many years later, "but if any woman can be called a lady while she is having an affair with a married man, Wally was that lady."[5]

The younger daughter, Joan, was more successful in coping with maturity and absentee parents — mainly by making herself also an absentee. After graduating from Radcliffe in 1945, she had visited her parents in Bern. When Allen and Clover left for home that autumn, Joan stayed on in Europe with Aunt Eleanor in Vienna. Joan had met a blond and attractive young Austrian named Fritz Molden, and they traveled together through the grim Soviet zone of Austria; he seemed very friendly with officers of the American occupation and was clearly on the way up in Viennese journalism. Molden knew that his new friend was the daughter of his OSS spymaster, and gradually Joan became aware that this dashing Austrian had been one of her father's top agents in the resistance. The couple entered upon a tempestuous relationship, with Eleanor as sympathetic chaperon. It ended, Joan thought, when she abruptly decided to leave Vienna and return home to graduate school at Harvard. Then, unexpectedly, Molden appeared in America and proposed marriage; Joan accepted. Allen had known nothing of this romance, but he was happy to give his daughter's hand to one of his favorite agents. Joan's marriage to Molden ended after six years, but Allen had no problem continuing to work on intelligence matters in Austria with his former son-in-law, just as they had done before Joan entered the picture.

It was Allen's third child and only son, Allen Macy Dulles, who suffered most from his parents' itinerant life. Young Allen went home from boarding school to the care of three servants while his mother stayed in Switzerland with her husband. The family was briefly reunited in New York for the 1945 Christmas vacation after Clover and Allen returned from Europe, but then Allen returned to Exeter, where one of the masters called him "the brightest student I ever had."

A schoolboy's loneliness shows through the guarded letters exchanged with his father during his final year at prep school, but Allen senior was never able to find the delicate line between encouraging and pressuring a son. After young Allen was named the best speaker in a school debate on China, his father wrote from his law office, "It seems to me that you took a constructive line in a situation which I must admit is far from clear. . . . Is there anything we should be doing about making sure that you can get into Princeton?" Allen congratulated his son on winning a one-hundred-dollar Latin prize. "We are all proud of you and suggest you hold this money and spend it in some special way. . . . However, it will be yours to deal with as you see fit." Mindful of the proprieties, the proud father sent a hundred-dollar contribution to the Exeter scholarship fund.

The son tried hard to keep his father's attention by writing precise letters about world affairs. In return Allen sent him press clippings about his speaking appearances and a copy of *Germany's Underground*, with reviews. The boy well knew how much his father enjoyed long working dinners with Hamilton Fish Armstrong, so for his fifty-fourth birthday, young Allen sent a poignant greeting: "I hope that you and Mr. Armstrong get together on your birthday to have a good time."

Allen was accepted into Princeton for the fall of 1947. He completed his degree requirements in three years, then went off to Balliol College, Oxford, to write a thesis on political science. With the outbreak of the Korean War in 1950, he enlisted in the Marines; his sisters look back on that decision as his way to demonstrate that he had indeed "toughened up." Uncle Foster maneuvered to get him a pleasant temporary duty after he completed basic training at Quantico; one weekend Allen booked a room for his son at the Metropolitan Club, but regretted that he would be away on business when the young Marine was passing through. With a tragedy looming that neither could foresee, father and son never again had occasion to spend any meaningful time together.

— * —

In January 1947 an obscure newsletter from an organization calling itself the Society for the Prevention of World War III began circulating around New York and Washington; it attracted attention for the explosiveness of its charges. Allen Dulles, the newsletter said, had represented pro-Nazi business interests in the years before, and even possibly after, the outbreak of World War II. Evidence was the list of German clients who had retained Sullivan and Cromwell in the 1930s, plus Allen's place on the board of the J. Henry Schroder Banking Corporation of New York, which was allied with the London house of Schröder, called a pro-Nazi firm with close ties to the notorious Baron Kurt von Schröder, then under indictment at Nuremberg as a war criminal. The strains of the last prewar years within Sullivan and Cromwell were brought out in a light that made Allen look like a Nazi apologist.

Among the incidental pieces in the newletter's evidential puzzle was the fact that while serving the OSS in Switzerland, Allen had met frequently with "a Dr. Schulte," representative of mighty German mining interests in Upper Silesia. True enough, and interesting that the newsletter's sources knew of those meetings. What they did not know, of course, was the intelligence about the Holocaust and the Nazi eastern front that Schulte had provided Allen and the U.S. government. Building up its case that international capital and the long-standing corporate interests of Wall Street and Germany were again at work together to surmount the setbacks of the Nazi downfall, the newsletter asked rhetorically "if it is purely coincidental . . . that Allen Dulles should be found in the vanguard of those who advocate the rehabilitation of Germany's industrial potential?"

Allen was livid at the collection of half-truths and innuendos in the obscure tract. To get to the bottom of the matter, he engaged a private detective he had known in the OSS New York office to look into this "Society for the Prevention of World War III." The old safecracker, pursuing his wartime skills at what they called surreptitious entry, reported back that a "brief examination" of the society's files revealed the financial backers to be certain European refugees who, if not "actual communists" had "sponsored extremely liberal views." This sort of loose talk was not what Allen considered intelligence, and he promptly terminated the investigation.

Then the liberal Democratic senator Claude Pepper of Florida repeated some of the charges, and Allen put out a public statement of rebuttal. Sullivan and Cromwell had been "for many years counsel of J. Henry Schroder Banking Corporation, a highly respected New York banking institution, in which the London Schröder family have a large stock interest. . . . We are not counsel for Schröder of London," Allen stated. But, he said, neither of these venerable banks had close connections with the Nazis.

> The Nazi Schröder was a distant relative of one of the partners of the London firm. Neither I nor my firm has ever had any dealings, direct or indirect, of any nature whatsoever, with this Kurt von Schröder, nor have we seen the man. . . . It is pushing innuendo rather far to impute moral guilt to an American lawyer, for giving advice about American law to an American banking institution, merely because it is related to a British firm which, like most New York banking houses, had, as part of its normal business, some German transactions during the prewar period.

Nonetheless a Moscow propaganda paper, *New Times*, picked up the newsletter's charges a month after their airing in New York and Washington, and they were repeated periodically from then on. And within the United States, as party politics took hold, Democratic candidates kept alive the notion of alleged pro-Nazi interests of the Dulles brothers.

— * —

Allen, in demand on the lecture circuit, was also pulled into service as legal adviser to a committee of the new United Nations that was seeking a permanent headquarters site. "I would prefer the location to be in Europe," he told a Connecticut audience in February 1946, "near its first great problems."[6] Delegates to the U.N. General Assembly, then meeting in London, decided otherwise, voting for an interim headquarters in New York City, to be followed by a permanent site in nearby Westchester or Fairfield, Connecticut. (In fact, of course, the United Nations never left Manhattan.)

The central issue looming for American foreign policy was the future of relations with Soviet Russia. Allen had been pondering this problem ever since the year with Charles Seymour and Walter Lippmann at the Paris Peace Conference. During his World War II operations Allen kept the faith of Roosevelt and Churchill in preserving the Grand Alliance with Stalin. He gave no evident encouragement to his contacts within the German resistance who pleaded for a truce on the western front so that the Nazi war machine could be turned against the alleged common enemy to the east. In four-power Berlin just after the war Allen admitted enjoying some camaraderie with Soviet officers. "There wasn't great prospect that our actual theories of government and of society were being blended," he assured an inquiring American, but "there existed a fair measure of collaboration and good humor as between the Russians and the Westerners."

Just one minor development presaged what was to come. In April 1945, one month before V-E Day, Allen had learned from Fritz Kolbe of an obscure German intelligence officer on the eastern front, General Reinhard Gehlen, who was interested in turning over his massive anti-Soviet intelligence files to the Americans, confident that they would soon be called into use. Allen paid little attention to the idea, at the time.

During those last months the OSS had come across captured Nazi documents identifying anticommunist cells that were to be left behind in Balkan lands occupied by the Red Army. With Donovan's authority Allen offered to share this intelligence with his Soviet counterparts. The reply was "reasonably courteous," Allen reported, requesting that the information be submitted in writing to Red Army headquarters. Allen and Donovan agreed that such sensitive matters could be discussed only in a face-to-face meeting between intelligence professionals. That ended the matter. "It was clear that they had no desire for any meeting," Allen concluded and, further, that "in the field of intelligence, no business could be done with the Soviets." Once back in his office at Sullivan and Cromwell, Allen heard stories from one of his former officers, Peter Sichel, about the machinations of Russian agents to solidify Moscow's control in central Europe.

As a private citizen Allen was free to examine the Soviet problem in terms more lofty than those of operational intelligence. In the spring of 1946 Churchill paid Truman the honor of a visit to a small college town in the president's home state; at Fulton, Missouri, the former British prime minister warned of an "Iron Curtain" descending across the middle of Europe. Shortly thereafter Foster showed Allen a draft of his tentative thoughts about the Soviet threat and about how the United States might find an "accommodation" with Russia. Foster wondered whether differences with the Russians had been recently "created" or merely "revealed." For Allen, barely settled into his tedious law practice, discussing a pressing world issue was a welcome break. On May 14 he gave Foster a memorandum of his half-digested ideas. For all their spontaneity, they were ideas with an enduring power that neither of the Dulleses could at that moment imagine.

The "difference between us," Allen wrote, is that "you hold out the hope of some satisfactory accommodation being possible between the Soviet system . . . and the rest of the democratic world. I doubt this."[7] There need be no immediate confrontation, Allen hastened to assure; rather, the West should seek to "gain time within which a gradual change may produce a different kind of Russian government and social structure with which a permanent accommodation is possible." This was a novel idea at the time, so Allen felt it necessary to explain. "The fact that the dictatorship of the Communist Party has existed in Russia for almost thirty years does not necessarily mean that it will last forever. . . . Personally, I am inclined to feel that so long as Soviet Russia enforces . . . the policy of suppression of all liberties, they will consider that the existence of such liberties anywhere in the world is, as you more or less state, a menace to their system and therefore something to be fought to the end."

But there might be a more viable strategy than Foster's proposed "accommodation." Allen went on:

> There may be a method of insulating the two systems; I doubt whether there is a method of reconciling the two systems. . . . We may be able to achieve a measure of insulation sufficient to keep the peace for a considerable period of time, and it is always possible that during such period the Soviet system will undergo some fundamental change which will mean that liberty, rather than repression, will be the world-wide rule.

I see no objection, in fact I have always favored, sitting down with the Russians and seeing whether there was any basis of settling territorial issues, giving them better access to the sea and any necessary military protection if a way can be found to do this without it being another Munich appeasement.

I favor this because I feel that if we can have a period of a number of years of peace, Russia, whether it likes it or not, will be brought so closely in touch with the rest of the world that a modification of the communist system will result, which will mean that the liberties existing in the rest of the world will also be introduced into Russia.

The label Allen chose for a profound strategy was "insulation." Seven months later a promising Soviet specialist of the Foreign Service, on sabbatical at the National War College, set about independently to convey the same concept: that the Soviet system might evolve in a benign way if the democratic West would provide the time and space for history to do its work. Instead of "insulation" he called the strategy "containment."

The scholarly diplomat, George Kennan, presented his formulation at a Council on Foreign Relations study group. Ham Armstrong was in attendance, and he wrote Kennan a few days later to suggest that his ideas be developed into an article for *Foreign Affairs*. Kennan was ready to oblige, but between the submission of his manuscript and its publication he was named director of the State Department Policy Planning Staff; any statement under his name could be construed as official policy. Armstrong's managing editor proposed that the article be signed "X," and so it was, in July 1947.

"Containment" became the code word for United States policy toward communism for the next four decades. Kennan had no idea when he wrote the *Foreign Affairs* article that it would be so enduring — indeed, he spent subsequent decades trying to explain the subtleties of what he meant while he was "hacking away at his typewriter" (as he later described himself) in a corner office of the War College. Both doves and hawks of the Cold War poured out printers' ink explaining the inadequacies of containment, though they could come up with nothing better. History and rhetoric must constantly submit to review. George Kennan had a sense of literary style that his friend and colleague Allen Dulles never achieved. If containment moved generations, both pro and con, would anyone have chosen to plant the American flag on insulation?

Allen had no pride of authorship; he had filed away his memo to Foster without further efforts to develop insulation in any more compelling form. But once Kennan went public, Allen spotted a better job of conceptualizing than his own halting prose and rushed to embrace containment as a strategy for the United States against Soviet communism.

For doves critical of the concept, containment implied a militaristic posture, a determination that dominoes should not fall, that communist advances, wherever and whatever their origins, be met by force and reversed. This was not, in their view, a worthy American purpose in the world. On the other side, particularly in the heyday of "rolling back the Iron Curtain" in the early 1950s, Kennan's containment seemed too mild a strategy for asserting the primacy of the Free World. Why should the West settle for mere containment instead of striving for overthrow?

The most eloquent criticism of Kennan's concept came from Walter Lippmann, who declared "Mr. X's" idea to be "fundamentally unsound." Over a dozen of his columns Lippmann argued that the United States could never deploy sufficient military power to sustain a policy of containment at any point on the globe where the monolithic Soviet system might choose to advance. Surely not, but Kennan had never meant to suggest that communism had to be contained militarily.* The essential point was to keep the two opposing political systems apart, "insulated" from each other, to avoid military confrontation and allow the communist system time to decay from within.

Allen was one of the few who grasped this essence more clearly than Kennan himself had expressed it. In his various speeches after the "X" article, Allen avoided advocating any military action in pursuit of containment. Indeed, he argued, Soviet military aggression was not the primary threat: it was rather Moscow's ideological and political aggressiveness that the Free World should contain. "The Soviet Union does not want war with the United States," Allen told a meeting of New York businessmen. "The Russians, by means short of war, will exert themselves to destroy the capitalist system in Europe, and hence to win this particular contest now going on." The Cold War, in Allen's words, would be fought by "maneuver and pressure," not by force of arms in battle.

Military strategists and those used to traditional warfare thought they understood the terms "maneuver" and "pressure" as they had been used by battlefield generals since the wars of ancient Greece. But Allen and

---

* On the occasion of his ninetieth birthday in February 1994, Kennan told the Council on Foreign Relations that he had viewed containment as "primarily a diplomatic and political task, though not wholly without military implications. I considered that, if and when we had succeeded in persuading the Soviet leadership that the continuation of these expansionist pressures not only held out for them no hopes for success but would be, in many respects, to their disadvantage, then the moment would have come for serious talks with them about the future of Europe."

others of the emerging Kennan school meant something quite different; it was *political* maneuver and "pressure that had to be applied against the communist system. They began calling it "political warfare." As the American government regrouped after World War II, Allen was among a small band of political practitioners who understood that the government had no mechanisms, no established agencies or battalions in place, to conduct this new and unfamiliar form of Cold War.

— * —

Allen sailed to Europe on the *Queen Elizabeth* in April 1947 for business meetings with Sullivan and Cromwell's prospective international clients and for academic conferences to further the research projects of the Council on Foreign Relations. He had not seen his wife since January and, for all his petulance on her departure, he showed signs of missing her. It would not do to rush straightaway to Zurich, where Clover was engrossed in her Jungian studies, so Allen paused in London for meetings with Arnold Toynbee and took a leisurely side trip to Oxford "at its loveliest" for mellow conversations in the common room of All Souls, where matters of import could be considered over port and cigars.

Then came a sentimental return to Germany, to seek out and encourage his Good Germans as they struggled with the bureaucracy and suspicions of the American occupation authorities. With Gisevius and Kolbe Allen could have normal reunions. But he also took upon himself the task of contacting the widows and fatherless children of men he had never met, the conspirators of July 20. At this point even Allen succumbed to the need for emotional support.

On an impulse — or perhaps he had slyly planned it this way all along — he called Zurich to tell Clover that he needed her by his side. This was the message she had been waiting for through all the unhappy years of marriage. She dropped her studies and hurried north; together she and Allen roamed the German countryside in the weeks of May, following leads to the families of the anti-Nazi martyrs, most of them hanging on in a destitution even greater than that of ordinary Germans. The occupation authorities still had no sensitivity to subtle differentiations among the conquered populace, and the German people could not overcome their ambivalence toward countrymen who had been courageous enough to confront the Nazis. Ilse von Hassell, widow of the German ambassador to Italy, who would have been foreign minister had the July 20 coup succeeded, echoed Anne Morrow Lindbergh in writing rapturously of Clover's "kind eyes" and her capacity for understanding, which only "strengthened my belief that a spiritual link in the midst of vanishing material values will be the only hope for this world."

This trip of reunion was important; at last Allen had invited Clover to share in his working life, however briefly. Intellectual and passionate women like Mary Bancroft and Wally Castelbarco had been fine company, contributing useful ideas and comforts to "clear his head" when matters of state and politics consumed his daily life. But in dealing with real people whose emotional needs even Allen could recognize as legitimate, he needed Clover. And Clover was there to be needed.

In the years and decades to come, Allen would not often again invite Clover into his working concerns, nor did she need as much to be included. Allen's official life came to involve secrets of state, problems that wives did not expect to share; women attached to men in secret careers know better than to press too hard about what goes on in the office. As for Allen's personal interests, he continued to be attracted to various witty, well-born ladies, including a reigning queen and a powerful ambassador, but these were discreet and passing flirtations of no import or threat. As far as their intimate friends could tell, Clover and Allen talked no more of separation; rather, as mature adults, their dependency upon each other only grew.

From their German springtime they came home to the university commencement season. The Dulles family assembled on June 16 in Providence, where Allen was awarded an honorary degree from Brown, citing his "vast energy, the infinite resourcefulness, the sweep of imagination, the flawless discretion, and rare discrimination in reporting . . . wartime diplomatic intelligence work of the highest order." At the equivalent ceremony at Columbia, William Donovan was commended as "leader and tactician in the silent war of secret intelligence, directing with imagination and deadly efficiency the men who fought in the shadows across the world." To a friend in the academic procession, Donovan remarked, "Well, they've finally made intelligence respectable."

And at Harvard's commencement that June, Secretary of State George C. Marshall delivered a formidable policy proposal: a program of massive American financial aid to the hopeless millions of Europe, with a view to long-term economic reconstruction. It was an idea that began to focus American energies on the unfamiliar tasks of a world no longer at war but not yet at peace.

From that 1947 commencement season thus came a vision for postwar statecraft: economic reconstruction abroad and the building of a national security apparatus at home, including something for which Americans had not yet perceived a need — an efficient, imaginative intelligence service to keep policymakers informed about the world. With the agenda defined, the next task for government was to devise the means for following it.

— * —

The Dulles brothers were emerging as leaders of a postwar generation of men experienced and wise in the affairs of the world. Their mentors, the diplomatists of an earlier era, were leaving the scene. Hugh Wilson and Hugh Gibson, stalwarts of the old diplomatic club, had both retired from the Foreign Service. Norman Davis, with whom Allen had traveled on endless missions of disarmament in the 1930s, had died in 1944. Allen and Foster were in the forefront of those who took up the cause of European economic reconstruction, what quickly came to be called the Marshall Plan; Allen even drafted a book-length manuscript to "sell" the idea to the American public.[8] To a more select audience Allen's expertise was called into play on the parallel track of designing a national intelligence service to replace the OSS — discredited but too hastily abolished.

Americans late in the century can scarcely imagine the naiveté prevailing in the 1940s within the government, not to speak of the public at large, about how intelligence actually works. Spy stories and tales of espionage were ever popular, of course, but these were not taken to depict serious pursuits of a democracy. With the Central Intelligence Agency now firmly established as an instrument of government, latter-day Americans may have difficulty appreciating the concerns, the mood of puerile questioning in Washington, that preceded its creation.

To break the tedium of law practice Allen and some of the old crowd sought collegial refuge at Donovan's New York townhouse on elegant Sutton Place. Reminiscences about their wartime exploits were inevitable, but as early as August 1946 they also had a more serious purpose in mind: how, given the then current state of ignorance, to mobilize expertise in intelligence for a democracy at peace. The honorary degrees awarded to Allen and Donovan the following spring were steps in the right direction; given the right reception in Washington, wrote one OSS veteran to a fellow insider, "a great many of the best men we had in the old show could be persuaded to go back into the picture."[9]

Yet even highly sophisticated officials whose public service had not exposed them to the intelligence business needed a crash course, starting from the basics. Intelligence, wrote the first official historian of the CIA, is not merely information that is gathered: "The raw material of information has first to be verified and then appraised for its usefulness. It may be interesting but inconsequential. Subjected to analysis, it may however display elements, though insignificant in themselves, that associate in startling fashion with other bits of information. New evaluations follow. The readjustments of old elements become new syntheses that have significance. And intelligence has been produced for the policymaker."[10] Thus, if intelligence is to have any value at all it must come in a tightly forged chain from the source (secret or public) to headquarters, which receives all information and tests its accuracy, and then to the policy level, where decisions are made based on that information. No link in this chain is simple or straightforward; pitfalls of tradecraft and judgment abound at every turning. The surprise attack on Pearl Harbor in 1941 had shown some of the perils that arise when information available to one set of officials is not properly assessed in relation to other information and then disseminated.

The absence of a national intelligence capability after World War II was not even noted by most policymakers, eager to return to peacetime standing. And those few who made bold to argue that a democracy at peace still needed to keep watch on the world could not agree on the very first steps. Psychologically and organizationally the slate was clean. Congressional investigators began to perceive the desirability of a central "news desk" to assemble and present all relevant information, yet even in this profound (to that epoch) discovery, they still considered intelligence in a democracy primarily a military matter.*

Allen, therefore, appeared a sage of exceptional insight when he informed a committee of the United States Senate in April 1947 of what would later become a commonplace: "The prime objectives [of intelligence] today are not solely strategic or military. They are scientific — in the field of atomic energy, guided missiles, supersonic aircraft and the like. They are political and social. We must deal with the problem of conflicting ideologies as democracy faces communism, not only in the relations between Soviet Russia and the countries of the west, but in the internal political conflicts within the countries of Europe, Asia and South America." In case this point was too obscure, he explained to the bewildered legislators that "it may well be more important to know the trend of Russian communism and the views of individual members of the Politburo than it would be to have information as to the locations of particular Russian divisions."

Allen and other advocates of a national intelligence service had to confront primitive fears that it would become a Gestapo spying on American citizens in their daily lives. It was just this fear that had led Roosevelt to scuttle Donovan's intelligence plan in 1944 and Truman to abolish the OSS altogether.

Diverted by his law practice and foreign travels, Allen was on the sidelines when the Truman administration took the first halting steps to create a new intelligence authority. Called the Central Intelligence Group when it was established in January 1946, the new unit was tightly

* Army doctrine admitted that intelligence included political, social, and economic considerations — but only so far as they affected army operations.

circumscribed by the military establishment. Its total personnel — clerical and professional — numbered no more than one hundred people. It had three directors in its first sixteen months, all from the uniformed services, revolving their way through the door to military promotions. In February 1947 the State Department had been ready to recommend that Allen be named head of the CIG, but the Joint Chiefs of Staff had already picked their candidate from the navy.

The military intelligence services were deeply suspicious of civilian intrusions into a business that from the World War I days of Ralph Van Deman, they had considered their own preserve. Officers in uniform feared that civilians, lacking military discipline, could not be trusted to keep intelligence secrets. Decisions about disseminating information became matters of interagency rivalry: could the navy consider sharing intelligence with its army counterparts or, even worse, with civilians of the State Department? Could the military services tolerate having the president receive information that had been filtered through civilian analysis, overriding the presumed insight of the experienced military mind? Even the jealous military services conceded that "evaluation and dissemination" of information could well be centralized. But for the prior and more dramatic step called "collection" — the spies, networks, agents in the field running the risks and, as it was said, bringing in the goods — the military officers dug in their heels against civilian intrusion.

Equally suspicious was J. Edgar Hoover's Federal Bureau of Investigation; though charged with surveillance over "internal" security, the FBI interpreted the mandate so broadly that it maintained networks and field offices across South America — assets not to be surrendered without a struggle.

Generating even more heat was the suggestion that a new national intelligence service might be empowered not just to analyze but to collect secret intelligence, as Maugham's Ashenden did in World War I and Allen Dulles of the OSS did in World War II. Civilian amateurs might succumb to rumors that contradicted the conclusions of the military professionals.

These were the sorts of issues pondered in the closed circles of the executive branch and then in executive sessions on Capitol Hill. Allen always made himself available for expert testimony, though he carefully preserved his status as a private citizen, knowledgeable from his wartime experience, to be sure, but aloof from the interagency rivalries that cropped up whenever a new entrant sought a place on a clean bureaucratic slate. On this matter, Allen felt it was not yet time to go public.

On April 25, 1947, just before he left for Europe, Allen responded to an invitation from the Senate Armed Services Committee to submit his ideas for a central intelligence unit. His memo was hastily penned, disjointed, and not fully thought out. But in its nine pages appear Allen Dulles's basic concepts of an American intelligence service, uncomplicated by all the controversies that would later arise — and that he himself would generate.[11] For all Allen's lifelong love of the Great Game, to the Senate in 1947 he found it useful to demystify the process and portray intelligence as a relatively normal agency of government. Personnel for a central intelligence agency, he argued, "need not be very numerous. . . . The operation of the service must be neither flamboyant nor overshrouded with the mystery and abracadabra which the amateur detective likes to assume." In a lecturing tone, he tried to tell the senators how intelligence is actually assembled.

> Because of its glamour and mystery, overemphasis is generally placed on what is called secret intelligence, namely the intelligence that is obtained by secret means and by secret agents. . . . In time of peace the bulk of intelligence can be obtained through overt channels, through our diplomatic and consular missions, and our military, naval and air attachés in the normal and proper course of their work. It can also be obtained through the world press, the radio, and through the many thousands of Americans, business and professional men and American residents of foreign countries, who are naturally and normally brought in touch with what is going on in those countries.
>
> A proper analysis of the intelligence obtainable by these overt, normal, and aboveboard means would supply us with over 80 percent, I should estimate, of the information required for the guidance of our national policy.

This estimate of 80 percent from overt sources remained a fundamental feature of modern intelligence theory. When another early intelligence chief amended the figure to 90 percent, he conceded nonetheless that the clandestine 10 percent was usually the most important, and Allen himself, in later years, would dwell on the secret inputs in his briefings to policymakers.

Next Allen confronted the military services' assumption that intelligence was their particular preserve, staking his position on grounds where the uniformed services were most vulnerable. "To create an effective central intelligence agency we must have in the key positions men who are prepared to make this a life work," he explained. "Service in the agency should not be viewed merely as a stepping stone to promotion in one of the armed services or other branches of the government." While military men would not be disqualified from the key posts under Allen's concept, "once they take high position in the central intelligence organization they should, if military, divest themselves of their rank as soldiers, sailors or airmen and, as it were, 'take the cloth' of the intelligence service." Rare indeed, as Allen and the senators well knew, was the career military officer willing to surrender rank or standing in the scale of promotions. "Appointment as Chief of Central Intelligence should be somewhat comparable to appointment to high judicial office. In fact, the duties the Chief will have to perform will call for the judicial temperament in high degree."

It was beginning to look as though Allen might have a particular candidate in mind for leadership in intelligence. He went on: "An appointee must gain that critical facility which can only come of long experience and profound knowledge to enable him to separate the wheat from the chaff in the volume of information which will pass through his office. With the proper legislative backing, a correct technical set-up, and adequate leadership, all that is required for success is hard work, discriminating judgment, and common sense. Americans can be found who are not lacking in these qualities."

Allen was not being presumptuous in hinting at his own qualifications; he had learned enough about bureaucracy to appreciate the little trick of defining a compelling job description for a desired post, and for such a job description General Eisenhower himself lent support. "One of the difficulties ... comes in getting a man who will understand intelligence; he must show a bent for it rather early in life and be trained all the way up to become a true expert in the thing," Eisenhower told a House committee. "If I knew I could get a civilian I wanted and knew he would stay there ten years, I believe I would be content myself."[12] Eventually Eisenhower would have that chance. But in the early years the military hold on intelligence remained firm; not until 1953 would a civilian director of central intelligence be appointed — by Eisenhower — and he would stay on the job for nearly ten years.

The closest Congress had in those days to intelligence oversight (and it was not close at all) was the House Committee on Expenditures in the Executive Departments. This overworked body held an extraordinary secret session on June 27, 1947, for a necessary primer in intelligence on the little-understood process of clandestine collection. The first witness was Lieutenant General Hoyt S. Vandenberg, then head of the Central Intelligence Group. Vandenberg had been converted during his eleven months at CIG to the belief that to be effective and not wastefully competitive, clandestine collection should be the exclusive responsibility of a central service. As the congressmen bore in on the sensitive details of placing surely unsavory spies on the government payroll, Vandenberg took a deep breath and launched into a halting, plain-language portrayal of secret intelligence in the field, a depiction of reality remarkable in the annals of congressional testimony.

> The clandestine field, sir, is a very complicated one, as it is very difficult.... I have spent days going through the ramifications of it. Roughly, the way it works is that you have an expert in the clandestine field, or as near an expert as the United States has, and who we can hire for the money that we can pay.
>
> They go to a certain locality and live in that locality and build up an acquaintance and they know the politics and the intrigue that is going on in that nation. They pick a man, after very careful study with records back here, from what we know in G-2 [Army intelligence] and the Navy and State and from friends, and they start him out as a nucleus. He then builds a chain of people that he knows.
>
> Then, we have to have another man picked, in whom we have full confidence, who builds a chain alongside, who is just watching him. Then you have to keep these two people and their reports, to make sure that this man is not giving you information and receiving pay from a foreign government. Then, this man who has established this is pushed out in front here, and he then has a contact back with what we call the letter box or the place through which we got this information; and the man who originally set up the net ostensibly has no connection with any person or any department of the government. That is what we term a 'cut-out'; ... if he gets in trouble, we wash our hands of it. For that reason, his pay has got to be fairly good, because his throat is cut and we wash our hands of him, and we say we know nothing about him.
>
> That is a very rough description of a very difficult business.[13]

In this nervous and rambling statement, Vandenberg gave Congress a generic description (quite likely the most down-to-earth it would ever hear) of the intelligence collection process, including the parallel role of counterespionage. At this early stage the Central Intelligence Group had no agents in the field, no authority to engage in any Great Game. Collection in those early days was largely the preserve of shadowy freelancers under contract.

Foremost among these entrepreneurs was Colonel John V. Grombach, known to his West Point classmates ('23) as "Frenchie," who followed Vandenberg to the congressional witness table. Grombach was one of those unsubtle patriots who believed that intelligence was a rough, he-man business for hardened specialists and that civilian "intellectuals" had no business interfering. At the same time, Grombach declared, the men collecting the intelligence in the field had no business doing the job of the intellectuals in figuring out what it all meant or explaining it. "I am down here, and I am not concerned . . . with anything that happens to my reports, unless . . . it is discovered that something sinister is happening to them, they are being eliminated or being misinterpreted. . . . My job is collecting."* From this point on, Grombach's testimony became so lurid that it was put off the record.†

When Allen's turn came to testify, he minced no words in puncturing the simple-minded prescriptions of the freelance sleuths and the notion that collection of intelligence and its analysis could be so neatly disconnected. Drawing liberally on his exploits in Switzerland and with the charm of a raconteur, Allen worried about "these private collectors of information. . . . I think it is impossible to continue with a series of agencies engaged in the work of secret inteligence. . . . You are going to cross wires, and you are going to find that these various agents will become crossed." He urged that control of secret collection operations be assigned exclusively to the proposed central agency.

Vandenberg, though loyal to the uniformed services, went even further than Allen in complaining about contract entrepreneurs like Grombach.

> You hire somebody who thinks he is a very fine sleuth and who can establish nets, and you give him a lump sum, several hundreds of thousands of dollars, and tell him to go get you information in a certain area, and then you back off and wait for the information to come; and you hope it is good. . . . You have no assurance. In some cases it is excellent; and in some instances, you have to take it with a grain of salt, and you do not know whether it is good or not. You have no control over it.

Though Grombach and his mentors in military intelligence had strong political backing among right-wingers in Congress, the practical experience of Vandenberg and Dulles persuaded the committee. They were joined on this point, interestingly enough, by the chief of naval intelligence, Rear Admiral Thomas B. Inglis, who advocated a strong and broadly empowered central intelligence service.

With little subsequent debate on the matter, a loosely defined Central

* Operations like Grombach's were kept secret by the army contractors. The chief of naval intelligence testified that his service was never told about these collection operations, that their information was never shared with the navy, and that he had learned of them only by accident and to the army's displeasure.

† Apparently the stenographers did not even take notes of Grombach's stories. But elsewhere in the transcript, now declassified, is Vandenberg's description, in obvious disgust, of raucous goings-on in foreign barrooms where rival low-grade agents shared indiscretions.

Intelligence Agency was established by law on July 26, 1947. The new agency assumed the functions of the faltering CIG, and absorbed the few OSS veterans remaining in the field — the personal networks nurtured by the likes of Helms and Angleton, who had been conserving their intelligence assets in Germany and Italy under the supervision of the War Department. That venerable department was upstaged, in the same National Security Act that created the CIA, by the office of the secretary of defense, a civilian position in the president's cabinet. Public discussion at the time focused on the dramatic measure of unifying the uniformed services under a civilian chief; the ancillary provision of setting up a national intelligence service was scarcely noticed. Named the first director of central intelligence was not Allen — a civilian in such a post would have been too much for the uniformed services to accommodate — but Rear Admiral Roscoe H. Hillenkoetter, a likable Annapolis man who had been a naval attaché.

Scarcely noticed in the enabling act, except by Allen and those knowledgeable about intelligence, was that the new CIA was given authority over all clandestine collection abroad. Even more, the intelligence agency could pursue other undefined operations, as directed by the National Security Council. CIA functions that later generations took for granted were eased into public policy with what seems, in retrospect, an embarrassing degree of nonchalance.

Allen did not discuss these matters in public; indeed, the whole intelligence controversy seemed too arcane and sensitive to be publicly debated. Over the months to come some of the hotly contested issues of national intelligence filtered out through the writings of Hanson Baldwin, military correspondent of *The New York Times* and a well-informed insider at the study groups of the Council on Foreign Relations. Baldwin even persuaded Allen to be quoted on a few of the points he had made privately in congressional testimony.[14] But when Ham Armstrong pointedly remarked that *Foreign Affairs* needed a "first-rate" article on the nation's intelligence requirements, Allen uncharacteristically let his old friend's invitation drop.

— * —

The American republic was confronted with broader problems than the collection of intelligence. The central issue was whether the nation should pursue Marshall's vision of economic reconstruction in the countries of Europe that had been enemies and those further east that seemed on the way to becoming enemies, as a perceived Stalinist monolith took hold. Marshall's original plan had been to extend American aid even to the states of eastern Europe occupied by the Red Army; to the relief of those in Washington who saw an Iron Curtain descending upon the continent, Stalin ordered his new communist satellites to refuse the offer of imperialist dollars. Thus the proposed European Recovery Program came to apply only to the sixteen noncommunist countries of western Europe.

The Marshall Plan was a bold political and economic gamble. Isolationists rose in fury against this multibillion-dollar "giveaway," but among the Republican opposition was a faction ready to give its blessing to the Truman administration's farsighted venture. Leader of these moderate Republicans was Allen's Bern and Paris clubmate Christian Herter, who had abandoned diplomacy to enter Congress as a representative from Massachusetts. In the fall of 1947 Herter invited Allen to accompany a congressional investigating committee for a firsthand look at conditions in Europe.

Clover and Allen, in their new togetherness, had planned a Caribbean holiday with a view to shopping for Guatemalan textiles to cheer up the Lloyd Neck house. But a junket with Chris Herter, the chance to join an old friend in pursuing the central issue of the day, swept aside thoughts of domesticity. Allen sailed to Europe in September to meet the legislators as they convened to write their report. (Among the committee members he befriended on the trip was a young California congressman seeing Europe for the first time — "one of the greatest thrills of my life," wrote Richard M. Nixon, who became a staunch supporter of the Marshall Plan.)

Europe that autumn was engulfed in political turmoil atop economic disarray. Even as Allen and the congressmen were meeting, Moscow announced the formation of the Communist Information Bureau, the Cominform, to combat the Marshall Plan and orchestrate a Soviet version of political warfare. Allen had the experience to see more clearly than most how far ahead Moscow was in the tactics of pressure and maneuver. Soviet propaganda was neatly targeted to exploit every anti-American prejudice: the Coca-Cola invasion was depressing the French wine industry; a plague of Hollywood films was displacing Italian film art and leading good Italians into "moral decay." Not to mention the insidious influence of imperialist dollars flowing in under the guise of reconstruction aid.

In Washington one member of the Truman administration, the new secretary of defense, James V. Forrestal, was determined to make an issue of Soviet subversion. In striving to rouse the government to meet the challenge, he learned how Jay Lovestone, a renegade American communist who had turned sharply to the right, proposed to pump American labor union funds into the coffers of anticommunist unions in France and Italy and thus prevent a takeover by Moscow of the European labor movement. At the time the private funds at Lovestone's disposal were small.

That autumn of 1947 communist-dominated labor unions in France called a crippling general strike. More than two million French workers heeded the call, and the French government mobilized two hundred thousand troops to maintain order. Secretary Marshall warned of "grave concern, . . . a serious risk of losing France." Lovestone's $7,000 monthly subsidy to the noncommunist unions was a pitiful weapon in an all-out political war. Forrestal implored Truman to take a firm stand and send as ambassador to Paris an American who understood how to combat the Soviets on their own terms. Forrestal's candidate, though he did not yet know him well, was Allen Dulles.

Allen dared to hope for a return to public service. Foster was already established in Secretary Marshall's coterie as the token Republican member of official delegations. Military traditions having checked Allen's ambition for leadership of the intelligence service, he was left to help sell the economic recovery program on the lecture circuit, a pale substitute for government office. Becoming ambassador to France would be quite acceptable. Allen waited through Thanksgiving for a White House summons. But despite Forrestal's sponsorship, Allen was known to Truman only as one of the old Donovan team that he so distrusted, and surely one Dulles in the official family was bipartisanship enough. It was Clover, in a rare flash of political instinct, who first sensed the futility of Allen's aspirations. "Darling," she told her grumpy husband, "the President isn't for it, I tell you. He isn't for it." When the French general strike ended on December 2, so too did Allen's chance for a top diplomatic post.

The campaigns of political warfare, however, had just begun. Lovestone and his union men had shown the way, and Allen remembered, from his days in the OSS New York office, being impressed with this apostate labor leader building his European networks. As the prospect of a top diplomatic post hung in the balance, Allen had lunch with his OSS colleague Frank Wisner, equally bored with the life of a Wall Street lawyer. The two old pros shared their impatience at the government's foot-dragging in mobilizing an active, concerted campaign of propaganda, pressure, even outright sabotage against Soviet subversion. Forrestal favored such a campaign, as did Kennan at the Policy Planning Staff of the State Department. CIA, incredibly to Allen and Wisner, was proving timid.

Though empowered to collect intelligence on its own, the new agency was not ready to go the next step and seek authority to conduct covert operations aimed at changing the politics of foreign countries. Director Hillenkoetter argued that political warfare was still warfare and should be the responsibility of the armed services; the Joint Chiefs of Staff argued that political warfare was political and thus not their proper function. At State, Marshall supported Kennan in advocating covert actions — as long as the State Department did not have to dirty its own hands carrying them out. Wisner complained to Allen that intelligence was still in the hands of an unimaginative military bureaucracy.

In fact, the CIA's hesitation was due to more than lack of imagination. The agency's legal counsel, Lawrence R. Houston, wrote two formal rulings for Hillenkoetter, concluding that the empowering statutes gave the intelligence agency no authority to conduct covert operations such as propaganda, sabotage, and the like.

> Primarily designed for subversion, confusion, and political effect, [such operations] can be shown incidentally to benefit positive intelligence as a means of checking reliability of informants, effectiveness of penetration, and so forth. In our opinion, however, either activity would be an unwarranted extension of the functions authorized. . . . We do not believe that there was any thought in the minds of Congress that the Central Intelligence Agency, under this authority, would take positive action for subversion and sabotage.[15]

That was as of September 1947.

Allen, impatient and frustrated, could only advise Wisner to find some inconspicuous foothold inside the government and start quietly building networks of agents for the political warfare that somehow would be authorized in the future. Shortly thereafter Wisner accepted the post of deputy to the assistant secretary of state for occupied areas.

On November 14 the National Security Council followed Forrestal in deciding that the defense of the Free World required a high-powered counterattack against Soviet propaganda. For the next four weeks State, military, and CIA bureaucracies hashed over the means for implementation and policy direction. Once again the Pentagon and the State Department shunned responsibility for what would undoubtedly be sinister doings, and on December 17, under the most secretive precautions, the NSC assigned a reluctant CIA responsibility for covert political warfare. Only three copies of the top-secret directive, NSC 4-a, were typed; one remained at the White House, the second was passed to Kennan in the State Department, and the third given to CIA director Hillenkoetter, who kept it locked in his personal safe.*

The wary Hillenkoetter now had no choice; he established a CIA

---

* At moments of high tension the bureaucratic mind is revealed at its most petulant. Though NSC 4-a was never intended for publication, the drafters spent hours arguing whether Soviet propaganda should be termed "subversive and immoral" or "vicious." In the final draft "vicious" won out.

committee, the Special Procedures Group, to plan and carry out the orders of the National Security Council. Undersecretary of State Robert A. Lovett informed Kennan and his colleagues that the less State knew about the proposed campaign of political warfare the better. Dismayed at the leisurely pace of an effort he considered urgent, Kennan proposed that the Special Procedures Group be put under the aggressive direction of "a person of very high standing and with a broad appreciation of national policy matters." Like Forrestal before him, he proposed the name of Allen Dulles.[16]

An obscure post within an uncomfortable bureaucracy was not Allen's style, no matter how important he judged the cause. As it happened, he was already engaged in a more far-reaching assignment for the future of the Central Intelligence Agency.

— * —

One afternoon in February 1948 Allen and the secretary of defense had a long conversation in the Pentagon. Forrestal, once a wealthy investment banker known as the boy wonder of Wall Street, had chosen government service for the career fulfillment that had eluded him when he was only making money. The two men discovered that they had been undergraduates at Princeton together, though they hadn't really known each other; even now they were not close friends, though they shared many acquaintances in the financial community. Forrestal was countless millions ahead of Allen in the dollar returns accruing to those who made deals. But they found immediate comradeship in their eagerness to defend the Free World. Forrestal had been impressed by one of Hanson Baldwin's articles quoting Allen, and he agreed that the American intelligence capability was not being adequately used in the effort to combat communism.

Worried that the new CIA was stacked with "deadwood," Forrestal proposed a nonpartisan study of intelligence and national security.[17] Truman faced a daunting electoral challenge in 1948, the first time that he would run for president in his own right. Challenging him, with all the establishment credentials Truman lacked, was Dewey, elegant, accomplished, worldly. Dewey had already confided in Forrestal that when he became president he wanted to put national intelligence in the hands of a reliable professional who knew the business — someone like Allen Dulles, whose brother Foster was already being so helpful in the Republican election campaign.

Allen agreed on the spot to conduct a formal assessment of the CIA's first-year record, to be presented in January 1949, convenient to the timetables of the election and the installation of the new administration. After his recent years of commenting as a knowledgeable outsider, Allen accepted an official role in defining the intelligence capabilities of the United States. Forrestal named two of his friends to be Allen's partners on the survey: William H. Jackson, a fellow Princetonian and New York lawyer who had worked with Allen on military intelligence in France in the closing months of the war, and Matthias F. Correa, a Democrat from New York with experience in counterespionage against black marketing in postwar Italy. Allen was assured that he would be the one calling the plays.

That spring of 1948 marked a flash point in the threatening Cold War and a turning point in Allen's philosophy of intelligence. No longer would the judicious analysis of events suffice; henceforth, the American intelligence service he envisaged would be called upon to mount aggressive covert actions to turn back communism. The shift was fundamental and driven by events — or by the perception of events. Jan Masaryk, the noncommunist foreign minister of Czechoslovakia, died mysteriously, and Soviet puppets took over in Prague. Early in March General Lucius Clay, the American commander in occupied Germany, sent Washington a warning that war with the Russians, previously considered "unlikely for at least ten years," could now come "with dramatic suddenness." On April 1 the Russians imposed a ground blockade on Berlin, forcing the Western allies into a massive supply airlift. So high was the war tension that Secretary of State Marshall declared, "All I want from the CIA is twenty-four hours' notice of a Soviet attack."

The French general strike had provided a foretaste of the communists' power to subvert the frail democracies of western Europe; now attention turned to Italy, where the legal Communist Party was seeking power through elections, its coffers well larded with Cominform funds through Russian agents in Yugoslavia (still loyal to Moscow). With Forrestal and Kennan's Policy Planning Staff leading the way, the National Security Council approved on March 8 a campaign of covert action to fund and support the Italian Christian Democrats and Socialists in the forthcoming April elections.

Here was a nonmilitary test for the strategy of containment, and it gave the fledgling CIA its first opening into the realm of covert action. Angleton flew back from his intelligence base in Italy to alert Allen and other friends of the communist danger; he proposed to raise $300,000 in private funds for radio and newspaper advertising and the "personal expenses" of noncommunist candidates. That March, at Rome's stately Hotel Hassler atop the Spanish Steps, a satchel stuffed with millions of lire passed from American to Italian hands; the noncommunists were finally well endowed, and a lavish election campaign began in earnest. Though Angleton and the CIA's Special Procedures Group were coordinating the government's covert operation, private citizens generated a large part of the support. Forrestal campaigned among his Catholic and banking colleagues and tapped into the community of Italian-Americans to exert their influence with voters in the old country. "He raised hundreds of thousands of dollars to send successful Italians back to the land of their origin to promote the American cause," said an admiring colleague, Agriculture Secretary Clinton P. Anderson.[18] John Foster Dulles proposed the creation of a "Western Counter-Cominform," an idea to which Secretary Marshall promised "sympathetic consideration."

The first day of the Italian voting, April 17, Allen spent the evening at Forrestal's Washington home poring over reports from Rome. Voter turnout was heavy, violence and mob action at the polling places minimal. When all the ballots were counted, the Italian communists had suffered a sound defeat. America's political warriors had won their first engagement on the battlefield of the Cold War.

The Italian election of 1948 was a major defining point for American intelligence. As the new CIA evolved its own identity and culture, the success in Italy produced a sense of omnipotence, of confidence that the Free World could successfully engage in political warfare against communist subversion. Through his contacts with Angleton and Forrestal, as well as his official investigation of CIA effectiveness, Allen knew too well how haphazard and amateurish had been this first burst of enthusiasm for the anticommunist cause. If political warfare was going to become a factor in American foreign policy, he concluded, it would need more professionalism than was evident in that hasty Italian campaign. Kennan was thinking of setting up an entirely separate agency for secret operations to keep from contaminating the CIA's abilities to collect intelligence. Allen, however, was conceiving a bolder theory of combining the two seemingly separate functions in one agency. Both Cold Warriors were confident that in its intelligence service, America had a weapon more powerful than its early practitioners dared to wield.

A second event during the month of the Italian election, forgotten to later generations, assumed equal significance in defining the place of the young CIA in the exercise of foreign policy. In late March Secretary of State Marshall had traveled to Bogotá, Colombia, for an inter-American conference. On April 9, after ten uneventful days of diplomacy, a local left-wing politician was assassinated, and a two-day outburst of mob violence threatened the visiting dignitaries.* The CIA subsequently learned that the assassination had been only a personal vendetta, but Americans

---

* Witness to the rioting was a twenty-one-year-old Cuban student on a visit to Bogotá. As government police rounded up the "provocateurs," young Fidel Castro escaped back to Havana on a plane carrying a herd of bulls.

in and out of government jumped to the belief that the riot was yet another communist plot, this one threatening the United States in its own hemisphere.

The Bogotá incident, nicknamed the Bogotazo, was branded America's first great intelligence failure. Dewey denounced the "dreadful incompetence" of the Democratic administration for having "no idea what was going on in a country just two hours' bombing time from the Panama Canal." Congressmen and columnists demanded to know why the CIA had not given sufficient warning of communist unrest in a nearby country. Partisans of the military intelligence services gloated over the bungling of inexperienced civilians. President Truman himself did not help when he admitted that he was taken by surprise.[19]

Over the next days Hillenkoetter briefed congressmen in closed sessions about what his agency had reported before the Bogotá conference. He produced numerous intelligence reports that local communists might try to find a pretext for disrupting the proceedings. But he conceded his own error in failing to disseminate the strongest of these warnings, which foretold specific attempts to "humiliate" the American secretary of state "by manifestations and possible personal molestation." State Department representatives, including the ambassador in Colombia, had convinced CIA that such a warning might give undue alarm; the CIA director himself felt too insecure to override the diplomats' advice. Hillenkoetter's explanations mollified congressional critics. One prominent CIA supporter, Representative Clarence J. Brown of Ohio, contemplated legislation to protect the intelligence agency specifically from "censorship or intimidation." He declared, "Otherwise one might as well turn the intelligence agency over to the State Department and let those dumb clucks run it."

Allen's reaction to the Bogotazo was more measured and logical. He and his two colleagues on the intelligence survey seized upon the incident as a test case: how — and how much — to integrate the work of diplomats and of intelligence agents working under cover in American embassies? How to oil the creaky mechanism within CIA itself for evaluating raw reports and translating them into intelligence that policymakers would find meaningful? Personally, Allen was not as charitable as the congressmen toward Hillenkoetter's self-confessed error; he confided to various associates that nothing was wrong with the CIA that could not be fixed by appointing stronger, more competent personnel at the top levels.

The Bogotazo had a more fundamental impact on the architects of American intelligence in the CIA's first year. The reach of intelligence collection and analysis, Allen and his colleagues concluded, had to be worldwide; no riot, no assassination or coup d'état anywhere could be considered beneath notice.[20] This conclusion was not as self-evident in the spring of 1948 as it became later in the Cold War; a more primitive intelligence service might have been content simply to focus on the main targets without wasting resources on problems that seemed either tangential or irrelevant. Yet the application of the lesson was flawed over the years to come: it was not the facts of any local unrest that deserved consideration, it was their perceived connection with international communism — whether the evidence confirmed that connection or not.

Thus two central features of the American intelligence service fell into place: omnipotence and omniscience. Unlimited horizons of omnipotence were opened by the work of the pep squads that turned the tide in the Italian elections that April. At the same time, after the Bogotazo, the men of intelligence discovered the need to be omniscient. The intelligence agency that Forrestal assigned Allen to analyze was turning out to be something far grander than its founders had imagined.

Leaving the more prosaic parts of the enterprise to be surveyed by his partners and staff, Allen went to work on the two aspects that touched his own restless imagination: the collection of intelligence and the use of intelligence networks to influence events covertly. Others would disagree — with a vengeance, over the decades to come — but Allen's confidence was growing in the counterintuitive belief that these two starkly different functions could be performed by the same agents, the same networks, the same organization, at the same time. In effect, he was contemplating how the techniques of his OSS operation in Switzerland could be made to work the world over.

Allen assumed that Dewey would win the presidency in November. In surveying the intelligence service in place in 1948, Allen proceeded to design the intelligence mission he would like to take on as his own, someday soon.

— 12 —

REACHING

ALLEN WORKED AT DEWEY'S SIDE against Harry Truman in the heat of the 1948 election campaign. It was not an easy summer for him. His gout returned; Clover was startled one day to see her husband limping through the front door at noon, so tormented by the pain that he could not sit at his desk. Then he came down with a mild but lingering pneumonia and had to be hospitalized; upon his release the stubborn patient received stern medical instructions: "No wines, no champagne. One small whisky a day, well diluted; one cup only of coffee. One hour's rest before dinner, may have four pipes a day." Allen ignored the strictures.

Nothing could keep him away from the Republican National Convention assembled in Philadelphia that June. Gout or no gout, wearing the courtesy badge of honorary assistant sergeant-at-arms, he worked his way among the state delegations on the convention floor as a fabled spymaster and Dewey booster. Actually, though few at the convention knew it, he was already established in the campaign in a more sensitive role.

Dewey's criticism of an "intelligence failure" in the Bogotazo may have been good politics against the Truman administration, but even Allen — no defender of Hillenkoetter's CIA — saw a danger in injecting the problems of the struggling intelligence service into the election campaign. He persuaded the Republican challenger that failure or not, the CIA should be left out of campaign politics. Further, with his brother Foster as the symbol of bipartisanship in Truman's diplomacy, Allen became the confidential link on foreign policy matters between the Truman administration and the Dewey campaign.

Presidential campaigns in those days were relatively civilized, full of partisan charges but not about diplomatic negotiations in progress. Foster was a member of the United States delegation to the United Nations

General Assembly, meeting that autumn in Paris; there he served alongside Secretary of State Marshall. Everyone knew he would be Marshall's
successor in a Dewey administraton. Foster sent classified dispatches
from Paris to a secure government office in New York, where they were
decoded by military cryptographers and sent by messenger to the Hotel
Roosevelt, Dewey's headquarters. Allen or Chris Herter or a clever
twenty-nine-year-old campaign aide named McGeorge Bundy would assess the up-to-the-minute diplomatic news for the presidential candidate
on the campaign trail. It is not clear how much Truman knew of this
back-channel leakage, but Marshall had enough appreciation for the con-
tinuity of diplomacy to condone what his Republican colleague (and presumed successor) was doing.*

Allen joined the Dewey campaign train in mid-September for a two-
week, 8,000-mile swing through the Midwest. The American delegation
in Paris was pressing the Soviets for recognition of the West's rights
in divided Berlin, and Foster's cables warned of imminent breakdown
in the negotiations. Even though the artificial war scare of the spring
had abated, the Republican member of the delegation warned Dewey,
through Allen, that campaign speeches critical of Truman's policies toward the Russians could start a "chain of events" leading to an early military confrontation — not at all the way the next president would want to
start out his administration. Each evening on the campaign train Allen
would brief Dewey on the daily take from the diplomatic dispatches. "We
were pretty sure that Dewey could pick up a good hundred thousand
votes by pointing up the administration's poor handling of the Berlin situation," Allen remarked afterward, but Foster's warnings were taken to
heart.[1] On their side the Democrats knew that Truman was vulnerable
on the question of how tough to be with Moscow. "I was astonished that
Dewey did not exploit it," recalled Clark Clifford, one of Truman's campaign aides, "but, apparently feeling that the election was wrapped up, he
said virtually nothing about it beyond a few vague references" — just as
Foster and Allen advised.[†]

Between campaign trips Allen nursed his gout and entertained visitors from Europe. Daughter Joan and Fritz Molden came for a visit, full
of stories of Soviet intrigues in the Vienna that would haunt moviegoers

* Partisan recriminations erupted, however, when it was learned that Defense Secretary
Forrestal had met with Dewey during the campaign, even discussing the possibility of continuing in office in a Republican administration.
† This reserve did not hold on the charges that Truman was coddling communists within
his own administration or the simultaneous controversy over Palestine, which Dewey, to his
regret, injected into the campaign — giving Truman an opening to appeal for the votes of
American Jews.

through the zither themes of *The Third Man*. When Republican friends at the Council on Foreign Relations warned of "coming disaster" if Dewey did not abandon his stance of bipartisan aloofness, Allen merely smiled. "Not one untoward thing has happened," he told a reporter a few weeks before the election; "everything has been extremely smooth." Then, when the last polls began showing that Truman was pulling ahead, Allen complained to a visitor at campaign headquarters about the pollsters' "irresponsibility — everyone knows we're going to win." As the last campaign train rushed through Illinois, Ohio, and Massachusetts, Allen padded through the candidate's compartments in his stocking feet. They returned to New York on the eve of Election Day.

Clover had prepared a festive supper at Sixty-first Street on election night.* When the early returns began casting a pall on the Republican celebration, the party ended sooner than planned. Early Wednesday morning Allen went over to the Hotel Roosevelt and found his defeated candidate standing in his room in a bathrobe, somber and silent. "He took it like a man," Allen reported to his brother. Foster, waiting in Paris by his radio for the triumph, instead found himself stripped of the status he, and all those around him, had anticipated. He was able to summon up enough humor to present himself to a reporter the next day as "the former future secretary of state."

— * —

Allen's yearlong survey of the Central Intelligence Agency ended as an anticlimax for its principal author. Instead of a blueprint for reform that Allen could implement under President Dewey, the study landed almost irrelevantly on the crowded desks of the reelected Truman administration. Allen and his colleagues went through the motions of formal hearings on the report just two weeks after the election, but their work no longer seemed so germane. Over lunch in January 1949 Allen handed the Dulles-Jackson-Correa report personally to Forrestal, who praised the survey as a "guidebook" for a long time to come, "an example of how a report should be prepared." But even commendation from the survey's initial sponsor came with diminished impact, for the powerful unifier of the armed services was no longer the man he had once been. At lunch that day, apparently their last meeting, Allen found Forrestal morose and preoccupied. Exhibiting progressive signs of mental strain and irrational

---

* Among the guests was a California businessman who had recently worked on special projects for Forrestal; Allen met for the first time John McCone, the man who would ultimately succeed him as director of central intelligence.

behavior, the secretary of defense had to be eased out of office in March. Less than two months later, depressed and paranoid, James Forrestal of Wall Street and Washington committed suicide.

The Dulles-Jackson-Correa report nonetheless had a long-lasting impact on the organization of the intelligence service. Within the CIA the epithets ranged from "devastating" to "messianic."* In 193 pages, with fifty-seven specific conclusions and recommendations, it found that the CIA had failed in its responsibilities during its first year of operation.[2] That failure, moreover, the survey attributed directly to Hillenkoetter's lack of leadership and lack of understanding of the professional field of intelligence. "The Central Intelligence Agency has tended to become just one more intelligence agency producing intelligence in competition with older established agencies. . . . The departmental intelligence services were not only holding out 'operational' information and 'eyes only' reports and denying the Agency materials which required 'special security handling'; they also were resorting to intelligence memoranda plausibly serving their purposes alone."

Within the survey were signals of the combat under way in Washington between early Cold Warriors, who wanted to hit the Russians with all the political weapons that could be deployed, and careerists — military and civilian — who were happy to regard the new CIA as just one more government office. The perspective of Allen and his colleagues reflected the biases of Forrestal, Kennan, and their ilk in the State Department, impatient at the deadwood and timidity imposed upon the intelligence organization, frustrated over the Bogotazo failure, and eager for covert action against Soviet Russia. (Since the military intelligence services considered CIA a competitor, their officers delighted at the feuding among civilians.)

The most sensitive and substantive finding of the Dulles-Jackson-Correa survey involved the scope of an intelligence agency's operations. Allen and the professionals had won their point the year before that intelligence collection belonged in the same organization as analysis and dissemination. By the middle of 1948 the intramural controversy had ad-

---

* The first two institutional histories of the CIA differ in their assessment of the survey. Ludwell Lee Montague, author of the second history, uses the word "devastating" even as he concedes merit in its fundamental conclusions. Arthur Darling, however, author of the first history, is thoroughly protective of Hillenkoetter against the report's criticism, and when he calls its presentation "messianic," his language is unmistakably ironic. Darling completed his history in 1953, when Allen was director of central intelligence, and his irreverence to his boss won him no kudos; Allen was so annoyed with Darling's conclusions that he restricted circulation of the classified history even within the agency's top echelons.

vanced to the next level: should operations aimed at influencing the policies and actions of foreign governments — covert actions — be conducted by the same networks and organizations charged with gathering information about these governments?

As an intellectual matter, a clear distinction between these two conceptually different functions can be readily drawn. Intelligence collection, which seems relatively passive, seeks to photograph existing reality like a camera; covert operations, by contrast, are distinctly proactive, aimed at changing reality in a desired direction. The intellectual distinction breaks down, however, in the face of experience. The agents and networks in the best position to provide information are usually motivated by a desire to change the situation. Any intelligence service attempting to keep the two functions separate is likely to be in competition with itself for the control and loyalties of its agents. In their report Allen and his colleagues attempted to present this difficult argument in its simplest form.

> The collection of secret intelligence is closely related to the conduct of secret operations in support of national policy. These operations, including covert psychological warfare, clandestine political activity, sabotage and guerrilla activity, have always been the companions of secret intelligence. The two activities support each other and can be disassociated only to the detriment of both. Effective secret intelligence is a prerequisite to sound secret operations and, where security considerations permit, channels for secret intelligence may also serve secret operations. On the other hand, although the acquisition of intelligence is not the immediate objective of secret operations, the latter may prove to be a most productive source of intelligence.

This conclusion was not reached easily, and it grew from the actual bureaucratic experience of the early CIA.

At the start of their survey Allen's associates leaned toward the view that the most sensitive secret operations of both intelligence collection and covert political warfare were beyond the capability of the military CIA directors and their staffs, who, the cynics would say, failed to grasp the differences between socialists and communists. Secret operations, in this reading, belonged in the care of an anonymous elite, hidden within the government, its very existence unknown to outsiders. Forrestal and Kennan at the State Department were attracted to this option; heady from the success of the ad hoc effort in the Italian elections, they sought a permanent, flexible, and imaginative mechanism for covert intervention to contain Soviet pressures wherever they might occur. The CIA's Special Procedures Group only dragged its feet. Kennan formally proposed the secret creation of "a 'directorate' for overt and covert political warfare" that would be firmly under State Department policy control but just separate enough bureaucratically that the diplomats could disavow any responsibility for anything unseemly.

The Kennan initiative led to a fundamental policy decision by President Truman's National Security Council, spelled out in a directive that set American intelligence onto an ambitious commitment to covert action and political warfare for decades to come. Called NSC 10/2, prepared in the tightest possible secrecy, the directive of June 18, 1948, proceeded from the belief that the Soviet Union and its satellite countries were embarked on a program of "vicious" covert activities "to discredit and defeat the aims and activities of the United States and other Western powers." To counter and contain such pressures, NSC 10/2 gave the highest sanction of the government to a broad range of covert operations, spelled out as "propaganda, economic warfare, preventive direct action including sabotage, anti-sabotage, demolition and evacuation measures; subversion against hostile states including assistance to underground resistance movements, guerrillas and refugee liberation groups." This was stretching intelligence into the ominous realm of the paramilitary. All such activities, in the words of NSC 10/2, must be "so planned and executed that any US government responsibility for them is not evident to unauthorized persons, and that if uncovered the US government can plausibly disclaim any responsibility for them."

In later years, when the CIA's penchant for unaccountable covert action was likened to the maraudings of a rogue elephant, Kennan called his sponsorship of 10/2 "the greatest mistake I ever made. . . . It did not work out at all the way I had conceived it. . . . We had thought that this would be a facility which could be used when and if an occasion arose when it might be needed. There might be years when we wouldn't have to do anything like this. But if the occasion arose we wanted somebody in the government who would have the funds, the experience, the expertise to do these things and to do them in a proper way."[3]

Just as with his "X" article and the doctrine of containment, Kennan had to spend countless hours and pages trying to explain the meanings and intents of his initiatives. The doubts came only long afterward, however. For that small group of trusted officials privy to NSC 10/2, the question was not whether to engage in covert action but who should be doing the necessary.

As 10/2 was taking shape, Allen used his mandate on the intelligence survey to head off any intent of assigning the covert action function to an agency other than the one he hoped someday to direct; for all the inadequacies of the existing CIA, which made Kennan and others look elsewhere for leadership, Allen was confident that he himself would be able to put the situation right. Pulling Jackson and Correa with him, Allen rushed out an interim report, amounting to another intelligence primer, called "Relations between Secret Operations and Secret Intelligence." In this paper Allen insisted that all clandestine operations, whatever their purpose, must be centrally controlled.

> We do not believe that these types of operations can be "farmed" out to various existing agencies of the government without jeopardizing their effectiveness and involving serious security risks. . . . There would be duplication of effort, crossing of wires in the use of clandestine agents, and serious risk for the chains and agents used in the respective operations.
>
> The Director [of Central Intelligence] and his staff should have intimate knowledge of what is being done in the field of secret intelligence and access to all the facilities which may be built up through a properly constituted secret intelligence network. Secret operations, particularly through support of resistance groups, provide one of the most important sources of secret intelligence, and the information gained from secret intelligence must immediately be put to use in guiding and directing secret operations. In many cases it is necessary to determine whether a particular agent or chain should primarily be used for secret intelligence or for secret operations, because the attempt to press both uses may endanger the security of each.
>
> The special operations contemplated will require a staff operating abroad under [*words deleted:* probably "both diplomatic and unofficial"] cover, as in the case of secret intelligence. Unless the personnel for both operations is under one overall control in Washington, even though a measure of insulation is provided in the field, there is likely to be overlapping of activities and functions in critical areas which will imperil security.

The drafters of NSC 10/2 heeded Allen's advice; the directive established a special staff for covert operations, within the CIA but with policy and personnel under the control of the Policy Planning Staff of the State Department. This staff was eventually given the innocuous name Office of Policy Coordination, "to ensure plausibility while revealing practically nothing of its purposes."[4] Obviously a hybrid, the OPC did not fully meet Allen's requirements for tight centralized control, but it at least allowed for the exercise of more imagination and initiative than could be expected from Hillenkoetter's CIA.

For Allen and his kindred spirits within the government, NSC 10/2 started the United States on a bold new course for fighting the Cold War against communism. The new OPC, not totally within CIA, not exactly separate from it — the bureaucratic ambiguity to be dealt with later —

held the promise of becoming just the instrument of pressure and maneuver that Allen and others had long found lacking in the government.
Their heightened expectations were only fueled by the appointment of
Frank Wisner to head this strange new operation. Veteran of the OSS in
eastern Europe and Germany, enthusiast of the political war against
communism (and, incidentally, a registered Democrat), Wisner was quietly elevated from his modest position in the State Department to a new
post of scope and secrecy unprecedented within the United States government.

Allen had counseled his old colleague in espionage to find an inconspicuous slot in the government and start building up a network for political warfare from within. That part of their joint strategy worked —
unlike Allen's hope of becoming director of central intelligence under
President Thomas E. Dewey.

— * —

With Truman's surprising reelection, Allen's prospects for a return to
government service evaporated. He had designed a powerful and dynamic intelligence agency, but thanks to the electorate it would be run by
a Truman appointee. The old rumors of an appointment as ambassador
to Paris surfaced again, but this time Allen knew better than to suppose
that Truman might name him to a prestigious post. (The Paris embassy
went to his friend David Bruce.) At age fifty-five he had completed his
government assignment and was unlikely to receive another; his only
prospect was to resume the life of a prosperous New York attorney.

Among the more interesting clients Allen found on his return to Sullivan and Cromwell in the spring of 1949 was an enterprising engineering
group called Overseas Consultants, Inc. Their most promising venture
was the design of a long-range economic development program to feed
the aspirations of twenty-nine-year-old Mohammad Reza Pahlavi, shah of
Iran. Allen signed on as legal adviser to a team of technical experts guiding
the young ruler on his domain's ascent to Great Power status.

Tehran, when Allen first arrived in April 1949, was not an appealing
place. "Everything moves slowly," he wrote home; the streets were full of
mud. A small ruling class sat in nonchalance above the vast "undernour-
ished, disease-ridden, indigent and illiterate" masses. About the only
thing to be said for the place, and it was quite enough to occupy his attention for some years to come, was that Iranian wells pumped about
560,000 barrels of oil every day, a significant six percent of Free World
production. Allen and some three dozen other consultants trudged
through the mud and proposed to the young shah such novel innovations
as "social reform" and "private enterprise," particularly in the oil busi-

ness. They aimed thus to counter the program of a volatile opposition leader in the parliament, Mohammad Mossadegh, who was proposing to seize and nationalize the valuable properties of the Anglo-Iranian Oil Company. Allen listened and observed, not very sympathetically, the rumblings of a nation seeking the way up from obscurity.

Then came a message from New York that he received even less sympathetically. Clover, fed up with the role of wife at home while her husband went to exotic places, announced that she had arranged to join Allen in Iran. She had signed on for an organized tour designed for New York matrons, led by a venerable professor, to visit the antiquities of Persia. Allen replied swiftly by cable: "Travel here is most precarious." And the professor, he had learned, was not reliable. "I thought it best to warn you. . . . I wouldn't get involved in his plans, as I fear they won't work out. This is disappointing, but the facts of life here are more grim than they look in picture books." That did it. Clover was finished with the role of patient wife living in a doll's house. The woman who had worked an assembly line in wartime Brooklyn and joined a convoy of motor cars through warring France would not be patronized. Welcomed or not by her husband, she set off for Persia.

In the event, the trip turned out to be just the disaster Allen predicted. To her diary she described it as a "nightmare"; in reminiscing long afterward, she called it merely "cock-eyed." Allen met her at the Tehran airport but announced that he would be leaving the next day for Baghdad; she should busy herself with the tour as best she could. They would rendezvous in Paris, he said, at the end of May, a few weeks hence. Clover and her tour group pursued their curiosity, even having their own audience with the shah, whom she labeled "the gloomy prince."

Allen saw the Middle East as a devious place, torn between oil men, Zionists, and Arab nationalists. All of these people seemed to have good ideas worth supporting; the conflicts among them did not fit comfortably into his gentlemanly world view. On leaving the area he was likened by a friendly reporter to "a cultivated Roman Senator watching over imperial provinces. . . . [He] lay back on his bed and spoke with aloof nonchalance of events in the United States, Germany and Persia."

When Allen arrived in Paris and checked into the Ritz, he touched base with David Bruce, the new ambassador, and encountered a young Foreign Service officer who turned out to be Royall Tyler's son. "Where is Clover?" asked young William Tyler. To his sudden astonishment, Allen realized that he had no idea. She was supposed to have left Tehran for Athens about this time, but he had no schedule. When a telegram finally arrived informing him of her arrival time, Tyler took Allen out to Orly Airport to meet her. For two hours they waited; there was no explanation for the delay, no word whether the plane was even airborne. Tyler saw an Allen quite unlike the cheery man he remembered; he stood immobilized at the lounge window, staring at the sky, speechless, solemn, and withdrawn.[5] When the plane from Athens finally arrived and Clover stepped off, Allen instantly reverted to his hearty self, never letting his wife see he had passed some hours of genuine worry for her.

— * —

Back at home Allen used his prominence at the Council on Foreign Relations to further the interests of his Iranian client. The council, as always, provided elegant and subtle ways for its elite members to combine their professional and public interests. Allen arranged to introduce the shah to the American foreign policy establishment at a "small private dinner," attended by one hundred council members. The guests were a who's who of opinion makers: Nelson Rockefeller, Senators William Benton and H. Alexander Smith, William Donovan, Henry R. Luce of *Time*, commentators Larry Leseur and John Gunther. And as a host who could convene such luminaries, Allen won credit with the shah of Iran. By such means, over the generations, are forged contacts and loyalties among gentlemen engaged in world affairs.

More substantive for Allen's council work was a blue-ribbon study group of distinguished gentlemen presided over by Dwight D. Eisenhower, recently named president of Columbia University, to analyze America's newfound responsibility for Europe's political, economic, perhaps even military, survival. The group met regularly from 1949 into early 1951; Eisenhower chaired eleven of the fifteen meetings, and Allen was there for almost every session. This group, it was later said, was where the future President Eisenhower got his first serious taste of free-flowing discussions among civilians about international politics.[6]

The Marshall Plan and efforts to strengthen the democracies of western Europe against communist subversion commanded a consensus within the common rooms of the council, but a different problem shattered the confidence of the establishment. It involved the promising diplomat Alger Hiss, president of the Carnegie Endowment for International Peace, a faithful member of the Council on Foreign Relations, a sometime protégé of John Foster Dulles.* Hiss had fallen under suspi-

* Allen and Foster first encountered Hiss in the 1930s, when the young lawyer served on the staff of a congressional committee aiming to show how Wall Street financial interests had lured the United States into World War I. Allen accused Hiss of betraying a trust by revealing private papers of former Secretary of State Robert Lansing, of which Allen held custody.

cion of being a Russian spy in the State Department. As the espionage charges gained currency, Foster summoned Hiss for a frank discussion and subsequently reported that Hiss had categorically denied "any Communist connection or sympathy," and that Foster's own inquiries in Washington had assured him of Hiss's "complete loyalty."

Congressman Nixon of California, a member of the House Un-American Activities Committee, was still troubled. At the height of the Dewey campaign he had arranged a confidential appointment with the Dulles brothers. Secret testimony from a witness named Whittaker Chambers looked very damning for Hiss, and Nixon "wanted our advice as lawyers," Allen recalled, "whether we thought the committee had the basis of a real case." After studying the testimony that Nixon supplied, both Foster and Allen reluctantly conceded that Hiss had been lying in his testimony. Five weeks after the election a federal grand jury indicted Hiss for perjury; Allen telephoned Foster in Paris with what he called "a serious shock."[7]

Throughout 1949 the Hiss case filled the newspapers and consumed America's body politic; the complex proceedings had dramatic elements, including secret documents retrieved from a hollowed-out pumpkin and decisive evidence in the sighting of something called a prothonotary warbler, which bird watchers the world over found significant. As the evidence mounted, Hiss's onetime mentors backed off. Republicans sensed that the Democrats were vulnerable on the inflated issue of communists in government, with Hiss as the prime example. An obscure senator from Wisconsin, Joseph R. McCarthy, waited for his moment to pounce. Foster, finding his previous sponsorship of Hiss deeply embarrassing for his own political standing, declared that officials of the Truman State Department had deceived him by not revealing to him all they knew. Alger Hiss was finally convicted of perjury and sentenced to prison in January 1950 for five years.[*]

During the summer of 1949 Dewey, as governor of New York, had occasion to make an interim appointment to the United States Senate; he named John Foster Dulles. Foster said he had no intention of running for election, but once installed he found the Senate an attractive perch. State Republicans prevailed upon him, from the advantage of incumbency, to

---

* Of which he served forty-four months. After his release he fought the rest of his life for exoneration. He avoided former friends and colleagues in the New York international community, but the records show that Hiss never actually resigned from the Council on Foreign Relations. The council's rules specify that once a person has gone through the rigorous selection process, membership terminates only on one of three circumstances: resignation, death, or successive years' nonpayment of dues. In recent years council officers have enjoyed noting that the only two prominent members whose memberships were terminated for nonpayment of dues were Alger Hiss and Richard Nixon.

run against the liberal Democrat Herbert Lehman, a former governor and formidable candidate. The eight-week New York campaign of 1949 started off as reasonably polite. Then Foster, not fully comprehending the pitfalls of partisan politics, accused Lehman of accepting "undercover" communist support. The Dulles campaign thought the issue a sure winner, given a mood that found communists under every bed, and with Lehman's long record of backing progressive causes that procommunist groups also supported. The New York Republicans, however, did not reckon with the broadsides that an angry Democrat could deliver against a Dulles.

If Lehman was to be tarred with "communist" connections, the rumbling started, look at Dulles's unabashed, documented "fascist" — indeed, pro-Nazi! — connections. Out came Sullivan and Cromwell's business deals of the 1930s: the links with German industrialists in their efforts to preserve their capital from transitory misunderstandings among politicians; the overlapping directorates with the J. Henry Schroder Banking Corporation and that American firm's "obvious" connection to Baron Kurt von Schröder, Hitler's best fundraiser.

Lehman won the November election comfortably. "My brother made a good race," Allen, with upper lip stiff, wrote a friend, "but the odds this off-year were too much. Anyway, he ran well ahead of his ticket and gave the opposition quite a good scare." At the White House Harry Truman took note of John Foster Dulles's entry into, and exit from, the real world of politics. Truman recalled that he had warned his token Republican diplomat "not to get off the high international plain or he'd get licked." So he had, and Truman said, "I'm glad that duck lost." The Dulles brothers were clearly not cut out for elective office.

Allen's biggest loss in November 1949 came the day before the election. At campaign headquarters early Monday morning, he picked up an urgent call from a Lloyd Neck neighbor: their Long Island house was on fire. Sweeping past Sixty-first Street to pick up Clover, Allen drove his wife out to their country retreat in time to watch helplessly the final gutting of the old wood-frame residence. Gone up in smoke were the accumulations of a decade of summers, even the matching upholstery and draperies of vibrant Guatemalan textiles that Clover had lovingly assembled on their periodic trips to Central America. Gone also was Allen's first manuscript and notes for Operation Sunrise, his wartime memoir that would now be fifteen years delayed.

— * —

Bored in his law practice, Allen was already embarked as a private citizen on a mission of his own in a domain that the public mind could not yet recognize. He quietly conceived the idea of a network of "fronts" for the coming battle against communism, the national interest as Allen perceived it. With the zeal that came to mark the Cold War generation, he led a like-minded group of public citizens in creating the means for psychological warfare and subversion. Nothing useful could be expected from the sluggish CIA and its lackluster holdovers from abandoned careers. What was needed, instead, was a structure of public organizations that could carry to the world the virtues of democracy without the baggage of bureaucracy.

With fanfare he presided over the formation of such innocuous-sounding groups as the Free Europe Committee. He enticed Fred Dolbeare out of semiretirement to become the committee's vice president. Royall Tyler was ready to combine his work in international economic organizations with efforts to find useful employment for anticommunist émigrés from eastern Europe. Labor leader Jay Lovestone was enlisted for his experience in clandestine agitation; Carmel Offie, an old hand from the postwar diplomatic circuit, could always be relied upon to get things done quietly. Cornerstone of the committee was to be a radio station called Radio Free Europe that would beam news (and, incidentally, anticommunist propaganda) to the satellite countries occupied by the Red Army. These private efforts, far from the routines of Hillenkoetter's CIA, amounted to nothing less than the nucleus of America's Cold War clandestine services.

As an aspiring diplomat in Bern, Paris, and Berlin, Allen had been motivated by a sense of personal integrity about public service as opposed to the self-interest of the private sector. Those days had long passed. It was not self-interest that guided him at the outbreak of the Cold War but a public interest in combating communism that would lose its effectiveness were it publicly stated. Allen showed no sign of recoiling from the fact that the proposed Radio Free Europe was built on a deception — perpetrated not only upon the targets of its psychological warfare, but upon the American public as well. For the Free Europe Committee solicited funding from the general public, even at one point announcing that the campaign would be financed entirely by private contributions. Ignoring the patriotism of the modest Americans who were sending in their savings, Radio Free Europe was taken on as a creature of the United States government, through that top-secret NSC Directive 10/2.*

— * —

* Radio Free Europe's government sponsorship was officially acknowledged only in 1975 after an investigation of the American intelligence service headed by a leading Republican, Nelson Rockefeller; among the Rockefeller Commission's members were Ronald Reagan and Allen's colleague from Operation Sunrise, General Lyman Lemnitzer.

The American public was slow to pick up on what the respectable New York establishment was doing, but the Kremlin quickly drew a bead on this man Allen Dulles. Scarcely two months after 10/2 became policy, Soviet propaganda organs announced that the United States was about to set up a "special European bureau" for sabotage and terrorism in eastern Europe.* To that nugget of sound intelligence Tass added erroneous embellishment, extrapolating from World War II: Allen would be the head of this covert operation from Switzerland, and other OSS veterans would be assigned to duty in Berlin and Istanbul; William Donovan would be pulling the strings from Washington. Hillenkoetter was one who noticed the Tass report with interest. The CIA director wrote Allen the next day, "I see you are being all fixed up with a new job in Switzerland, and evidently this will move you up on the Soviet list to a place right near the top."

Russian agents tracked Allen on his travels to Europe and Iran in 1949, assuming that legal business for Sullivan and Cromwell was simply a cover. Though still a private citizen (a distinction dismissed in the Kremlin's view of reality), Allen enjoyed a continuing close friendship with Wisner, the new head of the 10/2 covert action office, and their frequent meetings and phone calls would not be difficult for any alert operative to discover. But again, once the nugget of good intelligence reached them, the propaganda organs got it a little wrong. A Romanian newspaper reported at the end of April that in pursuit of his sabotage mission, Allen had summoned a meeting in Rome of European representatives of the United States Information Service, clearly a high command of intelligence.

Though fanciful and wrong in the details, the communist propaganda apparatus was not wide off the mark in spotting the start of an American intelligence effort against communist eastern Europe and in pinpointing — prematurely — the role of Allen Dulles in its direction. A Czech report in August knew that the covert action effort had an inscrutable name, though they had not yet caught on to the "Office of Policy Coordination." They simply called it "Organization X," which aimed, they said, to create "disturbances" in eastern Europe and put out "a steady current of lies and slanders about the Soviet Union." "Lies and slanders" were not terms that gentlemen like Allen or Wisner would use about their public service, though their concept of psychological warfare certainly did not require slavish adherence to the truth. As for creating "disturbances" in eastern Europe, the Czech report was right on target.

Eastern Europe in the autumn of 1949 was more vulnerable to distur-

---

* Tass, the press agency of the Soviet Union, attributed this item of Aug. 22, 1948, to a British intelligence report sent to NATO. Donald Maclean, Moscow's double agent in the British Embassy in Washington, would have been the likely source for Soviet intelligence.

bance than any American could yet know. Even as the Cold Warriors persisted in seeing a communist monolith, cracks and strains within the eastern bloc were already growing. The summer before, Tito and his Yugoslav communists had declared independence from Moscow, an act of defiance that disturbed the frail satellite regimes more than anything the OPC would be able to contrive. In May of 1949 Noel Field disappeared behind the Iron Curtain — a defector? A captive? Field had been openly sympathetic with communists in western Europe during World War II; he also had known Alger Hiss in the State Department and was suspected of involvement in the same espionage cell.* With allegations against Hiss then mounting in the United States, Field found it prudent to move out of reach — "I was sure I would be convicted of espionage," he told Hungarian interrogators.[8] As he discovered, however, the communists of eastern Europe under the Kremlin's control were considerably more ruthless than those he had known during the wartime alliance.

This time the Moscow apparatus did not need even a nugget of accurate intelligence to elevate Allen to a central position in one of the most tortuous intrigues of Stalin's declining years. Field became the pretext; not only had this idealistic American been in touch with a number of communists whom Stalin wanted to purge, he had also run errands for his old family friend, the American spymaster known as 110 during the war. Field landed in a Budapest prison and, with no chance to speak for himself, was branded the key link in the treason of heretical Hungarian communists. His name and that of Allen Dulles were brandished in a publicized show trial in September, with abject defendants offering their fulsome "confessions" and succumbing to doctored evidence of an imperialist plot. "I'm quite sure I've never met any of the people on trial and I've never even heard anything about the alleged plot," Allen told newsmen in New York, a denial that impressed no one who wanted to believe the worst.

Then a chance exchange at the Budapest trial gave Allen an opening for a more convincing denial. One of the victims in the dock was unable to recognize a bespectacled gray-haired man, allegedly his partner in espionage, in an old World War II photograph. The presiding judge helpfully identified Allen Dulles, and the doomed defendant, his memory suddenly refreshed, explained that "in 1944, he did not wear spectacles." Allen could tell New York newsmen, truthfully, that he had worn glasses for twenty years.

Over the next three years — the last of Stalin's life — the shakedown

---

* When Hiss first tried to recruit him, Field recalled for his communist interrogators in later years, "I carelessly told him I was already working for Soviet intelligence."

of communist leaders in the satellite countries took its toll. Show trials followed a predictable pattern: abject confessions, lurid details of heresies and betrayals, prostitution to Western imperialism, death sentences, executions. Some of the most able and worldly of the eastern European communist party leaders were wiped out between 1949 and 1953 in favor of toadies all too ready to succumb to the Stalinist line from Moscow.

After collusion with Tito, the second most heinous crime in the Stalinist indictments was sympathy for Zionism. Here again there existed the beginning of sound intelligence, though no evidence has come to light that any Soviet agent in Washington could have known of it. In the drive to gain American support for the creation of the state of Israel in 1947–48, Zionist emissaries headed by Teddy Kollek (later mayor of Jerusalem) pleaded with America's inexperienced Cold Warriors to accept ready-made intelligence networks in eastern Europe and the Soviet Union.[9] So great was the hostility of Washington diplomatic (if not political) circles to Zionism that these offers were bluntly refused.*

As the Stalinist show trials intensified, conjectures spread that Noel Field was himself a double agent, that while appearing to defect to communism he was still following CIA orders. In this interpretation his mission was to enmesh the most sophisticated eastern European communist leaders in a murky guilt by association. So he did, but it is fanciful to credit the CIA with the deed. Efforts to "destabilize" (as the technique would later be called) the satellite regimes was certainly a goal of the new covert action arm of American intelligence, and the ruinous turmoil of show trials and purges within those regimes during Stalin's last years was certainly destabilizing. But to suppose cause and effect would require an assumption of skill that the fledgling service did not yet possess.

— * —

As well as omnipotence, CIA aspired to omniscience worldwide. On June 19, 1950, Hillenkoetter's CIA informed top policymakers that "northern Korea's armed forces . . . have a capability for attaining limited objectives in short-term military operations against southern Korea, including the capture of Seoul," the capital city just south of the thirty-eighth parallel, the dividing line drawn across the Korean peninsula at the armistice ending World War II. In the flawlessly hedged language of bureaucratic consensus, the major military and civilian intelligence agencies had reached

---

* Allen was not yet privy to operational opportunities offered by the Zionists' European networks, and the only position he took on the Palestinian controversy was to allow his name to be used by an organization of American Protestants more interested in the plight of Palestinian refugees than in the birth pangs of the Jewish state.

accord, after painstaking month-long negotiations, on a "National Estimate." This was a new type of intelligence document, highly classified, powerful in its intent and tone, aimed at bringing policymakers up to speed on world situations that would not show up on their daily crisis agendas.

The lessons of global coverage learned so awkwardly from the Bogotazo of 1948 had been taken to heart by CIA, though the concept of an "estimate" was not yet familiar across the government. From his earliest musings about the purposes of an intelligence service, Allen had placed the estimate function near the top of his priorities. The Dulles-Jackson-Correa report of 1949 explained that a National Estimate should pull together all of the best intelligence opinions, based on all available information, not just the judgments of one or two departmental intelligence services. Comprehensiveness was the key: "[Estimates] should deal with matters of wide scope relevant to the determination of basic policy, such as the assessment of a country's war potential, its preparedness for war, its strategic capabilities and intentions, its vulnerability to various forms of direct attack or indirect pressures."

That was the theory; in reality the early estimates were slapdash affairs. The first, called ORE 1, on the "Foreign and Military Policy of the Soviet Union," was whipped out over one sleepless weekend in July 1946 by a single intelligence analyst, Ludwell Lee Montague.[10] Over succeeding years the national estimates developed into an art form reminiscent of the papers of the Inquiry in World War I and composed by boards of distinguished academic figures led by William Langer of Harvard and Sherman Kent of Yale.

In June of 1950 intellectually immaculate estimates were not the same as current intelligence, and few of the few who actually read the analysis of June 19 appreciated the distinction. Nowhere in that consensus estimate, including its five detailed appendixes, did the intelligence community warn American policymakers that an attack by North Korea was imminent.[11]

Just six days later massed communist forces from the north invaded South Korea and, as it appeared to Washington, Soviet aggressive designs became reality. President Truman flew back from a family holiday in Missouri the morning after the invasion and immediately summoned Hillenkoetter for a briefing. To the president, newsmen, and irate congressional investigators, all the CIA director could do was recall the various signals of warning and possibility, including the estimate just six days before. "You can't predict the timing," the hapless admiral explained.

The specter of Pearl Harbor once again arose over the American intelligence service. "The timing"—even twenty-four hours' notice, as

Marshall had asked in another theater of war — was what American poli-cymakers expected of their spies and analysts, and the young CIA had again fallen short. "The North Koreans were capable of such an attack at any time, according to the intelligence," Truman wrote, "but there was no information to give any clue as to whether an attack was certain or when it was likely to come." Over the next weeks of tense policy confer-ences, as President Truman and his top advisers, military and civilian, mapped strategy for committing American air, naval, and ground forces to war on the Asian mainland, CIA was nowhere represented. The time when the director of central intelligence would be an intimate consultant to the policymaking process was a remote prospect indeed.

Allen happened to be in Europe when the Korean War began, tend-ing to the inauguration of Radio Free Europe, but he rushed home to dis-cuss the new danger with the staff of the Council on Foreign Relations. Scholarly members of the Eisenhower study group were preoccupied with their assessments of the situation in Europe, and their first instinct was to regard the Korean attack as an irritating distraction from the main theater of confrontation. Yet America was back at war, in an area where it had least expected it and scarcely understood.

Business as usual could not continue in the foreign policy establish-ment and the intelligence services. As a start, Hillenkoetter had to go; the CIA needed better. In the first days of the North Korean invasion he himself seized the pretext to request reassignment to duty at sea, where he would be free from the bureaucratic combat of Washington. (He was eventually assigned command of cruisers in the Pacific Seventh Fleet.) Truman had long been seeking a new man — even a civilian! — to bring the organization of national intelligence up to speed. Secretary of State Dean Acheson was one who knew that Truman would never consider the obvious qualified candidate, a veteran of the OSS who, alas, had worked openly for Dewey and the Republicans; Allen himself had long since reached the same conclusion. Bandied about were the names of Dean Rusk, then a deputy undersecretary of state, J. Edgar Hoover of the FBI, and even retired General Donovan. Taking none of these suggestions se-riously, the president discussed the CIA post with Robert Lovett, who had just resigned from the State Department to rejoin his New York in-vestment banking firm, and David Bruce, ambassador to France. Both declined the appointment.

It was Truman himself, as close advisers recall, who first said, "How would Bedell Smith do?"[12] For the subsequent history of America's intel-ligence service and, as it turned out, for the career of Allen Dulles, Tru-man's impulse was a stroke of inspiration.

— * —

Army Lieutenant General Walter Bedell Smith of Indianapolis had been Eisenhower's chief of staff during World War II, "the general manager of the war," as Ike described him, "a Godsend, a master of detail with clear comprehension of the main issues." When Truman proposed him for CIA, the fifty-five-year-old retired general had served three years as ambassador to Moscow. He was a man who knew how to fight wars both hot and cold. "We must anticipate that the Soviet tactic will be to attempt to wear us down, to exasperate us, to keep probing for weak spots," Smith warned, "and we must cultivate firmness and patience to a degree that we have never before required."

Not the least of "Beetle" Smith's qualifications, as Truman saw it, was that he had no background in the ossified ranks of military intelligence and that, as he made abundantly clear, he had no desire to head the CIA. But Truman's mind was made up; he held back only because Smith had a chronic stomach ulcer and was at that moment in Walter Reed General Hospital for an operation.* As the Korean War raged, the president waited for a postoperative report and then, without asking the patient's opinion on the matter, he simply ordered Smith to take the CIA position. Bedell Smith was confirmed by the Senate unanimously on August 28 and, after five weeks of recuperation, carried out his commander in chief's orders to enter on duty as director of central intelligence on October 7, 1950.

"I know nothing about this business," Smith told Truman's aides. "I shall need a deputy who does." Once again the name of Allen Dulles was raised. Smith discussed the matter with Sidney Souers, a crony of Truman's who had overseen intelligence management before the creation of CIA and who remained influential in the White House. Souers brought an instinctive insight. Allen, he told Smith, though experienced in the broadest practice of intelligence, had lately become too single-minded about clandestine operations against communism.[13] Much more should be involved in an intelligence service than covert action; Allen had argued as much in his 1947 memo to the Senate, yet a year later his interests had focused tightly on political warfare. Souers proposed instead, and Smith accepted, the name of William H. Jackson, Allen's partner in the intelligence survey two years before, to be Smith's knowledgeable deputy.† (In his retirement memoirs Allen refers only vaguely to the fact that Jackson was invited to Washington before him.)

---

* Two-thirds of his stomach had been removed, and the once husky general was down to 135 pounds.
† Jackson actually had no ambitions in intelligence or government service, and his tenure at CIA, though significant, was brief.

As Smith recuperated, gearing up in soldierly fashion for his new command, he studied the long-dormant Dulles-Jackson-Correa survey. He called Allen at Sullivan and Cromwell for advice on organizing clandestine operations, a subject of which he, like other newcomers to the intelligence business, had only the slightest understanding. Allen later found it useful to let colleagues believe that Smith had summoned him to implement the intelligence survey proposals. In fact, the new CIA director was not at all persuaded by Allen's eagerness for Cold War covert actions, and their subsequent work together was far more troubled than Allen liked to remember it. At the start Smith said he would need Allen as a consultant for about six weeks. For Allen those six weeks became a decade. That autumn of 1950 Allen jumped into the role of consultant to CIA, commuting to Washington on the overnight sleeper twice each week during November and early December — though he made a point of being back in New York for the final meeting of the Eisenhower study group at the Council on Foreign Relations on December 11.

The nation was moving to a war footing. To CIA's surprise, Chinese communist forces had joined the North Korean invaders, and General Douglas MacArthur's troops were in retreat. Fearing a worldwide communist offensive and eager to shore up his flanks against restive Republican opposition, Truman recalled Eisenhower to active duty to take command of the North Atlantic Treaty Organization in Europe, the area still feared as the main front for communist aggression despite the diversionary feint in Asia.

A few days before Christmas, as Allen's consultancy came to an end, Smith offered him the new CIA post of deputy director for operations, supervising both secret intelligence collection and the covert actions of Wisner's OPC. This posed a dilemma for a man of ambition. Allen had long wanted, and expected, to be the director of America's intelligence service; now he was being offered a secondary position in the organization he had worked to design. Yet the post as Smith framed it seemed tailor-made for Allen's new interests. When he discussed it with Clover, she would not let him consider his larger ambitions or the financial hardship of giving up his Wall Street law practice. "You must accept," she told her husband, knowing full well what he wanted to hear. "You owe it to the country."

Allen wrapped up his pending legal cases, resigned as president of the Council on Foreign Relations, and told friends and colleagues that he was moving to Washington to help in the war effort. As in 1942, he was taking on a mission that he could not describe in public; he even changed the title of his new appointment, to deputy director for plans, "a less revealing designation."[14]

For the preceding five years Allen had made a life outside the profession of intelligence. Through the constant flow of visitors, ad hoc consultations solicited by Congress and friends within the government, and finally the official assignment to survey the CIA in 1948, he had stayed engaged though still on the outside. In his pursuit of the Great Game Allen had moved from the bleachers to the bench. Finally, at the end of 1950, he got the nod from Beetle Smith to join the offensive team on the field.

— * —

With remarkable accuracy, the dynamism and effectiveness of a bureaucracy can be measured in inverse proportion to the physical elegance in which it operates. Mature agencies have the time and attention to acquire comfortable headquarters; new operations just feeling their way toward power have to make do.

The CIA at the turn of 1951 was housed in an ungainly sprawl of ramshackle buildings on the Foggy Bottom bank of the Potomac. The agency had started out in the old OSS complex at 2430 E Street, four masonry buildings on a hilltop shared with billets for senior navy officers, plus, at the foot of the hill, four ding321
y frame structures of wartime construction. Across the road was a brewery, a roller-skating rink that had seen better days, an abandoned gasworks, and the State Department. The setting for the burgeoning clandestine services within CIA was even worse: two dilapidated "temporary" buildings across the Reflecting Pool on the Mall. Labeled only "K" and "L," they marred the tourists' vista of the nearby Lincoln Memorial.

For all his eagerness to rejoin the Game, Allen arrived in a strangely tentative frame of mind. He would make no commitment beyond six months, during which he would accept a modest per diem but no salary. He obviously wanted to make it work, but the Wall Street lawyer, veteran of diplomacy and intelligence, was unsure of his ground with the new director. This uneasiness, as it turned out, was thoroughly justified.

The difficult relationship between Allen Dulles and Beetle Smith was a formative feature of the CIA that later events tended to obscure — and Allen, the ultimate victor in their disputes, found it useful to perpetuate the obscurity. Personal ambitions posed any number of problems, first with Allen's longtime partner Frank Wisner. Smith, after all, had given Allen a responsible post that Wisner had dared to expect for himself; between trusted colleagues that slight could be managed, though to the end of his career, Wisner's respect for Allen was mixed with a degree of sadness and rivalry.[15]

More troublesome for Allen was Smith's working style; in his decades of active duty the general had adopted some of the traits of a martinet. He expected subordinates — even civilians — to stand smartly when he entered the room. Allen was prepared to stand up as a courtesy, but the rigidity of military practice grated upon his habit of cordiality. One associate in those early days remembers Allen sauntering into a staff meeting two minutes after the appointed time and asking breezily, "What's going on?" Smith fixed him with a soldier's glare and declared that the meeting had ended one minute before.

Smith was one of the few associates whom Allen could not charm. Indeed, as one of Smith's aides recalled, Allen often "rubbed him the wrong way." Smith was not a West Pointer, and his rise through the army ranks had been constantly marked by slights from elitist officers. When Allen was fitting naturally into the leisurely life of a Princeton undergraduate, Smith was a buck private in the Indiana National Guard with nothing more than a high school diploma.* As they worked together crafting intelligence networks of prominent people in European and international society, too many of the names under discussion turned out to be Allen's old friends; Smith felt he was being constantly upstaged.

But the differences between the two managers of intelligence were also profoundly substantive. Though respectful of Allen's experience and expertise in a field that he himself did not always understand, Smith nevertheless saw through the veneer of integrity; he simply did not trust Allen's capacity for judgment or self-restraint in the exercise of powers that, by their secret nature, had to operate beyond the normal discipline of accountability.

Allen tried manfully to gain his new chief's confidence, making himself useful even in matters outside his own area of responsibility, with uncertain results. One of Smith's biggest problems early in the Korean War was MacArthur's jealous hostility to the CIA. MacArthur had distrusted civilian pretensions in intelligence ever since World War II; though the CIA was now to be directed by a fellow army general, Smith was lower in rank and not even a West Pointer. To counter MacArthur's rebuffs to any CIA presence in his command area, Smith tried an end run; he invited a retired Marine general and MacArthur's early comrade-in-arms, Pedro

* As a young lieutenant emerging from World War I, Smith had naively aspired to become an embassy attaché doing intelligence duty. Admitting that he had no private income, he was dismissed with a contemptuous, "Sorry, Lieutenant, you can't afford to be in intelligence." He was the first four-star general in the army who had not graduated from West Point or any other military school. In fact, Smith never graduated from any college, though no less than fifteen American and European universities awarded him honorary degrees.

A. del Valle, to set up a CIA office in Tokyo. The savvy Marine saw that he had been set up to "pull the rug out from under MacArthur." But Allen did not understand these sensitivities of the uniformed services. Allen welcomed del Valle on his way out of Smith's office; "he was all smiles and greeted me cordially, saying he was glad I was joining them," del Valle reported to MacArthur. "I disabused him of this erroneous conclusion."[16]

Allen was equally unsuccessful when Smith asked him to set up an effective working relationship with the FBI under J. Edgar Hoover, who was as distrustful as MacArthur of this new entrant upon a domain he considered his own by long right. For most of 1951 Allen was unable to gain Hoover's attention, but it must be said that Smith fared little better when he took over the task himself. About the most the CIA could extract from the FBI was Hoover's gracious wilingness to have lunch every month with Bedell Smith.

The most serious problem between Allen and Smith was on the fundamental matter of how intelligence agents should best be used. It was the old question, still not resolved more than three years after it was raised, of whether the clandestine collection of intelligence and the conduct of covert operations could be carried out by the same networks, the same agents under the same command. In the Dulles-Jackson-Correa survey Allen had insisted on the practical reasons for combining the two functions and the dangers of keeping them separate. Smith was willing to place both functions within the purview of one deputy director, Allen, and in a preemptive first strike of bureaucratic clout, he summarily terminated the OPC's ambiguous status; instead of being split between CIA and its other two ostensible masters, the State Department and the Joint Chiefs of Staff, the covert action agency would function under CIA direction. Smith informed State and Pentagon of this, though of course, he said, he would graciously welcome any policy guidance they chose to provide. But for many months subsequently he tried to keep the OPC budget out of the presentation he would have to make to Congress for "intelligence activities," arguing that State and Defense should pay for political actions. And within CIA he resisted Allen's efforts to combine the separate lines of command of intelligence collection and covert action into a unified clandestine service. Allen's two-year tenure as Smith's deputy was marred by tension over this issue, and though Smith ultimately succumbed to Allen's experience and determination, it was only with reluctance and foreboding for the future of the intelligence service.

— * —

The fact of history is that the Central Intelligence Agency was created to collect information about the Soviet Union and communism.* The United States had no intelligence assets at the end of World War II, no resources in place for acquiring even the most basic current information about its Russian ally.

In the turmoil of Europe right after the war, with millions of displaced persons roaming across disputed borders, where black-marketeers and entrepreneurs thrived in all pursuits, "intelligence" became a hot commodity. Detached veterans of defeated foreign armies found lucrative opportunities in providing naive American military intelligence officers with reports from "behind the Iron Curtain," supplied, they promised, by active chains of agents. Even American freelancers like the agile "Frenchie" Grombach capitalized on Washington's hunger for information about the new adversaries and on the widespread gullibility in measuring and assessing its veracity.

A few professionals in the early CIA were skeptical about these dubious sources. Many of the alleged networks turned out to be fictitious, the agents nonexistent or even mischievous communist plants; some prized items of information were shown to have originated in so-called paper mills, where imaginative entrepreneurs fabricated whatever tidbits they thought would sell. CIA veterans are still embarrassed to contemplate the faulty judgments drawn from phony information about the communist bloc in the early postwar years — to say nothing of the millions of dollars wasted in the collection of useless intelligence.†

Not all the intelligence assets developed at the end of the war, however, turned out to be worthless. Late in 1946 one of the stream of callers at Allen's townhouse on East Sixty-first Street was a lieutenant colonel in army intelligence, still in his twenties, named John Russell Deane, Jr.[17] He was the sort of young man Allen always enjoyed meeting, a West Pointer, son of the renowned chief of the American Military Mission in wartime Moscow. Deane had come to Allen, as an old hand, to sound

---

* This point, unexceptionable for the decades of the Cold War, became troublesome after 1989, when communism faded as a target of intelligence, and the CIA seemed ill-equipped to change its focus to other sources of unrest and instability.

† Early in Allen's time at the CIA, Walter Jessel of the clandestine services was assigned to conduct a thorough investigation of these first attempts at intelligence collection. His study, presented in November 1951, was devastating in its disclosures about the fabricators and paper mills. Even forty years later the CIA could not bring itself to open this embarrassing record to the public; a request for the Jessel study under the Freedom of Information Act was refused on grounds that it would reveal too much about intelligence "sources and methods."

him out about an interesting proposition that had come to the attention of military intelligence in occupied Germany: a captured Wehrmacht general was prepared to turn over a vast archive of data about the Soviet Union and eastern Europe collected by Nazi intelligence and stashed away at secret locations in the Bavarian Alps as the war ended.

To Allen the description immediately rang a bell. Just before V-E Day, on his last secret visit to Switzerland, Fritz Kolbe had mentioned an intelligence officer on the eastern front who was preparing to make a deal with the victorious Americans. At that time Allen had been of no mind to follow up on any transactions with Nazi generals, but when he heard Deane's briefing he grasped the situation exactly. Deane told of the organization General Reinhard Gehlen proposed to make available to the United States for the common cause against Soviet communism. Both the Germans and the Americans were so nervous about secrecy that the original schematic chart of the Gehlen organization Deane unfolded was disguised as an architectural drawing of the electric circuits in a big house. Allen had no qualms about encouraging Deane and his superiors in army intelligence to take the former Nazi general seriously as an asset for collecting current intelligence about communist eastern Europe.

When Allen arrived at CIA four years later, he found that Gehlen had been taken seriously indeed; his organization of some four thousand agents had overwhelmed every other CIA collection facility in Germany. Gehlen's original bounty, the trunks of card files and Nazi records secreted in the Alps, had long since been absorbed by hungry American intelligence. Once adopted by the occupation authorities, Gehlen had mobilized a genuine network; his best agents in the late 1940s were German soldiers held as prisoners of war in the Soviet Union. On their return they were systematically debriefed by their countrymen about conditions, topography, and observations — the sort of inquiry Allen himself had supervised for the OSS in New York at the start of World War II. Gehlen's organization seemed better able to provide this kind of intelligence data base than any other readily accessible source.

American relations with Gehlen were strained from the start. American intelligence officers attempting to develop their own networks, lest the United States become too dependent on this difficult and suspicious German general, found their new agents lured away by Gehlen's men, issuing dark warnings that the United States and the Soviet Union were still really working together to keep Germany down. And Gehlen's eagerness to target the communists did not preclude an ample measure of spying on the American occupation administration as well. Some of the American liaison officers were uncomfortable about, if not downright offended by, establishing relations of trust with Germans, so recently the enemy. Long afterward Colonel Deane, for one, justified his acceptance of the Gehlen organization by noting that many of his coworkers in army intelligence were Jews. "I never heard any one of them complain about working with [Gehlen]," Deane said. "Here they were, Jews, those most directly affected, and they weren't complaining."[18] Gehlen's American "handlers" tried to prevent former SS men or Nazi intelligence agents from gaining rehabilitation under Gehlen's protection, and the general appeared to accede to their demands. Yet to many Americans the Gehlen organization appeared as just a "bunch of Nazis." At the same time, however, uniformed and civilian intelligence officers alike were inclined — more so than they would later like to admit — to forgive the Nazi past of experienced operators who could be useful in the fight against communism.

The reliance upon Reinhard Gehlen remains one of the most controversial chapters in the early CIA. The general, forty-three years old at the end of World War II, was the son of an obscure Prussian army lieutenant; he spent his boyhood in Breslau, the same eastern province as Eduard Schulte, and married into a fine old Prussian family. He fell out of Hitler's favor by the end of 1944 for his defeatist prognoses. In January 1945 Hitler ordered him to a lunatic asylum, and only then did Gehlen make his move to break with the führer. Gehlen was never important enough to be counted among the Nazi high command, nor was he bold enough to assist the resistance movement among his Wehrmacht comrades that culminated in the July 20 plot. From the top down, the ranks of the organization he built for American intelligence after the war included many of high and low standing who could not have passed the tests for denazification.

Gehlen was too professional to be classed with the fabricators, but as his organization spread in scope and numbers, his quality control fell short. Into his networks were accepted agents whose discipline and integrity could be — and were — questioned, and among the intelligence collected was too much data that ranked with the output of the discredited paper mills. Then, when the purpose expanded from merely collecting information to waging political warfare and conducting covert operations, the Gehlen organization was found to have been penetrated by communist provocateurs, double agents marching to Moscow's orders under the guise of devotion to Germany.

By the time Allen assumed responsibility for the Gehlen organization, it was evident that Gehlen and CIA were operating on different agendas. The Americans needed intelligence about the Soviet enemy;

Gehlen was seeking to build a national intelligence service for the new Germany. While the American occupation wanted to rid Germany of the Nazi mindset, Gehlen wanted to rescue German officers from the ranks of the defeated, to give them jobs and dignity. Only in the cause of the crude anticommunism that prevailed at the start of the Cold War did the two sides find a common interest. For Allen in 1951 that was enough.

A remarkable personal rapport developed, which the shrewd German general systematically nurtured, between Gehlen and the CIA's new leaders, Allen and his top intelligence analysts like Sherman Kent of Yale. For all the differences in moral and national values, men of intelligence somehow do find ways of working together. Allen and Gehlen got along famously when they first met six months into Allen's term at the CIA. Allen called on the general at Pullach, a village on the outskirts of Munich, where the Gehlen organization was building its headquarters. The American and German spymasters found they shared an impatience at the rules and cautions that inhibit enthusiasm in pursuit of the Great Game. Neither Allen nor Gehlen cared about untidy peccadilloes in their agents' pasts, and both considered security precautions as annoyances that only pedestrian policemen of counterespionage — or politics — would consider worthy of attention.

Allen knew how to relate to upper-class Germans and those like Gehlen of the middle class who aspired to high social standing. In truth Gehlen manipulated Allen, even as Allen thought it was happening the other way. The general would sit in rapt attention as Allen expounded on pressing problems in his fluent but atrocious German; only afterward would Gehlen discreetly ask a CIA aide for "a little explanation" of what Allen had been trying to say.

In their conversations over the years Allen found Gehlen fascinating on theoretical matters of intelligence; they discussed principles and methods, the process of analyzing intelligence, the motivations of agents, the sorts of people who play the Great Game. Inevitably would come up the old adage attributed to Henry L. Stimson — "Gentlemen do not read each other's mail." Gehlen blurted out (or so Allen told young recruits to the CIA) something like, "*Only* gentlemen can be trusted to read each other's mail." Allen found the German general a most interesting and congenial sort.

— * —

CIA had neither time nor experience to build its own networks. Instead the new agency had to make do with cooperative ventures cobbled together in haste and trust: arrangements with foreign intelligence services professing similar targets and interests, as Gehlen offered in Germany.

Only gradually did the dangers in such collaboration become evident: the contrasting agendas of the two services, the ease with which the communist side could penetrate and manipulate the German networks, for instance, and the destructive effects of admitting former Nazis into the American Cold War effort.

Damage of a more surprising sort, much more unsettling to intelligence professionals, took a toll early in Allen's tenure, from a source thoroughly unsuspected. As the American novices sought strong shoulders to stand upon, who more natural than the British? It was under Whitehall's guidance, after all, that the OSS had been established. Allen may have been somewhat disillusioned with his British counterparts in wartime Bern, but that could be written off to troublesome personalities. Comradeship among intelligence men of the English-speaking world was too deeply ingrained to be questioned.

A formal Anglo-American intelligence partnership had begun as early as 1946; personal ties went back further. Eisenhower, as supreme Allied commander in World War II, had chosen a British officer, Major General Kenneth Strong, to head his intelligence staff. So intimate were Strong's relations with Chief of Staff Bedell Smith that when Smith became director of American central intelligence, he briefly considered appointing the British general as his deputy.*

Anglo-American cooperation survived a series of mishaps. In occupied Germany, the two intelligence services found themselves competing for the same networks and agents. British spymasters were distrustful of the Gehlen organization, preferring instead a survivor of the July 20 plot, Otto John, to spearhead a German intelligence effort. In 1949–50 Whitehall and Washington collaborated in a quixotic operation: the covert dispatch of agents into Albania to foment an anticommunist uprising and pierce the armor of the Iron Curtain in an obscure corner where it was thought to be weakest. That early foray into covert paramilitary action was a dismal failure because of bad planning and naiveté in the new tactics of Cold War. Trusting officials found no reason to detect a more serious flaw in the Anglo-American liaison, managed as it was by Whitehall's estimable and popular intelligence representative in Washington, Kim Philby.

Philby seemed a true and trusted professional in the Great Game when he arrived in the United States in 1949 representing Britain's MI-6.

---

*The idea of naming a foreign national to such a position raised eyebrows as a matter of legality, but so great was the confidence in Strong, and in Anglo-American cooperation, that it did not seem a ludicrous idea on its face. Strong later became head of Britain's military intelligence, only deepening his close working partnership with the American service.

He was welcomed by the early CIA, by the top executives on the hill above the Potomac and by the operators down on the Mall in the temporary "K" and "L" buildings of the clandestine services. His entrée was unchallenged, his access to the most sensitive operational details unlimited. With his wealth of experience in intelligence dating back, as far as was known, to the Spanish civil war of the late 1930s, his insights and opinions were gratefully received by his American apprentices. With his tousled manner and charming schoolboy stutter, he won Washington's confidence, including that of Allen Dulles, newly named to the CIA.

The two aficionados of the Great Game had met even before Allen went to CIA, though Philby recalled, "I had known him much earlier by reputation, from his days in Switzerland where he acquired his legend." Allen was just the sort of American that Philby made a point of meeting, an expert likely to assume high responsibility. Thereafter they met frequently, usually with two or three colleagues, for lunch or dinner "at the usual Washington eating places, the Colony, La Salle, Mayflower, Shoreham, etc." Once Allen joined CIA, Philby reminisced, "I would often call at AD's office late in the afternoon on business, knowing that he would soon suggest drifting out to a friendly bar for a further round of shop-talk."

Just five months after Allen assumed his CIA functions, two little-known British diplomats defected to Moscow: the outrageous Guy Burgess and the thoroughly correct Donald Maclean. There was said to have been a "third man" in the Soviet spy ring who alerted Burgess and Maclean that they were about to be uncovered. Gradually suspicion began to center, incredibly enough, on Kim Philby. When Philby fled to Moscow in 1963, he was exposed as having been a Soviet double agent throughout the early Cold War, reporting to the Kremlin from his unparalleled vantage point at the pinnacle of British and, by his liaison role, of American intelligence as well.

Allen never had the chance to confront Philby in person after his treachery became known. Nor was the full extent of the damage from this liaison with a contaminated British intelligence service known in Allen's lifetime. Doubts about and criticisms by American and British intelligence officers were hardly unknown in Allen's experience; it was the underlying community of interests of the two nations that was never in question. "Perhaps [Allen's] most impressive personal triumph was to rise above his detractors in Britain, often prove them wrong, and nurse no bitterness," Philby wrote. "He retained his Anglophilia, so far as I know, to the end."

The fabled British secret service never recovered from the succession of blows that started with Burgess, Maclean, and Philby. From the third man, suspicions grew of a fourth man, a fifth and a sixth, into a wide and respectable network of communist sympathizers recruited by a far-seeing

Soviet intelligence apparatus in their student days at Cambridge University in the 1920s and '30s. The disclosures marked the end of a golden age for British intelligence, as the wand was passed to the Americans. "Allen's people had ingenuity, drive and *high* technology," said a British veteran after one of Allen's London visits. "We supplied experience, geography and *low* cunning." And the old-time professional from wartime, Malcolm Muggeridge, wrote in reminiscence:

> From those Elysian days I remember so well in London when the first [American] arrivals came among us, straight from their innocent nests in Princeton or Yale or Harvard, in Wall Street or Madison Avenue or Washington, D.C. How short a time the honeymoon period lasted! How soon our British setup was overtaken in personnel, zest and scale of operations, above all, in expendable cash! . . .
>
> The OSS-CIA network, with ramifications all over the world, came to outclass our once legendary Secret Service as a sleek Cadillac does an ancient hansom cab.[19]

— ∗ —

The Anglo-American collaboration in intelligence left, as an incidental but fortuitous legacy, a pair of perceptive personal portraits of Allen Dulles as he was reaching toward the apex of his career. Kenneth Strong and Kim Philby knew Allen intimately as professionals in intelligence. Yet as officers of another nation, they never fell victim to the adoring legends that grew up among Allen's protégés. Strong's admiration was tempered by lingering reservations about Allen's intellectual depth. Philby could afford to be more outspoken — disdain was natural to his status as adversary — yet even he could express a telling measure of personal affection. Given their differences in outlook, the two portraits are clearly of the same person, viewed from individual perspectives.

> Dulles always remained an enigma to me [wrote Strong]. When I met Dulles in 1945 he presented me with a gold watch that he had brought from Switzerland, a kind and friendly gesture when watches were almost unobtainable in Britain. My chief memory of him from that time is his infectious, gusty laugh, which always seemed to enter a room with him. Even when I came to know him better in later years I was seldom able to penetrate beyond this laugh, or to conduct any serious professional conversation with him more than a few sentences."[20]

Strong admitted that initially he had not taken Allen altogether seriously in the business of intelligence. "My first intimation," he wrote of

Allen's rising stature, "was a comment from Bedell Smith that in future I might be well advised to treat Allen with a little more deference." And as he did, he came to perceive strengths as well as weaknesses.

> Allen Dulles was undoubtedly the greatest United States professional in-
> telligence officer of his time, although he was perhaps stronger and more
> interested in matters concerned with collection and short-term evalua-
> tion than in the business of long-range estimating. He was not unaware
> of his unique experience. In spite of the slightly bantering attitude with
> which he approached serious matters, there was a certain hardness in his
> character, and he knew that his position effectively made him the doyen
> of the free world's intelligence activity. . . . Competitors were not entirely
> welcome, and he had an active dislike of being associated with a failure.
> Nevertheless, he was generous in praise of others. . . .
>   He might without disrespect be described as the last great Romantic
> of Intelligence.

Philby, naturally, was more caustic about the Americans with whom he had worked. He described Bedell Smith, with that "cold fishy eye and a precision-tool brain. . . . I had an uneasy feeling [he] would be apt to think that two and two made four rather than five." Smith was "a boss of outstanding intellect and character. . . . With him, I had to do my home-work; with Dulles, it was desirable, but not necessary." Indeed, at one point, Philby wrote of "the bumbling Dulles." In memoirs and personal letters from his Moscow exile, Philby went on to explain.[21]

> Why did I call him "bumbling"? Well, it was the first adjective which oc-
> curred to me after our introductory meeting, and he gave me no cause for
> second thoughts. . . . Personally, I liked him a lot. He was nice to have
> around: good, comfortable, predictable, pipe-smoking, whisky-sipping
> company. . . . Dulles did nothing to play down his legend; his unprofes-
> sional delight in cloak-and-dagger for its own sake was an endearing trait.

> I find recurring, with inexorable insistence, the adjective "lazy." Of
> course, AD was an active man, in the sense that he would talk shop late
> into the night, jump into aeroplanes, rush around sophisticated capitals
> and exotic landscapes. But did he ever apply his mind *hard* to a problem
> that did not engage his personal interest and inclination; or was he basi-
> cally a line-of-least-resistance man? . . . I put it to you that Dulles enjoyed
> what he did and did what he enjoyed, no less, no more. Quite enough,
> you may retort, for a nice guy. Yes, but not for the post he held.

In Philby's view Allen was an executive who presided rather than directed, a man "who could never get his mouth around the essential 'No.'"

> He had a habit of talking round a problem, not coming to grips with it. Sometimes, he seemed to be ruminating aloud — and pretty diffusedly at that; sometimes, when several of us were present, he would talk at random until we had all spoken, then mull and mumble over verbal formulae which might cover all views, however conflicting they might be. In short, he was the genial chairman.

— * —

Institutional ties never inhibited Allen from nurturing his own private networks of diverse colleagues and friends, many dating back decades, upon whom he would call in his regular trips to Europe for civilized exchanges among men and, increasingly, women of the world. (In his late fifties Allen had not lost interest in attractive women, though the intellectual aspects of those encounters became more motivating, just as with his men friends.)

One such colleague was the Swedish banker and Wimbledon tennis champion Marcus Wallenberg, who had helped Allen understand the amoral, cross-borders network of high finance in the 1930s and had served as a discreet conduit to the German resistance during World War II. On a visit to Stockholm soon after joining CIA, Allen found some points of interest in an after-dinner discussion with Wallenberg and sent off a brief report to Washington, carefully concealing his informant's identity with an OSS-style pseudonym. A young CIA man based in Stockholm, William Colby, not yet the sort to be included at gentlemanly dinners, received an information copy of Allen's dispatch a few days later. With some impertinence but a closer grasp of Scandinavian affairs than his peripatetic boss, Colby asked Washington the name of the informant, so he could assess the significance of the dispatch. The desk officer at headquarters could find no one at his level to uncloak the pseudonym, and when Allen heard of the field inquiry he took delight in declining to name his source, even within the agency. With the familiar twinkle, he explained, "I've got to have my little secrets too."[22]

For Allen always placed great store in what men of affairs said to each other in their unguarded moments of talk over port or brandy and cigars. That, after all, was the appeal of the Council on Foreign Relations. Clandestine agents are not the only, or even the best, sources, Allen would explain to young recruits. "If you get an official to give you important information, that's intelligence," he explained. "If he leaves a classified document on his desk and you steal it, that's espionage." His own distinction, of course, made espionage the far more powerful tool. If the "owner" of the information does not know that the other person possesses it, he is at a strong disadvantage; the beneficiary of sound espionage has the clear edge.

If Allen found intelligence a comfortable pursuit for gentlemen, he was only too content to leave the tricks of espionage to others, and the less he knew of the details, the greater his comfort with the end result. Amazed coworkers who knew of Allen's own merry transgressions saw occasional flashes of prudery. Briefed on a plan for placing a willing and enticing émigré ballerina in a compromising position with a Russian military attaché, Allen suddenly stopped the briefing short: "Are you proposing that we *use sex?*" At least one hardened case officer never could decide whether Allen expected to be taken seriously as, jabbing the air with his pipe, he declared, "We will *not* do that sort of thing as long as I'm in this agency."

Allen always frowned on paying for information. "If you have to pay an agent, you might as well not use him," he would tell recruits, recalling the plight of old Colonel Redl. Men who turn against their country for money alone are notoriously unreliable; they will not hesitate to sell to both sides. A potential agent should at the very least be driven by some other motivation — hatred, passion, or revenge. Better still, in Allen's concept, an agent should find a community of interest with his case officers; whether by America's own networks and devices or through liaison with foreign services, that was how intelligence was best collected.

Intelligence collection was one part of Allen's charge when he entered CIA in 1951. The clandestine collection service, called the Office of Special Operations (OSO), consisted of survivors of wartime intelligence like Helms and Angleton, the rising master of counterespionage, who had continued under other bureaucratic covers after the OSS was disbanded. Old hands of the OSO considered themselves professionals of tradecraft, possessed of the skills and the patience to nurture networks and agents for the long haul.[23]

The other side of the clandestine services under Allen's direction was the aggressive covert action division, formed in 1948. After two years under the dynamic Wisner, the OPC was threatening to overwhelm the traditional intelligence collection function of CIA. From its first-year total of 302 employees, including those at seven overseas stations, by the time Allen settled in, the OPC had grown to 2,812 staff officers supported by 3,142 contract employees overseas at forty-seven stations. Its budget had gone from $4.7 million to $82 million, perhaps three times what the OSO received, and uncounted more was in the pipeline.[24]

NSC Directive 10/2 had called for measures to thwart international communism, not just to collect intelligence about its vicious activities. With the zeal of their Cold War generation, activists like Wisner and Kennan inside the government and Allen, outside, had set upon a task that the American republic had never attempted before on such a scale. Wisner seized upon the network of public organizations, the Free Europe Committee and related groups, that Allen had championed from New York and turned the innocent-seeming structure to the OPC's needs. The government agency built up to distribute Marshall Plan largess in Europe provided another ready-made structure in which operatives for covert action could be housed out in the field; the deputy administrator for European economic recovery, a brilliant academic named Richard M. Bissell, was readily drawn into devices for strengthening the politics as well as the economies of European democracies.*

Planting useful "news" articles in friendly publications, smuggling leaflets behind the Iron Curtain, sometimes by parachutes and balloons wafted by conveniently eastward winds, the OPC began its campaigns with propaganda. Radio Free Europe broadcast news and features of distinctly Western perspective to the satellite countries of eastern Europe; later Radio Liberty targeted the Soviet Union itself. The thirty-two-year-old Tom Braden, who followed Allen to Washington as his special assistant, formed the OPC International Division to provide CIA support for cultural activities and front groups of students and professionals, pursuing just the same tactics as the more experienced Soviet intelligence apparatus.

An Estonian-born cultural officer in the American occupation administration of Germany, Michael Josselson, was encouraged to activate the Congress for Cultural Freedom, an organization of left-wing but anticommunist intellectuals, the kind of Europeans Allen had sought to encourage in the first years after World War II. For two decades to come Josselson channeled CIA funding to high-quality magazines like *Encounter* in Britain and *Der Monat* in West Germany, into elaborate conventions and public organizations to promote the ideology of Free World democracy, countering the head start of communist cultural infiltrations. Again appeared that public deception, which left Allen untroubled, for ostensibly the Congress for Cultural Freedom was funded entirely from private sources.[25] Jay Lovestone, who had become head of the international division of the American Federation of Labor, and his European representative, Irving Brown, saw to it that the anticommunist labor

---

* Bissell had been invited to join the Eisenhower study group at the Council on Foreign Relations in early 1950, though at this time he had no notion of working for CIA.

unions of France and Italy were kept in line and in prosperity with secret and apparently unlimited CIA cash subsidies.

But the OPC did not stop with propaganda. As the Korean War raged and Washington strategists feared a more formidable military offensive in Europe, Wisner and his planners devised a variety of penetration missions to gain intelligence behind the Iron Curtain, support the surviving resistance movements within the satellite countries, and assemble underground paramilitary teams as "stay-behinds" to retard the Soviet invasion when it came. The Free Europe Committee had organized nine nationalist groups among the eastern European émigrés, and their field offices found ready volunteers in the camps of displaced persons among toughened fighters who had not hesitated to join Nazi and other fascist units against Soviet Russia during World War II. To regain respectability after the war, these discredited fighters needed protection from the prevailing mood of denazification; a shared anticommunism was just the vehicle for their rehabilitation. In 1950, five years after the fall of fascism, the strictures against employing former Nazis, initially imposed on Gehlen and other partisans of the Free World, disappeared under the pressure of the Korean War.

Starting in the late 1940s, hundreds of agents were dispatched into the Soviet Union and the satellite countries by air and through obscure border crossings from almost every point on the periphery between Scandinavia and Japan. Some were to contact and encourage anticommunist elements holding on in the Baltic states and Ukraine, others merely to place themselves (with their clandestine radio transmitters) at airfields or selected transportation points to give notice of unusual movement or to collect and analyze earth and water samples near suspected uranium-processing plants. Congress authorized a special $100 million fund in 1951 earmarked for forming eastern European anticommunists into military units "or for other purposes." CIA veteran Harry Rositzke wrote many years later, when it was safe to discuss these secret missions, "These cross-border operations involved enormous resources of technical and documentation support, hundreds of training officers, thousands of safehouses, and, above all, hundreds of courageous men who preferred to fight the Russians or the Communists rather than linger in the DP camps or emigrate to Brazil."[26] The fact that many of these Poles and Czechs and Hungarians had previously placed their courage and zeal in the service of Nazis and allied fascist factions against communism was of dwindling concern to the CIA clandestine services carrying out NSC Directive 10/2.

Bedell Smith, however, found himself increasingly uneasy about the weight and dynamism of the covert action branch, which he considered tangential, at best, to the proper CIA mission of collecting intelligence. "The presently projected scope of these [covert] activities has ... produced a threefold increase in the clandestine operations of this Agency," Smith told a budget review meeting early in 1952, "and will require next year a budget three times larger than that required for our intelligence activities."[27] Though one of his first acts had been to take the autonomous OPC under his authority rather than let it continue on dangerously freewheeling operations, he resisted Allen's plans for absorbing the covert action programs into the established collection networks. He could not dispute the logic of Allen's arguments, forged in sound experience and expressed in the Dulles-Jackson-Correa report and countless discussions. But he restrained Allen, hoping that this unwelcome activity could soon be transferred to another government agency, perhaps the military or some secret branch of the Defense Department.

Even when the ideological inevitability of the Cold War took hold, the acerbic director of central intelligence could not resist taking on the champions of "psychological warfare," the euphemism employed in polite company for subversive action. Addressing C. D. Jackson, an early activist in Allen's New York crowd and a leading figure in the Time-Life publishing complex, Bedell Smith drew upon his memory of World War II to praise "the most successful psychological warrior" he had ever known. As Jackson preened, Smith explained that "C.D. had planned a leaflet drop on Polish and Russian 'slave labor' camps in Germany. The bundle of leaflets had failed to open. It struck and sank a barge in the Rhine." That, said Smith, "was the greatest achievement of psychological warfare in Europe."[28]

A clear culture gap divided the two jerry-built CIA clandestine services, the OSO and the OPC, a gap of social class and working experience, between academics and policemen, liberals and conservatives, professionals of intelligence collection and elitists from the Ivy League — "enthusiastic but inexperienced amateurs" scornfully labeled "Park Avenue cowboys." "Collection is the hardest thing of all," said one survivor of the period; "it's much easier to plant an article in a local newspaper."

William Colby, a thirty-year-old New York lawyer but a veteran of OSS collaboration with the French and Norwegian resistance (called the Jedburgh missions), recalled reporting to duty, on his way to Scandinavia, at the temporary buildings of the OPC on the Washington Mall.

> The atmosphere there was once again that of wartime and the urgency of mobilization. The halls were full of earnest and worried men and women, rushing to meetings, conferring on the run, issuing crisp instructions to assistants trying to keep up with them. New people, full of enthusiasm, mingled with OSS veterans, Jedburgh colleagues with the elite of the postwar era, fresh from the Ivy League campuses in their tweed jackets,

smoking pipes, and full of daring, innovative ideas, who had flocked to the Agency as the most effective place for a non-communist liberal to do battle against the communist menace. . . . I was glad to be back within this dedicated and stimulating band.[29]

But more than class and culture separated the two hemispheres of Allen's clandestine services. The collection apparatus, OSO, had become an established service, with budget and pay scales adjusted only for inflation. The OPC, by contrast, had to recruit new people, and that meant offering higher pay. Performing the similar functions of running agents and exploiting targets of opportunity, the "amateurs" were better paid. Even worse, the OPC was expanding while the OSO was static; a bright recruit seeking reward and promotion knew where to turn.*

Most serious for Allen in balancing the two cultures was the operational fact that the OSO and the OPC marched to different drummers. Intelligence collection requires silent long-term care and commitment; covert actions demand immediate impact. A network that collects intelligence could — and should — go undetected for years; a successful sabotage operation is immediately obvious and provokes immediate countermeasures. The enthusiasts of the OPC seemed like "reckless adventurers" to OSO officers, who understandably feared that their own tediously nurtured networks would be blown by the demands for fast action.[30] The two branches were running separate networks on the same turf, bidding for the same agents. Gehlen, funded by the OSO, fought off lucrative offers from the newcomers of the OPC. Their separate operations to infiltrate East Germany often ended in the betrayal of one by the other. Competing subsidies to the same émigré organizations only resulted in separate files of worthless information.

Both of the clandestine services sought global coverage, and outside Europe the competition for local agents and resources became even more intense. On the defensive in Korea, General MacArthur finally lifted his ban on CIA field activity in his east Asian theaters, and both the OSO and the OPC rushed in with cash offers to any well-placed officer or entrepreneur who seemed to have good potential as an agent; needless to say, the world capitals were full of plucky souls capable of recognizing the Americans as a bonanza. CIA-funded corruption and competition rose to a crisis in the Bangkok station early in 1952, when Smith had to send top officials of both clandestine branches out to untangle a mess of opium trading under the cover of efforts to topple the Chinese communists.

* Helms, however, was farsighted enough to stand as an exception; he opted for the professional safety of intelligence collection, the OSO, rather than the more glamorous OPC. He followed Allen, after two short-timers, as director of central intelligence in 1966.

The flourishing of psychological warfare was carefully tracked in Moscow, where no one had any doubt about the identity of the American responsible. On the last day of 1951 Soviet publicist Ilya Ehrenberg remarked in *Pravda* that "if ever the spy Allen Dulles should arrive in Heaven, through somebody's absent-mindedness, he would begin to blow up the clouds, mine the stars and slaughter the angels." Bedell Smith sent the clip over to Allen, with the caustic note, "Wish we did all *Pravda* gives us credit for."

Allen gradually found his bearings in coping with his four-star boss's temper and skepticism. CIA colleagues remembered bruising confrontations, decorously called "fanny-chewing sessions": "If you talk back to [Smith], he'll bite your head off; if you cringe, he's like a lion drawing blood." A CIA official historian recalled: "In the security of his own office, Dulles would exclaim 'The General was in fine form this morning, wasn't he? Ha Ha Ha!' But Frank Wisner was always shaken. He likened an hour with General Smith to an hour on the squash court — and he did not mean by that to suggest that he enjoyed it."[31]

On the substance of their differences, Smith finally saw that his CIA could not shed the mission of covert subversion that had been thrust upon it and eagerly embraced by all below him. After sounding out two others, Smith on August 23, 1951, named Allen to replace Jackson as his top deputy. Wisner moved up to succeed Allen in the number-three post, deputy director of plans. The OSO and the OPC were finally integrated into one rich, omnipotent clandestine service.

Allen abandoned any pretense that his tenure in Washington was temporary. For the first months he and Clover had commuted from New York, then had rented the Georgetown home of Joseph Alsop during the influential communist's absence on an extended world tour. Allen and Clover, in turn, rented their house on East Sixty-first Street to their theater friend Gertrude Lawrence, who was settling in for a long run of the musical *The King and I*, a fantasy about nineteenth-century Siam that was drawing in the Broadway crowds just as the sordid realities of contemporary Bangkok were preoccupying the leading lady's landlord. When that one-year lease expired, the Dulleses sold the New York brownstone, their family home of two decades.

— * —

For Allen and all official Washington the early 1950s have to be considered the halcyon days of the Central Intelligence Agency. The service was young and adventurous; the men and women accepting its call were smart, dedicated, and with no reason to doubt their own integrity and that of their new organization. The enemy was clearly identifiable and clearly vicious. Public enthusiasm for the Cold War effort was high, with a corresponding readiness to sanction whatever seemed necessary to defeat the evils of Sino-Soviet communism. In Allen's circle and through all the eastern establishment, working for the CIA was the highest public service imaginable, far more inviting than the hidebound State Department or the crusty Pentagon. Allen had no trouble luring his old Bern aide, Tracy Barnes, back into the Game from his Boston law practice. A Sixty-first Street neighbor, Desmond FitzGerald, also a lawyer, a school buddy of Barnes's but a stranger to intelligence, was ready to drop everything to accept Allen's call to Washington. Disparaged by the old pros, the Park Avenue cowboys were highly intelligent and deeply motivated to do the public good.

The means for defeating international communism seemed relatively straightforward: imaginative propaganda, encouragement and organization of downtrodden eastern European émigrés to do what they wanted to do anyway, a little money invested here and there to ensure that the ideals of democracy triumphed. Some of what was being proposed, to be sure, might be a little close to the illegal, the unethical, or the downright immoral. Bedell Smith himself used to tell friends that his job required a man to leave his moral values outside the door — but the old general's rectitude asserted itself: "You'd damned well better remember exactly where you left them."[32]

Allen had long since overcome scruples about the means by which a grand and noble purpose is furthered, and with his ascendancy, practices that might have raised questions before became the acceptable norm. Examination of the international mails, for instance, to get the names and addresses of those who corresponded with people in the Soviet Union might turn up useful leads for espionage. Accordingly, late in 1952 the CIA asked the chief postal inspector in New York for a discreet facility inside the post office to study the international mail traffic. Only the envelopes would be examined, the CIA men implied, but their internal planning memo was more candid. "Once our unit was in position, its activities and influence could be extended gradually, so as to secure from this source every drop of potential information available." Within just a few months selected letters were being opened and analyzed by CIA in violation of all postal regulations; indeed, their actions were a crime under federal statute.*

Allen became intrigued, for personal reasons that his intimates understood only much later, with medical experimentation. During the eastern

* The illegal mail intercepts continued until 1973, and by the end nearly nine thousand pieces of mail passing through New York were being opened and analyzed each year, according to the Rockefeller Commission. When in later years CIA officers questioned the propriety of this program, they were assured that if an investigation came close to exposing it, the whole facility could be dismantled and removed on an hour's notice.

European show trials of the late 1940s, in which the names of Noel Field and Allen Dulles had been routinely invoked by muddled witnesses, American experts discovered the intelligence potential of drugs that influenced human behavior. Their ideas for using such drugs came to the Dulles-Jackson-Correa survey, but Allen resisted a special report on this delicate topic on grounds that the survey team was not competent in these "highly technical fields."[33] By the time he assumed responsibility in CIA two years later, drug research had become part of a much larger CIA program, with studies on the effects of radiation, electric shock, psychology, psychiatry, sociology, and harassment substances. The time would soon come, on Allen's watch, when human subjects would be submitted, without their knowledge or permission, to testing by agency scientists.

Practices like these would focus the outrage of a new generation on the CIA. Even in Allen's time an intrepid few within the clandestine services questioned their wisdom and legality. Yet the demands and authorizations from the White House seemed clear and forthright; the men and women of CIA in those halcyon days understood that ultimately they had the full support of the president of the United States. Bedell Smith went to the Oval Office every Friday morning for an unrecorded meeting. Whenever a special need arose he would call for an immediate appointment, then for his driver, and proceed to the White House unaccompanied.

Long after leaving CIA, in the last months of his life, Beetle Smith confided a remarkable exchange that occurred at one such meeting. The CIA director was troubled by a particularly audacious covert action plan that had come up through the normal channels for his authorization. Smith told Truman of his uneasiness, testing the outer limits of his authority against the potential wrath of the law. Hearing Smith out, Truman reached into his desk drawer, pulled out a single sheet of White House stationery, scrawled a few words on it, folded and handed it to the general without saying a word. As Smith unfolded the paper he saw his own name granted a blanket presidential pardon, signed by Harry S. Truman. The absolution before the law was unlimited and undated.[34]

No one could ask for a more dramatic confirmation of authority. The pardon was a typically Trumanesque gesture, an impulsive act to show Bedell Smith that the president stood firmly behind him. From then on Smith could fall back on his own judgments of circumstances and realities, on the needs of national security as he perceived it, without fear of reprisal. Future CIA directors would have welcomed such a safety net under their daily decisions.

Though many of the legal abuses that later undermined the CIA's integrity got their start through Allen's enthusiasm and under Smith's authority, the general did not hesitate to impose his own judgment against the heady clandestine services. Assassination of political figures as a means to promote the national interest was one matter on which Bedell Smith would not yield. Allen was no stranger to assassination, both in his long perusal of intelligence literature and in personal experience. It was, after all, a plan to kill Adolf Hitler that had consumed much of his attention during World War II in Bern.

The word "assassination" is seldom used when gentlemen in power contemplate the act; officials in the line of command seem to connive tacitly in polite euphemisms to conceal the level at which such an act is ordered. The concept of "plausible denial," enshrined in NSC Directive 10/2, led to situations, as later congressional investigators described them, in which "subordinates, in an effort to permit their superiors to 'plausibly deny' operations, fail to fully inform them about those operations."[35] Nonetheless, in the late summer of 1952, when Bedell Smith turned to one of the clandestine services' proposals reaching his desk, he recognized it as nothing less than a CIA operation to assassinate Stalin.[36]

Ever since the spring, the Four Powers had been pondering the idea of a summit meeting to learn what aspects of the World War II alliance could be rescued. In March 1952 Stalin offered a deviously hedged proposal for the reunification of Germany, and at the end of the month he suggested to American newsmen that a meeting of the four heads of state might be helpful. Secretary of State Acheson dismissed the idea as propaganda to split the Western allies — not a quixotic scheme, for British prime minister Churchill was immediately attracted to the idea and the French government was wavering over measures for Western unity.

Acheson's suspicions of Soviet mischief only increased in August, upon one of those cryptic signals that always set the diplomatic rumor mills whirring. For no evident reason Stalin suddenly received the French ambassador, newly arrived in Moscow. The British ambassador had waited nearly six months for such an interview; Kennan, just on the scene as envoy from the United States, had not even bothered to ask. Was the wily Soviet leader encouraging the French in their recalcitrance? There were even theories that Stalin might follow up by flattering French vanities with the proposal of Paris as the venue for a Four-Power summit. Churchill said he preferred neutral Vienna, but if Stalin proposed Paris, what would be the grounds for a Western refusal? The CIA played no role in these diplomatic discussions. But intelligence analysts thrive on speculation, and when the men in the clandestine services got wind of the possibility that Marshal Stalin might make a personal trip to Paris, their fertile imaginations were engaged.

The CIA's liaison with French labor unions was flourishing through

Allen's channel to Lovestone and the AFL International Department. The contacts with French motor vehicle maintenance workers were particularly close and agreeable. The cars and limousines for any visiting dignitaries would have to be serviced at known garages, where the work force could easily be influenced. The CIA clandestine services thus conjured up the possibility of easy access to a limousine that would be used by Stalin in Paris; the next step was to ask the technical branch what could be done with the car: routine sabotage as an irritant to the busy passengers? Contamination of the circulation system to make the air Stalin would breathe unpleasant or perhaps dangerous? Or should they consider an explosive to actually destroy the car and its passengers?

At the policy level were clear directives. The Psychological Strategy Board, Truman's overseer of CIA covert actions, sought to place "maximum strain on the Soviet structure of power." A top-secret planning document specified that "one of the most favorable occasions for furthering these objectives may be Stalin's passing from power."[37] The various options presented by the possibility of a visit by Stalin to Paris, and the means for implementing them, were considered within the buildings by the Lincoln Memorial. They were sent up to Wisner, who passed them on to Allen, who passed them up to Smith, all in the normal bureaucratic channel. At any level, of course, ideas can be rejected and not passed onward for further consideration; with the plans concerning Stalin in Paris, the proposals were not rejected.

It soon evolved that the proposed summit meeting with Stalin would never take place in Paris, Vienna, or anywhere else. Big Four diplomacy took another tack, and within six months the seventy-three-year-old Soviet dictator was dead anyway. But none of that was known when the director of central intelligence had to make a decision about setting in motion an operation to "deal" with Stalin should he arrive in Paris. "After two years of close personal observation," wrote the CIA historian of the period, "Smith lacked confidence in Dulles' self-restraint," to say nothing of the even less restrained Wisner. At most, in the director's view, Allen could be employed as "an enthusiastic advocate of covert operations — as long as the decision rested with Bedell Smith."

With scarcely a pause for consideration, and without any further inquiry, Walter Bedell Smith rejected out of hand any further planning by the CIA to assassinate Joseph Stalin.

— 13 —

HIS OWN MAN

THE YEAR 1952 WAS A GOOD ONE for Allen to stay out of politics. His was a professional, nonpartisan government post; he had done campaign-train duty in 1948 and then was in the thick of his brother's ill-starred bid for the Senate a year later. Given the strong possibility of a Republican presidential victory this time, and gratifying though it might be to work on the winning side for a change, it was far from clear at the start of the year that the flag bearer of his party would be a man Allen could support. For the Republicans, united during the past eight years under Dewey's leadership, were now split into two factions.

In 1950, in a forlorn effort to avert the split, Allen had contributed a hundred dollars to a short-lived Draft Dewey campaign, as if the twice-defeated candidate could be viable one more time. By the autumn of 1951 party professionals had concluded that they must turn to new leadership. One obvious candidate was the hero of D-day, Dwight D. Eisenhower, then commanding the European theater of the Western alliance in the Cold War, which even the Democrats feared could turn hot at any moment. Senator Henry Cabot Lodge of Massachusetts flew to Paris in September to alert the NATO commander of a drive by the liberal wing of the party to draft him for the nomination. Opposed were the conservatives, called isolationists by their foes, promoting the presidential candidacy of Ohio senator Robert A. Taft. On the Democratic side the question of Truman's successor was still wide open.

Allen was torn among these competing forces — Eisenhower, Taft, and the Truman Democrats. Both personally and ideologically, he was in the camp of the Republican liberals. Though not personally close to Eisenhower, Allen had worked with him in the Council on Foreign Relations study group, and he feared the isolationism of the right wing. But just as the intraparty tension heated up, Allen found himself engaged on an unanticipated and awkward personal level with the family and friends of Senator Taft.

On the eve of the Republican National Convention in July, Taft announced the engagement of his younger son, Horace, to Mary Jane Bancroft; the Taft family planned a September wedding in Washington. Allen had known Mary Jane as a schoolgirl in Switzerland during the war, when he was involved with her mother. Clover's friendship with Mary Bancroft had only ripened over the years, their shared love for the same restless man more a bond than an obstacle, so she found it only appropriate to offer the Georgetown house as social headquarters for Mary and her betrothed daughter as they came to know their new Taft in-laws. Since Mary Jane's father was long out of the picture, it also seemed natural when, for the ceremony, the bride turned to her mother's great friend Allen. The Taft family came to think of Mary Jane as Allen's "ward," for want of a clearer definition.[1] At the height of the election campaign, therefore, Allen was called upon to give in matrimony, to the son of Senator Taft, the daughter of his former mistress.

Politically supportive of Eisenhower, socially involved with Taft, Allen was at the same time serving the Democratic administration as deputy director of central intelligence. Truman and Allen carried a heavy load of old political baggage between them. It was Truman who had abruptly abolished the OSS just as Allen was helping to build the wartime organization into a peacetime intelligence service. And Truman was not one to overlook Allen's role at Dewey's side in the 1948 campaign. He had repeatedly scratched Allen's name from lists of candidates for high diplomatic posts, even as the bipartisan imperative led him to welcome John Foster Dulles into the outer reaches of his foreign policy circles.

CIA business with President Truman was normally conducted by the director, Walter Bedell Smith, but at least three times in the spring of that election year, Smith's absence from Washington propelled Allen into the position of briefing Truman at the weekly intelligence meeting.[2] Years later Allen made light of the mutual wariness between him and Truman. He enjoyed regaling worldly friends with the story that Truman had once asked him for a wall map pinpointing the location of every CIA secret agent in the world. Well, the president is entitled to any information the government possesses, but no intelligence professional could conceive of assembling — much less handing over for idle curiosity — such a dangerous and frivolous display. It was only in Truman's character to tease his Republican spymaster with a mischievous request and then watch Allen's discomfort in explaining why such a map would really not be appropriate for the wall of the Oval Office.*

Allen's balancing act that election year paled before that of his older brother; unlike Allen, Foster saw his political fortunes once again entirely dependent upon a Republican victory in November. In the name of party unity Foster deftly avoided being publicly identified with either Taft or Eisenhower. Within days of Eisenhower's decision late in April to seek the presidency, however, Foster flew over to Paris to brief the new candidate on the coming campaign and to press his own views for a Republican foreign policy. He left with Eisenhower an advance copy of an essay he had written for *Life* magazine, arguing that Republicans should not settle for "containment" of communism but should push for the "liberation" of captive peoples from the yoke of the Kremlin.[3] Eisenhower was willing to start his campaign without questioning Foster's foreign policy guidance.

Allen took a different tack to avoid the heat of partisan debate. Tracing a course that would serve him in good stead in future political years, he got out of town. The weeks at the height of the campaign, after the Taft-Bancroft wedding, were just right for his annual vacation in Europe. Election Day came a week after Allen returned home; the Republicans under Eisenhower finally succeeded in ending two decades of Democratic power, winning 442 electoral votes to Stevenson's 89.

— * —

The week after the election the Dulles family suffered a cruel blow. Clover and Allen's son, Allen Macy, a lieutenant in the Marines, was fighting in Korea. At boot camp he had volunteered for the dangerous position of forward artillery observer. On a November Friday afternoon a call from the Pentagon informed Allen that his twenty-two-year-old son had been critically wounded in combat. On a scarred mountainside exploding mortar shells had injured him twice in his arm and back, but the youth had refused medical evacuation. Then, as Lieutenant Dulles crept to within thirty yards of an enemy gun emplacement to direct his men's mortar fire, a third explosion hit. A shell fragment tore away part of his brain and lodged in his head. A comrade, son of an Italian-American grocer, risked his own life to drag him to safety. In critical con-

* As the campaign proceeded, the CIA arranged classified briefings for Eisenhower and for Truman's handpicked successor on the Democratic ticket, Adlai Stevenson of Illinois. The briefings of the two candidates were identical, with one exception. Only Eisenhower was told that the sources for certain items of intelligence were electronic intercepts of foreign communications. As a general of the army, he was already cleared for that most sensitive of secret information; the civilian Stevenson did not have such clearance.

dition, he was lifted by helicopter to an offshore hospital ship and flown to Japan for emergency care.

When he received the call from the Pentagon, Allen telephoned his wife in Switzerland, where she had stayed on to continue her Jungian studies. Clover flew forthwith to Japan. Successful brain surgery at the naval hospital at Yokosuka eliminated the threat of permanent blindness and, though still unconscious, the young Marine was removed from the critical list. But for nearly a month he was unable to recognize his mother. Allen flew to Tokyo from Washington in the middle of December, and for the next two weeks, except for a brief courtesy call on the prime minister of Japan, he stayed at his son's bedside.

Just before he left Washington, Allen received a letter from Harry Truman: "I was terribly distressed to learn of your son being wounded." Bedell Smith had informed the White House of the injury and had dictated on the telephone a letter for Truman to sign.[4]

— * —

Within days of his election Eisenhower began receiving contradictory advice about the Dulles brothers, both of whom were eager to join the incoming Republican administration.

Foster was better known to the president-elect. Early in the campaign Eisenhower had bought the Dullesian theme of "liberating the captive peoples" of eastern Europe for his first foreign policy speech, but less than a week later he delivered another address specifying that freedom from communism was to be sought only through "peaceful means," a clear softening of Foster's bellicosity. From that point on Eisenhower no longer turned to Foster for drafts of foreign policy statements, and the Dulles counsel was noticeably absent during the rest of the campaign.

Well known in international diplomatic circles, Foster was not universally popular — because of his abrupt personal manners as much as his belligerent policy positions. Among Churchill's men in Whitehall he was particularly disliked, and these were the allies whom Eisenhower took most seriously. Foreign Secretary Anthony Eden was not the only one who remembered Foster's support for the discredited policy of appeasement in the late 1930s. Ignoring the usual discretion of his position, Eden made bold to write Eisenhower as an old friend to express the hope that Foster Dulles would not be named secretary of state.[5] Some leading Republicans around the president-elect worried that Foster would be too sympathetic to the Taft wing of the party. Eisenhower's first impulse, accordingly, was to name John McCloy, a trusted civilian veteran of the Pentagon and the German occupation regime. But after keeping all concerned in suspense for three long weeks, he finally turned to Foster for the position. A gesture to the Taft wing—if that was how some interpreted it—would not hurt the new administration and, as Eisenhower remarked of his choice, "There's only one man I know who has seen more of the world and talked with more people and knows more than he does, and that's me."[6]

The motives and maneuvers that played out in those transition weeks of December and January remain topics of conjecture decades after the fact. Comfortable hindsight tends to blur difficult decisions, making them appear inevitable. But the outcome of a delicate calculation, the choice of John Foster Dulles as secretary of state, and the controversial personnel shuffle that ensued, determined the basic complexion of the Eisenhower administration in international affairs, and with it the foreign policy of the United States for the rest of the 1950s.

Eisenhower immediately surrounded his designated secretary of state with others in whom he had more confidence. He named his campaign manager, Henry Cabot Lodge, ambassador to the United Nations and, to Foster's reported annoyance, confirmed Lodge as a member of the cabinet with direct access to the president. He asked his old chief of staff, Bedell Smith, to leave CIA to become undersecretary of state, a vantage point that would permit keeping a close eye on Foster's stewardship. Two other tested Eisenhower loyalists, Douglas MacArthur II and Robert Murphy, were named to high State Department posts. The shift left the leadership of the intelligence agency open; Allen was the obvious candidate to succeed Smith, but the prospect of two brothers in sensitive high positions of government, with inevitable personal interests and loyalties beyond their allegiance to the president, had to give Eisenhower pause. Again he delayed for long and agonizing weeks before naming the younger Dulles director of central intelligence.

Documents finally declassified four decades later permit a new rendering of Eisenhower's calculations in making these appointments, a reconstruction that is at odds in significant respects with the memories of key participants as they chose to tell the story for history. This version comes, through a series of private conversations and remarks, from Bedell Smith himself, the swing man in the shuffle.[7]

Smith had not enjoyed his tenure at CIA, and he dared to hope that he could score his final answer to the snubs of the West Pointers if his wartime commander and comrade, now the president-elect, named him chairman of the Joint Chiefs of Staff. But Smith's ambition ran straight up against the rigid military tradition that the top post had to rotate among the services. Following army general Omar N. Bradley (who happened to be one of Smith's longtime detractors), it was the navy's turn, and even Eisenhower could not flout the practices of the uniformed services. Smith apparently was confronted with these realities on the night of November 21, when he secretly boarded Eisenhower's private railroad car at an unscheduled stop in Baltimore, en route to the capital. Leaving the train glum and shaken, unobserved by the official welcoming party in Washington, Smith told military colleagues he was ready "to get out and make some money" as a business executive, as so many of his retired army comrades had done. But Eisenhower had other designs, and he had explained to his loyal staff officer the problems of leaving Foster unguarded at State.

Smith raised two objections to Eisenhower's scheme. First, like others who had worked with John Foster Dulles, he did not like the man and could not foresee a working relationship of mutual confidence. Second, relieved though he would be to leave CIA, he saw an inexorable pressure to name his well-connected and experienced deputy to the post vacated. Smith lacked confidence in the younger Dulles brother as well as the elder. He had made no secret of his concern over Allen's enthusiasm for extravagant covert actions and, mirroring Eisenhower's hesitancy about Foster, he worried what Allen might do with the expanding resources of the CIA without a cool hand to restrain him. Smith urged alternative choices upon the president-elect, but Eisenhower knew the frailties and peculiarities of intelligence men as well as Smith did, and the departing CIA director realized it was futile to try to change his old friend's mind once it was made up.

Once Eisenhower made clear his intention, Smith was incapable of refusing the position of undersecretary of state. Before giving his final acceptance, however, he had one prior obligation of honor. Bedell Smith had been a loyal aide to Harry Truman, the commander in chief who had ordered him to the CIA and subsequently granted him, as he alone knew, the ultimate trust of presidential power. As the old administration departed, Smith went to Truman privately to ask if the outgoing president would be embarrassed should his director of central intelligence accept a post with the Republican succession. Truman had tears in his eyes as he later told a congressional friend about Bedell Smith's gesture.

In retirement Eisenhower offered the account that Foster had chosen Smith to be his undersecretary. Unlikely though that is, given the contrary contemporary evidence, Foster did indeed have good reasons for not objecting to Smith's presence at his side. He would have a trusted presidential intimate effectively within his own jurisdiction, a safety valve for bureaucratic combat. Furthermore, despite the later suspicions of his detractors, Foster Dulles showed no signs of wanting to pursue a foreign policy independent of the president's, so Smith's presence would cause him no inconvenience. At the same time, of course, the opening of the

CIA directorship would clear the way for his younger brother to realize his own ambition.

What is remarkable is that Allen's appointment, completing the roster of Eisenhower's foreign policy team, was so long in coming. On January 9 *Washington Post* columnist Marquis Childs reported flatly that Allen Dulles would be the new head of the CIA. "Marquis Childs is a good friend of mine," Allen, ever jaunty, wrote a New York friend the day before the inauguration, but "his very pleasant article slightly jumped the gun. No final decision has been reached here — however, it is always pleasant to read these things."

For Allen had his rivals in the bureaucracy of the Great Game having nothing to do with partisan politics, fraternal relationships, or his own enthusiasm in the increasingly aggressive business of intelligence. Most embarrassing was the once formidable figure of William Donovan. Like so many other OSS veterans, Donovan was practicing law in New York, but unlike the others whom he had sponsored, he had not succeeded in rejoining the Game when it heated up again. By 1953 this exile was grating on him, and he pressed his last chance to take over, even at the expense of the younger friend and colleague who seemed to have so effectively upstaged him. "Have been following 'Wild Bill's' efforts to himself secure the post with trepidation," wrote one of Allen's friends. "If he had squeezed you out, I would have tried to get a . . . bill in Congress to bar his world travelling for more than eleven months each year." Donovan was not Allen's only competitor. *Newsweek* reported that the Taft Republicans sought the CIA post for General Albert C. Wedemeyer, MacArthur's comrade in Korea and the Pacific. Theirs was the lingering belief that national intelligence was still a prerogative of the military, and a MacArthur man seemed more ideologically reliable than an Eisenhower "internationalist."

So insecure was Allen about realizing his aspiration that he looked about for a safety net in case he was not chosen. He set up a lunch date in New York for January 21, the day after the presidential inauguration, with his Council on Foreign Relations friend David Rockefeller. He learned that if he gave the word, he could abandon the Washington power game and return to New York to become president of the Ford Foundation — already usefully engaged as one of those organizations that Allen had years before mobilized for political warfare against communism.

Inauguration Day 1953, therefore, was not a time of celebration for Allen. He was respected for his experience in the business of intelligence; his brother was safely placed in the diplomatic eminence of their uncle and grandfather. But family sorrow continued to cast a pall. His son was still immobile in Japan, hovering on the edge of consciousness. Clover's letters to her husband from the hospital bedside during the transition period vacillated between a mother's exhilaration at the slightest sign of her son's recognition, followed by her despair at what the future held for a once brilliant young man. The father realized the meaning of conflict in all its cruelty, though his daughter Joan said he went on bottling up all the emotion. Powerless to help his son, even had he dropped everything to join the bedside vigil, Allen also saw his own life's mission hanging undecided. He had not yet been able to arrange a personal discussion with the incoming president about the leadership of the CIA.[8]

As they mingled with the dignitaries in the Senate Marble Room the morning of the inauguration, awaiting the summons to step out onto the inaugural stand, the Dulles brothers showed their contrasting personalities. Foster huddled in a corner, courteously receiving those persons who came to greet him. Allen, ignoring the precariousness of his position, played the room, moving from group to group with cheerful words and appropriate anecdotes. He was still only deputy director of central intelligence, and no one could say for sure what would follow. That night the Dulles family of Watertown converged for a reunion in Georgetown, with the sisters, husbands, and children from upstate New York joining their illustrious Washington relatives, Foster, Allen, and Eleanor. Robert Lansing Edwards, Margaret's son, remembers his uncle Allen as unnaturally testy over dinner, irritated about the refusal of Charles E. Wilson, the incoming secretary of defense, to divest himself of his General Motors holdings, worth $2.5 million, because of a heavy tax liability. Wilson distinguished himself a few days later with the statement that "what's good for our country is good for General Motors, and vice versa." Allen had always accepted as gospel, from his early years as a diplomat, that the interests of American business were synonymous with the interests of the American republic. But the "vice versa" never fit into Allen's scheme of things: personal profit was never to be considered in public service.

On January 23, *The New York Times* broke the story that Allen was indeed to become director of central intelligence; the official announcement came the next day. "The outlook for a purposeful and imaginative development of our intelligence service is excellent," commented the *Times* editorial page. Commendations came as well from Democrats who knew Allen's public record but not his controversial role within the clandestine services. Arthur Schlesinger, Jr., wary and weary from the Stevenson campaign, nonetheless hailed Allen as "astute and experienced, [one whose] counsel should be effective in cooling down the hotheads"[9]— those of the Republican right wing, yes, but those within the classified ranks of the high-spirited intelligence agency?

The weeks of suspense were over. Allen immediately paid a call on Donovan, "since I retain the greatest admiration and affection for him."* The next week, as Allen awaited Senate action on his nomination, Lieutenant Allen Macy Dulles was flown home from Japan and carried off the hospital plane on a stretcher, his torn head swathed in thick white bandages. His father waited at the foot of the steps at Andrews Air Force Base. Allen's CIA office had alerted the press; news photographers clustered around. Allen bent down and — as too seldom in happier times — lightly kissed his son's cheek. The photograph was in the morning papers the next day as Allen went up to Capitol Hill for his confirmation hearings. He was confirmed in office without opposition, and on February 26, 1953, began the decade that came to be known as the Dulles era at the Central Intelligence Agency.

— * —

The CIA was still an insecure branch of government in the early 1950s, and the era opened with challenges at home and abroad. The civilian intelligence service sought to be a responsible instrument of foreign policy, but its functions were misunderstood and often not welcomed by the traditional bureaus of power. Even in its own mission the agency was insecure — torn early in the Cold War between the tasks of providing intelligence about perceived enemies and the more dubious task of acting covertly against those enemies. Allen had the double task of securing the CIA's professional standing among policymakers in Washington and of organizing the agency for carrying out its defined missions abroad. The Washington challenge was public, a matter of perceptions as much as reality; the foreign problems, cloaked in necessary secrecy, became known to the public only gradually over many troubled years to come.

Whatever status the agency enjoyed in the closing years of the Truman administration derived from the stature of its director, Walter Bedell Smith, in contrast to his lackluster predecessors. Allen had none of

* Four months into the new administration Eisenhower appointed Donovan ambassador to Thailand, where he spent the next year generating covert activities against communist China. As always, he was careless in financial matters, and in January 1954 Allen offered him financial help from the CIA in managing the embassy. Donovan resigned the post six months later but continued to harbor hopes for higher responsibilities; he eagerly grasped at rumors that Eisenhower might name him chief justice, the appointment that went instead to Earl Warren of California. In February 1957 Donovan was diagnosed as suffering from arteriosclerotic atrophy of the brain, a progressive condition that was said to account for his erratic behavior for several years past. Retired to his Sutton Place residence overlooking the East River, he reported spotting Russian troops marching into Manhattan across the Fifty-ninth Street bridge outside his window. Donovan died on February 8, 1959.

the standing with his president that Smith had enjoyed with Truman, nor could he assert a commanding presence with the Joint Chiefs, who continued to distrust a civilian intelligence service. But through his long career Allen had come to know the Great Game better than most, and his intuitive sense of what he called the craft of intelligence was unmatched anywhere in the government.

Beyond that, the new director had a special status of intimacy with the secretary of state. This was a wild card that, in the bids for power and influence, could not be ignored. Each Dulles brother had credentials for his respective position without any patronage from the other. Separately they were formidable enough, yet in tandem they were able to influence the president and Congress, and thus guide the foreign policy of the United States, far more effectively than either could have managed on his own.

Foster, aged sixty-five, and Allen, five years his junior, had always been rigorously loyal to each other, even as they pursued separate professional and personal interests. Through their grandfather and uncle, both secretaries of state, the virtue of public service and the unquestioned righteousness of the American purpose in the world had been instilled in the brothers from boyhood. In the last year before World War II they had been uncomfortably on opposite sides of the greatest foreign policy issue of the day — Allen passionately arguing for American intervention in the European war against Hitler and Mussolini, Foster asserting his formidable intellect to argue for a national interest in appeasing the dictators. The brothers' mutual loyalty against all detractors never prevented either from asserting a position contrary to the other's; but they would fight out their tensions over the chessboard and proceed in their separate careers.

Surrounded by the others in Eisenhower's inner circles, they behaved as any colleagues would, respectful of each other's turf, free to assert differing views on an impersonal basis. They were seldom alone together on the job. They spoke on the telephone to each other daily, often many times, in quick, shorthand conversations that bypassed layers of bureaucratic staff, but after all, each of them also talked every day with many others in the high strata of government. They also shared a more personal meeting ground, which had the effect of bringing the director of central intelligence into the making of foreign policy more closely than any of his predecessors.

Eleanor Dulles, established in her own right as a desk officer in the State Department, had built a bungalow house in the pastoral Washington suburb of McLean, Virginia. Its central attraction was the swimming pool. Here on a typical Sunday afternoon the secretary of state and the director of the CIA, with or without wives and family, would lounge at poolside sipping highballs — two middle-aged Presbyterian gentlemen sporting baggy shorts and gaudy Hawaiian shirts, the casual chic of the day. No staff aides or protocol-minded eavesdroppers were present to record their conversations.[10] Eleanor also occasionally invited a friend for the afternoon. Any foreign diplomat who could manage an invitation to swim at Eleanor's pool had the satisfaction of reporting back to his capital that he had gained access to the heart of American foreign policymaking.

As they settled into their respective responsibilities, the brothers' long-standing personality differences became more pronounced. In conversation Foster sought refuge in intellectual abstractions; Allen engaged on the human level. Foster had a shy and nervous smile, and as he succumbed to an illness not yet diagnosed, his heavy frame diminished. Even when the gout hit, Allen remained hearty, buoyant, and expansive, his barrel-chested ho ho ho known to all. He remained fierce and competitive on the tennis court with men half his age; on a good day he could go around a golf course at 90. "He has the soaring forehead of a professor, and a thatch of white hair," wrote *New York Times* reporter Russell Baker. "Full gray moustache, slightly rumpled tweeds and bow tie, glasses perched jauntily above his eyebrows and ever present pipe round out the impression of a prep-school headmaster." But as this shrewd observer noticed, "the eyes are perhaps a bit too penetrating to go with the big booming laugh; the hands are certainly too broad, too strong for anyone but a man of action."

Allen enjoyed the Washington diplomatic circuit, frequenting embassy receptions with a careless ease that was never Foster's style. Often Clover would go with him, though she hated the officious impersonality of it all. A classic vignette came at a particularly tedious reception, when Allen and Clover, trying to sneak out through the garden door, found a daunting brick wall barring their escape route. "Dare you!" Clover said, and within moments the director of central intelligence and his wife were spotted climbing over the embassy wall to the street outside. To have Allen at a dinner party was a Washington hostess's dream, while Foster's presence tended to cast a pall of sobriety. Foster went solemnly to church every Sunday morning; Allen, more often than not, would stroll the darkened corridors of his CIA, seeking out any diligent officers on duty to ask, "What's going on?"

Allen responded to the intrusions of democracy quite differently from Foster. Protest demonstrations were not the art form in the 1950s that they later became, but once, as Allen was being driven over to the State Department for a routine meeting, he spotted a modest picket line of crew-cut university students. From his fifth-floor office window, Foster stared uncomprehending at the untoward display; Allen jumped out of his car and strode over to the demonstrators with a hearty "Hello! I'm Allen Dulles. What are you all doing here? What's your problem?"[11] Foster had always found difficulty remembering the names of his junior partners at Sullivan and Cromwell; Allen would spend an hour before a trip abroad with a list of the people he would be meeting, not only the CIA men but their wives as well, so that he could greet them as old friends. Whenever he could, he would take his favorite field officers with him to the White House and introduce them to Eisenhower with the hearty words, "Mr. President, here's my best man!"

The brothers' concepts of their duties were also quite different. Foster respected the techniques of covert action that CIA had developed, largely under Allen's prodding, in pursuit of a cold but holy war against communism. Yet he often chose to adopt the State Department mentality of knowing as little as possible about sordid operational details of intelligence. Allen, for his part, was nurtured in matters of foreign policy, but he always claimed that his duty was only that of a professional intelligence officer, leaving the policymaking to others — to his brother.

The line between intelligence and policy wore thin from the start. Allen was ever imaginative in devising intelligence operations that by their very nature determined the shape of national policy. CIA support for a detected underground of Polish democrats, for instance, would seem to commit the United States against the communist government of Poland. And not only diplomatic decisions were predetermined by Allen's action proposals.

Just two days after Eisenhower's inauguration the new president came under pressure to offer executive clemency to Julius and Ethel Rosenberg, under sentence of death as atomic spies for the Soviet Union. As the Rosenbergs waited on death row at New York's Sing Sing penitentiary, Allen joined those urging clemency. He proposed to use the couple for foreign policy advantage: "Communist parties throughout the world have built up the Rosenbergs as heroes and as martyrs to 'American anti-semitism,'" he argued. Given Stalin's own anti-Jewish policies, the voice of that notorious couple would have impact if they could be persuaded to launch a public appeal "to Jews in all countries to get out of the communist movement and seek to destroy it."

> Their recantation would entail backfiring of this entire Soviet propaganda effort. It would be virtually impossible for world communism to ignore or successfully discredit the Rosenbergs. The couple is ideally situated to serve as leading instruments of a psychological warfare cam-

paign designed to split world communism on the Jewish issue, to create disaffected groups with the membership of the Parties, to utilize these groups for further infiltration and for intelligence work.[12]

The idea, like so many of Allen's early schemes, went nowhere; Julius and Ethel Rosenberg were executed on June 19, 1953, without any statement to the Jews of the world.

Foster and Allen first displayed their divergent, though not necessarily conflicting, purposes early in the Eisenhower administration over the professional standing of George Kennan, who was a man of Allen's circle of friends, not Foster's. As Truman's ambassador to the Kremlin, he was in limbo as the Eisenhower administration took office. Stalin had summarily declared him persona non grata the previous October after he blurted out some injudicious remarks about everyday life in Moscow. Normally this expulsion would not have endangered his career in the American Foreign Service, but since it came at the height of the election campaign, it would fall to the incoming administration to decide on the ambassador's next posting.

Foster had been suspicious of Kennan since 1950 when, in a closed State Department meeting, the career diplomat had made bold to challenge a Dulles position as "emotional anticommunism" that made him "shudder" for the future of American foreign policy. Foster told a newsman he regarded Kennan as "a dangerous man."[13] Just four days before the inauguration, as Foster was preparing to become secretary of state, Kennan delivered what he considered a routine speech about confronting Soviet power — a text, incidentally, which he said had been properly cleared by the State Department. The next day the *Washington Post* carried the headline "DULLES POLICY 'DANGEROUS,' KENNAN SAYS."[14] Kennan promptly wrote Foster an apology, and in a brief personal meeting a week later the new secretary of state listened impassively to Kennan's explanation of what he had actually said. The State Department issued a statement that the matter was closed.

Foster avoided further contact with Kennan, but Allen promptly offered him a job at CIA. Finally in April, after news reports that Kennan was being involuntarily retired from the Foreign Service, Foster received him one last time at his State Department office and urged him to accept Allen's offer. It was, as Kennan described it, "a confused contest of wills" between two powerful egos, in which Foster Dulles attempted to "pawn me off on his brother. . . . I felt that if I was not wanted where I had grown up and belonged, i.e., in the State Department, I would rather not be anywhere, and I told him so."

Kennan spent the rest of the decade in academic life, though he was often summoned from Princeton for sensitive consultations with Allen and other government analysts. He returned to the diplomatic service as President John F. Kennedy's ambassador to Yugoslavia and remained a revered elder statesman into his nineties. In common with many others who knew both Dulles brothers, he stayed personally friendly with Allen but never patched up his differences with Foster.

— * —

The episode that in the public mind most sharply distinguished Allen's CIA from Foster's State Department erupted in the first months of the Eisenhower administration. The mood of witch-hunting for communists within the government did not abate after the Democrats were driven from power; even Republican Washington was immersed in waves of suspicion and recrimination, driven by the aggressiveness of its right wing — specifically, the demagogic power of Senator Joseph McCarthy and his supporters.

Ever since the day in 1950 when the junior senator from Wisconsin had found a crowd-pleasing line in his claims to have uncovered covens of communists in high places, redbaiting seemed a runaway adventure in malevolence. One of the most insidious sources of rumor and innuendo against public figures, it later came to light, was none other than Major General Van Deman, whom Allen had befriended long before at the Paris Peace Conference. Following his retirement in 1929, Van Deman had spent two obsessive decades in southern California, piecing together tidbits from the public press and what he claimed were his own networks of agents about subversive communistic influences in American public life. After his death in 1952 Van Deman's massive card files found their way to the Senate's Internal Security subcommittee and fueled many of the unsubstantiated charges by McCarthy and the other witch-hunters against prominent Americans. Congressman Emanuel Cellar, Democrat of New York, appeared in the files as a "Jew playing the Reds"; others deemed suspect were actresses Helen Hayes and Joan Crawford, Nobel Prize chemist Linus Pauling, and author Pearl Buck.[15]

As presidential candidate Eisenhower had taken a high road, apparently believing he could simply ignore the unseemly rumblings within his own camp. Once in office, Foster followed his president's lead, placing himself above combat even when the loyalty of his own professional diplomats was impugned. Foster had no abiding loyalty to the Foreign Service; he continued to blame the diplomatic club for having misled him years earlier into thinking that Alger Hiss was blameless. Prominent career diplomats were pilloried for their alleged communist leanings; personal grievances among coworkers assumed the status of "reliable reports"; unsubstantiated rumors and gossip were sufficient to destroy careers. The secretary of state allowed the rampage to run its course, judging that he could pacify the party's right wing by leaving the management of the department to McCarthy sympathizers — the senior official, for instance, who thought he had a good laugh line in assuring his audiences that "not *all* New Dealers are necessarily security risks."[16]

Allen took the McCarthy virus far more seriously, for he considered the morale and integrity of his CIA professionals to be a precious commodity in the Washington power struggles. At one point he told an assemblage of some six hundred agency officers that he would summarily fire anyone who went to McCarthy's investigators with malicious information about fellow employees, and he determined to use the agency's own internal security procedures to weed out anyone disloyal or unworthy of the public trust.[17]

Ironically, CIA first caught the redbaiters' attention from a gratuitous remark by Bedell Smith while he was still the CIA director. On September 29, 1952, during the election campaign, Smith voluntarily gave a deposition in a civil suit against McCarthy. Asked if he believed there were communists in the State Department, and seeking to deflate the charges, Smith blurted out, "I do. I believe there are communists in my own organization." Too late, the blunt-talking soldier realized the danger of his careless remark. The next day, with his quote making headlines in seeming confirmation of McCarthy's charges, Smith contacted Truman and both presidential candidates to make certain they understood what he had meant, that one had to assume penetration by communists in order to root them out. Eisenhower and Stevenson both promptly issued statements denouncing attempts to drag the intelligence service into partisan politics, though it took Smith weeks of congressional hearings to set his own record straight.[18]

The CIA's lingering vulnerability in the witch-hunt was threatened anew on July 9, 1953, six months into the Eisenhower administration. By chance, three senior CIA men arrived a little earlier than usual that morning: Robert Amory, the deputy director for intelligence analysis, and two officers of the analytical staff, William P. Bundy and Chester Cooper. The three exchanged a few words about the day ahead as they walked from the parking lot to the headquarters building, where Amory and Bundy had their offices. A short time later Cooper called Bundy to pursue the discussion and was told by his secretary, Anna Lee Haslett, that Mr. Bundy would not be coming into the office that day. Cooper had walked in with him just half an hour earlier; what was going on?[19]

What was going on was a hastily contrived delaying action against an attempt by McCarthy to penetrate the CIA. In the interval between the parking lot encounter and Cooper's telephone call, Roy Cohn, McCarthy's chief investigator, had called the CIA's legislative liaison officer, Walter Pforzheimer, to demand testimony from Bundy that very morning. A few days before, the file of a routine CIA internal investigation had been passed to Hoover at the FBI and apparently had found its way to the McCarthy committee; it disclosed that Bundy, a Democrat, had contributed four hundred dollars to Alger Hiss's legal defense fund. The CIA investigation had cleared the thirty-five-year-old analyst of any impropriety; indeed, Bundy himself had reported the contribution before joining the agency two years previously. Bundy was just the sort of young man that Allen would support with no questions asked: Groton, Yale, and Harvard Law, he was the son of Harvey Bundy, well known to the Dulles brothers, and the brother of McGeorge Bundy, Allen's colleague in the Dewey campaign. William's wife, Mary, was the daughter of Dean Acheson, the former secretary of state.*

That morning Allen decided, as a matter of principle, that CIA officers would not be allowed to testify before Congress. To gain breathing space he ordered Bundy to take a few days' personal leave; Cohn could thus be informed that the target of his inquiry was out of town and unavailable. As the day wore on, McCarthy's men suspected a ruse. Pforzheimer warned his superiors that if he himself were summoned to the McCarthy committee to explain Bundy's absence, he would have to tell the truth. When Cohn accused Amory of perjury in saying that Bundy was on leave when the congressional summons came, Amory replied blandly, "It wasn't perjury because I wasn't under oath; I just lied."[20] An irate McCarthy rose on the floor of the Senate to denounce the CIA director for a "most blatant attempt [to] thwart the authority" of Congress.

With Bundy safely away at his family's home on Boston's north shore, playing golf with his father, Allen proceeded to confront McCarthy on the substance of the matter. Taking the CIA's legal counsel, Lawrence Houston, with him, he drove up to Capitol Hill the next day to meet with the Republican members of the committee. After the usual pleasantries he startled the senators by stating flatly, "Joe, you're not going to have Bundy as a witness."[21] Allen promptly called Foster to report his determination. Then he called another man on whom he felt he could rely and who would have influence on McCarthy, Vice President Nixon. It was Nixon who finally managed to cajole McCarthy into backing off. "But

---

* Later Pforzheimer, for one, wondered if Allen would have been so quick to defend some other CIA officer of lesser background.

what about his contribution to Hiss?" McCarthy argued. Nixon replied, "Joe, you have to understand how those people up in Cambridge think. Bundy graduated from the Harvard Law School, and Hiss was one of its most famous graduates. I think he probably just got on the bandwagon without giving any thought to where the bandwagon was heading."[22]

McCarthy's charges, and the nasty exchanges that followed over the next weeks, went a long way to defining public perceptions of the CIA, with leading liberal voices heralding the rebuff delivered by at least one Dulles brother to the presumptions of the junior senator from Wisconsin. Allen's jaunty face made the cover of the newsmagazines; he and his CIA were accorded popular acclaim as a strong and independent agency of government, in sorry contrast to the State Department. (Amiable even in opposition, Allen refused to let political grievances fester in personal relations; that September, when the bachelor McCarthy finally married in a grand social ceremony at Washington's Saint Matthew's Cathedral, Allen and Clover were prominent among the wedding guests.)

The clash with McCarthy well served the first of Allen's purposes, enhancement of the intelligence agency's standing in Washington power circles. But in that moment of triumph came a negative note of enduring impact, from two commentators whom Allen considered his friends. In separate columns, Hanson Baldwin of *The New York Times* and the nationally syndicated Walter Lippmann heaped scorn on the McCarthy rampage. But they both questioned the premise of Allen's stand against congressional inquiry into the work of the intelligence agency. "Secrecy is not a criterion for immunity," Lippmann wrote. The CIA had to submit to congressional accountability just like every other executive agency. "The argument that the CIA is something apart, that it is so secret that it differs in kind from the State Department or, for that matter, . . . the Department of Agriculture, is untenable." Baldwin went further, warning of "a philosophy of secrecy and power, of the ends justifying the means, of disagreeable methods for agreeable ends."

Allen had known Lippmann since his first heady days in Paris in 1918; Baldwin had been a colleague in the study groups of the Council on Foreign Relations. From both he had expected a more sympathetic reaction. Allen wrote Lippmann a thoughtfully argued personal response, asserting that the CIA was indeed something apart. It was not only a matter of intelligence sources and methods, already enshrined in statute as privileged information not to be made public. Allen argued that "the mere disclosure that a particular person is working for us may destroy an entire operation." He added cryptically, "This has already happened to us in connection with other congressional investigations," and offered to discuss the problem in more detail with Lippmann after their summer vacations.*

The congressional anticommunist witch-hunt did not end with the Bundy case. While Allen was on vacation in Europe, another promising CIA officer was falling under suspicion. Cord Meyer, Jr., was an idealistic war veteran and founder of the visionary United World Federalists; among his offenses was that he had once shared a lecture platform with Harlow Shapley, a Harvard astronomer of leftist political views. Meyer was suspended from his CIA job in Allen's absence, and it was not until Thanksgiving Day 1953 that Allen could telephone him at home with the news that he had been entirely cleared of disloyalty charges.

Only those in the inner circles of the clandestine services could appreciate the special irony in the interruption of Meyer's work. His CIA assignment was to manage secret support operations among western European intellectuals, strengthening their voices against the lures of communist ideology issuing from Moscow. This was the kind of operation to which Allen referred in writing Lippmann, where knowledge of a CIA connection would likely undermine the whole effort. As director of the agency's International Division, Meyer's contribution to the defense of the European democracies turned out to be a dozen times more effective than all the campaigns of the anticommunist demagogues.

— * —

CIA's warfare against anticommunists was daunting, but also to be waged, after all, was warfare against communists. The one was carried on in public, the other only under cover.

Democrats and Republicans both believed that the Free World confronted a global adversary that would yield to nothing less than an overwhelming counterforce. This conviction had been enshrined in NSC 68, a momentous program document issued in 1950 by Truman's National Security Council, which perceived the world through a Manichaean prism. Only among a minority on the left in American politics, notably the followers of an eclipsed Henry Wallace, was there dissent from a view that later generations would judge tragically exaggerated and oversimplified. Looking back upon the mood of the Truman-Eisenhower transition period, William Bundy remarked that "the picture of a thrusting Soviet policy and acute threat entered into virtually every assessment, not only of military factors but of the political situation in countries all over the world"; the lesson of the 1948 Bogotazo still loomed large. "We believe

* Allen and Lippmann met early in October, but neither recorded any candor Allen may have shown in confiding examples of current intelligence secrets to his old friend.

that all Kremlin policies and courses of action are directed toward the attainment of the Kremlin's long-range objective of a communist world dominated by Moscow," concluded a CIA estimate the month of Eisenhower's election.[23]

These assessments were based on conjecture, not on hard intelligence data collected by CIA or anyone else. As Bundy put it, "The blunt fact was that almost everything about Soviet capabilities and, even more, Soviet intentions, as well as the economic and social condition of Soviet society, had to be a judgment extracted from frail or nonexistent evidence." Allen conceded as much at an early meeting of Eisenhower's National Security Council, when he confessed to "shortcomings of a serious nature . . . in securing adequate information."

The sources that had sufficed for earlier days had gone dry. Liaison and information-sharing with the experienced British intelligence services could no longer be fully trusted after the defections of Burgess and Maclean in 1951. Networks directed by the intelligence service of the new state of Israel were available in Russia and eastern Europe, but American policymakers were still too suspicious of Zionist politics to give high credibility to such sources. Gehlen's German agents continued to produce reams of reports, but his agents were low-level and parochial, colored by the old prejudices of former Nazis gaining strength within his organization. The other paper mills and fabricators claiming sources behind the Iron Curtain had been exposed as useless by the CIA's internal investigation, which was modestly classified secret when submitted in November 1951, then abruptly made top secret and withdrawn from circulation in March 1952 for its devastating judgment on the agency's intelligence collection capabilities.[24]

The CIA was in a desperate and experimental mood. Novel new techniques for collecting intelligence about the Soviet Union were being developed, but it would take years for them to become fully effective. The tapping of international telephone lines at unmanned switching boxes in obscure junctions had started on a small scale in the Soviet zone of Austria; in time Allen would find an ingenious way to expand the reach of the technique. The illegal surveillance of postal exchanges with the Soviet Union was still in its infancy. New technology in high-resolution photography raised the prospect that unmanned cameras, carried by balloons wafted eastward by the prevailing winds, might penetrate the secrecy of Soviet military and industrial installations; the CIA established an experimental photo interpretation division in 1953. The heart of intelligence collection, however, remained the agent networks, the human sources that alone could convey glimpses about policy and — what

Allen most wanted to know — the attitudes of the men in the Kremlin.

Bedell Smith had been tempted by the claims of CIA's old adversary of 1947, Frenchie Grombach. When Allen first arrived in Washington in 1951, he gave the Grombach organization a renewable one-year contract and a generous subsidy. "We had a great deal of difficulty in dealing with them," recalled Lyman B. Kirkpatrick, Jr., Grombach's senior CIA case officer. "They insisted on giving us their reports with no indication of the place of origin and flatly refused to reveal the sources on the grounds that the CIA was insecure. Further than this, they kept changing their source descriptions on the rather paranoid grounds that we would be able to discover the real source if they provided identical descriptions on each report from that source."[25]

Grombach's intelligence came from the bars and brothels of Berlin and Vienna — drunken statements by Soviet junior officers about march- ing to the English Channel, which were elevated in the reports relayed to Washington to weighty evidence of Soviet intentions. By the time he be- came director, Allen was satisfied that Grombach's organization had nothing of value to offer, and the agency subsidy was terminated. (Ever creative, Grombach promptly offered his organization's services to Mc- Carthy for security checks on the CIA.)

The upshot was that CIA's ability to collect accurate intelligence about Moscow's political intentions was pitifully meager just when the need for such data became crucial. For not only did the government of the United States pass to new leadership in the first months of 1953; so, by the chance of human mortality, did that of the Soviet Union.

— * —

Shortly after 2 A.M. on March 4, 1953, the official telephone rang at the home of the director of central intelligence. Joan Dulles Molden, who was staying with her parents after separating from her husband, answered and, on the urgent demand of the CIA watch officer, went upstairs to arouse her father, sound asleep after a formal dinner at the French Em- bassy. A flash message had come from Moscow: Stalin had suffered a stroke touching vital areas of his brain; the dictator of communism was unconscious, paralyzed, and dying.

Allen muttered a few sleepy orders to the duty officer to alert key Kremlinologists on his staff and start them preparing the assessments that would obviously be needed in the hours ahead. Clover and Joan sat in wonder before a restoked fire as Allen called the news to his brother Foster and the national security assistant at the White House. There was no need to wake up the president right away; not until a little after 6 A.M.

was Allen's call put through to awaken Eisenhower with the news that Stalin was dying.

Allen had summoned Wisner, Amory, and other top aides in from the night for the first of countless office skull sessions about a development both inevitable and unexpected. The way the news came over Moscow Radio — did that mean Stalin was in fact already dead? Had he been ill longer than anyone knew? Maybe the public appearances within the past two weeks were really a double? Had he really suffered a stroke, or could more ominous foul play be considered possible? Who — if indeed any-one — would assume the full power of the Kremlin after Stalin? These were questions that policymakers would naturally expect their intelli-gence service to answer, and the high command of that service was painfully aware how paltry was their ability to respond. "For all the money we spent on espionage, nobody knew a helluva lot about what was happening in Moscow," recalled one of the bleary-eyed participants in that first predawn meeting.[26]

No special insight was needed to confirm the historical importance of Stalin's passing. Yet the conversation among America's top intellig-ence officers in those first hours was deceptively banal. The easiest im-ponderable to focus on was the question of a successor. "I think old Molotov will be the one," Allen mused, jabbing the air with his pipe. (Someone made bold to mutter that veteran Bolshevik Vyacheslav Molo-tov was only two years older than Allen himself.) Others threw out the name of Georgi Malenkov, recently elevated to prominence in the Com-munist Party apparatus. No one knew what to make of the dreaded security chief, Lavrenti Beria. After more desultory conversation, some-one spoke up about the director's first hunch: "Allen, don't forget, Molo-tov has a Jewish wife." Given the antisemitic mania then gripping the Soviet power structure, Allen paused and said, "I guess I'd better hedge my bets."

Allen drove over to the White House early the next morning for a pri-vate meeting with Eisenhower before a larger session of the National Se-curity Council. He stressed the arguments just rehearsed, that Malenkov would be the man to watch rather than Molotov, and when this turned out in the coming days to be accurate, Allen's stock rose in Eisenhower's view.* But that morning the president quickly turned his attention away from intelligence and onto policy: what would Stalin's death mean for the

---

* Three months later Allen reportedly "stuck his neck out" once again in predicting the downfall of Beria, building on evidence assembled by the agency's Kremlinologists. When in early July this hunch, too, proved out, Vice President Nixon joined the ranks of admirers of the CIA.

United States, the Cold War, and world peace? And what should the president of the United States do about it all?

In the course of that day, as the world waited to learn whether Stalin was alive or dead, the State Department and the CIA collected their first, separate impressions. The CIA's reaction was alarmist. "It would be unsafe to assume that Stalin's successors will have his caution, his respect for the power potential of the U.S., or his control over all agents of the U.S.S.R.," declared Sherman Kent, head of Allen's National Estimates staff. Kent and his team warned that even though nothing might happen immediately, the next few months could see "a struggle for power within the ruling group and/or a shift of Soviet foreign policy which might result in reckless courses of action."[27] At the State Department top analysts considered the same factual evidence but came to more measured conclusions. Their estimate of that first day, March 4, noted recent "manifestations of disharmony" within the Politburo but declared, "It appears at present that there will not be a struggle for the succession of a nature to disrupt the regime. . . . Stalin's elimination will probably bring no early change in Soviet domestic or foreign policy."[28]

Which would it be — reckless change in Soviet policy or no change at all? Stalin's death was announced on March 5. When Eisenhower convened his full cabinet the next morning, he made no effort to hide his annoyance at the contradictory assessments and the lack of imagination within the government about the policy implications. He blurted out, "Ever since 1946, I know that all the so-called experts have been yapping about what would happen when Stalin dies and what we, as a nation, should do about it. Well, he's dead. And you can turn the files of our government inside out — in vain — looking for any plans laid. We have no plan. We are not even sure what difference his death makes."[29] Eisenhower was not alone in his impatience. Undersecretary of State Bedell Smith confided to the Senate Foreign Relations Committee that the Voice of America was in a state of "great disturbance" about how best to react to Stalin's death. After listening to all the handwringing over policy uncertainties, Senator Taft interrupted with the arch advice to the VOA that "for a week, they had better confine themselves to music."[30]

In fairness, the frustration of the politicians was misplaced; the secret high-level board that supervised the CIA's covert actions was many months into planning propaganda measures to exploit the inevitable passing of Stalin. But at the higher policy level, where Eisenhower naturally operated, there were indeed no profound ideas. With each passing day the analyses and estimates kept piling up, ever more subtle and carefully reasoned — also more detailed and longer, which was never the way to get Eisenhower's attention. What is startling is that none of the analysts or committees of government dared to contemplate that the passing of Stalin might be the moment for some fundamental rethinking — about the nature of the Soviet revolution and its ensuing political system, about the decades of confrontation between the democracies and communism. Indeed no one suggested that perhaps the basis of American policy in the Cold War should be reexamined, its underlying assumptions of an aggressive, expansionist Russia tested anew at that moment of profound change.

After more than a week of bureaucratic exercises that scarcely hinted at reappraisal, White House speechwriter Emmet John Hughes remembered, he had a late afternoon conversation with the president in the Oval Office. Malenkov had just delivered a second statement containing hints of a more conciliatory Soviet policy toward the West. Pacing the floor, Eisenhower was still in a waspish mood. Hughes wrote down his words. "Look, I am tired — and I think everyone is tired — of just plain indictments of the Soviet regime. I think it would be wrong — in fact, asinine — for me to get up before the world now to make another one of those indictments. Instead, just *one* thing matters: what have *we* got to offer the world? . . . Malenkov isn't going to be frightened with speeches. What are we *trying* to achieve?"[31]

An indication of Allen's mounting stature in Eisenhower's circle is that he was summoned, at a moment of high tension, along with Foster and C. D. Jackson, the president's psychological warfare aide, on a question of policy — to try converting the frustration of Eisenhower the man into a policy speech for the president of the United States. Hughes himself remarked on Allen's presence, a striking departure from the CIA director's usual scrupulousness in staying outside the circles of policy formulation. It was Allen, moreover, rather than Foster, who warmed up to the president's new mood.

Independent of all the learned Kremlinological analyses flowing out of CIA, Allen submitted a personal memorandum of tentative and rather random proposals to start clearing the heavy air of the Cold War. Just as he used to do with Foster in the old days, he poured out a series of ideas, admittedly half-baked, none of them fully thought out, but intended to stimulate the kind of new thinking that Eisenhower sought. His proposals ranged from the symbolic gesture of offering to hold the next United Nations General Assembly meeting in Moscow to the radical notion that the United States and the Soviet Union might embark on a joint cooperative program to supply basic economic assistance to communist China. None of these ideas went anywhere, of course, but they started the process of pushing the administration into a substantive response to the new situation created by Stalin's death.

Over the next month a small group of scholars and specialists — not the secretary of state or other responsible foreign policymakers — worked closely with Eisenhower on his administration's first major statement aimed at setting the Soviet-American relationship onto a new course. On April 16, 1953, Eisenhower delivered a notable speech to the American Society of Newspaper Editors, meeting in Washington. He called his address "The Chance for Peace," and he indulged in rare moments of rhetoric. "The world knows that an era ended with the death of Joseph Stalin," he began. He tallied up the cost of the arms race that even then, at the start of the Cold War, was draining the world's energies and wealth.

> Every gun that is made, every warship launched, every rocket fired signifies, in the final sense, a theft from those who hunger and are not fed, those who are cold and not clothed. . . . This is not a way of life at all, in any true sense. Under the cloud of threatening war, it is humanity hanging from a cross of iron. . . .
>
> This government is ready to ask its people to join with all nations in devoting a substantial percentage of the savings achieved by disarmament to a fund for world aid and reconstruction. . . . I know of only one question upon which progress waits. It is this: What is the Soviet Union ready to do?

Eisenhower's "Chance for Peace" address was heralded as "America's voice at its best" (*The New York Post*); "magnificent and deeply loving, . . . obviously undertaken to seize the peace initiative from the Soviets" (*The New York Times*).* Sherman Adams, the White House chief of staff, later called it "the most effective speech of Eisenhower's public career." It was published, with not altogether critical comment, in both *Pravda* and *Izvestia*, a rare signal of Soviet interest.[32]

For, contrary to the more alarmist instant analyses as Stalin lay dying, Soviet policy was indeed showing signs of change — and not at all in a "reckless" direction. A week after Eisenhower's speech, analysts at CIA and State compiled a list, some twenty single-spaced pages long, of "peaceful or friendly gestures by the Soviet Union since Stalin died." They ranged, as an intelligence briefing officer told a secret session of the House Foreign Affairs Committee, "from friendly overtures at cock-

---

* Ironically, the impact of the speech came in its written form, not in its delivery. As he rose to speak, the sixty-two-year-old president was stricken by acute stomach cramps, the first signs of his ileitis. Eisenhower broke into a cold sweat, gripping the podium lest he faint from the crippling pain. He omitted full paragraphs of the published text so that he could get off the platform quickly.

tail parties here and there, to adoption of a different attitude toward the trucks blocked up in Berlin." The briefing officer displayed a big map with little green buttons locating where in the world such gestures had occurred. "Actually, we couldn't get enough buttons on the map. . . . There is no doubt but that an across-the-board directive has gone out telling people to be pleasant. . . . Under Stalin you did not have such behavior. You do have such behavior now."[33]

CIA's mission for collection and analysis became one of judging whether those little visible gestures would add up to a fundamental break with Stalinism. The Communist Party functionaries, the Russian people, asked the same questions. Only three years later would there come a clear answer.

— * —

The CIA's deficiencies in collecting intelligence about the Soviet Union might be forgiven, for no one in or out of government was doing much better in unraveling the enigmas of the Kremlin. But on the other side of the CIA mission, mounting covert paramilitary operations to undermine Soviet power in the satellite countries, Allen confronted his first major disappointment. Simply put, the bold concept of "liberating the captive peoples" was turning out to be a dreadful — and costly — fiasco. This bitter lesson, furthermore, was being absorbed by the small circle of clandestine officers just as Foster and other Republican stalwarts were trumpeting the strategy of "rolling back the Iron Curtain," their foreign policy alternative to the "timidity" of Democratic containment.

Allen's enthusiasm for aggressive covert action dated from the spring of 1948, while he was still a private citizen. In those early days the strategy was called psychological warfare, political warfare, or, to insiders, 10/2 operations, after the authorizing NSC directive. "There was something of the little boy in Allen," wrote Sherman Kent of the Board of National Estimates. "He was much more attracted to the 'monkey business' side of the Agency."[34] To Allen, however, covert action was not monkey business. Through his New York–based Free Europe Committee and the broadcasting transmitters of Radio Free Europe, Allen started his crusade with propaganda to counter the infectious party line from Moscow and the Cominform. Wisner's OPC, the implementing agency of 10/2, and then the CIA itself endowed a community of academic centers, such as the Institute for the Study of the USSR in Munich and the Free Europe University of Strasbourg, ostensibly to give employment to intellectual émigrés from eastern Europe and mobilize their scholarly knowledge for the Free World in the coming battle with communist Russia. If at the start most of these scholars were remnants of democratic forces,

their ranks soon swelled to embrace wartime Nazi collaborators who had
their own pressing reasons for fighting communism.

Once inside the CIA, Allen learned that psychological and political
tactics had grown into paramilitary actions. Among the groups mobilized against communism were hardened fighters — guerrillas of underground factions from Poland, Ukraine, and Russia. Former prisoners of
war, slave laborers, or general malcontents, many of these men had
fought communism alongside the Nazis in World War II, and from the
postwar camps for displaced persons they were now ready to resume missions of infiltration, sabotage, and insurrection against the Stalinist enemy. These were the operations that Bedell Smith had sought, unsuccessfully, to transfer out of the intelligence agency into the arsenal and
control of the Joint Chiefs of Staff.

Wisner had built a web of networks among émigré organizations that
claimed to have agents surviving unnoticed under communist rule,
mainly in the Baltic states, Poland, and Ukraine.[35] For two years, starting
in the summer of 1950, the CIA smuggled gold, radio transmitters, and
weapons valued close to $5 million to a Polish network directed by émi-
grés in London called, after its Polish initials, WIN (pronounced "vine").
The émigré leadership claimed to deploy an active cadre of 500 men inside Poland, with 20,000 partially active, and fully 100,000 available to
fight in the event of a war against the communist regime. Managers of
the covert operation were a veteran of OSS guerrilla operations in Yugoslavia, Frank Lindsay, and his deputy, John Bross. Lindsay and Bross
felt the first tinges of doubt about the effort when their WIN contacts
asked that some experienced American military personnel be smuggled
in to guide the anticommunist resistance. "The thought of an American
general, hanging from a parachute, descending into a Communist country, gave us some pause," Bross recalled.[36] And rightly so: late in December 1952, Warsaw Radio triumphantly exposed the entire plot; WIN had
been a fiction from the start, a creature of communist security forces enticing the West into a compromising and wasteful scam.

Covert paramilitary operations in Ukraine and Albania had gone sour
in spectacular debacles, and both Lindsay and Bross began to wonder if
theirs was a harebrained effort. Lindsay had already decided to leave the
government at the end of 1952, but late in the year he met with the leaders of one of the Russian political factions eager for CIA support to reen-
ter their homeland. "If you had an ideal agent in Russia, perfect cover,
everything just right, how long would it be before you could enlist your
first resistance agent?" Lindsay asked. The answer came, "Six months before we could gain enough confidence to ask anyone." Lindsay pressed.
"And what are the chances of being penetrated by Soviet security men

once you start building the cells?" "About fifty percent" came the honest answer. That, for the CIA's retiring director of eastern European operations, was not good enough.[37]

Allen asked Lindsay to prepare a retirement memorandum summing up his experience in covert paramilitary operations. He was not happy with what Lindsay delivered. In mellower days Allen could have recalled his own skepticism about paramilitary penetration missions, his clash with William Casey in the closing months of World War II. But the autumn of 1952 was not a mellow season for the officers and ranks of the Cold War. Upon reading the first draft of the memo he had invited, Allen summoned Lindsay to his home on a Saturday, and together they went over the half-dozen pages line by line. "Frank, you can't say that," Allen protested. "Frank, we have to change this phrasing." For Lindsay's conclusions were uncompromisingly negative:[38] "The consolidated communist state, through police and political controls, propaganda and provocation, has made virtually impossible the existence of organized clandestine resistance capable within the foreseeable future of appreciably weakening the power of the state.... The instruments currently advocated to reduce Soviet power, either directly or by attrition, are both inadequate and ineffective against the Soviet political system."

Allen found himself caught between his party's (and his brother's) rhetoric about liberating eastern Europe from communist rule and the experience of his own operatives. It was not long into the Eisenhower administration before the issue came up for its first test.

Early in June 1953, workers in Czechoslovakia went on strike in protest against a harsh new economic program of the communist government. Security forces suppressed the demonstrations. Two weeks later, a strike of construction workers in the eastern (Soviet-occupied) zone of Germany turned violent and spread into East Berlin. Rioters broke into the jails, and freed political prisoners; they tore down red banners of communist authority, laid siege to the headquarters of the secret police, and set fire to the offices of the official newspaper.

Reports of the rampage poured into the CIA base in West Berlin headed by the German-born OSS veteran Henry Heckscher, a man of imagination and aggressiveness in the kind of "monkey business" that attracted Allen — and that his clandestine service deputies had come to distrust. Heckscher drafted a cable to Washington reporting the mounting unrest and predicting a prompt and bloody Soviet reaction. He proposed that his networks start smuggling firearms to the East Berlin insurgents.[39] Heckscher's cable arrived late Tuesday evening, June 16. Allen had gone for the night, leaving Wisner on duty. Bross had no hesitation in overruling his field agent's zeal, but he duly submitted his draft rejection cable to higher authority. Wisner easily spotted the distinction between providing arms for long-term resistance networks, which he had strongly advocated, and fueling bloodshed actually in process, which he had not yet dared to contemplate. Within the hour, and acting in Allen's absence, he initialed Bross's cable. Even as this exchange proceeded, a Russian armored division moved into East Berlin, dispersed the general strike of some fifty thousand demonstrators, and killed sixteen young Germans.

A *fait accompli* by the Russians — and by his own men — confronted Allen when he arrived in the office the next morning. "It was the one time that I saw Allen angry and disappointed in me," Bross remembered. A flash point for paramilitary covert action had come — and gone. The CIA had held back. C. D. Jackson, Eisenhower's most enthusiastic Cold Warrior, writhed in fury for weeks afterward that Allen had become a stick-in-the-mud. Even Bedell Smith over at State wondered if his old CIA could have done more to encourage the mounting political ferment in the satellites.

The only light moment during the whole tense week came when the CIA director was handed the text of an East Berlin radio report on the short-lived uprising. "The Fascist putsch was staged on the direct instruction, and under the guidance, of Allen Dulles." Allen, the radio said, had personally sneaked back into his old Berlin haunts in an American army staff car, "with a powerful radio," to orchestrate the conspiracy. The CIA director vented his frustrations in his ever-booming ho ho ho.

— * —

Just as both sides of Allen's clandestine services were languishing, there came a fortuitous harbinger of better days ahead. Known only to the director, his top staff, and a handful of field officers, an intelligence breakthrough was taking shape at the CIA station in Vienna. A Soviet military intelligence officer had walked in and offered to convey to the United States personal, professional, and technical data of authoritative authenticity.[40]

Lieutenant Colonel Pyotr Popov was a lonely, obscure officer of peasant origin who had worked his way up in the military ranks by causing no one any trouble. He fit the pattern of Allen's World War II agent Fritz Kolbe, a link in the administrative chain through whom sensitive information passed but who himself remained too insignificant to attract notice or suspicion. Assigned to the Soviet occupation force in Austria,

Popov used clever subterfuges learned through his years in military intelligence to make himself known to CIA operatives.*

Both at the station and in Washington, Popov's approach raised suspicions. American intelligence officers were not yet experienced with this kind of defector, a walk-in willing to stay on his job for the enemy even as he served the CIA. The self-effacing colonel's motives were never clear — though, unlike Kolbe, he expected payment for his services, a condition that made Allen particularly wary. A week or so after Stalin's death Popov helped his new CIA contacts identify obscure figures in the Kremlin funeral photographs, and he remarked, "Those bastards are sweating" — hardly news to any good Kremlinologist, but an interesting if obvious judgment from a source who had firsthand, albeit low-level, knowledge. When Popov left Vienna on home leave at the end of June, his case officers returned to Washington to brief Allen in person on the circumstances surrounding the extraordinary arrival of what intelligence officers call a defector-in-place.

For the next five years this obscure and lonely officer gave the CIA an unprecedented glimpse into the Soviet system, including its undercover activities directed against the West. He provided personal knowledge of Soviet intelligence procedures, organization, and personnel — hard data totally unknown to outsiders at the time. Beyond that, the officer corps through which he moved so inconspicuously was a ready source of informed gossip and loose talk, invaluable in helping the analysts in Washington decipher cryptic references and slang used in intercepted radio and cable communications. After a short vacation in 1954 at the Kaliningrad resort for military and naval officers, Popov reported off-duty conversations about Soviet atomic submarines and guided missiles; pieced together with signals intercepts and intelligence from other technical sources, Washington gained significant data on some of the most secret weapons in the Soviet arsenal.

Popov was never a high-living spy, nor did the modest sums of money

---

* In reports about agents and their recruitment, precise details of time and place are kept secret, for skillful counterespionage analysis can adduce sensitive information from seeming trivia. Knowing the date or even the hour of a recruitment, for instance, can give the injured side a good idea of what information has been compromised. Furthermore, counterespionage knows no statute of limitations. Decades after the fact some point of precision may lead to just the clue explaining seemingly unrelated events in the intervening years. Thus even in the 1990s many of the details about Popov are deliberately obscure. One knowledgeable source, case officer William Hood, puts the date of Popov's first approach as Thanksgiving Day 1952. Another source equally familiar with the case, Soviet defector Peter Deriabin, writes that it came on New Year's Day 1953. For present purposes, it is sufficient to know that Popov entered the CIA's environment on a holiday sometime between Eisenhower's election and Allen's appointment as CIA director.

he received from CIA lure him into the extravagant life of a Colonel Redl. He apparently grew to enjoy the secret relationship and the importance that his American case officers assured him he had acquired with the mighty Allen Dulles. Once, as he set off on home leave, he reported that he had used some of his clandestine rubles to buy his peasant family a cow; the children needed a steady supply of milk. He wanted "Mr. Dulles" personally to know of "a CIA cow grazing on the bank of the Volga."

The lowly Colonel Popov's defection-in-place was an unheralded intelligence coup for the CIA just when penetration into the communist system was most desperately needed.* Popov's access was far removed from the minds of the men in the Kremlin, but it was the first direct link the CIA would establish within the organization of its adversary, and the five years it lasted was an eternity in intelligence. Soviet counterespionage finally uncovered the treachery only in 1958. Before his escape could be arranged, Popov was arrested in Moscow, and his American case officer expelled from the Moscow embassy. The Soviet officer was executed, reportedly in a gruesome display in front of other officers, as an example of the treatment to be meted out to traitors.

Though he was valuable to the collectors of intelligence, Popov frustrated the "little boy" in charge. When the colonel first presented himself in Vienna, the cause of "liberation" was still high on the CIA agenda. Active covert operations were far more exciting to Allen than the plodding, mundane process of collecting information. Soon after Popov's bona fides were established, CIA headquarters sent the Vienna station instructions that the new agent should be encouraged to form a "small, tightly knit resistance group of like-thinking comrades." The Vienna officers were appalled at the notion of endangering a valuable source of intelligence with a different operation that would necessarily involve more people and thus be more vulnerable to exposure. The station protested the instructions. Within hours came back the firm reply that "high level" (presumably Allen himself) insisted that the suggestion be put to Popov. The Soviet colonel was just as irritated with the idea as his American case officers and flatly refused to play any such role. In retirement, case officer William Hood wrote that "headquarters' expression of 'a small tightly knit resistance group' was etched on the memory of everyone concerned with the Popov operation. . . . For years it was used as a pejorative, to describe any headquarters proposition that seemed to slight the operational facts of life as perceived by field personnel."[41]

---

* Obviously the case could not be officially revealed for many years. As late as the 1990s, CIA declined to acknowledge, in response to a Freedom of Information inquiry, that it knew of the existence of any such person as Popov.

In less pressured days Allen had understood better than anyone the distinctions to be made in using agents to best advantage. From Switzerland he had welcomed the active underground maneuvers of Gisevius and Waetjen, but he firmly forbade Fritz Kolbe — serving in place in Berlin — to have any involvement whatsoever with the anti-Hitler conspiracy, despite Kolbe's eagerness to make contact with "like-minded comrades." Allen knew then, and should have remembered a decade later, that the value of an agent in place comes from his obscurity, and that participating in any sort of plot was not a good way to remain inconspicuous.

In the intervening years, however, Allen had become embroiled in the politics of intelligence and had planted his position firmly on the proposition that intelligence collection and offensive covert operations could proceed in parallel, using the same assets. The model from his own experience that stayed in his mind was not Kolbe in Berlin but his networks within the French, Italian, and Austrian resistance — eager, intrepid guerrillas who readily gained and shared information even as they went about blowing up bridges. The Popov case came as a rude reminder that Allen's concept was not as tidy as he had chosen to believe.

— 14 —

A THIRD WORLD

BACK IN 1947, a time of relative innocence, Allen Dulles had issued a warning to America. The United States, he said, was in danger of succumbing to hubris in the aftermath of world war, the impulse to try managing the whole world in peace as in war, to shape other countries in America's own image of what was best for them. His speech to the annual congress of the National Association of Manufacturers was one of his most thoughtful and carefully crafted, yet it was strangely missing from the long record of his public statements prepared by the CIA at the end of his career. His central point did not sit well against his own subsequent performance in guiding America's intelligence service. "There is, as far as I know, only one certain rule in international relations," he lectured the crowded ballroom of the Waldorf-Astoria the morning of December 3. "Interference by one country in the internal affairs of another causes resentment. It is sure to produce a result exactly the opposite of that intended.... We must not build barriers between ourselves and a third world, namely, the world which may practice a measure of state socialism."[1]

Allen had just returned from Europe, where the first postwar governments were experimenting with socialist principles of economic planning. He had spoken with social democrats and with their conservative opponents as well. "It was the latter, the opponents of socialism, who warned me in the most pressing terms against our doing anything which could be interpreted as American interference in the political and social struggle between the proponents of socialism and their antagonists. Given half a chance, they said, Europe can handle this problem itself. 'If you in America try to handle it for us, you will be giving a propaganda weapon of immense value to the extreme left and to the communists.'"

Allen's context in 1947 was not, of course, his context half a decade later. Then he had been preaching the message of the Marshall Plan, confronting the opposition of the conservative business community to support for countries that were nationalizing private industries. The "third world" to which he referred included familiar countries like England and France, democracies embarked upon what was called "state socialism." But as he continued before the skeptical audience, his analysis became prophetic across a wider realm.

> Our attention is sometimes focused on the so-called Iron Curtain, which represents a particular line of pressure extending from the North Sea to the Adriatic. But this is only one part of the picture. There is the Middle East and Persia, the vast areas of the Far East and China, and there are the fifth columns within almost every country in the world.
>
> We must use our resources wisely and where they will achieve the greatest effect. We must avoid an economic Stalingrad which could befall any nation which takes on commitments beyond its capacity. Our resources are great but not unlimited.

By the time Allen became director of central intelligence, he had grown less wary of the limitations of American power and more enthusiastic about the latent capacities of his new instrument of government. Insulating the western European democracies from the lures of communism no longer seemed as daunting as in the 1940s, but containment of international communism was a priority in a broader world. If covert actions to weaken the satellite regimes of eastern Europe were not working well by 1953, the imagination and daring of his CIA might prove more effective elsewhere.

In two countries far removed from the central focus of American policy, Allen's CIA found opportunities to show what it could do, to flex its muscle and reach and thereby persuade its detractors in the older institutions of government. Iran and Guatemala were outposts of that Third World that had long been subservient to the capitalism of the industrial West and that was now perceived in Washington as vulnerable to the expansionist drive of communism. Both nations were in the throes of deepseated social change; the imperatives of colonialism may have brought material benefit to the "natives" (at least some of them), but the Third World was starting its struggle to emerge from the paternalism of foreign economic interests. If Washington had perceived the upheavals of 1953 and 1954 in that light, policymakers could have invoked an old American tradition — support for the downtrodden, equity for the work force, and the rise of popular democracy to replace the exploitation that came with the Industrial Revolution. At one time, after all, Woodrow Wilson and

Herbert Hoover had been alike in wondering if the working masses of Europe in 1918 might have had legitimate grievance against their anciens régimes.

But Washington in 1953 was in no mood to recall the ambivalence of Versailles. For CIA the lesson of the 1948 Bogotazo was that local unrest at any spot on the globe necessarily affected American interests, because it must have its origins in the "vicious" machinations of international communism. Allen and his CIA analysts were doing nothing more than articulating the conventional wisdom all across the political spectrum: political agitation in Iran and Guatemala, like the military aggression in Korea three years before, must amount to cynical probing tactics by the Kremlin to test the resolve and capacity of the Free World.

— * —

Crisis came first in Iran in the summer of 1953. Allen was still engaged in the fight against McCarthy when long-simmering tensions reached a climax between a populist demagogue in Tehran and entrenched British oil interests. What more fortuitous opportunity for the CIA to show that it had better things to do than respond to the ravings of a maverick anti-communist?

Operation Ajax has mythic resonance in the lore of American intelligence: the prototype of a neat, cheap, successful covert action to topple the unfriendly and dangerous head of a foreign government.[2] Compared with the covert actions that followed, however, the CIA's venture in Iran is more reminiscent of Viennese operetta. The stock characters strain credibility: the outrageous prime minister, dumb like a fox, who prances across the world stage in his pajamas; the brooding "gloomy prince" who cannot decide who his friends are; the clever spy from abroad who hides in a villa out of town as he flips wild cards and jokers like a street shark; assorted middlemen and go-betweens who find ever-shifting middles and betweens; a chorus of Persian urban peasants and sword-bearers who enter and exit on cue. In the last act the illustrious spymaster stumbles onto the stage, avuncular and pipe-smoking, blissfully unaware of all the improvisations and delighted to accept the ovation of the happy ending.

The Ajax plan originated with the British, who were determined to protect the lush holdings of the Anglo-Iranian Oil Company, third largest crude oil producer in the world. Their adversary was the populist revolutionary Mohammad Mossadegh, equally determined to nationalize the oil industry of Iran and bring the British exploiters to heel. A Persian aristocrat and wealthy landowner, Mossadegh had found the religion of radicalism in his youth; he had been one of those pleading the anticolonial position at the Paris Peace Conference. He became prime minister in 1951. After paying a call at the United Nations in October, he journeyed to Washington for medical treatment and incidentally (it was said) a visit with President Truman. Secretary of State Dean Acheson met Mossadegh at Union Station. "I watched a bent old man hobble down the platform supporting himself on a stick and an arm through his son's. Spotting me at the gate, he dropped the stick, broke away from his party, and came skipping along ahead of the others to greet us." In their subsequent meetings, Acheson found the quixotic Persian to have "a delightfully childlike way of sitting in a chair with his legs tucked under him." At home in Tehran he often would not bother to get dressed in the morning, thinking nothing of receiving official visitors in his nightclothes. Meeting Truman at Blair House, Acheson related, Mossadegh suddenly looked old and pathetic. He leaned toward his host. "Mr. President, I am speaking for a very poor country — a country all desert — just sand, a few camels, a few sheep —" "Yes," Acheson interrupted, "and with your oil, rather like Texas." Mossadegh burst into a delighted laugh, "and the whole act broke up, finished."[3]

In its last months the Truman administration had seemed somewhat attracted by this apparition from Persia, and the British oil men realized that they would do better to press their case when the Republican administration came into office. Their moment came five months into Eisenhower's presidency. On June 25, 1953, Secretary of State John Foster Dulles convened in his office his top aides on Middle Eastern affairs, his brother Allen, and their old friend Kermit Roosevelt, who had become one of Allen's most adventurous field officers. The point of the meeting, as Foster said when he finished his phone calls and glanced at the twenty-two-page briefing paper in front of him, was "how we get rid of that madman Mossadegh."[4]

The British plan, modified and massaged in secret meetings with Kim Roosevelt over the past year, was built upon the ambivalent position of the young constitutional monarch, Mohammad Reza Shah Pahlavi, whom Allen had come to know in 1949. Eisenhower, too, had been favorably impressed with this curious young monarch, still in his twenties, when he visited New York to address the Council on Foreign Relations. Against the capricious Mossadegh, the shah seemed to embody all the liberal impulses of social reform along the noncommunist path.

The plan called for American and British agents to reassure the young ruler with promises of support if he would assert his royal prerogative and fire his prime minister, the old man in pajamas, and name in his place the more agreeable Fazlollah Zahedi. Never mind that Zahedi had been a Nazi collaborator in World War II; unlike Mossadegh, he was a man who would follow orders. Neither Foster nor Allen, however, could commit any American resources to a plan to save the British oil industry. There had to be a communist angle — and so there was. Iran shared a long frontier with the Soviet Union; Mossadegh seemed to be flirting with Moscow and the local communist party, the Tudeh, to get financial aid that the West was reluctant to provide this Middle Eastern Texas.

If the British-American plan failed to topple Mossadegh, Kim Roosevelt briefed the Dulles brothers at the June 25 meeting, "Iran would fall to the Russians and the effect on the rest of the Middle East could be disastrous. But I must add this: these are the same consequences we face if we do nothing." The oil motive thus comfortably shrouded in the Cold War impulse that ruled Washington in 1953, Allen and Foster gave the green light to Operation Ajax.

The resident CIA man, who had served in Tehran for five years past, presented a problem for Allen. Though he held no brief for Mossadegh, this old hand reported his skepticism that any coup like Ajax could be pulled off. Naysayers were not what the CIA wanted at that juncture, so Allen resolved to send Roosevelt to manage the operation in person. He arrived early in July after a clandestine overland drive from Damascus, carrying a hundred thousand dollars in small Iranian notes — needed by his eager local networks to call out the street crowds in support of the power play from the throne.

At first the shah did not believe Roosevelt's claim that he could deliver the support of the British and American governments. Within twenty-four hours came a riveting display of the resources available to modern intelligence. Proving an undercover agent's authority has always been a problem in espionage; in the twentieth century the public shortwave radio offered an ingenious solution, both effective and innocuous. Roosevelt arranged with his cohort in Whitehall for a little code signal, and informed the shah accordingly: the next night the routine BBC Persian-language news broadcast would not begin with the usual pronouncement, "It is now midnight in London." Instead the announcer would say, following firm but unexplained instructions, "It is now [*pause*] *exactly* midnight."[5] On the American side, the means for reassurance were not yet so subtle. Roosevelt took the bold chance of telling the shah to heed carefully a speech that President Eisenhower would deliver the next day. Then he sent a cable describing the problem to Washington. Allen contacted the White House speechwriters and arranged a small departure from the prepared text. Speaking to the Conference of Governors about federal-state relations, Eisenhower interjected, apropos of nothing, that the situation in Iran was "very ominous to the United States." The Soviet drive to the Middle East "must be blocked and it must be blocked now," the president would remark (on Allen's instructions), "and that's what we are trying to do." What the shah heard on his shortwave radio from London and Washington was ample confirmation of Roosevelt's credibility.

Thus Operation Ajax was launched. Signing off on the final details, and giving Roosevelt considerable authority to carry it out as circumstances required, Allen set off on his annual August vacation to Europe. He joined Clover, involved in her Jungian studies, at the Hotel St. Peter in Zurich. There he lounged with his old wartime comrade Gaevernitz, pursuing German business interests, and made a show of relaxing on vacation.[6] In Tehran, however, the shah was still hesitating to make his move. Roosevelt arranged for an American brigadier general, who had known the monarch a decade before, to arrive as a tourist and, calling on the shah as an old friend, confirm Washington's interest in getting rid of Mossadegh.* Awaiting the ouster of the prime minister, Roosevelt hid out at a country villa, swimming the afternoons away with his host's small children and playing over and over a record from the current Broadway hit *Guys and Dolls*, "Luck Be a Lady Tonight." As the early August days passed, something was going wrong. The messenger carrying the shah's decrees firing Mossadegh disappeared; he was lost or abducted — Roosevelt did not know which. Pro- and anti-Mossadegh factions were agitating, and the CIA man did not bother to keep Washington informed of his frantic improvisations. Either in panic or thinking he had done his part, the shah set off on a vacation of his own, to Baghdad.

On August 13 Allen and Clover, accompanied by Gaevernitz, went to St. Moritz.[7] The director of central intelligence casually called the American Embassy at Bern but could get no meaningful reports from Tehran. Finally, after three days of ominous silence just when the coup was to be sprung, Allen announced to Clover that they were leaving for Rome, where he might be able to see the classified cable traffic. And he always found it refreshing to spend time with Clare Boothe Luce, the American ambassador. They arrived on Tuesday, August 18, checking into the hotel where royal and diplomatic visitors usually stayed, the Excelsior on the Via Veneto. Allen went straight to the American Embassy and learned that in Tehran street crowds brought out by the Tudeh were supporting Mossadegh; the putative new prime minister, Zahedi, was in hiding, and the shah had left the country. Roosevelt was on his own.

Wednesday morning, August 19, Clover sat in her hotel room planning a day in Rome — as usual, without her husband — when she heard a street commotion outside her window. In the middle of a ring of police and plainclothesmen was a young man with jet-black hair whom she im-

---

* This general, H. Norman Schwarzkopf, went on to raise a son in the American military who would play a significant role in the Persian Gulf four decades later.

mediately recognized, from her visit to Tehran four years before, as the "gloomy prince." The shah of Iran had flown from Baghdad to Rome, to the very hotel where the director of central intelligence was also stopping over.

Of all the conspiracy theories that later swirled around the personage of Allen Dulles, none has made a convincing case to accommodate this unfortunate proximity. Allen did not yet know it, but Roosevelt had left the children at the swimming pool and was setting his own agents to work bringing out throngs in support of the absent monarch. Zahedi's partisans pulled him out of hiding; in clashes between rival mobs more than three hundred people were killed. The next day Mossadegh abandoned the fight. The shah waited three days in Rome to be sure, then returned to Tehran in triumph. Years later, with Operation Ajax celebrated as an example of a CIA covert action that worked, Allen would respond only with a knowing twinkle when asked if he had used the hospitality of the Excelsior to persuade the reluctant shah to reclaim his sway over Iran.

The myth of the omnipotent spymaster was important to Allen; the realities of those August days in Rome argue the contrary. He spent little time at the Excelsior; his waking hours were passed at the embassy with Luce, keeping an eye on the diplomatic cables. The Wednesday when the shah arrived, Allen was up until 4 A.M. in the communications room with the local CIA man, Gerald Miller. Thursday he and Luce flew to the island of Ischia, returning to Rome only the next day. The shah and his queen, meanwhile, scarcely left the Excelsior; lacking the bank accounts and wardrobes that later followed wherever they went, they were reduced to wistful window-shopping and lonely meals in the hotel dining room. It was Clover, not Allen, who saw the shah at the hotel, and only from an impersonal distance. She spent her days at the gardens and art collection of the nearby Villa Borghese, and the night Allen was away, she dined with a big party of Americans at Rome's Square of the Three Fountains. In those critical days both Allen and the shah were out of touch with fast-moving developments a thousand miles from Rome, developments that would turn out to be crucial for their respective fates. No good could have come to either from being noticed in the other's company.

When Eisenhower himself finally heard a detailed briefing about the role of the CIA and Kim Roosevelt in deposing Mossadegh, he wrote in his diary, "It seemed more like a dime novel than an historical fact."[8] Operation Ajax succeeded in toppling a populist leader whom the United States suspected of being a stalking horse for communism and whom the British saw as the threat to their Persian oil interests.

But success has its statute of limitations. The reforming shah turned out to be not such a liberal leader of his people after all. And the throngs Roosevelt bought into the streets in August of 1953 were the parents of those who, a generation later, became the core of support for a rabid ayatollah who challenged and undermined the president of the United States. The most damaging long-term legacy of Ajax was the hubris that CIA, through a covert political action, could so easily (all things considered) change the politics of the world, shaping foreign societies to the American design. Kim Roosevelt himself remembers reporting to Secretary of State Dulles in the immediate aftermath of Ajax, "If we, the CIA, are ever going to try something like this again, we must be absolutely sure that people and army want what we want. If not, you had better give the job to the Marines."

Within a few weeks Roosevelt declined Allen's assignment to mount an intriguing new CIA operation in a different hemisphere. In the banana and coffee republic of Guatemala, another dangerously revolutionary leader was striving to find a new life and destiny for his people.

— * —

On March 12, 1953, the Congress of Guatemala stood for one minute of silent homage to the late leader of the Soviet Union, Joseph Stalin — one of the jarring incidents noted by Allen and the men of the CIA as they pondered the worldwide significance of Stalin's death. Guatemala was the only country in the Western Hemisphere to pay such respect. Two years earlier, as a thirty-seven-year-old army officer named Jacobo Arbenz celebrated his inauguration as the country's president, the Communist Party of Guatemala had emerged from underground to issue its manifestoes in public. In December 1952 the Guatemalan communists convened a formal party congress. In the rest of Latin America communists were proscribed or persecuted, but Arbenz granted them legal recognition. Within the month Guatemala implemented a sweeping land reform, confiscating the rich holdings of the major United States firms and parceling out the properties to the peasants and workers on the land.

Little wonder that policymakers in the Land to the North, as Guatemalans called the United States, saw red in what they considered their banana republic. Gripped by the paranoia of McCarthyism and embarked on a global crusade to contain communism, Americans across the political spectrum fulminated against what Democratic senator J. William Fulbright called "the communist-dominated government of Guatemala." They saw a bridgehead of Soviet infiltration in Central America, within easy reach of the Panama Canal.

Had they looked a little deeper, something the American public rarely did in Latin America, they would have discovered a rather more pathetic reality. That legislative homage to Stalin, for instance, came only after three hours of violent debate pro and con, hardly the sort of parliamentary proceedings that distinguished the Supreme Soviet. "The people of Guatemala had regarded Roosevelt, Churchill and Stalin as saviors of the world," Arbenz's dynamic wife lectured the United States ambassador over a six-hour dinner the one time they met. "Perhaps when Mr. Churchill passes on, Congress will hold memorial services for him" as well.*

As for the Communist Party of Guatemala, it was a modest, homespun affair. No foreign delegates had joined the little band of teachers and university students at the secret organizing meeting in 1949, and when the party met openly in 1952 foreign delegates came only from Cuba, Mexico, and Costa Rica, hardly an international recognition of a global conspiracy. CIA sources suspected that funds were coming in from Soviet front agents in Paris, but the party's financial dealings with Moscow itself amounted to a bill for $22.95, which the Guatemalans actually paid to the Moscow supplier of Marxist literature. "You people are crazy," said a delegate from the Mexican Communist Party. "We haven't paid them a cent for at least ten years." By the time the CIA was called into action against Guatemala, card-carrying communists numbered about five thousand in a population of three million. "Yes, Guatemala has a very small minority of communists," an iconoclastic friend of Eisenhower's informed the president in 1954, "but not as many as San Francisco."[9]

It was not only at Versailles or on Wall Street that the word "communist" resonated among those who sought to preserve their wealth and privileges. Communism had been the scare-word of the Guatemalan landed elite since the 1930s, used to brand anyone who uttered the words "trade union, strike, labor rights, petitions" — the interests of the unnoticed working class. The dictator then ruling Guatemala, Jorge Ubico, worried about the "communistic activities" of the New Deal under Roosevelt.

The notion of an indigenous communism — college teachers and graduates studying (and paying for) the Marxist tracts that came in the mails, reacting to generations of foreign paternalism — was something Washington could not fathom in the early Eisenhower years. "There is no communism but the communism which takes orders from the despots of the Kremlin in Moscow," declared Republican senator Alexander Wi-

* Maria de Arbenz was being disingenuous. As she conceded to Johns Hopkins historian Piero Gleijeses after years of widowhood, she and her husband were indeed inclined to communism; as they tried to explain events to the suspicious ambassador, they were "in a difficult situation."

ley. "It is an absolute myth to believe that there is such a thing as home-grown communism."[10] Wiley was chairman of the Senate Foreign Relations Committee, though he made no pretense to intellectual depth in world affairs. But those who knew more shared his view. The United States "knew that communists the world over were agents of Soviet imperialism," wrote a senior State Department official. And John Foster Dulles himself, whom even detractors recognized as a man of superior intellectual power, saw little reason for subtler distinctions. "It will be impossible to produce evidence clearly tying the Guatemalan government to Moscow," he conceded to a South American diplomat in May 1954, but the United States might act anyway, "based on our deep conviction that such a tie must exist."[11]

Inference before the fact was nothing new in American policymaking. George Marshall had been quick to see communists behind the unrest in Bogotá in 1948. Kennan tried to introduce a subtlety into policy judgments in 1950 when he noted that "most of the people who go by the name of 'communist' in Latin America are a somewhat different species than in Europe." Their bond with Moscow was only "tenuous and indirect." This argument fell on deaf ears. A Council on Foreign Relations study group met six times over the winter of 1952–53 to discuss the premise that Guatemala represented "quite simply the penetration of Central America by a frankly Russian-dominated communist group."

Thirty years after the 1954 CIA operation in Guatemala, after the seal of secrecy was finally broken open on parts of the official documentation, a key American diplomat in the Arbenz years made a revealing admission. The retired deputy chief of mission in Guatemala City, Bill Krieg, recalled that most of the various Guatemalan revolutionaries were "bums of first order, lazy, ambitious; they wanted money." Just a few of the men around Arbenz "had a sense of direction, ideas, knew where they wanted to go." These were the communists. "They were very honest, very committed," Krieg concluded. "This was the tragedy — the only people who were committed to hard work were those who were, by definition, our worst enemies."[12]

— * —

Guatemala had been a favorite vacation retreat for Allen and Clover over the years. For Clover the ancient Mayan ruins held endless fascination, relics of the superior civilization that thrived in Central America before the firepower of the Spanish conquistadors reduced the Mayans to a local Indian work force for foreign capitalist enterprise. Even Allen appreciated the Guatemalan Indian textiles woven in distinctive, vibrant colors, which Clover collected to decorate their Lloyd Neck country home. Allen could always find a business reason to cover his visits to Guatemala, for in the 1930s Sullivan and Cromwell represented the country's most powerful American interests, notably the United Fruit Company. Between remote ruins and the urbane social life of the country's ruling elite, Allen and Clover found in placid Guatemala a respite from their busy New York life.

Late in 1952 Allen encountered his old friend Adolf A. Berle, who brought him up to date on the activities of the Council on Foreign Relations. Of particular interest was the Guatemala study group. Though social reforms were clearly to be welcomed, Berle told Allen, what Arbenz was doing simply disguised "a Russian-controlled dictatorship."[13] Berle, a former member of FDR's Brains Trust, was only one of the prominent liberals whose interest in Guatemala had been stirred by the tender influences of the United Fruit Company long before Arbenz appeared in office. The banana company's chief lobbyist was Thomas G. Corcoran, another early New Dealer and consummate Washington power broker; working with him was former senator Robert La Follette, heir to an illustrious progressive name in American politics. To gain popular support United Fruit had retained the sophisticated services of Edward Bernays, America's top public relations man. Bernays had gained a respectful reputation among the most liberal voices in the American press over a long career that began in his apprentice days at the Paris Peace Conference. The warnings about Arbenz thus came not from the radical anticommunists of the right but from the heart of the American liberal establishment.

It was nevertheless the Nicaraguan dictator Anastasio Somoza who persuaded the Truman administration during the summer of 1952 to consider a covert action in Guatemala. Through well-placed contacts in the White House, Somoza presented the plan to overthrow Arbenz. Truman casually initialed the idea and ordered CIA director Bedell Smith to get on with it. This was in July. By October, when Secretary of State Acheson learned what was afoot, a United Fruit freighter loaded with weapons and ammunition (the boxes were marked "agricultural machinery") was already en route to the Nicaraguan staging base. Acheson rushed over to the White House to argue the risks and pitfalls of such a move and, as casually as he had approved it, Truman scuttled the Somoza-inspired operation.

When Eisenhower and the Republicans came into office, the little community of foreign policy specialists who had any interest in Latin America was well primed to contemplate action against "communist Guatemala." Ever agile in finding the levers of power, United Fruit shifted from its liberal moorings to mobilize Republican supporters — Henry Cabot Lodge and Senator Wiley, for instance — to ensure that the company's interests were well recognized by the new powers in Washington.* Bernays found sensitive chords in warning that Arbenz's proposed land reform had all the potential for investment disaster of Mossadegh's nationalization of British oil interests. The State Department noted that once the reform was fully implemented, more than half of the total private acreage in the country would be confiscated. The new smallholders, moreover, would give the communists "an excellent opportunity to extend their influence over the rural population." This was the communists' "greatest opportunity to supplement their tough city cadres with peasant battalions," wrote Sydney Gruson of *The New York Times*, the best informed of the American correspondents who passed through Guatemala. In dispatches late in February Gruson described the local communists in terms reminiscent of those an official like Bill Krieg could not use on the record until many years later, stressing their "missionary zeal and devotion to party causes rather than self-enrichment."

Berle submitted a sixteen-page memorandum to the White House that began, "The United States cannot tolerate a Kremlin-controlled communist government in this hemisphere." In Eisenhower's National Security Council, Allen was one who needed no convincing on this score, though at that early stage he shared in the general uncertainty about the best means to confront Guatemalan communism. Once the United States could enforce the Monroe Doctrine by simply sending in the Marines; the NSC in March 1953 thought it better for the United States to "avoid the appearance of unilateral action" against countries of the neighborhood.[14] As one American diplomat put it, "We must be careful in our own minds to distinguish between intervention and being caught at it."

— * —

The CIA's capacity for covert operations in Latin America was still in a primitive stage.[15] Even before World War II the Western Hemisphere had been considered the preserve of the Federal Bureau of Investigation, and Hoover was not about to share his proprietary networks with a rival intelligence service. When Bedell Smith took over CIA and finally managed to assert the agency's responsibility in Latin America, he found the FBI veterans accustomed to classic espionage and intelligence collection but unschooled in the new techniques of active covert operations.

* The company's lines of access in Washington were nothing short of extraordinary. Eisenhower's personal secretary, Anne Whitman, was the wife of United Fruit's publicity director. United Fruit was one of the companies that Bedell Smith looked over for the retirement days when he could "make some money." Hoping to become its chief executive officer, he had to settle for a seat on the board of directors.

Smith recruited a man of his own to direct CIA clandestine services for the Western Hemisphere, Colonel Joseph Caldwell King, a West Point graduate and classmate of both Hoyt Vandenberg, an early manager of American intelligence, and Frenchie Grombach, a perennial CIA detractor. King, settled into a business career, had been a prewar hand at ferreting out Nazis in South America; he was a man who, it could safely be said, knew the territory. "J.C." (as he was invariably called) was never quite part of the Eastern Establishment crowd that Allen brought into CIA. But his region was a world apart; while the Ivy Leaguers busied themselves in Europe and Asia, King built himself into a formidable presence amid the dictators, generals, and expatriate businessmen of Latin America. It was King who provided American support for Somoza's various regional designs. Then, once Eisenhower's NSC focused on Arbenz in March of 1953, King's networks mobilized their right-wing contacts within the Guatemalan officer corps. Armed with the cash and logistical support of United Fruit, they staged a short-lived mutiny in one of the provincial capitals. Arbenz's loyalists within the army held firm; the rebellion was crushed, and King's network of conservative officers was decimated.

If Allen's CIA was to prove itself in Washington, he would have to mount a better campaign. He had men who knew a thing or two about sedition and covert action —Wisner, for one, who jumped at the opportunity to grab a piece of the action in the Western Hemisphere and revive his reputation after the failures of his eastern European operations. But the assignment in Guatemala was more brazen than any Wisner's men had taken on in Europe — nothing less than the overthrow of a duly elected government without getting caught. (Later, of course, subtle techniques were devised for "destabilizing" governments, but that concept was well beyond the CIA's sophistication at this stage.) Over the summer of 1953 came Kim Roosevelt's success in Operation Ajax, and Allen promptly asked his old Middle East hand back to test his skills — and luck—in the less familiar terrain of Central America. When Roosevelt declined, Wisner took virtual full-time charge, and J. C. King saw his fiefdom slipping away from him.

The first idea proposed by Wisner's clandestine services — a straightforward plan to assassinate Arbenz—was discarded, for no reason beyond fear of turning the Guatemalan reformer into a martyr.[16] Allen and Wisner then devised a more comprehensive operation, buoyantly calling it Operation Success.* They would start with familiar techniques of psychological warfare to generate a mood of fear and uncertainty in

* Actually, the official name was the unpronounceable PBSUCCESS, the first two letters being what CIA called a digraph for operations of political action.

Guatemala and nearby republics. Without being told the full scope of the operation, attachés at the American military mission in Guatemala City would continue to probe for anti-Arbenz sentiments within the armed forces, encouraging and buying potential allies for a post-Arbenz regime. King's men had failed in this effort back in March, but the new operators of the clandestine services thought they might do better.

Then, with the ground prepared as it had not been the last time, a limited paramilitary "invasion" would be launched from Honduras and made to look like a spontaneous uprising by Guatemalans who had fled the communism of Arbenz. At this point the CIA strategists showed they were still amateurs in the business, at least compared with what they later became. Their plan assumed that Arbenz and his inexperienced communist advisers would simply lose their nerve and flee the country without a fight. In the event that is what happened. But the CIA was naive to stop its planning with the invasion, making no preparations for the variety of contingencies that might have ensued.

Operation Success was devised and elucidated by a tight circle of clandestine service officers with no reference to the analytical experts in the agency or regional specialists in the State Department or Pentagon. Such officials outside the clandestine services, J. C. King observed, tended not to be "in sympathy with our way of doing things." Buoyed by the CIA's success in Iran, Allen won NSC approval in September to mount the necessary preparations under conditions of tightest secrecy. Longtime station chiefs in Guatemala and Honduras, veterans from the plodding FBI days, were quietly replaced by men more experienced in paramilitary operations and covert action. Through Allen's personal back channel to the secretary of state, new ambassadors were named to Honduras and Costa Rica, diplomats whom the CIA men had reason to believe would be sympathetic.[17] As ambassador to Guatemala itself, the Eisenhower administration sent the swashbuckling figure of John Peurifoy, a career diplomat who nonetheless enjoyed carrying a pistol on his hip.*

Armed with the full support of Eisenhower and the NSC, Allen moved to build up the team that would actually carry out Operation Success. With King hovering in the background, disgruntled at being cut out of a mission in his own domain, Allen and Wisner scoured the ranks of officers who knew how to assemble a paramilitary force and make it look

---

* Historian Gleijeses called Peurifoy the "embodiment of imperial hubris," the sort of diplomat who would have been sent to Vietnam in the 1960s. After Operation Success he was named ambassador to Thailand, replacing Donovan in the management of covert actions against communist China. On Aug. 18, 1955, he was killed in a crash of the car he was driving.

convincing. They came upon the name of Colonel Albert Haney, a thirty-nine-year-old veteran of army intelligence just then finishing his tour as CIA station chief in Korea. Haney had helped arrange the emergency evacuation of Allen's son to the hospital in Japan after his war injury late in 1952. Strikingly handsome, curly-haired and tanned, the six-foot-two Haney was one of those dynamic and daring young men who always caught Allen's eye. His limited knowledge of Central America was unimportant; he had experience in training and operating guerrilla units in hostile territory. In the culture of CIA at the time, someone could always be found to handle the "local problems."

Allen summoned Haney to Washington early in November. Swelling in the role of military theater commander, the CIA director briefed him on the concept of Operation Success. Earlier attempts to provoke a military uprising in Guatemala had been bungled, Allen said; the networks of J. C. King and United Fruit had only "contaminated" the officer corps. Haney would have to start from scratch and report his progress to no one but Wisner and Allen himself. King, however, was still in charge of the CIA's Latin American division; he was not a man to leave the battlefield without a fight. He summoned the wary Haney to his office down the stuffy corridors of the clandestine services, by the Lincoln Memorial, and ordered him, first, to set up a meeting with Corcoran, the United Fruit fixer in Washington, and second, to cash in on the company's ability to ship arms to a Guatemalan underground. To Haney this seemed like just the old and discredited planning that Allen had warned him against. He remembered King snorting at him, "If you think you can run this operation without United Fruit, you're crazy!"[18]

Just before Christmas Haney left Washington for the Marine air base of Opa-Locka, north of Miami, to establish a training center for the Guatemalans who would lead the "spontaneous uprising" against Arbenz. He was on his own in mounting a high-level CIA covert operation with few precedents and little experience. The walls of his new office, right above the children's nursery for Marine dependents, were soon covered with a forty-foot-long chart, a time line of efforts in propaganda, exile organizations, defecting officers, and paramilitary logistics.

Haney returned to Washington in January 1954 to present his detailed plan. At the airport to meet him was an aide of Wisner's, who warned, "There's going to be a fight; Frank is with you, but keep your lip buttoned." For King was geared up to assert his expertise against this newcomer from the Far East. "Do we want another Korean War right at our doorstep?" King stormed, hitting where he thought Haney was vulnerable. "Korean-style guerrilla tactics could start a civil war in the middle of Central America." J.C. proposed the familiar alternative of relying on the Guatemalan military itself, "killing 'em with kindness," with extravagant funds that would induce them to make their own revolt against Arbenz. Haney kept obedient silence as Wisner said, "J.C., you've had four years to try that approach and now the situation is worse than ever." Wisner recessed the meeting until the afternoon, to reconvene in Allen's office.

Jaunty as ever in moments of tension, fiddling endlessly with his pipe, Allen gave no indication of his own view as he listened to the opposing strategies of Haney and King for crushing communism in Guatemala. "There's only one person who can make this kind of policy decision," he said finally. "That's the secretary of state."* Allen would be seeing his brother later in the day; the CIA men should assemble early that evening at the new home Allen and Clover had rented on Wisconsin Avenue, called Highlands.

At 7 P.M. the intelligence crowd gathered nervously over cocktails, which Clover set out before dutifully leaving the room. Allen walked into the library with unusual solemnity and went straight to Haney. "Colonel, just one question. Do you *really* think you can pull this off?" "Sir, with your help, we will win," Haney replied. Allen broke into his broad smile, gripped Haney's shoulders with both hands, and said, "Then go to it, my boy, you've got the green light!" King, the old West Pointer, walked out of the library at Highlands without a word.

— * —

The operation began inauspiciously. Early in March 1954, a furtive visitor arrived in Guatemala City, sporting a straw hat and dark glasses but otherwise alien to the ingrown social landscape. The night before he had carefully cut the labels and laundry marks off all the clothes in his single suitcase in case he was searched. He presented himself as a European coffee merchant and, with his German-accented English — he spoke no Spanish — found his way into the company of German émigrés who had much to lose under the Arbenz land reform. Through such kindred spirits he sought access to congenial officers in the armed forces. The visitor's real name was Henry Heckscher; he was the CIA man whose plea to inflame the East German riots the year before had been rebuffed by Washington.

Now he had been transferred to Central America to penetrate the Guatemalan military establishment. An old-style Latin American approach to the president himself had failed; word had been given to Arbenz

---

* Interestingly enough, Allen did not think it necessary at this juncture to seek the view of the president, who did have some experience in military operations.

of a secret bank account in Switzerland available to him if he would just leave his capital — for good — to claim it. Arbenz let the offer drop. So Heckscher was sent in to find the Guatemalan military officers who could be induced to turn against Arbenz when the time came. Though an old hand in Europe, Heckscher's approaches to members of the General Staff turned out to be as crass as King's had been; he was rebuffed with such antagonism that the "coffee merchant" fled the country in fear of arrest.[19]

Meanwhile, in Washington and Florida, Allen's Guatemala task force was taking shape for the next phase. Rivalry continued between Haney, training the paramilitary cadres at Opa-Locka, and King at CIA headquarters, still determined to keep his hands on any Western Hemisphere operations. Wisner brought in as mediator and troubleshooter Tracy Barnes, veteran of the OSS and of early CIA exploits, who could pull rank on anyone below Allen himself. For general administrative and logistical supervision, those aspects of the Great Game that neither Allen nor Wisner had the patience to oversee, Allen assigned his new special assistant, forty-four-year-old Richard Bissell. A newcomer to intelligence, Bissell was an academic economist who had found his métier in government as a deputy director of the Marshall Plan aid organization in Europe. These three, Wisner, Barnes, and Bissell, were the Washington high command of Operation Success; they brainstormed with Allen at least three times weekly through the spring, and Allen was on the telephone daily to Foster.

But Allen always needed input and stimulation from his officers on the ground. Haney would fly in from Florida every week for a secret meeting with the CIA director at his home. Their relationship became that of father and son. Haney was rubbing many of his coworkers the wrong way, with his arrogance and certitude of manner — they called him "Brainy Haney" — but he managed beyond all doubt to ingratiate himself into Allen's deepest confidence. Strolling the garden of Highlands, mentor and protégé would share their fears and anxieties about the evolving mission; Allen wanted to know every detail, every question mark. Inspired by the eagerness of the young officer, Allen found himself drifting into mellow reminiscences of his own exploits in the old days.

To prepare the ground with propaganda, Wisner and Barnes pulled an inventive young writer and editor named David Atlee Phillips out of his private-sector job as a journalist in Chile. Though he had done contract work for the agency, Phillips was still a novice at big-time covert action, so one of King's longtime field operators, E. Howard Hunt, was brought into the circle; together Phillips and Hunt set up a clandestine radio station in the Nicaraguan jungle to pump out inflammatory "news" reports to confuse the government and people of nearby Guatemala. Inevitably careful observers began noticing ominous developments in Central America. When he returned to Guatemala to cover the situation, Gruson of *The New York Times* was expelled, along with an NBC reporter, a self-defeating act by the Arbenz government that only added to the artificial tension the Americans were trying to generate.

A key effort in this direction was unfolding on the diplomatic level, though at the State Department only Foster and his deputy, Bedell Smith, were fully aware of how everything fit together into Operation Success. Given the injunction against getting caught in a unilateral intervention, United States diplomacy sought a consensus among Latin governments that could provide multilateral cover for the American coup. Secretary Dulles, geared up to press for a bold concerted stand against Guatemalan communism, flew to Caracas at the beginning of March for a conference of the Organization of American States. Arbenz's delegation, naively reveling as pioneers in the hemisphere's social revolution, expected enough support to prevent a two-thirds majority on the question. By softening the proposed resolution, Dulles succeeded in winning the votes — lukewarm, but sufficient — of seventeen states. Argentina and Mexico abstained; Guatemala, alone in opposition, denounced the Caracas Resolution as the "internationalization of McCarthyism."

The deadline for Operation Success was the month of June 1954, after which the summer rains would make even a token "uprising" impossible to pull off. As the preparations and tensions mounted, isolated voices within the agency were heard expressing skepticism about either the efficacy or the wisdom of this bold venture in overthrowing a government. A newcomer to King's division, just returned from Rome, a veteran of OSS operations in Europe whom Allen held in high regard (and who happened to be a cousin of Clover's), was allowed an inspection tour of the Opa-Locka training base and came back aghast. "This is the most stupid, asinine thing — what Teddy Roosevelt did in Panama will pale in comparison with what you're planning in Guatemala," he warned. "You'll start a civil war — you'll have the blood of thousands on your hands!" After outbursts like this, Haney complained to Allen, "I'm not worried about the enemy in Guatemala — what worries me is the enemy in Washington."

Another skeptic was Wisner's deputy in the clandestine services, Richard Helms. As Wisner himself was consumed by Guatemala, it fell to his deputy to supervise all the other field work of the agency. Helms would duly report at Allen's morning staff meetings, but when discussion turned to Operation Success, Helms would quietly leave the room — a move that did not pass unnoticed.

A lucky break came in mid-April, triggered by a report from one of the discredited eastern European networks that only Helms was monitoring. A Polish agent in the port of Szczecin (Stettin) reported that weapons and military gear from Czechoslovakia had been loaded onto a Swedish vessel, the *Alfhem*, bound for the Western Hemisphere. The CIA unfortunately lost track of the *Alfhem* as it plied a leisurely route across the Atlantic. The ship quietly docked at the Guatemalan port of Puerto Barrios on May 15 and started offloading its 2,000-ton cargo for Arbenz's military command. "The deception . . . was excellent," Wisner later told Foster Dulles in flustered explanation.[20] The *Alfhem* incident seemed one more proof of Soviet communist mischief in the Western Hemisphere. The day the arms shipment was confirmed, Allen chaired a meeting of the Intelligence Advisory Committee, consisting of military intelligence men alongside the civilian CIA, and directed them to the conclusion that the new Czech arms would give Arbenz enough firepower not only to crush his neighbors but also to sweep into the Panama Canal Zone.

Tension was just what the PBSUCCESS team wanted, but the secrecy of their plot constrained them from explaining what was afoot. An outspoken right-wing Republican, Senator William Knowland of California, telephoned Foster Dulles the morning of May 18. If the communists are supplying arms to the Guatemalan military, Knowland asked in uncomprehending outrage, why is the United States supporting the Guatemalan military with an American mission on the spot? Foster knew, of course, that the American attachés were there specifically to undermine Arbenz's military support, but he dared not give a quick reply. When he spoke to his brother later that day, Allen offered to turn his persuasive charm on Knowland, telling the powerful senator just enough to convince him that the issue should not yet be raised in public.[21]

In response to the crossing of the *Alfhem*, the United States imposed a naval quarantine in the Gulf of Honduras. This, to old hands at international law, was nothing short of an act of war; James Hagerty, Eisenhower's press secretary, noted in his diary that the War of 1812 with Britain was fought over the issue of freedom of the high seas.[22] The State Department's legal adviser, well outside the circle of those privy to PBSUCCESS, warned of international legal implications. Then a more formidable figure weighed in, a man whose perspective revealed better than anyone else's how far Allen's CIA was drifting from the established moorings of intelligence. Robert Murphy, veteran of Vichy France and North Africa, and a colleague of Allen's in clandestine action in World War II, was holding on as deputy undersecretary of state. He learned of the quarantine decision only through "a casual reference" over lunch. Murphy went back to his office and dictated a memo to Foster:

Now that the President and you have decided on this action it, of course, must be seen through, but I would like you to know that I believe the philosophy back of the action wrong and that it may be very expensive over the longer term. . . .

Instead of political action inside of Guatemala, we are obliged to resort to heavy-handed military action on the periphery of the cause of trouble. While I do not question the usefulness of a display of naval force in the Central American area under present circumstances, forcible detention of foreign-flag shipping on the high seas is another matter. . . .

In the past we asserted our right to deliver arms to belligerents. Our present action should give stir to the bones of Admiral von Tirpitz.[23]

Only an old hand like Murphy could so provoke memories of the naval blockades in World War I. Yet the principles of international law had no place in CIA's concept of covert action. The same day Foster received Murphy's incautious memo, he turned the historical point around when the British ambassador, Sir Roger Makins, called to complain about the quarantine. "The British would forgive us if we learned some lessons from British blockade practice in the First World War," Foster archly informed Makins.[24] Later Eisenhower himself let his wartime allies know what he thought of their protests: if they persisted in taking an independent line, the United States would feel no reason to be helpful with "their colonial problems in Egypt, Cyprus, etc."

This was political hardball, and if Operation Success was in danger of overreaching, it was too late to turn back. The tension in Washington — to say nothing of Guatemala — showed. At an NSC meeting on May 27, Foster complained about the "communist line" in Sydney Gruson's dispatches. Never mind that this respected correspondent had unwittingly prepared the ground by offering confirmation of Arbenz's inclinations toward communism. Now, as the operation reached its climax, Gruson's capacity for independent witness was found inconvenient. Allen picked up on his brother's remark and arranged a friendly dinner with his Princeton classmate Julius Ochs Adler, cousin of Arthur Hays Sulzberger, publisher of *The New York Times*. He could have called any number of friends at the *Times* directly, of course, but he felt that this matter should be handled more discreetly. He and Foster would feel more comfortable, Allen told Adler, if Gruson were not to cover the delicate story gathering in Guatemala. Allen gave no reason, but such was the climate of trust between the CIA and the *Times* in those days that Sulzberger promptly called Gruson off his beat.[25]

On Sunday, June 13, 1954, Allen delivered a routine speech to a Princeton class reunion; his topic was "The Worldwide Battle for Men's

Minds." The next morning Allen approached Eisenhower privately and alerted him that it might be necessary to prepare "some statement on Guatemala." Haney's advance patrols were already probing the country's paltry border defenses. Allen drafted a stern presidential statement warning of communist inroads, but the State Department's ranking officer for Latin America, Henry F. Holland, not yet briefed on the enormity of what was about to occur, protested the appearance of a unilateral American action. Foster Dulles concurred in his aide's show of caution and telephoned Allen to cool him down. As press secretary Hagerty understood it, the secretary of state "was afraid if the President supported the CIA, it . . . would place the President in the dangerous position of appealing to citizens of a foreign country to revolt against their leaders." That was, of course, exactly what Eisenhower, Foster, and Allen were doing, but perhaps it need not be said so openly.

On June 16 Allen met with a representative of the American companies that supplied all of Guatemala's imported oil to discuss "the small country down south." The CIA was preparing its full panoply of pressure devices, as the president desired. Eisenhower, as his closest aide, General Andrew Goodpaster, once said, "had a great inventory of principles, in order (some would say) to rationalize whatever he wanted to do." Press correspondents picked up the military moves afoot in Central America and alerted their editors, if not yet their readers. The canny columnist of *The New York Times*, James B. Reston, overcame the caution of his publisher by opening his next column with a disingenuous hypothetical: "John Foster Dulles, the secretary of state, seldom intervenes in the internal affairs of other countries, but his brother Allen is more enterprising. If somebody wants to start a revolution against the Communists in, say, Guatemala, it is no good talking to Foster Dulles. But Allen Dulles, head of the Central Intelligence Agency, is a more active man. He has been watching the Guatemalan situation for a long time."[26] Allen had long since learned that Reston was one Washington reporter who was immune to the charm treatment that kept the rest of the American press at bay.

The carefully crafted cover of PBSUCCESS as a spontaneous local uprising was in danger of being blown. Early on the morning of June 18, Allen called the White House with advance word that an anticommunist uprising in Guatemala was imminent; news of the invasion broke that night. First thing the next morning Allen complained that the news reports — unmarked planes overflying Guatemala City, bombings — were "greatly exaggerated." Those things were indeed happening, but they did not conform to the cover story. Press aside, reports from Allen's own men were not as reassuring as he and Wisner hoped. On June 20 a CIA analysis warned: "The outcome of the efforts to overthrow the regime of President Arbenz of Guatemala remains very much in doubt. The controlling factor in the situation is . . . the position of the Guatemalan armed forces, and thus far this group has not given any clear indication of whether it will move, and if so, in which way. . . . If the effort does not succeed in arousing the other latent forces of resistance within the next period of approximately 24 hours, it will probably begin to lose strength."[27]

On June 22 the invading rebels reported that two of their three old airplanes had been knocked out of action. One had actually been hit by ground fire, and the other was out of gas. Allen sought an urgent meeting with Eisenhower to ask for two additional American planes.* The president remembered the discussion vividly. After hearing the legal objections of the State Department's Holland, he turned to Allen: What would the chances of success be without the planes?

> His answer was unequivocal: "About zero." Suppose we supply the aircraft. What would the chances be then? Again the CIA chief did not hesitate: "About 20 percent.". . .
>
> I walked to the doorway with Allen Dulles and, smiling to break the tension, said, "Allen, that figure of 20 percent was persuasive. It showed me that you had thought this matter through realistically. If you had told me that the chances would be 90 percent, I would have had a much more difficult decision."
>
> Allen was equal to the situation. "Mr. President," he said, a grin on his face, "when I saw Henry [Holland] walking into your office with three large law books under his arm, I knew he had lost his case already."[28]

Jacobo Arbenz surrendered on the night of June 27, crushed by what his limited imagination perceived as a revolt of his own military. CIA men on the spot were scornful of the beleaguered president's lack of political savvy. "If they had had the common sense to truck in 5,000 Indians to demonstrate in the streets of Guatemala City, the State Department probably would have buckled under 'pressure of Guatemalan public opinion,'" said one of Allen's psy-war hands.[29] That, after all, is what partisans of both Mossadegh and the shah had done in Iran. In Guatemala, by contrast, only the American side was geared up for the psychological warfare of anxiety and confusion. "The entire effort," noted a formal CIA report as Operation Success moved to its climax, "is thus more dependent upon psychological impact rather than actual military strength."[30]

---

* When interviewed by Richard Smith, Haney specified that the new planes would augment, not replace, what his force already had. In making his case, Allen glossed over this point, letting the president and others believe that they were simply making good on combat losses.

It was CIA ingenuity, matched by his own lack of guile, that defeated Arbenz. He and his openly Marxist wife sought refuge in Mexico, then drifted through Paris, Prague, and Moscow. Only in 1957 were they allowed to return to the Western Hemisphere, to Uruguay. There Arbenz officially joined the Communist Party of Guatemala. When Fidel Castro came to power in Cuba in 1959, he offered the couple a temporary home. But because he had given in, Arbenz was not a heroic figure to Fidel. Arbenz died in Mexico in January 1971, a lonely man of fifty-six; his restless wife was traveling in El Salvador.

To the men of the CIA clandestine services, the episode was splendid "monkey business." Allen walked away from Guatemala in pride; he never saw any reason to express regret about the consequences of his "little-boy mentality." The caution that had marked the judgments of a young diplomat, his capacity for nuance on complex political matters, paled before the devices of covert action that were now his to deploy. "Communism" in Central America had been vanquished; the new military rulers installed under CIA guidance removed all but two hundred of the peasants trying to settle the newly confiscated lands. The old elite families returned to their paternalistic ways. Of the ancien régime, only United Fruit failed to prosper. Despite the company's fabled access to Washington's power brokers, the Eisenhower administration hit United Fruit with an unrelated antitrust suit shortly after Arbenz's overthrow, and the company never regained the patrimonial domain it had long enjoyed over Guatemala.

Guatemala's decade of social revolution was over. New generations of CIA men improvised their way through a series of harsh and dreary military dictatorships for three decades to come. More then one hundred thousand Guatemalan peasants, heirs of the culture of the Maya, were killed in the American-trained army's antiguerrilla rampages through the countryside. All that was beneath notice about the land that Allen and Clover had so enjoyed. In the sardonic words of the American historian Gleijeses, Guatemala became once again "the joy of American tourists, with its pro-American elite, its Mayan ruins and its smiling, humble Indians who lived their quaint traditional life."[31]

— * —

Sorting through the archives of the fallen Arbenz regime in Guatemala City a few weeks after the coup, David Atlee Phillips came across a single sheet of paper about a twenty-five-year-old Argentine physician who had arrived in town the previous January to study medical care amid social revolution. "Should we start a file on this one?" his assistant asked. The young doctor, it seemed, had tried to organize a last-ditch resistance by Arbenz loyalists; then he sought refuge in the Argentine Embassy, eventually moving on to Mexico. "I guess we'd better have a file on him," Phillips replied. Over the coming years the file for Ernesto Guevara, known as "Che," became one of the thickest in the CIA's global records. In Mexico Guevara met Fidel Castro and joined the circle of Cuban revolutionaries who made their way to the Sierra Maestra en route to power in Havana. All the while CIA was maintaining a watch on him, at one point even infiltrating an agent, under cover of being a freelance journalist, to sleep in the same tent with him for a week. Long after Che became an international revolutionary martyr, his first wife noted that "it was Guatemala which finally convinced him of the necessity for armed struggle and for taking the initiative against imperialism."[32]

The American side drew other lessons, starting with unabashed euphoria among the little group within the government that knew the full story. Allen's CIA had shown, in Guatemala as in Iran, how easy it could be to overthrow an unfriendly government in the Third World, where the risk of direct confrontation with the Soviet Union was absent. Kim Roosevelt's was a lonely voice in warning that such operations should not be attempted without the support of "army and people." In Operation Success the CIA seemed to have shown that both these social forces could be neutralized — manipulated by modest paramilitary pressure in combination with clever psychological warfare. Che Guevara and Allen Dulles were alike in drawing a straight line from Guatemala in 1954 to the Cuban Bay of Pigs in 1961.

Allen, acting out his pride in covert action, paraded the men of his task force before Eisenhower. On that festive occasion only his golden protégé Haney let him down. Gathering the team the night before in the garden at Highlands, Allen asked each to rehearse the presentation he would make to the president. Barnes, King, Heckscher, Phillips — all related their daring missions. For some reason Haney insisted on dwelling on his experience in Korea, as if that would be relevant or apt. Allen listened in silence, then delivered himself, as Phillips recalled it, of the closest to an expletive in his vocabulary: "I've never heard such crap." Turning to the psy-war scriptwriter, Allen ordered Phillips to work through the night on a new statement for Haney to deliver at the White House.*

---

* Phillips rose in the clandestine services eventually to become chief of the Western Hemisphere division, J. C. King's old job. After retirement in 1975 he emerged into the public eye as a prominent advocate for the intelligence profession against the hurtful exposés of the 1970s. E. Howard Hunt, his psy-war colleague in PBSUCCESS, fared less well. An Ivy Leaguer but hardly a liberal, Hunt passed through a series of "black propaganda" assignments, including one in the Bay of Pigs operation. He retired from the agency but went on doing dirty tricks for other masters; he was caught among the burglars sent by the Republicans to the Watergate office of the Democratic National Committee in 1972.

Eisenhower, in a reminiscing mood about his long army career, found his own way to tease the CIA team in the afterglow. Hearing Heckscher's detailed report of the intrigues at the Guatemala military academy, he stopped the celebratory proceedings short with the question, "Do you know who founded that school? Who was the founder of the academy?" On that historical point a puzzled Heckscher admitted he was unprepared. "Well, by god, I did!" Eisenhower said, immensely pleased with himself.

— * —

The CIA was no rogue elephant in the early 1950s. In both Operation Ajax and Operation Success, at virtually every step along the way, Allen's fledgling agency was responding to orders from the highest levels of government. Indeed, the initiative for action against communism in Iran and Guatemala had come from the president and his top advisers in the National Security Council. There were, as yet, no secret "findings" (the euphemism later adopted for authorizations of covert actions), no deceptions of the highest responsible authorities in the executive branch. Congress and the public, of course, were not informed of any covert action in process, but, starting with the senators of the Foreign Relations Committee and the publisher of *The New York Times*, these good Americans did not wish to be. That was the mood of the times.

CIA was establishing itself in a realm where it had not before been taken seriously, as an instrument of power integral to the foreign policy of the United States. That, it seems clear, was Eisenhower's deliberate conception. "Part of CIA's work is extension of work of State Department," he told a military critic of the growing intimacy between the two agencies.[33] To be sure, the State Department seemed a junior partner at times during the year of Operation Success, when diplomacy merely extended the CIA's mission of subversion. But the president's retort was a telling indicator of how far the civilian service had come from the days when intelligence was regarded as primarily a military matter, when only disciplined men in uniform could be trusted with the secrets of espionage.

The Dulles brothers were the visible symbol of this new partnership in foreign policy, but the working reality went much deeper. A key figure in building the partnership was Bedell Smith as he moved from CIA to State. Though not actually spelled out, that may have been one of Eisenhower's purposes in moving him. From army general to director of central intelligence to the second-ranking official of the State Department, Smith bridged the bureaucratic cultures and encouraged an interchange of personnel and facilities unthinkable to previous generations.

Just half a decade before, the State Department and its elite Foreign Service officers had been skittish about identifying too closely with men

386 GENTLEMAN SPY

on mysterious missions of intelligence. Military attachés had been tolerated in embassies, of course, since the days of the Dulleses' grandfather, Secretary of State John Watson Foster. But venturesome civilians interested in political matters were not welcomed in diplomatic communities.

By the time Smith completed his tour at State in 1955, ambassadors routinely, if grudgingly, accepted onto their diplomatic staffs personnel designated by CIA. As a matter of protocol the CIA men reported to their respective ambassadors like other political officers; in reality their missions were quite separate from the official embassy representations, and many an ambassador lamented that activities about which he or she knew all too little were being directed from within the embassy. Indeed, in more than a few capitals the CIA men enjoyed a more candid and confidential relationship with the head of state or key figures of the host regime than did the official diplomats, who sometimes were even ordered not to interfere. The CIA established streamlined communications with the field, parallel to but separate from the normal diplomatic channels. With fewer layers between the field and headquarters, this link often brought news of diplomatic developments to Washington faster than the regular embassy traffic. Because of their presumed exclusivity and candor, the CIA cables often were scanned by the few top State Department officials privy to the channel ahead of their own diplomatic reports.

Most Wednesdays Allen went over to lunch at a private State Department dining room, sometimes with his brother, always with his brother's blessing in conferring with high officials of State, White House, and Pentagon, to review covert CIA actions under way and to prevent accidents of cross-purposes from arising. Foster, with no record of respect for Foreign Service professionals, often seemed to trust Allen's men more than his own. On the most sensitive assignments his special assistants were often of CIA background rather than Foreign Service. Foster offered to name Allen's Middle East expert, Kim Roosevelt, assistant secretary of state for the region; Bedell Smith advised Roosevelt to stay in CIA, "where the action is."

When Eisenhower convened his National Security Council every week, he generally turned first to Allen's report on world developments; it was always concise and trenchant but, in character for Allen, nicely interspersed with colorful anecdotes that seized the attention of preoccupied officials. Later presidents often ignored the NSC as a policymaking body, but Eisenhower took these sessions with the utmost seriousness.

Just as in Bern, Allen wanted his CIA—and himself—to be highly visible. He seethed on recalling the day when Milton Eisenhower, the president's brother, set out in a White House car for an appointment with him, "but could not find the office until a telephone call was put through to me for precise directions. . . . Sight-seeing bus drivers made it a practice to stop outside our front gate. . . . Every taxicab driver in Washington knew the location. As soon as I put up a proper sign at the door, the glamour and mystery disappeared."[34]

Prominent journalists like Walter Lippmann and Joseph Alsop were Allen's steady social contacts. As much as his brother, he received foreign dignitaries and American ambassadors on home leave, people who would normally confine their meetings to the official diplomatic circle. Indeed, Allen constructed his office with several doors of access and separate waiting rooms so that secretive CIA field operators would not be seen by the next visitors, and self-important callers would not be reduced to the indignity of waiting with others. It was all part of Allen's concept of intelligence and the image of the genial spymaster.

Allen was ever annoyed with security precautions about his own doings. When he could, he would travel to a lecture date or an academic meeting without a bodyguard. "I've never been shot at," he could claim, pride mixed, perhaps, with disappointment. "I don't know that anybody has ever tried to kidnap me." His personal security detail was always told, "Don't worry about anyone shooting the Old Man, just make sure he doesn't leave any classified cables lying around." Once during a raging snowstorm in Washington, Allen carelessly left an office window open; a stack of top-secret cables blew out the window, to be frantically retrieved by CIA security men tramping through the snowdrifts.

Secure telephones, which garble conversations against eavesdropping, were beyond his comprehension. To activate the jamming, the user had to press an extra toggle switch. No matter how many times he was instructed "Press to talk, Open to listen," Allen never got it right; he would loudly complain, "The guy can't hear me!" and end up bellowing out the most sensitive information on the open line. Or, in a chatty mood, he would convey his information with twinkling eyes, silly code words, and circumlocutions utterly transparent to anyone with the slightest knowledge of what he was discussing.

A young recruit to the CIA in 1954 remembers being angrily challenged in his own security interview when he asked about taking a lie detector test. "Where did you learn about that? That's classified information!" The new man stuttered that he thought he had read about it in an interview that Allen Dulles gave to *U.S. News and World Report* the previous March. No one in authority had noticed; at that time no CIA man, not even the director, was supposed to refer to the lie detector in public.

Allen cared about the institutional role of intelligence in the American system of government. "What interested me," he told Russell Baker of *The New York Times*, "was the idea of building up a new kind of struc-

ture in the American government, creating a good intelligence organization and giving it its momentum, its start." David Phillips remembers the
director visiting the ramshackle buildings of the clandestine services on a
Sunday morning. Stepping into the dingy corridor and taking a look
around, he forgot his errand and snorted, "This is a damned pig sty."
Allen started nurturing the bold idea of designing a big and imposing
building to house a secret intelligence agency.

John Bross, a stalwart of covert action in Europe who survived with integrity intact, said shortly before his death in 1992, "Allen gave a sense of
permanence to CIA. He established the traditions which guided us all."
Another officer of those early days, Wayne G. Jackson, wrote, "If one
were to ask who was generally considered the incarnation of intelligence, . . . the answer would inevitably be Dulles."[35] Allen was not the first,
and ultimately maybe not the most effective, director of central intelligence. But working in the uneasiness and uncertainties of his times, he
left no one in doubt that henceforth in the American system of government, for better or worse, there would always be a CIA.

— 15 —

OTHER GAMES, OTHER RULES

ONE OF THE PIONEERS of intelligence technology looked back, with more than a tinge of bitterness, at the Eastern Establishment character of the OSS and the CIA, the Ivy League tone set by Allen's donnish personality. Individuals recruited for key positions came from similar backgrounds, he wrote, and were inclined toward "the more traditional liberal-arts-based 'substantive' intelligence. . . . The ultimate result was a bias against scientific and technical intelligence."[1] The irony is that the Dulles era at CIA marked the transformation of intelligence from a liberal art form into an undertaking of high scientific and technological genius. Allen's personal technical skills had their limits, giving grief to anyone trying to work a telephone or recording system with him, but from his first years of conceiving a peacetime intelligence service, he acknowledged, with all the insouciance of a humanist, the importance of science for the security of the United States.

At the end of 1946, when contemporaries were speaking of the dawn of the atomic age, Allen had been one of the civilian intelligence experts invited to participate, along with Donovan and Hoyt Vandenberg, in the planning of government research and development programs. This group, chaired by Professor I. I. Rabi of Columbia, concluded without reservation that "scientific intelligence," that is, accurate knowledge of the scientific and technological advances made by any possible adversaries, was a prerequisite for determining America's own research and development programs.[2]

A year later, during the Dulles-Jackson-Correa survey, Allen pleaded ignorance about biological warfare, though he acknowledged it to be "second only to atomic warfare among the evils of the future." The young CIA itself, under Hillenkoetter, conceded its incompetence as

well. "Only meager information" had been obtained about Soviet capabilities in chemical warfare, Hillenkoetter admitted; "installations to produce vaccines were so like those for making biological weapons that espionage agents would have difficulty in detecting the latter, even if they
were able to penetrate . . . [*twelve lines deleted*, probably location of secret
facilities]."[3] Defense Secretary Forrestal, just before leaving office in
March 1949, nonetheless proposed the creation of a "medical intelligence
unit" within CIA. Rival intelligence bureaus of the army and navy, as well
as the State Department and the Atomic Energy Commission, derided
the proposal.

But "Wild Bill" Donovan was, typically, less timid. His adventurers in
the OSS had conducted their own clumsy experiments with exotic drugs
with the idea of somehow poisoning Hitler. In 1949, as a private citizen,
Donovan seized upon Forrestal's interest to conduct his own survey of
biological warfare.* He discovered that the CIA knew less about what
the Soviet Union was doing in this field than American intelligence had
known about Germany in 1939. His report to Forrestal of April 20, 1949,
was full of phrases like "limited information" and "there is no definite
knowledge," and concluded, "Nothing is known regarding political or
military policy with respect to use of BW [biological warfare]." He
warned that "the United States was vulnerable to a number of operations
in which the Russians had displayed expertise."

One such operation involved the substance lysergic acid diethylamide,
known by the initials LSD. The meager intelligence reports indicated
that Soviet scientists were engaged in intensive efforts to produce this obscure drug which, it was said, led to "odd physiological activity."[4] The
Swiss chemical firm Sandoz was the only producer of LSD in the West;
CIA doctors feared that the Soviet Union was trying to buy up the total
available supply.†

After the decade of the 1960s, when the so-called drug culture became
an American commonplace, a CIA veteran testified to a Senate investigating committee: "It is awfully hard in this day and age to reproduce how
frightening all of this was to us at the time, particularly after the drug
scene has become as widespread and as knowledgeable in this country as

---

* Among Donovan's partners in this survey was his junior law associate, William Colby,
who later became director of central intelligence.
† The American military attaché in Switzerland reported that Sandoz was prepared to sell
the Russians 10 kilos (22 pounds) of LSD, enough for 100 million personal doses! Years
later Sandoz chemists told the CIA that their entire inventory of LSD was never more than
40 grams, about 1.5 ounces. The discrepancy was explained by the attaché's confusion between a milligram (1/1,000 of a gram) and a kilogram (1,000 grams). Thus all his calculations were off by a factor of one million.

it did. . . . We were literally terrified, because this was the one material that we had ever been able to locate that really had potential fantastic possibilities if used wrongly."[5] When Allen entered CIA in 1950, the government had gone no deeper into these matters than to acknowledge finally the need for Forrestal's interagency program of medical intelligence.

Not that the early CIA was entirely ineffectual in the scientific field; the traditional intelligence methods that Allen championed did score one modest success. It came after the shocking disclosure that on August 29, 1949, the Soviet Union had detonated an atomic bomb, fully three years ahead of the timetable estimated by American intelligence. The CIA's director of scientific intelligence promptly sent Hillenkoetter a memo defining the deficiencies in the American intelligence assessment of the Soviet atomic and technological threat.[6] But from agent networks in Europe, interrogations of returning German prisoners of war, and such, CIA analysts were able to pinpoint a plutonium factory in Kyshtym, in the Ural Mountains between Sverdlovsk and Chelyabinsk. The agents' reports noted that some leading Soviet chemists and physicists had been transferred to the obscure site.* Learning of this, a skeptical U.S. Air Force demanded that the CIA show its stuff by producing a detailed map of the area for potential targeting guidance.[7]

Allen, then still in law practice, was arguing that the private sector had a wealth of technical information available if intelligence analysts only knew where to look. Accordingly CIA analysts found out that a young American mining engineer had done surveys in the Kyshtym area in the years before the 1917 Bolshevik Revolution. This engineer, Herbert Hoover, had since given all his papers to Stanford University. In the voluminous files of the thirty-first president of the United States, CIA found a map of Kyshtym, located the probable factory site on the shore of Lake Irytash, and promptly submitted the data to the Strategic Air Command.†

But Allen had little opportunity to gloat about this vindication of traditional methods. In his first month in office as Bedell Smith's deputy, he received an alarming report from the chief of the agency's new medical staff. Six months of war in Korea had provided a window into the capabilities of communist-bloc countries in biological warfare, and liberated prisoners of war were telling stories of a technique called brainwashing.

There is ample evidence in the reports of innumerable interrogations that the communists were utilizing drugs, physical duress, electric shock, and

---

* After the fall of communism the Moscow media revealed in 1989 that Kyshtym had indeed been its major plutonium production plant.
† Kyshtym was a target to be photographed by U-2 pilot Francis Gary Powers in his final surveillance mission of May 1, 1960.

possibly hypnosis against their enemies. With such evidence it is difficult
not to keep from becoming rabid about our apparent laxity. We are forced
by this mounting evidence to assume a more aggressive role in the development of these techniques, but must be cautious to maintain strict inviolable control because of the havoc that could be wrought by such techniques in unscrupulous hands.[8]

In retrospect of the drug-testing program that ensued under Allen's
leadership, two points of this early memo are especially significant. First,
research that up to this time had been defensive, to protect American
agents — military and civilian — against enemy devices should give way
to "a more aggressive role" in devising ways to use biological warfare on
the offense. Second, from the start Allen and his CIA colleagues were on
notice about the need for "inviolable control" over the use of drugs like
LSD.

As the program developed, the CIA adopted the first point, embarking upon its initial major foray into the unfamiliar realm of biological intelligence. On the second point, the demand that mind-altering drugs be
kept under "inviolable control," for reasons that can only be inferred after
the fact, Allen fell into an uncharacteristic carelessness.

— * —

On April 4, 1953, in his second month as head of CIA, Allen received a
comprehensive proposal from Wisner's deputy in the clandestine services, Richard Helms. Helms sought Allen's approval for a major project
"to develop a capability in the covert use of biological and chemical materials, . . . the production of various physiological conditions which could
support present or future clandestine operations. . . . The development of
a comprehensive capability in this field . . . gives us a thorough knowledge
of the enemy's theoretical potential, thus enabling us to defend ourselves
against a foe who might not be as restrained in the use of these techniques
as we are."[9]

Helms called the project Operation MKULTRA. Detailing the types of
covert operations for which the results might be used, he minimized the
dangers. "We intend to investigate the development of a chemical material which causes a reversible non-toxic aberrant mental state, the specific
nature of which can be reasonably well predicted for each individual. This
material could potentially aid in discrediting individuals, eliciting information, and implanting suggestions and other forms of mental control."[10]

From the start, therefore, CIA officers made no pretense that this project would be an innocuous matter of pure science. The research would
have to proceed "without the establishment of formal contractual rela-

tions," Helms advised Allen; the existence of signed contracts would reveal the government's sponsorship. Moreover, the scientists qualified to do research in this field "are most reluctant to enter into signed agreements of any sort which connect them with this activity, since such a connection would jeopardize their professional reputations."[11]

Clandestine operations involving extraordinary precautions were nothing unusual for CIA; it was all part of the Great Game. Yet Allen took ten days to consider MKULTRA. His interest in the subject was not casual. On April 10, with the Helms proposal fresh in mind, he devoted a public speech to the topic of what he called brain warfare. "We in the West are somewhat handicapped in getting all the details," he told a Princeton alumni conference. "There are few survivors, and we have no human guinea pigs to try these extraordinary techniques."[12]

On April 13, Allen approved Operation MKULTRA, with a budget of $300,000. He concurred in Helms's recommendation that security considerations precluded handling the research through the contractual agreements that CIA used for other scientific research. Fully five years later a CIA audit justified the extraordinary secrecy of the project: "Precautions must be taken not only to protect operations from exposure to enemy forces but also to conceal these activities from the American public in general. The knowledge that the Agency is engaging in unethical and illicit activities would have serious repercussions in political and diplomatic circles."[13] For years to come CIA auditors defended the absence of normal accountability on grounds of professional discretion within the scientific community, dubious legality, and the dangers of public disclosure. Neither Congress nor the president was informed about MKULTRA.*

Less than a month after Allen gave his approval to the program, Helms informed his staff meeting that he considered the drug LSD to be "dynamite, and that he should be advised at all times when it was intended to use it." He must have reported this concern to his superior, Frank Wisner, who sent a memorandum to the medical director of the project, stat-

---

* The 1975 Senate committee investigating the CIA, headed by Frank Church, was officially informed that documentation of the experiments had been destroyed in 1972 by the project director, Sidney Gottlieb. Yet in any complex bureaucracy duplicate or related memos have a way of surviving in secondary archives or the personal papers of individuals. Two years after the Church Committee investigation, CIA found another archive, earlier overlooked, that told much of the story. These documents were made available to joint hearings of the Senate Select Committee on Intelligence and a subgroup of the Committee on Human Resources on August 3, 1977. Gottlieb himself, retired and working in a leper colony in India, pleaded that illness prevented him from testifying in public about his drug experiments for CIA.

ing that not only Helms but Wisner himself must personally approve any use of LSD.

On November 27, 1953, seven months into MKULTRA, an American physician engaged in the project, Dr. Frank Olson, was found dead under a broken tenth-floor window of the Statler Hotel in New York City. Eight days before, he had swallowed 70 micrograms of LSD, administered by a CIA colleague without his knowledge, in a glass of Cointreau as the team sat discussing their researches in New York. Olson apparently did not know that a week earlier the directors of MKULTRA had concluded, at a semiannual review conference at a secret hideaway, an old Boy Scout camp at Deep Creek Lake in western Maryland, that "an unwitting experiment would be desirable."[14]

Olson's CIA colleagues observed their unwitting subject closely after that drink of liqueur. Father of three, happily married to a woman he had met at the University of Wisconsin, Olson was intermittently boisterous and cheerful, they noted, then depressed. At 2:30 on the Saturday morning, the CIA officer sharing Olson's hotel room was awakened by a loud crash of glass and saw that his partner had jumped to his death.

Allen and Wisner were preoccupied with the launching of Operation Success against Guatemala at the time. Despite his specific instructions, Helms had not been informed of the LSD experiment. After their subject's death, however, the CIA swung into action at the highest level, first to ensure that Olson's widow would receive death benefits equal to two-thirds of her husband's base pay, but second to ensure that no one — not even the family — would know of the CIA's involvement.

An internal CIA investigation into the circumstances surrounding Olson's death took two months. The medical and scientific sponsors of MKULTRA tried to plead the normal risks of casualties in war. In his role as the agency's conscience, Lawrence Houston, the general counsel, testified:

> I'm not happy with what seems to be a very casual attitude on the part of [Technical Service] representatives to the way this experiment was conducted and the remarks that this is just one of the risks running with scientific experimentation. I do not eliminate the need for taking risks, but I do believe, especially when human health or life is at stake, that at least the prudent, reasonable measures which can be taken to minimize the risk must be taken and failure to do so was culpable negligence. The actions of the various individuals concerned after effects of the experiment on Dr. Olson became manifest also revealed the failure to observe normal and reasonable precautions.

Allen received the investigation report early in February 1954. Inspector General Lyman Kirkpatrick recommended that the technical experts involved be formally reprimanded for the fatal experiment, but the agency's research director appealed to Allen personally. A reprimand, he said, would hinder "the spirit of initiative and enthusiasm so necessary in our work." Allen struggled through six drafts of a formal response, each one more watered down. On February 12 he wrote a letter officially criticizing the chief of technical operations, under whose responsibility the LSD experiment had been conducted, for "poor judgment . . . in authorizing the use of this drug on such an unwitting basis and without proximate medical safeguards." The same day he wrote the medical doctor who had actually carried out the experiment that "unwitting application of the drug . . . did not give sufficient emphasis for medical collaboration and for the proper consideration of the rights of the individual to whom it was being administered." Allen thus protected the written record with a critical verdict.

But the CIA director then ordered an unusual procedure. Allen's signed letters were to be hand-carried to the two recipients, read in the presence of the official delivering them, and immediately returned to Allen's files with no copies made. Overnight Allen decided on a further step; he instructed Helms to tell the individuals concerned orally — not in writing — that "these are not reprimands and no personnel file notation[s] are being made." In effect Allen endorsed the human risks taken by his men; none of the participants in the experiment leading to Olson's death suffered any adverse consequences in their careers.

In the months and years to come Allen took no steps whatever to halt the testing of LSD on subjects without their knowledge or consent. Indeed, MKULTRA went on for at least ten more years; as many as fifty persons were given the drug without being told what was happening to them. At safe houses in New York's Greenwich Village and San Francisco's Telegraph Hill, hired prostitutes and hustlers secretly administered LSD to their varied (and still unnamed) clientele as CIA men watched for reactions through one-way mirrors.[15]

When they finally penetrated the details of MKULTRA in the mid-1970s, congressional investigators issued a rebuke, remarkable in the record of legislative-executive relationships, to the CIA and by implication to Allen Dulles personally (and by then posthumously).

From its beginning in the early 1950s until its termination in 1963, the program of surreptitious administration of LSD to unwitting non-volunteer human subjects demonstrates a failure of the CIA's leadership to pay adequate attention to the rights of individuals and to provide effective guidance to CIA employees. Though it was known that the testing was dangerous, the lives of subjects were placed in jeopardy and their rights were ignored. . . . Although it was clear that the laws of the United States were being violated, the testing continued.[16]

None of this sorry episode became known to Congress or the public during Allen's lifetime, so he was never confronted with the need to explain his "carelessness," putting it tactfully, in imposing "inviolable controls." But Allen's known frame of mind in these years permits speculation about a personal interest in mind-altering drugs. His son had recovered physically from the critical brain injury suffered on that hillside in Korea in November 1952; he was strong, active, and handsome in a winning fashion once again. But in his mind he was not well. In spite of medical and psychiatric treatments, he showed no signs of becoming a whole person.

From his desk at CIA Allen carried on extensive correspondence with knowledgeable family friends and specialized psychiatric clinics in Switzerland to discover a cure for his son's illness, without success. Even as Dr. Olson's suicide was under secret investigation, Allen summoned to the CIA a world-renowned neurologist from the Cornell Medical Center in New York, Dr. Harold Wolff, who was at that time treating young Allen. Wolff had political as well as medical credentials. He was a close friend of Adolf Berle, who was being so helpful to Allen in Operation Success. Wolff continued to work under a lucrative but secret contract with the CIA for the rest of the 1950s, pursuing his research on the human brain and central nervous system.

Grasping at any signs of medical progress that could restore a son to mental health, a father would perhaps pause before imposing restrictions on scientific research that might provide an answer. His son never regained his full mental capacities, but the CIA drug program proceeded in such secrecy that Allen's successor, John A. McCone, was not informed about it until his second year in office. McCone ordered the research halted.

— * —

Part of the allure of scientific intelligence is the hope of an "antiseptic" method of gaining information, without the frailties, dangers, and tedium of running networks of human agents. As early as 1951 CIA experts had seized upon a careless habit of communications security, the practice of securing sensitive telephone and cable lines at their points of origin and destination but leaving unsecured other points along the way. British and American experts collaborated in tapping an old telephone junction box under the highway to Schwechat, outside Vienna, through which passed communications to Moscow from the Russian occupation headquarters in Austria.* By 1953 Vienna was supplanted as a center of East-West espionage by Berlin, which was divided into sectors of the three Western occupying powers and the Soviet zone of East Germany. Historically Berlin was the metropolis of central Europe; "everything came to Berlin," a CIA specialist explained. "When the Soviet commandant in Bucharest or Warsaw called Moscow the call went through Berlin."[17]

Physical infrastructure, such as telephone cables, sewers, and railroads, tends to endure through changing political regimes. If British and American intelligence could locate, just a foot or so underground, the critical switching points of Vienna's communications links, surely they could do the same in Berlin. The networks at the CIA's disposal through Gehlen included any number of technicians familiar with the telephone system of Nazi Berlin; there would be no reason to suppose that the Soviet occupiers of the city's eastern sector had altered the basic configuration.

In 1953 CIA technicians were exploring the possibilities of tapping into Berlin's land lines, using the decoding technology that had performed so admirably in Schwechat. As he learned about it, Allen insisted that "as little as possible concerning the project would be reduced to writing." It is probable, said the CIA historian, "that few orders have been so conscientiously obeyed." The mission was named Operation Gold.†

At twilight on November 13, one of Gehlen's agents was spotted on West Berlin's Kiefholtzstrasse sailing a model sailboat across a branch of the Heidenkamp Canal, which flowed eastward from the American sector. The little battery-driven toy was invisibly dragging an underwater cable, which Gehlen's men hoped could be connected to a land line that would make the tap at the critical switching point eighteen inches under the verge of Schoenefelder Chaussée, a busy highway linking East Berlin

* The listening post above the switching box was disguised as a shop selling Harris tweeds; unfortunately for the intelligence mission, Harris tweeds promptly became popular with the Austrians and the operation had to divert some of its resources into the retail clothing business. See David C. Martin, *Wilderness of Mirrors* (New York: Ballantine, 1980), pp. 76–85, 102.

† The exact dates of the following episode's origins are among those factual precisions that the counterespionage mind insists must remain vague. The official CIA history blacks out all dates in the version declassified in 1977. The project started sometime in Allen's first six months as head of CIA. Whether the first inspiration came from the British or the Americans, or from Gehlen's German networks, remains an obscurity of the rivalry among competing national intelligence services. "While it should perhaps be possible to credit one individual with the initial concept," the official history states cautiously, "it appears to be a bit difficult to do so" (CIA, *Berlin Tunnel*, p. 5). As for the code name, CIA was naive in those days: operational code names should be neutral, revealing nothing of their purpose. The Vienna wiretap operation was code-named Silver; any alert counterespionage officer could guess that Gold was something of a similar nature.

to the main Soviet air base in the eastern zone. The agent and his accomplice were seized, tried, and executed in East Germany.[18] Clearly the connection could not be made in a simple way; there would have to be another route of access from the American sector to the junction box under the shoulder of the highway.

Gehlen then contacted Allen in Washington, according to German accounts of the operation, and the CIA director approved the ambitious idea of a man-sized tunnel from the American sector to the edge of Soviet East Berlin. A month later, in December, the head of CIA's Berlin operations, an old-time espionage manager named Bill Harvey, went to London for a planning session with his British counterparts. Specifications for an underground passage were laid out in detail, along with the tapping technology, the method of recording the data, the costs, and the methods of assessing the information received. Avidly taking notes of the entire plan was a promising young officer of British intelligence named George Blake.[19]

Exactly when the idealistic and innocent-seeming Blake became a double agent, reporting to Moscow what he discovered in London, is another counterespionage secret. But by April of 1955, when British intelligence sent him to their Berlin base, the tunnel he had learned about at its very inception was fully operational. Three hundred yards long, with six feet of headroom fifteen feet below the surface, the tunnel was packed with electronic equipment, but also with air conditioning, heating, and noise-muffling equipment. After a year of clandestine burrowing under the cottages and gardens of the Berlin suburb of Rudow, with elaborate cover techniques for removing vast quantities of dirt without attracting notice, German and American army engineers had managed to make contact with an electronic box no larger than a tennis ball, through which passed three telephone cables, a total of 172 individual circuits, each capable of carrying at least eighteen channels simultaneously.

A year later, on April 21, 1956, Soviet and East German soldiers broke into the eastern end of the tunnel in the neighboring village of Alt-Glienicke. American technicians at the most exposed reach dropped their gear and their warm coffee cups and fled to the western access point. The CIA's Berlin Tunnel was blown. When Foster Dulles twitted his sister Eleanor, the State Department's Berlin desk officer, about the debacle in her city (though it is unlikely that she had known of the tunnel), she replied defensively, "It's all Allen's fault."[20] Moscow and the East German press trumpeted the "gangster act" of the West, an "international scandal, . . . breach of the norms of international law, . . . such a vileness."[21] News media in the West, together with knowing officials of East and West alike, were impressed not so much with the audacity as with the display of superior intelligence technology.

For fourteen months virtually every section of CIA had been engaged in handling the output of this sophisticated listening post — without knowing, of course, the nature of the source. One of the clandestine services buildings, called T-32, was renovated for teams of translators and analysts. Intelligence officers across Washington, military and civilian, knew only that T-32 had an "incredible source." The analysis center was inundated with information about Soviet troop movements and industrial activity in East Germany and the other satellite countries.

For years following, Allen loved to reminisce about the glory days of his tunnel. On his next visit to Berlin he made bold to visit Rudow and the tunnel's western access point, concealed in a military supply dump, where rings of barbed wire provoked no suspicion. Newsmen following him asked for his reaction to this show of technological prowess and, with his eyes twinkling but otherwise poker face, he replied, "Tunnel? What tunnel? I don't see any tunnel!" He loved recalling the mishaps that threatened exposure during construction and operation. With the first snowfall in the winter of 1954–55, for instance, he wrote that "the snow just above the tunnel was melting because of the heat coming up from underneath. In no time at all a beautiful path was going to appear in the snow, going from West to East Berlin, which any watchful policeman couldn't help but notice." An alert inspector on the western side gave the alarm, the tunnel heat was turned off, and cooling ventilation substituted. "Fortunately it continued to snow and the path was quickly covered over."*

Analysis of the material from the tunnel intercept went on in T-32 until the end of September 1958, so great was the backlog. From the hard data on the flow of military material could be constructed intelligence on Soviet military production. Clues to progress in rocketry and missile research came through fully two years before the launching of Sputnik, man's first artificial satellite. Conveyed also was a wealth of personal gossip among the men at Soviet outposts concerning the black-marketeering and womanizing of their officers.

* By the 1990s, the prosperous Berliners living in upscale Rudow had forgotten about the old tunnel, a relic of the irrelevant Cold War. But the administrator of a local cemetery, by chance an amateur of history, proudly took me to the various tunnel sites on Mother's Day in 1993. His daughter laughed as we climbed through little garden plots, saying, "There is not a single other person in this village who could have told you about all this old stuff." Crossing the all-but-forgotten border into East Berlin, we stopped a middle-aged man mowing the lawn around his little detached house, and he, with amusement, pointed out the back yard two houses away where the Russian soldiers had dug down to the tunnel's eastern edge. The Chaussée itself, now that a superhighway goes to the Schoenefeld airport, was that day being repaved as a pleasant residential access road. Naturally the residents had no idea whether the telephone lines to their homes were still strung underneath the garden verge.

George Blake was arrested in 1961 and confessed to spying for the Soviet Union, including the alert to the tunnel intercept. Ever since, CIA men have debated the obvious question. If Moscow knew about this breach in their communications security, why did their officers go on using a compromised channel? In the nature of modern counterespionage lie several answers.

First, any abrupt or even gradual change in routine would be detected by those listening in. No more attention would be paid to the tunnel intercept, and the Americans might even have been able to discover the source of the leak and thus blow a valuable Soviet intelligence asset. Blake acknowledged as much after he escaped from Britain in 1966 and settled in Moscow. Although the Soviet side knew about the intercept, he told *Pravda*, "it continued 'not to notice' the outflow of information." Only after many months did the Russians contrive another excuse for altering their communications patterns. "I was working in West Berlin so you can understand how important it was for me," Blake explained, that the tunnel analysts be led to detect innocuous reasons for the change in communications patterns.[22]

A second factor may have influenced the Soviets. Although the intercept may have been known from the start, Moscow did not know of American code-breaking technology. That intensely sensitive "detail" had not figured in Harvey's original meeting with the British, where Blake was taking notes. Thus the Russian command may have believed that even if their messages were being intercepted, they were still unintelligible.

Finally, historical retrospect permits a speculative explanation that Allen and his colleagues would probably not have taken seriously at the time. It involves a reading of the state of the Cold War in 1955 and the nature of the information passing through the switching box on the Schoenefeld Chaussée.

East-West tensions in Europe had eased following the death of Stalin in 1953. The United States and the Western alliance remained concerned about the possibility of a Soviet invasion of Europe through Germany, and World War III was not an empty threat. But for that year of the Berlin Tunnel the strategists of the West could feel secure against a Soviet surprise attack. George Marshall's successors could have the twenty-four hours' notice he had demanded in an earlier era. No matter how much Soviet deception had been engaged, tunnel intercepts of signals from field commanders would necessarily have provided some clues to advance preparations and mobilizations for any aggressive design.

All that time reassuring public and private signals were coming from Moscow arguing against any surprise attack. The post-Stalin leaders were seeking a new basis for competition with the West. Instead of continuing to expand communism into the Western democracies, the Kremlin seemed to be content with the more modest effort of preserving the East-West status quo. Their problem was to convince suspicious policymakers in the West that this new motivation was sincere. Guarded public statements and uncharacteristic courtesies at diplomatic receptions were hardly definitive in the deceptions of the Great Game.

The information allowed to pass through the Berlin Tunnel provided a fortuitous solution, according to this logic. Though in themselves interesting, assessments of military production and deployments, and even embarrassing evidence of the corruption of the Soviet officer class, were not fundamentally threatening to the security of the Soviet Union or its satellites. The signals from the tunnel would only indicate the absence of any aggressive designs on the part of the Kremlin and the Red Army. If this indeed was the message that the Soviet leaders wished to convey, what better way of convincing the strategists of the West than by letting them hear secret military communications? Arguably, CIA technology in devising a bizarre communications intercept may have served as a building block of détente.

— * —

The collection and evaluation of intelligence is a never-ending process. Many of the most critical questions of concern to policymakers are not likely to be answered in interrogations of prisoners or through intercepted communications. After 1953 the CIA and the military intelligence branches had reason to believe that the Soviet Union was embarked on the production of long-range bombers and even intercontinental ballistic missiles, which would threaten the United States more directly than a conventional invasion in Europe. How could an adversary acquire accurate information from within a closed totalitarian society? It was a society, moreover, far more sophisticated than the United States on the matter of deception.

"As a technique, deception is as old as history," Allen mused in his retirement writings. To professionals of intelligence it is only naive to equate "deception" with "lying," but that, of course, is what it means — and at a level of technique that requires spending countless millions of dollars and man-hours. Compared with the American democracy, the Soviet Union in its heyday of the 1950s enjoyed a distinct advantage. "With their centralized organization and complete control of the press and of dissemination of information," Allen wrote, "they can support a deception operation far more efficiently than we can."[23]

The techniques available to CIA and military intelligence in the early

1950s to penetrate the deceptions were primitive. In the rehearsals for the Kremlin's May Day parade of 1954, for instance, American military attachés photographed the practice flybys of a new Soviet bomber, using rooftop cameras with long-focal-length lenses. Enlargement of the film revealed serial numbers on the planes, and these were interpreted by air force intelligence (which had its own agenda to pursue) as a vast production line; when civilian analysts argued that the Russians might simply be etching misleading numbers on a small number of planes, their equally self-interested skepticism was overruled. "Often the Soviets put armaments on display with a certain amount of fanfare," Allen wrote, "in order to draw attention away from other armaments they may have in their arsenal or may plan to have. Sometimes they exhibit mock-ups of planes and other equipment, which may never see the light of day as operational types." By Aviation Day 1955 the flybys again suggested operational wings far more numerous than Western estimates. Only later did it emerge that a single squadron had been flying around in circles, with the same planes, this time unmarked by serial numbers, reappearing every few minutes.

Strategic intelligence needed more than the numbers and types of weaponry; military and civilian evaluators alike wanted to know the location of the Soviet military production facilities and their size, configuration, and potential output. Western intelligence knew that since the end of World War II, more than 1,500 Soviet manufacturing plants had been dismantled and moved from the regions of Moscow, Leningrad, and the western USSR deep into the interior in advance of the Nazi armies. Where had they been relocated? A lucky chance had produced intelligence about the plant at Kyshtym; no such luck could be expected for all the others.

From the end of the war, Eisenhower had become a champion of aerial reconnaissance for collecting otherwise unattainable intelligence; he frequently cited the postwar assessment by the Strategic Bombing Survey that aerial reconnaissance, amazingly accurate, had produced 80 to 90 percent of American military intelligence during the war. On becoming president in 1953 he spurred the air force to greater efforts. Reconnaissance aircraft, loaded with cameras, flew along the sensitive Siberian borders for oblique observations, but the tactic was dangerous.* At least four planes were shot down, and coverage was limited to the border areas.

The CIA did not see itself in the business of flying high-technology aircraft, but that April Allen took the initial step of establishing a photo

---

* Actually the tactic involved two planes: one to make a hostile pass, a second to follow and observe the ensuing countermeasures.

interpretation center, previously a preserve of the navy, and hiring for the job a young geology professor from the University of Chicago, Arthur C. Lundahl, who had wartime experience in making maps from aerial photographs. Whatever his own limitations in technology, Allen knew how to pick the right man for a job.

Allen met Lundahl personally only many months after he had joined CIA. Early in 1954, at one of the numerous dinner parties that consumed his evenings, Allen heard a guest talking about the amazing capabilities of modern photography and techniques of interpreting still pictures. Back in his office he summoned Lundahl and gave him a specific test. Just then an American general had been captured in Korea, and a demeaning photograph of him as a prisoner displayed to the world. The army suspected that the captive on display was not the real American officer at all. From the general's wife Allen obtained pictures of him, which he gave to Lundahl to compare with the communist photographs. Lundahl subjected both sets of photos to his most exacting analysis and returned to Allen with the unwelcome judgment that they were indeed the same man. When the general was later released, Lundahl was proved right, and Allen was convinced that he had a valuable new tool of intelligence analysis.

Meanwhile Eisenhower was following the modest results of aerial reconnaissance with mounting dissatisfaction. He summoned a meeting of civilian scientific advisers on March 27, 1954, and told them that "to anyone bearing the responsibility for the security of the United States, the situation was highly unsatisfactory." Under his prodding the president of Massachusetts Institute of Technology, James R. Killian, assembled a formidable team to develop more sophisticated photoreconnaissance techniques. Notable among them was the forty-five-year-old Edwin H. Land, who had dropped out of Harvard in his freshman year but had gone on to found an innovative corporate venture called Polaroid and to eventually claim 164 patents in photographic technology. Another civilian, Clarence L. "Kelly" Johnson, chief aircraft designer at Lockheed Aircraft Corporation in Burbank, California, submitted to the air force a design for a new concept in reconnaissance aircraft — as he described it, a jet engine mounted inside a glider — that could fly long distances at unprecedentedly high altitudes, out of the reach of Soviet antiaircraft. The air force, with its own conventional aircraft to maintain, was dubious about this unorthodox intrusion into its domain. Pressed into more innovative thinking, the best the air force could devise was a project to send unthreatening balloons over eastern Europe, armed with automated cameras and programmed to drop parachutes carrying the exposed films, which conventional air force planes would recover.

Eisenhower, no novice at Pentagon politics, was not so quick to reject the idea from Lockheed, and he encouraged his ad hoc civilian team to keep working on it. Aside from imposing the tightest secrecy, he specified that the project "should be handled in an unconventional way so that it would not become entangled in the bureaucracy of the Defense Department or troubled by rivalries among the services." Land, as skillful in bureaucratic rivalries as in innovative technology, took Eisenhower's interest as a marching order. He wrote Allen on November 5, 1954: "This seems to us the kind of action and technique that is right for the contemporary version of CIA; a modern scientific way for the Agency that is always supposed to be looking. . . . Quite strongly, we feel that you must assert your first right to pioneer in scientific techniques for collecting intelligence — and choosing such partners to assist you as may be needed. The present opportunity for aerial photography seems to us a fine start."[24]

Allen's affable nature always led him to avoid confrontation; when he could, he shied away from interagency rivalries. But he never shrank from an opportunity to enlarge his agency's scope, whether he understood the mechanics or not. Kelly Johnson's proposition fell into three distinct phases: designing and building the novel "jet-glider," planning for its actual deployment at forbiddingly high altitudes, and finally interpreting the photographs brought back. The able executive director of CIA, Colonel Lawrence "Red" White, who tended to all the administrative matters that bored Allen, suggested that while the agency might be uniquely qualified to surmount interservice obstacles to building the plane, perhaps it should be left to the Defense Department to draw the strategic meaning of the intelligence collected. White remembers Allen pushing his little wire-frame glasses up onto his high forehead and saying, "Red, you don't think that after I've taken all those photos, I am going to let someone else tell me what they mean!"[25]

Allen went to Eisenhower on November 22 with the proposal that CIA take over the high-altitude reconnaissance plane in all its aspects, and two days later he replied to Land, confirming the CIA's interest. He sent his special assistant, Richard Bissell, and general counsel Lawrence Houston to talk it all out with Johnson and his Lockheed team.

Bissell, the same age as Land, had just proved himself in his first big intelligence undertaking, Operation Success in Guatemala; his was a quick and agile mind that could grasp complexities on first hearing. Houston put a price tag on the project from the start: "We have $22 million." Johnson went back to his Lockheed executives, who bargained for $26 million at the outside. They struck a tentative deal for $22 million, with a little more if required along an ingenious time line of delivery schedules and permitted profit margins, a novel arrangement the likes of

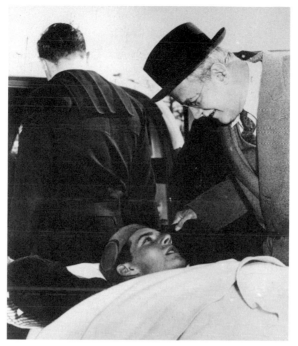

Allen with his son, Allen Macy, arriving home from service in the Korean war in 1953. This photo appeared in the American press the day Allen went to Capitol Hill for hearings on his confirmation as director of central intelligence.

Allen congratulates his son as Allen Macy receives a Marine Corps medal for bravery in action; brain injuries suffered on a Korean hillside in November 1952 marred the youth's intellectual capacities from that point on. His father struggled to find appropriate psychiatric treatment. (*National Naval Medical Center, Bethesda, Maryland*)

No. A-1

THE

UNITED STATES OF AMERICA

CENTRAL INTELLIGENCE AGENCY

2430 E STREET, N.W.

WASHINGTON, D.C.

This is to Certify that

Allen W. Dulles

WHOSE PHOTOGRAPH AND SIGNATURE APPEAR HEREON, IS AN ACCREDITED SPECIAL REPRESENTATIVE OF THE UNITED STATES GOVERNMENT ENGAGED ON OFFICIAL BUSINESS FOR THE CENTRAL INTELLIGENCE AGENCY

HEIGHT   6
WEIGHT   190
EYES   BLUE
HAIR   GREYING

SIGNATURE OF SPECIAL REPRESENTATIVE

DIRECTOR OF CENTRAL INTELLIGENCE

COUNTERSIGNED:

CHIEF, INSPECTION AND SECURITY STAFF

Above: Allen's CIA ID card, number A-1, when he became director of the CIA under President Eisenhower, 1953. *(Collection of H. Keith Melton)*

Right: Allen's campus of intelligence. He supervised the planning and construction of the new CIA headquarters in Langley, Virginia, down to the last detail, but before he could occupy the new quarters he was replaced as director.

John Foster Dulles and Allen, 1956. Allen saw his brother off to con-
valesce in Florida after the secretary of state's first cancer operation,
just at the height of the crises at the Suez Canal and in Hungary.
(Allen Dulles Papers, Princeton University Library)

Allen with his long-time friend Clare Booth Luce, wife of Henry Luce of Time, Inc., in 1954. Mrs. Luce served as Eisenhower's ambassador in Rome, where Allen would often visit her at the embassy. *(UPI/Bettmann)*

Allen at leisure, in dinner dress and sockless slippers to ease the pain of his never-ending gout. "His style was always to pick out one lady at the start of an evening," said his daughter Joan, "and devote his full attention to her until the end, a way of avoiding annoying small talk." His dancing partner on this occasion is not identified.

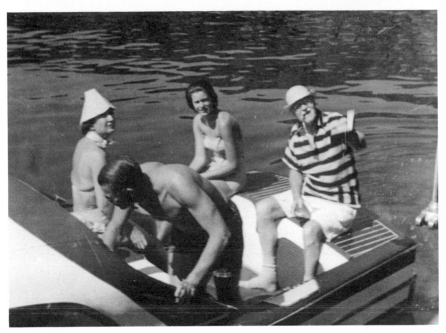

Allen (right) and Clover (left), yachting off Greece with Stavros Niarchos in 1956. "Allen would always chase after rich men," said Clover; he lamented that he would probably never be able to afford a yacht of his own.

Grandfather Allen with Toddy's children, Joan, Clover, and Allen Jebsen.

Above: Richard M. Bissell, manager of the U-2 spy-plane operation. Allen was grooming him to be the CIA director — until the 1961 disaster at the Bay of Pigs, for which Bissell had to accept responsibility. *(UPI/Bettmann)*

Above right: Reinhard Gehlen, the former Wehrmacht general who became CIA's protégé in the anticommunist campaigns in West Germany. The secretive Gehlen autographed this rare photograph, which he sent as a special token of his esteem to colleagues in Cold War intelligence. *(Allen Dulles Papers, Princeton University Library)*

Below: Allen as field marshal, reviewing CIA mercenaries hired for combat against communist China, in Thailand in 1956.

Allen Dulles with his last president and his successor, John A. McCone, at the Newport Naval War College on the day in 1962 when Kennedy announced Allen's retirement.

Allen with Richard Helms in 1968, the year before Allen's death. Helms, named director of CIA by President Johnson, invited Allen back to the campus at Langley to accept the tribute of a new generation of American intelligence officers at the unveiling of his portrait in bas-relief in the CIA reception hall.

After Allen's death James J. Angleton (left) carried the testimonial program of his funeral to the retired prime minister of Israel, David Ben-Gurion. Acquiring Nikita Khrushchev's secret speech of 1956 was only one of the joint ventures by CIA and Israeli intelligence. Angleton and Ben-Gurion posed for a snapshot in their moment of tribute to Allen. *(Allen Dulles Papers, Princeton University Library)*

which defense contractors were not accustomed to accepting from the Pentagon.*

On Wednesday, November 24, the day before Thanksgiving, Eisenhower reviewed the idea with his top military and civilian aides. General Nathan Twining of the air force remembered thinking that the CIA men were getting "too big for their britches"—they would not know how to handle this kind of operation. But he was not about to voice his reservations in the Oval Office against a presidential mind already made up. Properly concerned with the political and diplomatic implications of intelligence missions, Secretary of State Foster Dulles spoke up to say, "Of course, difficulties might arise out of these operations, but we can live through them."[26]

The week after the Thanksgiving holiday Eisenhower ordered the CIA to move ahead on developing the spy plane, to be called the U-2. That week Lundahl, poring over the paltry photographic evidence coming in from the conventional air force reconnaissance missions, received a call from Allen's secretary. Without warning he was informed that he was relieved of all previous duties, and would he please come to the office of the director of central intelligence at once. There a beaming Allen introduced him to Bissell, his new partner in an enterprise that in the next six years would turn out to mark the greatest achievement, and the worst political disaster, of Cold War intelligence.

The contract signed by CIA and Lockheed on December 9, 1954, has been called "the biggest intelligence bargain in history." Lockheed would develop and build the innovative spy plane, and the photographs taken would be analyzed and interpreted by the CIA's hungry assessors of Soviet military and industrial potential. Except for Foster's offhand remark at the Oval Office meeting just before Thanksgiving, no attention was paid to any possible political costs in the operation.

— * —

General Twining was not the only officer in the Pentagon to take a dim view, once the word got around in the rarefied circles of clandestine operations, of Eisenhower's decision to turn the CIA loose in aerial photo-reconnaissance. General Curtis LeMay, chief of the Strategic Air Command and renowned in his day for tough-talking bravado, told a staff meeting, "We'll let them develop it and then we'll take it away from them." They tried; even a year later, in July 1955, as a prototype U-2 was checked out for its first test flight, Bissell warned Allen that the air force

---

* The contract was completed for $22 million, without the permitted overrun being invoked.

still had designs on the project. As the CIA men left the briefing room, Bissell remembers giving a final message to the director: "Don't let Le-May get his cotton-picking fingers on the U-2." Having brought his agency this far, Allen needed no such reminders.[27]

A remarkable reversal of roles had taken place in the power struggles of Washington. In the 1940s the military services had argued that intelligence was a secretive business, that undisciplined civilians could not be trusted to protect clandestine espionage operations. Then came pressure for cutbacks in the defense establishment; in the fight for budgets and prerogatives the uniformed services became what CIA men called "bugle lips," ever ready to leak sensitive information — helpful to their particular cause, of course — to Congress, the press, and the public.[28] By 1954 the simple fact was that for keeping secret operations secret, Eisenhower had more confidence in the CIA than the Pentagon.

The military services and their champions in Congress lost no opportunity to embarrass their civilian intelligence rivals. The U-2 project was too highly classified to be discussed, of course, even by the loudest bugle lips. But some secrets of espionage, when they went wrong, could not be concealed. Exposure of the Berlin Tunnel was one such, though its audacity and technological genius redounded to the CIA's advantage. Far more troublesome to Allen and his various clandestine operations was an untoward incident that broke out in public the summer of 1954.

Otto John, forty-five years old, survivor of the 1944 conspiracy against Hitler and, ten years later, head of West Germany's internal security apparatus, disappeared in Berlin on July 20, the anniversary of the anti-Nazi bomb plot. He turned up a few days later in East Germany, an apparent defector to the communists. John was not a CIA protégé; indeed, he was a political rival of Gehlen, whom the CIA had established as German spymaster against the communist East. But John had visited the United States just a few weeks before he crossed over, and the CIA had briefed and entertained him warmly as a responsible official of an allied government. He and Allen had walked the gardens of Highlands together, conferring about the politics of Konrad Adenauer's Germany in the Cold War.[29]

After John's defection, Allen's detractors pounced on the incident. To the headline and editorial writers, who had no way of understanding that the CIA was working with Gehlen rather than John, it looked like another CIA blunder. As damage-limitation investigations proceeded, an even more awkward circumstance came to light. On John's last night in America, over dinner at the home of a senior CIA officer, the host's wife had casually asked if John might convey greetings to her relatives in the zone of Russian occupation should he ever have the opportunity. This he was able to do on July 19, calling on the German in-laws of a high CIA officer the very day before his disappearance. The coincidence was too suspicious for eager anticommunist investigators in Washington to overlook.

Notably on the offense against CIA was Frenchie Grombach, pursuing his eight-year vendetta against the presumptuous civilian intelligence service. The agency, having tired of Grombach's flow of unevaluated barroom gossip, had canceled the contract that had kept him in business for the past three years, and he was seeking new buyers for the secrets uncovered by his private networks. The FBI, McCarthy, and the other Senate internal security investigators were on his lists of prospects. In an angry sixteen-page memo, Grombach outlined all the warnings his agents had filed over years previous against John and his "left-wing" leanings. All of these, Grombach told his potential clients, the CIA had ignored and suppressed. Pressing his advantage, he reminded his readers about Allen Dulles's friendships with German socialists and devoted a special appendix to the suspicious postwar activities of Allen's wartime agent Hans Bernd Gisevius; according to Grombach the Prussian Gisevius was advocating dangerous "neutralism" as a foreign policy principle.[30]

Allen feigned indifference to John's defection when he was asked about it, and the CIA eventually weathered the frail coincidences of his visit to America.* But the incident only irritated the tensions between CIA and military intelligence, which came to a head the summer of 1955. The chief of army intelligence at the time was Major General Arthur Trudeau, an engineer and gifted battle commander from World War II and Korea, who had no particular background in intelligence. An admirer of MacArthur, he fell easily into his service's suspicions of CIA.[31] Numerous reports were coming in from Grombach and similar sources that the Gehlen organization had been penetrated by the communists of East Germany. Knowing of Allen's respect for Gehlen, Trudeau believed that the CIA was turning a blind eye to the danger.

Early in 1955 Trudeau had asked the West German ambassador in Washington for an opportunity to discuss intelligence concerns with a counterpart from Bonn's armed forces. As the general remembered what ensued, a call came from the ambassador the third week of June, inviting Trudeau to meet an unnamed guest staying at the embassy. When he arrived he was escorted into the embassy garden and introduced to the ambassador's house guest, Konrad Adenauer. Trudeau plunged in, confiding

---

* John reappeared in West Berlin a year later, claiming he had been kidnapped and framed. He served close to four years in a West German prison, where he prepared memoirs to clear his name, which made a good story but hardly cleared up all the mysteries. Allen, for his part, took little further interest in the case and never revised his opinion that John was in fact a traitor.

to the West German chancellor his concerns about Gehlen and the dangers of NATO secrets being passed to Moscow. He pulled a packet of seven index cards from his uniform jacket and read out some of the derogatory reports coming in to military intelligence. Adenauer heard him out, then asked to have the general's cards for his own review.

Returning to Bonn, Adenauer and his aides went through Trudeau's file cards with the local CIA station chief, James Critchfield, who recognized familiar half-baked accusations that had already been checked out and dismissed. He cabled a report to Allen, who reacted with a rare burst of outrage — not so much at the slurs cast on Gehlen, but at the audacity of the Pentagon general in passing unevaluated field reports, on his own initiative, to a foreign head of state.* In July the new army chief of staff, General Maxwell Taylor, summoned Trudeau for an explanation, and they went over the same seven index cards, which Adenauer had since returned to Washington. "I said I recognized that Allen Dulles might have lost confidence in me," Trudeau recalled, "but that I wanted [the Army] to know that I had also lost confidence in Dulles and the CIA." A power struggle between a journeyman chief of army intelligence and the revered head of the CIA was no contest at all, and within days Trudeau was transferred to another command in the Far East.[32]

Through all these bureaucratic battles with members of Congress, the uniformed services of the Pentagon, and all others who doubted the legitimacy of a civilian intelligence service, Allen found he could ultimately count on the support of the one man who mattered, President Eisenhower. Seeking to deflect criticisms of CIA by McCarthy and his allies, the president had asked retired air force general James H. Doolittle to conduct a new confidential survey of intelligence activities. Eisenhower spent an afternoon with Doolittle in October 1955 to hear his report. At each passage that was critical of Allen the president argued back. Doolittle remarked that the intimate relationship between the secretary of state and the director of central intelligence was "unfortunate"; Eisenhower interrupted to say he thought the relationship was "beneficial." Doolittle persisted, telling Eisenhower that he and his colleagues had found Allen "too emotional" for the serious business of intelligence. This was the military professional commenting on a civilian, but he tried to press upon the president that Allen seemed driven by emotions — implicitly, by Cold War ideology — "far worse than it appeared on the surface." Again Eisen-

---

* Whether or not Trudeau was right to go straight to Adenauer, the point of his concern was well taken; six years later the West German intelligence service was shown to have one high-level Soviet agent working closely alongside Gehlen and countless others lower in the networks.

hower would hear none of it. He interrupted his comrade with a defensive retort, which missed Doolittle's point: "I have never seen him show the slightest disturbance. . . . Here is one of the most peculiar types of operation any government can have, and it probably takes a strange kind of genius to run it."[33]

For the rest of his presidency Eisenhower would hear complaints about Allen, including some from his own son, John S. D. Eisenhower, who became a special presidential assistant on sensitive national security matters. Allen's administrative skills were less than impressive; in his little-boy fascination with covert operations, he failed to take firm control of the broader intelligence community that could have fallen within his purview had he chosen to exercise the necessary guidance. Eisenhower listened; but, as he once told his national security adviser, Gordon Gray, "I'm not going to be able to change Allen. . . . I have two alternatives, either to get rid of him and appoint someone who will assert more authority, or to keep him with his limitations. I'd rather have Allen as my chief intelligence officer, with his limitations, than anyone else I know."[34]

— * —

Take cadres of bright and adventurous men (in those days, Washington was still a man's town, where the wives set the table and provided a gracious ambiance in which the men could do their work), build upon their classical education, high idealism, and sense of mission, give them whatever funding they need, and then send them off uninhibited by administrative controls or accountability.

This was the CIA as it hit its stride in the mid-1950s, and the range of operations around the world was too diverse for even a strong central authority — which Allen certainly was not — to manage. Allen loved to meet his men when they came in from the field and pump them for stories and ideas, often to the despair of the staff trying to schedule his time around more important callers and demands. "His was not an orderly way of doing business," complained the CIA history of the Dulles era. "There is no collected record of what he did with his days."[35] Allen kept close watch on the operations that interested him most, but for the rest he allowed the leash to grow long.

Allen never felt he knew the territory in the Far East, though he would never miss an opportunity to reminisce about the year of his youth in India and China. He had not returned to Asia and, indeed, that whole region had not been hospitable to CIA's early attempts to extend its reach. MacArthur ran his own intelligence service from Japan, and neither Bedell Smith nor Allen had much success at moving in. The Chinese Nationalists, from their offshore base on Taiwan, took the lead in mounting covert operations against the communist mainland, often with disastrous effects, while the CIA's Far Eastern operatives served in supporting roles.*

Only in the Philippines was the CIA a force to be reckoned with; in 1950 a paramilitary advisory mission was begun to help the American-trained civilian leader Ramón Magsaysay put down a long-simmering communist guerrilla uprising. "Where there begins to be evidence that a country is slipping and communist takeover is threatened," Allen explained in Washington, "we can't wait for an engraved invitation to come and give aid." Unlike his role in Iran and Guatemala, however, Allen left the Philippine effort largely in the hands of a freewheeling man on the spot, Lieutenant Colonel Edward Lansdale. Technically on active air force duty, Lansdale was loaned first to OPC and then to CIA, but he operated independently even of the CIA station chiefs in the same country — not a unique pattern in Allen's agency.[36]

Allen viewed the other great communist guerrilla campaign, in Indochina, as primarily a French problem. In December 1953 he blandly asked colleagues for all available intelligence "respecting the existence of Ho Chi Minh."[37] He kept Eisenhower and the NSC informed on the final agony at the French fortress of Dienbienphu the spring of 1954, but he admitted he lacked independent insight into the Vietnamese enemy. Eisenhower heard his briefings with impatience about the mistakes of the French. "Who could be so dumb as to put a garrison down in a valley and then challenge the other guy, who has artillery on the surrounding hills, to come out and fight?"[38] When Allen tried to get his president's attention, Eisenhower dismissed him with the words, "Do you think I have to be bothered with that god-forsaken place?"[39] Only after the fall of the French colonial regime did Washington turn its attention to the successor state of South Vietnam.

A reputedly charismatic Vietnamese political exile, Ngo Dinh Diem, was sent home from America, providing an opportunity that looked somewhat analogous to the nation-building task Magsaysay had accomplished with such gusto. Allen's reaction was to send Lansdale to Vietnam to repeat the successes he had scored in the Philippines. Diem's first test of strength came in early 1955, not against the communist regime in North Vietnam but against a Vietnamese secret society known as Binh Xuyen, which had cornered Saigon's lucrative market in drugs, gambling,

---

* One such support was a civil airline, established by the CIA, called CAT, a gun- and agent-running facility started by Claire Chennault for the Chinese Nationalists. The CIA's so-called proprietary companies — ostensibly independent ventures, in reality wholly owned by the agency — caused numerous legal problems over the years, which Allen chose to ignore. "Allen just loved the idea of owning an airline," said one CIA aide, "but he never knew a damned thing about how it was run."

and prostitution. Lansdale served as the new president's special adviser in successfully putting down the Binh Xuyen rebellion and went on to represent the United States in promoting a democratic South Vietnam.*

To pull together the Asian operations left after the Korean War, Allen sent out one of his favorite Park Avenue cowboys, Desmond FitzGerald. The Chinese Nationalists on Taiwan and their champions in America, the so-called China Lobby, were seeking to return to the communist mainland. FitzGerald found a bewildering array of dubious CIA covert operations in Laos, Thailand, and other unmarked lands on the Chinese periphery; the American interest in these fiefdoms was not all that clear, but they figured in the CIA mission of omniscience and omnipotence. When a conference of nonaligned leaders convened at Bandung, Indonesia, in April 1955, the most inventive proposal of the CIA's Asian stations — vetoed by Washington — was a plot to blow up the aircraft flying Chinese premier Chou En-lai to the conference and thus "neutralize" another troublesome communist leader.[40]

— * —

For his sixty-second birthday, in 1955, Allen allowed himself an Easter vacation, a week with oil magnate Charles Wrightsman at his magnificent "cottage" on North Ocean Boulevard in Palm Beach. Always "he was drawn to dumb millionaires," admitted one longtime aide. The Wrightsmans kept two virile young tennis pros on their staff, and that would be quite enough to keep Allen pleasantly occupied. In fact, however, the director of central intelligence had another purpose as well that Easter week. Between Lansdale and FitzGerald his agency's interests in Asia seemed well in hand; he wanted to look in on a troubled region where he felt more knowledgeable. After arriving at the Wrightsmans' on April 7, he excused himself the next morning and, without advance notice, boarded a commercial plane for the one-hour flight to Havana.

The CIA station chief in Cuba, an FBI veteran and protégé of J. C. King's, had been pleading for Allen to come down in person to help persuade Cuban dictator Fulgencio Batista that he needed help in setting up a counterespionage bureau to target communist subversives within Cuba rather than his political opponents. But the CIA man was dismayed when

---

* Lost to history are the friendly off-duty dialogues in the early 1950s between Lansdale and Kim Roosevelt, two early pioneers of CIA paramilitary operations. When interviewed by Richard Smith, Lansdale remembered taking the high road, arguing that Asians whom the United States wanted to support would be moved only by the argument that "*your* country should come first." Roosevelt, old hand in the intrigues of Persians and Arabs in the Middle East, argued that only money, liberally disbursed, could make local factions pliable to American interests.

Allen suddenly arrived, for Batista was off on his yacht for the holidays. No one knew when he would return, and there was no one else around worth meeting. Allen shrugged, took a quick tour around the city, and returned to Florida on the afternoon plane without a complaint. It was silly to try visiting anyone important in Cuba on Good Friday.[41]

Settling in for a relaxed Florida weekend, Allen agreed to pay a neighborly social call the next day on Joseph P. Kennedy, former ambassador to the Court of St. James's. Allen knew Kennedy mainly by reputation; he had never forgiven the ambassador's isolationist stance in the troubled years before World War II. They may have met casually in the 1930s but had found no basis for a friendship. One always observed the social courtesies, however, and Allen's willingness to be correct turned to pleasure when a dramatic, lovely young lady opened the door of the Spanish-style beach residence down the road from the Wrightsmans'. She introduced herself as Ambassador Kennedy's daughter-in-law Jacqueline.

Moving into the study, Allen greeted Kennedy and then saw a young man lying on the sofa, flat on his back, whom he immediately recognized as the junior senator from Massachusetts. John F. Kennedy was convalescing from a serious spinal operation. "He was in a good deal of pain," Allen recalled of this first meeting, "but he was just determined that he was going to make a comeback, that he was going to conquer his physical ills. . . . He would get up and walk a few paces, [but] he was wincing with pain." The three men talked for nearly two hours that Saturday morning about current international problems, the state of the world. The young senator "obviously wanted to learn . . . he was very respectful . . . he was trying to find out what the facts were," Allen remembered.[42]

When Allen returned to the Wrightsmans' cottage, he found waiting an urgent message from Havana: Batista would be happy to receive Allen on Easter Sunday. No commercial flights were available, but the American Embassy plane would fly in the next morning to pick him up. Allen scratched the tennis game he had anticipated, arrived at the airport just as the terminal gift shops were opening, and boarded the plane with a large basket under his arm. Upon arriving in Havana he insisted on meeting the children of his CIA station chief right away. The avuncular old man to whom their father reported presented them with an array of brightly colored Easter eggs and chocolate rabbits.

With Batista, dressed in a gleaming white suit as he welcomed Allen to his office in the presidential palace, the conversation was gentlemanly. Both men lit up the finest Havana cigars, and Allen pressed his point about the dangers of communist subversion in the Caribbean. Batista agreed to establish, with CIA help, a Bureau for the Repression of Communist Activities.

Allen needed little urging to stay on for dinner at the embassy with the

Cuban foreign minister and other hastily summoned officials before returning to Palm Beach. The Easter basket for the children was already the talk of the American community, and before letting the men start their business talk, the ambassador's wife confronted the CIA director. "Allen, I can't believe you're a master spy," she gushed; proceeding with slightly skewed images, she said, "You seem more like Santa Claus than Dick Tracy!" For the carefully cultivated image of a lovable spymaster, it was a holiday weekend's work well done.

— * —

Diplomacy was proceeding in Washington along a track that did not involve the director of central intelligence. Pressure for a Four-Power summit conference had built up again. John Foster Dulles was apprehensive about letting action on foreign policy leave the hands of knowledgeable diplomats, but Eisenhower went ahead to propose a meeting of the American, British, French, and Soviet heads of state, to be held at Geneva in July 1955. If nothing else transpired, it would be helpful to know which of the Soviet leaders who had taken over Stalin's office and powers was actually calling the shots of foreign policy — the plump and courtly Nikolai Bulganin, nominally head of state, or perhaps the equally plump but most uncourtly Nikita S. Khrushchev, leader of the Communist Party.

Heads of state do not generally parade their intelligence chiefs at diplomatic encounters, so Allen was not among the advisers who accompanied the president to Geneva.* But as it turned out, it was a secret venture of Allen's that indirectly became the central business of the conference. After two days of ineffectual jousting with the Soviet leaders, Eisenhower found himself frustrated with the briefing books prepared by his secretary of state. Nowhere was there a positive program for reducing international tensions. On his own initiative he turned to a novel idea developed by an ad hoc group of unofficial advisers.

Since early June a seminar of private academics had convened at the Marine base at Quantico, Virginia, to design a new American foreign policy. Foster naturally took a dim view of policymaking by amateurs. Allen, however, was never one to pass up an academic seminar where interesting ideas might be floated. The CIA director attended the opening meeting at Quantico on Sunday evening, June 5, and returned for the close on June 9. Telephone logs of the brothers' conversations on those days reveal Foster's uneasiness about the goings-on at Quantico; Allen was defensive about being a part of it, even as a silent observer. "The Sec. wants to play

---

* Because of the conciliatory mood to be set, Defense Secretary Charles Wilson did not attend either.

it down, doesn't think much of it," notes the log of a telephone call on June 9. "AWD wondered too. . . . They agreed nothing would probably come of it. . . . AWD will report."[43]

From this seminar came a proposal for authorized reconnaissance flights over the United States and the Soviet Union to provide mutual reassurance against a surprise attack or first-strike capability by either superpower. The program was called Open Skies. Allen, alone among the participants, knew that the United States already had a project under way for aerial reconnaissance of the Soviet Union, his own U-2 program. Obviously he would say nothing about it to uncleared academics.

During the Geneva summit Eisenhower plucked the idea out of his memory, and on July 21 he blurted it out before the heads of state assembled in the splendor of the Palais des Nations. Eisenhower remembered the truly Wagnerian effect of his remarks.

> As I finished, a most extraordinary natural phenomenon took place. Without warning, and simultaneous with my closing words, the loudest clap of thunder I have ever heard roared into the room, and the conference was plunged into Stygian darkness; . . . in our air-conditioned and well-lighted room there had been no inkling of an approaching storm. For a moment there was stunned silence. Then I remarked that I had not dreamed I was so eloquent as to put the lights out. This was rewarded with laughter.[44]

Responding for the Soviet Union, Bulganin expressed cautious interest. But as the statesmen filed out to the lounge, Eisenhower found himself walking alongside Khrushchev, who said simply, "I don't agree." As Eisenhower noted, "I saw clearly then, for the first time, the identity of the real boss of the Soviet delegation."

Open Skies, as a device to soften the tensions of Cold War, went dark almost as definitively as the lights in the conference room upon its presentation. Khrushchev told Eisenhower he regarded the idea as a "bald espionage plot against the U.S.S.R." He apparently could not comprehend the reconnaissance plan as an occasion for each side to be reassured against the other's hostile intentions. Eisenhower, of course, knew what the planners at Quantico, and presumably the Soviet communists, did not know just how far the United States had gone toward a unilateral capability in aerial reconnaissance, whether the other powers agreed or not.*

The U-2 made its first test flight on August 1, 1955, eleven days after

---

* Open Skies, as a technique to reduce tensions, reemerged upon the diplomatic agenda nearly forty years later, when the Soviet Union had imploded and the surviving nations were eager to build their own security.

the American president offered to open the skies of the world against hostile intent. The jet-powered glider worked; the CIA was launched into a bold new era of intelligence collection and evaluation.

— * —

Challenges to CIA's role in government continued in Washington. Not for five years would the bold U-2 become known to the public, and then, unlike the Berlin Tunnel, it would be exposed in a political crisis, scarcely deserving popular applause. The agency's ingenuity in combating "communism" in Iran and Guatemala was no more than suspected, and soon the judgments of hindsight would cast those operations in negative terms. The crucial CIA support for media, labor unions, and other institutions in western Europe, Latin America, and South Asia had to go unheralded if the efforts were to succeed — and when that program was blown in the 1960s, it also became public in the worst possible light.

Even Allen's personal life was suffering upheavals; he and Clover had to leave their grand home, Highlands, with its private gardens where statesmen and spies alike could stroll unbothered. The Sidwell Friends School, long seeking to expand onto the estate, which adjoined its own property, succeeded in evicting the illustrious tenants. For a year or so Allen and Clover rented Chris Herter's house in Georgetown while their friend was abroad. Finally they found a Georgetown house of their own. At this classic townhouse, with every available wall lined with bookshelves, and a garden backing up to the grounds of the home of Lamot Belin, their first friend in Constantinople, Allen and Clover achieved permanence; 2723 Q Street remained their home for the rest of their life together.

In Congress the challenges were no longer from the likes of McCarthy and the primitive anticommunists but from the liberal side of the political spectrum. Allen had come to rely on a clique of southern Democrats and northeastern Republicans, whom he could massage into compliance simply by dropping in after hours, puffing at his pipe, and telling spy stories. Meeting Clarence Cannon of Missouri, chairman of a House appropriations subcommittee, Allen would take care to be smoking the corncob pipe that Cannon had given him. When he introduced his favored officer Kim Roosevelt to conservative Republicans, Allen would pointedly explain that he was "an Oyster Bay Roosevelt — not one of those Hyde Park liberals." If the introduction was made to a Democrat, the formula was reversed. After one appropriations hearing, Gerald Ford of Michigan happened to stroll out of the room with Allen and asked, "What was that meeting about?" A CIA aide explained that it was a budget hearing. "That's what I thought," Ford replied, "but the word 'dollar' wasn't even mentioned."[45] Leverett Saltonstall, Republican from Massachusetts, was one who, when pressed on the need to exercise closer super-vision over intelligence matters, demurred, warning that "we might ob-tain information which I personally would rather not have." But outside this little club reservations voiced by Lippmann and other independent-minded critics were starting to take hold.

It was a maverick Democratic senator from Montana, Mike Mansfield, who led the liberal charge. Mansfield introduced a resolution in January 1955 calling for a formal procedure of congressional intelligence over-sight; he was soon joined by thirty-five other senators, Republicans as well as Democrats. Allen found himself preoccupied for a year by the en-suing legislative hassle, until the Mansfield resolution was finally de-feated, fifty-nine to twenty-seven, in April 1956. More than a dozen of the original sponsors withdrew their support for the resolution upon ex-posure to Allen's charm and persuasion.

The lesson for Allen was that CIA, to achieve permanence, needed more secure support in politics and in public. He embarked on a discreet form of public relations for the agency — showing its achievements, not its mishaps, of course. The most ambitious in-depth portrait of American intelligence came in a three-part series in *The Saturday Evening Post* late in 1954, called "The Mysterious Doings of CIA." The author was a re-spected radio journalist named Richard Harkness, whom Allen had come to know during the 1948 Dewey campaign.

It is too much to say that Allen fed his friend the material for the laudatory article; Harkness was a shrewd enough reporter to understand the techniques of gathering ideas from anyone in the know, CIA men who in turn understood that they had the boss's permission to talk. But once the articles were written, Allen accepted Harkness's invitation to dinner at his home, and he affected casual interest in looking over the page proofs, making a few corrections or suggestions here and there. As the di-rector left the house, Harkness noticed that Allen had left his briefcase on a chair in the entry hall. He rushed after his departing guest, wondering about all the secrets of espionage in his hands, and the man from the CIA played his role. As Harkness told the anecdote, Allen accepted the forgot-ten briefcase sheepishly, conceded his carelessness, then opened it to show the eager journalist a crumpled shirt from the office and a day-old copy of *The New York Times*.

Such stories made the rounds in Washington, like that of the Easter eggs presented to the children in Havana, and even the old story of dodg-ing a meeting with Lenin back in 1917 Switzerland. The Allen Dulles legend was on its way.

— * —

On September 24, 1955, when Eisenhower suffered a heart attack, concern arose that he would not be able to run for reelection in 1956. Allen had every reason to worry, not only about his own tenure but about whether CIA would be able to sustain the momentum he had so carefully built up.

Particularly worrisome was the popular image of intelligence as a secret activity of unsavory spies, rather than a respectable instrument of government. John Bross recalls Allen turning red in the face, a rare moment of visible anger, when a German visitor remarked on the difficulty of getting good men to go into the service, "for intelligence is so . . . ," he searched for the distasteful word, ". . . *schmutzig*," a barely polite word for "filthy." To Allen intelligence was anything but *schmutzig*, and he was determined to overcome that image by his own public persona and the public appearance of his agency. To be sure, there were *schmutzig* things to be done. But Allen persisted in seeking to reverse what he called the unfortunate trend of focusing on the spying; instead he presented CIA as an agency that coordinated and evaluated information from many sources — including, but not limited to, networks of spies.

As long before as the Dulles-Jackson-Correa survey of 1948, Allen had been intrigued by the idea of a headquarters building for intelligence work, which by the rule of bureaucracy would establish an enduring presence for CIA. The setting of the 1950s, with the clandestine services operating from temporary buildings on the Washington Mall, was not only unpleasant for the staff, it undermined security. Shrewd counterespionage agents could see people coming and going, and the license plates of cars in the parking lot could be recorded and investigated. Allen argued, "Secret operations of this nature should preferably be located at a building having so many services and visitors that the identification of a secret staff and their visitors would be rendered difficult. Further, the staff could more easily cover the explanation of its work by giving a well-known and relatively innocuous address."[46]

In the ensuing years Allen clashed regularly with some colleagues, like Wisner, who clung to what they considered the British concept of "lurking in scrubby old hideouts, with peeling plaster and toilets stopped up."* The various elements of the CIA were parceled out among thirty-nine government buildings across Washington; an annual budget line of $3 million was required just for secure maintenance and shuttles connecting the offices. Allen developed the contrary vision of a veritable college

---

* Actually the British secret service was relatively well ensconced in sturdy, though characterless, buildings in Whitehall, on Broadway, adjoining St. James's Park underground station.

campus for intelligence, where diverse activities could be performed in a creative bustle, and where the agency could present a respectable and dignified face to the world. In the political insecurity of 1956, Allen turned with some urgency to this vision. "I don't know if I'll be here after November," he said. "I've got to get this building project started." He set out on an extended campaign of congressional testimony to justify a $56 million appropriation for a new CIA headquarters.

In his memory were the parties that he and his bride had attended in Coolidge's Washington, deep in the rolling Virginia hills across the Potomac, in a rural village called Langley. By the 1950s many of the old estates had passed to government ownership by one means or another. One spring morning Allen piled several aides into his car for a tour of rural Virginia, to scout out a site for his projected campus. When his plans became known, the few gentlemen farmers remaining around Langley allied with suburban newcomers to block a massive and dubious intrusion into their bucolic countryside; President Eisenhower himself had to intervene to persuade local planning boards to allow the necessary building permits.

Allen absorbed himself in every detail of the planning. He and Clover would stroll the hillsides together on weekends, Clover being particularly attentive to find old trees that must not, under any circumstances, be removed. Allen was more than ready to humor his wife. Bypassing the normal government construction procedures of the officious General Services Administration, Allen insisted on hiring architects from his own networks, one a friend of the Rockefeller family, the other a former military intelligence agent in Czechoslovakia. These were the architects of the rebuilt Dulles summer home at Lloyd Neck and the redesigners of the old Harold Pratt house on Sixty-eighth Street to become the headquarters of the Council on Foreign Relations. They were the sort of people Allen could work with, and whatever the demands of government bureaucracy, he was not going to let the design of his campus out of his own hands — any more than he would surrender control of his U-2 photographs.

After giving formal testimony to the various congressional subcommittees, Allen fell back on his own ways of dealing with Congress, the after-hours chats over highballs with the men who mattered.[47] "Well, this looks like one fine building," drawled one of the southern legislators who could always be relied upon to support CIA. "Going to cost about $25 million?" Allen muttered the more likely figure of $50 million. The congressman replied with a knowing smile, "I'm sure this will be a *very* fine building."

— 16 —

ERUPTIONS

OVER TWO DAYS, February 24 and 25, 1956, the Twentieth Congress of
the Communist Party of the Soviet Union heard a momentous statement
of policy and history, delivered by the intemperate new first secretary,
Nikita Khrushchev. The speech was a sweeping denunciation of the late
communist autocrat Joseph Stalin, delivered with emotion and corrobo-
rative detail, alleging crimes of the entire Bolshevik era from the death of
Lenin. Only the Soviet delegates assembled in the Kremlin heard the report; all foreign comrades were excluded from the secret session that
concluded the eleven-day congress. But typescript texts of Khrushchev's
speech and shorthand transcripts, of varying accuracy, began circulating
among the party faithful.

The communist world was still in a state of political turmoil three
years after Stalin's death. The party line had lost the clarity of a single
voice; political jockeying and factional infighting were the norm, both in
Moscow and in the satellite capitals of eastern Europe. On those two days
Khrushchev staked his claim to power in the Kremlin, using the bitter
memories of his predecessor's reign to assert his own authority for the era
to come. Though protocol and the impact of his message required him to
speak under precautions of secrecy, Khrushchev's interest was that de-
Stalinization should become the new party line and that the word should
get out, at least to the fraternal communist parties he sought to bring under his control. Versions of the Soviet leader's statement were soon on
their way to the national communist Politburos, where any lifting of the
old Stalinist hand was only welcomed.

Allen and the CIA received the first fragmentary reports of Khrushchev's secret speech within a fortnight of its delivery, the most credible
source being the humble defector-in-place, Pyotr Popov, then in his

fourth year of supplying sensitive technical intelligence and gossip from the officer corps of the Soviet armed forces.

Popov's value to the CIA and the West had soared since his first discreet approach to the American intelligence base in Vienna late in 1952. As long as he remained on station with the Soviet mission in Vienna and then later in East Germany, his CIA case officers could be confident of secure contact with their prized agent, a system of efficient "drops" for documents, and even occasional personal meetings under circumstances that aroused no suspicion. But late in 1955 Popov was rotated back to Moscow, where clandestine drops were far more dangerous. On Washington's orders his contacts with the CIA became infrequent and more circumspect.* For news of a denunciation of Stalin from the podium of the Kremlin, Popov was ready to take risks. He sent word that he could get a text of the Khrushchev speech from his Soviet military comrades.

When Popov had first come forward, Allen had been attracted to the idea of using him to organize "a small tightly knit resistance group" to undermine Soviet authority. But by early 1956 the director had regained his sense of intelligence priorities; this agent was too valuable to be risked on political matters. Just as he had instructed the Berlin bureaucrat Fritz Kolbe in 1944, Allen ordered Popov to avoid political entanglements. The CIA would find other devices for getting the Khrushchev text.

The talk Popov was hearing in the officers' clubs spread quickly to the diplomatic community. On March 10 at a French Embassy reception, American ambassador Charles E. Bohlen heard rumors about the speech from the perennial party-lining gadfly of Moscow's foreign community, Ralph Parker, correspondent of the London *Worker.* Bohlen immediately concluded, and so informed the State Department, that key Soviet officials were deliberately leaking the story.[1] At the next NSC meeting, on March 22, Allen reported with some skepticism on Khrushchev's "plain attempt to blast Stalin to pieces." Indeed, in his inevitably colorful language, he sparked lengthy discussion among Eisenhower's top policymakers when he speculated that de-Stalinization might become "a Trojan corpse" introduced into the defenses of the Free World.[2] Still he had to admit that no one yet knew exactly what had been said at the closed-door meeting.

The prize for any self-respecting intelligence service was obvious, both for potential policy implications and for honorable pursuit of the Great Game. Once before, in wartime Switzerland, Allen had made a ma-

---

* Popov's methods of contacting his CIA case officers in this delicate period are still held in tight secrecy. One version put about is that contact was completely broken off, but this could be a protective cover to preserve the official position that CIA had no officers stationed in the Soviet capital.

jor effort to obtain a secret document and arrange for its publication: the gossipy diaries of Mussolini's foreign minister, Count Ciano. Now a far more profound document was circulating behind the Iron Curtain; hundreds of Russians and other communists were gaining access to it. How could the CIA obtain the document, authenticate it, and then decide how the United States should use what was surely the most explosive document of the Cold War?

Allen looked back on the clandestine intrigues that ensued from March to May of 1956 as "one of the major coups of my tour of duty in intelligence." For three decades the precise train of events was murky; personal and bureaucratic rivalries clouded the reminiscences of the key players, and the inevitable need of counterespionage officers to cover their tracks added further obscurities. But with the fall of Soviet communism, a fair reconstruction of a complex series of encounters became possible.

As the first rumors reached Washington, Allen summoned his top deputies and issued a challenge. Robert Amory, deputy director for intelligence analysis, recalled the merry mood of that staff meeting. "In the words of the ancient bawdy ballad, [Allen] offered 'half his kingdom and the royal whore, Hortense,' to whoever brought him home the bacon."[3]

The text of Khrushchev's speech was being passed around in Moscow, but since Western intelligence agents were isolated from the Soviet party elite, more promising sources would likely be found in the eastern European satellites. Yugoslavia was the natural place for CIA to start.

Tito's maverick communist regime had long since broken with Stalinism and even enjoyed some cooperative relations with the United States. Bohlen learned that the Yugoslav ambassador to Moscow had personally hand-carried a detailed summary of the proceedings to Tito in Belgrade. The Yugoslav communist party newspaper began dropping hints that the Khrushchev text was well received because it confirmed Tito's own line. Amory had good contacts among the Yugoslavs, so Allen promptly sent him off to Belgrade on a scouting expedition. In a two-hour meeting with the foreign minister Amory argued that after all the economic aid Yugoslavia had received from the West, this was a good occasion to return the favor. Furthermore, promotion of a de-Stalinization campaign would serve Yugoslavia's interests. The diplomat saw merit in Amory's argument, but the old-style Marxist-Leninist in charge of the security services could not bring himself to accommodate Western intelligence. Amory returned to Allen empty-handed. The fact of his mission, however, provided a useful cover story in the months ahead.

Yugoslavia was not the only eastern European communist regime to welcome relief from Stalinist rigidity. Poland was well on its way toward a more moderate, indigenous communism free of the Kremlin's total con-

trol. No thanks to CIA's clumsy maneuvering with the fictitious WIN resistance movement four years before, measures of de-Stalinization were
already under way in Warsaw that winter of 1955–56, even before the
Kremlin's official sanction. "Week after week, people whose existence
had no longer been a certainty were showing their prison-pallid faces on
the streets," wrote an American correspondent in Warsaw, Flora Lewis.
"Some of them came out of rapidly emptying Polish jails, others wandered back half blinking from distant Russian camps which they still
hated to mention."[4]

The CIA was not well positioned to make contact with these former
prisoners of Stalinism as they sought to regain political stature in Poland;
the WIN debacle was still remembered with derision. But other nations'
intelligence agencies, eager to collaborate with the CIA, were in place and
building contacts with potential agents. On the chase for the Khrushchev
document, Allen and his deputies recognized these networks as assets to
be encouraged.

Among the most resourceful of the third-party assets were the successors of the old Zionist networks, now directed by the intelligence services
of the new state of Israel. Some two dozen Israeli diplomats in eastern
Europe were in fact representatives of Shin Beth, the Israeli counterintelligence service. Allen had not shared the suspicions of the State Department or his early predecessors at CIA about cooperation with Zionist
intelligence, and by the 1950s the old political controversies that had discouraged collaboration in the late 1940s no longer applied. In the spring of
1951 a meeting had finally been arranged between the director of central
intelligence, Walter Bedell Smith, and the prime minister of Israel, David
Ben-Gurion, at which the foundation was laid for intelligence liaison.

For an odd reason, supervision of the new Israeli connection fell to
James Angleton, whose principal responsibility at CIA was counterespionage. Angleton had known the diverse Zionist networks in postwar Italy,
but an incidental fact propelled him into this special assignment: the
more natural case officer for the Israeli connection, the director of CIA
Near Eastern operations, was an Arab-American and thus not congenial
to Tel Aviv. Angleton, an austere intellectual from Idaho, was not at all
one of the Park Avenue cowboys; but he was an old hand at conspiracy
from the OSS, and he carried these talents to the CIA. In April 1952
Allen dispatched him on a visit to Tel Aviv to meet the agency's Israeli
counterparts; the Shin Beth chief, Amos Manor, returned the visit in October, when he conferred about joint anti-Soviet operations with both Bedell Smith and Allen, walking the gardens at Highlands like all the other
foreign visitors whom Allen entertained and debriefed.[5]

Angleton was among those top deputies whom Allen challenged to bring in Khrushchev's secret speech. As Amory set off for Belgrade, Angleton put the inquiry to his Israeli friends. Never living in a vacuum, both Shin Beth and the Israeli foreign intelligence branch, the Mossad, were already on the trail; competing rivals within the Israeli establishment, they needed no direction from Washington to proceed with the vigor and ingenuity that came to distinguish Israeli intelligence.

Shin Beth in Warsaw was already in congenial contact with a circle of former political prisoners gathered around the figure of Wladyslaw Gomulka, a promising but independent-minded communist politician who had been purged by Stalin in 1948, spending four years in a prison for dangerous social misfits. Liberated after Stalin's death, Gomulka and his comrades were a center of excitement and innovation. They talked loosely, with the frenetic energy of the eastern European intelligentsia that had been stifled under Stalinism. They even talked with Westerners, taking foreign diplomats into their confidences. Gomulka's wife, who was Jewish, readily accepted the friendship of the Shin Beth representative in Warsaw, known as "Victor," as her husband was maneuvering his way to the top of the post-Stalinist communist party of Poland.

One day in April 1956 a responsible intimate of the Gomulka circle handed their Shin Beth friend a bulky typescript. After taking one look at the papers, Victor drove straight to the airport to catch the first plane out. Landing in Vienna, he called Tel Aviv to say that he would be on a connecting flight to Israel. He arrived late on a Friday afternoon at the onset of the sabbath, as the work of the Jewish state was closing down for the weekend. Amos Manor recalls daring to suspect the reason for his agent's sudden return to headquarters, but until he could be sure he did not immediately alert Allen or Angleton in Washington. The head of Israel's Shin Beth, then only thirty-seven years old, was a seasoned conspirator in the post–World War II campaigns to rescue the surviving Jews of eastern Europe and transport them, against British colonial regulations, to Palestine.

Born in Transylvania, Manor was comfortable in Hungarian, Romanian, English, and German, for a start. The one eastern European language he could not handle was Polish — and to his dismay that was the language of the papers thrust before him by his Warsaw agent. Sabbath or not, Manor ordered his secretary, who did read Polish, to start typing out a quick translation into Hebrew. After just three paragraphs, he knew what he had; he grabbed the rest of the text and drove off to show it to the one man in Israel who had the right to see it, who had the sense of history to assess its contents, and who, important at that moment, could read Polish: David Ben-Gurion.

The prime minister of Israel had already left for his kibbutz in the

Negev desert, two hours or so from Tel Aviv. By the time Manor arrived at Sde Boker, it was close to 7 P.M. on the sabbath, and Ben-Gurion was not pleased to be disturbed. As he started turning the pages handed to him, his testy mood softened. He settled down to read in silence, ordering his intelligence chief to go away and leave him alone. Early Saturday morning, when proud Israeli Jews consider it improper to use the telephone, Ben-Gurion called Manor at his home and asked a few general questions about the provenance of the text he had spent the night studying. He authorized Manor to pass it immediately to his CIA contacts, then, before hanging up, he made a simple statement that the Shin Beth chief long remembered. "If this document is authentic," Ben-Gurion said, "Russia is on her way to democracy — only twenty or thirty years away." His prediction missed by five years.

A courier carried the typescript to Washington by the first plane after the sabbath, and with a flourish that his detractors would later disparage, Angleton declared to Allen that he had "brought home the bacon." Two days later he called Manor personally, speaking in the guarded tones required on the international circuits, with the unadorned message, "Thank you." A leading CIA analyst, Ray Cline, later wrote that the agency acquired the Khrushchev secret text "at a very handsome price."[6] Manor and his Israeli associates deny that they asked for any compensation, though Cline was right in the sense that over the years to come the Israeli intelligence liaison, having proved its mettle in the global Great Game, was able to demand extensive favors from the CIA in recompense.

Allen's next step was to test the purported transcript for authenticity. Translating teams immediately started to produce an English text from the Polish version, itself a translation from Russian. They were aided by extracts and partial texts coming in from other sources among the outlying communist parties, notably a French language version, which arrived early in May and which turned out to be the hasty notes of a French intelligence officer in Warsaw who had been allowed an hour to scrutinize the Polish text. Verifiable errors of fact in this version were not present in the text that arrived from Tel Aviv, enhancing its authority.

Allen ordered Wisner and Helms of the clandestine services to share their text with the analytical side of the agency, headed by Amory, where the Russian experts could apply disinterested scrutiny. "I was able to provide convincing, and most welcome, internal evidence that the text we had was an authentic account of what happened at the Twentieth Party Congress," Cline recalled, "and that much of it was Khrushchev's own colorful prose. This made everyone happy." Allen sent another of his top Soviet experts, John Maury, to hand-carry the text to George Kennan, then absorbed in academic research at Princeton but still recognized as a sage on Soviet matters. Kennan perused the text and declared to Maury, "It's pure gold." When the CIA finally dared to send the text through secure diplomatic channels to Bohlen in Moscow, the ambassador also pronounced it genuine.

By the end of May Allen realized that his men had indeed delivered the goods, but he faced conflicting ideas within his CIA ranks over what to do about it. Angleton and his counterespionage officers wanted to squirrel the text away, dribbling out little bits and pieces of the anti-Stalin evidence when it suited the purposes of resistance groups in the eastern European satellites. The mentality of counterespionage, in the words of operations officer David Atlee Phillips, is that of "information misers, gloating over their stashed jewels, but never doing anything with them."[7] But Bohlen also advised against making the text public, on different grounds; he argued that a confirmed anti-Stalinist stance might enhance the credibility of the new Soviet leadership and thus weaken the West's propaganda themes.

Others in CIA made strong arguments for publishing the entire Khrushchev text immediately, for its historical value and as a political fact. If the maneuvering and pressures of the Cold War sought to take advantage of this development within the Kremlin walls, let its exploitation come in the aftermath of the evidence. Even before receiving the text, Allen had remarked in public on the rumored de-Stalinization campaign. "It seems to me that the Soviet leaders, without fully realizing what they are doing, have posed an almost insoluble problem for themselves," he told a San Francisco audience on April 13. "It is not easy to wipe out the memory of their great hero. . . . Their entire history must be re-written."

Once the authenticated text was in hand, Allen confronted his dilemma. He owed "half his kingdom" to Angleton, the man who had actually brought home the bacon, and to Wisner, his covert action enthusiast, who was already conjuring up ways to exploit the shock value of a turn-around in the party line. But Allen had his own ideas. On Saturday, June 2, he was conferring privately with Cline on another matter; the senior analyst recalled the conversation:

> Suddenly, in the way he often moved from one topic to a quite unrelated one, Dulles swung his chair around to look intently at me and said, "Wisner says you think we ought to release the secret Khrushchev speech." I related my reasons for thinking so, and the old man, with a twinkle in his eye, said "By golly, I am going to make a policy decision!" He buzzed Wisner on the intercom box, told him he had given a lot of thought to the matter, and wanted to get the speech printed. Frank Wisner agreed, a little reluctantly but graciously, and Allen then phoned

Foster Dulles at State.*. . . The speech was sent over to State and given directly to *The New York Times.*

On Monday, June 4, the *Times* headlined the news that Washington had received, through "diplomatic channels," the text of Khrushchev's long-rumored secret speech. Harrison Salisbury, the newspaper's Moscow correspondent, who had returned to New York in March to try piecing together fragmentary reports unrestrained by Soviet censorship, recalled the weekend of journalistic anxiety that led to the stunning news story.[8]

The Shin Beth representative in Warsaw, about whom Salisbury and his editors knew nothing, was not the only outsider to whom the Gomulka circle had entrusted their prized text. Through its Warsaw stringer the *Times* had received its own text of the Khrushchev speech just a few days earlier but had not yet had time to translate or authenticate it. More ominously for journalists interested in a historic scoop, the *Times* learned that an Associated Press correspondent in Warsaw might also have the document, which, once carried on the AP wires, would be available to newspapers all over the world.

The offer of an authoritative leak from the State Department, therefore, was not unwelcome. But it was a practical impossibility to get a massive text ready over the weekend for immediate publication. Salisbury and the *Times* took the chance in its Monday editions of announcing possession of the document. Then ensued one of those tense deadline cycles that thrill working journalists. Upon seeing the *Times*'s headline, other news media demanded official publication; the State Department could hardly admit to playing favorites among the competitive media, so despite the *Times*'s reputation as a newspaper of record the department also handed the text to *The Washington Post.* "We were mad as hell," Salisbury conceded, "but that was the risk we took." The *Times* printed the full Khrushchev speech over four dense pages on Tuesday, June 5.

Salisbury and other correspondents were led to believe that it was the maverick communists of Yugoslavia who had leaked the explosive document. A little digging could disclose that a top CIA official had paid a secret visit to Belgrade. This was a calculated move for protecting sources; unlike all the other eastern European communist regimes, Tito's Belgrade was already beyond the reach of the Kremlin should there be reprisals for the disclosure of Soviet state secrets.

"I was then expecting that the Kremlin, either directly or through its controlled press, would declare the published text a fake," Allen recalled.

---

* Actually, Foster was at that moment on vacation, so the call would have gone to him at Henderson Harbor.

No such word came from Moscow. Bohlen met two Politburo members, Malenkov and Molotov, at a reception a few days after the speech was published and reported that they smiled in response to his questions, saying simply that versions circulated abroad were "not accurate." The next day he encountered Khrushchev himself, who launched into subdued comments about various pending problems. When the American ambassador gingerly brought up de-Stalinization, "Khrushchev started to deny he had made the speech, then broke off in mid-sentence and said, 'Versions have been circulated which do not correspond to the truth.'... He then switched the subject."[9]

The text published in the United States remained largely unchallenged as the authentic Khrushchev statement, but Allen let his disinformation teams work a little mischief for foreign consumption. CIA circulated abroad an expanded version containing some additional paragraphs doctored by the inventive staffs of Angleton and Wisner to stir up doubts and insecurities among outlying communist parties.[10]

In all the excitement and commentaries the United States government maintained the polite fiction that the State Department had obtained the text through "diplomatic channels." This was a euphemism that most people were willing to accept; at the time Americans and foreigners who had any sense of how the Cold War was conducted were under no illusions about which branch of government was charged with uncovering facts about the communist enemy. It was still considered impolite to pinpoint achievements of a secret intelligence service, and for all his interest in promoting the work of his agency and his men, Allen would not be so gauche as to claim in public the credit that was the CIA's due. The men of power whom he cared about understood full well that America's civilian intelligence service had lived up to expectations. True to its statutory mandate of protecting intelligence sources and methods, the CIA has never disclosed the sequence of events that revealed a major Kremlin policy statement to the American, and world, public.

— * —

Within the intelligence community events in Moscow and eastern Europe had stirred understandable confusion. One estimate reached the conclusion that Khrushchev's speech and the subsequent de-Stalinization campaign would not, after all, lead to ferment in the satellites. Allen, as he listened to the discussions, was disappointed. A friend of his, a law client from the 1940s, had just returned from a tour of eastern Europe and, in one of the skull sessions that so delighted Allen, had reported vivid impressions of political and social change, of the startling new freedom of expression being enjoyed — and not only by the Gomulka circle. Allen let his experts detail the evidence against any break in the Stalinist monolith, but interrupted to say, "I just have a feeling. . . ." Nothing is so irritating to experts immersed in evidence as executives who "have feelings," but Allen went on to wonder if the communist bloc might in fact be on the verge of a "coming explosion."* At the NSC he focused discussion on the question, which he admitted CIA could not yet answer, of whether the confusion within the satellites was "simply the result of confusion in the Kremlin, or . . . the result of a deliberate design."[11]

Deliberate design was what Washington suspected of the Soviet Union around the world, particularly upon the nonaligned countries, the former colonies that had gained independence and were busy flexing their new status as members of the Third World (the capitalist and communist countries being the first and second). The charismatic military leader of Egypt, for example, Gamal Abdel Nasser, concluded a suspicious arms deal with communist Czechoslovakia, acting as an industrial front for Moscow. Playing its own hand, the United States entered into a deal to help Egypt build a massive dam across the Nile at Aswan to spur economic development. But in May 1956 Nasser's Egypt recognized communist China, as vivid a red flag of hostility to Western interests as Washington could then imagine.

In mid-July Eisenhower's National Security Council, meeting at Camp David, decided to punish Nasser by withdrawing American financing for the Aswan Dam. Two weeks later Nasser nationalized the Suez Canal to gain the transit revenues as a substitute for Western development aid. At the end of the month Allen listened in relative silence as the policymakers of the Eisenhower administration, led by his brother, the secretary of state, debated how to handle this audacious challenge from the Third World.

Allen saw merit, in that time of uncertainty, in getting out of town. This was the political season in the United States. With the onset of a presidential election campaign, the director of central intelligence wanted to put all past partisan politics behind him. President Eisenhower had suffered a heart attack the previous September; then, on June 7, as world attention was riveted upon the secret speech, the president was stricken by a recurrence of ileitis, the stomach ailment that had so unpleasantly cut short his delivery of the conciliatory message to the Soviet Union immediately following the death of Stalin. Eisenhower and the Republicans were still favorites for a second term, but even more than in

---

* In a display of intuition, rather than from hard data supplied to him, Allen later that year recalled a private conversation with Senator Mansfield in which he cited Hungary, not Poland, as the likely flash point.

1952, Allen wanted to stay aloof from electioneering. He envisaged an adventurous foreign tour to CIA stations not yet well known to him, where he might broaden his own perspective. Early in August, with a flight plan of over thirty thousand miles, Allen and Clover set off to go around the world in fifty-seven days.

— * —

This was surely "one of the most highly publicized clandestine expeditions ever made," wrote Ray Cline. Anyone who remembered Allen's style in Bern, the style of the big bell and the flypaper, would not be surprised that the head of a secret intelligence service would tour the world like a renowned statesman. Grandson and nephew of secretaries of state, preempted in his own ambitions to that stature by his older brother, Allen would not be inhibited from acting like a secretary of state whenever the opportunity arose.

The air force gave Allen its most luxurious aircraft, a four-engine, VIP-configured cargo DC-6, the Cadillac of the pre-jet era. To the crew was added a medical officer in case gout should interfere with his schedule. Allen invited Cline to record official conversations and provide the analytical branch of the agency with a record of the meetings. To Cline's relief an even more junior officer came aboard to carry briefcases and change currencies; this was a rising academic specialist on the Soviet Union and a Princetonian, James H. Billington.* Devoted to Allen — Billington called him "Mr. D" — this was another of those young men whom Allen could lure into the endless skull sessions he never enjoyed with his own son. Completing the official party were a code clerk and a communications man to make certain Allen was never out of touch.

Though all aboard remember it as a joyful trip, Allen's world tour of 1956 was no frivolous junket.[12] His first purpose was to make personal contact with his field officers, men on the spot who could easily feel neglected by Washington. The stopovers were carefully selected where, as Cline put it, Allen's "presence would not expose and endanger" CIA field operations. The mission was supposed to proceed under blackout communications without any indication of the name of the principal traveler. "Of course, once Allen Dulles arrived in countries where heads of state and prime ministers started throwing formal state dinners for him, the press picked up what was happening," Cline noted. Allen was not averse to official welcoming parties — indeed, he expected them at each new airport. He "liked to make a grand arrival, modest-appearing but with style. . . . He

* Billington soon left the CIA to pursue a distinguished academic career, culminating in the post of librarian of Congress.

was a little vain about his appearance, especially when women were to be in the reception line at the foot of the aircraft landing steps."

All went well at the first stop, London, where Allen and Clover checked in at Claridges and renewed acquaintances among the British intelligence and intellectual establishment. But in Paris there occurred a mishap that Allen considered serious. Mistaking the arrival time, the CIA welcoming party was fifteen minutes late. Allen's anger recalled his seemingly irrational reaction to the secret agent who arrived in wartime Switzerland with shoes unpolished. Then he had explained that dirty shoes would tip off the Swiss security guards that the man had crossed the fields along the border. This time he lectured the men in Paris that headquarters arranged its operations precise to every detail; the field officers might not know the reasons for every exact instruction, but for their safety and the success of the operation, every detail should be double- and triple-checked. Cables went out to every post along the rest of the journey that the welcoming party should be in place one hour before the scheduled arrival of the Dulles party.

General Gehlen greeted Allen at Frankfurt; his security men unscrewed telephone receivers and kept bathroom faucets running loudly in the guest house to guard against enemy eavesdropping. Then the party flew on to Rome for three days as guests of Ambassador Clare Boothe Luce.* At the beginning of September Henry and Clare Luce accompanied Allen's party to the next stop, Athens, where all pretense of a secret mission was abandoned. In the welcoming party were Prime Minister Constantine Karamanlis and Queen Frederika. A weekend on the 190-foot yacht of shipping magnate Stavros Niarchos provided a break from official meetings. Allen, as Clover remarked, was still chasing after rich men. But to Clare Luce, Allen confided, "You know, all my life I've wanted a yacht like this. And I just know I'll never have one." From Greece the party flew to Turkey. Allen's first request was for a reunion with Betty Carp, his Constantinople colleague from the 1920s, who was still an efficient stalwart at the American Embassy. Then Tehran, where the younger Dulles daughter, Joan, was living with her second husband, the Austrian ambassador to Iran. They had just had a baby, and Allen met his new grandson, Matthew.

---

* From all surviving evidence, it can be judged that Allen's relationship with Luce was surely more than platonic but less intense than the affairs of his younger days, for instance with Wally Toscanini Castelbarco. His supportive wife had long since found her caring place in his diffuse life, but Allen ever enjoyed the company of hearty, opinionated women who talked tough. It may be worth noting that Clare Luce's husband, Henry Luce of Time Inc., was finding much interest at this time in a relationship with Allen's former mistress, Mary Bancroft.

By the second week of September the "clandestine" party reached Dhahran for a luncheon stopover with the friendly intelligence chieftains of Saudi Arabia. The Saudi hosts were preoccupied with plans detected in London and Paris to counter Nasser's assertiveness at the Suez Canal, but not a word of this was spoken, by either the Arabs or Allen, at their luncheon. Over the next stops, Pakistan and India, Allen regaled Cline and Billington with tales of his elephant rides along the Ganges years before. On this visit to India he had to submit to a lecture from Prime Minister Jawaharlal Nehru about the horrid treatment John Foster Dulles was meting out to Nasser, Nehru's Egyptian partner in nonalignment. *The New York Times* called the meeting with Nehru a courtesy call.

With his code clerk and communications man, Allen was hardly unaware that major diplomatic developments were under way that autumn among Washington, London, Paris, Tel Aviv, and Cairo. But the director of central intelligence played no role in the mounting crisis around the Suez Canal, nor did he seek to involve himself. When the party stopped in the Cambodian capital of Pnompenh, Allen humored Clover in making a side trip to Angkor Wat, but once there the vast and eerie palaces of another civilization made an impact. Billington remembers Allen's pensive mood as they drove away from the sprawling ancient site. "Whoever can figure out what they were trying to tell us here," Allen said, peering out the car window, "may hold the secret for this entire region."

By now the entire complement of the round-the-world tour knew the drill. Allen's neverending stock of stories consumed the hours of flight. "When he was amused and threw back his handsome gray head to laugh, as he frequently did, he let out a booming, stagy ho ho ho!" Cline remembered. "Listeners laughed at his laugh, if not always at his stories." As the aircraft touched down at each stop, Allen would bark, "Clover, are you ready?" In her ethereal voice she would invariably respond, "Oh, Allen, just a minute." At Bangkok the airport reception (on time) surpassed all that had come before. Assembled were an honor guard of troops, a bagpipe band, the Thai security chief extending the hand of welcome with a .45 pistol bulging from his hip pocket, as the local CIA staff lurked nervously. Three days of banquets followed, with white-gloved waiters and dancing girls; Allen had to wear slippers with his dinner jacket to ease the nagging gout. As Allen immersed himself in official meetings, Clover was taken on a tour of Bangkok. She watched Thai women paddling their little boats in the Menam River; she thought aloud, and her Thai hosts heard her say, "They seem so carefree—I wish I could live my life like that, rowing a sampan down the Potomac."

The next day's departure was slightly delayed; airport crews were laboriously removing the sides of the air force "Cadillac" for a huge consignment: a full-sized sampan, gift to Clover from the Thai police chief. "I will not go back to Washington with a gift as big as my plane," Allen thundered. With as little offense as possible to his Thai hosts, but to Clover's dismay, Allen ordered the boat removed to the American Embassy where for years to come, CIA men said, it adorned the lawn of the ambassador's residence.

At Saigon Allen had an audience with the puzzling South Vietnamese president, Ngo Dinh Diem, sponsored by the United States as the architect of democracy in Southeast Asia, but turning increasingly autocratic with his grip on power — achieved largely through the ministrations of Allen's own CIA officer, Edward Lansdale. Allen listened in noncommittal silence to Diem, then to briefings from Lansdale, who was just winding up his tour of duty, and other Americans who conveyed their concern about the police-state atmosphere building in the supposed democracy. Diem's brother, Ngo Dinh Nhu, assigned a special legion of bodyguards to follow Allen as he wandered through the city.

Stopping next in Australia, Allen wondered aloud about the National League pennant race back home, and Australian intelligence sent an urgent query to the States. "The answer came back very quickly," recalled the brigadier in charge (the Brooklyn Dodgers would meet the New York Yankees in the World Series), "and only enhanced our efficiency in Allen's eyes."

Manila, Hong Kong, and Taipei followed in quick succession into October. Allen's security was especially tight in Hong Kong, lest Chinese communist agents create an incident. But another of those silly unforeseen circumstances interfered with the precautions. Clover had sent one of Allen's suits to a local tailor to measure for a new wardrobe, and a personal fitting was arranged at the home of the CIA station chief. As it ended, the Hong Kong tailor bowed and said, "Thank you, Mr. Dulles, for giving us your business." This was a gross breach of security, but upon interrogation the tailor noted that the name "Allen Dulles" was sewn into the pocket lining of the old suit.

Allen returned home the second week of October after final stops in Tokyo and Seoul, to conclude an adventure that CIA old-timers would never forget. The head of the bold new American intelligence service, far from engaging in a *schmutzig* business, was greeted as a statesman. "I never saw him in later years without our reminiscing about this famous trip, unique in the annals of the CIA, until tears of laughter came to our eyes," wrote Ray Cline. Allen had indulged the sense of fun from the old days. He had turned his diplomatic charm upon world statesmen he had not known before, as well as boosting the morale and camaraderie of his own men. The colorful Allen Dulles image was made useful. Then, immediately upon his return home, his agency and his own standing in the policymaking of the Eisenhower administration were put to their most severe tests yet.

— * —

On Monday, October 8, as Allen reached the end of his world tour, his seasoned Middle East hand, Kim Roosevelt, dropped in on some British friends at the United Nations. Through the guarded language that intelligence officers use among themselves, Roosevelt picked up hints of a major military operation in the offing, which Prime Minister Anthony Eden was deliberately keeping secret from his American friends — indeed, as it later emerged, from much of his own government as well. Roosevelt returned from New York to CIA headquarters that day with the flat prediction that by the end of the month Britain would dispatch an expeditionary force to reclaim the Suez Canal, nationalized by Nasser the previous July.[13]

The Dulles brothers had been at odds over Nasser for the past year, ever since Egypt concluded the communist arms deal. As Foster saw it, not only was nonaligned Egypt drifting dangerously into the Soviet camp, but Moscow was itself stirring up trouble in the Third World. The secretary of state had been incredulous when CIA told him about the arms deal; Roosevelt, who hand-carried the intelligence alert, remembered Foster asking, "Do you really believe this, Kim? It would be contrary to the spirit of Geneva." When Foster then confronted Allen directly, asking him to send his man to Egypt to "straighten out" Nasser, Allen replied bluntly, "If you want Kim to go out to Egypt again on this, you send him. CIA will take no responsibility."

Allen argued in the NSC that the United States might still "do business" with Nasser, that he might even represent a "wave of the future"; certainly he should not be relegated to the status of a colonial minion.[14] This position came from papers developed by his intelligence analysts, Robert Amory and Robert Komer. Foster vigorously opposed his brother, and Allen returned to his disappointed aides with the news that they had been overruled, that they were obliged to follow the anti-Nasser policy line laid down by the secretary of state. It was one of the early occasions in which a fundamental difference between Foster and Allen on the substance of American policy flared into open debate within the Eisenhower circle. As he had since their boyhood, the senior Dulles brother ultimately prevailed.

By July of 1956 the aim of American policy was to check Nasser's growing appeal to radical Arab nationalists. Allen had taken several of his key aides, including Roosevelt and Angleton, over to Foster's house at 2740 Thirty-second Street in Georgetown to brainstorm the Nasser phenomenon. Given his pretensions as a Muslim leader, perhaps the atheism of communism could be explored as one theme, one CIA man suggested. On the operational level Allen and Roosevelt had devised plans, and coordinated them carefully with the British, to engineer a coup d'état in Syria, politically unstable and torn between pro-Nasser factions and more "reliable" military officers. As for Nasser himself, Eden and his British colleagues were determined simply to overthrow him. Even Foster, reflecting Eisenhower's own caution on the matter, had been nervous about going that far. The Sunday before he left on his world tour Allen met with the president and Foster in the Oval Office to agree on a message to Whitehall to sooth British anxieties over Nasser's perceived affront to the imperial world order. One of Allen's first missions on his tour was to argue in London against a dangerous power play; in this he obviously failed. When Foster received his report on Allen's talks with the British, he complained to Wisner, acting in his boss's absence, that Allen "hadn't put his point across."[15]

Foster's irritation increased during the weeks of his brother's travels. It was not only Eden and the British who were acting mysteriously. The French and the Israelis were somehow involved, but none of his diplomatic counterparts from these friendly governments would tell him what they were contemplating. "I do not think that we have really any clear picture as to what the British and French are up to" in the Middle East, Foster told Allen upon his return. Were these allies "deliberately keeping us in the dark?" Allen, still unpacking from his trip and trying to move into his new Georgetown house, could not pretend to be on top of the situation. He replied only that his CIA was "fairly well" aware of developments in Egypt.

But Egypt was not the source of anxiety for American policy: it was Britain, France, and Israel. The British intelligence services had "crawled into a shell," Allen learned from his liaison officers; they were unwilling to share anything with their American counterparts. Nor was the CIA learning much from the French or the Israelis, though the Israeli military commander, Moshe Dayan, was said to have made a quick trip to Paris, and reliable reports were coming in that France had hurriedly provided Israel with a fleet of Mystère fighter aircraft, suitable for an offensive operation. The CIA sent its U-2 planes on regular reconnaissance flights over the Middle East starting August 29. Four passes in quick succession were followed by seven more in September, ten in October, and fourteen in November, photographing the area from Spain to Saudi Arabia, observing in particular air and naval movements in the eastern Mediterranean.[16] The American military attaché in Tel Aviv reported ominously that his driver, an Israeli of fifty still suffering an old war wound from 1948, had suddenly been mobilized into the army reserve. Angleton, confident of his close liaison with Israeli intelligence, dismissed the possibility that Israel could be mounting any action, for he had not been informed.

Around October 23 American intelligence came up with something specific — not word from a human source like that provided by Kim Roosevelt earlier in the month, but an indication from high-technology monitoring of radio communications. Suddenly there was detected an enormous increase in the volume of secret coded communications between Paris and Tel Aviv on the frequencies used by the military and security bureaus.* Electronic intercepts were one of the most important innovations in modern intelligence collection; the early players in the Great Game had no idea of the devices that would come to be employed in its pursuit. During World War II, in both the European and the Asian theater, clever codebreakers had figured out how to decipher what enemy commanders were saying to each other. By the 1950s cryptography and communications were more sophisticated; but even if the heavily coded messages could not be read, the mere fact of radio traffic in sensitive channels was significant. American analysts could not yet decipher what the French and Israeli military strategists were saying, but the fact that they were engaging in intensive exchanges had to be considered important.

— * —

The next weeks of October and November 1956 brought to Allen a fundamental transformation of a mature man's prospect upon the world. Political instincts built up over a lifetime, assumptions underlying his professional standing, even his personal composure among family and friends — all were suddenly under assault in an extraordinary time of stress, the likes of which he had not known before. Affability wore thin as the burdens of responsibility mounted.

At sixty-three, successful in spirit and generally healthy in body, Allen was no stranger to work under pressure. At many previous junctures he had thrived under competing demands. As an apprentice diplomat he had anguished over the impotence of the democracies in meeting the threat of Bolshevism. In the last months of World War II he had persisted in engineering the surrender of German forces against the skepticism, suspicions, and geopolitical imperatives guiding the policymakers whom he served. As director of central intelligence he had presided over American operations to overthrow communist-inclined governments in Guatemala and Iran.

---

* This is called "indications intelligence" — not meaningful on its own, but an important clue when combined with hints from other sources.

But the pressures that accumulated in the autumn of 1956 seemed different. Always before, Allen had held the initiative; as much as any man in a world of complexity, he was in control of his choices. This time forces and reactions bore down without Allen's anticipation, understanding, or control. Added to a human explosion in eastern Europe and an act of colonial desperation at the Suez Canal was a personal foreboding: at the height of these international tensions, he confronted intimations of mortality within his own protective family.

The first flash point was sparked in the restive Soviet satellite of Poland. Starting on October 19, popular disturbances sought to overturn the Kremlin-dominated regime; acceding to power was the reforming Gomulka, denounced by the Kremlin as a Titoist. Gomulka brazenly declared, "There is more than one road to Socialism." Three days later students and frustrated workers in Hungary seized the mood, demanding in street demonstrations the withdrawal of Soviet troops, the release of political prisoners, and an independent communist regime for their country as well.

"It is a well-known phenomenon in the field of intelligence," wrote the top CIA man for eastern Europe, Peer de Silva, in Vienna, "that there often comes a time when public political activity proceeds at such a rapid and fulminating pace that secret intelligence, the work of agents, is overtaken by events publicly recorded."[17] Such was the case of Hungary in October 1956. For over a year an increasing flow of defectors from the Soviet Union and satellite countries, including intelligence officers, had filled out CIA's knowledge of political factions and sentiments behind the Iron Curtain, as well as military dispositions and technological progress. The era was well past when the CIA could parachute agents into hostile societies in hopes of sparking "small, tightly knit resistance groups" to take action against communist power. By 1956 the CIA had succeeded in making tentative contacts with little cells of dissidents within the satellites — the operations bore the cryptic code name Red Sox/Red Cap — but Wisner, with his émigrés and defectors, and Angleton, with his Israeli networks, were not sanguine about their prowess. The Hungarian resistance, when it came, started spontaneously from within.

On October 23 another renegade reformer in the once subservient satellites, Imre Nagy, was swept into power in Budapest. When Soviet tanks and armored troops moved into the capital to restore order, youths and their parents alike hurled homemade grenades, ironically called Molotov cocktails, at the tanks.

The National Security Council meeting of October 26 began with the president courteously welcoming Allen back after his world tour, an absence in which his intelligence insights had been sorely missed. Ever seek-

ing drama, Allen read out dispatches from Budapest filed at the height of
the anti-Soviet uprising by a CIA officer lying on the floor of the U.S.
Embassy as bullets whizzed overhead.[18] And though it does not show in
the official minutes, he offered his intuitive feeling that Khrushchev himself might be a victim of the anti-Kremlin anger. "His days may well be
numbered," one participant remembers Allen saying. (His intuition was
not infallible; Khrushchev survived in office four years longer than Allen.)

Nonetheless, it looked as though the Soviet empire was finally crumbling, that the day of eastern Europe's liberation was at hand, four years
after John Foster Dulles had made it the Republican battle cry against the
Democrats' policy of containment. Options for response conjured up by
CIA's clandestine services ranged from overt Western military intervention to the smuggling of weapons (just as Heckscher had proposed in
1953 in East Germany), to the infiltration of trained saboteurs from
among the restive émigrés. De Silva's CIA station in Vienna reported
contacts with well-informed Hungarian railroad conductors at Austrian
border crossings, who were eager to pass on the signals they were hearing
on their internal traffic communications about an unusual concentration
of rolling stock along the Hungarian border with the Soviet Ukraine. If
there was to be a massive invasion by Soviet troops, this logistical move
would be an essential preparation. Amory and the Joint Chiefs of Staff
consequently worked out a contingency plan to bomb three key railroad
junctions through which any invading force would have to pass.

Allen decided against taking any of these measures to the NSC. Eisenhower, having long since pulled away from Foster's vision of liberation,
made it clear that he had no interest in aggressive tactics. He instructed
the CIA to maintain caution and avoid giving Moscow any reason to suppose that the United States had either instigated or would support the
Hungarian rebels. He expressed concern about the Soviet reaction to any
real or imagined American moves; confronted by acts of defiance from
the satellites, might the Kremlin be "tempted to resort to extreme measures . . . even to start a world war?" the president asked. Given the mood
of the Oval Office, Allen contented himself with the cautious suggestion
that a mobile hospital unit be flown into Budapest to establish an American presence. Doing his own job far from the White House, the CIA psychological warfare director, Cord Meyer, went on churning out policy directives to the newscasters of Radio Free Europe, guiding them in the
subtle process of encouraging the Hungarian rebels without — as he later
insisted — inciting them to revolution.

When Allen finished his report to the NSC on October 26, Foster
took his turn. His focus was not the rebellion in eastern Europe but rather
the looming threat in the Middle East. The Dulles brothers had settled

upon their respective spheres of interest. The secretary of state described the tension along Israel's eastern border and shared his suspicion that an Israeli attack on Jordan was imminent.[19] The NSC adjourned with the sense that by the next week's meeting, momentous events would confront American policymakers as they watched nervously from the sidelines.

Three days later, on October 29, Israel attacked — the target was not Jordan but the Egyptian Sinai Peninsula to the west. Eisenhower, reassured by Foster the day before that war pressures were being contained, had gone off on a campaign trip to Miami, Jacksonville, and Richmond — he was, after all, up for reelection in just eight days. Allen awaited his return to the White House that evening to deliver the latest intelligence reports from the Israeli-Egyptian front. Since his trusted contact with the Israelis, Angleton, had still not given hints of a major war under way, Allen called the Sinai invasion merely a "probing action."

Foster, meanwhile, had done his own intelligence check, using the methods of the men of Wall Street to exchange confidences without pangs of indiscretion. He learned from John McCloy, by then an executive of the Chase Bank, that no Israeli accounts had recorded any sudden withdrawals. (McCloy had failed to notice that the Israelis had made precautionary withdrawals weeks before.)[20] Yet as he took his turn in briefing Eisenhower that night, the secretary of state reversed his earlier advisories and took the news far more seriously than the director of central intelligence. The U-2 photographs revealed an Anglo-French naval armada moving through the eastern Mediterranean toward Egypt. Foster foresaw a scenario in which the Israelis would reach Suez overland; Egypt would close the canal, and the Arab allies would shut down all the oil pipelines of the area. Then, faced with an obvious threat to economic and political stability, Britain and France would seize the pretext for a military intervention. "They appear to be ready for it, and may even have concerted their action with the Israelis," Foster informed the president, as the realization dawned of what had been secretly building during the past weeks.[21]

The contrast, or rather comparison, between the Soviet power play in Hungary and an apparent Western intervention against Egypt was deeply disturbing to the policymakers of the Eisenhower administration. The Anglo-American special relationship was "facing one of the greatest tragedies, not only for our trust in each other but also for the world situation," Foster told the British chargé d'affaires the next morning. To Eisenhower on the telephone he was more explicit: "Just when the whole Soviet fabric is collapsing, now the British and French are going to be doing the same thing over again. . . . I'm afraid we will be back in the same pasture as the Soviets in Hungary."

On the last day of October Allen arrived for his early morning briefing of the president with startling good news: the Soviets had announced withdrawal of their forces from rebellious Hungary. The Kremlin apologized for past imperious behavior and pledged noninterference in the internal affairs of other countries. "This utterance is one of the most significant to come out of the Soviet Union since the end of World War II," Allen declared. "Yes," replied Eisenhower, "if it is honest." This time it was Eisenhower's intuition that was the wiser; though American intelligence could not yet be sure, both in Hungary and at Suez the worst was yet to come.

That same day an attack force of 250 British and French aircraft launched a bombing raid on Egyptian airfields and port and communications facilities. The U-2 made two fortuitously timed passes over the Egyptian front. The first recorded photographs of a calm and quiet Cairo military airport; the second pass, just ten minutes later, showed the same airfield to be a scene of destruction. In that interval had come the bombardment. Eisenhower remembered those contrasting photographs as the most dramatic visual intelligence ever placed before him.[22]

The president was awakened on November 1 with reports of the Anglo-French raid on the Cairo airport. "Bombs, by God! What does Anthony think he's doing?" Eisenhower placed an angry telephone call to his old friend Eden in London. The NSC met at 9 A.M. Allen tried to focus attention on what he called the "miracle" evolving in Hungary. The announced Soviet withdrawal disproved the theory "that a popular revolt can't occur in the face of modern weapons," he said. "Eighty percent of the Hungarian army has defected; except in Budapest, even the Soviet troops have shown no stomach for shooting down Hungarians." Eisenhower listened courteously to the intelligence report but stopped Allen with the firm injunction that Hungary was not his interest at that moment. The topic for this meeting, he said, had to be the Middle East and an act of unilateral belligerency by America's closest allies.

Foster took over where his brother was cut off. Britain and France, he reported, "have acted deliberately contrary to the clearest advice we could possibly give them. They have acted contrary both to principle and to what was expedient from the point of view of their own interests. . . . It is nothing less than tragic, at this very time, when we are on the point of winning an immense and long-hoped-for victory over Soviet colonialism in eastern Europe [that] we should be forced to choose between following in the footsteps of Anglo-French colonialism in Asia and Africa or splitting our course away from their course."[23] Allen interjected that the United States had been inhibited from condemning Russian force in Hungary "when our own allies are guilty of exactly similar acts of aggression."

Foster and Allen, talking privately that day on the telephone, agreed that Nasser's downfall was imminent, given the destruction of his air force and the defeat of his Sinai defenses by the advancing Israelis. Amid international calls for a cease-fire, Allen suggested that Eisenhower could step in with an offer of mediation. Foster let the idea drop.

For all the anguished rhetoric about the juxtaposition of two major world crises, American policymakers ultimately admitted to ambivalence toward the Anglo-French-Israeli power play of 1956. From Eisenhower on down they resented the secrecy — indeed, deception — in which three close allies had hatched a war plan without consulting the United States.[24] They harbored serious doubts that such an imperial show of force could be effective against a hero of the Third World. But once engaged, a power play has to be followed through. It was Robert Amory who best conveyed this ambivalence over the transatlantic telephone with Chester Cooper, who had become a CIA liaison officer with British intelligence. "Tell your friends to comply with the goddam ceasefire or go ahead with the goddam invasion," Amory blurted. "Either way we'll back them up if they do it fast. What we can't stand is their goddam hesitation, waltzing while Hungary is burning."[25]

These were days to try the souls of men doing their jobs. "Life gets more difficult by the minute," Eisenhower wrote his military comrade Alfred Gruenther four days before the election that would determine the fate of his presidency. "Sleep has been a little slower to come than usual. I seem to go to bed later and wake up earlier — which bores me."

Allen also suffered a painful intrusion on his already difficult days. A few minutes after midnight on November 2, he was awakened by a telephone call. Foster, back in Washington after addressing the United Nations General Assembly, had been rushed to Walter Reed Hospital with severe stomach pain. The doctors made no attempt to conceal their concern. Allen paced away the morning of November 3 in the hospital lounge outside the operating room. Aged sixty-eight, Foster was diagnosed as suffering from cancer of the colon. A five-hour operation was successful, as far as the doctors could tell, but recuperation would take two months. Stricken down in the midst of two international crises, the secretary of state could manage no more than a few telephone calls each day from his hospital bed.

- Sunday, November 4, at daybreak, Russian tanks returned to Budapest in a full-fledged invasion, belying the soothing messages Allen had so buoyantly reported to a skeptical Eisenhower less than a week before.
- Monday, November 5, a British and French expeditionary force landed at the Suez Canal to assert the old colonial powers' authority over a rebellious leader of the Third World.

· Tuesday, November 6, the American electorate went to the polls to
pass judgment on the Eisenhower administration.

Allen showed up at the White House at 8:30 A.M. on Election Day. Before flying to New York to cast his vote, he briefed Eisenhower about an
urgent special estimate made by his CIA staff. The situation in the eastern Mediterranean would not likely involve the engagement of Soviet
forces "on a large scale"; combat volunteers and military aid to Egypt
might well be forthcoming, however. On the other crisis front, Hungary,
Allen reported that the heroic freedom fighters stood no chance whatsoever against a determined Soviet show of force. Foster was resting comfortably, Allen could report.

That night the election returns gave the Republican Eisenhower-
Nixon ticket forty-one of the forty-eight states, 457 electoral votes to
the 74 electoral votes of the second-time Democratic challenger, Adlai
Stevenson.

— * —

Allen's worries about his tenure at CIA were resolved by the electorate. But
a chance to overthrow Soviet power in eastern Europe had evaporated. Simultaneously the American government had been deceived by its closest
and oldest allies in Europe. And the life of his brother had to be considered
in jeopardy — even if the cancer was caught this time, the unspoken reality
was that it would likely come back, perhaps sooner rather than later.

Allen arrived late for a secret hearing of the Senate Foreign Relations
Committee on November 12. Eisenhower had authorized him to give the
senators a general picture of developments in the Middle East but not to
reveal the nature of Washington's knowledge in advance of the Suez invasion, nor certainly the various clandestine means — including the U-2 —
by which that fragmentary knowledge had been collected. In Foster's absence a next-ranking State Department officer was holding the senators'
attentions as best he could about the twin reversals suffered by American
foreign policy. When Allen finally took the stand, he was treated with deference and respect. Even the most querulous senators listened intently as
he spun out an eloquent intelligence assessment of all that had been going
on.* A sense of tragedy permeated his testimony. He got muddled about

* One fact he could not reveal was the aborting of yet another American endeavor, the
covert action to trigger a coup d'état in Syria. In one of his last telephone conversations
with his brother before Foster went into hospital, he had remarked that good though it
would be "to have an anticommunist government" in Syria, given the tensions at the Suez
and in Hungary, "it would be a mistake to try to pull it off" at this time.

the Soviet aircraft supplied to the Egyptian air force — "did I say MiG 15s or MiG 18s?" — and he summed up with a sorry verdict on the autumn crises. Across Africa and Asia, he told the senators, "from Japan to Casablanca, the reaction to the British-French-Israeli attack on Egypt has been one of virtual unanimous opposition. Earlier doubts as to Nasser's ambitions and the outrage over the tragic events in Hungary have tended to be drowned out by a wave of the revived, age-old hatred of Western imperialism and colonialism."[26]

Scarcely had the Soviet grip been reimposed on Hungary when the CIA's Radio Free Europe came under criticism for allegedly misleading the Hungarian freedom fighters to expect supportive military intervention from the West. The frantic pleas on their radio transmitters gave pathetic testimony that they hoped for such a show of force. But CIA's Cord Meyer, feeding guidance to Radio Free Europe, was pressed to defend the record at an interagency meeting at the State Department on November 13. RFE had never promised Western armed assistance, he insisted, nor could any of the broadcasts be interpreted as implying that such assistance would be forthcoming. The confusion apparently arose from the fact that RFE had agreed to relay rebel Hungarian broadcasts on its more powerful transmitters to give them a wider audience. Meyer insisted that the State Department had approved this measure.[27]

Given the mounting political charges — particularly in West Germany, host country to the RFE transmitters — the matter could not be disposed of at a closed meeting of second-ranking American officials, and on November 20 Allen sent the White House a fuller report to justify Radio Free Europe's broadcasts. "If this does not meet the requirement," he advised Goodpaster, "please let me know." Allen suggested that the problem was not the judiciously worded news scripts but the emotions of the émigré announcers, who may have been carried away in offering tactical advice to the rebels as the uprising spread across the country. "As soon as these deviations from policy were noted," Allen reported, "steps were taken to insure rigid supervision of broadcasting content."[28]

Allen and the CIA were thrown on the defensive by critics on both sides — for being too inflammatory in their reporting of the Hungarian events and, conversely, for not doing enough to support the uprising, so long awaited by the most radical Cold Warriors. Eisenhower's great champion of aggressive anticommunist psychological warfare, C. D. Jackson, weighed in with angry complaints of American inaction as the Soviet empire was crumbling. The president responded in a personal letter to his old friend, saying, "To annihilate Hungary, should it become the scene of a bitter conflict, is no way to help her."[29]

Most painful to Allen was the anguished reaction of his colleague in covert action Frank Wisner, who had struggled for years to bring about a break in the Iron Curtain. Wisner had set off on his own world tour just as Allen returned; in London and with Gehlen in Frankfurt he watched helplessly as the reports from Hungary came in. He rushed to Vienna and lingered, grieving at the Hungarian border, where thousands of refugees were pouring across into Austria. The strain got to him at his next stop, Rome, where the local CIA men had to nurse him through drunken evenings. At Athens he gobbled down half a dozen raw clams, from which came hepatitis, high fever, and delirium atop the emotional distress of the failed anticommunist revolution. Wisner's family and friends date his eventual decline as Allen's chief deputy to the agonies of that autumn.

Foster recovered from his cancer operation in remarkably spruce form, and the Dulles brothers would spend the next two years of service together at the crest of American foreign policy. But a misunderstanding in the first days of Foster's return as full-time secretary of state was a harbinger of the problems that lay ahead, in policy differences as well as their brotherly working relations.

Early in January 1957 Foster testified at a Senate hearing about the course of American foreign policy during his illness. America's close, trusted allies — Britain, France, and even Israel — he said, had given Washington no advance information about the imminent Suez invasion. True enough as stated, but senators privy to earlier classified testimony from Allen recalled a different view of the recent events. "We were quite well informed with regard to the events leading up to the — informed, I mean, through intelligence sources — of the events leading up to the Israeli attack," Allen had testified, under Eisenhower's careful instructions. "We were not caught by surprise, from the intelligence angle, when the British and French forces moved in."[30] A discrepancy of testimony from Eisenhower's highest foreign policy aides or not? The reality was that American intelligence collection *had* worked, though only at the very last stages before the invasion, while American diplomatic relationships within the Western alliance were mired in a fundamental deception. Foster made the larger point; his brother had defended the turf and capabilities of his own operation.

But in that same season the other side of intelligence, the networks for covert action and political warfare, was also coming under assault. Well hidden from public or congressional view, the function Allen considered his personal charge was challenged, and from a particularly hurtful source.

— * —

Disquiet within the White House over CIA covert action, even as the president went on authorizing it, can be traced to a most unlikely stimulus. On June 18, 1954, just as Operation Success was being sprung in Guatemala, Eisenhower had a private lunch with Herbert Hoover, his predecessor twice removed. Hoover, then approaching his eightieth birthday, was no public hero; his one-term presidency from 1929 to 1933 was remembered even by a new American generation as the Depression era. But Hoover's grace and good nature during his years of retirement made him a personage of stature, at least among Republicans.

Over lunch that day Hoover suggested that Eisenhower's presidency might benefit from an independent inquiry into the workings of CIA, then in its seventh year of existence. Hoover knew something about the way intelligence people worked, from the years after World War I when he had reluctantly allowed agents into his European relief and reconstruction teams. Senator McCarthy had just renewed his flamboyant attack on the civilian intelligence agency. Hoover made clear that his proposal for a blue-ribbon inquiry would preempt any damage that the unruly Wisconsin senator might cause; indeed, a precondition of such an inquiry would have to be the calling off of McCarthy's assaults.[31]

Discussion of Hoover's initiative kept the critics at bay for almost a year. But as congressional nervousness about the CIA mounted, Eisenhower set up a formal covert action control committee in March 1955. Comprising the second-ranking officers of the State and Defense departments, his national security adviser, and Allen himself, the committee was called the 5412 Group, after the number of the enacting NSC directive. The director of central intelligence was put on notice that his secret political operations would have to submit to a modicum of accountability to non-CIA overseers. Allen had long since learned the art of manipulating committees of busy and preoccupied officials and legislators, techniques for alternately titillating and boring them so that they would lose sight of the sticking points and let him go his own way without hindrance. So it worked out with the 5412 Group.

Eisenhower, however, did not let Hoover's broader concern drop. One weekend late in 1955 a presidential helicopter flew Allen to Gettysburg, where Eisenhower was recuperating from his heart attack, so the two men could have an uninterrupted — and unrecorded — chat as they drove back together to Camp David. The president's latest idea, he informed Allen, was to name a high-level board of distinguished but discreet private citizens to keep an ongoing monitor on intelligence operations. Allen had no choice but to agree, probably assuming that he could manage this group as he had all the others that had looked in upon the unfamiliar plays of the Great Game. The President's Board of Consultants on Foreign Intelligence Activities held its first meeting with Eisenhower on January 24, 1956.[32]

Under the persistent leadership of James Killian, president of Massachusetts Institute of Technology, the consultants set upon their charge with unexpected diligence. They tackled the problems still plaguing CIA relations with the military intelligence services and sought to nudge the civilian director into a more forceful role in the bureaucratic confrontations that Allen always sought to avoid. They examined the various directives guiding the work of the intelligence services and the status of CIA representatives in relation to the American ambassadors in foreign capitals. Inevitably they turned to the psychological and political warfare programs, which they found to be consuming much of the agency's resources: more than half of CIA personnel and over 80 percent of the budget were said to be dedicated to clandestine operations. Killian delegated two of his consultants, Robert Lovett and David Bruce, to investigate yet again Allen's covert action programs, the 10/2 operations against vicious communism.

Nothing about Lovett and Bruce could have upset Allen as he assembled his defenses against this latest inquiry into matters he preferred to keep hidden from outsiders. Both men were of the Eastern Establishment and had been privy to the 10/2 concept from the start. Lovett, a partner in the investment banking firm of Brown Brothers Harriman and a protégé of Henry Stimson in the War Department during World War II, was a sophisticated Wall Street colleague of Allen's and an old hand at political warfare.

As for David Bruce, he was among Allen's oldest and closest friends. His older brother had been a classmate at Princeton, and as a young diplomat in Paris, Allen had helped the younger Bruce get his first job in diplomacy, as a courier to the Peace Conference. Bruce was not yet part of the elite diplomatic club of Bern and Paris, but in Calvin Coolidge's Washington he and Allen spent countless bachelor weekends together while Clover and the girls were escaping the summer heat. Independently wealthy, Bruce had remained in the diplomatic profession after Allen went off to make money on Wall Street.* Pressures of time and distance had separated the two friends in recent years, but Allen had little reason to doubt Bruce's reliability in assessing the sensitive matters that had become so central to his, and CIA's, preoccupations.

Allen could hardly have been more wrong in his nonchalance. Lovett later recalled that Bruce "was very much disturbed" as he started looking into the CIA; he asked, presaging the questions of generations to come, "What right have we to go barging around into other countries, buying

_____
* To Bruce had gone the post of ambassador in Paris that Allen himself had briefly hoped for in 1948.

newspapers and handing money to opposition parties or supporting a candidate for this, that or the other office?" As Lovett reported:

> We felt some alarm that here was an extremely high-powered machine, well endowed with money, and the question was how could any Director of Central Intelligence navigate, fly, drop the bomb, get back and say what he had seen and everything else. . . . The idea of these young, enthusiastic fellows possessed of great funds being sent out in some country, getting themselves involved in local politics, and then backing some local man and from that starting an operation, scared the hell out of us.[33]

If any living man was capable of measuring how far Allen had drifted from his beginnings as a cautious and judicious diplomat, it was David Bruce. "He got me alarmed," Lovett said, "so instead of completing the report in thirty days we took two months or more."

The 1956 Bruce-Lovett report on covert action stands decades later as the most sweeping official assault on the CIA's propensities to dabble in the politics and social frameworks of other lands. "We are sure that the supporters of the 1948 decision to launch this government on a positive [psychological and political warfare] program could not possibly have foreseen the ramifications of the operations which have resulted from it. No one, other than those in the CIA immediately concerned with their day-to-day operation, has any detailed knowledge of what is going on."[34]

Covert actions were in the hands, Bruce and Lovett asserted, of "a horde of CIA representatives (largely under State or Defense cover), . . . bright, highly graded young men who must be doing something all the time to justify their reason for being." In a particularly cruel dig at Allen's penchant for favoring his special protégés, they added that "by the very nature of the personnel situation" many of these CIA men were "politically immature." Mindful of recent experiences in Iran and Guatemala, they concluded:

> The CIA, busy, monied and privileged, likes its "kingmaking" responsibility. The intrigue is fascinating — considerable self-satisfaction, sometimes with applause, derives from "successes" — no charge is made for "failures" — and the whole business is very much simpler than collective covert intelligence on the USSR through the usual CIA methods! . . . There are always, of course, on record the twin, well-born purposes of "frustrating the Soviets" and keeping others "pro-Western" oriented. Under these, almost any [psychological and political] action can be, and is being, justified.

As a general salvo, this would have been quite enough to rivet attention. But then Bruce and Lovett plunged without mercy into specifics.

For any given project, they said, final pro forma approval from outside the agency came only at informal luncheon meetings. "In most instances, approval of any new project would appear to comprise simply the endorsement of [Allen's] proposal, usually without demurrer, from individuals preoccupied with other important matters of their own."

The two intrepid investigators did not hesitate to raise the personal circumstance that even Eisenhower chose to resist, the fact that Allen and Foster were, after all, brothers, in a relationship of unique access and mutual trust. "At times, the Secretary of State/DCI brother relationship may arbitrarily set 'the US position,' . . . whether through personal arrangement between the Secretary of State and the DCI (deciding between them on any one occasion to use what they regard as the best 'assets' available) or undertaken at the personal discretion of the DCI."

They elaborated on the grievance of State Department professionals, frustrated careerists in diplomacy who could seldom get Foster's attention in the office.

> The State Department people feel that perhaps the greatest contribution this Board could make would be to bring to the attention of the President the significant, almost unilateral, influences that CIA [covert] activities have on the actual formulation of our foreign policies. . . .
>
> CIA support, and its maneuvering of local news media, labor groups, political figures and parties and other activities, are sometimes completely unknown to or only hazily recognized by [the local ambassadors]. . . . It is somewhat difficult to understand why anyone less than the senior U.S. representative . . . should deal directly with [the head of a foreign government]. . . . One obvious, inevitable result is to divide US foreign policy resources and to incline the foreigner, often the former "opposition" now come to power (and who knows with whom he is dealing) to play one US agency against the other, or to use whichever suits his current purpose.

The report concluded with a call for " 'unentanglement' of our involvements, and a more rational application of our activities than is now apparent."

> Should not someone, somewhere in an authoritative position in our government, on a continuing basis, be counting the immediate costs of disappointments, . . . calculating the impacts on our international position, and keeping in mind the long range wisdom of activities which have entailed our virtual abandonment of the international "golden rule," and which, if successful to the degree claimed for them, are responsible in a great mea-

sure for stirring up the turmoil and raising the doubts about us that exist
in many countries of the world today? What of the effects on our present
alliances? What will happen tomorrow?

The Bruce-Lovett report was submitted in top secrecy the autumn of
1956, just as the triple crises of Suez, Hungary, and Foster's illness were
smothering the agendas of harassed policymakers. Though its immediate
effect was thus muffled, its impact endured, anticipating the charges of an
"invisible government," the criticisms of irresponsible procedures and inept personnel that would resound against the CIA in the eras of Watergate in the 1970s and the Iran/Contra deception of the 1980s. To be sure,
other branches of the agency—the National Estimates staff, the intelligence collection operations, and such—emerged relatively unscathed,
even praised. But the centerpiece of Allen's CIA, the "Plans" Directorate
for Cold War covert action, was mercilessly exposed to the scrutiny of
Eisenhower's top policymakers.

Allen's first reaction, at a moment of policy and personal crises, was as
muffled as his friends' assault, but when the full board of consultants under Killian adopted the Bruce-Lovett report at the end of the year, he responded with a deft diversionary tactic. He was considering, he told the
president in January 1957, hiring one of Eisenhower's trusted military
colleagues to manage intelligence administration and collection, so he
himself could concentrate on covert action programs. Eisenhower muttered merely that he would prefer it the other way around, and Allen
dropped the idea. Goodpaster told historian Michael Beschloss years later
that the president realized he had to make a choice; "if he wanted Dulles
to stay, he wasn't going to be able to force this upon him. At that point, he
decided it would be better to have Dulles stay, and keep the pressure on
him."[35]

— * —

Allen was not alone in feeling pressure as the Eisenhower administration
began its second four-year term. The tone of cordial collegiality among
the like-minded businessmen of Eisenhower's inner circle was beginning
to fray. In the formal deliberations of the National Security Council, in
congressional hearings, in private memos exchanged within the executive
branch, and in the conversations of Eisenhower himself—in all these exchanges is revealed a growing testiness among trusted colleagues.

Allen tried to be his usual jaunty self as the NSC convened for its first
meeting in 1957. Might the president or other members, he asked, have
any comments about the content and style of the intelligence briefing
with which he regularly opened the weekly meetings? Eisenhower quickly

disposed of the gratuitous opening, replying "with a smile," according to the minutes, "that he had nothing critical to say, for the very good reason that he had just come back from church."

Over time the president would admit his irritation with the style of the Dulles brothers. He expressed "real impatience" with Allen in one private memo, saying that he found the intelligence briefings "too philosophical, laborious and tedious." But, he added, "one must recognize the personality of the individual involved." About Foster, Eisenhower was less tolerant; the secretary of state's discourses "were frequently too long and in too much detail in historical account."[36] Having explained something once, Eisenhower recalled, Foster "was apt to forget that he had, and, within a day or so, [would] tell it over again." As a general of the army, Eisenhower was accustomed to military briefings from subordinates who confronted immediate decisions and did not bother with background.

Other pressures were converging. Starting immediately upon his return from convalescence in January, Foster was under virtually continuous fire from Congress and the public. Inadvertently he had himself provided the opening — and enduring — ammunition. In an interview with *Life* magazine before the election, Foster had sought to distinguish vigorous Republican foreign policy from the Democrats' mere "containment" of communism. "You have to take chances for peace, just as you must take chances in war. Some say we were brought to the verge of war. Of course we were brought to the verge of war. The ability to get to the verge without getting into war is the necessary art. If you try to run away from it, if you are scared to go to the brink, you are lost. . . . We walked to the brink and we looked it in the face." Foster never actually used the word "brinkmanship," but the label stuck to him as the legacy of a diplomatic strategy that was reckless for the nuclear age.[37]

Less on matters of ideology than on specific issues, Allen found himself disagreeing with his brother — not exactly in public but within the inner circle. At one NSC meeting late in 1957, for instance, Foster opined in his decisive way that a recent assassination attempt on President Sukarno of Indonesia, a situation with which the NSC was increasingly concerned, had been perpetrated by communists. Allen knew exactly the intelligence reports Foster was interpreting — presumably he had sent them over to his brother himself — but he interrupted with doubts as to the reliability of the information. Some time later, as Foster held forth about communist influence over public opinion in Latin America, Allen took issue, noting that less than one-tenth of the media in the Western Hemisphere were under communist control.[38] At another point, when Foster argued that the Kremlin was simply turning on a hard line in dealing with the West, Allen said he thought the change was "more fundamental" than his brother had just stated. As the NSC minutes recorded, "the President looked mildly astonished."

Walt W. Rostow, then at MIT but on call as an administration consultant, remembers being summoned to Washington to work on a forthcoming bellicose speech by the secretary of state. To Rostow's surprise Allen met him at National Airport to warn about the substance of the speech, concluding with the admonition that "if my brother has his way, I'll have to resign." Foster's rhetoric was softened.[39]

Eisenhower kept the pressure on Allen in the specific matter of organizing the intelligence community. The military and other intelligence agencies were apparently not responding to the director's instructions. Allen argued that he preferred to work things out on a cooperative basis (that is, without confrontation), but according to the NSC minutes, "The President did not agree, and emphasized that the Director of Central Intelligence must *direct* the cooperation, not *ask* for it."

Allen preserved his sangfroid within his own shop. Lawrence Houston, the CIA general counsel, remembers once walking out of Allen's office in something of a daze and remarking to John S. Earman, the omniscient assistant outside the director's door, that his days at CIA were surely numbered: it seems that he had engaged Allen in a heated argument on a point of law. Earman called Houston back a short time later, telling him not to pack up his desk just yet. Allen had emerged beaming after Houston left the field of lawyerly combat, saying, "I haven't had that much fun in years!"[40]

And then, late in 1958, a most welcome visitor to CIA provided Allen with a moment of relief from the pressure bearing down from his colleagues in government. Among the countries where the CIA was most influential was Greece; Athens, with the third largest CIA station in the world, was one of the capitals cited in the Bruce-Lovett report where the station chief enjoyed more power than the ambassador. The most important center of power in Athens was the German-born Queen Frederika, manipulative queen mother of the future King Constantine. Allen had encountered members of the royal family during cruises with Stavros Niarchos and other wealthy Greeks. Frederika was just the sort of intense and intelligent woman who had always intrigued Allen. For her part, the queen found in Allen a magnetic, powerful man worthy of royal attention. Their friendship was immediate — if necessarily discreet.

Queen Frederika, then forty-one, brought her teenage crown prince and his older sister, Sophie, to see the United States from coast to coast that autumn. Just as the royal party was about to leave for home on December 6, Frederika received word that she would be privately welcomed in Washington. Without announcing the reason, she extended their visit by a week. President Eisenhower received her at the White House on December 9; the meeting was called "strictly off the record," but their conversation was tape-recorded. They spoke of "spiritual values," which alone could preserve the peace of the world. Three days later the president shared his impressions of the glamorous queen, remarking that her novel plans for dealing with the Soviet Union would be "the trick of the week."[41]

Queen Frederika then called upon the director of central intelligence, where a most untoward incident occurred. The CIA officer responsible for relations with Greece ushered the royal visitor into Allen's office and left them alone. After forty-five minutes without a signal from inside, he tentatively knocked and peeked into the office. It was empty. He heard a muffled sound from behind the closed door of the adjoining dressing room, which Allen used to change for dinner or, when the gout hit, put his feet up on the couch. With even more nervousness, the officer knocked and unlatched the dressing room door. Inside Allen and Frederika were laughing in obvious embarrassment. The door had apparently slammed closed behind them, and they were unable to open it from within. Driving back to the embassy, the CIA escort remembers the queen's afterglow. "We just love that man!" she said.[42]

— * —

Allen's intimates, particularly Mary Bancroft, had noted him undergoing a distinct change between the two phases of his World War II operations in Bern — the first when neutral Switzerland was isolated and the OSS spy chief was operating on his own, and the final year, when support staff and colleagues poured in with the liberating Allied armies. A similar change marked the mid-1950s. The 1953 overthrow of Mossadegh in Iran had been essentially a one-man operation; more personnel were engaged in the ousting of Arbenz in Guatemala a year later, but the operation had still been a tidy and inexpensive affair, as Allen saw it. Now the CIA was firmly established in the Washington power structure, and the various covert actions he had launched with just a handful of daring aides had become vast bureaucratic enterprises, engaging military and naval staffs, the Defense Department, and oversight panels, all of which required care and handling.

Allen always found the greatest satisfaction in working through a few favorite lieutenants, men in the style of Kim Roosevelt, Tracy Barnes, and Ed Lansdale, leaving the larger bureaucratic enterprises to others — Bissell for the U-2 reconnaissance operation, Helms for overall intelligence collection. No longer derided as Park Avenue cowboys, Allen's protégés nonetheless commanded special stature within the secret world of the clandestine services.

Notable within the special circle was Alfred C. Ulmer, Jr., a fellow Princetonian (class of '39) and gracious southerner, whom Allen had first encountered in the Italian operations of the OSS. Ulmer showed promise as the powerful station chief in Athens in the 1950s, deftly guiding Allen through the turmoil of Greek politics and facilitating friendships with Niarchos and Queen Frederika. When CIA needed a fresh hand to take over disparate Far Eastern operations, spinning aimlessly under the pressures of the Korean War, Allen turned to Ulmer — typically ignoring his man's total unfamiliarity with Asia. Ulmer, after carrying out a sweeping reorganization of the CIA's Asian assets, awaited reassignment to a European base. Instead, in 1957 he found himself the central figure in the most ambitious covert action yet launched, a separatist rebellion across the sprawling archipelago of Indonesia.

The problem of this former Dutch colony, rich with the oil of Sumatra, had first come to Allen's serious attention two years before, in an approach from the heart of the Republican establishment. Thomas E. Dewey, twice-defeated presidential candidate, telephoned from his New York law office to ask if a CIA representative might be interested in meeting a certain Indonesian politician, an opponent of the mercurial national leader Sukarno. The politician, who represented a conservative Muslim faction, sought American support in the effort to topple Sukarno, regarded in Washington as a dangerous champion of nonalignment. Over the next two years the CIA set out to dabble in Indonesian politics for the perceived benefit of the Free World.

Allen sent Ulmer to Djakarta in the autumn of 1957 to size things up. When the United States ambassador argued that the conservative opposition's scheme to overthrow Sukarno was futile, he was promptly replaced. Happily remembering the similar circumstances of Guatemala, and his avuncular relationship with Al Haney four years earlier, Allen gave Ulmer the green light — and a $7 million budget — to launch a revolt of military officers in Sumatra.[43]

Operation Hike, as the Indonesian venture was dubbed, would follow the pattern of Operation Success: a deliberate campaign of psychological insecurity, followed by a contrived military uprising that would strike fear into the ruling regime. But in 1958 neither Washington nor the rest of the world was living in the naive environment of 1954. Sukarno was no Arbenz: he was not cowed by a murky military rebellion, and he fought back. Eisenhower's policymakers had grown wary of giving the CIA clandestine services a free hand in foreign ventures; from the first moves the secret Indonesian operation figured high on the agendas of the National

Security Council, the State and Defense departments, and the liaison staffs of British and Australian intelligence, both of which had their own interests, for reasons of geography and oil economics, in the fate of Indonesia.

At the start Allen anticipated the midnight phone calls from Ulmer, just as he had savored Haney's recitation of the details about Guatemala. But preoccupied with other concerns as 1957 turned to 1958, he had less time for Ulmer. As in Bern, he found that a vast bureaucracy was driving an operation he had counted as his own: Bissell dispatched U-2 planes for reconnaissance of military installations across the archipelago; Des FitzGerald, his most dynamic Asian hand, supervised establishment of American air and naval supply bases in the Philippines. The Joint Chiefs of Staff offered submarines to guard the waters around Sumatra; an ad hoc air force of unmarked planes appeared to strafe key targets.

In such circumstances Allen withdrew into aloofness. He had learned to handle paramilitary operations, but a massive deployment of firepower, ships, and planes was not his style. Ulmer found his putative boss less available for briefings and decisions on the burgeoning operation; instead the detailed planning was hammered out, not in the CIA buildings by the Lincoln Memorial but across the Mall in Foggy Bottom, at daily meetings in the office of the secretary of state. To the NSC Allen affected a posture of bemused detachment. "If there was to be a climax in Indonesia, we were on the point of reaching it," noted the minutes of his report on February 6. "But one has to be very skeptical about the Indonesians and about any climax." After uprisings and invasions, bombardments and rebellious rhetoric, Operation Hike foundered, and Allen kept his distance. "The dissidents had moved rather too fast and made their decision . . . without carefully counting their military assets," he blandly informed the NSC late in the month.[44] Sporadic military operations continued without a decisive outcome.

On May 18 one of the unmarked aircraft was shot down after a strafing raid that killed a dozen Indonesian sailors. Parachuting into a palm grove, an American pilot named Allen Lawrence Pope was captured by soldiers loyal to Sukarno. In the hapless prisoner's kit were found papers linking him to the CIA and records of previous bombing raids ostensibly by Indonesian rebels. The administration, including Eisenhower himself, tried to portray Pope as a freewheeling "soldier of fortune," but the reality was stark. Ulmer was summoned to the secretary of state's office and, as he recalled the meeting, Foster said, "Sometimes you win, and sometimes you lose. Can your people cut your losses and get out fast?" Official instructions to terminate CIA aid to the dissidents had to come from Allen himself. "This is the most difficult message I have ever sent," he ca-

bled his Indonesian field officers. "It is sent only under impelling necessity and in what we all view here as the highest national interest." The
clandestine CIA team was ordered to abandon positions with the dissidents; they were evacuated by submarine.[45]

Operation Hike in Indonesia had started as yet another CIA covert
action in which "politically immature" activists, in the words of the
Bruce-Lovett report, sought to show their mettle. But Allen had long
since abandoned the role of kingmaker for Indonesia. When the president's board of intelligence consultants made a retrospective study of Operation Hike, it concluded that the venture was carried out in "catch-as-
catch-can fashion."

> On different occasions it was considered by the President, by the NSC,
> and by assorted ad hoc groups for various purposes. There was no proper
> estimate of the situation, nor proper prior planning on the part of any-
> one, and in its active phases the operation was directed, not by the direc-
> tor of central intelligence but personally by the secretary of state, who,
> ten thousand miles away from the scene of operation, undertook to make
> practically all decisions down to and including even the tactical military
> decisions.[46]

— * —

His brother may have been been responsible for the most spectacular failure of American covert action (to that date), but Allen's grip over the intelligence service he had built was faltering. By 1958, Allen could no
longer sustain his chosen part of the spymaster; he had become a bureaucrat, a rold for which he was ill suited, enmeshed with competing bureaucracies across the government. "You're taking the fun out of intelligence!" he would complain to aides confronting him with administrative
or technical decisions.[47]

Even when CIA was right, it could not always prevail. One Sunday
morning early in May, just before Pope was shot down, Allen wandered
into his office to catch up on the incoming cables from world trouble
spots: riots in Lebanon, Beirut an armed camp, the CIA's favorites in the
last elections in trouble. More alarming for his standing in Washington
was the advisory that Vice President Nixon would encounter angry left-
wing mobs when he arrived in Caracas on a good-will visit — and that the
military junta of Venezuela was not prepared to prevent it.

Weeks before, the CIA station chief in Caracas, Jacob Esterline, had
learned of the plan for violent demonstrations during Nixon's visit. It
threatened to be a repeat of the disastrous Bogotazo of a decade before,
though this time the CIA was alert to the danger. The American ambas-

sador in Caracas, however, refused to take the intelligence seriously, and on his own authority Esterline took the next plane to Washington. He laid out his evidence, pleading for a change in the vice president's itinerary. Allen shook his head sadly, the CIA man recalled, and said, "It's a political decision; Nixon's going and that's that. You'll just have to make the best of it."[48]

That Sunday morning in May, Esterline urgently asked Allen's authority to intercept Nixon, then in Bogotá, with word of the danger ahead at his next stop. Allen cabled his approval, but the ambassador in Caracas refused to let Esterline leave on his alarmist mission, instead sending one of his diplomatic staff to assure the vice president that the Venezuelan police "had everything under control." When Nixon and his wife landed in Caracas Tuesday morning, they were immediately set upon by yelling, spitting mobs brandishing iron pipes against the motorcade of the American vice president.

In the Washington uproar that followed — Eisenhower personally went to National Airport to greet Nixon on his triumphal return — Allen kept up the facade of a team player. "You can't predict when a mob will go berserk," he told critics. "We had to take some chances; you can't cancel a trip like that except for extraordinary reasons — you can't let people blackmail you." Only long afterward did Nixon concede that Allen had given him advance warning — against the State Department's judgment — that there might be trouble in Venezuela.[49]

But another crisis in the coming months revealed the CIA's shortcomings in the world reach to which it aspired. The CIA officer in Amman, Jordan — another capital where the station seemed more influential than the embassy — had been alert to left-wing pro-Nasser attempts to topple King Hussein. Similar plots were being reported against Hussein's cousin, King Faisal in Baghdad, but Iraq was not as high on CIA's watch list as Jordan. The CIA's Near Eastern division briefed Allen about a looming crisis in Jordan as he prepared for an NSC meeting in July.

During the night before, the division chief, Norman Paul, awakened by a call from the CIA watch officer, heard the words, "They're marching on the palace." Paul rushed into the office to update Allen's NSC brief on the Jordan crisis, only to learn that "the palace" was in Baghdad, not Amman. The violent fall of the seemingly stable, pro-Western royal regime of Iraq provoked a Middle East panic that led Eisenhower into the impulsive decision to dispatch the Marines to the placid beaches of Beirut. Allen had urged caution in Lebanon two months before, but the president made his decision to commit American troops without meaningful consultation; at the crucial NSC meeting on July 14, no minutes were kept.[50] CIA had been caught completely unawares by the coup in Iraq. It was little consolation that British, Israeli, and even Soviet intelligence had been equally ignorant of the plotting in the barracks of the Iraqi armed forces.

The CIA's sense of its own wisdom was checked. A decade earlier, in 1948, an outburst of rioting in Bogotá during an international conference had stirred the fledgling agency to the quest for omniscience: no political situation the world over should be considered beneath notice or irrelevant to American national security. At that same formative moment a few clandestine operators in Italy, mobilized by Angleton, had succeeded in swinging an election and preventing the rise to power of the Italian Communist Party, thus provoking CIA aspirations to omnipotence in political warfare.

Over the experience of the ten subsequent years, even the most adventurous of CIA men had adequate reason to look wryly upon their early ambitions. With the debacle in Indonesia and the surprise in Iraq, Allen's CIA was shown to be neither omnipotent nor omniscient.

— 17 —

ALONE

ALLEN, CLOVER, AND THEIR SON spent Thanksgiving of 1958 at his sister Eleanor's home in McLean, Virginia. Foster and Janet were there, along with assorted children of the Watertown Dulleses, making it a traditional festival. The readiness of Allen Macy to attend made the occasion special for Allen and Clover. Then twenty-eight, still under intensive medical care to overcome the effects of his brain damage, the serious young man was striving to lead a normal life on his own. The gathering was cheerful, Eleanor recalled, and at least on the surface, carefree. "The family group around the table filled the dining room, which was almost a part of the outdoors with its sliding glass panels between the warm inside and the frost-touched field and garden outside. Foster carved the large bronze turkey and exclaimed in mock surprise at the bounty as the traditional American dishes were brought in — the chestnut and other dressings, the candied sweet potatoes, the vegetables, the salad, pies, ice cream."[1]

Scarcely had young Allen finished saying grace when the telephone started ringing, first for Allen, then for Foster, as watch officers of the American government reported the latest moves in a Soviet challenge to the status of Berlin, still controlled by the Four Powers. After this rare, brief interlude of family time Allen excused himself to check in at CIA headquarters, Foster departed to meet diplomatic aides converging at his Georgetown home, and Eleanor left for her office in the State Department.

Foster had turned seventy in February. His birthday had started with a White House breakfast and would have ended in a family dinner given by his brother — except that Foster had an important official function that evening, and by the time he showed up at Allen and Clover's home the birthday dinner was over. Foster seemed to be constantly on the move. It was by now a controversial commonplace for the secretary of state to be supervising American foreign policy from his airplane more than from his desk in Foggy Bottom. Even Eisenhower had grown diffident about intruding upon Foster's demanding schedule; he worried at one point about telephoning, since "people chase him around if they know the president is calling." He assured the State Department staff that the president would always be available whenever Foster could manage to call him.[2]

Right after Thanksgiving Foster flew to Mexico City for the inauguration of a new president. Only three or four people closest to him knew that Foster was in constant abdominal pain. On December 6, the day after he returned from Mexico, he entered Walter Reed Hospital. Suspecting a hernia, the physicians put him on a restricted regime. Nevertheless, on checking out of the hospital six days later, the secretary of state was driven directly to the airport, where the presidential plane was waiting to fly him to Paris for a conference of NATO foreign ministers.

This Presbyterian family seldom discussed matters of health. Foster "felt embarrassed to discuss matters so personal and so delicate," Eleanor explained. "He did not think that what affected him personally ought to intrude on serious business." By the start of 1959, after the conference in Paris and a Christmas holiday in Jamaica, Foster's pain was too severe to continue ignoring. Unspoken were the worries about his colon cancer, discovered two years before.

Foster tried to maintain his schedule of meetings, diplomatic receptions, and news conferences, but on February 9 he officially informed Eisenhower that a "recently developed hernia" would require surgery and a few weeks of recuperation.[3] He returned the next day to Walter Reed, where Eisenhower had placed the presidential suite at his disposal. The operation took place on February 13; Clover joined Janet and Eleanor in waiting for the results. The pain was not a hernia.

Eisenhower visited his secretary of state at the hospital the next day, and in the president's subsequent press statement the word "malignancy" was used for the first time. "I express the thoughts and prayers of all of us that the results of [Foster's] operation and the further course of treatment will be successful." In the private circle there were no such illusions. Eisenhower confided to an aide that same day, "It seems so wrong somehow that a man who has given of himself, as has Dulles, must die in such a painful fashion."[4]

Allen and the State Department staff agreed to full public disclosure of the postoperative biopsy results. The treatment recommended involved injection of radioactive gold; Allen authorized an explanatory public statement. When Foster left the hospital on March 30, Allen took him to the airport for a flight to Hobe Sound, Florida, and a period of sunny convalescence. On arrival the attending physicians quietly informed Foster's personal assistant, Joseph N. "Jerry" Greene, Jr., that the cancer was spreading out of control. Greene concurred in the medical judgment that this disclosure would sap the patient's will to survive and, with misgivings, they kept the final diagnosis secret from him.[5]

Clearing his own schedule for an Easter holiday, Allen went to stay with the Wrightsmans in Palm Beach, forty-five minutes from Hobe Sound. He visited his brother late in the afternoon of April 5; a fraternal chess game was clearly beyond Foster's capacity by this time, but Allen indulged him in an hour's desultory conversation about the matters he knew his brother would find most diverting — Nasser's latest posturing, the Berlin confrontation, an embassy staffing problem in India. The main point, Allen told Foster, was to regain his strength. Foster insisted that the tumors were under control; Allen said nothing to disabuse him. They could wait two weeks or so, Allen said, before facing any decisions about Foster's future as secretary of state.

Two days later, on his sixty-sixth birthday, Allen had to leave Florida for a quick visit to Lubbock, Texas, where he had promised to deliver a speech called "The Immediate Communist Peril." (Lubbock was the hometown of a key member of the CIA's congressional oversight clique.) On his return to Palm Beach he found that the moment of decision was arriving sooner than he had anticipated. Foster's condition was deteriorating quickly, to the point that Greene felt he had to inform the White House, but without Foster's knowledge; he worried that his boss would not authorize the call.

The morning of April 11 Foster made the decision himself to resign as secretary of state. On a pad of yellow paper he drafted a letter to the president, which he read slowly for Janet to take down in her clearer handwriting, for his secretary to type. Allen arrived, learned of his brother's decision, and in a brief conversation discovered the futility of trying to change his mind. He and Jerry Greene arranged for a chartered plane to fly them that afternoon to Augusta, Georgia, where Eisenhower was vacationing, to hand Foster's letter to the president in person. "The secretary is a very sick man," Allen informed the president. "He has grown weaker rather than stronger. . . . Large doses of sedatives have helped him, but his spirits have also been declining." Eisenhower, apparently sensing a brother's difficulty, asked if Greene wished to continue the report. The faithful aide, who had scarcely left Foster's side for weeks past, had little further to say. Allen produced the letter Foster had dictated a few hours before. The president read it and quickly folded it into his pocket. He tried small talk, remembering his own back pains in 1936, which had been caused by, of

all things, an infected tonsil. Allen replied that the president would find
Foster very stubborn in his decision to resign.

Foster had asked to return home to Washington and Walter Reed the
next day, "while the going was good," he said. Eisenhower immediately
summoned his own presidential plane to transport the dying secretary of
state back from Florida, but he sought to avoid any public announcement
of Foster's condition until he could discuss the situation in person. Leaving the president's vacation home, Allen and Greene devised a cover story
with Press Secretary James Hagerty about "CIA business" that had
brought Allen to Augusta; Greene's presence was not announced, for it
would have signaled the reason for the sudden visit. Allen instructed
Greene to telephone the acting secretary of state, Chris Herter, of the
imminent resignation, while he himself continued on the chartered aircraft straight back to Washington, and Greene returned to Hobe Sound
to help prepare for Foster's final journey home.

Eisenhower called on Foster for the last time on May 5, bringing with
him the unlikely personage of Sir Winston Churchill, who was in Washington on a private visit. Churchill was no admirer of Foster, after his
stance of appeasement in the late 1930s and the more recent Anglo-
American crisis over Suez. But dying men deserve respect. Down the corridor in Walter Reed Hospital, as it happened, was another dying man
who figured memorably in the lives of the two statesmen, George C.
Marshall. The seventy-eight-year-old general, hero of World War II and
the postwar era, was immobilized by strokes; he could not talk or even
recognize callers, but Eisenhower and Churchill looked in on him anyway.* Foster, wearing a robe loosely thrown over his pajamas, was wheeled
into the sitting room where the president and the retired British prime
minister waited for him. The three men talked, the official communiqué
stated, of international affairs.

"We are going through some tough days," Allen wrote his daughter
Joan. "Unfortunately, there is very little that can be done." Allen approved a medical bulletin disclosing that Foster had contracted pneumonia, adding, "There has been some further decline in his general condition." The family from Henderson Harbor maintained vigil during the
helpless weeks that followed.

John Foster Dulles died in his sleep early Sunday morning, May 24,
1959. To his funeral came British Prime Minister Harold Macmillan,
Chancellor Konrad Adenauer of the Federal Republic of Germany, Foreign Minister Andrei A. Gromyko of the Soviet Union, and foreign ministers from eleven other lands. Among the pallbearers were Thomas E.

* Marshall held on to life until October 16, 1959.

Dewey, C. D. Jackson and, from a retirement as testy as his active life, Walter Bedell Smith. The final tributes, at Washington's National Cathedral, proceeded with all the ceremony and honor accorded to a head of state.

— * —

Allen recorded a strangely colored memory of his last days with his brother.

> [Foster] had only days, maybe hours, to live, and he knew it. Speech came hard as the cancer gripped him. I saw there was something very special he wished to tell me. Every word of what he said was a struggle and cost pain. This was his last legacy of thought to me:
>
> "Would this nation of ours and our allies ever thoroughly understand the scope of the peril, the unchanging goals of communism and its subtle and subversive techniques to accomplish them? The tempo of action changed but the threat was constant, the advance and then the retreat, the probing, now here, now there, each weakness of the Free World tested, its strong points bypassed.
>
> "Here was no ordinary antagonist. The ambitions of the Soviet leaders were not limited like those of the tsars of old to reaching out for warm waters and free oceans. The Soviets sought not a place in the sun, but the sun itself. Their objective was the world. They would not tolerate compromise on goals, only on tactics. And, as each advance was consolidated into the communist system, there was to be no turning back, no choice for the people enslaved.
>
> "A Grand Alliance of the free nations could meet and turn back this threat. In power, moral, economic, as well as military, we of the Free World, if united, stood head and shoulders over the communist world. But would we have the steadfast purpose and the understanding, the skill and the fortitude, to use our strength wisely, meaningfully, successfully? And how could our people here in the United States be brought to understand the issues, their responsibilities and the need for American leadership anywhere, maybe even everywhere, in the world?"
>
> This is what my brother said to me on that May day. This was his last message to me.[6]

That was how Allen chose to remember and record the Foster Dulles legacy for posterity. The memory is uncharacteristically maudlin. It also seems self-conscious and contrived — almost as if Allen were trying to invoke Foster's authority in confronting some perceived but undefined new crisis. For the dogmatism of this alleged last message stands in stark contrast to the outlook that Foster had actually expressed in his last year of life before the final illness. That year Foster had generated a series of spirited ideological arguments within the closed circle of the National Security Council. The declassified records of these weekly meetings reveal somber intellectual exchanges, not at all the operational discussions that this body came to represent in later administrations.

Foster's views on communism, as expressed in these meetings, were far more nuanced than the Manichaean caricature Allen attributed to him in memory. Foster, as Eisenhower concluded, was ever the advocate "not of the perfect or the theoretical best, but of the possible."[7] Soviet behavior on the international scene was actually improving, Foster argued. "The Soviet Union no longer dares try to reduce other countries to its control by direct and forceful action, but feels obliged to use more subtle approaches." The United States was clearly unable to prevent this change, but should we want to prevent it? "Doubtless the ultimate intentions of the Soviet Union were still bad, but their behavior, at least, was better, and ultimately the Soviets may become more civilized."[8]

Others in Eisenhower's inner circle persisted in taking an ideological approach to foreign policy even as Foster was relaxing his own dogmatic perspective. Against such rigidity Foster argued strenuously, for instance, that Moscow was no more willing to take risks in provoking local aggression than was the United States. For the sake of argument Allen cited the Hungarian invasion of 1956 as an example of the Kremlin's continued aggressive designs. Foster brushed aside invocation of past grievances and retorted that in the local crises "which most greatly concern the United States today, . . . the directing forces [are] not communist, but primarily forces favorable personally to a Sukarno, a Nasser or the like. Developments in these areas had not been initiated by Soviet plots."[9] This, of course, had been Allen's position in countless earlier arguments with his brother. The irony is that after Foster had come around to Allen's more measured perspectives, and after his death, Allen chose to perpetuate his brother's original dogma. It was almost as if he sought to draw a straight line from the rabid anti-Bolshevism of Uncle Bert Lansing forty years before, ignoring the turnings and shadings that he himself had been so quick to detect in the intervening years.

The interaction of the Dulles brothers was central to the human fabric of the Cold War. Over the years and the crises Foster enjoyed defining principles; Allen sought to take useful steps. As at chess, Foster preferred to open, but Allen could deploy the winning response. Through their careers they would confront, challenge, humor, respect each other, trimming a little here and there to preserve the family ties, ultimately sticking together against all detractors. The paths along which they guided their respective instruments of government power were congruent; neither could have made the same impact upon his times in the absence of the other.

Then, at age sixty-seven, Allen found himself bereft of his partner, his guide and foil. Once before this had happened, in adolescence, when Foster, who always set the pace for the neighborhood games, went off to college. Allen then had compensated by making himself affable and popular in his own right. Advancing age lacks the resilience of youth; Allen was less successful in compensating for loneliness the second time. He seemed to assume an obligation to carry on his late brother's anticommunist mission in its purest form. Without Foster, as Allen found himself alone in carrying the legacy of a proud Presbyterian family dedicated to public service, his instincts dulled, his zest at work lost its edge.

Allen remained a responsible member of the Eisenhower administration, of course, and his public celebrity soared within his own country and the world outside, where his name was revered and reviled by anti- and procommunist voices, respectively. He had built his CIA into a formidable instrument of government, but the civilian intelligence service was growing too big and too diffuse for one man to handle. For all the public respect he had brought to the business of intelligence, criticism of his gentlemanly leadership continued in the private councils of the White House. Eisenhower began excluding Allen from small meetings of his inner circle. Eventually, the president told his staff, in an ominous signal of dwindling confidence, that he did not want to meet with Allen unless at least one other person was also present.

One by one Allen's natural moorings were dropping away. His old diplomatic clubmates, with whom he had learned and taken his ease for decades, had long since dispersed. None of them achieved the eminence of "our Allen," but the loss of old colleagues is never easy. His sophisticated friend Royall Tyler, who always had seemed to find enduring value in transitory circumstance, had decided to end his life in 1953. William J. Donovan, the man who brought Allen into intelligence as a profession, died in February 1959, a pitiful invalid of hopelessly clouded mind, unable at the end to appreciate how much he had contributed to the workings of American government. Allen gave a thoughtful testimonial address in Donovan's hometown of Buffalo just two weeks after Foster's resignation. Frank Wisner, enthusiastic partner from the birth of covert actions against "vicious" communism, never fully recovered from the failures of 1956 and his bout with hepatitis. Though he served two more years as head of the clandestine services, colleagues found him increasingly irritable and irrational. Late in 1958 Wisner suffered a nervous breakdown; Allen could delay no longer in replacing his longtime deputy.

The decision he made was fateful for the future of the American intel-

ligence service. Wisner's natural successor would have been Richard
Helms, who had been acting head during the months of Wisner's inca-
pacity. But Helms represented the traditions of intelligence collection, of
espionage, rather than the mounting of positive covert actions, which had
come to dominate Allen's concept of the CIA in the Cold War. Except for
the ill-starred medical research programs, Helms pointedly absented
himself from discussions of covert actions to roll back the tide of communism.

To the astonishment of CIA professionals, Allen passed Helms over as
director of the clandestine services and chose instead Richard Bissell,
from Yale and MIT, once the key administrator of the Marshall Plan. Dynamic, efficient, and unquestionably brilliant, Bissell was not a man of the
intelligence business. His U-2 air reconnaissance program was thriving as
a logistical and technological feat, but he showed no aptitude for the traditional expertise of building networks and running agents. Allen apparently saw the future of the intelligence service in the crisp style of man-
agerial efficiency, not the professional skills of Helms. To Bissell he
passed effective leadership of CIA, reserving for himself only the tasks he
most enjoyed and could do best: avuncular and nostalgic meetings in a
haze of pipe smoke with officers in from the field, intelligence briefings to
the National Security Council, and public speeches to secure the agency's
image.

For just as Allen was withdrawing from the most sensitive tasks of intelligence, he was becoming the mythic symbol of the Cold War in communist propaganda. "Foster Dulles died," Khrushchev was quoted as saying, "but Allen Dulles lives on. One shuddered at the thought of what a
great force was in such hands." Such an expression of anger from the
Kremlin was not at all inconvenient for the image and the legacy that
Allen sought to sustain.

— * —

Eisenhower faced an unwelcome decision in choosing a successor to John
Foster Dulles to be his secretary of state for the remaining twenty-one
months of his presidency. Just a few days after his operation and the discovery of the malignancy, Foster himself had discussed the problem with
Herter, who had been filling in as acting secretary during his illness. They
mentioned some possible names; Herter said he would eliminate himself
as a candidate on grounds of his physical handicap.

The courtly sixty-four-year-old former diplomat, publisher, and two-
term governor of Massachusetts was crippled by osteoarthritis; through
all his public duties he carried his six-foot-five frame around on crutches.
(It was suggested to White House photographers that they might honor

the precedent set for President Roosevelt in his wheelchair and avoid pictures of Herter's difficulty in walking.) Herter had long since made peace
with his infirmity and managed his daily life comfortably. But he understood that his was not the most confidence-inspiring image for the
spokesman for American foreign policy. Also Herter hailed from the liberal wing of the Republican party. Eisenhower understood that Nixon,
for one, did not fully trust these Republicans, and with some reason:
Herter had actually been proposed as replacement for the controversial
Nixon as Eisenhower's running mate in 1956.* Eisenhower always de-
ferred to his vice president on such party matters. "Our good friend Chris
Herter [put on] a pretty stupid performance," Eisenhower once remarked
after Herter appeared in a television interview. With Nixon obviously
concurring, the president said, "They tied him in knots."[10]

Over the next years, however, as Herter took over much of the work of
the State Department in Foster's frequent absences, Eisenhower grew
comfortable with him. Two days after hearing of Foster's determination
to resign, the president discussed the options for succession. The Brah-
min Herter insisted that he "did not want the President to feel obliged in
any sense to offer the job to him." Eisenhower brushed this aside, saying
that he was being "very cold-blooded" in considering his options. As
Goodpaster recorded the conversation, "he first wishes Mr. Herter to go
to a competent medical clinic and have a thorough and completely objective medical examination, . . . the whole bevy of doctors, . . . [to] give a report that he will not be too seriously handicapped in getting around the
world readily and quickly to carry out the duties of the office."[11]

Eisenhower mentioned a few other candidates for his next secretary of
state: Treasury Secretary Robert B. Anderson or Henry Cabot Lodge, his
ambassador to the United Nations. Douglas Dillon, undersecretary of
state for economic affairs, was also on the president's list, along with a career diplomat with whom he felt particularly friendly, Livingston Merchant.[12] One name did not figure in these conversations, though after the
decision was made Eisenhower admitted that he had given brief thought
to another person of his official circle. Outsiders, at any rate, considered
this silent candidate an obvious choice.

"There are private indications that Mr. Allen Dulles, who has worked
hand-in-glove with his brother, is foremost in the President's mind,"
wrote *The Times* of London. "The remarkable impact on the contemporary scene of the Dulles brothers, both specialists whose separate paths
brought them to positions of power, would certainly be dramatized." In

---

* Yet Nixon was one of those said to have asked the press not to photograph Herter on his
crutches.

Paris press organs of both right and left commented favorably on the possibility of Allen's succession. *Newsweek* joined in saying that Allen had "both a sound strategic grasp of the world struggle and intimate knowledge of the various specific problems confronting us in all parts of the world.... His appointment would be interpreted worldwide as proof of the basic stability of American policy."

From his journeyman days in Constantinople, Allen had confided his ambition to be secretary of state, following in the path of his grandfather and his uncle. At a crucial point of combat in the incipient Cold War, he hoped for the interim step of ambassador to France. But once he "took the cloth," as he put it, of a career in intelligence, he gave every sign of having abandoned the ambitions of boyhood. The work of maturity had superseded the dreams of youth.

Foster had discussed the succession candidly with his brother, saying he would not choose to disrupt the work of CIA. He told Allen he would recommend Herter. Allen accepted the decision without recording any comment.[13] Nor could Allen begrudge the choice of Chris Herter, a friend since Armistice Day of 1918, when the new clubmate from Boston had nursed Allen through the near-fatal grippe.

The National Security Council met on April 17, two days after Foster's resignation was announced, to discuss the continuing problems of Iraq, a discussion too sensitive to be recorded in official minutes. The next day Eisenhower received satisfactory medical reports and announced the selection of Christian A. Herter to be America's fifty-third secretary of state.

— ∗ —

Fidel Castro arrived in the United States on a "friendship visit" the day of Foster's resignation. Herter, for one, was relieved that Eisenhower was off in Georgia so the question would not arise of the president either meeting or refusing to meet the thirty-two-year-old revolutionary who had overthrown Batista's corrupt Cuban regime in the first days of 1959.

The new secretary of state gave a luncheon, and Vice President Nixon spent three hours with Castro, intent on sizing him up and steering him in the direction of democratic leadership. "He is either incredibly naive about communism or under communist discipline," Nixon informed Eisenhower.[14] "My guess is the former."∗ Herter recorded his own impressions as the Cuban leader departed for home. He was "sorry, in a way,"

∗ Faithfully reprinting this memo of his first impression in memoirs written twenty years later, Nixon — by then an ex-president — quickly added that subsequent developments convinced him that Castro "was indeed a communist."

that Eisenhower had not had the opportunity to meet this puzzling person. "Despite Castro's apparent simplicity, sincerity and eagerness to reassure the United States public, there is little probability that Castro has altered the essentially radical course of his revolution. . . . Castro remains an enigma." In the margin of Herter's report Eisenhower scrawled the note: "File. We will check in a year!! D.E."[15]

That summer of 1959 Castro was only one of the enigmas, persons who grandly or humbly defined the world that confronted Allen in crises at the climax of his career:

- A thirty-year-old test pilot from Kentucky read in *Stars and Stripes* about astronauts selected to fly to the moon, and he felt a tinge of envy. Not that Francis Gary Powers was leading a meaningless life: over the past three years he had flown twenty-seven government missions more secret than any other, in a plane called the U-2. He never considered himself a spy. "I was a pilot flying an airplane," he wrote long afterward. "It just so happened that *where* I was flying made what I was doing spying."
- The idealistic George Blake was transferred back to British intelligence headquarters in London. During the very days that Foster Dulles learned of his cancer, Blake informed his Soviet case officers that he would remain their double agent, no longer in the outpost of Berlin, but in the central preserve of Whitehall.
- A troubled ex-Marine, separated from the service that summer and barely twenty, figured on building a new life for himself in Moscow. He renounced his American citizenship and lived in the Soviet Union, in uncertain status, until June of 1962. His name was Lee Harvey Oswald.

Allen had elevated himself above the day-to-day workings of intelligence by that summer of 1959. He had put Bissell in place to run the shop, and even if he was not to be the secretary of state, there was no reason why he could not act like it. Prime Minister Macmillan had led the West in offering respectability to Nikita Khrushchev by visiting Moscow in February of 1959. Nixon followed in July, and the ambitious vice president found his moment for spontaneous debate with Khrushchev during a photo opportunity in a model kitchen at an exhibition of American consumer life. In September Khrushchev paid a coast-to-coast visit to the United States and, at a state dinner at the White House, he came face to face with the mythic Cold Warrior of communist propaganda.[16]

Allen had muffed the chance to meet Lenin, but four decades later he could not resist the delicious moment, under the conviviality of protocol, for banter with the head of world communism. "You may have seen some of my intelligence reports from time to time," the director of central intelligence told the leader of the Soviet Union at their handshake. A startled Khrushchev responded with the instincts of a professional in dealing with adversaries. "I believe we get the same reports, and probably from the same people." Allen pressed the riposte. "Maybe we should pool our efforts." Yes, Khrushchev replied before moving on to the next guest. "We should buy our intelligence data together and save money — we'd have to pay the people only once!"*

Apart from such splendid moments, Allen's consuming interest was the new CIA "campus" under construction in Langley. The headquarters of his civilian intelligence service would not be ready for another year or so, but Allen insisted on a formal ceremony, with full protocol and publicity, to lay the cornerstone. When the architects proposed a bronze plaque with Allen's name as director of central intelligence, he protested. A plaque could later be removed, he feared; he wanted his name etched deeply into the quartz aggregate finish of the stone. Eisenhower reluctantly agreed to participate in the ceremony that seemed to mean so much to his intelligence director, but the president expressed hope that no one would ask him to deliver any kind of address.

Involved in every detail, Allen arranged that the text of his testimonial to Donovan be among the archives sealed inside the cornerstone. On November 3, Allen and Eisenhower used five silver trowels to place the stone; Eisenhower two, Allen the other three. The protocol guide assured participants that a professional mason "will spread the mortar to the correct depth." Eisenhower gave a brief speech.[17]

— * —

In the early years of CIA, as the public and government alike were being brought up to speed on the culture of modern intelligence, Allen liked to argue that "the mindset of Stalin" was a more important factor to discover than any data on military or industrial strength. It was a quaint way of defining a perennial debate among intelligence analysts, between assessing an adversary's "intentions" and its "capabilities."

Estimating capabilities often involves setting up a series of "worst-case scenarios" depicting what an enemy has the means to do if it wants to. It is only prudent to be prepared for the worst, but these kinds of estimates were found to have particular value at budget time for justifying ever-ex-

---

* This exchange, apparently overheard in the receiving line, was reported in *Time* magazine, September 28, 1959. As Khrushchev traveled across America, he remarked that he had indeed read "most of the stuff Allen Dulles puts out," but, he added, he would prefer to read good novels.

---

panding defense appropriations. Probing intentions is far more subtle, requiring a clear reading of a policymaking process that may not be easily discernible, even by the participants themselves. Capabilities and intentions are not altogether unrelated, of course. In a complex industrial and military establishment, hard evidence of deployments, of production and mobilizations, can become soft evidence of what that regime may have in mind to do, whether or not the decisions to go ahead have been made.

The CIA—along with the rest of the world—never succeeded in penetrating the mind of Stalin, and did only marginally better with the Soviet leaders who succeeded him. Acquiring such intelligence would ideally require a "mole," a well-connected agent within the Kremlin who could accurately and confidently report out his findings.* Though such a boon sometimes appears in the history of intelligence, it generally belongs in the category of what Allen called "story-book stuff."

But for nearly four years, from July 1956 to late April 1960, CIA wielded an extraordinary tool of intelligence, collecting evidence beyond all previous expectations of Soviet strategic capabilities, if not the Kremlin's actual intentions. Through this secret means Washington strategists could estimate with eerie accuracy the deployments of Soviet missiles, heavy bombers, and fighter aircraft, the testing and storage arrangements for nuclear warheads, and the capabilities of the air defense system that would have to be penetrated should the dreaded global confrontation come about.

American intelligence had come a long way from the first years after World War II, when the geography of Russia was essentially an unknown void. In older, simpler days intelligence was collected by networks of lone agents who would fade into the landscape at critical sites. Their mission might be to count the flatcars on trains rolling by or the smokestacks on an unmarked factory; early in the atomic era, an important task for American intelligence networks was to collect water samples downstream of suspected nuclear installations, for clues to what might be going on upriver.

By the 1950s high-definition photography and remote sensing technologies held promise of rendering obsolete such primitive and dangerous means of intelligence collection. Eventually technology would permit remote surveillance from cameras in orbit high above the globe, but it was Allen's successors in intelligence who would perfect those even more remarkable devices in the 1960s. The transition stage from human agent to spy satellite was the era of the U-2.

---

* The term "mole" is a relatively recent addition to the lexicon of espionage. It was coined by the British novelist John le Carré.

"This operation was one of the most valuable intelligence collection operations that any country has ever mounted at any time," Allen declared of the high-altitude U-2 reconnaissance plane. To which Senator J. William Fulbright, a Democrat and no partisan of Allen's, could only concur. "What I regret more than anything else," Fulbright later told his Foreign Relations Committee, "is that we seem to have finally gotten ourselves into a position where we are committed as a country not to do it any more."[18] For the U-2 program ultimately exposed CIA—and the trusted president of the United States—as perpetrators of a blatant and destructive lie on the international scene.

— * —

The U-2 spy plane, a miracle of the technology of the day, made its first operational flight over the Soviet Union at the beginning of July 1956. Richard Bissell recalls walking into his boss's office with the words, "Well, Allen, we're out and running." That flight was a quick and tentative feint over only Moscow and Leningrad, but Allen expressed nervousness nonetheless. "The first time is the safest," Bissell replied. "We should hear within another hour."* That first flight brought back dazzling aerial photographs of the Kremlin and of the Winter Palace in Leningrad, sites known to generations of tourists but now defined with an unprecedented clarity of detail, down to the lines separating parking spaces around familiar buildings.

From that relatively innocuous beginning and for nearly four years to come, the fleet of ten U-2s deployed at secret bases around the Soviet periphery made at least two hundred passes over the Soviet Union's most secret military and industrial facilities, returning their priceless photographs to Arthur Lundahl's photoanalysis laboratory in Washington.† Unwieldy on the runway because of their astonishing wingspan, the U-2s were painted black to make visual detection difficult. Since it could cruise for hours at a far higher altitude than any known winged aircraft, American strategists were confident that Soviet interceptors could not come anywhere close to it in flight. For three years and nine months they were right.

The fundamental purpose of the U-2 program was to eliminate the threat of a Soviet surprise attack upon any point of the globe. During the

---

* Bissell remembers the date of this first flight as July 4, but testimony to Congress suggests that it may have occurred two or three days earlier—perhaps another example of the vagueness about dates that intelligence men like to perpetuate.

† The exact number of U-2 flights over the Soviet Union remained a secret of counterespionage for many years. As Allen later explained, a precise number would allow the Russians to reexamine their radar records and correlate flight patterns with surface facilities, and thus gain insight into exactly what the United States had learned.

year of the Berlin Tunnel, just before the U-2 became operational, Washington had field intelligence giving reassurance against such a possibility in central Europe. By the later 1950s, however, the potential theater of war was becoming global; the feared attack would not necessarily be by ground divisions invading Germany but by intercontinental missiles armed with nuclear warheads, launched from remote areas of Russia or Khazakhstan, and capable of striking cities and targets within the United States or any other country. Those were the capabilities. Though the U-2 could never discover whether the men whose cars were so neatly parked within the Kremlin walls actually intended such a strike, at least it could discern whether they had the capability. The CIA analysts asked the question, "How many missiles would the Soviets want?"[19]

Fear of surprise attack was the impetus for Eisenhower's Open Skies proposal at the Geneva summit of 1955. "If the proposal had been carried out," Allen explained in retrospect, "it is very possible these [U-2] planes would have been used to implement it. They would have been ideally suited for it."[20] Khrushchev, however, just then assuming the reins of power, saw Open Skies as a ruse for gathering intelligence rather than a means for mutual reassurance — missing the natural connection between the two. His brusque rejection of the Eisenhower initiative allowed the CIA to launch its own program to open the skies of the Soviet Union without Khrushchev's agreement.

The hard intelligence collected by the U-2 amounts to a catalogue of Soviet strategic capabilities in the Cold War:

· Kapustin Yar, east of Stalingrad, known to American Soviet watchers as "K Y," was the Kremlin's original missile test range. Its experimental firings were soon vulnerable to surveillance by electronic sensing from the Soviet periphery rather than photographs from overhead.
· Plesetsk, in the Arctic 600 miles north of Moscow, became the more crucial target for the U-2 cameras. Here was fired the first intercontinental ballistic missile (ICBM) in August 1957; it would be four months before the United States could match it. Allen informed Eisenhower that the Soviets would probably have ten such ICBMs ready by 1959 or 1960, and Bissell determined to keep a close watch on Plesetsk.
· Tyura Tam, deep in central Asia, became the center of the Soviet space program. Here was launched *Sputnik*, earth's first artificial satellite, on October 4, 1957. The black U-2 had found the site the previous summer and, in modest recompense for the public outcry over the Soviet advantage in space flight, the CIA's Lundahl was able to show nervous American strategists a complete scale model of the launching facility. The United States launched its first satellite only in January 1958.

- Novaya Zemlya, near Murmansk, was the site of the first Soviet nuclear tests; it was succeeded by the facility for underground testing at Semipalatinsk. The U-2 and other American sensing devices were able to report Soviet nuclear explosions even before Moscow made them known.
- The most intense U-2 scrutiny was focused along the Ural Mountains, the geographical frontier between Europe and Asia, where analysts expected to find long- and medium-range missiles in operational deployment. From here, if the deployments actually existed, nuclear warheads could be fired toward any target on the globe.

The method of pinpointing sites in the Urals gives a revealing example of the analytical techniques used in U-2 reconnaissance. American strategists had determined that the booster rocket for the Soviet ICBM was so massive that it could be transported to a launching site only by rail. Thus U-2 flight plans were designed to follow railroad tracks, particularly obscure spur lines leading to uninhabited areas. Such otherwise meaningless spur lines could be important clues to missile deployments at the railhead. To those designing worst-case scenarios, the end of a railroad track in a barren field might tip the strategic balance of the Cold War.

During its clandestine four-year life span, the CIA's fleet of black spy planes was dispatched not only over the Soviet Union but wherever American policymakers needed hard intelligence. U-2 photographs of the Cairo airport showed the Anglo-French bombing raids during the 1956 Suez crisis. A subsequent flight that November put to rest fears of a dangerous Soviet military presence in Syria. A U-2 was dispatched to report on the military rebellion in Indonesia during the CIA's abortive Operation Hike early in 1958, and Allen used his U-2 photos of Cuba to try persuading Eisenhower that sabotage of the Cuban sugar refineries might be an effective covert action against Castro.

The U-2 pictures, were not, to be sure, infallible. When Bissell sent one of his jet-powered gliders from the base in Taiwan to overfly communist Chinese nuclear test ranges, the photos revealed a suspicious missile deployment, a silo ominously pointing a ballistic missile toward Taipei. Only after more learned analysis was the conclusion reached that the "silo" was actually the ruins of a watchtower erected by a twelfth-century Chinese warlord.

— * —

Allen and Bissell were as close a partnership as any Allen had enjoyed before. Bissell was hardly of the "golden boy" category of Allen's previous protégés, Barnes, Haney, Ulmer. But Allen had concluded that the der-ring-do of traditional espionage was no longer what CIA needed. Bissell was an iconoclast with a brilliant analytical mind, capable of discerning immediately the nature of the task to be accomplished and then the means for getting the job done, no matter how unfamiliar it was. The in-scrutable human factors were not particularly relevant, in his methodical way of thinking.

Allen gave Bissell broad authority in making the U-2 program effec-tive, asking few questions and reserving to himself only the final step of gaining Eisenhower's approval for each proposed flight. Even then he would often take Bissell with him to the White House to add expertise in the final briefings. Early in the program only three men in the White House, other than the president, even knew that something called a U-2 was flying.* The results of the intelligence collected were properly passed to a wider circle of policymakers and analysts, but the means by which the information was collected was not revealed, a standard practice in intelli-gence. Eisenhower was adamant on this point of secrecy, but it led his ad-ministration into an awkward and unnecessary political debate concern-ing the so-called missile gap of 1960.

Starting in 1956 an unlikely alliance had arisen between Democrats seeking a campaign issue and Pentagon stalwarts eager to inflate defense appropriations with worst-case scenarios of Soviet strategic capabilities. First it was a "bomber gap," a supposed Soviet advantage in bombing power, based in part on those deceptive ceremonial flybys over Red Square. When shrewder intelligence disproved the gap, critics turned to the scary next stage of strategic weaponry, the mighty new ICBM, on which Soviet research seemed clearly ahead of the American coun-terpart.

Thanks to the growing stash of U-2 photographs, Allen and the presi-dent had good reason to conclude that in spite of their admitted advan-tage in heavy rocket boosters, the Russians were nowhere near deploying an operational ICBM force that could threaten the United States. But more conventional intelligence sources, which were available to a wider number of strategic analysts, permitted predicting an alarming superior-ity for the Soviets by 1960. These predictions were discreetly passed to defense partisans in Congress.

On August 30, 1958, a year after the Russians' first ICBM test, the leading Democratic expert on strategic warfare, Senator Stuart Syming-

---

* They were Gordon Gray, the national security adviser; Andrew Goodpaster, Eisenhow-er's closest military aide; and John Eisenhower, his son, who worked as Goodpaster's deputy.

ton of Missouri, confronted Eisenhower directly on the apparent gap. Symington, a former secretary of the air force, challenged the president on the quality of the intelligence that was reaching the Oval Office; he expressed astonishment, for instance, "at the things Allen Dulles did not seem to know."[21] Eisenhower made a tactical error, putting Symington off with the patronizing jibe that the senator's informants deep within the Pentagon bureaucracy could not possibly know everything available to the president. Since he was flatly unwilling to let Symington in on his own superior sources, his reassurances about America's relative strength were unconvincing.

Eisenhower sent Allen up to Capitol Hill to brief all those concerned about Soviet strategic capabilities. From his years at disarmament talks in the 1930s, Allen could play the games of rearranging numbers as well as any of the latter-day strategic analysts. But in these briefings he could reveal no hint of the evidence collected by the U-2s, and since vague reassurances could not be backed up with hard data, the hawks remained skeptical. The alleged missile gap became an issue in both the 1958 and 1960 elections, with Democratic candidates accusing economy-minded Eisenhower Republicans of being soft on defense.

Eisenhower claimed in his memoirs that the U-2 "provided proof that the horrors of the alleged 'bomber gap' and the later 'missile gap' were nothing more than imaginative creations of irresponsibility." This was an overstatement. The U-2 did not "prove" a negative, that the Russians had no operational ICBMs; it was always possible that they had successfully camouflaged the missiles. The most that could be said was that as of January 1960, neither the U-2 nor any other American sensing device could confirm the fears arising from analytical speculation. In all its ingenious reconnaissance of railroad spurs in the Urals, the U-2 never spotted a single ICBM deployment. This was enough to give the president pause about the most alarming scenarios. But for those from whom this intelligence was withheld, it was not irresponsible to consider the hypothesis of the worst case.

— * —

Though most of the United States government, and all of the public, was in the dark about the U-2, the Russians knew about it from the start. Soviet air defense radar alerted Moscow to the first overflight in July 1956, and American electronic sensors detected the Soviet radar detecting the U-2. But the Soviet sighting was imprecise; reasonably enough, Moscow apparently could not believe that a dangerous penetration mission would be attempted on just a single engine. When Khrushchev ordered his ambassador in Washington to deliver a protest on July 10, he misdescribed both the plane and its mission, calling the intruder a U.S. Air Force two-engine bomber. The next day Foster drafted a quick reply, correctly asserting that no such military plane had violated Soviet airspace. The secretary of state read his draft over the telephone to the director of central intelligence, who replied, "Fine, perfect, good luck." Eisenhower then added a further flourish; standing orders "carefully exclude such overflights as the Soviet note alleges." As Allen later explained, "It was easy to deny what [Khrushchev] said because what he said was mostly wrong."[22] No deception or cover story had to be invoked — yet.

The U-2 was not a harmless, sanitary venture in intelligence collection. From the start Eisenhower was concerned over the terrible danger that overflights would be interpreted as prelude to a military attack. He insisted that the U-2 pilots fly as civilians. Should a pilot be captured, he was to identify himself as an employee of CIA, Allen explained, "to make it clear that he was not working for any branch of the armed services and that his mission was solely an intelligence mission" — not an aggressive act of war. In preparation for the U-2 flights Eisenhower ordered the Pentagon to halt the more clumsy penetrations of Soviet border areas by conventional aircraft, and he made the air force abandon the balloon reconnaissance missions the service had devised as a pallid alternative to the CIA's U-2.[23]

The inner circle privy to the U-2 program calculated that Khrushchev would face a dilemma in complaining about the flights even as he learned about them. Foster assured the president that even if a U-2 should be shot down, "I'm sure they will never admit it, . . . [that] we have been carrying on flights over their territory while they . . . had been helpless to do anything about the matter."[24]

As they commenced their bold plan to intrude upon Soviet airspace, Allen and Bissell gave the U-2 two or three years of effective operation before the Soviets devised countermeasures. But after some one hundred or more overflights and the anticipated three years passing without incident, they considered announcing the technological triumph to gain a propaganda benefit such as the CIA had enjoyed in the disclosure of the Berlin Tunnel. At home they could also lay to rest lingering suspicions of a missile gap. Foster joined in advocating announcement that "the United States has the capability of photographing the Soviet Union from a very high altitude without interference," to reassure Americans after the launching of *Sputnik* in October 1957.

Even without public disclosure, Allen argued, Moscow's knowledge of the U-2 flights removed some of the danger from the Cold War, making the Kremlin "far less cocky about its ability to deal with what we might bring against them." He defended the U-2 venture on theoretical grounds as well, within his philosophy of intelligence:

> I see no reason whatever to draw an unfavorable distinction between the collection of information by reconnaissance ... in the air, and espionage carried on by individuals who illegally operate directly within the territory of another state.
>
> In fact, the distinction, if one were drawn, would favor the former. The illegal espionage agents generally attempt to suborn and subvert the citizens of the country in which they operate. High-level reconnaissance in no way disturbs the life of the people, does not harm their property. They do not even notice it.[25]

Eisenhower was never persuaded by such sophistries; his record through the years of the U-2 is full of reservations about the political costs of intruding upon hostile airspace, no matter how far above the ground. How would Americans feel if Russian planes were overflying the United States at will? Less than five months after the first U-2 flight, for instance, he asked Allen if the overflights would "cost more than we gain in the form of solid intelligence." Repeatedly he challenged proposals for a new set of overflights with the question, "How much good will it do?" At small group meetings in the Oval Office, State Department representatives remarked, "If we lost a plane at this stage, it would be almost catastrophic."[26]

At one point in the autumn of 1958 Allen tried a little stratagem to test the president's support for CIA's prized technique of intelligence collection. He tentatively raised the old idea of transferring the U-2 program to the air force; given Eisenhower's injunction against sending military aircraft on overflights, such a move would surely end U-2 surveillance of the Soviet Union. To Allen's dismay the president did not shrink from an idea the CIA considered preposterous. Allen had to send Bissell back to the White House a few days later — better to leave personal confrontation to others — with a reasoned argument about why national security would be best served by keeping control and management of the U-2 within the small CIA circle where it had always been.[27]

The question facing the president, recorded John Eisenhower, was "whether the intelligence which we receive from this source is worth the exacerbation of international tension which results." After the NSC meeting of February 12, 1959, Eisenhower told the small group lingering behind that he wanted U-2 flights held to a minimum, for he considered them "undue provocation." A fortnight later he specifically ordered suspension of all U-2 flights "in the present abnormally tense circumstances." He was "concerned over the terrible propaganda impact that would be occasioned if a reconnaissance plane were to fail."*

Through all this record, Eisenhower showed persistent concern about his own stature, his reputation for integrity on the international scene and in history, established in the triumph of World War II. To his board of intelligence consultants, which was strongly supportive of the U-2, Eisenhower said, "This is one of the most 'soul-searching' questions to come before a president." He spoke of his "one tremendous asset, . . . [my] reputation for honesty. If one of these aircraft were lost when we are engaged in apparently sincere deliberations, it could be put on display in Moscow and ruin the president's effectiveness."[28]

The fact remains that every single overflight of the CIA's U-2 was conducted only upon Eisenhower's personal authority — if not down to the precise hour of takeoff, at least upon his authorization of the flight plan, the designated targets for photography, and the time period for conducting the mission. Allen confessed to a measure of annoyance at Eisenhower's caution. Proposed flights were stopped in times of tension, he later complained, "because they might increase tension; in times of sweetness and light, they should not be run because it would disturb any 'honeymoon' in our relations with the Soviet Union."[29]

Eisenhower's trump card in restraining Allen and Bissell in the later years of the U-2 was a further technological advance in 1958, providing the prospect of artificial satellites that could overfly the Soviet Union and all other quarters of the globe from orbit, at altitudes far higher than the single-engined black spy plane but with camera equipment that could provide even better definition. In February 1959 the president ordered U-2 flights "held to a minimum pending the availability of this new equipment." No satellites would be operational for eighteen months to two years, Eisenhower was told, but the U-2 had already given evidence that no danger was anticipated from Soviet ICBM deployment in that time period.

---

* There is something strange about all these forebodings as preserved in the presidential archives declassified in the 1980s. Revisionist historians have built from them a case for Eisenhower's wisdom and prescience, in light of the disaster about to befall his presidency. But these archives are heavily censored. The staff of the Eisenhower Library in Abilene, Kansas, removed a large portion of the documents before opening the relevant files, and those that remain contain heavy deletions. Eisenhower's reservations about the U-2 are there on the record, but there is no way yet of knowing whether the censored materials contain remarks less conducive to the image that the promoters of the Eisenhower legacy wish to perpetuate. Perhaps historical judgment on the sum total of Eisenhower's contribution to the U-2 program should be withheld, just like the missing documents.

In the politics of the Cold War as well as in the technology, reconnaissance satellites came to be quite distinct from high-flying aircraft—though the distinction had no place in Allen's concept of nonintrusive surveillance. The practical difference was that the Russians could launch satellites into orbit as well as the Americans. No one in the West yet knew how sophisticated the Soviet photographic analysis was, but orbital passes seemed less offensive to international law than winged aircraft—or at least that was how Khrushchev saw it. Since intelligence collection by satellites was a feat in which the Soviet Union could compete, Khrushchev told his Western adversaries that "anyone might take all the pictures he wished from satellites over Soviet territory."[30]

— * —

At the turn of 1960, as Eisenhower's presidency entered its final year, Allen's (and Bissell's) CIA was on the defensive on all fronts. The dismal failure of covert paramilitary action in Indonesia occasioned continuing criticism; the president's consultants on foreign intelligence activities persisted in their harsh judgments about Allen's leadership of the agency. Within closed circles the old idea was being revived of separating covert actions from intelligence collection, establishing a new and secret branch within the Pentagon for the former, leaving the CIA as a traditional collection and analysis agency. Allen had fought against such a separation when it was first proposed in the late 1940s, but the idea had remained alive.*

Among the major CIA programs the U-2 remained CIA's greatest asset. And even here were signs of fraying. In one of his last reports before his arrest, Lieutenant Colonel Popov, the CIA's most effective mole within the Soviet military establishment, reported that Soviet weaponry could intercept aircraft to altitudes of 60,000 feet, perilously close to the U-2's highest, supposedly safe altitude. Bissell, discussing this information with his rival, Helms, acknowledged that it could be serious for the future success of the program.

When the U-2 overflights began in 1956, Allen and Bissell had persuaded Eisenhower on a contingency plan in the event of failure, a cover story to be put out should one of the reconnaissance planes be intercepted and shot down. The U-2 could provide valuable data on conditions in the upper atmosphere for scientific study, alongside its primary purpose of detecting Soviet missile developments. Allen found it only natural, therefore, to invoke the cover of space research. It was the

* Vice President Nixon reportedly had decided that if he became president after Eisenhower, he would implement such a reform.

National Aeronautics and Space Administration (NASA) that provided
cover for the presence of U-2 planes at bases throughout the world. Hugh
Dryden, the key administrator at NASA, knew that the U-2 was not primarily a "weather plane," but he shared this information with only three
or four other people in his agency. "I think we regarded it as a responsibility to cooperate with another agency of government."[31] For nearly four
years there was no occasion to pull out the contingency cover story.

As the charges of a missile gap continued to fester, Eisenhower authorized Allen to dispatch the U-2 on a new series of flights early in April
1960 for a concerted probe into Soviet progress in ICBMs. The missile
testing ranges and potential launching sites in the Urals and central Asia
were prime targets for up-to-date photography. Eisenhower did not specify precise dates for these flights, nor did Allen request them in advance,
for even the most sophisticated technology of the day was crucially dependent on the weather.

Cloud cover, high-altitude winds, the possibility of conspicuous con-
densation trails, and the angle of the sun over the target areas (lest some
medieval watchtower be again mistaken for a missile silo) were key elements in the timing of U-2 reconnaissance. Furthermore, flights from
Pakistan to Norway covered two distinct weather areas, the southern lati-
tudes and those closer to the North Pole. It was fortuitous when good
forecasts came in from both weather areas simultaneously.

The overflight of April 5 brought new photographs of Tyura Tam, revealing construction of a new two-pad launch area complete with access
roads.[32] Eisenhower authorized a second flight within the next two weeks,
but for those fourteen days cloud cover prevented effective photography.
The president reluctantly agreed to a one-week extension, but set May 1
as an absolute deadline for any U-2 flights over the Soviet Union. A Four-
Power summit meeting was scheduled to open in Paris on May 16, and
Eisenhower wanted to take no chances of any incident that might complicate his meeting with Khrushchev.

Late Saturday afternoon, April 30, Allen was shown the latest weather
reports over the key areas of the Soviet Union. Around 5 P.M., acting under his authority from the president, he ordered the U-2 field base in
Adana, Turkey, to dispatch a flight from Peshawar, Pakistan, over the Soviet Union the next day.

In the aftermath a myth developed about some special reason for
sending an overflight on May 1, the Soviet national holiday. For weeks
past rumors had circulated that the Kremlin would attempt a spectacular
display on that day, perhaps the launching of a new space probe. The U-2
flight plan would carry the American cameras directly over Tyura Tam to
reexamine that two-pad launch site. Hanson Baldwin of *The New York*

Times later reasoned that the CIA had been attempting to photograph a Soviet space launch as it actually occurred. Since Baldwin was one of the best-informed military analysts (and also an old friend of Allen's from their Council on Foreign Relations study groups), his speculation was taken seriously on Capitol Hill. Allen acknowledged that Baldwin "has pretty good contacts, . . . he is a pretty able reporter — and he is a pretty good guesser, too." But the denial that the May 1 flight had such a dramatic purpose never caught up with the titillating speculation, and fully two years later Allen's successor at CIA, John A. McCone, and general counsel Lawrence Houston had to deny once again that the U-2 had that kind of special mission.[33]

With his order given, Allen took off for New York, where he was to be the honored guest at a Sunday breakfast at the Waldorf Astoria, to accept the New York Police Department's Golden Rule Award for "distinguished government service and dedication to Christian ideals." As he was being feted, the CIA base at Bodø, Norway, notified Washington that the expected U-2 flight was overdue. Electronic intercepts of Soviet military communications detected clear efforts to thwart an intruding aircraft. "Our boy isn't there," CIA watch officers reported as the day wore on. "We don't know what has happened to him."

For the first time the officers responsible for the U-2 operation pulled out the four-year-old cover plan. Bissell and CIA aides met with State Department officers to prepare a bland statement, to be issued from the U-2 base at Adana, that a NASA high-altitude weather plane was missing. Goodpaster showed the cover story to the president, who handed it back to his aide in wordless approval.[34] Early Monday morning the Adana air base commandant announced that an American research plane "engaged in upper air studies" was missing, believed downed after incurring oxygen problems, and a search was under way in remote regions to the east.

That first announcement of a U-2 aircraft missing in Turkey attracted little press attention. As the hours passed without any word of the plane, the handful of officials in Washington who understood the problem grew more nervous. Monday morning Goodpaster walked into the Oval Office, his face like "an etching of bad news," as Eisenhower described him. "Mr. President, I have received word from the CIA that the U-2 reconnaissance plane I mentioned yesterday is still missing. . . . With the amount of fuel he has on board, there is not a chance of his being aloft." Over at CIA Bissell assured Allen, on his return from New York, that it was "impossible" for the U-2 pilot to have survived a crash.

The next two days passed uneasily, with no information whatever about the fate of the spy plane or its pilot. On Wednesday CIA and State

Department officials prepared a few pages of "talking points" for NASA spokesmen to use if further questions arose about the missing aircraft.*

In official business no less than private life, there are days when nothing seems to go right. Thursday, May 5, 1960, was such a day. Shortly after 7 A.M. top officials of the National Security Council were ordered to proceed immediately to special helicopter pads around Washington for sudden evacuation to a secret NSC underground shelter at High Point, North Carolina. The order had nothing to do with the missing U-2; it was simply a test of civil defense procedures, a "fire drill" to see how quickly and efficiently the highest officers of the government, the president included, could be transported to a secure site in the event of a nuclear crisis, without any advance notice.

Not in the meanest of neighborhood schools or city office blocks has a fire drill come off in such shambles. Eisenhower himself was transported to the secret site without incident and, as it happened, Allen fared better than some of his NSC colleagues: his official Cadillac was already waiting at 2723 Q Street to take him to his office. But on this day of all days the government car broke down. The president's science adviser, George B. Kistiakowsky, who lived nearby, found the director of central intelligence and his driver peering incredulously under the hood of the car; Kistiakowsky offered Allen a lift.[35] The limousine of the secretary of defense, Thomas Gates, had not yet arrived to pick him up; Gates's wife had to drive, in her nightgown, to the designated point, where her husband found he had forgotten to bring his ID card permitting access. The chairman of the Joint Chiefs of Staff, General Nathan Twining, whose presence in a strategic emergency would presumably be of some importance, never got to the evacuation point at all.

After this inauspicious beginning, the NSC meeting at High Point was an anticlimax. Allen's routine briefing mentioned problems expected in the Belgian Congo, which was soon to be granted independence; an "irresponsible" African leader named Patrice Lumumba was making trouble, "supported by the Belgian communists." And, Allen went on, "there is some possibility that a movement might develop in the rich Katanga area for separation from the Congo and union with Rhodesia." All such problems were for the future. Allen then touched briefly on a

---

* "Talking points" are a revered bureaucratic device, in style falling somewhat short of a speech or formal statement. In tightly worded single sentences, talking points codify specific and often sensitive phrases in a form that an official or spokesman can use in responding to questions, seemingly off the cuff, without straying from a policy line determined in advance.

speech that Khrushchev was at that moment delivering in the Kremlin; he had only teletype reports of the opening passages, which he said seemed tough.

The subject of the missing U-2 was not even raised at the High Point meeting — few of the twenty-two NSC members and advisers had any reason to suspect a problem. But Allen and a small group of others stayed behind with the president. The question, to which there was yet no answer, was what Khrushchev and the top Soviet leadership actually knew about the incident. "We didn't know exactly where we stood," Gates later testified. In such uncertainty the inner circle simply agreed to let stand the cover story of a weather research aircraft, to keep the CIA and certainly the president out of the news. "We were still living under conditions where the cover story was the story," the secretary of defense said.

As reports of Khrushchev's speech continued coming in, the Eisenhower administration learned that what they had feared was true. The Soviet leader confirmed that an intruding American plane had been shot down; he accused "American aggressive circles" of trying to sabotage the forthcoming Paris summit meeting, scheduled to begin just ten days later.

When the acting secretary of state, Douglas Dillon, returned from High Point, he joined a meeting of working-level officials to design a response to Khrushchev's charges. Clearly the cover story needed some refinement. Dillon called Allen and Goodpaster for help in preparing a new story for public release. "We were talking back and forth, trying to draft a statement as to what we were going to say about this damn thing," Dillon told historian Michael Beschloss. "We were having a helluva time."

Shortly after noon on May 5 the State Department issued the modified cover story in response to Khrushchev's allegations, continuing the line of "weather research" on behalf of NASA but adding a spurious, if tentative, concession to the reality. "It is entirely possible that, having a failure in the oxygen equipment which could result in the pilot losing consciousness, the plane continued on automatic pilot for a considerable distance and accidentally violated Soviet airspace." Allen was not alone in knowing how "accidental" the intrusion actually was, and that a "considerable distance" really meant more than a thousand miles.

The space explorers at NASA were not as devious in dealing with the subtleties of deception, espionage, and high diplomacy. The talking points prepared by CIA and State the day before, when the old cover story was still the story, were issued as an official statement: high-altitude weather research; a flight plan only over Turkey; cameras not for intrusive reconnaissance but only to measure atmospheric conditions. "This statement was absolutely crazy," Dillon said later, for he and Allen now knew the Russians had enough evidence to disprove it in detail. As a rueful Dryden put it, the men of NASA were like "a piano player who didn't know what was going on upstairs."[36]

The damage to official credibility did not stop with NASA. On the same dismal day of May 5 the State Department gave two "background" briefings to select correspondents, providing further information to be attributed to "informed sources," without the authority of an official statement. Lincoln White, the trusted State Department spokesman, assured his correspondent friends that there was "absolutely no deliberate attempt to violate Soviet air space and there has never been." White didn't know what was going on upstairs either; he naively assumed that the talking points, prepared by his most responsible seniors, had some basis in fact.

When he was later thrown on the defensive, Allen insisted that even after Khrushchev's speech there was no reason to depart from the original cover story as refined by the circumstances then known. "We still did not know whether the plane or any recognizable part of it, or the pilot, were in Soviet hands or whether the pilot was dead or alive. Furthermore, we did not know whether Khrushchev desired to blow up the incident, as he later did, or put it under the rug and spare his people the knowledge that we had been overflying them."[37]

Angry congressmen began denouncing Khrushchev for shooting down an American plane, which made Allen and Bissell nervous, for once the full truth came out — and they were beginning to suspect that it would — the congressmen would turn their anger on their own government for misleading them. They urged Eisenhower to take at least the congressional leaders into confidence, if only to muffle statements that might later prove embarrassing. Eisenhower flatly refused, on grounds that "these congressional fellows will inevitably spill the beans."[38]

Following his speech Khrushchev distributed photographs purporting to be the wreckage of the U-2. American experts were relieved to discover that the pictures showed only a miscellaneous pile of junk, pieces of an old Soviet fighter plane.

There remained the matter of the pilot's fate. A quick review of the records revealed him to be one Francis Gary Powers, a thirty-year-old air force veteran who had resigned his commission to fly as a civilian for CIA. Allen and Bissell had never met Powers; he was simply one of the skilled test pilots, and in fact was one of two airmen on duty when the order for the May 1 flight came through. His military record and reliability were exemplary. In reviewing his credentials for a subsequent congressional inquiry, Allen invertently revealed a note of defensiveness about the eastern European émigrés the CIA had long employed for intelligence missions. Powers, Allen emphasized, was a fourth-generation American.

Allen had repeatedly assured Eisenhower that if the Soviets ever downed a U-2, the pilot could not escape alive from a crash. This was "a complete given, a complete assumption as far as we were concerned," said John Eisenhower. "There was not one scintilla of doubt in our minds that [Powers] was dead."*

At an Ethiopian Embassy reception in Moscow that evening (still the miserable May 5), American ambassador Llewellyn Thompson picked up a most unexpected item of diplomatic gossip. Casually eavesdropping on a conversation between the Swedish ambassador and the Soviet deputy foreign minister, Jacob Malik, Thompson heard the words "we are still questioning the pilot." An urgent message to Washington sent the creators of the cover story reeling. Allen was called to the telephone in the middle of a black-tie dinner at Washington's Alibi Club (an appropriately named location) with news that ruined the rest of his mellow evening. To the CIA aide sitting next to him when he returned, ashen-faced and shaken, he muttered, "The pilot's alive."

Khrushchev confirmed the government's worst fears the next day, as he gave, with relish, yet another speech to his Supreme Soviet. He admitted that he had been twitting the American warmongers; he had not told the whole truth in his first speech two days before. "I deliberately refrained from mentioning that we have the remnants of the plane — and we also have the pilot, who is quite alive and kicking! We did this quite deliberately, because if we had given out the whole story, the Americans would have thought up still another fable." He mocked the cover story, the flight over Turkey, the automatic pilot, the mission of weather research. "The whole world knows that Allen Dulles is no great weatherman!" Khrushchev exclaimed to wild Kremlin applause.

In Switzerland Mary Bancroft had marveled at her lover's ability to justify his work in espionage within a strict moral code. Perhaps unsavory deeds were necessary toward a "higher good," reasons of state taking precedence over individual morality. Allen certainly accepted the notion, attributed to his German colleague Reinhard Gehlen, that "gentlemen" are entitled to transgress upon the moral codes of civilized mankind. Whatever such gentlemen think to themselves, they invariably employ euphemisms in referring to activities that would not stand up to scrutiny. With Khrushchev's latest disclosure, in Allen's phrase, "the cover story was outflanked."[39] "No longer suitable" was the State Department's locution in a confidential memo to Secretary Herter. Less worldly folks, per-

* The president's son distrusted Allen from that moment onward. "Allen Dulles lied to Dad," he told Beschloss years later. Whether or not a considered judgment about a future eventuality can properly be considered a "lie," the anger against Allen was enduring.

ceiving reality as it was, saw that the United States government had lied and been caught at it.

Saturday morning, May 7, Allen convened the U-2 working circle in his office — Bissell, Herter's men from State, and Goodpaster from the White House. The immediate business was a new statement to be issued to the public. Their draft displays, at its most crafty, Allen's accomplished (if cumbersome) style of the precise half-truth, misleadingly arranged to deceive. "Insofar as the authorities in Washington are concerned, there was no authorization for a flight of the kind described by Mr. Khrushchev. . . . It would appear either that Mr. Khrushchev is exaggerating what actually happened with regard to this U-2 plane for his own purposes, or that somehow standing instructions to avoid incursions over Soviet territory were, in this instance, not observed."[40] Individual elements of this statement were not actually false, though they were obviously deceptive. The flight was not intended as an aggressive military act, as Khrushchev had described it. "Standing instructions" might indeed forbid incursions upon Soviet airspace, but it is a commonplace of the Great Game of intelligence that standing instructions exist to be over-ridden.

With the new cover statement completed, Allen raised the possibility of a more fundamental step. To help President Eisenhower escape the odium of a public lie, he offered to resign as director of central intelligence. This assumption of personal responsibility was in the British tradition that Allen so respected; it also responded to the political imperatives of statesmen accountable to the public and before history. In the U-2 case, however, Allen's resignation would simply have set up a new cover story, compounding the lie. For though Allen's CIA was indeed the perpetrator of both the U-2 operation and its cover-up, President Eisenhower himself had been knowledgeable and engaged at virtually every step along the way. The high officers of state responsible for maintaining American national security, through war scares and missile gaps, had been the knowing and willing beneficiaries of everything the U-2 program had provided. When Allen presented his sacrificial offer, Goodpaster reportedly interrupted, "That's the last thing the president would want." Without pausing to consult his boss, he said, "The president isn't in the business of using scapegoats."

John Eisenhower and Douglas Dillon were among those who later believed that Allen should have been allowed to resign. "We would have thought he was a greater hero," Dillon told Beschloss long afterward, "and a lot of people would have known underneath that he was just taking the rap for somebody higher and would have admired him for it." Allen maintained a sense of personal detachment, remarking when it was all over that his resignation "was rejected because of the many elements making it highly incredible over the long run."[41]

The draft statement prepared that morning went over to Secretary of State Herter, just returned from his official travels. Herter called Allen to discuss whether there might be some further way "to get the president off the hook." Allen patiently explained to his old friend, continuing in the art of euphemism, "There is an inconsistency." Allen offered to do whatever he could to help, but for the crisis at hand it was a little late in the day.

The statement finally issued on May 7 reflected Eisenhower's willingness to assume at least general responsibility. Contrary to all previous statements, now "outflanked," the U-2 flight of May 1 was acknowledged under "a very broad directive from the president given at the earliest point of his administration to protect us from surprise attack." Goodpaster argued that this might at least give Khrushchev "a certain degree of satisfaction." Eisenhower said it was "worth a try." But the artful last sentence of Allen's draft was hardened, against his will. "It appears that in endeavoring to obtain information now concealed behind the Iron Curtain, a flight over Soviet territory was probably taken by an unarmed civilian U-2 plane." This statement, of course, amounted to nothing less than a government's admission of a deliberate act of espionage, and Allen was offended by a breach in the rules of the Great Game.

Defense Secretary Gates called Herter Sunday morning, May 8, to complain that the new story opened his military establishment to charges of irresponsible initiatives down the line of command, which was clearly not the case. "We should say that it is a matter of national policy and we have been doing it because everything else has failed," Gates said. "Somebody has to take responsibility for the policy and while the president can say he didn't know about this one flight, he did approve the policy." Herter replied simply that "we have been trying to keep the president clear on this."

Monday morning, May 9, Allen and Herter went up to Capitol Hill to brief the eighteen-man leadership group of Congress on the real situation. Eisenhower had finally authorized the briefing, but Allen had insisted that he must show a few of the U-2 photographs, since no one outside the inner circle had the slightest notion of what this black spy plane could accomplish. If he could not show the pictures, Allen argued to Goodpaster early that morning, he would "rather not do it at all." It would be "disastrous, . . . accomplish nothing," he said. Eisenhower reluctantly authorized the display, in a classified setting, of no more than three U-2 photographs.

Reporters accosted the director of central intelligence as he entered the hearing room. "Any statement?" they asked. "About the usual," Allen replied, and everyone laughed. Herter opened the secret briefing with an explanation of the diplomatic problems. Then Allen took the stand; he introduced Arthur Lundahl, his "best man" in photoanalysis, to the legislators assembled behind tightly guarded doors. "You've got to be good," Lundahl remembered Allen whispering as he stood up with his three photographs and briefing boards.

Lundahl was good. The disclosure, at long last, of what the CIA had learned about Soviet military and ICBM capabilities came as a stunning surprise. Senators and congressmen of both parties listened in astonished silence, then, at the conclusion of the briefing, rose to their feet in spontaneous applause. Allen had been chewing on his pipe as he also listened to Lundahl, and in his surprise at the standing ovation he dropped the burning pipe onto his lap. Those next to him had to help the director bat out the embers scattered across his tweed suit.[42]

"We will now just have to endure the storm," Eisenhower told his aides. On May 9 Secretary of State Herter issued the fourth statement in five days on the U-2. At last the president's personal responsibility for the mission of the spy plane was clearly stated, without verbal artifice.

> The President has put into effect . . . directives to gather by every possible means the information required to protect . . . against surprise attack. . . .
>
> Programs have been developed and put into operation which have included extensive aerial surveillance by unarmed civilian aircraft, normally of a peripheral character but on occasion by penetration. . . . The fact that such surveillance was taking place has apparently not been a secret to the Soviet leadership, and the question indeed arises as to why at this particular juncture they should seek to exploit the present incident as a propaganda battle in the Cold War.

Khrushchev maintained the public pressure with a series of angry denunciations of American warmongers. Eisenhower held his own news conference on May 11. He offered no apology, expressed no regret for the U-2 overflights. For Khrushchev to carp on the "flight of an unarmed nonmilitary plane can only reflect a fetish of secrecy," Eisenhower said. The nature of the closed Soviet system makes spying "a distasteful but vital necessity." But to say that the single aircraft amounted to a provocation to war, "this is just — it's absolutely ridiculous, and they know it is."

Eisenhower had a big stake in the forthcoming summit meeting. After years of feints and false starts, the leaders of the United States and the Soviet Union, Harold Macmillan of Britain, and Charles De Gaulle of France were about to gather to ratify the sense of détente, the so-called spirit of Camp David that had been achieved with Khrushchev during his visit to the United States the year before. And the Paris summit was to be followed by a triumphant visit of the American president to Moscow and the Soviet Union. It was Eisenhower's final chance to leave office on a record of a major understanding with the Cold War adversary, his goal ever since those first frustrated sessions with his speechwriters after the death of Stalin.

The question now was whether Khrushchev would compound his public outrage with a bold move to scuttle the summit and cancel Eisenhower's trip. For intelligence men it was the old question of attempting to perceive the adversary's intentions. Sometimes a trivial tidbit of intelligence can provide a vital clue. The CIA learned that the forthcoming issue of the glossy Soviet propaganda organ, USSR, had been pulled back from the press as early as May 6; it would have contained a glowing article about the welcome to be accorded Eisenhower on his Moscow visit. As Allen later explained, this was the first clue to a Soviet intention to wreck the summit. But that same day the Soviet ambassador to Paris had assured De Gaulle that the summit would go on.[43]

Nonetheless the analytical side of the agency, well outside the loop of the U-2 program and other clandestine operations, struggled to put the best possible face on the situation. A special Current Intelligence Memorandum for Eisenhower's attention the day before he left for Paris stated: "We do not believe Khrushchev will seek to exploit the U-2 incident in Paris to a point that might endanger his higher priority goals of obtaining some satisfaction on Berlin, disarmament, and a nuclear test ban. We would expect him to state his case in relatively moderate terms for the record and then stress the need to restore the 'Camp David spirit' in international relations."[44]

On the flight to Paris John Eisenhower went to his father's cabin in fury at the beating of the last seven days. He put the blame squarely on Allen. "You ought to fire him!" John Eisenhower told his father. The president replied in equal fury to his son, "I am not going to shift the blame to my underling!"

Allen might have loved the prospect of sitting in at the Paris summit, no matter how awkward the circumstances, but that was not protocol; the spymaster may have become a public figure, but he did not belong in a ceremonial presidential delegation. To keep the CIA inconspicuously informed of the developments in Paris, Allen sent the head of his National Estimates staff, Sherman Kent, the crusty Yale historian whose incisive analyses and caustic wit had brought him into Allen's circle of personal intimates (though not, of course, into the classified realm of clandestine operations).

The chaos of the abortive Paris summit of May 1960 gave Kent little opportunity for trenchant analysis but ample room for his sense of the absurd. Eisenhower, Macmillan, and De Gaulle, mighty statesmen accustomed to elegance in protocol, were left staring into space as Khrushchev threw tantrums and stormed out of the conference room at the preparatory meeting. Kent delighted in regaling Allen with his accounts of how the statesmen spent their subsequent unscheduled days in Paris.

It emerged that Marshal Rodion Malinovsky, Khrushchev's dour defense minister, knew the French capital better than any other Russian in the delegation. As a young officer in World War I he had actually lived in a village on the Marne, part of an Imperial Russian contingent allied with Britain and France against the kaiser. Malinovsky remembered "young Marie Louise," the French lover of his Russian roommate. Khrushchev was delighted to learn of this long-forgotten peccadillo and welcomed the pretext to view the French countryside while his Western counterparts struggled with the diplomatic tatters of his walkout. A linden tree had fallen across the road leading to the village of Malinovsky's memory; the Soviet leader jumped out of his limousine, grabbed an axe, and helped workers clear the road. Marie Louise still lived in the village and vaguely remembered the young Russian soldier.

Kent's next dispatch informed Allen of Eisenhower's reaction to days of enforced leisure in Paris while the staff tried to reassemble the summit. To fill the time Ike proposed a cookout at the American Embassy. Ambassador Amory Houghton and his wife had some difficulty locating the necessary grills and barbecue paraphernalia, but on Wednesday evening, May 18, the president of the United States stood in the gardens behind the Rue St.-Honoré in white apron, broiling steaks for a bemused gathering of American officials who had nothing else to do. Kent's reports of the Paris non-summit served Allen well for the after-dinner stories of his retirement.

The KGB wasted no time in pressing its advantage within Khrushchev's Kremlin. On June 7, Soviet intelligence informed the Central Committee it planned "to make use of this newly complex situation and to carry out . . . measures targeted at further discrediting CIA activity and compromising its leader, Allen Dulles." In retrospect, three decades later, George Kennan observed that the downing of the U-2 put an end to Khrushchev's hopes for a relaxation of international and Soviet internal tensions. "The episode humiliated Khrushchev and discredited his relatively moderate policies," Kennan wrote. "It forced him to fall back, for the defense of his own political position, on a more strongly belligerent anti-American tone of public utterance."[45]

Meeting with his National Security Council in the aftermath of the Paris trip, Eisenhower bristled at the suggestion that the United States had lost its leadership role in world affairs. He ordered associates never to draw such a conclusion again. Allen's old rivals in the air force could not contain their smugness at the fate of the U-2. "We might have got caught," remarked General Twining, "but we wouldn't have got caught that way, a disgraceful way."[46] In retirement, reminiscing endlessly about the disaster, Allen remarked only that "if one stops gathering intelligence because some day something should be a little out of place, you wouldn't be doing anything!" Bissell attempted to keep his U-2 in readiness for situations less threatening than Soviet airspace, but in August 1960 the United States succeeded in placing a photoreconnaissance satellite into orbit, and technology brought to an end the era of the black spy plane.

Allen and Francis Gary Powers were to meet for the first and only time in 1962. By then they were both symbolic figures of the Cold War, relegated by different circumstances to retirement; Powers had been freed from Soviet captivity in exchange for Soviet spy Rudolph Abel; Allen had been retired by President Kennedy after the massive CIA failure at Cuba's Bay of Pigs.

From the first signals of May 1, 1960, questions were raised about Powers. Was he a double agent hired by Moscow to deliver a U-2 intact? The evidence in American security files argued against such a suspicion, but it prodded Allen into defending Powers as a "fourth-generation American." Then it was suggested that when the pilot found himself in trouble, he should have taken his own life rather than provide living evidence of American perfidy. Allen always denied issuing any order for self-destruction. But the kit of the U-2 pilots contained a suicide pill, with instructions for its use should any situation become unbearable. "We said, here, you have this," Allen explained long afterward. "If you get into a situation where you think death is better than what awaits you, use it."[47] C. L. Sulzberger, the statesmanlike columnist of *The New York Times*, who had unparalleled access to persons of prominence over decades, but who also had a way of imposing his own views upon what he heard, remarked after a conversation with Allen, "Dulles left me with the impression that Powers should somehow have knocked himself off. He said Powers had been brainwashed. . . . I gather Dulles is unhappy with Powers' behavior, but doesn't like to say so."

The two men finally met face to face after Powers had completed his debriefings upon his release into American hands and Allen was packing up his office files, heading for private life. The retired director summoned up the jauntiness of a lifetime to tell Powers he had "heard quite a bit" about him. Powers recorded his own confusion about meeting the legendary spymaster. He quoted Allen as saying, "We are proud of what you have done."

— 18 —

FADING FAST

ALLEN SOUGHT EVERY PRETEXT for vacation weekends in Palm Beach, to stop over at the welcoming "cottage" of Charlie and Jane Wrightsman. Newly acquired paintings by Renoir and Vermeer adorned the entrance hall; off the drawing room was displayed a collection of porcelain birds. Allen never tired of the company of his rich friends, and whenever the nagging gout did not interfere too painfully, he enjoyed the availability of a ready tennis pro. It also became routine to visit the nearby villa of retired Ambassador Joseph Kennedy and any members of his engaging family who happened to be around.

On one such call late in 1957 Jacqueline Kennedy handed Allen a new novel she had just finished, with a coy admonition: "Here is a book *you* should have, Mr. Director." It was *From Russia with Love* by Ian Fleming, Allen's first introduction to the outrageous master spy James Bond. Nurtured on *Kim* and *Ashenden*, Allen could only be intrigued by a more timely image in spy fiction and by the twisting plot in the sleaziness of Istanbul, so familiar from his early years in diplomacy.* As each new James Bond adventure appeared, Allen savored the series, often sending copies over to Jacqueline Kennedy's husband with his own arch comments. Allen and the future president found endless fascination in the insatiable man of romance and intrigue — a personage, needless to say, unlike anyone Allen had ever known in the real-life business of intelligence. "The modern spy could not permit himself to become the target of luscious dames who approach him in bars or come out of closets in hotel rooms. Good spies are too valuable, their training is too long and costly, and they are

---

* Allen remembered the Pera Palace Hotel, where many of James Bond's doings occur, as "infamous mainly for its bedbugs, rather than its blondes."

too hard to find to warrant undue exposure. I fear that James Bond in real life would have had a thick dossier in the Kremlin after his first exploit, and would not have survived the second."[1]

Allen and Fleming did not meet until some years later.* Both men had apparently forgotten — if they ever knew about it — an earlier, impersonal tangent in the lives of Allen Dulles and the creator of James Bond, whose background was more profound than that of the run-of-the-mill pulp novelist. Had they remembered, it would have made too good an after-dinner story to pass up.

Navy Commander Ian Fleming of British intelligence was the man unwittingly responsible two decades earlier for arranging Allen's entry into the profession of espionage. In June 1941 he was one of the British experts advising William Donovan on the requirements for setting up the government agency that became the OSS. It was Fleming who defined that a man of "absolute discretion, sobriety, devotion to duty, languages and wide experience" was needed to manage intelligence collection from a New York office — the post that Donovan offered Allen, starting him on his career in professional intelligence.[2] Allen apparently never knew how his name first came up for the OSS job, and Fleming, moving on to other assignments, never followed up to inquire what had happened to his recommendation.

Allen's mind seldom drifted far from the Great Game. Palm Beach was a place to take his ease but also to focus on a situation just ninety miles away. Cuba posed an ominous problem to American policy in the Cold War, so close to the continental United States yet rattled by a revolutionary movement springing from the remote mountains of the Sierra Maestra, led by the charismatic Fidel Castro. "Communists and other extreme radicals appear to have penetrated the Castro movement," Allen informed the National Security Council in December 1958, a week before the corrupt and wasted dictator Fulgencio Batista fled Havana and left the way open for Castro's triumphal entry into the capital.

The CIA's agents in the field had upset the more conservative diplomatic establishment with warnings of Castro's mass appeal among the oppressed Cuban populace. In reporting to a closed hearing of the Senate Foreign Relations Committee the month of Batista's downfall, Allen was cautious. Castro himself did not seem to have communist leanings, Allen said, nor was he at that time known to be "working for the communists."

* A luncheon was arranged by the CIA London station chief, Archibald Roosevelt. To keep the conversation going, Roosevelt tactlessly remarked that he found the American dialect of the CIA men in the 007 books "absolutely terrible." Fleming replied, a little defensively, "I can't see why. I had it reviewed by an American friend who's been a professor at Oxford for twenty years."

Indeed, the revolutionary leader "apparently has very wide popular backing throughout the island." A State Department analysis concurred. "The communists are utilizing the Castro movement to some extent, as would be expected, but there is insufficient evidence on which to base a charge that the rebels are communist-dominated."[3]

The CIA's Western Hemisphere division was still tightly controlled by J. C. King, whom Allen had relegated to the sidelines during Operation Success in Guatemala five years before in favor of the new blood of his own protégés. But a sad fact of twentieth-century Washington — CIA included — was that high-level interest in Latin America was seldom sustained. The old regional hands had the patience to survive and reassert their influence once the top policymakers' attention turned elsewhere. King's division inherited the colonial outlook of the old FBI networks in Central and South America; their contacts and values were with the conservative traditional elites. "The glamour of the Sierra Maestra and the straggly beards is rapidly wearing off as the realities of the situation daily become more apparent," advised a Current Intelligence Report on February 4, 1959, one month after the Castro takeover. The report warned even that "the Hilton and perhaps other luxury hotels may be forced to close."[4]

Eisenhower led the NSC on March 10 in considering the varying assessments of the Castro phenomenon, triggered in part by the imminent visit of the new Cuban leader to Washington. In the course of a meandering discussion, the NSC raised the prospect of "bring[ing] another government to power in Cuba," but it was all hypothetical, and no decision was reached.

As Castro tightened his hold on Cuban society through 1959, Allen clung to his cautious line that "the Castro regime could not be described as communist-dominated," but he warned repeatedly that communist influence within the Cuban labor unions, armed forces, and such "have a potential for even greater penetration in the future."[5]

Allen felt he could best concentrate on such developments at Palm Beach. "Here I am sunning by the pool, playing tennis, swimming in the sea — doing just nothing but a bit of thinking," Allen wrote his daughter. He took Clover with him that Christmas of 1959; she may not have liked the *nouveaux* Wrightsmans, but her husband had also planned a few days in the Bahamas just for the two of them. Clover could read, Allen could think about the challenge of Castro.

J. C. King was raising the alarm of a "far left" dictatorship in Cuba, which if permitted to stand would threaten United States holdings in other Latin American countries. Clearly something more than Easter eggs for his station chief's children would be required of the director of central intelligence. King proposed a broad program of sabotage, assassination, and paramilitary subversion to "eliminate" the Castro regime. The example of Operation Success, the relatively painless "elimination" of the Arbenz regime in Guatemala five years before, stood as a reminder of happier days in Allen's CIA stewardship, when covert actions could be accomplished by, as he saw it, a merry band of like-minded clandestine warriors, without all the nuisance of the Pentagon, the Joint Chiefs of Staff, the bureaucratic maneuvers and compromises that had made the disastrous Indonesian operation of 1958, for instance, so unwieldy.

Upon his return to Washington Allen specifically rejected the most extreme tactic implied in King's proposal, the assassination of Fidel. At the January 13, 1960, meeting of the 5412 Committee, the watchdog group that Eisenhower had established to keep his CIA operatives under policy control, Allen emphasized that the "quick elimination of Castro" was not CIA's intent, "but rather actions designed to enable responsible opposition leaders to get a foothold." He was no longer ambivalent about the motives of the Cuban revolution, advising the committee that "over the long run the U.S. will not be able to tolerate the Castro regime in Cuba." So, he concluded, "covert contingency planning to accomplish the fall of the Castro government might be in order."[6]

For such planning the entrenched CIA networks were not viable. "We've got to start working with the Left," Allen told his closest associates. King's agents knew every military strongman, actual and potential, in the hemisphere, but younger social democrats and reformers who might be useful were still documented in King's files as "subversives." To circumvent the existing operational lines of authority, Allen established a special Cuban task force led by Bissell, his dynamic deputy for the clandestine services, and Tracy Barnes, veteran of Guatemala and countless previous covert operations. King was admitted to the group as a matter of bureaucratic necessity, but he saw himself once again upstaged by Ivy League newcomers moving into the Latin American scene, with their academic models of group behavior in an area that, as far as he was concerned, knew no such nuances. "Unless Fidel and Raul Castro and Che Guevara could be eliminated in one package — which is highly unlikely — this operation can be a long, drawn-out affair and the present government will only be overthrown by the use of force," he informed the new task force.[7]

Allen tried to interest Eisenhower in modest measures of sabotage. He brought in some of Bissell's U-2 photographs of Cuban sugar refineries, suggesting that a few saboteurs could put them out of operation. The president, no stranger to sabotage operations in his own military career, noted that any damage could be quickly repaired; he sent his director of central intelligence back to come up with a more serious program.

Who should arrive in Washington at this juncture but Ian Fleming, riding the crest of his publicists' wave for the latest James Bond thriller. A casual Sunday dinner on March 13 at John and Jacqueline Kennedy's Georgetown house numbered among the guests columnist Joseph Alsop, the painter William Walton, John Bross of CIA, and Fleming. Under Alsop's prodding the creator of James Bond held forth after dinner about how "007" would handle the problem of Fidel Castro. Fleming's imagination soared; Bond would print up handbills warning that radioactivity from American nuclear tests reacted with facial hair to render men with beards impotent at the essential moment of romance. Cubans to a man, including Fidel himself, would promptly shave off their beards, and that, for James Bond, would be the end of the Cuban revolution.[8]

When Bross related the story to the director's staff meeting Monday morning, he was puzzled that Allen's amusement was not as hearty as he had anticipated. Unbeknownst to Bross, the CIA that very day was to present a program of action against Castro, including measures uncomfortably similar to those in the impromptu 007 fantasy. Eisenhower had made clear his scorn for the gimmicks that delighted the little-boy mentality of the clandestine services, so Bissell rephrased the various subversive ploys into a formidable "Program of Covert Action Against the Castro Regime" for approval by the 5412 Committee.

The president did not like to discuss covert intelligence operations with the full National Security Council, so after receiving the watchdog committee's recommendation, he convened a special meeting three days later, on March 17, of thirteen top advisers, including Vice President Nixon, Secretary of State Herter, Admiral Arleigh Burke of the Joint Chiefs of Staff, Treasury Secretary Robert Anderson, and John Eisenhower of the NSC staff.

Allen led off the briefing, but when Eisenhower started boring in with questions about the details of a comprehensive action program, he turned the meeting over to Bissell. The first step was to be the formation of a moderate Cuban opposition group in exile that would agitate under the slogan "Restore the Revolution," which, the Cuban émigrés would argue, Castro had betrayed. Allen predicted that this political action phase could be accomplished in about one month.

Next would come broadcasts from a medium-wave radio station of deceptive or "black" propaganda designed to provoke unrest within Cuba. At the same time CIA agents would mobilize networks of agents inside the country, Cubans who would be "responsive to the orders and directions of the exile opposition." This phase would come into play by month two. In the meantime CIA would start organizing and training paramilitary contingents at bases outside Cuba "for future guerrilla action." Allen warned that this aspect of the program might take as much as eight months, meaning that the proposed CIA overthrow of Castro might not occur until after the presidential election in November, a point of importance for Nixon, the likely Republican candidate, as the months wore on. Nixon hoped for a major foreign policy triumph before the election.

According to the available record, nothing was said to the president at this stage about any assassinations, though the idea had been raised at the earlier 5412 Committee meeting without decision.* Hearing Allen's and Bissell's briefing, Eisenhower emphasized his understanding that the CIA covert action program was aimed "to undermine Castro's position and prestige.... The president said that he knows of no better plan for dealing with this situation." But, he went on, according to the official minutes, "our hand should not show in anything that is done.... The great problem is leakage and breach of security. Everyone must be prepared to swear that he has not heard of it. He said we should limit American contacts with the groups involved to two or three people, getting Cubans to do most of what must be done. Mr. Allen Dulles said [here is the crucial one-and-a-half-line deletion in the record]. The President indicated some question about this."9

Once everyone in the closed circle had said his piece about the program to overthrow the Castro regime — no one in the group that met that day opposed the idea — "the president told Mr. Dulles he thought he should go ahead with the plan and the operations." The United States was launched on the bumpy road that ended at the swamp of Zapata, inland from the Bay of Pigs.

— * —

Allen turned sixty-eight in April. "I hope he won't carry on too much longer," Clover told her friends. The Eisenhower administration was in its last year, and although Allen conceived of the CIA directorship as a nonpartisan position, he often mused that the time was coming for fresh leadership. Though he did not want to step down in that way, his offer to resign in responsibility for the U-2 disaster that May was not altogether disingenuous. His sprawling CIA, moreover, was becoming fractured and fragmented, diffuse in the chores it had taken on and too complex for any one man to dominate with the chummy, collegial tone Allen had set at the start of the Dulles era a decade earlier.

* This statement may have to be modified as further documents are declassified. The available memo of the March 17 meeting contains a single deletion of one line and a half in a context that could conceivably have included a hint of "radical" or "executive" actions, common euphemisms for assassinations. Participants recall no such hint, but on subjects like this Allen's language was often so circumspect that an uninitiated listener would not understand what he was really saying.

Any intelligence operation is necessarily compartmentalized, with an officer's or section's "need to know" defining access to information. But the various CIA divisions had grown so accustomed to operational autonomy that their independence spilled over into their sense of identity and purpose. Sherman Kent's Board of National Estimates, for instance, functioned in Olympian isolation from operations, producing masterful estimates, precise and internally cohesive, but of doubtful relevance to harassed policymakers under the pressures of daily decisions. Robert Amory's analysts of current intelligence were kept in the dark about the agency's covert actions, even those under way in the regions they were watching. Officers of the clandestine services, the elite of the agency, seemed not to care much about insights from mere analysts, which might confuse their visions of derring-do.

Alongside the necessary divisions to handle administrative, financial, legal, and logistical support for CIA's wide-ranging activities were two areas special to the intelligence business: the scientific and technological research branches, continually devising new devices and techniques for eavesdropping, penetration, and communication, and the most secretive and sensitive section of all, counterespionage, charged with protecting the agency against hostile penetration, a task that generated among its officers a habitual suspicion of all coworkers. Independent-minded operators like Sidney Gottlieb of the medical staff and the powerful James Angleton of counterespionage were not accustomed to accepting supervision from anyone listed as their superior on an organizational chart.

By naming Bissell as head of the clandestine services, Allen was putting in place one potential successor. But Bissell had yet to prove his grasp of the intelligence profession, in whose subtleties others were far more experienced. The most obvious alternative as the next director was still Richard Helms, once bypassed for promotion in favor of Bissell, but not to be ruled out when Allen's time came to retire. Another potential candidate had been the experienced Lyman Kirkpatrick, but he had contracted polio while on an agency mission in Southeast Asia and could manage only a reduced workload. Allen's easygoing attitude toward the office politics of ambitious deputies was simply to let everyone find his own orbit around his center — which in the case of Bissell and Helms involved each staying out of the other's way.

Since Allen had never shown aptitude or interest in the workings of a large bureaucracy, the centrifugal forces accelerated unchecked. The seeds were planted in the Dulles era for habits of operating and spending without careful accountability — the sorts of abuses that would lead to disaster for the agency after Allen had left the scene. This state of fragmentation was not widely understood outside the agency, but the uneasiness stirred up by the Bruce-Lovett report of 1956 and by the subsequent inquiries of the president's board of consultants lingered on. Bruce had become ambassador to West Germany, and upon learning that the CIA men in his embassy were contriving to build another Berlin Tunnel, he ordered the station chief not to put "a shovel in the ground without telling me first."

In sum, the CIA Allen had built was not as confident as it seemed; despite his longtime insistence on combining intelligence collection, analysis, and covert actions into one professional service, the different activities were in fact being conducted in isolation from each other, with only his personal, and sporadic, leadership holding them together. The old idea of removing the covert action function to another, more secret agency of government was, therefore, not far-fetched. The fun was indeed going out of intelligence.

Allen and Clover's life together had settled into a routine. Home life scarcely existed, for all the comfort of the book-lined townhouse in Georgetown. Once, as guests were about to arrive for Sunday brunch, Allen stomped through the living room saying, "This house looks too un-lived in!" He accordingly scattered opened newspapers around the neat furniture. Husband and wife had little to talk about when alone; he was naturally inhibited from discussing his problems at the office, and she well knew her husband's lack of interest in her own concerns. Clover had moved beyond her Jungian studies into a reforming zeal common among intelligent ladies of privilege; the woman who had relished playing poker with ex-convicts became passionate about penal reform. The one common pleasure the couple enjoyed was long hours of reading together, about their separate interests. Clover had prevailed to shrink the number of large and impersonal diplomatic receptions on their social calendar in favor of small and intimate dinner parties with their social friends, the Wisners, the Bohlens, and others of the Georgetown set.

Their three children had moved away into their own lives: Allen Macy, tragically, was in and out of intensive medical care, while Joan and Toddy were raising families far from the worlds of politics and publicity. With Foster's death the ties to the Watertown family grew tenuous. Allen urged his sisters and their husbands to sell the old houses at Henderson Harbor. Though Allen and Eleanor were both in Washington, theirs was not the closest of relationships and, without the older brother there to mediate, they found it pleasanter not to spend much time together.

An illuminating glimpse of life at 2723 Q Street came from Philip Moore, the Princeton undergraduate who had lived with the Dulles family at Lloyd Neck that last summer before Pearl Harbor. Late in 1959 Moore, by then launched on a career in finance, called at the Dulles home. Clover invited him to tea in a little sitting room, while beyond closed doors in the next room he could hear Allen and several male visitors talking in some foreign language. Moore was impressed at the way the Georgetown house was set up to accommodate parallel meetings in privacy and discretion. When the foreign visitors left, Allen popped in to greet his old tennis pro, and Clover announced that she had just asked Moore to stay for a family dinner. The three went into the kitchen; the help were off that night and, as it emerged, there was nothing for dinner. As Moore described it, "I went about setting the table for three, with elegant candelabra and place settings, but the meal consisted of frozen peas and scrambled eggs — which I remember whipping up myself!"[10]

Allen's waking hours were devoted to work, but he often enticed younger officers of the agency into fiercely competitive tennis games on the Q Street court. "What's the matter with getting exhausted?" he would respond to those who complained. He "gave the impression of not knowing what exhaustion was," wrote Sherman Kent. "Yet of all the men of our experience, . . . none more consistently courted it. How did he stay fresh for all those years?"[11]

Allen's public image was growing so glamorous that the CIA set up a special clipping service to compile articles from the world press about the director. An Italian magazine called Allen "the most influential man in Washington, . . . secretly directs the entire foreign policy of the United States." A British profile dubbed him "the man most hated by Khrushchev." At the annual spring dinner of the Gridiron Club the elite of the Washington press corps roast the elite of Washington political society. The theme one of these years was "A Sewer in Old Vienna," and the chorus was composed of spiffy young crew-cut men in flannel suits, naturally bedecked in cloaks and carrying daggers. The central figure was the spymaster himself, portrayed by a prominent Washington columnist wearing baggy slacks, a battered hat perched on the back of his head, directing his agents from underground. Allen laughed, ho ho ho, with the rest of the crowd at all the fun poked at the CIA and himself.

Allen was never one for the vision of a statesman, musing over grand schemes for American responsibilities in the world — one of the reasons why the idea of assuming Foster's mantle after his death must have seemed so daunting to him. His passion was practical covert action to undermine the communist foe, and information, up to the minute and precise. He made a point of listening every morning, while being driven to the office, to the CBS World News Roundup. As this habit became known around the agency, his deputies would listen to the same newscast to be sure they were not taken by surprise at the morning staff meeting. Official overnight briefing memos would convey all the agency news needed for the coming day's business, but Allen had learned the necessity of knowing also the latest news available to the public.*

Allen regarded dealings with the president and the NSC as his own preserve. For eight years past he had been the steady weekly briefer on world matters; NSC meetings were "very high church," said one participant, "with Allen's briefing the opening litany."[12] As the years went on, his CIA aides noted, Allen began winging these briefings to an extent that he would not have considered proper in younger days. Often he would read an estimate or a current intelligence memo in the car to the White House, quickly absorbing enough of it to be able to ramble on in his entertaining and convincing anecdotal style. A favorite trick was to seize upon one point in a complex memo, read that section carefully, and then guide the entire discussion to that point, without regard to all the rest.

Often enough, however, his seasoned instinct on political intelligence compensated for the lack of homework — as, for example, the early notice he took of the crisis building in the unfamiliar Belgian Congo. Unlike the decolonization process in the British, and even the French, African territories, the Belgians proceeded in haste and without adequate planning for an orderly transfer of power. Within a month of independence day, June 30, 1960, the Congo turned into a morass of pillage, rape, and anarchy. To wary Washington policymakers the disorders seemed to offer a Cold War testing ground for Soviet inroads into the heart of Africa. A multinational United Nations force was set up to try restoring order. Not merely a little-known tribal society was at stake, but, in the province of Katanga, the strategic source of minerals for the Western world. Presiding unpredictably over the chaos was the mercurial Congolese leader, Patrice Lumumba.

— * —

Political assassination was foremost among those topics that Allen would obviously never discuss with Clover. The security of any such plan natu-

---

* Richard Helms had also learned this lesson early in his Washington career, in an embarrassing way. One morning in February 1952 Helms had to address a breakfast seminar of aspiring intelligence officers. Instead of listening to the radio news on his way to the meeting, he drafted notes for his remarks on the business of intelligence. All went well until the first question, about the CIA's reaction to the death of Britain's King George VI and the accession to the throne of the twenty-five-year-old Princess Elizabeth. This was not a matter of particular CIA concern, and the duty officers had seen no reason to include the news in the overnight brief. But the ranking CIA officer for collection of world intelligence was left dangling in ignorance about a news event that was all over the air waves and late editions. He could draw little consolation from the fact that CIA had earlier been the first to alert Washington that Princess Elizabeth was pregnant; many months later she gave birth to a son, whom she named Charles.

rally required the tightest secrecy. But there was perhaps another reason. Mary Bancroft defined it: "I personally think the reason Allen went to such lengths to exclude her was that he had such a high regard for her moral and ethical values that he did not dare risk the unsettling effect of her possible disapproval."[13] Allen's personal code of ethics allowed him to assume moral responsibility for his acts toward a higher purpose; he would not want his wife to share in this burden.

Allen had called attention to Lumumba's dangerous instability well before independence. Then, two weeks after the Belgian withdrawal he told the NSC that Lumumba was another Castro "or worse. . . . It is safe to go on the assumption that Lumumba has been bought by the communists."[14] When the NSC next met, on August 1, Allen declared that the United States might at any time have to "take appropriate military action to prevent or defeat Soviet military intervention in the Congo."*

To the officers of the clandestine services one solution would be simply to assassinate the offending political figure. They had already proposed such actions against Stalin, Chou En-lai of China, and Sukarno of Indonesia, to name a few. Allen had no compunctions about contemplating assassination; his first major intelligence mission, after all, had involved the attempt to murder Adolf Hitler. In a public speech after the war he had said, "Assassination may be the only means left of overthrowing a modern tyrant."[15] The problem, he had learned, was not whether to do it, but how, and this was never an easy matter — not for the German plotters of the July 20 movement nor, two decades later, for the imaginative operatives of the clandestine services in the Congo, Cuba, and elsewhere.

On August 18 the CIA station chief in the Congolese capital of Leopoldville cabled that "there may be little time left in which [to] take action to avoid another Cuba."† The head of CIA's Africa division, Bronson Tweedy, replied the next day that he was seeking approval for a political operation based upon "your and our belief [that] Lumumba must be removed if possible." An artful ambiguity in the word "removed" was left standing at that point. The next day Bissell cabled Leopoldville, "You are authorized [to] proceed with operation."[16]

* Long after these events, the Republic of Congo was officially renamed Zaire; the old capital of Leopoldville became Kinshasa.
† In a gesture to the determination of clandestine officers to keep their identities secret, the Church Committee report called the CIA station chief Victor Hedgman, without acknowledging that this was a fictitious name. Those familiar with the Congo knew that the CIA man's real name was Lawrence Devlin, and in her 1982 study Madeleine Kalb identified Devlin as the man behind the Hedgman pseudonym. Bronson Tweedy, however, was the headquarters officer's real name.

Allen presented the 5412 Group on August 25 with a plan to arrange (presumably through bribery) a vote of no confidence by the Congolese parliament. Speaking for Eisenhower, Gordon Gray said the president "had expressed extremely strong feelings on the necessity for very straightforward action in this situation, and he wondered whether the plans as outlined were sufficient to accomplish this." This, in the euphemisms of bureaucracy, was a strong statement indeed. Allen's recorded reply to this top-secret council indicated that he well understood the serious — if guarded — import of the national security adviser's remark. "Mr. Dulles replied that he . . . had every intention of proceeding as vigorously as the situation permits or requires, but added that he must necessarily put himself in a position of interpreting instructions of this kind within the bounds of necessity and capacity."[17] A little careful thought was necessary to figure out what Allen was really saying, but bureaucrats learn how to decipher the phrases their colleagues use to avoid blunt language. The 5412 Group concluded that day "that planning for the Congo would not necessarily rule out 'consideration' of any particular kind of activity which might contribute to getting rid of Lumumba."

No one in attendance could honestly claim any lingering ambiguity. "When you use the language that no particular means were ruled out, that is obviously what it meant, and it meant that to everybody in the room," Bissell later explained. "You don't use language of that kind except to mean in effect, the director is being told, get rid of the guy, and if you have to use extreme means up to and including assassination, go ahead." And Allen's reply meant that the men of the CIA would have to figure out, on the spot and on the fly, whether they could actually pull it off.

During this period Allen had delegated to Bissell all the detailed planning of parallel assassination operations against Fidel Castro. He was not even aware, for instance, that agents of the clandestine services had approached members of organized crime syndicates who had formerly been active in Batista's Cuba about assassinating Fidel in Havana. Informed of the action only as it was being triggered, Allen abruptly called it off.[18]

But in the attempt to "remove" Lumumba Allen's personal responsibility is on record, not once but repeatedly. According to CIA practice, the director seldom signs the cables to his field officers personally; operational instructions usually go out over the name of an official a step or two down in the hierarchy. On August 26, the day after the 5412 Group meeting, the CIA station chief in Leopoldville, Lawrence Devlin, received an extraordinary cable over the signature of Allen Dulles.

In high quarters here it is the clear-cut conclusion that if [Lumumba] continues to hold high office, the inevitable result will at best be chaos and at worst pave the way to communist takeover of the Congo with disastrous consequences for the prestige of the UN and for the interests of the free world generally. Consequently we concluded that his removal must be an urgent and prime objective and that under existing conditions this should be a high priority of our covert action.

The cable went on to grant Devlin "wide authority" to pursue operations previously planned, but also "even more aggressive action if it can remain covert. . . . We realize that targets of opportunity may present themselves to you." Allen's signature on this cable assured that Devlin would take the instructions very seriously indeed.[19]

Shortly thereafter Lumumba was voted out as prime minister, but he remained a powerful force in Congolese politics. "Lumumba in opposition is almost as dangerous as in office," the CIA station reported to Washington. At a White House meeting Gray drove home his previous point, telling Allen he "hoped that Agency people in the field are fully aware of the top-level feeling in Washington that vigorous action would not be amiss." Allen briefed Eisenhower and the NSC on September 21 that Lumumba "would remain a grave danger as long as he was not yet disposed of." Hearing no dissent or caution from the president, Allen sent a second personally signed cable to Devlin three days later. "We wish [to] give every possible support in eliminating Lumumba from any possibility [of] resuming governmental position," either in Leopoldville or as leader of a breakaway province.[20]

Meanwhile a secretive CIA executive set out from Washington for the Congolese capital. Devlin was informed that one "Joseph Braun" would arrive about September 27, and would announce himself in a telephone call as "Joe from Paris." "It [is] urgent [that] you should see [Joe] soonest possible after he phones you. He will fully identify himself and explain his assignment to you."

"Joe from Paris" turned out to be none other than Sidney Gottlieb from Washington, head of the CIA medical division, who for a decade had studied the effects of lethal drugs on unwitting subjects.* In his personal baggage, protected by diplomatic seal, was a supply of an ingenious biological poison that would leave no traces upon a corpse. In case such things were unavailable in the chaos of Leopoldville, Gottlieb also handed Devlin a pair of rubber gloves, a mask, and a syringe. If the experienced station chief had not yet fully understood his instructions from Allen, "Joe" made the mission perfectly clear. One of Devlin's team

* Gottlieb is identified in the Church Committee report under the pseudonym Joseph Schneider.

recalled his reaction when the brute fact of his orders from headquarters sank in: "Oh, shit!"

All of Allen's cables were dispatched through a special communications channel, code-named PROP, between Washington and Leopoldville, established for the sole purpose of discussing this singular operation. Devlin was the only authorized recipient; though he was ostensibly one of the political officers in the United States Embassy, not even the ambassador was entitled to see the PROP traffic. In Washington only Allen, Bissell, Tweedy, and one other officer in the Africa division were even aware of the PROP channel.

The administration's designs upon Lumumba became so devious that on one day in October a cable went to Leopoldville through normal — but still highly classified — channels, addressed to the ambassador and available to other responsible political officers on the third floor of the embassy building. This directive specified that, desirable though it would be to "immobilize" Lumumba, "any action taken would have to be entirely Congolese." Within a few hours a second cable arrived for Devlin alone, in his separate office suite on the second floor, through the PROP channel: "So you [will] not [be] confused. . . . [The] specific purpose you discussed with colleague . . . remains highest priority."[21] "Colleague," of course, was Gottlieb, and the "specific purpose," of which the ambassador and all the rest of the diplomatic establishment was not to be informed, was the assassination of Patrice Lumumba.

As it happened, even with all of Gottlieb's paraphernalia Devlin could not arrange for access to Lumumba's toothbrush, breakfast food, condoms, or any other personal equipment through which the poison might be administered. In the turmoil of the Katanga secession and the UN battle for the Congo, Lumumba died shortly after January 17, 1961, while held captive by his tribal enemies. The exact circumstances of his death have never been clarified, but the record is clear that ultimately all the CIA's PROP plotting was irrelevant. As the death of Lumumba was announced, Allen happened to attend a White House correspondents' dinner in Washington; while mingling with the guests he was accosted by C. D. Jackson, Eisenhower's old Cold Warrior, who had never forgiven CIA for its tepid reaction to the Hungarian uprising of 1956. "I see you boys finally got Lumumba," Jackson said as he worked the room. Allen replied in earnest defense, "C.D., we didn't do that." Jackson retorted, "You didn't have the guts to do it."[22]

A decade or so later, after Allen's death, the American public finally learned enough about the activities of the CIA clandestine services to be anxious. The fact that political assassinations were contemplated at the highest levels of the American government provoked outrage among public and officialdom alike. Testifying before the Church Committee in 1975, Devlin confirmed all the instructions he had received—the personal cables from Allen, Gottlieb's arrival with the merchandise in his suitcase, the CIA's attempts to penetrate Lumumba's motley entourage. In ostensible sincerity, matching the mood of that season, Devlin said, "Never in my training or previous work in the agency had I ever heard any reference to such methods"—a remark under oath that only brought cynical smiles to the faces of CIA colleagues who remembered Stalin, Chou En-lai, and the rest.

Was it Allen personally who had conjured up the mission of assassination, or could President Eisenhower himself have given the green light? Douglas Dillon, a trusted figure in both Eisenhower's and Kennedy's political establishments, testified that it was "perfectly plausible . . . perfectly possible" that Allen would have taken Eisenhower's strong language about "getting rid" of Lumumba to mean presidential authorization for assassination. Dillon went on, "I think that Allen Dulles would have been quite responsive to what he considered implicit authorization because he felt very strongly that we should not involve the president directly in things of this nature. And he was perfectly willing to take the responsibility personally."[23]

But the Eisenhower legacy cannot evade the responsibility, either of the chief executive in general or of his own personal role, in the decision to assassinate Lumumba. In fact the Congolese leader was only one of three Third World figures whose proposed assassination figured high on Eisenhower's foreign policy agenda that summer and autumn of 1960. Along with Castro, Rafael Trujillo of the Dominican Republic was also a target. George Kistiakowsky, the White House science adviser, who managed to sit in on all kinds of high-level discussions, wrote of Eisenhower's reaction whenever the "use of force" against offending foreign politicians was raised at the NSC or other large forums. "The President got very angry and said that he won't let even his own agency heads take action, . . . that all plans should be brought to him for decision."[24] It is inconceivable, in such an atmosphere, that a man with Allen's political sense could have proceeded without what he considered proper presidential authority.

Andrew Goodpaster and John Eisenhower expressed to the Senate committee their incredulity that anyone could imagine Dwight D. Eisenhower authorizing an act of political murder. So even did Gordon Gray, whose own interventions had confirmed Allen on the course of assassination. "Nobody wants to embarrass a President of the United States by discussing the assassination of foreign leaders in his presence," said Helms long afterward. "We're hired out to keep those things out of the Oval Office." Even in briefings to Allen, officers of the clandestine services "deliberately avoided the use of any 'bad words'" when discussing

assassination plans. "The pointed avoidance of 'bad words' emphasized
... the extreme sensitivity of the operation."[25]

In government or wherever sensitive matters are afoot, a good staff is
expected to give a chief executive just enough information to allow him or
her to stop an action, but not so much that "plausible deniability" — the
ability to deny knowledge of an embarrassing secret undertaking if it ever
becomes public — is lost.* Defenders of presidential virtue only insult
Eisenhower's intelligence in suggesting that he did not understand the intimations he was receiving from his aides and the signals he was sending
when he let the opportunities pass without a negative response. At any
point between July and October of 1960 Eisenhower could have told
Allen or Bissell that their efforts to immobilize Lumumba should stop
short of actual assassination. This he did not do.

— * —

On Wednesday night, July 13, 1960, the Democratic Party nominated
Senator John F. Kennedy of Massachusetts as its candidate for president.
Eisenhower promptly offered a series of global intelligence briefings for
Kennedy and his running mate, Senator Lyndon B. Johnson of Texas.
Nixon, the likely Republican candidate, was already a member of the National Security Council as vice president; it seemed only prudent that
both candidates should be aware of current world problems, lest something said during the campaign complicate the foreign policy of the nation or the task of the next president.

President Roosevelt had taken the unusual step in 1944 of giving
his Republican opponent, Thomas Dewey, secret information that the
United States had broken Japanese military codes, alerting him to the
danger of inadvertent remarks that might compromise strategy in the Pacific war. In 1948 Allen himself had acted as informal liaison between the
Dewey campaign and the Truman administration to prevent campaign
mischief that might upset negotiations then in progress.

But Allen understood better than anyone that the offer of secret brief-

---

* This cynical but thoroughly practical lesson was stated in textbook form in Bissell's testimony to the Church Committee in 1975. Allen had had the obligation to brief two successive presidents on assassination plans, Bissell observed. He would indicate "the general objective of the operation that was contemplated, to make that sufficiently clear so that the
president — either President Eisenhower or President Kennedy — could have ordered the
termination of the operation, but to give the president just as little information about it as
possible, beyond an understanding of its general purpose. Such an approach to the president would have had as its purpose to leave him in the position to deny knowledge of the
operation if it should surface" (Church Committee, *Alleged Assassination Plots*, pp. 111,
118).

ings in a campaign season was not as straightforward a process as it may have seemed. "I have found candidates, on the whole, not anxious to get briefings in depth," Allen said long afterward. Too much inside or tactical information "could restrict the freedom of action of a candidate in a very important situation, or make it very uncomfortable for him." Nowhere was this more true than in the management of covert operations. No matter how careful or discreet the candidate, he went on, "in the heat of a campaign, if you fill his mind full of all kinds of information, this is going to come out. . . . I did not brief candidates on secret operations which were destined to come out only in the future. . . . The candidate, if he became president, would then have complete control of the situation"— power to stop an operation, that is, if it did not respond to his own foreign policy choices.

On the last Saturday of July a CIA courier plane flew Allen up to Hyannis, where the Democratic candidate was assembling his forces for the campaign. The senator's brother, Robert, met the director of central intelligence at the airport and, with some difficulty, inserted him into a family convertible already packed with assorted squirming and hyperactive Kennedy children — it was Allen's first operational exposure to the Kennedy style. Allen and John Kennedy spent more than two hours together. The candidate had asked if two of his foreign policy advisers, Adlai Stevenson and Chester Bowles, could attend the intelligence briefings; Eisenhower refused. The briefings were for the candidate alone.[26]

What was said at this and subsequent briefings became a point of angry contention between Allen and Nixon, his friend of thirteen years' standing. Allen and Kennedy had discussed politics and world affairs over the years, starting with those weekend visits in Palm Beach. The difference on this July day on Cape Cod was that serious purpose was engaged. Kennedy let Allen ramble on in his entertaining way, about this country and that, ripening crises and those merely in the offing. Asking few questions, the young candidate was apparently interested only in seeing whether Allen Dulles would volunteer more candor than he had shown on the Palm Beach weekends. Apparently not.

Eisenhower may have hoped that Allen's briefings would soften the Democrats' charges of a missile gap. Allen was not a man to take chances on a partisan issue; when Kennedy asked him bluntly, "How do we stand in the missile race," Allen deflected the question to the Pentagon and avoided a direct answer.[27] This was the first point that irritated Nixon, that Allen did not protect the Republican candidate from campaign accusations.

As the two men emerged for a photo opportunity amid the listening ears of the waiting press, Kennedy jauntily inquired, "Haven't you got any good news in that black bag of yours?"— a gentle barb at Eisenhower's foreign policy, which Allen was in no position to answer. As he repaired for the rest of the weekend to play tennis at the nearby Cotuit home of a CIA friend, Allen said, "I just told Kennedy what he could've read in the morning *Times*." Kennedy said precisely the same to his close adviser Theodore Sorensen. Three days later Allen flew to Texas, prepared to give a similar briefing to Johnson. This time even less of substance came up, as Johnson spent the day driving Allen across his 1,800-acre ranch, pointing out herds of prize breeding cattle and wild deer. Allen and Johnson sat outside the ranch house after dinner listening to the Republican convention.

Covering the range of world problems from Berlin to Laos, Cuba to the Congo, Allen was careful at this and subsequent briefings to omit any references to covert operations. He warned of dangers to American policy posed by Castro and Lumumba but said nothing of the plans under way to deal with the offending dictators. The closest he came was at an October briefing to Kennedy about "a capability, on the back burner, to bring covert political pressure on Castro." He added a few words about the agency's psychological warfare operations involving a medium-wave radio station on an obscure little Caribbean island. Allen never explained that CIA was also training an exile paramilitary force to invade Cuba or at least to stir up guerrilla operations. Kennedy asked no questions, and Allen went no further in discussing the Eisenhower administration's covert action program of March 17.

On October 19 Kennedy's campaign staff, eager for an issue on which their candidate could appear aggressive in defending American interests around the world, prepared a statement declaring: "We must attempt to strengthen the non-Batista democratic anti-Castro forces in exile, and in Cuba itself, who offer eventual hope of overthrowing Castro. Thus far these fighters for freedom have had virtually no support from our government." The statement was reportedly written by Richard Goodwin, drawing on ideas his candidate had voiced in the past, but without knowledge of anything Kennedy had learned from his CIA briefings. Goodwin's colleague, Arthur Schlesinger, claims that Kennedy never saw the statement before it was issued to the press; he had gone to bed and his staff did not want to awaken him.[28]

When Nixon saw the Kennedy statement in the news the next day, "I could hardly believe my eyes," he wrote. "I knew that President Eisenhower had arranged for Kennedy to receive regular briefings by Allen Dulles, . . . precisely so he would be as well aware as I of what our policies and programs were." Nixon asked a campaign aide, Fred Seaton, to call the White House on a secure line to learn whether or not Dulles had briefed Kennedy about the administration's covert action program.

Seaton, who knew nothing about the CIA planning, apparently asked if Allen had briefed Kennedy "on Cuba." Allen's side of the story was that when asked if he had briefed Kennedy "on Cuba," of course he had — but in general terms, about overt assessments and developments. "I did not tell Mr. Kennedy that there was a project to arm some of these Cuban refugees, to help the underground in Cuba," Allen explained later. "Nixon thought that I had briefed Kennedy on these secret operations."[29]

"For the first and only time in the campaign, I got mad at Kennedy personally," Nixon recalled. "I thought that Kennedy, with full knowledge of the facts, was jeopardizing the security of a United States foreign policy operation." The two presidential candidates met for a television debate the next day, and Nixon found himself in a corner — forced by a questioner to criticize his opponent for advocating just the course of action that the Republican administration, and Nixon himself, was promoting but could not acknowledge in public. He called Kennedy's statement of support for anti-Castro Cubans "the most dangerous, irresponsible recommendation that he's made during the course of this campaign." Nixon confronted Allen angrily at the next NSC meeting, saying, "You never should have told him! Never!" It took Allen a moment to realize what had provoked the vice president's fury, but when he did, he could say in full candor that he had given no information whatever on secret operations planned against Castro.

Both candidates found it prudent to drop the Cuba issue for the rest of the campaign. But Nixon's suspicions, about Kennedy and perhaps even Allen, were not easily overcome. They might have been fueled even more had he known of a casual meeting between Kennedy and Bissell, the CIA officer masterminding the Cuban covert operation.

Bissell saw himself as a political independent, though he had voted Democratic more often than Republican. A change from a Republican to a Democratic president was not at all disagreeable to him; indeed, earlier that year he had sent discreet messages through his old friend Adlai Stevenson that he could work on the Democratic campaign if they wanted him to take leave from his CIA service. Columnist Joseph Alsop, always ready to oblige persons of power, quietly arranged for Bissell to meet and chat unofficially with Kennedy. The Democratic candidate was aware of Bissell's background in the Marshall Plan and economic development programs but knew little of his current work in the CIA clandestine services. For Kennedy this was only a meeting with a man who might be useful in the economic planning of the New Frontier. Bissell said even less than Allen about the Cuban operations.

Whatever the political consequences of this confusion between Allen and Nixon, the clash revealed a particular danger in hasty discussions among men of affairs. Imprecise communication does no harm when both parties are on the same track, with the same information, assumptions, and goals. Such imprecision, however, is destructive between people who do not have the same information or do not share goals and assumptions. The problem would only get worse for Allen as the presidency passed from Eisenhower to Kennedy.

— * —

Allen and Clover arrived home from their annual European vacation on election night, November 8. As usual, the director of central intelligence liked to be out of the country during the election campaign. He also found it pleasant to visit his dear friend Queen Frederika in Athens and to withdraw from the world on a yacht cruising the Greek isles. (The CIA station chief in Athens could always drum up a Greek millionaire to lend a yacht for Allen's enjoyment.)

That year a potentially untoward incident interrupted the placid island-hopping holiday. Sitting at a tavern overlooking the temple of Poseidon, Allen and Clover were startled by an American stranger approaching their table. "Aren't you Allen Dulles?" came the sudden greeting. "I'm an American citizen and a taxpayer"—the CIA security guard accompanying the director bristled in readiness—"and I just want to shake your hand and thank you for all the things you've done for our country." Allen's holiday, and pleasure in his job, was complete.

Just before his departure Allen had greeted a class of new CIA recruits. One young man asked innocently if Allen would be staying on at the agency after the election. Leave it to youth to confront elders where they are most vulnerable. The director, who had no idea of his prospects under a new president, replied to the question with an informative ho ho ho. Allen voted, by absentee ballot from New York, for Nixon. Neither he nor anyone else at CIA was surprised that Bissell voted for Kennedy. The election results were about as close as any in American history, but during the next day Allen and his colleagues reckoned with the results and the expectation that the Dulles era at CIA was about to end.

In Hyannis that Wednesday evening the newly chosen president-elect spent a boisterous evening with old friends, expansive in the opportunity that was now theirs. What was the first thing he should do? Kennedy asked. Someone said he should fire J. Edgar Hoover, the powerful but ever suspicious chief of the FBI. Someone else added the name of Allen Dulles to the initial Kennedy hit list. "Kennedy, listening with apparent interest, egged his friends on," recounted Arthur Schlesinger.[30] He kept to himself the fact that just a few hours before he had placed a telephone call to the director of central intelligence.

Allen was back at work on his first day after vacation when his secretary came in with a message. As Allen remembered the moment, "The president-elect, I guess she said, wanted to speak to me. He went right to the point. 'Allen, I'd like to have you stay on as director of central intelligence when I take over next January twentieth.'"

"I admit I was surprised," Allen told Tom Braden a few years later, "and I was flattered and I was pleased." Foster had become a symbol of the Republican foreign policy of "brinkmanship" that the Democrats wished to revise, and yet here was the younger Dulles brother ranking first among the appointees of the new Democratic administration. "Senator, I'm beyond retiring age," Allen replied to Kennedy. "There are a lot of young men in this shop that are coming along, and a lot of able people, and I would like to see a change come about in an orderly way and be around when it was made. But if you want me to stay on, I'll certainly stay on for a period—[a] year or so—whatever you want, and then I think I probably ought to retire." Kennedy replied impatiently, "We can talk about the other later. What I'd like to know is and I want to announce it, I'm also communicating with J. Edgar Hoover, and I would like to announce that both you and J. Edgar Hoover will continue on in your present functions, respective functions, after I take over as President." Allen promptly sent a message to the supervisor of new CIA recruits: tell that young man who had put the impertinent question to him a few weeks before that "the Director is here to stay."[31]

The hearty advice Kennedy received from his buoyant friends that first night after the election had been rejected before it was even proffered. As Schlesinger later explained the president-elect's impulsive first decision, "This was part of the strategy of reassurance. Hoover and Dulles were still national icons in 1960. Since the political cost of discharging them would have been considerable, reappointment enabled Kennedy to get full credit with their admirers for something he had no real choice but to do anyway." Kennedy knew Allen, whose orientation was undeniably Republican, as a social friend but also as a professional who had won the respect of friend and adversary alike. Hoover, for his part, was a political, if not a personal, asset.

Ten days after the election Kennedy began learning the cost of his pragmatic decision. Allen arrived in Palm Springs to brief the president-elect on the intelligence matters that he had deliberately withheld from him as candidate. The setting by Ambassador Kennedy's swimming pool was familiar from their mellow previous encounters, but the substance of the discussion this time was different. On November 18, 1960, Kennedy was briefed for the first time on the CIA's covert paramilitary planning to overthrow Fidel Castro.[32]

— * —

Allen's task during the interregnum was to tell the president-elect all the things he could not tell a mere candidate, who might, after all, return to the ranks of the opposition. Until the inauguration the president-elect did not have responsibility, but he would inherit it. "We want you to know this is going on," Allen would say. "We're not asking for any final decisions on your part now. When you've taken over as president, you can turn these things off, or you can let them continue."

Allen did not see fit to brief Kennedy about the attempt to assassinate Lumumba, for if anything came of that it would surely happen before the new administration took office on January 20.* Nor was there any talk of the plotting by the clandestine services to "immobilize" Castro by one means or another. Allen himself was not clear on all the details of these schemes, and there seemed little reason to burden Kennedy then with knowledge of something that might or might not happen to Castro during the anticipated four years, at least, of his presidency.

But after his *tour d'horizon* of world trouble spots, Allen turned to Bissell, whom he had brought along to Palm Beach, for a few words on Cuba in general. Bissell said guardedly that CIA was contemplating some form of "significant strike force to act as a catalyst" in ultimately provoking an anti-Castro uprising on the island. Kennedy listened to Bissell's briefing in silence, though he later confided his astonishment at the "magnitude and daring" of the operation. Allen came away confident he had received "a go-ahead to continue to plan, but without any commitment to act." As Schlesinger wrote later, the incoming president "did not yet realize how contingency planning could generate its own momentum and create its own reality."

Anyone familiar with the evolution of CIA designs over the past eight months would have caught the subtle embellishments upon Eisenhower's cautious program of March 17 in Bissell's presentation to Kennedy. The original program had said nothing about a "significant strike force," and an anti-Castro resistance within Cuba was something that would have to come about *before* any covert paramilitary infiltrations from outside. The changes in the operation had come about incrementally during the summer of 1960, and neither Allen nor Bissell had seen fit to apprise Eisenhower or any of his advisers of it.

---

* By a couple of days, and in ways CIA did not anticipate, it did.

The starting point in Eisenhower's thinking had always been the establishment of a Cuban opposition in exile to give legitimacy to any future military moves. In retrospect, the futility of this first step was foreshadowed by the staffing of the Cuba task force. Bissell, always independent and secretive in his hands-on management, had no taste for the old hands of J. C. King's Western Hemisphere division; these men were not accustomed to dealing with the politicians of the moderate left, whom Allen regarded as the most promising alternative to Castro. Bissell's deputy, Tracy Barnes, brought in one of the field veterans of Guatemala, E. Howard Hunt, who, with his Puerto Rican sidekick Bernard L. Barker, could mingle convincingly in the émigré community — they, at least, spoke Spanish.

The challenge they faced among no less than 113 Cuban political factions in Florida should have come as no surprise. As an earnest young diplomat named Allen Dulles had written in 1917, "Refugees from oppressed countries are always singularly jealous of fellow countrymen in a like position, and are very given to suspect each others' motives and activities." After only a few months Bissell gave up on the prospect of forming a united Cuban front that could work effectively against Castro. "If the operation was to be continued," he said, looking back on the whole experience, it would have to be "a U.S. organization that, in effect, made all the decisions." But this judgment was never shared with Eisenhower. Into the autumn, when the matter came up in the Oval Office the president's first question was always about progress in creating "our government-in-exile." Once, as Allen and Bissell tried to explain the difficulties, Eisenhower stormed, "Boys, if you don't intend to go through with this, let's stop talking about it!"[33]

Rather than argue on that level, Bissell quietly turned his attentions to the paramilitary component of the program, where things could be made to happen without getting squabbling exile factions to agree. The CIA station chief in Havana, an old hand in King's division, had managed to smuggle out of Cuba some forty anti-Castro activists. Once organized in Florida, these men were to be the core of an infiltration effort; teams of half a dozen saboteurs were trained in partisan warfare and dispatched to generate resistance cells on the island. Such was the efficiency of Castro's internal security forces, however, that after being smuggled into little fishing villages on Cuba's north coast, none of these teams survived intact for more than forty-eight hours.

In frustration Bissell's task force turned to the training of a serious strike force, numbering as many as three hundred Cuban fighters armed with bazookas, mortars, and artillery, who would be landed on the coast in force to secure a beachhead that would attract dissident Cubans to the resistance. Training of this force began at the old Opa Locka base in Florida, where Operation Success first got under way, but political and security considerations quickly made it desirable to transfer the training base outside the United States. The Guatemalan military government, put into power by the CIA in 1954, agreed to return the favor by hosting a new covert operation; a wealthy coffee planter offered his 5,000-acre plantation in the mountains of southwestern Guatemala as a training site, which became known as CIA's Base Trax.

To drill the unseasoned little brigade, Barnes called upon the paramilitary instructors he knew best, hardened anticommunist fighters from Europe. "They were a strange bunch of people with German experience, Arabic experience," said Robert Amory, "pretty goddamned good at blowing up barns and power stations, . . . absolutely no sense or feel about the political sensitivities." Speaking no Spanish, the drill sergeants spent their days shouting Hungarian and Russian obscenities at boys from Cuba in the mountains of Guatemala.[34]

In contrast to Eisenhower's caution, other pressures were coming from Washington for an early show of anti-Castro force.[35] A working-level operative remembered storming into Barnes's office one day in September, demanding, "What's the hurry? . . . Why are we working our asses off on this?" Barnes had the political savvy to understand that the person pressing the urgency was Vice President Nixon, eager for a dramatic action to propel him into the White House.*

One key person was largely absent from the CIA's available records of this planning. Against Arbenz's Guatemala in 1954 Allen had kept on top of every detail of a bold covert operation, debriefing his protégés in from the field, relishing the adventure of the war on communism. This time Bissell's Cuban task force was dealing in such matters as aircraft procurement, drop-zone identification, and materiel stockpiling, things that took the fun out of intelligence. Six years older and jaded by covert actions that had not worked out, Allen had lost touch. He became the Cuban opera-

---

* For a decade to come Nixon remained edgy about his relationship to the anti-Castro operation that aborted at the Bay of Pigs, even after he finally became president and won re-election to a second term in 1972. The old CIA hands Hunt and Barker were on the team of burglars arrested at the Watergate office building in July 1972; in the ensuing scandal, Nixon demanded immediate recovery of the CIA's Bay of Pigs files for fear of some undescribed but adverse disclosure. Secret tape recordings made in the Oval Office just after the burglary contain such cryptic remarks by Nixon as: "You open that scab, there's a helluva lot of things, and we just feel that it would be very detrimental to have this thing go any further. . . . If it gets out that this is all involved, the Cuba thing, it would be a fiasco. . . . It is likely to blow the whole Bay of Pigs thing." Without the parts of the CIA record that remain classified, Nixon's role remains murky.

tion's high-level advocate even as he dropped the reins of the operation itself. When the Havana station chief returned to Washington expecting to
brief the director, as in the old days, he found Allen "pretty foggy about the
whole thing." Angleton, whose overarching responsibilities for counterespionage gave him access to pending matters withheld from all others, remembers raising problems about the Cuban operation in a private meeting and being alarmed at how little Allen seemed to know about the
activities of Bissell and his task force.[36] In another context Stuart Symington, critic of the so-called missile gap, had remarked in astonishment of
"the things Allen Dulles did not seem to know." In the matter of the missile gap, the impression of ignorance had really been Allen's forbearance
about discussing the reassuring intelligence received from the still secret
U-2. With Angleton and the work of the Cuban task force, the ignorance
was real — Allen had not bothered to inquire what his trusted deputies
were doing.

Only in the weeks after the presidential election did Allen turn his attention to the strategy that had evolved incrementally since the previous
March. There had been no progress in forging an anti-Castro alliance
among the Cuban émigrés. The clandestine infiltrations and air drops
were achieving no success in stirring up an indigenous resistance. Early in
December he briefed the retiring president and the 5412 Group on the
revised planning. He fleshed out the "strike force" that Bissell had mentioned to Kennedy in their first postelection briefings, the concept that
only an amphibious invasion to secure a beachhead would suffice to trigger the resistance to Castro. From the initial three hundred in the incipient Cuban brigade, the number of fighters under training by European
émigrés had reached seven hundred and was still growing.

Though not spoken at the time, this was the moment of the first great
mistake in the debacle that became known as the Bay of Pigs. "By about
November 1960, the impossibility of running . . . a covert operation under
CIA should have been recognized and the situation reviewed," concluded
President Kennedy's review board after the fact. "Failing such a reorien-
tation, the project should have been abandoned." In his own postmortem,
Bissell conceded the point: "Wishful thinking about maintaining the oper-
ation's covert nature persisted among all those involved in the planning."[37]

State Department representatives did raise the suggestion that perhaps the training base could be moved out of Guatemala, where newsmen
were already getting wind of the purpose. They suggested airlifting the
Cuban brigade to the more secure training camp in Saipan, in the northern Marianas of the far Pacific. There the CIA was training Chinese nationalist fighters for action against the communist mainland; perhaps the
Cubans could fit in? The idea fell flat.

Eisenhower, a lame-duck president and weary, voiced none of his earlier cautions when Allen told him of the new concept; had he been interested, his own experiences might have offered some insight into the difficulties of an amphibious landing. On January 19, Eisenhower's last full day in office, he invited Kennedy and his aides to sit in at a final NSC meeting. The outgoing team surveyed the world for the new administration. Clark Clifford took notes for Kennedy's reference. When the discussion got to Cuba, Clifford sensed no reluctance or hesitation. "President Eisenhower said with reference to the guerrilla forces which are opposed to Castro that it was the policy of this government to help such forces to the utmost. At the present time we are helping train anti-Castro forces in Guatemala. It was his recommendation that this effort be continued and accelerated."[38]

On assuming office, therefore, Kennedy inherited "contingency" planning that had set up its own imperatives for action. Bissell admitted his own culpability in limiting the options before the new president. "It's only fair to say that the Kennedy administration did inherit a military organization here that would have been difficult to dispose of, and embarrassing to dispose of, in any way other than by allowing it to go into action." Allen did not demur. "We either had to go ahead or we had the alternative of demobilizing these people," he said after it was all over. Had the Cuban brigade been demobilized, "to the world it would have meant that we were not behind these people who were trying to over-throw Castro."[39]

— * —

From his first days in office, an uneasy President Kennedy challenged the contingency planning that had been bequeathed to him. "It was a sort of orphan child JFK had adopted," Allen wrote, looking back. "He had no real love and affection for it . . . [he] proceeded uncertainly toward defeat, unable to turn back, only half sold on the vital necessity of what he was doing."[40] More than eight hundred Cuban fighters were now gathered under the CIA leash at Base Trax in Guatemala. McGeorge Bundy, the new president's national security adviser, said Kennedy "was informed that the force must leave Guatemala within a limited time, and that it could not be held together in the United States for a long period. It would begin to deteriorate; its existence could not be kept quiet; and if it were disbanded within the United States the results would be damaging."[41]

On January 28, a week after the inauguration, Kennedy and his foreign policy aides reviewed the CIA's plans in detail; he authorized continuing propaganda, political action, and sabotage efforts. Though they would never be raised at a large meeting, the plans included at least two different plots to assassinate Castro and key figures around him. "Assassination was intended to reinforce the plan; there was the thought that Castro would be dead before the [paramilitary] landing," Bissell declared long afterward. "Very few, however, knew of this aspect of the plan. . . . There was a reluctance to spread, even on an oral record, some aspects of this operation."[42] "Bad words" were inevitably avoided; Kennedy, just as much as Eisenhower, had to have his "plausible deniability."

At this first meeting Kennedy reserved judgment on the proposed invasion itself; he ordered the Joint Chiefs of Staff to give him their expert assessment. Bissell and the task force had been reluctant to engage the Defense Department up to this point, mindful of the Pentagon's penchant for extensive staff work and analysis, which to the CIA mentality only stifled initiative and daring. The army staff officer assigned to the JCS study, Brigadier General David W. Gray, was appalled to find that the CIA task force had never committed the full plan to paper. The CIA men gave the Pentagon team only a spoken rundown of the complex training, equipping, and deployment operation. Working around the clock for six days, the JCS produced a guarded assessment. In his first briefing to the chiefs Gray cautiously gave the proposed invasion a "thirty percent chance" of succeeding. For their final report to Kennedy the Joint Chiefs preferred a less precise formulation: "the plan has a fair chance of ultimate success."[43]

In this exchange is a textbook example of the problem of communication within a bureaucracy, particularly acute when the officials involved are new to their jobs, not yet intimately familiar with each other and with the system working around them. The chiefs used the word "fair" as compared to "moderate" or "good" — better, that is, than "poor." But to those unfamiliar with the discussion leading up to the assessment, the measure could easily be interpreted as "reasonable," which was how Kennedy and his civilian advisers took it. Apparently no one saw fit to inquire further.

The problem of communications had serious implications; indeed, it plagued Allen's relations with the new president despite their previous friendship. For eight years Allen had been accustomed to Eisenhower's crisp style of staff work, with careful minutes of meetings circulated, reviewed, and parsed for possible misunderstandings. That, to be sure, was not the style within CIA, but it was the operating procedure on the high level where Allen functioned. Kennedy operated differently. Robert Amory, personal friend to both John Kennedy and Allen Dulles, summed up the problem. Kennedy, he said, was "used to dealing with guys . . . over the years that he knew exactly what they meant by a shrug of their shoulders or the way they phrased a sentence." But with Allen, Kennedy later confided, "I can't estimate his meaning when he tells me things." Sorensen explained, "The President, on more than one occasion, felt that

Mr. Dulles, by making rather vague and sweeping references to particular countries, was seeking tacit approval without ever asking for it, and the President was rather concerned that he was not being asked for explicit directives, and was not being given explicit information."[44]

Allen had the same difficulty. Early in his career, as a spymaster running agents, he had developed a sensitivity to indirect communication on delicate topics. But now, in his later years, he would often remark upon his problems in discerning Kennedy's meaning. "Now about this Cuban operation . . . " he might say, to which Kennedy would say, "Yeah . . ." in what Allen took as vague impatience. "If Eisenhower had said that," Allen explained, "it would have signified, 'Yes, I know all about it and let's go on to something else.'" Too late, as Allen told it, "I learned that Kennedy had intended to express, not understanding or assent, but only, 'Yes, I'm listening. . . .'"

In this subtle problem of communications may lie the answer to a question that troubled Americans a decade later: did President Kennedy authorize, or even know about, CIA attempts to assassinate Castro? Allen may have thought Kennedy grasped the underlying meaning of his deliberate circumlocutions, and he proceeded accordingly. To protect the president and his "plausible deniability," Allen would not ask for a specific directive. But in avoiding "bad words" he may also have deprived the chief executive of the opportunity to call it off. It may well be that Kennedy, new to the job and confused by Allen's manner, simply did not understand what Allen thought he was communicating.

Allen did try to adapt his style. Pleased, as a Republican, to have been reappointed by a Democratic president, he made a special effort to engage his CIA team with the Kennedy circle, and this was appreciated on both sides. In the first weeks after the inauguration Allen arranged a mellow dinner at the private and discreet Alibi Club for a dozen of his top CIA officers and the equivalent number of new White House aides, including Sorensen, Lawrence O'Brien, and others. Amory long remembered the occasion. "It was a pleasant three-cocktail dinner, but then a serious discussion went on until one o'clock in the morning. . . . Why did we get in such a mess in Indonesia in 1958, and that kind of thing. . . . From then on out, there was nobody in the key White House staff I couldn't pick up the phone and say, 'Hey, Larry . . . this is Bob' . . . a very sensible thing for Allen to have done and, I think, sat well."[45]

Allen accommodated the spirit of Kennedy's New Frontier. The Peace Corps, for instance, reminded Allen of his postgraduate year teaching in India. But to the officers of the clandestine services, the idealistic program offered a tempting opportunity to place undercover agents in difficult places around the world. Allen convened his staff; one officer recalled his words. "You are already looking at the Peace Corps for your own purposes. I want you to understand that if *anyone* in this agency tries to recruit a Peace Corps volunteer for CIA, that man will be immediately fired." For once, and for as long as Allen remained in office, his pious stricture was taken seriously.

— * —

The Bay of Pigs plan was conceived upon two major premises, both of which were misunderstood by President Kennedy and the people closest to him: the so-called guerrilla option for the invading force and the need for an air strike to accompany the landing. A further misreading, most serious of all, became fully evident only in Allen's troubled reflections years later.

A guerrilla campaign against the Castro regime was inherent in the Eisenhower plan from the start. Before Kennedy came into office this had been abandoned in favor of an outright invasion, but the notion was not dead. "In approving the operation, the president and senior officials had been greatly influenced by the understanding that the landing force could pass to guerrilla status, if unable to hold the beachhead," concluded the Kennedy administration's official inquiry.[46]

Conceivably this was a valid option in the first plan presented to Kennedy, calling for landing the invasion force near Trinidad, at the foot of the Escambray Mountains. Under questioning afterward from Robert Kennedy, Bissell explained that the invading force "would administer a strike which could lead to a general uprising or a formation of larger guerrilla units in the mountains with which dissidents could join forces. The strike force was not in repudiation of the guerrilla concept but in addition to it."[47]

But when the president and his policy advisers considered the Cuban operation again on March 11, Kennedy vetoed the Trinidad plan as too "spectacular"; he asked instead for a more obscure site for a "quiet" landing, "without having the appearance of a World War II–type amphibious assault."[48] The myth that the invasion could be kept covert died hard. Within the next five days Bissell and his team shifted the proposed landing site to a little bay near the thinly populated swamp of the Zapata Peninsula, the Bahía de Cochinos, or Bay of Pigs. Never was the eager informality of the CIA's operating culture shown up to such disadvantage. In later years Bissell was admirably candid in a critique of his own lapse:

It was rather lightheartedly assumed . . . that the swampy regions around the Bay of Pigs, while utterly different geographically from the mountains near Trinidad, could support guerrilla operations. With hindsight, this assumption was highly questionable and, in any event, was not carefully researched in the planning of the operation.

The implications for the "guerrilla option" of the shift from Trinidad to the Bay of Pigs were never made clear to the President.... Those in charge of the operation must accept a serious responsibility for having ill-informed the President on this aspect of the operation.[49]

Allen covered his own admission of fault in jauntiness. "Actually, I blame myself a bit on the guerrilla thing," Allen told the official inquiry. "I think we were misled by the fact that Zapata was a traditional guerrilla area." The only "fact" was that guerrillas had operated at Zapata during the Spanish-American War and then again early in the twentieth century, before roads and villages had spread across the island — but not more recently. As Allen acknowledged after the debacle, "the only real course of action in the event the operation didn't succeed was sea evacuation" — a course totally contrary to everything he had outlined before.[50]

Then on April 16, as the ships carrying the Cuban brigade were approaching the Bay of Pigs, Kennedy decided to cancel the air strikes by CIA-hired Cuban flyers that were to begin at dawn, aimed at neutralizing Castro's modest air defense forces. He had failed to understand the significance of air support; as late as that last week the orders for the action were not pulled together into a coherent framework. Secretary of State Dean Rusk was a strong advocate of canceling the air strikes, arguing from his own experiences in World War II that air support was not essential to guerrilla infiltration operations — for that is how, at the core, the Kennedy team still erroneously conceived the Bay of Pigs mission. Allen looked back in harsh judgment on his own culpability: "I should have said, 'Mr. President, if you're not willing to permit us to take the steps necessary to ... substantially immobilize the Cuban air force (which was a very small and crotchety and defective air force at that time), the plan to get this brigade ashore with its equipment and supplies is a faulty one.'"[51]

But Allen did not say this to Kennedy. Nor did Bissell or General Pearre Cabell, Allen's principal deputy, as they sat in the secretary of state's office late Sunday night, April 16, when Rusk called the president to present their arguments for reinstating the air strike. Kennedy was unpersuaded. Rusk removed the telephone from his ear and held it out across the desk, inviting Cabell or Bissell to make their case to the president directly. Weary and discouraged, they declined.[52]

"I had the strong feeling," McGeorge Bundy said afterward, "that if the military had said that calling off the air strikes would have caused the operation to fail, the president would have reversed his decision." For the

CIA men were not the only ones keeping silent at crucial moments. Admiral Arleigh Burke, chief of naval operations, conceded the Pentagon's complicity without presuming to state the reasons. "We did have an opportunity to say that we thought this plan was not feasible, and we did not say so."[53]

— * —

A far more serious malfunction of policy and intelligence occurred in the experience of the Bay of Pigs. Some officials at the time may have harbored their private suspicions, but the official inquiry that Kennedy ordered immediately after the disaster took scant notice of it. Only twenty-three years later did vague suspicion become admitted fact, through the study of handwritten notes Allen made in retirement. In 1965, after Kennedy's death, Allen wrote about the Bay of Pigs, in effect replying to criticism of CIA's mismanagement of an operation gone wrong. But when it came to submitting the manuscript for publication, he held back. Clover noted after Allen's death that he decided against publishing his account "because there was so much more in his favor he could have said, if he had been at liberty to do so."

Perhaps, but the fact remains that for decades to come CIA was accused of violating the trusts of the democracy that created it, of arrogance in the absence of accountability, of operating like an "invisible government." CIA stalwarts scoffed at the charges, but it can now be argued convincingly that in the Bay of Pigs operation the clandestine services were behaving just as the critics charged.

From the start and throughout, both Eisenhower and Kennedy had been adamant that no United States military personnel would be permitted to participate in any combat action against Cuba. Kennedy had said as much in a press conference on April 12, the week before the landing: "There will not be, under any conditions, an intervention in Cuba by the United States armed forces." The leadership of CIA ultimately did not accept the president's words. Whatever the stated policy, Allen and those around him adhered to the comfortable belief that the armed forces of the United States would back them up in preventing the failure of a covert action, no matter how botched or ill conceived it turned out to be.

Evidence for this serious charge appears in Allen's typed and handwritten, coffee-stained notes, which were preserved with his personal papers at Princeton. In this tentative form he voiced candid explanation for his failure to disabuse Kennedy of the key misunderstandings, about the guerrilla option and the supposed covert nature of the invasion.

[We] never raised objections to repeated emphasis [by the President] that the operation: a) must be carried through without any "combat" action by

U.S.A. military forces; b) must remain quiet [and] disavowable by [the] U.S. gov[ernment]; c) must be a quiet operation yet must rouse internal revolt vs. Castro and create a center to which anti-Castroites will defect.

[We] did not want to raise these issues ... which might only harden the decision against the type of action we required. We felt that when the chips were down — when the crisis arose in reality — any action required for success would be authorized rather than permit the enterprise to fail. . . .

We believed that in a time of crisis we would gain what we might have lost if we provoked an argument [in advance].

Thus a CIA agenda, hidden but apparently long-standing, emerged in the retirement musings of its director. "I have seen [a] good many operations which started out like the B of P," Allen's notes continued, "insistence on complete secrecy — non-involvement of the U.S. — initial reluctance to authorize supporting actions. This limitation tends to disappear as the needs of the operation become clarified." But in the Bay of Pigs the stated policy prevailed; the nation's commander in chief did not back up the CIA clandestine services when the operation faltered. In his more defensive moods, Allen faulted Kennedy for lack of "determination to succeed." But another way of putting it was that the president was unwilling to let his policy be held hostage to a CIA covert action.

These long-ignored notes were analyzed by a research fellow at the Brookings Institution of Washington, Lucien S. Vandenbroucke, early in the 1980s. Before the academic quarterly *Diplomatic History* would publish his analysis, the journal's editors turned to the retired Bissell for a reply (Allen was long since deceased). Displaying the cool academic detachment with which he could analyze errors, including his own, Bissell conceded that he and Allen had allowed Kennedy to persist in misunderstandings about the nature of the Cuban operation. As to why they did so, he grew uncharacteristically vague.

"The profound hope and the expectation in the CIA was that there would not be a crisis which would call for such a drastic policy change," he wrote. "There was never any trace of a conspiratorial alternative operational plan based on the assumption that the President's hand would be forced." Perhaps not in the formal way Bissell depicted; but if the worst-case scenario became real? Bissell's cautious language did not negate the underlying point. "Many of us, like Dulles himself, believed there was a possibility that, in the event of trouble, restrictions would be relaxed, possibly even on the use of U.S. aircraft."[54]

Even in the immediate aftermath of the aborted invasion, Allen conceded having put pressure on the new president in the prior discussions of what Kennedy still thought was a contingency plan. "The President was faced with hurried and difficult decisions," he said. "We had made it very clear to him that to call off the operation would have resulted in a very unpleasant situation"—a situation, however, of the CIA's own making. Allen told Kennedy, for instance, at the March 11 meeting, "Don't forget that we have a disposal problem. If we have to take these men out of Guatemala, we will have to transfer them to the United States, and we can't have them wandering around the country telling everyone what they have been doing."[55]

Searching his memory, Robert Kennedy recalled a point made when the CIA first presented the plan to the new administration but then dropped as the discussions proceeded: "We were told that it would be impossible to successfully overthrow Castro, unless you had the invading force backed up by intervention by U.S. forces."[56] The Kennedys also discovered that before the inauguration the Joint Chiefs of Staff had analyzed possible levels of U.S. involvement in a military operation against Cuba; this study paper was never called to the new administration's attention. As late as April 18, as the Cuban brigade was fighting for the beachhead, Admiral Burke dispatched two battalions of Marines to ships cruising off Cuba in case Kennedy did, after all, order United States combat action to salvage a botched invasion.[57]

Perhaps none of this adds up to what Bissell scorned as a "conspiratorial alternative operational plan," but it is clear evidence that the CIA's hidden agenda at the Bay of Pigs was more than fantasy. The option of American military intervention, held in reserve to be invoked only *in extremis*, would supersede the declared policy of the president to meet the CIA's needs.

— ⋆ —

As president, Kennedy had every right to expect his intelligence service to provide impartial input into the formulation of policy and then impartial evaluation of the likely effects of various policy options. Instead he was confronted, at the very start of his administration, with the consequences of Allen's argument that intelligence collection and assessment should be performed by the same service as the parallel challenge of covert action. The team advocating an operation was also responsible for assessing and evaluating the situation in which it would be played out.

"Mistakes were made in this operation by a lot of people whom the President had every right to trust," McGeorge Bundy said. "In the future any such plan should have much more careful preparation and evaluation, and the President should have intelligence estimates presented to him by others than advocates."[58]

Allen remembered expressing some short-lived misgivings to Kennedy, and inside the CIA inner circle he would regularly warn his aides against overselling the project. "We've got to underplay it," one aide remembered him saying. But later he conceded the difficulty of sustaining that reserve; he became, in effect, a salesman for the operation his clandestine services had conceived. As he told Tom Braden, "Obviously, you present a plan and it isn't your job to say, well, that's a rotten plan I've presented. You can only say, here are the merits of the plan, and in presenting the merits of the plan the tendency is always to . . . be drawn into more of a salesmanship job than you should."[59]

To be fair, Kennedy's own memory played tricks when he recalled the extent of Allen's advocacy. After the debacle the president told both Sorensen and Schlesinger that Allen had said to him in the Oval Office, "I stood right here at Ike's desk and told him I was certain our Guatemalan operation would succeed, and, Mr. President, the prospects for this plan are even better than they were for that one."[60] Allen said no such thing to Eisenhower at the time of Operation Success; on the contrary, what impressed Eisenhower so much was that Allen put the chances of success at only about twenty percent. Allen vehemently denied that he had every promised Kennedy more than "a fighting chance" for the Bay of Pigs operation.

Before there was a CIA, before he had taken up the profession of intelligence, Allen had warned a committee of the U.S. Senate against the "human frailty of intellectual stubbornness." The measure of how far he himself had succumbed to that frailty came early in the planning for the Cuban invasion, when one of his old protégés, Edward Lansdale, appeared at a meeting of the 5412 Group to discuss the prospects of an operation against Castro. Lansdale, veteran manager of guerrilla warfare in the Philippines and the early stages of the Vietnam War, challenged the CIA's plan.

"Initially there was thought of doing what Castro had done, go up in the hills, get some people — including some who had been with him — to fight the Castro government," Lansdale said. "I went [along] with that." But now the CIA seemed to be contemplating an invasion. "You can't do that in a country where the army is as alert [as in Cuba]. We're going to get clobbered! What's the political base for what you're going to do?" he asked Allen directly. "How popular is it going to be?" Allen interrupted his old comrade with angry remarks of his own. "You're not a principal in this!" he said, trying to silence Lansdale, who retorted firmly, "In policy meetings, you have got to be very honest. You should have talk."[61]

As the meeting dispersed, Allen pulled Lansdale aside and quietly asked his old hand, as a favor for past efforts, to be more discreet in the future about voicing objections.

— * —

Historians, including those in government with access to the classified record, have searched in vain for a clear-cut decision by President Kennedy to invade the Bay of Pigs. There was no such decision. All the operational meetings of March and early April 1961 concerned a CIA plan that would proceed unless or until a decision was made to call it off. As often happens in sensitive clandestine actions, a chief executive is spared the need to go on record authorizing an operation that might later backfire; the only decision forced is a passive one: to refrain from calling off actions that have acquired their own momentum. That was the decision made by Kennedy for the last time the morning of April 16. "No diversion being ordered," reported the CIA internal record, the landing was authorized to proceed.[62]

As dawn broke on April 17, the invasion force landed on the western shore of the Bay of Pigs. In two days of fierce fighting, deprived of air cover and supply support, the Cuban brigade was unable to secure a beachhead. A thousand or so of the trained fighters were captured by Castro's defense forces; only a hundred were able to escape out to sea to be rescued by U.S. Navy and commercial ships. By 5 P.M. on April 19, the Bay of Pigs invasion was over.

The days of April 16 to 20 saw the proud CIA humbled as never before. Allen "looked like living death," wrote Robert Kennedy in the aftermath. "He had the gout and had trouble walking, and he was always putting his head in his hands."[63] Surprisingly, Allen had provided no guiding hand through that week of crisis; he hovered between helplessness and irrelevance.

Although the aging director had lost touch with the details of his clandestine services' operations, he preserved the front. Early that month James Reston of The New York Times had learned enough from the correspondents in Central America to confront Allen directly. He went to 2723 Q Street after hours. The setting was beguiling; Reston expected to come upon "the late George Apley reading eighteenth-century novels." Allen airily dismissed with a wave of the hand all the journalistic suspicions of skullduggery against Castro; Reston, a canny Scotsman long immune to Allen's English ways, concluded that "he was lying like hell."[64]

On April 5 word that the Times had the story had reached Edward R. Murrow, the distinguished radio and television journalist whom Kennedy had just made head of the United States Information Agency. Not yet comfortable operating through bureaucratic channels, Murrow called on the director of central intelligence personally for guidance. Allen received his bold new colleague with smiles and cordiality amid the cloud of pipe smoke. When it came to the business at hand, he said that much as he regretted it, he was simply in no position to give the USIA any information about covert operations. Murrow left Allen's office in less than fifteen minutes. As a crack journalist, he understood that absence of denial probably meant confirmation — of something. But the CIA invasion of Cuba caught the USIA unprepared and without guidance.[65]

As D-day at the Bay of Pigs approached, Allen simply left town. Months before, he had accepted one of the speaking engagements he so enjoyed, to a convention of the Young Presidents' Organization in Puerto Rico. To cancel the engagement, he argued, would only alert interested observers of some looming intelligence crisis. (Actually, a plea of illness and the provision of an equally illustrious substitute would have been a thoroughly respectable dodge.) The unstated fact was that there was nothing left for Allen to do in springing the covert action to dislodge Fidel Castro. He trusted Bissell, as did Kennedy, in any last-minute decisions. As the armada of the Cuban brigade — now 1,200 strong — moved toward the coast of the Zapata Peninsula the weekend of April 15–16, Allen and Clover flew to Puerto Rico for a public show of conviviality, golf, and swimming. "It is highly unlikely that [Dulles's] presence in Washington would have made any difference," concluded the CIA official history, "although in hindsight there is the appearance of the captain's not being on the bridge at the time of a major engagement."[66]

In overall charge of CIA Allen left his unimaginative deputy, General Cabell, who knew the ropes but would not presume to try untangling them; Bissell and his task force were fully capable of handling the final decisions in a complex paramilitary operation. Amory, head of intelligence analysis, whom Bissell had not included in the Bay of Pigs planning, confronted Allen alone as he was leaving his office. "You know I've got the duty tomorrow; whether you know it or not, I know what's going on. What should I do if anything comes up?"[67] Allen replied impatiently, "You have nothing to do with that at all; General Cabell will take care of anything."*

Without secure telephone contact with Washington, without any source of information more sensitive than the public news media, Allen spent the crucial weekend, as planned, playing golf with the young business executives. Before leaving he had arranged a primitive telephone code; he might call Washington to report catching "three marlin today." A congratulatory response would mean that all was going well at

* So when the trouble started, Amory went home and played five sets of tennis. "I said, screw 'em!"

the Bay of Pigs. No code was set for news that things were going badly.

On Monday morning, April 17, reports of the landing led the radio news. The Young Presidents heard a panel discussion with Margaret Mead and Dr. Benjamin Spock on the topic "Are We Letting Our Children Down?" Then Allen gave his address on doing business behind the Iron Curtain. He had no time to call Washington about the three marlin; when newsmen confronted him with reports of an invasion of Cuba, he was able, jauntily and accurately, to say that he knew nothing about it except what he had heard from the press.

Allen and Clover flew home from Puerto Rico at the end of the festivities that evening. One of the deputies in the Cuban task force, Richard Drain, met them at Baltimore's Friendship Airport to brief the director on the struggles of the invading force, against unexpected resistance and the lack of air and sea support, before he could learn about the imminent collapse from any other source.

Descending from the plane, still in his dinner jacket, Allen expressed pleasure at seeing one of his fondly remembered field officers (Drain had earlier been station chief in Athens). Allen sent Clover home in Drain's Chevy and settled the officer into his own CIA Cadillac for a good chat. Drain told him about the cancellation of the air strike. "The president must be a little confused," Allen remarked. Drain marveled at his boss's sense of detachment from the human drama being played out at that very moment on Red Beach and Blue Beach of the Bay of Pigs. The invaders had landed, but two of their support ships, carrying ammunition and supplies, had been knocked out of action by three planes of Castro's air defenders. The rest of the twenty-five-minute drive to Georgetown passed largely in silence.

As the car pulled up to the house on Q Street, Allen invited Drain in for a nightcap. Now would come the moment for a private briefing, Drain supposed. But all Allen wanted to discuss was the personality of the prime minister of Greece, who, Allen learned from looking at his schedule, was to pass through Washington the next day.[68] There was no further discussion of the tragedy on the beaches in Cuba.

All the next day came the news of despair, and Allen circulated between Foggy Bottom and the White House almost in a daze. Castro's ground forces were moving in against the invaders. Allen mechanically reported the dispatches of failure to Kennedy; Bissell provided energetic briefings and presented the dwindling options. This was the moment to invoke the hidden agenda, an escalation with United States combat troops to save the Cuban brigade and the national honor. President Kennedy would have none of it. "We're not going to plunge into an irresponsible action just because a fanatical fringe . . . puts so-called national pride above national reason," he said.[69] So much for the presumed safety net under the CIA's paramilitary operation.

Tuesday was the night of the annual White House congressional dinner. Kennedy stayed in the Oval Office as late as he could, then went up to the residence to change for dinner. He and Jacqueline danced elegantly through the evening. Only a little after midnight could he make his escape; still in white tie and tails, he gathered around him those of his aides he could find at the party, Rusk, Bundy, Defense Secretary Robert McNamara, Vice President Johnson, the Joint Chiefs in their full-dress uniforms. Allen had been at the dinner but had gone home early, to bed. Bissell joined the group and made his final plea for U.S air support; the chiefs proposed landing a company of Marines. Kennedy agreed only to a one-hour overflight, without any combat engagement, to cover a landing of supplies or an evacuation.

When Kennedy faced a news conference at the end of the week, he made no attempt to put a positive face on the human and political disaster that had overtaken his administration. "There's an old saying," he said, "that victory has a hundred fathers and defeat is an orphan." The Kennedy brothers had an amazing ability to recall lines they had read over their lives and to summon up spontaneously just what the occasion needed. All the intellectuals who fed the president ideas for speeches were taken aback at this "old saying." When he was writing his memoir of the Kennedy presidency, Schlesinger actually called the editor of *Bartlett's Familiar Quotations* in an unsuccessful search for the origin of the line. Belatedly the source was identified, and it turned out to be just about the only positive contribution Allen Dulles made to that week of disaster. Though Kennedy himself probably had no notion of where he had first read it, the line was finally traced to an entry in the Ciano diaries, which the OSS spymaster had unearthed in Switzerland at the end of World War II.

Kennedy was naturally concerned at what his Republican opponents would make of the disaster. He personally called Eisenhower, Nixon, Nelson Rockefeller, and Barry Goldwater, just to share his anguish with his opponents. On Thursday Allen himself went to the home that Nixon still maintained in Washington, to give his old friend a personal accounting of the week's events. For all his partisan anger at the bungling of an operation that he himself had helped initiate, the former vice president found himself feeling genuine concern for the well-being of a professional colleague he had known ever since the days of the Alger Hiss investigations. Allen was an hour and a half late for the appointment. "He was under great emotional stress," Nixon wrote. He limped into the house in slippers, despondency all over his normally buoyant face. This, Allen said, "has been the worst day of my life."

— 19 —

SIR ALLEN

ALLEN HAD TO GO. As the new Kennedy administration surveyed the political wreckage of the Bay of Pigs, none of the key policymakers were in any doubt of that. Settling in to the four years that the voters had given him, Kennedy needed his own leadership at CIA, a director in whom he had confidence, who would be there when needed, and whom he could understand when they talked. The question about Allen's retirement was only when, and how.

As her gout-stricken husband staggered home each night that week in April, the extent of the disaster becoming ever clearer, Clover pleaded that he take matters into his own hands and resign immediately — not just offer it, do it! She, for one, had long been looking forward to a time when Allen might have more time and energy for her. Allen apparently gave serious thought to taking this preemptive step to spare the new president (and himself) an unpleasant confrontation.[1] After all, he had agreed at the outset to serve for only a year of transition; a few months less would not make a big difference to him, and it might help clear the sour air.

On Friday, April 21, Allen called at the Oval Office to see Kennedy alone; he was prepared to accept whatever fate the president presented. Kennedy received him in a matter-of-fact mood, without a hint of recrimination. For half an hour they reviewed pending intelligence situations, just as they had done over the past three months. The subject of resignation was never raised.

One consideration that held Allen back over the coming weeks was the storm of criticism resounding through the American and international press against his CIA. For the director to step down under pressure would seem to confirm that the errors had been his alone. That did not correspond to the reality and was not an impression he wished to promote. Nor did Kennedy. The day after the beachhead collapsed, when Vice President Johnson started criticizing the CIA at a White House meeting, Kennedy cut him off. "Lyndon, you've got to remember we're all in this, and that when I accepted responsibility for this operation, I took the entire responsibility on myself. . . . We should have no sort of passing of the buck or backbiting, however justified."[2] The last two words, of course, may be more revealing than Kennedy intended of his personal judgments on the matter but, like Eisenhower after the U-2 disaster, the president was determined not to use Allen as a scapegoat. Allen and Kennedy had many talks in the following weeks, "and while I did have a feeling that maybe he thought I had let him down," Allen said, "there never was one harsh or unkind word said to me by him at any time thereafter."

A small incident conveyed the president's generosity of spirit more than any reassuring words. Allen's (and Kennedy's) old friend from Palm Beach, Charles Wrightsman, appeared in Washington shortly after the crisis; as he normally would, he telephoned Kennedy to ask if he could stop by. He pointedly told the president he would not be making an effort to see Allen on this visit. Kennedy was offended at this crude show of disloyalty to a longtime friend. He invited Wrightsman over to the White House for a drink that afternoon, and he invited Allen as well. When Allen walked in — Wrightsman was already settled down — Kennedy stood up and, in case the rich man from Florida still did not get the message, the beleaguered president put his arm around Allen's shoulders to lead him to a comfortable chair.

High in the political demonology of Kennedy's administration was the late Republican secretary of state, John Foster Dulles, branded as the rigid apostle of "brinkmanship," which the Democrats of the 1960s sought to overcome. Remarkable, therefore, that none of this odium was transferred to Foster's brother. "Allen Dulles handled himself awfully well, with a great deal of dignity," Robert Kennedy told a friend after the Bay of Pigs. "The President was very fond of him, as I was."[3]

British notables who had known Allen over the years often remarked upon an unfortunate omission when the American colonies adapted the English paraliamentary model — the absence of an honors system, knighthoods or elevation to a lordship. This elegant device allowed distinguished public servants to be removed from the political fray once they had passed their prime but retained their luster and experience within the system. Allen, the British would say, was a prime candidate to be a viscount, or at least a knight of high degree.

Leaving no one in doubt that Allen would be relieved of his CIA leadership, Kennedy nonetheless held to his own calculations of how and when to do it. "We will have to do something about [CIA]," he said privately the week of the crisis. "I must have someone there with whom I can be in complete and intimate contact — someone from whom I know I will be getting the exact pitch." On the Tuesday of the Bay of Pigs fighting, Kennedy had a long-scheduled luncheon with the venerable publisher of *The New York Times*, Arthur Hays Sulzberger. As was customary in such courtesies, the publisher brought along his Washington correspondent, James Reston, lest a valuable opportunity for off-the-record discussion with the president degenerate into empty pleasantries.

Kennedy seemed open with his guests. "I probably made a mistake in keeping Allen Dulles on," he said. "It's not that Dulles is not a man of great ability. He is." But, he went on, "Dulles is a legendary figure, and it's hard to operate with legendary figures." That remark found its way into the public domain and added yet another lustrous strand to Allen's image. But a short time later the president was more candid with Schlesinger, who had also attended the Sulzberger luncheon; as long as Allen held office, Kennedy said, the Republicans would be inhibited in their attacks on his administration.[4]

— * —

President Kennedy sought to learn from the experience of the Bay of Pigs. The Friday of the crisis week he asked McGeorge Bundy to telephone retired General Maxwell Taylor in New York. The former army chief of staff, only fifty-nine, was establishing himself in the illustrious post of president of Lincoln Center for the Performing Arts. Bundy asked Taylor to clear his weekend and fly down to Washington for a serious meeting the next morning.

Allen, also summoned to the White House that Saturday, was surprised to see among the NSC regulars not only Taylor (a longtime tennis partner) but the attorney general, Robert Kennedy. The president declared his need for a detailed investigation of how his administration had gone wrong in Cuba. He ordered Taylor to manage the inquiry, giving the army careerist no room for hesitation. To make clear that he was seeking only information for his own presidency, not a witch-hunt or a scapegoat, Kennedy informed Taylor that his partners in the inquiry would be Admiral Burke, an early advocate of the Bay of Pigs action, and Allen Dulles, director of the agency that had carried out the operation. They would surely know exactly what had gone on and, for all their instincts to preserve their own turf, Kennedy regarded them as men of integrity. The final member named to the Taylor commission was the president's brother.

Taylor had no choice but to take his assignment seriously. The presidential board of inquiry held its first meeting for four hours the afternoon of that same Saturday, then resumed Monday morning and met twenty times during the month to come. Allen sat in pipe-smoking silence as surviving Cubans testified about how they had been misled by their CIA handlers. When one said that whoever planned the operation "must have been crazy," Allen just looked through him. He argued, always politely, with his old comrade from Operation Sunrise, General Lyman Lemnitzer, who had become chairman of the Joint Chiefs of Staff, about the role of the military establishment in the debacle.[5]

Occasionally he would steer the inquiry away from delicate subjects, such as the schemes to assassinate Castro. In a closed meeting of presidential confidants who had been through the wars of government and occasional misdeeds, a simple remark from the director of central intelligence was sufficient. "We don't really need to pursue this point much further," was a typical Allen Dulles formulation, and for the Taylor board it served to silence further inquiry.*

Theatrical relief came when General Walter Bedell Smith appeared before the board to deliver what turned out to be his final judgment on the civilian intelligence service he had pioneered before Allen. The crusty old soldier's health was failing, but nothing could prevent him from sounding off. "You have to be immoral," he said about covert operations. "When you are at war, Cold War if you like, you must have an amoral agency which can operate secretly and which does not have to give press conferences." But to the CIA as it had become, he showed no mercy. "Beetle" Smith had not changed his mind about separating covert actions from intelligence collection and assessment.[6] "I think that so much publicity has been given to CIA that the covert work might have to be put under another roof. . . . It's time we take the bucket of slop and put another cover over it."†

The final report of the Taylor board was harsh in its criticism, not only of the CIA but of the State Department and the Joint Chiefs of Staff as well, as they had performed in the first months of the Kennedy administration. With responsibility thus diffused, Allen's CIA survived intact. Kennedy's basic judgment, however, remained; Allen had to be retired, with as much respect and dignity as the young president could arrange.

It is not clear whether Allen knew it or not, but both the president and Robert Kennedy were vetting Taylor carefully throughout this period with the idea of naming him to be Allen's successor. Kennedy's first choice had been his own brother: "I made a mistake in putting Bobby in

---

* So it would also for a future presidential commission on which Allen was called to serve, the circumstances and purpose of which could not yet be imagined.

† Smith died in August, just three months after his appearance before the Taylor board.

the Justice Department," Kennedy confided to Schlesinger, even as the Cuban invasion was still in process. "He is wasted there . . . he should be in CIA." But the younger Kennedy argued against the move and, impressed by the way the board of inquiry was proceeding, turned the president's attentions to Taylor. The career army officer had retired prematurely over disagreement with the strategies of massive retaliation espoused by Eisenhower and John Foster Dulles. He was not eager to return to Washington, and certainly not to take responsibility for CIA. "I insisted that this was just not my dish," Taylor explained. "I really felt that I would be justified in coming back to the government only if I utilized my military experience."[7] Kennedy promptly created a White House military post for him, which he accepted. It included stern policy supervision of the CIA's covert operations.*

The Bay of Pigs effectively ended the Dulles era at CIA. With neither the will nor the clout to embark upon any significant new ventures, Allen's remaining months in office were consumed by the one project that he could still control: completion, to the point of perfection, of the new CIA campus on 140 acres of once placid farmland in Langley, across the Potomac from Washington. Even this venture provoked a measure of friction with the Kennedys. As it happened, the attorney general drove past the new site every morning on his way into Washington from his farmlike home in McLean; he began getting irritated with large signs on the highway that told the world exactly how to find the inner sanctum of the CIA. He complained to his brother. The next time Kennedy saw Allen he casually asked if road signs announcing the CIA headquarters were really consistent with the character of a secret service. Allen, of course, had always regarded publicity and accessibility as assets for an intelligence service. He replied to Kennedy's gingerly concern only with banter — without direction signs, he said, the teams of contractors and movers then at work would never find the place! Ho ho ho!

A week passed, with Robert Kennedy's annoyance mounting on the drive each morning. The president pressed Allen again; surely his was an agency that should not stand out for attention. This time Allen tried an-

---

* None of the criticisms in the inquiry report threatened the friendship between Allen and Maxwell Taylor. Indeed, Taylor nervously used Allen as his stalking horse when the two were asked to give Eisenhower a courtesy briefing on the board's conclusions. Taylor and his whole military generation were still in awe of the World War II supreme commander. Yet he had resigned from Eisenhower's administration and was now taking a post in the Kennedy White House. On the helicopter to Gettysburg, not entirely in jest, he asked Allen to go in first and drop Taylor's amply decorated general's hat on Ike's desk, just to see how it was received. Only then would Taylor dare to enter the presence. As it happened, Eisenhower bore no grudge and even congratulated Taylor on his new post in the White House.

other tack, mentioning that since CIA included many overt employees and functions, their place of work should not be secret. Indeed, the overt side of an intelligence service even provided useful cover for the clandestine branches, in case anyone was watching license plates and arrivals and departures in the two sprawling parking lots that accommodated 3,000 cars.

The Kennedys were not to be pacified. Two days later the president picked up his Oval Office telephone and called Bissell: "Who the hell do I have to talk to, to get those damned signs taken down!" A man of loyalty but also of politics, Bissell presumed to bypass his director. The attorney general reported to his brother the next morning a heartwarming victory in their joint effort to rein in the CIA.*

Allen ordered the brigades of contractors and movers about on every last detail, like the field commander he never was. Fearing communist penetration of the American labor movement, he ordered all union workers out of the building while the agency's sensitive telephones and internal communications were installed. The director decreed that he would stay aboard his Foggy Bottom command post until the last of the ranks had been moved and installed. It was a fateful grand gesture, for it meant that Allen would never occupy the new office suite he had designed, with open doors and easy access, for his own cheerful style.[8]

Although he had briefly considered resigning immediately after the Bay of Pigs, Allen's zest for the Game returned; that summer he told colleagues he would like to remain as director two more years, until he reached the age of seventy. Thus his dejection showed one day in August when he returned from the White House with the news that it was not to be. As he bluntly told his executive assistant, John Earman, "I've been fired."[9]

After vetting numerous other candidates through the summer, Kennedy settled in September on a wealthy California businessman, John McCone, to take over the CIA. A Republican, a hard-liner, McCone had served in the Pentagon during the Truman administration and had been chairman of the Atomic Energy Commission for Eisenhower. Allen, who had made known his displeasure over other possible candidates, was relieved that Kennedy had chosen a man of anticommunist credentials as impeccable as his own. "Successor and predecessor are worthy of each other," was the snide comment of the Soviet magazine *Life Abroad*. The *Times* of London remarked that "both men have white hair, wear the same rimless glasses and are the same age, but those similarities are misleading." McCone was a tough and thorough administrator who knew how to pound heads together; the trouble was that at the start he knew nothing

---

* The victory did not endure. After both the Kennedys and Allen had left the scene, modest direction signs to the CIA were restored along the verge of busy Route 123.

about espionage. One CIA station chief was astonished when, on taking the incoming director of central intelligence to meet his counterparts in Europe, McCone turned to him with the bland question, "What, exactly, is a double agent?"

CIA was not a happy ship as Allen hauled down his flag of command. Old hands like Helms and Amory, who had been excluded from the Bay of Pigs operation, had trouble concealing their satisfaction at the downfall of Bissell, Allen's last favored protégé; for all his virtues, Bissell was always an outsider in their eyes.* But Allen himself in his last months took a step that inadvertently led to a season of backbiting and recrimination that endured long after his departure.

As the Taylor board was being constituted, Allen asked his inspector general, Lyman Kirkpatrick, to conduct an internal investigation to see what the CIA had done wrong in the Cuban operation. Kirkpatrick had once been a favored player in the Great Game; as he was repeatedly passed over for higher responsibility, colleagues sensed that bitterness came to dominate his capacity for judgment. Pursuing his investigation with a vigor that also seemed to include the settling of old scores, the inspector general produced a 170-page critique even more scathing against his CIA colleagues, implicitly including Allen, than the Taylor report.

Kirkpatrick then made a fatal misstep in the game of bureaucracy. Completing his work the week before McCone was to be sworn in, he handed the report personally to the new man. McCone read the text on the plane to California, where he went to close out his private affairs over the Thanksgiving weekend. He telephoned Kirkpatrick the morning after his arrival. This document, he said, must go to Allen, who was still the director of central intelligence, and it must go to him "immediately." Allen, predictably, was outraged, both at Kirkpatrick's ugly personal judgments and at the seemingly devious manner in which he had presented them to the new director rather than to the executive who had commissioned it; gentlemen may or may not read each other's mail, but they do not strike at one of their number when he is down. The Kirkpatrick report, surreptitiously circulated within the agency, became a gleeful testimonial for those outside the loop of the Bay of Pigs operation. Despite lengthy lawsuits brought by retired officers, Allen's successors at CIA refused even thirty-three years later to release it for public information.[10]

— * —

* A still admiring President Kennedy offered Bissell senior posts in foreign aid and other economic development positions. Bissell, always his own man, declined, and spent the rest of his years contentedly in private business at his family home in Farmington, Connecticut. He died in 1994.

President Kennedy chose a ceremony at the Naval War College in Newport, Rhode Island, on September 27, 1961, to announce the appointment of McCone. He had waited until Allen's return from his late summer vacation in Europe — actually not only a vacation, for Allen and Clover had the sad task of placing their thirty-one-year-old son, Allen Macy, in a Swiss sanitorium at Kreuzlingen, near the Lake of Constance, which specialized in long-term care for difficult psychological cases. The weekend of their return they went to dinner at the home of Republican senator Prescott Bush, taking a guest with them. "I want you to meet my successor," Allen said cheerfully as he introduced McCone. "We tried to make a pleasant evening of it," Bush reminisced, "but I was rather sick at heart." All the company knew that the spymaster's illustrious career was ending.*

The change of command was to come in November, exactly one year after Allen had accepted Kennedy's invitation to remain as a transition figure in the Democratic administration. True to his inclinations, and his affection for Allen, Kennedy saw to it that he left office with dignity and respect. Though his was the responsibility for the Bay of Pigs debacle, the Kennedy circle took special care, following the president's lead, to avoid casting Allen in the role of scapegoat.

In the season of testimonials that followed, one Pentagon general with whom Allen had clashed during the Taylor inquiry wrote to the retiring director with the words of his beloved Kipling: "'If you can meet both triumph and disaster and treat those two imposters just the same' is still the measure of a man. I am grateful for the example you have been to me and to others in this."

Allen held to the values of a patrician without making an unnecessarily obvious point of it. Thus another letter received on his retirement was most meaningful. It came from David Bruce who, with Robert Lovett in 1956, had delivered one of the government's most damaging assessments of the covert action philosophy on which Allen had built his leadership in intelligence. Such differences were ignored when the end came. Bruce wrote Allen a careful letter, extraordinary in the correspondence of the era, between gentlemen.

> I only want to say, which I could never do orally, so reticent are we all when our affections are truly tugged, how much I have always admired you, and how sorry I am to reflect that I believe you to be irreplaceable. . . .
>
> Through sheer force of ability, and the loyalties that you so com-

---

* Thirteen years later, it would be the host's son, George Bush, who took over as Allen's successor, six times removed, as director of central intelligence.

pletely and unconsciously evoke, you have performed, in my estimation, one of the really significant duties in government, with the greatest of skill and, throughout, with what can only be described as supreme "chic," in every sense of the word.[11]

Allen took McCone to Europe late in October to introduce his successor to the foreign intelligence services with which the CIA had built liaison relationships. In all the capitals were muted signs of the deterioration in Western intelligence cooperation that would plague Allen's successors. The British service was still struggling to undo the damage of Philby's treachery. In Paris Gaullist intelligence officers were still suspicious, despite Allen's denials, of an imagined CIA role in the plotting of the French generals in Algeria against De Gaulle. The most awkward encounter of all came in Bonn, where Allen presented McCone to the spy chief of West Germany the very day that Gehlen's top lieutenant was exposed as a communist double agent of ten years' standing. (This was the happenstance that prompted McCone's naive question about one of the oldest dangers in the world of espionage. McCone demonstrated in the next three years the capacity of a fast learner, becoming one of the most effective directors the CIA ever knew.)

On their last evening in Germany, CIA old-timers who had worked with Allen over decades past convened at the Bonn station chief's home for an evening of reminiscence and nostalgia. McCone tactfully left early to not detract from Allen's last night with his men. About 11:30 Allen himself went up to bed as the CIA men settled down for nightcaps. A few minutes after midnight the assembled company was startled by an apparition on the stairs, descending in pajamas and dressing gown. There was no way Allen could settle into sleep while his comrades in espionage were savoring one final skull session together.

— * —

As the CIA's moving day to Langley approached, Allen stayed in his old office in Foggy Bottom, puttering with his files and old friends.* Allen kept his silence as he heard that McCone, moving into the Langley campus, set about rearranging the architecture of the director's office; the multiple doors, through which Allen had planned to receive all manner of

---

* Among the papers kept in his office safe was a packet of letters exchanged in earlier years with Mary Bancroft. Only after Allen's death did the CIA's general counsel, Lawrence Houston, retrieve the letters. Glancing quickly at undisguised expressions of long-standing affection, the lawyer reluctantly decided he had no choice but to honor a widow's wish to see letters from a woman who was her dear old friend as well as Allen's. Houston supposed that Clover destroyed the packet, but he never asked whether she read the letters first.

visitors without attracting attention, were boarded over. At an early staff meeting McCone interrupted J. C. King as he launched into one of the spy stories that would have intrigued Allen; "Damn it, J.C.," he said, "shut up!" The telephone buzzer system by which CIA officers could speak with Allen directly, without intervention by a secretary, was turned off.

Kennedy came to Langley on November 28 to preside over the dedication of the CIA's new home. Allen greeted the presidential helicopter at the landing pad hidden among the trees of the campus. Interrupting the carefully scripted ceremony that followed, with more than six hundred CIA professionals in attendance, Kennedy turned to the dais behind him. "Would you step forward, Allen." On his lapel he pinned the National Security Medal. Short of knighthood or lordship, it was the highest honor of the United States government.

McCone was sworn in as the sixth director of central intelligence the next day. After the White House ceremony Allen and Clover were driven back to his old office. As he stepped out of the official Cadillac, Allen suddenly realized his loss of status. He told Clover, "I'll come home in a taxi tonight." A CIA aide heard the remark and insisted that the government limousine was his as long as he needed it. "We'll find another car for Mr. McCone," he said.

— * —

Once he found himself truly retired as he approached his sixty-ninth birthday, Allen made the mistake of all energetic men, past and future. He accepted too many obligations, sat on too many boards, and gave too many speeches of diminishing substance. As always he revealed little of importance, but in such a charming and entertaining way that he would invariably be invited back. "I'm just amazed," he wrote an old friend. "They're actually paying me — a lot of money — to give a speech!" To others he wrote, "I work on the theory that if you relax, the hobgoblins of old age overtake you. . . . I have seen too many business tycoons who have rotted away in retirement that they thought they wanted. I shall start work at nine in the morning instead of eight, and get away at six instead of God knows when." To Cass Canfield, the New York editor who pressed him for his memoirs, he wrote, "I shall have to persuade myself that I have the aptitude and the skills to do effective writing, as I am not much of a believer in 'ghosts.'"

His speaking engagements involved travel, and finally he enjoyed taking Clover with him. He used Henry Luce's guest rooms in Arizona, the Bahamian villa of a retired ambassador, the Swiss chalet of an old OSS comrade. His two daughters had growing families, and Allen fit into the role of grandfather with an affection and attention span that had eluded him when his own children were young.

When he tried to interest publishers in his views on the communist menace to free societies, he was informed that his only marketable book would be a now-it-can-be-told account of his world of espionage. He compromised on a slim volume called *The Craft of Intelligence*, published in 1963, which contained a few favorite stories and more of his theories about communist perfidy in the Great Game. For all his distrust of "ghosts," he asked one accomplished writer of his acquaintance, E. Howard Hunt, to draft a few chapters. The book failed to live up to the promise of its title as a distillation of his experience, either theoretical or practical, for a public still uninformed about the role of ongoing intelligence as an essential instrument of government. "In or out of office," wrote the most friendly reviewer, "Allen Dulles is incorrigibly discreet, unfailingly gentlemanly."

Allen was a pioneer in the emerging television fixture of the talk show. Did he think Fidel Castro had a future? asked one host in late-night conversation. "I hope not," Allen replied. "I rather think he might fade away." What would the CIA do, asked another, if a foreign agent threatened the national security of the United States. Allen answered disarmingly, "We'd kill him." He relit his pipe and reassured everyone that question and answer were entirely hypothetical; he "could not possibly conceive" of such a situation actually arising. Helen MacInnes, an author of thrillers that Allen admired second only to Fleming's, wrote that Allen was "either very shy or so accustomed to concealing his emotions that it was very difficult for him to relax his guard.... I thought of him as a rather splendid stoic, with an impish sense of humor, quite a collection of opposites."

Allen watched helplessly as his CIA became enmeshed during the first years of his retirement in what became the agency's most crippling internal controversy. In December 1961, a month after Allen left, a minor KGB officer on the rolls of the Soviet Embassy in Helsinki, Anatoly Golitsyn, defected to the United States and started pouring out lurid tales of Soviet penetrations into the CIA's inner ranks. Angleton, head of counterespionage, with ever greater power over his colleagues, seized upon the Golitsyn testimonies to pursue, for years to come, an imagined Soviet mole within American intelligence.*

Golitsyn was a difficult man to handle, radiating airs and demanding

* Only in the 1980s, long after Angleton had left the scene, did the Soviet Union manage to "turn" an American headquarters officer, Aldrich H. Ames, uncovered in 1994 as a Soviet mole in CIA.

courtesies and perks far beyond his status. Successive CIA case officers (other than Angleton) found him impossible to manage. One in the series was a veteran of covert actions against the Soviet Union, Donald F. B. Jameson, known among those who never knew his real name as "Jamie." In an inspired effort to soften up the difficult defector, Jamie took Golitsyn to the townhouse on Q Street in August 1962 to meet fabled spymaster Allen Dulles.

This might have been an encounter worth recording; as it happened, the conversation was banal. Over drinks on the terrace, Allen asked whether the Kremlin had ever placed an informer within the CIA. Golitsyn dodged, then finally replied categorically, "No, I know of no penetration." (Under Angleton's prodding the defector later modified his story.) The next day, when Jameson called at Golitsyn's safe house for their day's work, the defector turned on his CIA handler: "I won't talk to you until you apologize for letting that old man interrogate me." Jamie, a loyal product of the Dulles era at CIA, could no longer contain his anger at his difficult charge. "Hell no," he said. "*You* apologize to *me* for your rudeness to an 'old man' who was a far greater figure in all the history of intelligence than you will ever be!"[12]

— * —

Allen was flying to his Long Island country home toward noon on Friday, November 22, 1963, after giving an early morning interview in Boston. Arriving at Lloyd Neck for a relaxed weekend, he heard the news that jolted an entire world to attention, and to grief. Like countless others in a hundred nations, he could say for years to come, "I shall never forget when I first heard the news of the Dallas tragedy."

John F. Kennedy "was a man who hadn't had a chance really to show his full capabilities," Allen told Tom Braden in his oral history for the Kennedy Presidential Library. "He'd gone through the very difficult days . . . ," and here Allen had to recall his own part in making those difficulties. "All that, he had put behind him," Allen said. "He was at a point to move forward and show us the full possibilities of a very extraordinary man."

Seven days later, about 5:30 in the afternoon of November 29, Clover called Allen to the telephone. A harassed White House operator said they would have to call back in a few minutes. "This gave me a brief chance to puzzle out what it was." In the news were proposals for a high-level investigation of the Kennedy assassination and the public shooting two days later of Lee Harvey Oswald, Kennedy's presumed murderer. Allen wondered if the call might have some relation to that.

Allen settled down in front of the fire, and in five minutes the phone rang again. On the line came the familiar Texas drawl of the new president, Lyndon Johnson. Allen took notes of the ensuing conversation.

> I told him how much my thoughts had been with him in recent days. He thanked me. . . . He said he wished me to do a job for him. I asked him what it was. He said he was appointing a commission to look into all the circumstances surrounding the assassination and the later killing of the man believed responsible for the assassination. . . .
> I told the President without hesitation that I was prepared to serve . . . I said that I assumed that he had considered my recent job [at CIA] and that he did not consider that this service was in any way an impediment. He said he had carefully considered it and he felt that, on the contrary, it would be helpful.[13]

Allen's was the first name raised in composing the inquiry that came to be known as the Warren Commission, after its chairman, Chief Justice Earl Warren.* The double killings in Dallas had set the nation, the world, on edge. Secretary of State Rusk had warned Johnson of mounting, though unspecified, "international complications" in explaining the tragedy. There were real fears that the assassination of the president of the United States could be the first shot in a world war. Then, when the presumed assassin himself was murdered, in full view of the television public, Johnson came under pressure from all sides to take extraordinary steps to calm a troubled nation.

Oswald had been shot while in police custody. Within the hour Eugene Rostow of Yale Law School called Johnson's aide, Bill Moyers, to say that "world opinion and American opinion is just now so shaken by the behavior of the Dallas police that they're not believing anything."[14] The new president resisted the idea of a special investigation since the FBI and the Texas attorney general were already on the case. "Sometimes a commission that's not trained hurts more than it helps," he complained to J. Edgar Hoover on November 25, the morning after Washington and the world were immobilized by the Kennedy funeral. "We can't be checking up on every shooting scrape in the country."

Public pressure mounted over the succeeding four days, however, and by the morning of November 29 Johnson was canvassing his old colleagues in the Senate for guidance. He told Republican leader Everett

---

* Lyndon Johnson later wrote that Robert Kennedy himself had asked that Allen Dulles be part of the investigation into his brother's assassination. Decades later, as the archives of the day were opened to public scrutiny, there was no evidence that the younger Kennedy played any role in the composition of the commission.

Dirksen of Illinois, "Seems to us we might ask the members of the [Supreme] Court, might even ask Allen Dulles, might ask a couple of members of the House, a couple from the Senate, and wrap up the three divisions of government, . . . just so we would have a very high caliber, top-flight, blue-ribbon group that the whole world would have absolute confidence in."

At 4 P.M. that day Johnson got through on the telephone to Richard B. Russell, Democrat of Georgia and a respected dean of the Senate. He said he would "try to get Allen Dulles" to serve on an investigating commission. Russell concurred: "Dulles is a good man." Secretary Rusk had also commended Allen: "Dulles, on this kind of an issue, I think would not be partisan. I think that would be good." Then the president put the call in to Allen.[15] An hour later Johnson was confiding to trusted congressional friends that the Kennedy assassination "has some foreign complications, CIA and other things. . . . We just can't [have] House and Senate and FBI and other people going around testifying [that] Khrushchev killed Kennedy or Castro killed him — we've got to have the facts."

At 8:55 P.M. Johnson was back on the phone with Russell, demanding that the Georgia senator serve on the commission despite his dislike for Earl Warren (the chief justice had led the court in ordering the desegration of public schools). They jousted over the foreign implications of the assassination. Russell dismissed suspicions of Soviet involvement but started to add, "I wouldn't be surprised if Castro —" Johnson cut him off. "Okay, okay, that's what we want to know."

Over the years Russell had been privy, probably beyond any other member of the Senate, Johnson included, to the most secret of Allen's CIA operations; the Georgia dean was one of the handful in whom Allen would confide and thus secure congressional authorization for whatever the CIA wanted to do. Russell would have known, if anyone on Capitol Hill knew, about the faltering attempts to assassinate Castro. And from their Senate years together, Johnson understood that Russell knew things on which no one else dared to speculate. With Russell and Allen together on the Warren Commission, there would be no chance that unspecified "international complications" would be allowed to interfere with a soothing, straightforward, and useful verdict.

Executive Order 11130 of November 29, 1963, created the President's Commission on the Assassination of President John F. Kennedy, under the chairmanship of the seventy-two-year-old chief justice of the United States, a former Republican governor of California and candidate for the vice presidency in 1948. Johnson had assembled a carefully constituted panel — two senators, Democrat Russell of Georgia and Republican John Sherman Cooper of Kentucky; two members of the House, Democrat

Hale Boggs of Louisiana and Republican Gerald R. Ford of Michigan; and two public figures from the private sector, both international lawyers of broad government experience, both Republicans: John McCloy and Allen Dulles.[16]

Subtle psychological judgments go into the composition of ad hoc commissions, whether in government or private institutions; the nature of the membership often determines the nature of the outcome. The Warren Commission was diverse in obvious ways among the branches of government and between the political parties; actually, counting Warren and the two public commissioners, five of the seven members were Republican. Less obvious but far more meaningful were character traits common to all the members. Only within a circumscribed establishment were they diverse. Each had acquired distinction among his fellows, a judicious outlook, integrity in public affairs such that they all commanded respect even from adversaries. From the Warren Commission would come no sudden surprises; there would be no grandstanding by its members, nor would any of them go off on idiosyncratic tangents. These were men of the establishment middle, for whom the importance of sticking together was a conviction more compelling than any other.*

Furthermore, they were all busy men, little inclined to drop other commitments to pursue an energetic inquiry that might head off in unpredictable directions. Rather, their function as they saw it—and as President Johnson intended—was to invoke their collective integrity and long experience in issuing a report designed to calm a restive public. They set out not so much to examine every clue that might turn up as to "dispel rumors," for, as Allen reportedly put it, "an atmosphere of rumors and suspicion interferes with the function of government, especially abroad."[17] Joseph Alsop, influential columnist and presidential confidant, told Johnson in the formative days that the commission "doesn't need to use the things that the FBI says can't be used," and still, Alsop said, its conclusions "will carry absolute conviction."[18]

The task before the Warren Commission thus was totally different from the last ad hoc panel on which Allen had served, the Taylor board of inquiry into the Bay of Pigs disaster. That 1961 inquiry had served not to soothe the public but to inform the president about shortcomings in his policymaking process. It sought cold judgments, not reassuring rhetoric. From the first meeting, Maxwell Taylor and Robert Kennedy had made

* Early evidence of the commission's determination to be cautious came when the members rejected Warren's first choice for general counsel and staff director as "too controversial," according to Edward Jay Epstein's interview with McCloy (*Inquest*, p. 6). They chose instead a former solicitor general of the United States, J. Lee Rankin, who became the workhorse of the commission.

it clear that this would be a working board; the members, not the staff, would carry the load. For the month of hearings the Taylor board demanded its members' full attention.

The Warren Commission, by contrast, worked for ten months, but its plenary meetings were intermittent and poorly attended. Allen proved to be the most diligent of the group. He sat through nearly three-quarters of the oral testimony, about 180 out of 244 hours of hearings, conducted on forty-nine days between February and September of 1964. Only two other commissioners were present to hear more than half the witnesses, though presumably all studied the transcripts; Russell, never overcoming his scorn for Warren, attended no more than fifteen hours of oral testimony.

"Although we faced a difficult and perhaps unprecedented task," Allen said, "each of us had had a lifetime's experience in dealing with extraordinary problems, and we knew what had to be done."[19]

— * —

Well, Allen knew what he had to do himself, and his role would provoke speculation and conjecture for decades to come. To him fell the function of managing the Warren Commission's relations with the CIA, of simultaneously investigating and protecting government secrets. Records made public only in 1993 finally document the finesse with which he performed this double role; he would advise his colleagues on the commission about how best to pose questions, then advise his former colleagues at the CIA about how best to answer them. This turned out to be a delicate task indeed, for it quickly emerged that investigation of the Kennedy and Oswald assassinations would touch upon secret CIA operations at many points. The open question is which master, the Warren Commission or the CIA, claimed Allen's first allegiance.

Over the coming months Allen systematically used his influence to keep the commission safely within bounds, the importance of which only he could appreciate. He sought with utmost subtlety to neutralize the impulses of his fellow commissioners to pursue lines of inquiry that might expose CIA operations, even though they had nothing to do with the Dallas shootings. And from the start, before any evidence was reviewed, he pressed for the final verdict that Oswald had been a crazed lone gunman, not the agent of a national or international conspiracy.

The Warren Commission opened deliberations on December 5, two weeks after Kennedy's death. Allen took his first initiatives of leadership at the second meeting, December 16. Supported by the commission's cautious counsel and staff director, J. Lee Rankin, he urged that the panel confine its work to a review of the investigation already being made by the FBI. In taking this stand he implicitly turned his back on the sentiments of his old friend, Hamilton Fish Armstrong, who wrote Allen that the truth must come out, "no matter who it affects, FBI included." Allen argued, to the contrary, that a new set of investigations would only cause frictions within the intelligence community and complicate the ongoing functions of government on unspecified matters of national security.

Then Allen submitted to the commission an academic study of seven attempts on the lives of American presidents, all of them apparently by lone gunmen acting out their own fantasies. "You'll find a pattern running through here that I think we'll find in this present case," Allen said. A lonely note of skepticism came, surprisingly enough, from McCloy, with whom Allen had worked on sensitive matters of international law and diplomacy for three decades past. McCloy remarked that the assassination of Lincoln had been a conspiracy, not the act of a lone gunman. Allen brushed aside this untoward challenge: "Yes, but one man was so dominant that it almost wasn't a plot."* Warren quickly turned the discussion to procedural matters.

The Warren Commission did not meet again until January 21. By that time the FBI had presented a five-volume report, said to be based on 25,000 interviews and 2,300 investigative summaries.[20] It reached just the conclusion that Hoover — and Allen — had settled upon from the start, that Oswald had acted as a lone assassin.

The very next day information came to the commission staff from Dallas that Oswald may have served as some kind of FBI informer. If confirmed, this tip could call into question the fundamental integrity of the FBI investigation. The commission convened an emergency meeting that same afternoon. Gerald Ford said it was "the most tense and hushed meeting" he could remember.[21] After deciding to seek further information about the rumor — the sort of independent investigation that Allen had sought to forestall — the panel reassembled on January 27. Allen led off by reading press reports of FBI denials of any relationship with Oswald. McCloy again spoke up in skepticism, this time about the validity of official denials.

---

* Allen's point was not vapid at the time he made it. In the immediate aftermath of Lincoln's death, dark suspicions spread that John Wilkes Booth had acted in collusion with partisans of the southern Confederacy. They were quickly discredited. Seven decades later an even cruder conspiracy theory, involving Secretary of War Edwin Stanton, captured the public imagination, though mainstream historians convincingly refuted it. Allen's rebuttal to McCloy reflected the consensus academic judgments of his day. Ironically, a new generation of scholars reexamining the evidence in the 1980s began to speculate that Booth's many connections to the Confederacy may have been instrumental after all in the assassination. The Lincoln precedent thus offers titillating parallels for all who go on seeking a conspiracy against Kennedy.

Then ensued a remarkable little seminar among men of the world. Allen found himself pushed into a corner to explain things that intelligence professionals do not like to discuss with outsiders. Russell extracted Allen's acknowledgment that the FBI, or the CIA for that matter, would routinely deny any connection with a person engaged as an undercover agent. Boggs persisted that surely the case officers would know whether or not a specific individual was an agent. Allen replied, "Yes, but he wouldn't tell." This provoked lawyerly incredulity from the chief justice. "Wouldn't tell it under oath?" Warren asked. "I wouldn't think he would tell it under oath, no," Allen replied blandly. "Wouldn't he tell it to his own chief?" asked McCloy. "He might or might not," Allen said, adding the ambiguous remark, "If he was a bad one, then he wouldn't."[22]

Allen's attempts to make the uncomfortable discussion more abstract only boxed him in further. He said there would be no written records of undercover agents to confirm or refute allegations. Then he offered a personal statement that in light of subsequent disclosures became more revealing than he could possibly have intended. The president of the United States was the only person, he said, to whom a true professional of intelligence would impart all information in his possession, and to him only if asked. A responsible American sypmaster would confide in no one else — not the secretary of state nor the secretary of defense, not the national security adviser in the White House. And by Allen's reasoning, though he never said it, not a commission chaired by the chief justice of the United States.

Boggs expressed the general exasperation. If this was the way secret services operate, he said, it "makes our problem utterly impossible, because you say this rumor can't be dissipated under any circumstances." "Under any circumstances, I think Mr. Hoover would say, certainly, he didn't have anything to do with this fellow," Allen said. "You can't prove what the facts are; there are no external evidences. I would believe Mr. Hoover. Some people might not." And that was that for the meeting of January 27.

In the next weeks Allen found his role becoming even more uncomfortable as the Warren Commission began probing for Oswald's possible links, not to the FBI but to the CIA. A disturbed ex-Marine, Lee Harvey Oswald had defected to Moscow in October 1959. He lived in Soviet Minsk for nearly three years, married a Russian woman (the niece, it emerged, of a Soviet intelligence officer), then returned to the United States with his wife in June 1962. Why had these strange circumstances not attracted the CIA's attention? As the commission started questioning witnesses, Oswald's widow and mother testified to their assumption that Oswald had worked for the CIA before, during, or after his time in the Soviet Union. Neither was a particularly credible source; they had no real information. It was just an assumption, one that ordinary people sometimes make about those who wander about in foreign countries.

The fact is, in the rules of the Great Game as played in the Cold War, Lee Harvey Oswald was about as unsuitable for the role of undercover agent as James Bond. His character traits were questionable; his life was loose and undisciplined. He stood out from his environment; his strange odyssey only invited questions from all around him. This is not the sort of person that those who build intelligence networks seek for their agents. On March 17 commission counsel Rankin wrote Allen for personal guidance on how best to assess, and perhaps put to rest, allegations of Oswald's links to the CIA.

Thus began Allen's delicate role of liaison between competing loyalties. He met discreetly with a representative of the clandestine services three days later.* Allen stated that he would have no difficulty in assuring the commission that up to the time he left the CIA in November 1961, "as far as [I] could remember [I] had never had any knowledge of Oswald at any time prior to the date of the assassination."[23] The weakness in this assurance was obvious, however. The director of central intelligence would not normally bother to know the names of agents within networks, and Allen's personal experience had ended long before Oswald made his way back to the United States.

Rankin asked if Allen might himself review CIA records and give the Warren Commission an assessment about Oswald. Allen told his CIA contact that he could invoke "good and sufficient reason" for not undertaking such a review. As he had told the commission weeks before, the names of undercover agents would not appear in the written records. More to the point, however, scrutiny and discussion of the records that did exist about espionage operations and covert actions against the Soviet Union would raise genuine problems for United States policy in pursuing the Cold War.

Three weeks later, on April 11, Helms sent his officer back to ask Allen what information the Warren Commission would be seeking from CIA. Allen's liaison role was engaged in earnest.[24] He informed the CIA contact that the commission intended to submit a summary of Mrs. Oswald's garbled testimony about her husband's alleged CIA connections. For its reply Allen suggested that the agency provide not personal testi-

* In these records of Allen's talks with CIA representatives, declassified in 1993, the names of the CIA officers are deleted. They were officers on the staff of Richard Helms, then deputy director for plans, official name of the clandestine services.

mony but a sworn statement. That, after all, was as far as Hoover had gone about any FBI connection. Allen dictated for the agency's use a draft assertion that "neither CIA nor anyone acting on CIA's behalf was ever in contact or communication with Oswald."*

The CIA man wondered if the assurance might be more credible if it were accompanied by a description of CIA procedures for agent assessment and handling, "to show that it would have been unlikely for Oswald to have been chosen as a CIA agent to enter Russia." Allen considered the idea, then rejected it on grounds that "there are always exceptions to every rule, and this might be misunderstood by members of the commission with little background in activity of this sort." As with the U-2 cover story, "standing orders" exist to be invoked for concealing countermanding orders in specific covert actions.

Next, Allen informed his CIA contact, the commission would put the question of whether Oswald had been a Soviet agent sent back to the United States under deep cover. From his own knowledge of intelligence procedures, Allen seemed to have no reservations in dismissing this possibility. But he expressed concern about issuing a categorical denial, for subsequent questioning could elicit too much detail about the CIA's knowledge of communist practices in recruiting agents. Allen proposed, therefore, a simple reply "that CIA possessed no knowledge, . . . tending to show that Lee Harvey Oswald was an agent of the Soviet intelligence services, or the services of any other communist country, or for that matter of any other country."

Finally Allen warned that the agency should be ready to answer commission inquiries about why the CIA had not investigated Oswald's standing once he defected. The CIA man told Allen that this question had already been discussed with Rankin, who seemed to understand that as a practical matter it would be awkward for the agency to investigate Oswald inside the Soviet Union. Allen agreed to argue that the commission should not seek "to place matters of this sort in the public record."

That, as far as Allen then acknowledged, was the extent of the Warren Commission's curiosity about any Soviet involvement with the Kennedy assassination. He did not see fit to raise, nor did the CIA man, discussion of the most important evidence about Oswald that had come from

---

* For what it is worth, the head of the Soviet KGB at the time, Vladimir Semichastny, offered his own confirming opinion when the era of *glasnost* permitted him to speak. In a 1993 interview with NBC, quoted in Gerald Posner's book *Case Closed* (p. 56), the retired Semichastny asked, "Would the FBI or CIA really use such a pathetic person [as Oswald] to work against their archenemy? I had always respected the CIA and FBI, and we knew their work and what they were capable of. It was clear Oswald was not an agent, couldn't be an agent, for the U.S. secret services, either the CIA or the FBI."

Moscow, evidence in a form that was at that very moment tearing the CIA clandestine services apart.

Fear of a Soviet plot had been foremost among the "international complications" raised when Kennedy was shot. Knowledgeable insiders, including even Senator Russell, gave little credence to such fears, for all developments in East-West relations argued against such a conspiracy. The Russians, moreover, seemed as distraught when Kennedy was killed as the Americans. Panicky diplomatic signals came in from all quarters to persuade the United States that the Kremlin had nothing to do with the murder of the president.

One Soviet official, in all likelihood for his own reasons, stepped forward with formidable evidence about the man accused of shooting Kennedy. Yuri Ivanovich Nosenko, a lieutenant colonel in the KGB, had been a double agent for the United States since 1962. In February 1964 he told his CIA case officers that he could not go on; he demanded political asylum as a defector. Under interrogation he declared that he had happened to review the KGB file on Oswald during the years when the young American had lived in the Soviet Union. He could affirm without hesitation that Soviet intelligence, while keeping Oswald under surveillance, had judged him unfit for service, had never interrogated him, and certainly had never engaged him as an agent, under deep cover or any guise whatever, to perform any acts upon his return to the United States.

Nosenko was at that time the highest-ranking officer of the KGB to fall into CIA hands. Hoover's FBI grabbed at the reports of his first debriefings and urged that the Warren Commission summon him as a witness, for he would confirm that Oswald was a loner, not serving any conspiracy. But within the CIA were men suspicious of this fortuitous circumstance. James Angleton had become convinced that the Kremlin was embarked on evil designs against the United States, and his suspicions were eagerly fed by his protégé, Golitsyn. In the view of this CIA faction, Nosenko was a fraud, an agent of Soviet disinformation, whose conveniently timed defection was another step in a devious smoke screen.

Understandable, therefore, that discussion of the defector Nosenko was never raised at Allen's April 11 planning session with his CIA contact. The matter was still too tentative to be presented to the Warren Commission, and it raised emotions among Allen's old agency colleagues that would take time to analyze and sort out. Richard Helms could later sit back and explain the tension.

It is difficult to overstate the significance that Yuri Nosenko's defection assumed in the investigation of President Kennedy's assassination. If

Nosenko turned out to be a *bona fide* defector, if his information were to be believed, then we could conclude the KGB and the Soviet Union had nothing to do with Lee Harvey Oswald in 1963 and therefore had nothing to do with President Kennedy's murder.

If, on the other hand, Mr. Nosenko had been programmed in advance by the KGB to minimize KGB connections with Oswald, if Mr. Nosenko was giving us false information about Oswald's contacts with the KGB in 1959 to 1962, it was fair for us to surmise that there may have been an Oswald-KGB connection in November 1963, more specifically that Oswald was acting as a Soviet agent when he shot President Kennedy.[25]

Helms called on Chief Justice Warren on June 24 to explain the problem about Nosenko's credibility. Warren was visibly annoyed, for he had planned the commission's work on the FBI assurance that Nosenko was worth a hearing, if for no other reason than to put the Soviet connection to rest. The full commission met that same day to discuss Helms's warning and the responsible way to handle Nosenko. Allen conducted his own quick review of what Nosenko had told his interrogators, working from a staff summary of the FBI reports. By this time Allen had been briefed by his old friend Angleton, and his notes on the staff memorandum showed considerable skepticism about Nosenko's testimony.[26] On some points, however, he saw a legitimate problem, one that weakened his own case against Oswald: the KGB information from Minsk, for instance, that Oswald's hunting club friends had considered him a bad shot. Allen penciled in the margin, "Find a way to use that."*

Allen resumed his discreet role of liaison between the CIA and the Warren Commission at a meeting two weeks later with the chief of the Soviet division of the clandestine services.[27] The problem, as the two men discussed it, was stark. If the commission ignored Nosenko's information, it would be open to subsequent charges that important evidence had been suppressed. If, however, it gave credence to a defector's testimony, and later that defector was shown to be a Soviet plant, the commission's integrity would be in far worse danger. A disclaimer "that doubt existed regarding the source of the information" would be one way out of the commission's dilemma, but it would bring great damage to CIA counterespionage, for it would give Moscow a clue to the CIA's attitude toward Nosenko.

---

* Critics have seized on the rumor from Minsk about Oswald's poor marksmanship. Other information acquired by the commission and subsequent investigators is convincing that whatever he showed in Minsk, he was certainly good enough with a rifle to have made the three shots from the Texas Book Depository on November 22.

In a particularly cynical aside the CIA man dismissed fears that one day Nosenko might reveal he had given information which the Warren Commission ignored. Unlike other defectors, he told Allen, "it would be less likely that Nosenko would be allowed to surface." Less likely indeed, if Angleton's wishes remained dominant. Since April Nosenko had been kept in solitary confinement, treated as a captured spy rather than a defector, and submitted to psychological duress that might break his story—or might destroy him as a human being.*

Nosenko's testimony would have supported the basic case that Allen sought to make, at least insofar as it eliminated a Soviet plot, but the commission seemed ready to accept that argument anyway, so the testimony would be superfluous. Allen persuaded his colleagues to withhold any reference to Nosenko in the final report. Against Hoover's recommendation and Warren's intentions, Nosenko was not called to testify, and his name was not even mentioned in the twenty-six volumes of commission records.

— * —

Allen withheld other CIA information from his colleagues on the Warren Commission. Certain things he would convey only to the president, and then only if asked.† That was the ethical code of conduct he had devised for himself as a professional of intelligence. The issue for the historical record is whether any of the information he withheld about CIA secret operations was materially relevant to the assassination of President Kennedy.

In 1978 commission member Gerald Ford, by then the former president, could tell a committee of the House of Representatives, "To the best of my recollection, I think we got from any and all of the federal agencies all of the information they had as to Oswald's connection with any foreign government."[28] That guarded assurance did not go far enough. Congressional investigations had finally documented the CIA plots to assassinate Fidel Castro, and Oswald had been party, at least tangentially, to Cuban émigré politics. At the same 1978 hearing, commission counsel Rankin conceded disillusionment. "I have been very much disappointed with some of the things that have been revealed.... When I learned that [the FBI was] supposed to have known about plans for an assassination that were under way in the CIA, ... and did not report it to

* The CIA kept Nosenko incarcerated in subhuman conditions for five years, finally releasing him in 1969. His evidence is now regarded as far more reliable than all that Angleton's protégé Golitsyn ever provided.
† The interesting question arises whether a professional like Allen would have confided in the president if another person were also present, as Eisenhower insisted on in the later years of his administration.

us, and that we didn't receive any such information from the CIA, it was quite disheartening to me to know that that kind of conduct was a part of the action of our intelligence agencies at that high level." Nicholas deB. Katzenbach, assistant attorney general under Robert Kennedy, was blunter. "I am surprised that the FBI did not seize the opportunity to embarrass the CIA."[29]

Katzenbach, who later became attorney general and was deeply concerned with intelligence abuses, conceded the naiveté of those days: "I thought that the appointment of Allen Dulles to the [Warren] commission would ensure that the commission had access to anything that the CIA had. I am astounded to this day that Mr. Dulles did not at least make that information available to the other commissioners." Years of plotting to assassinate Castro were clearly something that should have been made known to the Warren Commission, Katzenbach testified.[30]

Allen was not alive to answer the suspicious judgments of hindsight. The contemporary record shows that his fear, shared by President Johnson and Senator Russell at least, had been that investigation of the Kennedy assassination would ineluctably lead into unrelated CIA secret operations. On suspicions of a possible Soviet involvement, Allen guided his fellow commissioners into a fair judgment of no complicity — though he did so without revealing all that could have been presented to make the case. A possible Cuban connection was more diffuse in the perspective of the times.

It is now documented that the day Kennedy was shot, a CIA case officer met one of his Cuban agents and handed over a poison pen to be used to kill Castro. But also that day a confidential emissary from President Kennedy was meeting Castro to discuss how relations could be improved.[31] Allen would not have known of either of these developments, for he was long out of government, and both transactions were being held in tightest secrecy.

He did know of past assassination plots against Castro, but nothing he would have been likely to recall on the day of the assassination could have led in any line, straight or crooked, to Dallas. Then, however, when Oswald himself was shot by Jack Ruby, a nightclub operator with known contacts in the underworld of organized crime, Allen would have been entitled to wonder whether this person Ruby was linked to any CIA contacts in the crime syndicates. The underworlds of crime and espionage often intersect, as Allen had learned decades before. But they always work on separate agendas; a close working relationship on one operation gives neither partner the right or ability to know what else might be going on in the other side's diverse activities. Yet once suspicions are raised, once investigators start asking questions, no one can control where they might lead. Reason enough, therefore, for Allen to argue at the Warren Commission's second meeting against an independent investigation, and to urge acceptance of the evidence already assembled by the FBI. Hoover's men, it was known, had their own contacts within organized crime, and they also knew how to keep things from unraveling under investigation.

Nothing was ever straightforward about the CIA's efforts to assassinate Castro, and the principals involved were as burdened by false rumors and misinformation as were curious outsiders.* If Allen could consider his conscience clear in withholding his limited information about old CIA secret operations, it is worth speculating about what he would have done had the commission turned up any evidence of a direct CIA connection to the Dallas assassination. On his own testimony, he might have gone to the president with what he knew — but no one else. More likely he would have let his successors at the agency take the initiative, for they knew much more about names and details than he ever had. And if, as later conspiracy theorists suspected, the CIA men themselves had something to hide, that would have been beyond Allen's competence to report.

In all his subsequent writings and discussions, Allen never admitted to the slightest possibility that he possessed any information to modify the Warren Commission's fundamental conclusion that Oswald had acted alone in killing President Kennedy. Nor, it must be said, have three decades of conspiracy theories come up with any convincing evidence, other than fanciful conjectures, that Castro was somehow instrumental in Oswald's action.

But lack of interest in the supposed Cuban connection was one factor among many that tended to discredit the Warren Commission. The panel chose not to examine medical photographs and x-rays of Kennedy's body. Analysis of ballistic evidence, which so exercised future critics, was also beyond the commissioners' patience, though Allen tried on several occasions (without recorded success) to sort out the conflicting theories about bullets and trajectories. The perfunctory attendance record of the commissioners — not widely noted at the time — did not inspire confidence in those who subsequently analyzed their work.

Allen's top priority throughout the ten months of the commission's study was to press for endorsement of the FBI's conclusion that Kennedy was murdered by a lone assassin; a finding of any international or domes-

* Fourteen years later Castro gave an American visitor a list of twenty-four alleged plots to assassinate him in which he said the CIA had been involved. The Church Committee submitted this list to the CIA in 1975, and in a fourteen-page response the agency demonstrated to the committee's satisfaction that in not a single one of the alleged plots was CIA implicated. The actual CIA assassination operations that the Senate committee did discover never appeared on Castro's list.

tic conspiracy might compromise all of American foreign policy. McCloy and, apparently, Senator Cooper were the last skeptics of the lone-assassin hypothesis.

The second weekend of May Allen, McCloy, and Cooper flew to Dallas for an extraordinary personal inspection on behalf of the Warren Commission.[32] For two days the three men visited the obscure locales that have since been immortalized in the memories of November 22. Starting Friday afternoon, May 8, the commissioners first followed the bus and taxi route taken by Oswald immediately after the assassination to the movie theater where he allegedly killed Dallas police officer J. D. Tippit an hour later. Their staff escort wrote:

> We went to the parking lot where the Oswald light-tan zippered jacket was found. Then we drove to the vicinity of the Hardy Shoe Store and the Texas Theater. We first went into the shoe-store lobby, where the testimony of Johnny Brewer was reviewed. The commissioners then walked to the Texas Theater and talked to the ticket cashier, Julia Postal, who was on duty on November 22. Then the commissioners walked inside and talked to the usher and concessionaire. . . . We then walked into the lobby and inspected the theater itself.

Allen and his colleagues went to the house on Neely Street where Oswald had been photographed with the rifle, but they could not get inside; no one was home. Finally they arrived at the police station where Oswald was interrogated, and viewed his cell and place of arraignment. They walked the path of Oswald's transfer, down the jail elevator and into the underground garage where Jack Ruby had moved into position to fire point-blank at the prisoner. That closed their first day. McCloy spent the evening alone at the hotel, reading a detailed description of Dealey Plaza, where Kennedy's life ended.

At 8:30 Saturday morning Allen, McCloy, and Cooper left their hotel for the final task of their mission. They inspected the Texas Book Depository. From the laconic notes of their staff escort:

> We first went to the sixth floor and looked out the assassination window. . . . The Secret Service provided a telescopic sight, and the commissioners each took the position of Oswald and sighted down Elm Street. . . . We completely went through the sixth floor and looked at the place . . . where the pop bottle and chicken bones were found. We inspected the place where the long paper sack was found. Then we took the route that the assassin took: across the sixth floor and down the stairs. . . . We inspected the place where the rifle had been found. . . .

When we got to the fifth floor, we went to the place where the three

Negro men had been located. . . . Then, empty gun shells were dropped on the sixth floor and a bolt action rifle was operated while the commissioners were at the window, so that they would have an opportunity to learn whether or not these sounds could be heard.* . . . We then went to the windows on the west side of the fifth floor where the three men went shortly after the assassination. It could readily be seen that one could not see the stairway from the west windows because of the obstruction of permanent cabinets.

On and on through the haunted warehouse they trudged. Then outside they stood just where different witnesses had been standing at lunchtime on November 22. A Secret Service agent placed himself in the southwest corner window so the three commissioners could see the problems witnesses had in identifying someone seated there, as Oswald had been. Dallas police diverted traffic from the middle lane of Dealey Plaza. Allen and his colleagues stood in the middle of the roadway and paced back and forth over the place where Kennedy's open car had moved along at the final moments. Then they walked to the grassy knoll. This was "the spot where Abraham Zapruder had taken his moving pictures, and then [they] went behind the fence to see what kind of a shot could be fired, and then went to the triple overpass. We not only looked at the problems confronted by any potential assassin from the triple underpass, but in addition we pointed out why the motorcade did not proceed down Main Street — there was a median strip which would have necessitated a hairpin turn."

McCloy, when he arrived in Dallas, had warned commission staff members that he still found insufficient evidence to conclude that Oswald was the lone assassin. After the weekend with Allen and the examination of the critical sites, the last skeptic announced himself convinced that no other hypothesis fit the evidence available. "I personally traced every step that I think that Oswald took after he committed the crime," McCloy testified later. "I sat there in the little cubbyhole. . . . I worked and reworked the bolt of the rifle. I have had a good bit of experience with firearms, and I knew a good bit about ballistics. . . . I tested for myself what I thought a man could do in terms of firing that particular rifle."[33]

As he looked back on the whole ordeal of John Kennedy's assassination, even Allen had to concede the fragility of the verdict he had pressed upon the Warren Commission. He told Tom Braden:

---

* Allen let his skeptical colleagues reach their own conclusions on this point of evidence; McCloy acknowledged hearing the empty shells falling, but Cooper admitted he was so hard of hearing that he could not be sure.

Here was a man, Oswald, who had been a failure at everything he had done, yet he carried through successfully the intricate details of this mad act.

As I studied all that record, I could see literally hundreds of instances where if things had been just a little different, . . . if the employees of the Book Depository had eaten their lunch in a little different place, if somebody had been at one place, where he might easily have been, instead of another at one particular time . . . the "ifs" just stand out all over it. . . . If any one of the chess pieces that were entered into the game had been moved differently, at any one time, the whole thing might have been different.[34]

— * —

While the Warren Commission was winding up its formal hearings in June 1964, a drama of a different sort was unfolding in America. Student volunteers from the north were organizing to go south for a summer of demonstrations and community work to register black voters in pursuit of their civil rights. On June 20 two white students from New York joined a black activist from Meridian, Mississippi, and the next day they set out toward a village near the Mississippi town of Philadelphia, where a black community church had been destroyed in a mysterious fire. The three civil rights workers, Andrew Goodman, Michael Schwerner, and James Chaney, were never heard from again.

The news galvanized the nation. Civil rights organizations demanded that the federal government provide protection for the next waves of student volunteers heading south. As he sat in his Georgetown garden a few evenings later, Allen was not prepared for yet another portentous call from the White House operator. President Johnson came directly on the line and said, without preliminaries, "Allen, I want you to go to Mississippi. I want you to talk to the governor down there."[35]

For all his engagement in international crises over decades past, Allen had absolutely no experience of the civil rights movement in America. "Mr. President," he protested, "I couldn't even tell you who the governor is!" The president said, "He's a man named Johnson, but no relation." The two men laughed. Allen said he had no credentials whatever for such a sensitive mission, and Johnson replied that this was precisely why he must go; Allen Dulles would be welcomed in Mississippi as a respected figure of the northern establishment who was not "tarred" by public statements supporting the civil rights movement. A special air force jet was being lined up to transport him the next day.

"Now hold the line a minute," the president said, and to Allen's further surprise, the next voice he heard was that of the attorney general. Again without any preliminaries, Robert Kennedy asked Allen to come to his office for a briefing before he took off. The next morning, after discussing the situation with Kennedy and J. Edgar Hoover, Allen flew to Jackson, Mississippi.

Wearing the dark, double-breasted suit he affected for diplomatic and official appointments, Allen stepped off the government plane and flashed his customary smile to curious reporters waiting for him in a light rain. He was not there to interfere in investigating the disappearance of the three civil rights workers; fresh from his meeting with Hoover, he said, "That is in good hands." He was whisked away by his host, Mississippi's commissioner of public safety, Colonel T. B. Birdsong, and driven straight to the governor's mansion.

Governor Johnson could not have been more cordial to this veteran Cold Warrior who, though a Yankee, would surely understand revolutionary agitation when he saw it. These well-meaning but misguided northern students, the governor explained, really had no idea what they were getting into. They had been hoodwinked by their leaders, "known communists . . . beatnik types" who encouraged student "orgies, wild debauchery and immorality." Since the local police were sympathetic to the Ku Klux Klan, Governor Johnson admitted, he was not optimistic about preventing further violent incidents.

After two hours with the governor, Allen was driven to his room at the Sun and Sand Motel, where he changed for a dinner with white community leaders, including the mayor of Jackson, the editor of the local newspaper, president of the bank, and the heads of the chamber of commerce and the utility company. These men filled their visitor's attention with assurances of the progress made by the Negroes of Mississippi; civil disorders, they insisted, were the work of cynical carpetbaggers from the north. The federal government should persuade them to go back home. No, Allen said, he doubted that would be possible, nor did he think it realistic to expect the president to urge black leaders to "restrain" their demands for civil rights. He left the dinner disturbed that, as he later described it, with the naiveté of an alien from space, there was "no real willingness to acknowledge the legitimacy of Negro demands for greater equality."

The next morning, June 25, Allen met black Mississippians for the first time, two ministers in an interdenominational delegation with three whites. "They're not our 'plantation darkies' any more," declared the white Catholic bishop. "They're different people now, and they want their rights." Allen was impressed. He was moved even more when he met later in the day with some of the young black activists of the civil rights movement, who related their experiences of cross burnings, of collusion between the Klan and the local police. Finally he spent an emotional half hour with Michael Schwerner's mother from New York.*

Allen flew back to Washington that night and assembled a report to give the president the next morning, factual and detached like the NSC intelligence briefings of years past. The American south was torn by a dangerous polarization, he informed Lyndon Johnson of Texas, between diehard segregationists and the "new breed of Negro agitators ... provoking incidents" to force federal intervention. He urged the president not to send federal troops, as Eisenhower had done in Little Rock the decade before; that would inflame the situation further. He said the "wisest and most reasonable Negro leaders" concurred in this judgment; only the more rabid and radical sought direct federal intervention. Washington should cooperate with Mississippi law enforcement officials in controlling white terrorism, strengthen the FBI presence in troubled areas and, finally, give "discreet encouragement" to whatever forces of moderation — white or black — might arise. It sounded, almost to the letter, like a plan for political covert action in the old days of CIA.

Johnson sent Allen out to the White House press with a statement warning northern civil rights workers of the dangers they would face in their summer voter registration drive. But whatever his white southern hosts might have expected from him, Allen did not even hint that the northern youths should abandon their effort. One telegram he received from a woman in New York in response to his public statement touched him where he was most sensitive. "Greatly encouraged that you are trying to protect these brave young people. . . . My daughter is in Hattiesburg working for the Mississippi summer project. Hope she will not have the same fate as her uncle in Nazi Germany." The young woman's uncle had been Peter Yorck von Wartenburg, tortured and hanged by the Gestapo after the abortive plot to kill Hitler twenty years before, almost to the day.

Allen's lifetime of experience in revolutions overseas was of no avail as he tried to comprehend the social revolution in America. Perhaps, he told an astonished television interviewer, the young volunteers, with their "high motives," would be more effective if they were "very well chaperoned by older people." The legendary figure had lost his grasp on the country's evolving realities.

— * —

* Only on August 4 did FBI agents, tipped off by a paid informer, find the bodies of the three young men hastily buried on a farm near Philadelphia, Mississippi. All three had been shot; Chaney, the local black, had been beaten, his bones crushed.

The Warren Commission's report, released in September 1964, was acclaimed by a relieved American public, but in Europe skepticism resounded from the first readings. Allen used his annual late summer vacation to try convincing friends from his own era that they should not pursue a search for conspiracy behind the acts of a sole crazed gunman. Over civilized dinners with the likes of Dame Rebecca West and the chiefs of British intelligence, he encountered unending resistance. "I offered them roast beef, but they preferred soufflé," he complained. Only among the opinion leaders of Switzerland did he seem to make headway. He reported to Rankin and the commission staff on his return that "the editor of the leading Swiss paper, *Neuer Zuericher Zeitung*, told me that the report had changed the earlier skeptical attitude of his paper."

For his remaining years Allen resisted all efforts to reopen the Warren Commission investigation or even reply to the mounting chorus of critics, who persisted in finding conspiracies where the commission had found none — or, rather, had chosen not to look. Yet he could never close his door to visitors, the lesson learned from Lenin's halfhearted attempt to see him in 1917. In September 1965 he blithely agreed to discuss the Warren Commission report with a young graduate student from Cornell University, Edward Jay Epstein, and they had an apparently pleasant conversation.

Epstein's book, *Inquest*, published the next year, quickly won wide acclaim as the first responsible critique of the superficiality in the Warren Commission's work. Taken aback, Allen tried ad hominem rebuttals in private correspondence. "What disturbs me most," he wrote Rankin, "is the fact that certain people seem to be accepting, without serious consideration, the judgment of writers who have little reputation and no particular expertise." A month later, as the questions raised by Epstein, and less persuasively by a lawyer named Mark Lane, survived the expressed contempt of the old political establishment, Allen confessed that he had found the attacks "so frivolous" and the authors "so undistinguished ... that it was better to ignore them. I now see that I was wrong." Nonetheless he refused to appear on television programs with the likes of Lane. He wrote an old law partner, "For the commission to attempt to reassemble would merely bring down on our heads every crackpot who had any ideas about the assassination. . . . I personally still feel that the report is a good one and, if carefully studied, would furnish the answers to most of the queries and critiques that have been addressed to it."

As late as November 1967 he could write a young lawyer from the commission staff, Arlen Specter, that he could "find nothing in the way of new evidence which would affect the conclusions." And there, after nearly three decades of heated analysis, of conspiracy charges conjured up against CIA and Allen himself, the fundamental verdict of the Warren Commission stands.

— * —

When Allen turned seventy-two on April 7, 1965, he had time to reflect that he had lived two years longer than his brother. He told friends of Foster's dismay at the words of Psalm 90: "The days of our years are threescore years and ten; and if by reason of strength they be fourscore years, yet is their strength labor and sorrow, for it is soon cut off." Allen remembered that Foster had been so disturbed by this prophecy that he had summoned the ambassador from Israel for expert exegesis. The diplomat in Washington was caught unbriefed on this unexpected matter, but his urgent query to Jerusalem brought the diplomatic reply that the most recent interpretation of the passage, a rabbinical commentary of the fourteenth century, declared that the psalmist's "strength" meant a steady moral balance that would carry a man to the age of eighty.

During the winter of 1964–65 Allen apparently suffered some kind of stroke. Clover was of a breed that did not discuss medical matters, even (perhaps especially) with family; the Dulles daughters were never certain about exactly what happened. But after the mission to Mississippi and his return from Europe to defend the Warren report, Allen's reactions to life around him clearly slowed.

Inevitably, as his years of retirement lengthened, a sense of dismay over the failures assumed greater prominence. Tom Wicker, Reston's successor in the Washington bureau of *The New York Times*, called at Allen's home on Q Street early in 1966 to discuss the impact of the CIA on American democracy. Allen received him cordially, of course, wearing his donnish tweed jacket but limping about in bare feet and slippers. The conversation touched upon the Bay of Pigs, and Allen launched into a painful confession. "I confronted an inexperienced President Kennedy directly with the argument, 'Do you want to be perceived as less anticommunist than the great Eisenhower?'" The notion may have been implicit in all the CIA arguments during those early Kennedy months, but Sorensen, for one, who was as close to Kennedy as any of his staff, did not remember hearing of any such blunt challenge from the head of CIA.[36]

Allen always stalled off the official CIA historian seeking to record his memories of incidents of his tenure. "I am too old, I have forgotten so much," he would plead.[37] The raconteur of times past had lost his zest for the Game. When he finally agreed to an oral history interview for the John F. Kennedy Presidential Library, the setting was as conducive to mellow reflection as could be arranged. The interviewer was his old protégé in the early CIA, Tom Braden, who prompted Allen as best he could about some of the most revealing episodes in his experience. But Allen got mixed up on names, places, and time frames to such an embarrassing degree that the transcript was kept locked away long after the others in the Kennedy collection had been opened to scholars and the public.

— * —

Allen had endorsed Lyndon Johnson against the convervative Republican Barry Goldwater in 1964, the first time since Woodrow Wilson's day that he had supported a Democratic presidential candidate. Upon election in his own right, Johnson found his vision cruelly diverted from the civil rights struggle and his Great Society program to the mounting war against a communist guerrilla threat in Vietnam.

Allen had actually visited the small American military units in South Vietnam shortly after retiring from CIA in 1962, on a relatively silly mission. A newly aggressive right-wing organization called the John Birch Society had complained that the Kennedy administration was muzzling their attempts to circulate "instructional materials" among American servicemen abroad. To pacify the Birchers Allen was sent out to review "nonmilitary instruction" offered at military installations. Beyond this stated purpose, however, the junket let him see for himself some of what his old protégé Ed Lansdale had been telling him about, a campaign of so-called irregular warfare against the Vietcong guerrillas.

Allen's three days in Saigon were not particularly noteworthy. The CIA station chief, William Colby, took him to the presidential palace for another meeting with the American-backed leader, Ngo Dinh Diem, and they toured military outposts together. Allen's subsequent recommendations on nonmilitary instruction were quickly relegated to rightful obscurity, but during his talks with American military officers he began forming some disturbing impressions that endured. Allen found too many servicemen "confused about American aims in Southeast Asia"; this, he told associates on his return, could be a "growing problem of serious proportion."

The problem did assume serious proportions in the later 1960s, but Allen's voice was strangely absent from the public dialogue. By his instincts he was always supportive of United States efforts to resist the spread of communism. What few public statements he made about Vietnam classed him as a "hawk." But in private musings he admitted to uneasiness about where the American commitment in Vietnam was heading. Perhaps word of this ambivalence reached President Johnson, or perhaps the president and his advisers simply concluded that the voice of Allen Dulles carried less weight for a new generation. It is nonetheless noteworthy that as Johnson was soliciting public expressions of support from establishment luminaries of past wars, Allen was not among those called upon to stand prominently at the president's side.

An eager recruit to the CIA took it upon himself to call on the legendary spymaster at his Georgetown home in the spring of 1967, hoping for inspiration at the start of a career. Allen received the young man with his unfailing amiability, but his words could not match his visitor's enthusiasm. "Oh," he said, "perhaps we have already intervened too much in the affairs of other peoples."

These were years for attending to unfinished business. Through the mid-1960s Allen gave his name and occasional presence to a major study group of his beloved Council on Foreign Relations. The topic under study was evolving American attitudes toward communist China, and Allen worked with old colleagues like John McCloy and Arthur Dean of Sullivan and Cromwell. Even within this older generation the bitter hostility of the 1950s toward Mao Tse-tung's regime was softening. Allen had not counted China policy among his personal interests; Uncle Bert had warned him in another era that the China problem would not be solved in his lifetime, and Lansing was right. But Allen spoke up to defend his turf against criticism within the study group. "We may not always have drawn the right conclusions from the intelligence available," he said, "but we have not been woefully ignorant." To the astonishment of an old guard still steeped in the rigidities of John Foster Dulles, the council study group advocated recognition of the communist mainland regime and the opening of an era of peaceful coexistence. Allen wrote the foreword to the council's trailblazing report.

Early in 1967 Allen's CIA (now finally headed by his old comrade Richard Helms) suffered its worst public assault. Opening shots came from the left-wing magazine *Ramparts*, in a disclosure of CIA covert operations in the agency's heyday nearly two decades before. The program targeted was the secret financial support for the National Student Association and related intellectual groups in western Europe, considered by those in the know at the time to be the most liberal and visionary of the CIA's ventures into anticommunist political warfare.

In public response to a storm of criticism, Allen wrote, "If we had sat down and done nothing in those days, where would we be today?" East-West tensions had indeed softened since the height of the Cold War, and Allen argued that "I think what we did was worth every penny. If we turned back the communists and made them milder and easier to live with, it was because we stopped them in certain areas, and the student area was one of them."

Old friendships foundered upon the burgeoning disclosures of CIA covert political action. Allen had long since fallen out with the mentor of his youth, Walter Lippmann, on their differing philosophies of intelligence in a democracy. After the still-influential commentator joined the choruses lambasting the CIA for devious maneuvers among unwitting intellectuals, Allen gave up the friendship and never saw Lippmann again.

A more emotional blow came, however, from Allen's first bright young man of CIA, the man who had actually created the program of secret subsidies, Tom Braden. Long out of government, Braden decided to break the silence imposed on players of the Great Game with a ringing defense of the fifteen-year subsidy program. In a major article for *The Saturday Evening Post* called "I'm Glad the CIA Is 'Immoral,'" Braden only fueled the criticism with new disclosures of hitherto secret elements of CIA political warfare. "I think Tom meant well," Cord Meyer, Braden's successor in charge of the program, wrote Allen, "but obviously it is going to be very damaging. I really can't understand why he did it." Nor could Allen. When he chanced to encounter Braden's wife at a Georgetown social occasion, Allen lashed out with angry charges of Tom's betrayal.

"What you said," Joan Braden wrote Allen the next day, "hurt more deeply than you perhaps know.... Disagree with his judgment, but not with his motive." Her letter sat on the crowded desk in the study on Q Street for a month before Allen could rouse himself to compose a reply. When he wrote back, it was upon the sorrow of a lifetime scorned. "You speak of his feelings for me, and your own, but if what you say about Tom is true, why, oh why, did he have to do this without any consultation or without attempting to find out what those with whom he had worked so closely, and who had vouched for him in the past, would feel about his action.... He has hurt many of us, and my feelings for Tom have been deeply affected."

Another long friendship was broken. Allen never spoke another word to Tom Braden.

— * —

As Clover had hoped, in Allen's last years he turned his attentions to family. He and his sister Eleanor, retired from her long career as the Berlin desk officer at the State Department, began seeing more of each other in Washington. They flew together, with a large official delegation, to the funeral of West German chancellor Konrad Adenauer in April 1967.

Allen even rediscovered the family home at Henderson Harbor on Lake Ontario, where his sisters and their children and grandchildren, from whom his intense official life had estranged him over the years, still spent the summers. "He was glad we hadn't sold it," said a nephew. Though uneasy of movement — there apparently were a couple more little strokes — he rediscovered the joys of fishing, particularly with small boys of the family, whom he took out in a catboat, just the way Grandfather Foster and Uncle Bert Lansing had spent happy days with him and his brother Foster eons ago.

One summer day in 1966, just after Allen and his ten-year-old grandson Matthew Buresch had set out on the lake together, a sudden storm arose. The family waited anxiously for the fishermen to return. Finally at nightfall, with pride on their faces, Allen and Matthew stomped wearily into the cottage, bearing a huge catch of trout.

The following year Helms set up an occasion to boost the morale of his agency against the siege of public outrage. He invited Allen back to the Langley campus for a large ceremony in the imposing entrance lobby. Pale, walking with difficulty, the seventy-four-year-old former director broke into an expression of delight as the veil fell from a plaque on the wall. Next to his name was his profile in bas relief, and the words deeply graven in stone:

ALLEN WELSH DULLES
Director of Central Intelligence, 1953–1961
His monument is around us

— * —

Richard Nixon was elected the thirty-seventh president of the United States in 1968, as national outcry over Vietnam overwhelmed the Democratic ascendancy of John Kennedy and Lyndon Johnson. Allen was among those Republican notables invited to emerge from the wilderness to attend the inauguration of January 20, 1969. He declined. "I have attended my full share of inaugurations over the past few decades, and will make way, this time, for others."

Allen puttered around the Q Street house. In his sunny study he worked through the days, albeit with the "ghosts" whom he had once scorned, on two anthologies of intelligence lore, *Great True Spy Stories* and *Great Spy Stories from Fiction*. Of all his published writings, these books have had the most enduring audience.

On Christmas Eve 1968 a mild case of the flu turned serious. The Angletons and other guests from the old days were celebrating downstairs as Clover took her husband up Reservoir Road to Georgetown University Hospital for the last time. Allen never returned home to Q Street.

Clover had been unfailing in maintaining a gracious home. Serving tea from a silver salver, she was also eager for stimulating conversation on the metaphysical realms of Carl Gustav Jung or the worldly problems of prisons and halfway houses for young delinquents. Homely details were bothersome. The daily mail piled up on the table in the entrance hall; for weeks it went not only unanswered, but unopened. Once Allen went into the hospital the house fell apart, literally. On that Christmas Eve of her husband's pneumonia, Clover threw the bedclothes into the bathtub; as she rushed to the hospital she forgot to turn off the faucets. Water flooded the bathroom, overloaded the plaster walls and floor, brought the ceilings crumbling down. As emergency workmen struggled to clean up the mess, she pleaded with friends that no one must tell Allen about the disaster in his absence.

From his hospital room Allen listened to Richard Milhous Nixon taking the oath of office. Ten years before, Foster Dulles had spent his long final months in coma and suffering as Allen and the other relatives waited in anguish. Allen's wish, he told his doctors, was that he should not lose consciousness of all that was happening around him; he wanted to remain mentally active and alert to the end.

Allen died an hour before midnight on January 29, 1969, three months short of his seventy-sixth birthday. He never fell into a coma, but he did not suffer. President Nixon issued a statement from the White House. "He was a man who brought civility, intelligence and great dedication to everything he did. In the nature of his task, his achievements were known to only a few. But, because of him, the world is a safer place today."

Angleton, for all his obsessions with counterespionage, remained a man of sentiment and erudition. He prepared the eulogy for a private ceremony at the Georgetown Presbyterian Church. Allen Macy was flown in from his new home in New Mexico for his father's memorial. Richard Helms offered his arm to Clover Dulles to accompany her to her place, surrounded by some two hundred unnamed and unheralded veterans of intelligence from around the world. They heard Angleton's words read by the pastor: "It is as a splendid watchman that many of us saw him, a familiar and trusted figure in clear outline on the American ramparts. But Allen Dulles was much more than a watchman. He was the least passive of humans, the most active and open of men. He stood in full view and was ever accountable in our good society." At the Council on Foreign Relations in New York, Hamilton Fish Armstrong led a special meeting. He called the former president of the council, his friend from pre–World War I Princeton, a chivalrous knight, a man *sans peur et sans reproche*.

Testimonials flowed in from across the world. Veterans of the French resistance gathered at the American church in Paris for their own memorial service. From the Middle East David Ben-Gurion and Teddy Kollek of Israel expressed their grief; King Faisal of Saudi Arabia said he had lost a friend. Moscow noted the passing of a man who had "fiercely hated the Soviet Union and was the advocate of unscrupulous ideological and propaganda activity by the United States." The most eloquent spokesman of the American right wing was, by contrast, more reserved in assessing Allen's measured stance against communism. "Even if he did not know how finally to cope with the enemy," wrote William F. Buckley, "he knew at least who the enemy was, and that, those days, is practically a virtuoso performance."

In his own country Allen never attained the prominence of his brother Foster.* But across the restive Third World, where the CIA had acquired a reputation larger than life, in Guatemala and its Central American neighbors, for instance, Allen Dulles became the symbol of all the oppression they had suffered from the early and later days of CIA meddling.

That was all the public figure. Allen had also lived a private life of merriment and pleasure, and that side endured. During her five years of widowhood, Clover turned the Q Street house (suitably repaired after the flood) into a haven for youths during the years of protest in Washington. Her four grandchildren, their cousins, and friends came in flocks, appreciating no irony whatever in crashing at a warm Georgetown home after a day of demonstrating against the misdeeds of the ruling elite. Allen's widow knew how to make endless supplies of sandwiches as well as pour tea, and she kept impassioned conversations flowing.

Others were also enriched in their lives by their friendship with Allen. Among the condolences Clover received upon his death was a warm, thoroughly correct message from Milan, from Wally Toscanini Castelbarco. She flew to Washington for the memorial service. Clover herself telephoned Mary Bancroft with the news of Allen's death. The indomitable Mary, with her neverending flair for the changing scene, had plunged into a new life of New York Democratic politics. Mary remembered that Clover's call interrupted a popular song then blaring from her radio, "Those were the days, my friend, we thought they'd never end."[38]

Eleanor Dulles was waiting on Q Street when Clover came home from the Georgetown hospital after the end. The sisters-in-law stood together in the entry hall, the little table piled higher than ever with unopened mail. Clover finally broke the silence, saying, "All the fun is over."

---

* Dulles Airport outside Washington is named for Foster, not Allen.

ACKNOWLEDGMENTS

NOTES ON SOURCES

INDEX

ACKNOWLEDGMENTS

This biography could never have been written without the interest and cooperation of the three children of Allen and Clover Dulles. Over many hours of conversations, Clover Dulles Jebsen ("Toddy"), Joan Dulles Buresch, and Allen Macy Dulles were generous in speaking with me about their father and mother and about the family culture in which they grew up. They emptied their attics of family papers, as they had never done before, for the personal records of a man they recalled, by and large, with great affection. Allen Macy and I talked in his sunny New Mexico garden, and I am grateful to him for welcoming me to his home and for sharing his ideas. Toddy came to see me in New York from her retirement home in Connecticut. Joan, a Jungian analyst in Santa Fe, opened the family trunks for my inspection and then educated me in countless discussions about the mood and presence of her parents.

In no way and at no time over four years of contact did these stalwart individualists, worthy inheritors of deep family values, ask for the right to approve what I would write. I can offer only simple words to convey my respect for them and my gratitude for the confidence they showed in their father's biographer.

Allen's knowledgeable sister, Eleanor Lansing Dulles, was kind enough to invite me to her Washington apartment early in my researches and guide me onto the most fruitful paths for further inquiry. Allen's nephew Robert Lansing Edwards was also gracious in letting my wife and me visit his home in West Hartford and peruse his family scrapbooks and files.

Close to two hundred other busy people gave of their personal time and attention to help in the preparation of a biography long awaited. Many were approached fully two decades ago for interviews and correspondence with my colleague Richard Harris Smith, shortly after Allen's death. At that time it was too early to summon the perspective necessary for a proper assessment of a rich lifetime. But Dick Smith wisely filed away the notes of those unparalleled conversations for use at an auspicious time, and I am ever grateful to him for his tireless cooperation throughout the preparation of this book. I offer apologies to many individuals who may well have wondered, until now, if they had wasted their time in sharing their memories of Allen and his diverse ventures. To those who have not survived to read the results of their assistance, my apology is meaningless. My debt, and that of the readers of this biography, endures to:

Max Abramovitz, Richard Aldrich, Joseph Alsop, Stewart Alsop, Robert Amory, Nicholas Andronovitch, James J. Angleton, Christa Armstrong, Louis Auchincloss, Mary Bancroft, Moyra Jacobsson Bannister, Janet Barnes, Tracy Barnes, Philip Bastedo, Peter Belin, James Billington, Richard Bissell, Paul Blum, Lynn Bollinger, John Bonnell, Tom Braden, A. Spencer Braham, Henry Brandon, John Bross, David Bruce, James Bruce, Margaret Bryan, McGeorge Bundy, William P. Bundy, Ellsworth Bunker, Arleigh Burke, Michael Burke, William Caldwell, Laughlin Campbell, Cass Canfield, Rhoda Clark, Clark Clifford, William Colby, Chester Cooper, James Critchfield, Hugh Cumming, F. R. Cummings, Hugh Cunningham, Arthur Dean, Sir Patrick Dean, Brewster Denny, William Diebold, Richard Drain, Gerald Droller, Dana Durand, Walter Elder, Jacob Esterline, Douglas Fairbanks, Jr., Ladislas Farago, Barbara FitzGerald, Polly Wisner Fritchey;

Gero von Schulze-Gaevernitz, Thomas Gates, Val Goodell, David Gray, Gordon Gray, Joseph Grazier, John Greaney, Joseph N. Greene, Jr., Ernest Gross, Fowler Hamilton, Albert Haney, Chester B. Hansen, Averell Harriman, John Hazard, Richard Helms, Loy Henderson, Enno Hobbing, Lawrence Houston, William G. Hyland, Vane Ivanovic, Wayne Jackson, Donald F. B. Jameson, Walter Jessel, Peter Jessup, Howard Jones, Lem Jones, Robert Joyce, James Kellis, Walter Kerr, J. Caldwell King, William Kintner, Lyman Kirkpatrick, Jr., Teddy Kollek, Robert Komer, Edward Lansdale, Joseph Larocque, Edward Lilly, Frank Lindsay, H. Gates Lloyd, Arthur Lundahl, Helen MacInnes, William Macomber, Amos Manor, H. Freeman Matthews, John Maury, Gerald Mayer, Thomas McCoy, Kenneth McDonald, Livingston Merchant, Cord Meyer, Marjorie Miduch, Gerald Miller, Fritz Molden, Philip Moore, Robert Myers, James Noel, John B. Oakes, Thomas Parrott, Norman Paul, Claiborne Pell, Walter Pforzheimer, Herman Phleger, Henry Pleasants, George Pratt, John Ranelagh, F. Garner Ranney, James Reston, Archibald Roosevelt, Kermit Roosevelt, W. Arthur Roseborough, Harry Rositzke, Walt W. Rostow, Merritt Ruddock;

Arthur Schlesinger, Jr., Herbert Scoville, John Shephardson, Peter Sichel, John Simpson, Sidney Slomich, Bradley Smith, Edward Smith, Joseph Smith, Theodore Sorensen, Wallace Sprague, Sir Charles Spry, John Temple Swing, Tad Szulc, Barbara Taft, Maxwell Taylor, Clare Torrey, Bronson Tweedy, William Tyler, Alfred Ulmer, Gerhard Van Arkel, Clifton Von

Kann, Benjamin Welles, Dame Rebecca West, Sir Dick Goldsmith White, Lawrence K. White, David Wise, Henry Wriston, Ghosn Zogby. A few veterans of the CIA clandestine services asked not to be identified, for all their generous cooperation.

I am grateful to Nancy Bressler and the Seeley G. Mudd Manuscript Library, Princeton University Archives, for assistance in consulting Allen's personal papers and related records. Similar gratitude is due to curators of other manuscript collections across the country; among the most useful of these collections were the following:

The Hanson Baldwin Papers, Yale University; Mark Bristol Diary, Library of Congress; Norman Davis Papers, Library of Congress; James Russell Forgan Papers, Hoover Institution, Stanford University; James V. Forrestal Diary, Princeton University; Gero von Schulze-Gaevernitz Papers, Hoover Institution, Stanford University; Hugh Gibson Papers, Hoover Institution, Stanford University; George D. Herron Papers, Hoover Institution, Stanford University; Arthur Bliss Lane Papers, Yale University; Robert Lansing Papers, Library of Congress; John Simpson Oral History Interview, Bancroft Library, University of California at Berkeley; Henry Stimson Papers, Yale University; Walter Trohan Papers, Herbert Hoover Presidential Library; Hugh Wilson Papers, Herbert Hoover Presidential Library.

The great presidential libraries of those chief executives whom Allen served are natural treasure troves, particularly the Truman, Eisenhower, and Johnson libraries, and I appreciate the help of the research staffs of these overworked centers for their cooperation in my arcane inquiries. I owe special and long-standing gratitude to William R. Emerson, retired director of the Franklin D. Roosevelt Library at Hyde Park, New York. Under his guidance at Yale I took my first plunge into military and diplomatic history with an audacious undergraduate thesis on the Herron-Lammasch talks of 1918— little knowing that this "covert operation" would appear again in my later life. Bill Emerson never tired of my enthusiasms. At the National Archives in Washington I am only the latest in a long line of researchers to recognize a unique national resource in the person of John D. Taylor, who valued the fundamental freedom of information long before it became recognized in law.

The reference staff at the Council on Foreign Relations in New York was ever patient with my questions. I acknowledge particular gratitude to Janis Kreslins, Leigh Gusts, and Barbara Miller. Also at the council my colleagues Rosemary Hartman, Mae Bennett, and Lisa Ann Buono kept me organized and moving in the right directions. Mark Piel and his staff at the New York Society Library in Manhattan provided comfort and resources for research. When I visited Switzerland to pursue Allen's traces, my old friend Morris Abram opened doors, as he always does; I am also grateful for the welcome given me by the American ambassador in Bern, Joseph B. Gildenhorn, and his wife, Alma. The Harriman Institute at Columbia University provided an accommodating base as I completed my work, and I will always appreciate the welcome and generous hospitality offered by our friends in Colebrook, Connecticut.

For the concept of this biography and the encouragement to keep it moving, I am ever obliged to Michael Janeway, now dean of the Medill School of Journalism at Northwestern University, my father's old home; Janeway, Tom Powers, and Tom Wallace were "present at the creation," and without them I could not have proceeded. An estimable editor, Dick Todd, brought the insights of an ever alert mind, and Peg Anderson at Houghton Mifflin enforced discipline when it was necessary — holding back when it would have hurt. Mindy Keskinen provided good cheer and practical aid as we moved into publication. Bernice Colt is responsible for the index, which is readable as well as useful.

Numerous friends have humored my interests and helped disentangle the problems over the years. I look back with gratitude on the general and specific research assistance provided by Adam Dixon, Jim Hester, Michael Mandelbaum, Dankwart Rustow, Ted Smith, and Enzo Viscusi. I gave portions of this manuscript in early draft to several colleagues whose opinions I respect, and I have benefited from their sensitive readings: they include Bill Bundy, Brewster Denny, Bill Diebold, Jim Hoge, Bill Hyland, Nick Rizopoulos, Dick Smith, and Peter Tarnoff. Of course, they bear no responsibility for what I ultimately chose to write, but their reflections were valuable as I moved along.

A man blessed with a close family knows not where to begin. From the start, my two growing daughters found themselves in the middle of a father's obsession. At the library of Middlebury College I romped through early systematic looks at the literature on the times of Allen Dulles; Carolyn and her friends parked me comfortably in the stacks as they went off to rehearsals of the college musical before we reassembled for extended family dinners. A couple of years later Kim deposited me at the Hoover Institution day after day while she went off for sailing practice; when she returned weary and sweaty, I was more than ready to spend carefree evenings with a bunch of Stanford undergraduates. These two splendid young women make a father's life worthwhile. After completing my first book long ago, I acknowledged an endeavor shared with Claudia that had given a married couple "our happiest years, so far." A decade has now passed; the happiness and sharing have only grown.

A final note for the record: a few of the traditionalists among my friends have asked whether I am entitled to call the subject of this biography "Allen," as if to claim personal intimacy. I make no such claim; I had to use the first name to avoid confusion with "Foster" and others of the Dulles family. But as it happened, I did have a personal encounter with Mr. Dulles when I was a Senate page boy in 1953. The circumstances were trivial but to me memorable, for a reason anyone versed in intelligence will understand: I knew who he was, he did not have the slightest idea who I was.

Thinking back upon Allen Dulles and his life, I want to pay the only tribute I can to four people who mattered, for they cannot join in celebrating the American epic to which they so contributed. They are Toddy Jebsen, Bob Amory, Dick Bissell, and John Bross.

New York and Vineyard Haven
August 1994

NOTES ON SOURCES

The records of Allen Dulles's public and private life are scattered. A rich stock is now finally unsealed and available; other materials are not open at all—and in all likelihood never will be.

In May 1994 the Central Intelligence Agency released a massive record of the Dulles tenure at the agency, in delayed response to my request of March 1989 under the Freedom of Information Act. This long classified historical study, completed only in 1973, draws upon contemporary internal documents that remain secret; though much is still withheld, it provides important new evidence for key episodes in the CIA of the 1950s, as well as conveying the Dulles lore as his colleagues knew it at the time. (As the second volume in CIA's records of successive directors of central intelligence, it is listed in the notes that follow as CIA, DCI-2. Details of other recently declassified CIA studies are given in the introduction to the source notes for Chapter 11.)

Four months earlier, on the twenty-fifth anniversary of Dulles's death, the last remaining restrictions were lifted on the use of his voluminous personal files, collected at the Seeley G. Mudd Manuscript Library of Princeton University (abbreviated in these notes as AWD Papers). These miscellaneous papers of a multifaceted man contain notes of his prolific writings and an extensive personal correspondence, including letters to and from his wife, children, and other family members, notably his brother, John Foster Dulles, whose own papers are also available at Princeton (JFD Papers).

Beyond the materials at Princeton, this biography draws upon more personal records held by his three children. Correspondence is also found in the files of many of Allen's friends and colleagues, in collections across the country. Allen lived at a time when busy men still wrote long letters, and many of these survive intact.

Allen's early career is documented in the diplomatic records and the newly opened files of the World War II Office of Strategic Services, at the

National Archives in Washington. The presidential libraries of the various presidents whom he served also contain much of interest for Allen's official career.

If the CIA itself is still constrained from making matters in the internal record available for public discussion, that is not the case with many retired officers who knew and worked with Allen, who realized that much of historical importance would be lost forever if they did not tell of their experiences. Most, after initial hesitations arising from lifelong habits of secrecy, agreed to be interviewed on the record. With the exception of a few who argued good reason not to be identified, their names are listed in the Acknowledgments.

A special word about the timing of these interviews. Many were conducted by Richard Harris Smith in 1973 (except as noted) and kept in his personal files until now. Some of the people who were interviewed are no longer alive, and of those still hearty, memories may be, from the perspective of a historian, flawed. In intelligence, where so much is never put in writing, people tend to remember incidents just the way they want to remember them, confident that nothing will show up to contradict. The later years of the 1970s were a time of turmoil for intelligence veterans, when congressional and journalistic investigations opened the floodgates on previously secret CIA activities. Forced to speak in public, habitually secretive people found themselves converging upon an accepted wisdom. The Smith interviews (indicated in the notes with the notation RHS) were conducted *before* the established wisdom was settled; they are, therefore, as close to a primary source of many of the incidents of Allen's life as we are likely to have.

A chronic weakness in the literature of intelligence is a reluctance to identify sources of sensitive disclosures. I have done my best to minimize use of such "confidential" sources, occasionally to the point of hesitating about reporting specific details simply because I could not verify them responsibly.

Episodes in Allen's rich public life have been the subject of analysis by many sound authors (as well as by some less sound). A comprehensive bibliography thus would have to embrace the entire foreign policy experience of the United States in the twentieth century and would be superfluous here. Yet it would be presumptuous of a biographer to ignore diligent and enlightening work that touches upon the life of his subject; references to the most important of those secondary works are cited in the notes.

My rule of thumb in citations has been to assist further research along the many trails that can benefit from continuing inquiry, to indicate sources that may not be obvious, but not to clutter the pages of narrative with references that would serve only the interests of pedantry. For the AWD Papers, for instance, I have tried to provide enough information in context to guide serious researchers; thanks to the admirable finding aids at the Mudd Library, they will have no trouble locating the boxes and file numbers. Virtually every paragraph of this biography could be accompanied (and is, in working drafts) by extensive citations to primary sources and interesting secondary discussion. At this point I will rest on a good-faith effort to be sparing and selective, yet, I hope, helpful.

Book One: Prologue

Diplomatic records of the emperor's funeral are in the Correspondence File of the United States Embassy in Vienna, vol. 43, RG 84, National Archives, Washington, D.C. For the Redl case, somewhat fictional but clear for the main lines, see Robert Asprey, *The Panther's Feast* (New York: Carroll & Graf, 1986). Allen comments on Redl in *The Craft of Intelligence* (New York: Harper & Row, 1963); and in his introductions as editor, *Great True Spy Stories* (New York: Harper & Row, 1968).

1. In Prep

The background on Allen's parents comes first from the unpublished "Sketch of a Life" by Edith Foster (Mrs. Allen Macy Dulles), dated Feb. 14, 1934. I am grateful to the Reverend Robert Lansing Edwards, Mrs. Dulles's grandson, for interviews at his home in West Hartford, Connecticut, where he shared this and other family papers with me. See also General Foster's published memoirs: John W. Foster, *Diplomatic Memoirs* (Boston: Houghton Mifflin, 1909).

Dulles family background is found in Samuel Gaillard Stoney, *The Dulles Family in South Carolina* (Columbia: University of South Carolina Press, 1955). For family life in Watertown and Auburn, see Eleanor Lansing Dulles's vast Oral History at Butler Library, Columbia University, and her two published memoirs, *Chances of a Lifetime* (Englewood Cliffs, N.J.: Prentice-Hall, 1980); and *John Foster Dulles: The Last Year* (New York: Harcourt, Brace & World, 1963).

1. Eleanor Dulles, *Chances of a Lifetime*, p. 9.
2. Allen Welsh Dulles interview, May–June 1965, John Foster Dulles Oral History Collection, Seeley G. Mudd Manuscript Library, Princeton University.
3. Eleanor Dulles, *The Last Year*, p. 161.
4. Eleanor Lansing Dulles, Oral History, p. 32.
5. Washington's Birthday Oration and Class History, *The Nassau Herald, Class of 1914*.
6. George Stewart, ed., *The Letters of Maxwell Chaplin* (New York: Association Press, 1928), pp. 36–57.

7. Hamilton Fish Armstrong, *Peace and Counterpeace* (New York: Harper & Row, 1971), pp. 17–18.

2. *War and Peace*

Allen's early diplomatic life is described throughout the Vienna correspondence file for 1916 and 1917, particularly vols. 29 and 47, and the Bern correspondence file for 1918, vol. 51, RG 84, National Archives, Washington, D.C.; see also the papers of Hugh R. Wilson at the Herbert Hoover Presidential Library, West Branch, Iowa; and those of Hugh Gibson at the Hoover Institution, Palo Alto, California. The unpublished papers of Allen's uncle, Robert Lansing, in the Library of Congress contain numerous letters from Allen over the years, well indexed.

The Peace Conference of Paris is documented across many volumes of the official series *Foreign Relations of the United States* (hereafter abbreviated *FRUS*), including two additional volumes, *Lansing Papers*, published later. See also Harold Nicolson, *Peacemaking 1919* (London: Constable, 1933); Lawrence E. Gelfand, *The Inquiry* (New Haven: Yale University Press, 1963); Arno J. Mayer, *Politics and Diplomacy of Peacemaking* (New York: Knopf, 1967); and Arthur Walworth, *Wilson and His Peacemakers* (New York: Norton, 1986).

Important published memoirs of Allen's colleagues are Hugh R. Wilson, *The Education of a Diplomat* (New York: Longmans, Green, 1938) and *Diplomat Between Wars* (New York: Longmans, Green, 1941); and Pleasant Alexander Stovall, *Switzerland in the World War* (Savannah, Ga.: Mason, 1939).

1. State Department personnel officers dutifully placed Penfield's signal, effusive for the diplomatic traffic of the day, in Allen's Foreign Service personnel file, where it remains to this day. No. 123.D88, box 1330, RG 59, National Archives.
2. Foster, *Diplomatic Memoirs*, vol. 1, p. 163.
3. Dulles, *Craft of Intelligence*, pp. 72–73.
4. Definitive untangling of this episode required a delightful romp through records in Switzerland, the Diplomatic Branch of the United States National Archives, and the Marxist-Leninist archives in Moscow. I am grateful to my friends Bill Hyland, Kirk Kraeutler, and Bob Goldsmith for helping me in the fun of this investigation.
5. Wilson, *Education of a Diplomat*, pp. 209–10.
6. Frederic Dolbeare, memorandum attached to Hugh R. Wilson's letter of Dec. 20, 1939, Dolbeare file, Hugh R. Wilson Papers, Herbert Hoover Presidential Library.
7. Wilson, *Diplomat Between Wars*, pp. 13–14.

8. W. Somerset Maugham, *Ashenden, or The British Agent* (Garden City, N.Y.: Doubleday, 1927).

9. Ralph E. Weber, ed., *The Final Memoranda of Major General Ralph H. Van Deman* (Wilmington, Del.: SR Books, 1988), particularly pp. xvii and 21; and the Hugh Gibson Diaries, at the Hoover Institution; see particularly box 68, Feb.–Apr. 1918.

10. Gibson Diaries, July 1918, p. 133.

11. Lippmann, *New Republic*, Sept. 17, 1919, p. 195.

12. This and the following dispatches are reprinted in *FRUS, Paris Peace Conference*, vol. 1, pp. 194–203.

13. *FRUS, Paris Peace Conference*, vol. 1, p. 121; see also *FRUS, 1918, Supplement I*, vol. 1, pp. 485–86.

14. Weber, ed., *Final Memoranda*, pp. 82–84.

15. Jordan A. Schwarz, *Liberal: Adolf A. Berle and the Vision of an American Era* (New York: Free Press, 1987), p. 25.

16. Gibson Diaries, Dec. 1918.

17. C. K. Leith of the University of Wisconsin, who developed a hearty dislike of the dilatory style of the State Department. See Walworth, *Wilson and His Peacemakers*, p. 22.

18. Cited in Walworth, *Wilson and His Peacemakers*, pp. 62–63.

3. Banquo's Ghost

In addition to the Peace Conference literature cited above, see George F. Kennan, *Russia and the West under Lenin and Stalin* (Boston: Little, Brown, 1961); and Inga Floto, *Colonel House in Paris* (Princeton: Princeton University Press, 1973).

1. Quoted in Kennan, *Russia and the West*, p. 123.

2. *FRUS, Lansing Papers*, vol. 2, pp. 352–53.

3. Lansing MSS, Library of Congress, quoted in Gelfand, *The Inquiry*, pp. 212–13.

4. Van Deman letter of Nov. 13, 1918, in Weber, ed., *Final Memoranda*, Appendix G.

5. Herbert Hoover, *Memoirs: Years of Adventure* (New York: Macmillan, 1951), p. 411.

6. *FRUS, Paris Peace Conference*, vol. 2, pp. 481–82.

7. Charles Seymour, *Letters from the Paris Peace Conference*, ed. Harold B. Whiteman (New Haven: Yale University Press, 1965), pp. 61–62, 92.

8. AWD letter, Feb. 3, 1919, Walter G. Davis Papers, Sterling Library, Yale University.

9. Nicolson, *Peacemaking 1919*, p. 107.

10. Gibson Diaries, Jan. 1919.

11. A useful study of the Béla Kun episode is George W. Hopkins, "The Politics of Food: The United States and Soviet Hungary, March–August 1919," *Mid-America* 55, no. 4, Oct. 1973, pp. 245–70.

12. *FRUS, Paris Peace Conference*, vol. 12, pp. 416–24.

13. This text, from the Woodrow Wilson Papers, Library of Congress, is reproduced in Mayer, *Politics and Diplomacy of Peacemaking*, pp. 577–78.

14. Bliss to Wilson, Mar. 26, 1919, cited in Hopkins, "Politics of Food," p. 248.

15. Gibson Diaries, Mar. 27, 1919.

16. Hoover's memo was found in Colonel House's papers and is reproduced in Mayer, *Politics and Diplomacy of Peacemaking*, pp. 474–78.

17. *FRUS, Paris Peace Conference*, vol. 2, pp. 376–77.

18. For Wilson's interest in the New Czechoslovakia, see Victor S. Mamatey, *The United States and East-central Europe, 1914–1918* (Princeton: Princeton University Press, 1957), pp. 13–14; and Kennan, *Russia and the West*, p. 101; also D. Perman, *The Shaping of the Czechoslovak State* (Leiden: Brill, 1962).

19. Seymour, "Czechoslovak Frontiers," *Yale Review*, Winter 1939, pp. 273–74; Allen's letter of Nov. 7, 1938, is in the Charles Seymour Papers, box 5, Sterling Library, Yale University.

20. AWD Oral History, JFD Collection.

21. Ibid.

22. *FRUS, 1919*, vol. 2, pp. 137, 241–43.

4. Finding Himself

Allen's papers at Princeton contain extensive personal and family correspondence, including Clover's diaries and memoirs.

1. Eleanor Lansing Dulles, *Chances of a Lifetime*, pp. 80–81.

2. AWD personnel file, July 29, 1920, RG 59, National Archives.

3. Interviews with Margaret Bryan and John Sutherland Bonnell (RHS).

4. Constantinople Post files, vol. 16, Mar. 9 and 12, 1921, RG 84, National Archives. For the next dispatch, see vol. 17, July 26, 1921.

5. For the following episode, see Allen's Constantinople dispatch of Aug. 31, 1921 (over Bristol's signature) and related correspondence, in file 800.4016/12, RG 84, National Archives; also, for Graves's reports, see *The Times* (London), Aug. 16, 17, and 18, 1921.

6. This episode is described in CIA, DCI-2, vol. 1, pp. 6–7.

7. Interviews with H. Gates Lloyd (RHS) and Lawrence Houston.

5. Man of Affairs

Beyond the papers of Allen and John Foster Dulles at Princeton, see Arthur II. Dean, *William Nelson Cromwell* (New York: privately printed, 1957); and Nancy Lisagor and Frank Lipsius, *A Law unto Itself* (New York: William Morrow, 1988). The business of Sullivan and Cromwell is discussed in Ronald W. Pruessen, *John Foster Dulles: The Road to Power* (New York: Free Press, 1982); and Townsend Hoopes, *The Devil and John Foster Dulles* (Boston: Little, Brown, 1973). Often overlooked is James Stewart Martin, *All Honorable Men* (Boston: Little, Brown, 1950).

1. Edmund Hugo Stinnes, *From New York to Chicago* (Berlin: privately printed, 1929), p. 8.
2. Allen remembered this episode as he was playing tennis at Hobe Sound in February 1963 and promptly recorded it for his papers at Princeton.
3. Joseph Retinger, *Memoirs of an Eminence Grise*, ed. John Pomian (London: Sussex University Press, 1972), p. 138.
4. Harold Bartlett Whiteman, Jr., "Norman H. Davis and the Search for International Peace and Security," unpublished dissertation, May 1958, Sterling Library, Yale University, pp. 71–72, 491, 547–48.
5. Interview with Teddy Kollek.
6. *Documents on German Foreign Policy, 1918–1945: The Third Reich: First Phase*, vol. 1 (Washington: U.S. Government Printing Office, 1957), pp. 256–60.
7. The American report of this meeting is in *FRUS, 1933*, vol. 1, pp. 85–89. No German memorandum of the conversation has been found.
8. Armstrong, *Peace and Counterpeace*, pp. 526–27, 535.
9. Whiteman, "Norman H. Davis," p. 551.

6. On the Way to War

Helpful for this chapter were the archives of the Council on Foreign Relations, at the Harold Pratt House in New York, and the papers of John Foster Dulles at Princeton.

1. Notes of the speech of Oct. 30, 1935, are found in AWD Papers and are cited in Lisagor and Lipsius, *A Law unto Itself*, pp. 135–36, also 272.
2. The saga of Dr. Albert is explained in Martin, *All Honorable Men*, pp. 52–53.
3. Quoted in Lisagor and Lipsius, *A Law unto Itself*, p. 133.
4. Allen W. Dulles and Hamilton Fish Armstrong, *Can We Be Neutral?* (New York: Harper & Brothers, 1936), pp. 5, 117.
5. John Foster Dulles to Henry Leech, Sept. 30, 1937, JFD Papers.
6. Dewey Oral History interview, JFD Collection, quoted in Hoopes, *The Devil and John Foster Dulles*, p. 47.

7. For instance, his speech to the Economic Club of Detroit, Dec. 14, 1936.
8. Interview with Philip Moore.
9. Charles Lindbergh, *The Wartime Journals of Charles A. Lindbergh* (New York: Harcourt Brace Jovanovich, 1970), p. 283.
10. Allen W. Dulles and Hamilton Fish Armstrong, *Can America Stay Neutral?* (New York: Harper & Brothers, 1939), pp. 108, 154.
11. Albert to JFD, Dec. 8, 1939, quoted in Lisagor and Lipsius, *A Law unto Itself*, p. 141.
12. This memorandum is reproduced in ibid., pp. 339–40.
13. Interview with Joan Dulles Buresch.
14. Interview with William P. Bundy, Acheson's son-in-law.
15. John L. Simpson Oral History, Bancroft Library, University of California at Berkeley.
16. *The Secret War Report of the OSS* (New York: Berkley Medallion, 1976), p. 10.
17. *The New York Times*, April 5, 1942.

Book Two: Prologue

1. *Secret War Report of the OSS*, pp. 9, 17, 39, 41–42; see also Thomas F. Troy, *Donovan and the CIA* (Frederick, Md.: University Publications of America, 1981), p. 91.
2. Interview with Clover Dulles Jebsen.

7. Networking

As of the early 1990s, the working papers of the OSS are open, with extensive finding aids and cross-referencing, which can at least start research, in RG 226, National Archives. Some of Allen's more important dispatches can be located more easily in the archives of the Franklin D. Roosevelt Presidential Library. Allen's account of his journey to Bern is in AWD Papers. An important memoir of his life in Bern is Mary Bancroft, *Autobiography of a Spy* (New York: William Morrow, 1983).

1. Interviews with Gerald Mayer and George Pratt (RHS).
2. Dulles, *Craft of Intelligence*, p. 48.
3. Nelson Douglas Lankford, ed., *OSS Against the Reich: The World War II Diaries of Colonel David K. E. Bruce* (Kent, Ohio: Kent State University Press, 1991), p. 193.
4. The following episode is drawn from the papers of the Soviet historian Lev A. Bezymenski, Hoover Institution, Stanford University. See also Jon Kimche, *Spying for Peace* (London: Weidenfeld and Nicolson, 1961).
5. These cables are found in the Diplomatic Branch of the National Archives; the first is in a comprehensive assessment of Nazi activity in

Latin America from the U.S. Embassy in Uruguay, Aug. 12, 1942, file 851.20200/6; the second is in the folder "Hohenlohe-Langenberg, Maximilion Egon/3," May 20, 1943, file 862.20200.

6. Mary Bancroft, "Jung and His Circle," *Psychological Perspectives* 6, no. 2 (Fall 1975), p. 115.

7. Bancroft, *Autobiography of a Spy*, pp. 142–43.

8. C. G. Jung, *Collected Works* (Bollingen Series XX), vol. 7, paragraphs 296 and 330.

9. See, for example, OSS Bern files, entry 123, box 10, RG 226, National Archives.

10. Gerhard Van Arkel, interview by John Ranelagh, Washington, Nov. 11, 1983. I am grateful to Mr. Ranelagh for sharing with me his record of an interesting conversation.

11. Until the records of the eastern European communist regimes are fully available and properly triangulated, the best general portrayal of Noel Field is Flora Lewis, *Red Pawn* (New York: Doubleday, 1965), pp. 57–58, 76, 83–84, 121.

12. An interesting collection of documents concerning the Bank for International Settlements during World War II is available in the archives of the Foreign Research Division of the Federal Reserve Bank of New York. See particularly BIS President to Harrison, N.Y. Federal Reserve, Dec. 12, 1939; "Nature and Status of the Bank for International Settlements," Mar. 3, 1944; Moore to Sproul, "Current Status of the B.I.S.," May 5, 1944; "The Bank for International Settlements—Wartime Activities and Present Position," revised June 11, 1947. See also Martin, *All Honorable Men*, pp. 136–37, 281.

8. Into the Reich

Along with the scattered OSS records in the National Archives and at the Franklin D. Roosevelt Presidential Library, useful sources for the personalities and incidents in this chapter are Allen Dulles, *Germany's Underground* (New York: Macmillan, 1947); and Hans Bernd Gisevius, *To the Bitter End* (Boston: Houghton Mifflin, 1947). Two recent studies are Bradley F. Smith, *The Shadow Warriors* (New York: Basic Books, 1983); and Anthony Cave Brown, *The Last Hero* (New York: Times Books, 1982).

1. Felix Gilbert, *A European Past* (New York: Norton, 1988), p. 61.

2. Bancroft, *Autobiography of a Spy*, p. 134.

3. On Adam Trott zu Solz, see Christopher Sykes, *Troubled Loyalty* (London: Collins, 1968); and Dulles, *Germany's Underground*, pp. 131–33.

4. House Committee on Expenditures in the Executive Department, *Hearings on the National Security Act of 1947*, 80th Cong., June 27, 1947 (declassified and released 1982). See AWD testimony, p. 20.

5. Dulles, *Germany's Underground*, pp. 130–31.

6. Gisevius, *To the Bitter End*, p. 481.

7. The following discussion of challenges to Allen's information is drawn from William Donovan's OSS Papers in the National Archives, important parts of which are quoted and reproduced in Cave Brown, *Last Hero*, pp. 277–86.

8. Bancroft, "Jung and His Circle," p. 123.

9. See the interesting monograph by Collum A. MacDonald, *European Studies Review* 8, no. 4 (Oct. 1978), pp. 443–64.

10. An authoritative account of the following episode was finally made public late in 1993: Anthony Quibble, "Alias George Wood," from the classified in-house journal of CIA, *Studies in Intelligence*, pp. 69–90, RG 263, box 4, 38-1, National Archives. This invaluable essay also provides important insights for the study of counterespionage techniques in confirming the reliability of a secret source. Allen gives his own account in *The Secret Surrender* (New York: Harper & Row, 1966); and a somewhat romanticized version by Edward P. Morgan, "The Spy the Nazis Missed," apparently drawn from Gerald Mayer's guarded reminiscences, appeared in *True* magazine, July 1950. For the perspective of a new German generation, see *Die Zeit*, May 2, 1986, pp. 33–36. I am grateful to Barbara Ungeheuer for calling this study to my attention.

11. In fact, he remained so proud of this venture into literary diplomacy that he reproduced the excerpt verbatim in *Secret Surrender*, pp. 23–24.

12. Bruce diary entry, July 14, 1944, in Lankford, ed., *OSS Against the Reich*, p. 109.

9. The End

The July 20 conspiracy against Hitler is now the subject of a vast literature, though Allen's role as its secret contact with Washington has not been previously explored. The basic dispatches are in the OSS records, RG 226, National Archives, and in the Map Room files, Roosevelt Presidential Library. Some of these dispatches were excerpted in *FRUS*, though in difficult context. See Fabian von Schlabrendorff, *The Secret War Against Hitler* (New York: Pitman, 1965). A useful cross-reference, embarrassing to its authors, is F. H. Hinsley, *British Intelligence in the Second World War* (New York: Cambridge University Press, 1988), vol. 3, part 2, appendix 22.

1. Allen describes this incident in *Germany's Underground*, p. 69. For other attempts on Hitler's life, see Peter Hoffmann, *The History of the German Resistance, 1933–1945* (Cambridge: MIT Press, 1977).

2. Quoted in Walter Laqueur, *The Terrible Secret* (Boston: Little, Brown, 1980), pp. 98–99.

3. OSS Bern files, entry 123, box 13, Castelbarco file, RG 226, National Archives.

4. OSS Bern files, entry 165, contains operational cables to and from 110, particularly for this period: box 14, folder 129. See also entry 190, boxes 25–30.

5. Quoted in Hoffmann, *History of the German Resistance*, pp. 243–44.

6. Bancroft, "Jung and His Circle," pp. 122–25.

7. Bruce diary entry, in Lankford, ed., *OSS Against the Reich*, pp. 183–84.

8. William J. Casey's posthumous memoir, *The Secret War Against Hitler* (Washington: Regnery Gateway, 1988). See also Joseph E. Persico, *Casey* (New York: Viking Penguin, 1990).

9. Clover's account is in her diary, starting with the entry for May 6, 1943, AWD Papers.

10. For example, see entry 180, roll 159, item 16, RG 226, National Archives.

11. Discussion in Smith, *Shadow Warriors*, pp. 292–93.

12. These figures are from *Secret War Report of the OSS*, pp. 541–44. For once this official history—which normally did not hesitate to inflate the agency's achievements—may have minimized the record. At least Casey himself offers far higher effective figures in *The Secret War*, pp. 22, 198, and in the anecdotal accounts in Joseph E. Persico, *Piercing the Reich* (New York: Viking, 1979).

13. Some of the Flute cables are found in entry 180, rolls 22, 38, 62, RG 226, National Archives. I am grateful to Tom Powers for pointing them out to me. See also *Secret War Report of the OSS*, pp. 325, 331; interview with Philip Bastedo (RHS), 1973; and memorandum of Jan. 24, 1945, RG 226, box 26, folder 3, National Archives.

14. Fritz Molden, *Fire in the Night* (Boulder, Colo.: Westview Press, 1989); also interview with Joan Buresch.

15. Wally's relations with her father are discussed in Harvey Sachs, *Toscanini* (Philadelphia: Lippincott, 1978), p. 169; and George R. Marek, *Toscanini* (New York: Atheneum, 1975), p. 93.

16. Cable of Dec. 6, 1943, Castelbarco file, entry 159, box 3, folder 45; also entry 123, box 13, folder 147, RG 226, National Archives.

17. Discussion of Black and Vessel are found in Donovan Papers, entry 180, roll 2, particularly item 27; also roll 5, item 1, RG 226, National Archives.

18. Max Corvo, *The OSS in Italy* (New York: Praeger, 1990), especially pp. 301–2.

19. Howard McGaw Smyth, *Secrets of the Fascist Era* (Carbondale: Southern Illinois University Press, 1975), pp. 43–69.

20. Interview with Paul Blum (RHS).

21. Allen described this finding in an interview by Howard Smyth, Jan. 1966.

22. See Hugh Gibson's introduction to the published version: *The Ciano Diaries* (Garden City, N.Y.: Doubleday, 1946).

10. Cold Sunrise

The primary account of Operation Sunrise is the classified forty-page report by Allen and Gaevernitz, written in May 1945, in the OSS files at the National Archives and in AWD Papers. This document provided the basis for Allen's memoir *The Secret Surrender*, published after his retirement from the CIA. Where these two accounts have minor discrepancies of time and detail, I have used the earlier version. A skeptical, somewhat revisionist study of the operation is Bradley F. Smith and Elena Agarossi, *Operation Sunrise* (New York: Basic Books, 1979).

1. Clover's diary of this adventure is in AWD Papers.
2. Mary Bancroft gives a more sympathetic version of this encounter in *Autobiography of a Spy*, p. 241, but she, of course, learned of it only second-hand.
3. Bancroft, *Autobiography of a Spy*, pp. 243–44.
4. For details see Urs Schwarz, *The Eye of the Hurricane* (Boulder, Colo.: Westview Press, 1980), pp. 104–5.
5. Quoted in Ronald Steel, *Walter Lippmann and the American Century* (Boston: Little, Brown, 1980), p. 416.
6. Dulles, *Secret Surrender*, pp. 66–80; see also Eugen Dollmann, *Call Me Coward* (London: William Kimber, 1956).
7. Dulles, *Secret Surrender*, p. 114; Bancroft, *Autobiography of a Spy*, p. 289.
8. Dulles, *Secret Surrender*, p. 206.
9. Casey, *Secret War*, p. 201.
10. Rodney G. Minott, *The Fortress That Never Was* (New York: Holt, Rinehart & Winston, 1964).
11. Allen's correspondence with Minott in 1962 and 1963 is cited in Minott, *Fortress That Never Was*, p. 89; quoted passage is from Casey, *Secret War*, pp. 205–6.
12. "The Secret History of a Surrender," *Saturday Evening Post*, Sept. 22 and 29, 1945.
13. Dulles, *Secret Surrender*, p. 147.
14. *Secret War Report of the OSS*, p. 3.
15. Robert Thayer Oral History, JFD Collection. Thayer, in whose office Allen took the call, quotes Foster directly, though it is not clear how he would have heard Foster's actual words. Perhaps the phrase should be considered apocryphal, but Foster's enthusiasm for the lucrative side of law practice and his wish to have Allen back at Sullivan and Cromwell were not in doubt.
16. Interview with Philip Bastedo (RHS).
17. Jacobsson's account of this episode appears in *The Per Jacobsson Mediation*, edited by his daughter, Erin E. Jucker-Fleetwood (Basel Centre for Economic and Financial Research, series C, no. 4).

18. Allen Dulles, introduction to Jucker-Fleetwood, ed., *Per Jacobsson Mediation*, p. vii.
19. See Michael Balfour and Julian Frisby, *Helmut von Moltke* (London: St. Martin's Macmillan, 1972), Appendix.
20. Schlabrendorff, *Secret War Against Hitler*, p. 325.
21. Morgan, "Spy the Nazis Missed," p. 108.
22. Interview with Philip Bastedo (RHS).

11. Attorney in Waiting

The creation of the civilian intelligence service is authoritatively documented in the early volumes of the CIA's historical series, prepared starting as early as 1951 and classified, when written, either secret or top secret. The various authors conducted lengthy contemporary interviews with the officials involved and were granted full access to CIA and other government archives, most of which remain classified. At the end of 1989, the CIA History Staff began opening these professional studies for academic and public scrutiny. For all their limitations, they open an invaluable new resource for serious historians of intelligence. They are: Arthur B. Darling, *The Central Intelligence Agency: An Instrument of Government to 1950*, cited in the notes that follow as CIA, HS-1, and Ludwell Lee Montague, *General Walter Bedell Smith as Director of Central Intelligence*, cited as CIA, DCI-1 (these two documents have been reprinted by Pennsylvania State University Press, 1990 and 1992, respectively, with annotations by Bruce D. Berkowitz and Allan E. Goodman; page references are to the published editions); George S. Jackson and Martin P. Claussen, *Organizational History of the Central Intelligence Agency* (CIA, HS-2), declassified in 1992; and Wayne G. Jackson, *Allen Welsh Dulles as Director of Central Intelligence* (CIA, DCI-2), declassified in 1994 (page references for the latter two are to the typescript versions available for consultation at the Modern Military Branch of the National Archives).

1. Interview with Louis Auchincloss.
2. Published in 1976 as *Secret War Report of the OSS*.
3. AWD to Heinrich Brüning, Apr. 22, 1946, AWD Papers.
4. Interview with William E. Jackson.
5. Interview with Clover Dulles Jebsen.
6. *Stamford Advocate*, Feb. 13, 1946.
7. AWD to JFD, May 14, 1946, AWD Papers.
8. This was finally published as a historical document only in 1993: Michael Wala, ed., *The Marshall Plan* (Providence, R.I.: Berg Publishers).
9. Forgan to Magruder, Nov. 18, 1946, J. Russell Forgan Papers, Hoover Institution, Stanford University.
10. CIA, HS-1, p. 163; CIA, DCI-1, pp. 13, 17.

11. Senate Committee on Armed Services, *Hearings on the National Defense Establishment*, 80th Cong., 1st Sess., 1947, pp. 525–28.

12. House Committee on Expenditures in the Executive Departments, *Hearings on the National Security Act of 1947*, 80th Cong., 1st Sess., May 8, 1947, p. 301; also CIA, HS-1, p. 179.

13. House Committee, *Hearings*, pp. 10–11, 52. The transcript of this secret session was finally opened to the public only in September 1982, after congressional and CIA staffs had struggled to figure out the most responsible way to handle it. See also CIA, HS-1, pp. 181–82; CIA, DCI-1, p. 34.

14. Baldwin, *Armed Forces*, Oct. 18, 1947; *The New York Times*, July 20–25, 1948. See also CIA, HS-1, pp. 300, 318–19.

15. CIA, HS-1, pp. 247–49, 256–57.

16. Ibid., pp. 245–64, traces this entire process.

17. Steven L. Rearden, *History of the Office of the Secretary of Defense, The Formative Years 1947–1950* (Washington: Historical Office, Office of the Secretary of Defense, 1984), pp. 142–44; also CIA, HS-1, p. 302.

18. Quoted in Townsend Hoopes and Douglas Brinkley, *Driven Patriot* (New York: Knopf, 1992), p. 315.

19. CIA, HS-1, pp. 240–44, 309–10.

20. This conclusion is explored more fully in the CIA historical study on the Office of Policy Coordination by Gerald Miller, head of covert operations in Europe in the early 1950s. For all the promise of the Freedom of Information Act, this study has not yet been opened to the public.

12. Reaching

Supplementing the CIA's own historical studies, a reliable chronicle of these early years appeared in the work of the Church Committee (so called after its chairman, Senator Frank Church, Democrat of Idaho) in 1976. The committee's *History of the Central Intelligence Agency* was published as Book Four of the *Final Report of the Senate's Select Committee to Study Governmental Operations with Respect to Intelligence Activities* (Washington: Government Printing Office, 1976). Because its author, Anne Karalekas of the committee staff, had access to numerous historical studies and other internal CIA documents that remain classified, her brief account remains valuable and authoritative (cited in the following notes as Church, FR 4).

Of all the secondary writings about the early CIA, two are generally useful: John Ranelagh, *The Agency: The Rise and Decline of the CIA*, rev. ed. (New York: Simon & Schuster, 1987); and Thomas Powers, *The Man Who Kept the Secrets: Richard Helms and the CIA* (New York: Knopf, 1979).

1. AWD, Oral History interview, John F. Kennedy Presidential Library, Boston, Mass.; Clark Clifford and Richard Holbrooke, *Counsel to the President* (New York: Random House, 1991), p. 233.

2. The Dulles-Jackson-Correa report and its associated interim reports were declassified in phases. Though they have been excerpted and quoted in published anthologies, the full text is in the Modern Military Branch of the National Archives, as well as at the Harry S. Truman Presidential Library, Independence, Mo. A ragged declassification process produced one of those aberrations that reward careful researchers. Security review of classified documents usually results in the deletion of words or passages still considered sensitive even many years later. The review of Interim Report No. 2, of May 13, 1948, was not consistent in the several typescripts in different collections and in the CIA official histories—words, even whole paragraphs, deleted in one version remain in clear text in another. The passages quoted here, therefore, are a composite of several declassified texts.

3. Quoted in Church, FR 4, p. 31, Oct. 28, 1975; see also the fuller discussion of Kennan's role in the origins of covert action in Wilson D. Miscamble, *George F. Kennan and the Making of American Foreign Policy* (Princeton: Princeton University Press, 1992).

4. CIA, HS-1, p. 273.

5. Interview with William Tyler (RHS).

6. Record of groups, vol. 30, Archives of the Council on Foreign Relations, New York. See also William Diebold memo of Sept. 4, 1990, CFR archives.

7. AWD Oral History, JFD Collection.

8. Field's interrogation in Hungary was unearthed in the secret police files in 1993 by a Hungarian researcher, Maria Schmidt. Her findings were reported on the Op Ed page, *The New York Times*, Oct. 15, 1993.

9. Interview with Teddy Kollek.

10. CIA, HS-1, pp. 130–31.

11. *FRUS, 1950*, vol. 7, pp. 109–21.

12. CIA, DCI-1, pp. 55–56.

13. Ibid., pp. 42, 56–57.

14. Ibid., p. 91.

15. Interview with Polly Wisner Fritchey.

16. D. Clayton James, *Refighting the Last War* (New York: Free Press, 1993), p. 46.

17. Deane's mission is described in Mary Ellen Reese, *General Reinhard Gehlen: The CIA Connection* (Fairfax, Va.: George Mason University Press, 1990), pp. 73, 90–91.

18. Ibid., p. 73.

19. Malcolm Muggeridge, in *Esquire*, Jan. 1973, p. 48.

20. Sir Kenneth Strong, *Men of Intelligence* (New York: St. Martin's Press, 1972), pp. 125, 128, 135.

21. These quotations from Philby are collected from several sources where he is directly quoted: Kim Philby, *My Silent War* (New York: Ballantine

Books, 1968; reprint, 1983), p. 185; Philip Knightly, *The Master Spy* (New York: Knopf, 1989), p. 154; Leonard Mosley, *Dulles* (New York: Dial Press, 1978), pp. 505–15.

22. Interview with Thomas McCoy (RHS).
23. CIA, DCI-1, pp. 221–22.
24. Church, FR 4, pp. 31–32.
25. The only historical study of the Congress for Cultural Freedom is Peter Coleman, *The Liberal Conspiracy* (New York: Free Press, 1989), particularly pp. 40 ff.
26. Rositzke, *Foreign Affairs* (Jan. 1975), p. 336.
27. CIA, DCI-1, p. 203.
28. Ibid., p. 214. Tantalizingly, the four lines following this delightful anecdote were deleted by the CIA when the official history was declassified.
29. William Colby, *Honorable Men* (New York: Simon & Schuster, 1978), p. 80.
30. CIA, DCI-1, p. 222.
31. Interview with Clifton von Kamm (RHS); also CIA, DCI-1, p. 92.
32. Interview with Brewster Denny.
33. CIA, HS-1, p. 316.
34. Denny interview. As a young Senate staff man in 1961, Denny was assigned to discuss intelligence matters with Smith in the last months of his life. Now a professor at the University of Washington, Denny is chairman of the Twentieth Century Fund.
35. Select Committee to Study Governmental Operations with Respect to Intelligence Activities (Church Committee), *Alleged Assassination Plots Involving Foreign Leaders*, interim report, Nov. 20, 1975, p. 11.
36. This episode is based on interviews with a former CIA staff aide to Smith and a retired officer of the Soviet section of the clandestine services.
37. *FRUS, 1952–1954*, vol. 8, p. 1059.

13. His Own Man

1. Interview with Barbara Taft; see also Bancroft, *Autobiography of a Spy*, p. 290.
2. Files of Matthew J. Connelly, Harry S. Truman Library.
3. John Foster Dulles, "A Policy of Boldness," *Life*, May 14, 1952.
4. President's personal file, Nov. 21, 1952, Truman Library.
5. Dwight D. Eisenhower, *Mandate for Change* (Garden City, N.Y.: Doubleday, 1963), p. 142.
6. Quoted in Robert A. Divine, *Eisenhower and the Cold War* (New York: Oxford University Press, 1981), p. 21.
7. This reconstruction is found in CIA, DCI-1, pp. 262–66.
8. Interview with Stuart Hedden (RHS).

9. *New York Post*, Feb. 1, 1953.

10. But see CIA, DCI-2, p. 83.

11. Interview with Arthur Lundahl (RHS).

12. Blanche Wiesen Cook, *The Declassified Eisenhower* (New York: Double-day, 1981), pp. 162–63; see also Ronald Radosh and Joyce Milton, *The Rosenberg File* (New York: Vintage, 1984), pp. 359, 373–80, 562–63.

13. Hoopes, *Devil and John Foster Dulles*, pp. 155–56.

14. George F. Kennan, *Memoirs, 1950–1963* (New York: Pantheon, 1972), pp. 168–78. Kennan noted that he had not used the word "dangerous" in the relevant portion of his speech, nor had he mentioned Dulles by name.

15. An account of Van Deman's influence appeared in *The New York Times*, Sept. 7, 1971.

16. The official was the head of State Department security, Scott McLeod, a former FBI agent and onetime reporter for the Manchester, N.H., *Union-Leader.* Quoted in Hoopes, *Devil and John Foster Dulles*, p. 157.

17. Lyman B. Kirkpatrick, Jr., *The Real CIA* (New York: Macmillan, 1968), p. 139.

18. House Committee on Un-American Activities, *Hearings*, Oct. 13, 1952, held in Philadelphia. Smith's testimony is pp. 4283–98.

19. The following account is based on interviews with Chester Cooper and Robert Amory (RHS) and with Lawrence Houston, Walter Pforzheimer, and William Bundy.

20. Interview with Amory (RHS).

21. Interview with Houston.

22. Richard Nixon, *Memoirs* (New York: Grosset and Dunlap, 1978), pp. 139–40.

23. "U.S. Perceptions of Soviet Policy and Behavior" (paper delivered at a colloquium on the Cold War, Woodrow Wilson School, Princeton University, July 29, 1990); *FRUS, 1952–1954*, vol. 2, p. 195.

24. Letter to the author from Walter Jessel, Boulder, Colo.

25. Kirkpatrick, *Real CIA*, p. 150.

26. Interview with Amory (RHS).

27. Kent to AWD, Mar. 4, 1953, box 1, folder 24, RG 263, National Archives.

28. *FRUS, 1952–1954*, vol. 8, pp. 1088–89.

29. Quoted from cabinet notes, in Emmet John Hughes, *The Ordeal of Power* (New York: Atheneum, 1963), p. 101.

30. Senate Foreign Relations Committee, *Hearings*, Executive Session, Mar. 5, 1953, published Feb. 1977, p. 264.

31. Hughes, *Ordeal of Power*, p. 103; see also W. W. Rostow, *Europe after Stalin* (Austin: University of Texas Press, 1982), pp. 46–60.

32. Eisenhower, *Mandate for Change*, pp. 145–47; Hughes, *Ordeal of Power*, 113–14.

33. House Committee on Foreign Affairs, *Hearings on U.S. Foreign Policy and the East-West Confrontation*, Executive Session, Apr. 24, 1953, pp. 470, 479.
34. Sherman Kent, *Reminiscences of a Varied Life* (posthumously privately printed, 1991), p. 273.
35. Harry Rositzke, *The CIA's Secret Operations* (Pleasantville, N.Y.: Reader's Digest, 1977), pp. 166–73.
36. Interview with John Bross.
37. Interview with Frank Lindsay.
38. The actual memo Lindsay submitted to Allen is either "lost" from the files of CIA or held in an area immune to the probings of the Freedom of Information Act. The CIA officially rejected my request for the Lindsay memo on June 26, 1990, explaining that they had not located such a record. These quotations come from a parallel memo, prepared in necessarily vaguer form, to be read by Allen's friends who did not have the highest security clearances; Lindsay indicated to me that these passages are similar in substance to what he wrote to Allen. Lindsay found the unclassified memo in the Eisenhower Presidential Library and gave it to me from his personal files.
39. Interviews with Bross and Michael Burke (RHS).
40. Among the guarded sources on the following episode are William Hood, *Mole* (New York: Ballantine, 1983); Jerrold L. Schechter and Peter S. Deriabin, *The Spy Who Saved the World* (New York: Scribners, 1992); David Wise, *Molehunt* (New York: Random House, 1992); and Richard Harris Smith, "The First Moscow Station," *Intelligence and Counterintelligence* 3, no. 3, pp. 333–46.
41. Hood, *Mole*, pp. 93–97, 155.

14. A Third World

The CIA's covert actions in Iran and Guatemala have been the subjects of a vast literature, but none of it has been based on authoritative documentation, which CIA has been unwilling to make public. Allen's personal role emerges from memoirs, from interviews with surviving participants, and between the lines in a few notable scholarly studies, from which his interests can be pieced together.

On Iran, Clover's diary, AWD Papers, Aug. 1953, provides reliable evidence for a crucial episode. Two published accounts are useful: Mark J. Gasiorowski, "The 1953 Coup d'Etat in Iran," *International Journal of Middle East Studies* 19 (1987), pp. 261–86; and the controversial memoir by Kermit Roosevelt, *Countercoup* (New York: McGraw Hill, 1979), which detractors find self-serving; it nonetheless remains a necessary source to consider on the matters that Roosevelt knew about. A Duke University scholar, Bruce

Kuniholm, has led the charge against what he calls "fraud" in presenting American foreign policy toward Iran in *FRUS, 1952–1954*, vol. 10; see *Perspectives* (newsletter of the American Historical Association, May/June 1990), pp. 1, 11–12.

For Guatemala, the analytical situation is a little better, though much remains to be discussed about the whole impact of the CIA's role. Historical studies built upon extensive interviews and the Eisenhower presidential records when they were first declassified provide insight: Richard H. Immerman, *The CIA in Guatemala* (Austin: University of Texas Press, 1982); Stephen Schlesinger and Stephen Kinzer, *Bitter Fruit* (New York: Anchor Books, 1982); and Cook, *Declassified Eisenhower*. Above all is the masterful history by Piero Gleijeses, *Shattered Hope* (Princeton: Princeton University Press, 1991), which draws with great sophistication onthe Guatemalan sources when the official American records were not available.

1. "The Challenge from Abroad" (speech delivered to the annual Congress of American Industry, Dec. 3, 1947). I am grateful to the reference staff of the Hagley Museum and Library in Wilmington, Del., for digging the all-but-forgotten text out of the archives of the National Association of Manufacturers. Allen's remarks were briefly noted in *The New York Times*, Dec. 4, 1947, p. 1.

2. This account of Ajax draws in significant part from interviews (RHS) with Robert Amory, Richard Bissell, Loy Henderson, James Kellis, Tom McCoy, Gerald Miller, and Kermit Roosevelt.

3. Dean Acheson, *Present at the Creation* (New York: Norton, 1969), pp. 503–4.

4. Roosevelt, *Countercoup*, pp. 1–8.

5. Ibid., pp. 156–57.

6. See *ZüricherWoche*, Aug. 14, 1953, p. 5.

7. This reconstruction of the crucial days comes from Clover's diary (AWD Papers) and what she later told her daughter Joan Dulles Buresch; and Miller interview (RHS).

8. Quoted in Stephen E. Ambrose, *Eisenhower* (New York: Simon & Schuster, 1984), p. 129.

9. Eisenhower's friend was William Prescott Allen, publisher of the *Laredo Times*, quoted in Immerman, *CIA in Guatemala*, p. 183.

10. Quoted in ibid., pp. 102–3.

11. *FRUS, 1952–1954*, vol. 4, p. 1106.

12. From an interview by Piero Gleijeses with Krieg, in Gleijeses, *Shattered Hope*, p. 193.

13. Jordan A. Schwarz, *Liberal* (New York: Free Press, 1987), p. 314; see also Edward L. Bernays, *Biography of an Idea* (New York: Simon & Schuster, 1965).

14. Mar. 18, 1953, *FRUS, 1952–1954*, vol. 4, pp. 6–10.

15. Primary sources for the following account of Allen's engagement in the Guatemala of Arbenz are a series of comprehensive interviews (RHS) with J. C. King, Robert Amory, Albert Haney, William Caldwell, Tom Braden, and Enno Hobbing, between the autumn of 1973 and August 1974.
16. Schlesinger and Kinzer, *Bitter Fruit*, p. 111.
17. Interview with King.
18. Interview with Haney.
19. An amusing account of Heckscher's arrival is in David Atlee Phillips, *The Night Watch* (New York: Ballantine, 1977), p. 46. At the time Phillips was writing, CIA men were still trying to conceal their real identities: Heckscher is given the name "Peter" in the published account; Haney is "Brad."
20. JFD telephone log, May 17, 1954, Eisenhower Library.
21. Ibid., May 18, 1954, Eisenhower Library.
22. Robert H. Ferrill, ed., *The Diary of James C. Hagerty* (Bloomington: Indiana University Press, 1983), p. 68.
23. Cook, *Declassified Eisenhower*, p. 267.
24. Quoted in Trumbull Higgins, *The Perfect Failure* (New York: Norton, 1987), p. 27.
25. This story was finally pieced together years later by Harrison E. Salisbury, *Without Fear or Favor* (New York: Ballantine, 1980), pp. 477–80.
26. *The New York Times*, June 20, 1954.
27. *FRUS, 1952–1954*, vol. 4, pp. 1174–76.
28. Eisenhower, *Mandate for Change*, pp. 425–26.
29. Interview with Hobbing (RHS). This perspective from the field was not off base; on June 24, at the height of the tension, Foster called Allen to warn of anti-American sentiments in other Latin American capitals: "Our people . . . are frightened by reactions all over."
30. *FRUS, 1952–1954*, vol. 4, p. 1176.
31. Gleijeses, *Shattered Hope*, pp. 381, 383.
32. See Phillips, *Night Watch*, p. 68; Schlesinger and Kinzer, *Bitter Fruit*, p. 184; King interview.
33. Eisenhower to Doolittle, Oct. 19, 1954, quoted in Gleijeses, *Shattered Hope*.
34. Dulles, *Craft of Intelligence*, p. 48.
35. Interview with John Bross; CIA, DCI-2, p. 138.

15. Other Games, Other Rules

1. Dino A. Brugioni, *Eyeball to Eyeball* (New York: Random House, 1991), p. 6. Unknown to the public through his thirty-four years of CIA service, Brugioni was free after his retirement in 1982 to publish incisive discussions of aerial and spatial imagery, as used not only in intelligence but also in environmental protection.

2. CIA, HS-2, folder 6, p. 12.
3. CIA, HS-1, pp. 316–17.
4. The CIA drug research program is carefully traced in John Marks, *The Search for the "Manchurian Candidate"* (New York: McGraw Hill, 1980), which contains detailed references to the various reports of the Church Committee in 1975–76 and a later joint hearing of the Senate Select Committee on Intelligence and a subgroup of the Committee on Human Resources, Aug. 3, 1977. See also *Sandoz 1886–1961: Seventy-five Years of Research and Enterprise*, a report published by the Sandoz Company.
5. Church, FR 1, pp. 392–93.
6. CIA, HS-2, folder 6, p. 20.
7. Brugioni, in *Bulletin of the Atomic Scientists* (Mar. 1990), p. 12.
8. Church, FR 1, p. 393.
9. Memo of Apr. 3, 1953, quoted in ibid., p. 390.
10. Church, FR 1, p. 399. The digraph MK referred to an operation of CIA's Technical Services.
11. Ibid., pp. 404–5.
12. This speech was published in *U.S. News and World Report*, May 8, 1953.
13. Quoted in Church, FR 1, p. 394; see also pp. 405, 390.
14. The Olson case is described in ibid., pp. 394–99; and Marks, *"Manchurian Candidate,"* pp. 73–84, 220.
15. The personal papers of a flamboyant federal narcotics official, George H. White, containing lurid details of the experiments, survived the purge of the CIA program's records. They were unearthed after the Church Committee's investigation and formed a basis for an extensive article in *The New York Times*, Sept. 20, 1977.
16. Church, FR 1, p. 403.
17. The following episode is drawn from interviews with Michael Burke and Lyman Kirkpatrick (RHS). See also CIA, *The Berlin Tunnel Operation*, CS Historical Paper no. 1 (Aug. 25, 1967), p. 2 (available in typescript from CIA under Freedom of Information Act procedures); see also Heinz Höhne and Hermann Zolling, *The General Was a Spy* (New York: Coward, McCann & Geoghegan, 1971), p. 329.
18. E. H. Cookridge, *George Blake: Double Agent* (New York: Ballantine, 1970), p. 150. CIA, *Berlin Tunnel*, p. 3, refers only to "negative results" in the early efforts.
19. Blake's later account of his personal role in the Berlin Tunnel appeared in *Pravda (International)* 2, no. 11/12 (1988), pp. 9–11, and *Moscow Magazine* (Oct./Nov. 1991), pp. 50–54.
20. JFD to ED, May 11, 1956, quoted in Michael R. Beschloss, *Mayday* (New York: Harper & Row, 1986), p. 115.
21. CIA, *Berlin Tunnel*, appendix D, pp. 2, 4–5, 9.
22. Blake, *Pravda (International)*. CIA, *Berlin Tunnel*, clings to the belief, at

least in the sanitized version that has been declassified, that the Russians discovered the tunnel only by chance.

23. Dulles, *Craft of Intelligence*, pp. 136–39.
24. Brugioni, *Eyeball to Eyeball*, pp. 9–17.
25. Interview with Lawrence White (RHS).
26. Quoted in Beschloss, *Mayday*, p. 83.
27. Brugioni, *Eyeball to Eyeball*, p. 24; Beschloss, *Mayday*, p. 105.
28. Interview with Arthur Lundahl (RHS).
29. Otto John, *Twice Through the Lines* (New York: Harper & Row, 1972), p. 226; also interviews with John Bross and Michael Burke (RHS).
30. The inability of Grombach and his ilk to draw distinctions between "communists," "socialists" and "neutralists" indicates the level of the analysis, which allowed CIA to conclude that such sources could be dispensed with. Christopher Simpson of American University came upon this remarkable memo in his researches into postwar intelligence activities. I am grateful to him for providing me a copy from his files.
31. The following confrontation is constructed from interviews with James Critchfield and by RHS with Robert Amory, John Bross, and Lyman Kirkpatrick. Trudeau's side of the story is told in Reese, *General Reinhard Gehlen*, pp. 139–41. See also CIA, DCI-2, vol. 2, pp. 126–36.
32. The incident was prominently recalled thirty-six years later in the obituary on Trudeau's death at the age of eighty-eight, *The New York Times*, June 8, 1991.
33. Quoted in Ambrose, *Eisenhower*, p. 227.
34. CIA, DCI-2, vol. 4, p. 84.
35. Ibid., vol. 1, p. viii.
36. Interview with Edward Lansdale (RHS); also Cecil B. Currey, *Edward Lansdale: The Unquiet American* (Boston: Houghton Mifflin, 1988), p. 61.
37. CIA, DCI-2, vol. 1, p. 92.
38. Quoted in Stephen E. Ambrose with Richard H. Immerman, *Ike's Spies* (New York: Doubleday, 1981), p. 245.
39. Interview with Robert Amory (RHS).
40. See analysis of this plot in Arthur M. Schlesinger, Jr., *Robert Kennedy and His Times* (Boston: Houghton Mifflin, 1978), p. 481.
41. The following account is based on an interview with William Caldwell (RHS).
42. Oral History interview, Kennedy Library.
43. Quoted in W. W. Rostow, *Open Skies* (Austin: University of Texas Press, 1982); also interviews with Livingston Merchant and Sidney Slomich (RHS).
44. Eisenhower, *Mandate for Change*, pp. 521–22.
45. CIA, DCI-2, vol. 4, p. 145; David Atlee Phillips, *Secret Wars Diary* (Bethesda, Md.: Stone Trail Press, 1989), p. 177; CIA, DCI-2, vol. 1, p. 52.

46. Dulles-Jackson-Correa report (typescript), p. 123.
47. Interview with Lawrence White (RHS).

16. Eruptions

Eisenhower's faithful personal assistant, Anne Whitman, admirably organized the Oval Office files for the Eisenhower Presidential Library, Abilene, Kansas. She divided them into several categories, such as the diary series, the National Security Council, staff memos (particularly in General Goodpaster's files), and telephone logs. These are well catalogued and readily accessible—but with inevitable deletions on alleged security grounds. John Foster Dulles's telephone logs and official papers are available at the Eisenhower Library as well as in his papers at Princeton. After Whitman finished her work, the lesser files remained in somewhat haphazard form—and for the work that concerned Allen, these more obscure collections deserve greater scholarly attention. The Walter Bedell Smith papers, though taciturn and spotty, befitting their creator, remain to be triangulated with evidence from other quarters.

1. Charles E. Bohlen, *Witness to History* (New York: Norton, 1973), pp. 396–97.
2. *FRUS, 1955–1957*, vol. 24, pp. 73–75.
3. Quoted in Ranelagh, *The Agency*, p. 286.
4. Lewis, *Red Pawn*, p. 16.
5. The following account is pieced together from interviews with Amos Manor, then head of Israel's Shin Beth, who kept his silence on intelligence matters for many years after his retirement, and from the memories of key CIA players. A more tentative version appears in Dan Raviv and Yossi Melman, *Every Spy a Prince* (Boston: Houghton Mifflin, 1990), pp. 85–89.
6. Ray S. Cline, *The CIA under Reagan, Bush and Casey* (Washington: Acropolis, 1981), pp. 185–87.
7. Phillips, *Night Watch*, p. 65.
8. Interview with Harrison Salisbury.
9. Bohlen, *Witness to History*, pp. 400–401.
10. Ranelagh, *The Agency*, p. 287.
11. NSC minutes, June 29, 1956, Eisenhower Library.
12. This account is drawn from an interview with James Billington, and from Cline, *The CIA*, pp. 187–92.
13. An important new documentary source for the role of American intelligence in the Suez crisis became available in May 1994: CIA, DCI-2, particularly vol. 5, pp. 1–38, which had been assigned the high top-secret classification (the four previous volumes of this historical study were classified secret). This source, noted in specific references below, augments

an already vast primary and secondary literature. The following account also draws from interviews with Kermit Roosevelt, Robert Amory, Robert Komer, Gordon Gray, Herman Phleger, Loy Henderson, and Norman Paul (RHS). The most useful recent scholarly study is W. Scott Lucas, *Divided We Stand* (London: Hodder & Stoughton, 1991).

14. CIA, DCI-2, vol. 1, p. 95.
15. See staff memos series, Aug. 1956, Eisenhower Library; CIA, DCI-2, vol. 5, pp. 6–8; *FRUS, 1955–1957*, vol. 15, p. 383; Lucas, *Divided We Stand*, pp. 110, 181.
16. CIA, DCI-2, vol. 5, pp. 8–9; Senate Foreign Relations Committee, *Hearings*, Executive Sessions, Nov. 12, 1956, p. 619.
17. Peer de Silva, *Sub Rosa* (New York: Times Books, 1978), p. 120.
18. Diary series, NSC meeting 301, Oct. 26, 1956, Eisenhower Library.
19. Dwight D. Eisenhower, *Waging Peace* (New York: Doubleday, 1965), pp. 67–73.
20. Lucas, *Divided We Stand*, p. 255.
21. CIA, DCI-2, vol. 5, pp. 20–36.
22. Richard Bissell, Oral History, JFD Papers; also interview (RHS).
23. Diary series, NSC meeting 302, Nov. 1, 1956, Eisenhower Library.
24. CIA, DCI-2, vol. 5, pp. 37–38.
25. Quoted in Lucas, *Divided We Stand*, p. 282.
26. Goodpaster memorandum, staff secretary (alphabetical) series; JFD telephone logs, Oct. 30, 1956, Eisenhower Library; AWD testimony to SFRC, Nov. 12, 1956, pp. 621–22.
27. CIA, DCI-2, vol. 3, p. 101; *FRUS, 1955–1957*, vol. 25, pp. 436–37.
28. AWD to Goodpaster, staff secretary (alphabetical) series, Nov. 20, 1956 (box 7), Eisenhower Library.
29. Diary series, Nov. 1956 miscellaneous folder, Eisenhower Library.
30. AWD testimony to SFRC, Nov. 12, 1956, p. 641; see also AWD Oral History, JFD Collection; and, in the same collection, oral histories of Richard Bissell and General C. P. Cabell.
31. Eisenhower to Sherman Adams, diary series, June 1954, Eisenhower Library.
32. Diary series, Nov. 1955, folders 1 and 2; DDE personal, 1955–56 folder 2, Eisenhower Library.
33. Lovett to the subsequent Taylor Board of Inquiry, May 11, 1961; the transcript of this session remains classified, though the bulk of the ensuing report has been made public. Arthur M. Schlesinger, Jr., found a copy of the secret transcript in the Robert Kennedy Papers before they were deposited at the John F. Kennedy Library under restricted access; see his *Robert Kennedy*, p. 455.
34. The Bruce-Lovett report is still tightly classified; the reference staff of the Eisenhower Library told me they have no knowledge of such a document. Once again, it was only because of Professor Schlesinger's unrestricted access to the Robert Kennedy Papers that these excerpts can be

published. I am grateful to him for providing me with the notes he took from this rich file of intelligence matters. His own discussion of the report is in *Robert Kennedy*, pp. 454–57.

35. Memorandum of conversation, Jan. 17, 1957, diary series, Eisenhower Library; Beschloss, *Mayday*, p. 133.

36. Quoted in Ambrose, *Eisenhower*, p. 469; the next quotation is from Eisenhower, *Waging Peace*, p. 366.

37. Eleanor Dulles provides a characteristically defensive explanation for her brother's remarks, in *The Last Year*, pp. 50–52.

38. Vice President Nixon interrupted to say that Allen's facts were accurate but misleading; the real point was not press ownership but the origin of the opinions printed. The journalists who supplied press content, Nixon said, were mostly anti-American. See NSC minutes, meetings 347, 358, 369, and 370, Eisenhower Library.

39. Interview with Walt Rostow.

40. Interview with Lawrence Houston.

41. Staff notes, Dec. 1958, folder 2, Eisenhower Library.

42. Interview with Hugh Cunningham (RHS). Queens know how to sanitize the records as well as government archivists; in her memoirs Frederika describes the room where the couple was trapped as "a small passage with a staircase." Frederika, *A Measure of Understanding* (New York: St. Martin's, 1971), pp. 174–75.

43. Interview with Alfred Ulmer (RHS). An official CIA view of the Indonesian operation is found in CIA, DCI-2, vol. 3, pp. 108–13.

44. NSC minutes, meetings 354 and 356, Eisenhower Library.

45. CIA, DCI-2, vol. 3, pp. 112–13.

46. Minutes of meeting of presidential intelligence consultants with Eisenhower, Dec. 16, 1958, in Schlesinger's notes from Robert Kennedy Papers and his *Robert Kennedy*, p. 457.

47. CIA, DCI-2, vol. 1, p. 56; also interview with Wayne Jackson (RHS).

48. Interviews with Jacob Esterline and Gates Lloyd (RHS).

49. Richard Nixon, *Six Crises* (New York: Doubleday, 1962), p. 186.

50. Interview with Norman Paul (RHS); NSC minutes, Eisenhower Library; see discussion in Ambrose, *Eisenhower*, pp. 463–67, and Divine, *Eisenhower and the Cold War*, p. 99.

17. *Alone*

1. Eleanor Dulles, *The Last Year*, pp. 214–15.

2. DDE phone calls, Oct. 1956, Eisenhower Library.

3. Dulles-Herter series, Feb. 1959, Eisenhower Library.

4. This quotation, along with others following not otherwise cited, is found in Ambrose, *Eisenhower*, p. 510.

5. Unless specifically cited otherwise, this account of Foster's illness and

death is from the various contemporaneous notes and memos of Joseph
N. Greene, Jr., his personal assistant, JFD Papers, 1951–1959, and interviews with Greene; see also the Dulles-Herter series and the DDE diary
series, Apr. 1959, Eisenhower Library. Eisenhower gives his own account
in *Waging Peace*, pp. 357 ff.

6. Unpublished notes, 1959, AWD Papers.

7. Eisenhower, *Waging Peace*, p. 365.

8. NSC minutes, Mar. 20, 1958, Eisenhower Library.

9. NSC minutes, meeting 359, Eisenhower Library.

10. Diary series, copies of DDE personal, Mar. 13, 1956, Eisenhower Library.

11. Goodpaster memorandum, Apr. 14, 1959, diary series (staff notes),
Eisenhower Library.

12. Eisenhower to Merchant, Dec. 28, 1960, diary series (dictation), Eisenhower Library.

13. Unpublished note, Apr. 15, 1959, AWD Papers.

14. Richard Nixon, *Memoirs* (New York: Grosset & Dunlap, 1978), pp. 201–3.

15. Ambrose, *Eisenhower*, p. 527.

16. See Beschloss, *Mayday*, pp. 194, 199.

17. CIA, DCI-2, vol. 1, pp. 81–82, which reveals that the "mortar" was really
only a mixture of sand and sugar, later to be set right. Also interview
with "Red" White (RHS).

18. Senate Foreign Relations Committee, *Hearings*, Executive Session, May
31, 1960, pp. 282, 285, 292.

19. CIA, DCI-2, vol. 2, p. 43.

20. SFRC, *Hearings*, May 31, 1960, p. 357.

21. Goodpaster memorandum, staff notes, Aug. 1958, Eisenhower Library.
A full discussion of the various analytical techniques that permitted hypothesis of a missile gap is found in the formerly top-secret historical
study, CIA, DCI-2, vol. 5, pp. 39–138. See also McGeorge Bundy, *Danger and Survival* (New York: Random House, 1988), pp. 337–48.

22. SFRC, *Hearings*, May 31, 1960, p. 299.

23. Staff secretary series (alphabetical subject "Intelligence Matters"), Mar.
13, 1956, Eisenhower Library; see also testimony of Thomas S. Gates,
Jr., secretary of defense, SFRC, *Hearings*, June 2, 1960, p. 402.

24. This and the following are quoted in Beschloss, *Mayday*, pp. 8, 148–49.

25. SFRC, *Hearings*, May 31, 1960, p. 282.

26. See notes in Goodpaster's quick handwriting, Nov. 15, 1956, staff secretary series ("Intelligence Matters"), Eisenhower Library; see also Ambrose, *Eisenhower*, p. 374.

27. Goodpaster memo, Sept. 9, 1958, staff secretary series ("Intelligence
Matters"), Eisenhower Library.

28. Goodpaster memo, Feb. 8, 1960, staff secretary series ("Intelligence
Matters"), Eisenhower Library.

29. SFRC, *Hearings*, May 31, 1960, p. 287.

30. NSC minutes, May 24, 1960, Eisenhower Library. Khrushchev was reported as speaking during preliminaries to the abortive Paris summit meeting that month.
31. For this and following quotations, see SFRC, *Hearings*, May–June 1960, pp. 365, 377, 313–17, 325, 283, 301–2, 335.
32. CIA, DCI-2, vol. 5, p. 113.
33. SFRC, *Hearings*, Mar. 6, 1962, pp. 255, 266–67.
34. Beschloss, *Mayday*, pp. 31–37. Beyond the official history declassified in 1994 (CIA, DCI-2, vols. 4 and 5), useful documentation of the May 1 flight is contained in the staff secretary series (alphabetical subject "U-2 Incident"), Eisenhower Library. These files also contain a detailed, if somewhat defensive, chronology of events prepared in the State Department for Secretary Herter, who was out of the country during the crucial days.
35. Kistiakowsky's memoir, *A Scientist at the White House* (Cambridge: Harvard University Press, 1976), is another interesting source for the U-2 incident; see p. 317.
36. SFRC, *Hearings*, June 1, 1960, p. 370.
37. Ibid., *Hearings*, May 31, 1960, p. 291.
38. Kistiakowsky, *Scientist at the White House*, pp. 318–19.
39. SFRC, *Hearings*, May 31, 1960, p. 291.
40. This meeting is reported in Beschloss, *Mayday*, pp. 243–44.
41. SFRC, *Hearings*, May 31, 1960, p. 291.
42. Interview with Arthur Lundahl (RHS). Lundahl and Alfred Ulmer, by then CIA station chief in Paris, gave the same briefing a few days later to General De Gaulle, host to the abortive Paris summit conference.
43. Reported to the NSC: see NSC minutes, May 24, 1960, Eisenhower Library.
44. CIA assessments of this sort are not yet declassified at the source. This Current Intelligence Memorandum of May 13, 1960, was found in the staff secretary series (alphabetical subject), Eisenhower Library.
45. The June 7 memo was unearthed in the Communist Party's archives in 1994 by the Cold War International History Project of the Woodrow Wilson Center in Washington. I am grateful to Benjamin Aldrich-Moodie and Jim Hershberg for calling it to my attention. Kennan's remarks, OpEd page, *The New York Times*, Oct. 28, 1992.
46. Oral History interview, Columbia University, quoted in Beschloss, *Mayday*, p. 260.
47. AWD, interview by Eric Sevareid of CBS News, Apr. 26, 1962.

18. Fading Fast

1. Allen's memoir of Fleming, *Life*, Aug. 28, 1964.
2. Troy, *Donovan and the CIA*, pp. 81–82.
3. Quoted in Ambrose and Immerman, *Ike's Spies*, p. 505.

4. CIA memo to the director, found in Dulles-Herter series, JFD Feb. 1959 folder, Eisenhower Library.
5. NSC minutes, Mar. 26, 1959, Eisenhower Library.
6. This episode is discussed in Church Committee, *Alleged Assassination Plots*, pp. 92–93.
7. Quoted in Ambrose and Immerman, *Ike's Spies*, p. 509.
8. John Pearson, *The Life of Ian Fleming* (New York: McGraw Hill, 1966), pp. 321–23.
9. Goodpaster memo of Mar. 18, 1960, staff secretary series (alphabetical subject "Intelligence Matters"), Eisenhower Library. See also the declassified report of the Taylor Board of Inquiry, published as *Operation Zapata* (Frederick, Md.: University Publications of America, 1981), pp. 3–4.
10. Interview with Philip Moore.
11. Kent, in *Studies in Intelligence*, the classified professional journal of CIA, spring 1969.
12. Interview with Maxwell D. Taylor (RHS).
13. Bancroft, *Autobiography of a Spy*, p. 242.
14. The CIA experience with Lumumba is documented to a degree unparalleled in the history of covert actions, thanks to the investigations of the Church Committee. Entire folders of operational cables, down to working instructions to the officers in the field, were turned over to the committee. Deserving (indeed, given the chaotic narrative flow, demanding) careful study is the Interim Report, *Alleged Assassination Plots*. For a wider perspective on United States policy in the Congo, see Madeleine G. Kalb, *The Congo Cables* (New York: Macmillan, 1982).
15. Speech to the New York Bar Association, June 20, 1947.
16. Quotations in this and the following two paragraphs are from Church Committee, *Alleged Assassination Plots*, pp. 14–15, 61.
17. CIA, DCI-2, vol. 3, pp. 87–88.
18. Church Committee, *Alleged Assassination Plots*, pp. 91, 97.
19. Ibid., pp. 15–16.
20. Ibid., pp. 17, 62, 52–53, 23–24.
21. Ibid., p. 31.
22. Interview with Richard Clurman.
23. Church Committee, *Alleged Assassination Plots*, p. 59.
24. Kistiakowsky, *Scientist in the White House*, p. 377. The science adviser's memoirs were published a year after the Church Committee completed its work; had this notation been known to the committee, its tortured analysis of remarks by lower-level officials would have been greatly eased. See Church Committee, *Alleged Assassination Plots*, pp. 55–70.
25. Church Committee, *Alleged Assassination Plots*, pp. 149–50, 95.
26. Theodore C. Sorensen, *Kennedy* (New York: Harper & Row, 1965), p. 176.
27. AWD memorandum to Eisenhower, quoted in Ambrose, *Eisenhower*, pp. 598–99.

28. Arthur M. Schlesinger, Jr., *A Thousand Days* (Boston: Houghton Mifflin, 1965), pp. 74–75.

29. Nixon's side is in his *Six Crises*, pp. 353–55; Allen's is in his Oral History interview at the Kennedy Library.

30. Schlesinger, *Thousand Days*, pp. 121–22.

31. AWD Oral History, Kennedy Library; Tom Gilligan, *CIA Life* (Guilford, Conn.: Foreign Intelligence Press, 1991), pp. 54–55.

32. CIA, DCI-2, vol. 3, pp. 117–18.

33. Quoted in Ambrose and Immerman, *Ike's Spies*, pp. 311–13.

34. Robert Amory, Jr., Oral History interview, typescript pp. 123–24, Kennedy Library.

35. Interview with Thomas McCoy (RHS).

36. Interviews with James Noel, Lawrence White, and James J. Angleton (RHS).

37. Taylor Board, *Operation Zapata*, p. 40; Bissell, "Reflections on the Bay of Pigs," *Strategic Review* no. 12 (Winter 1984), pp. 66–71.

38. Quoted in Schlesinger, *Robert Kennedy*, p. 444.

39. Taylor Board, *Zapata*, p. 110; see also Ambrose and Immerman, *Ike's Spies*, p. 315.

40. Unpublished notes, box 244, p. 2, AWD Papers.

41. Taylor Board, *Zapata*, pp. 176, 110, 224.

42. Church Committee, *Alleged Assassination Plots*, p. 95.

43. Interview with David Gray (RHS); Taylor Board, *Zapata*, p. 10; see also the careful history by Peter Wyden, *Bay of Pigs* (New York: Simon & Schuster, 1979), p. 89.

44. Schlesinger, *Thousand Days*, p. 276; *Robert Kennedy*, p. 447; Sorensen is quoted in Church Committee, *Alleged Assassination Plots*, p. 120.

45. In Oral History interview, pp. 21–22.

46. Taylor Board, *Zapata*, pp. 41–42.

47. Ibid., p. 59.

48. Ibid., p. 13; see Allen's discussion in his Oral History, p. 22, Kennedy Library.

49. Bissell, "Reflections," pp. 69–70.

50. Taylor Board, *Zapata*, p. 182; AWD Oral History, p. 19.

51. AWD Oral History, p. 31.

52. CIA, DCI-2, vol. 3, pp. 124–25; this meeting is also described in Wyden, *Bay of Pigs*, pp. 199–200.

53. Taylor Board, *Zapata*, pp. 182, 110.

54. This discussion appears in the journal of the Society for Historians of American Foreign Relations, *Diplomatic History* (Fall 1984), pp. 365–80: Lucien S. Vandenbroucke, "The 'Confessions' of Allen Dulles," followed by Richard M. Bissell, Jr., "Response to Lucien S. Vandenbroucke."

55. Taylor Board, *Zapata*, p. 147; Schlesinger, *Thousand Days*, p. 242.

56. Taylor Board, *Zapata*, p. 102.
57. Burke revealed this in a 1983 interview with Vandenbroucke; see "'Confessions,'" p. 371.
58. Taylor Board, *Zapata*, pp. 179–80.
59. AWD Oral History, p. 24.
60. Wyden, *Bay of Pigs*, p. 308.
61. Currey, *Lansdale*, pp. 211–12.
62. CIA, DCI-2, vol. 3, pp. 121–22.
63. Quoted in Schlesinger, *Robert Kennedy*, p. 446.
64. Interview with James Reston.
65. Taylor Board, *Zapata*, p. 19; Wyden, *Bay of Pigs*, pp. 144–45.
66. CIA, DCI-2, vol. 3, p. 127.
67. Amory, Oral History, p. 122.
68. Interview with Richard Drain (RHS); Wyden, *Bay of Pigs*, pp. 265–66.
69. Some months later, as he reflected upon the tensions of that April week, Kennedy remembered making remarks to that effect. Quoted in Schlesinger, *Robert Kennedy*, p. 453.

19. Sir Allen

1. AWD Oral History, p. 28.
2. Schlesinger, *Thousand Days*, pp. 288–89.
3. Schlesinger, *Robert Kennedy*, p. 459.
4. Schlesinger, *Thousand Days*, pp. 276, 290.
5. Taylor Board, *Zapata*, pp. 332–33.
6. Ibid., p. 277.
7. Maxwell Taylor, *The Sword and the Pen* (New York: Doubleday, 1989), pp. 234–35.
8. Interview with Max Abramovitz (RHS).
9. CIA, DCI-2, vol. 4, p. 135.
10. See ibid., vol. 3, pp. 128–41, for discussion of the Kirkpatrick investigation and the agency's angry reactions to it. Kirkpatrick conveyed some of his substantive conclusions, though none of the personal venom, in a speech, "Paramilitary Case Study: The Bay of Pigs," published in *Naval War College Review* (Nov.–Dec. 1972), pp. 32–42.
11. Bruce to AWD, Sept. 1961, AWD Papers.
12. Interview with Donald Jameson, 1989. A full biography of Angleton has so far eluded those of his friends and detractors who have tried to write one; pending something more definitive, see Tom Mangold, *Cold Warrior* (New York: Simon & Schuster, 1991).
13. Diary notes, Nov. 29, 1963, Allen Dulles Papers, John F. Kennedy Assassination Records, RG 200, National Archives.
14. The following, unless otherwise noted, are found in the Lyndon B.

Johnson telephone transcripts for November and December 1963 at the National Archives, opened to public inspection in 1993.

15. The presidential logs coincide closely with Allen's diary entry about the conversation, with the only addition that Johnson called his request to Allen "a little unpleasant news."

16. Of all the discussions of the Kennedy assassination, the most measured is Gerald Posner, *Case Closed* (New York: Random House, 1993), which includes a brief analysis of the work of the Warren Commission. Standing out among the numerous critiques is one of the earliest, Edward Jay Epstein, *Inquest* (New York: Viking, 1966).

17. AWD, interview by Epstein, *Inquest*, pp. 32–33.

18. LBJ telephone transcript, Nov. 25, 1963, National Archives.

19. Interview by Epstein, *Inquest*, pp. 5–6; see also pp. 105, 107, 110.

20. Posner, *Case Closed*, pp. 406–7.

21. Epstein, *Inquest*, p. 16.

22. The internal records of the deliberations of the Warren Commission are a morass for researchers. The twenty-six published volumes of hearings contain formal testimony; other passing remarks appear in the final report. Private or executive sessions were poorly recorded, but information filtered out in various stenographic notes that have been generally unchallenged. See, for example, David S. Lifton, ed., *Document Addendum to the Warren Report* (El Segundo, Calif.: Sightext Publications, 1968); Harold Weisberg, ed., *JFK Assassination Transcript* (Frederick, Md., 1974); Extensions of Remarks, *Congressional Record*, May 14, 1975, pp. 14438–40.

23. Memorandum of Mar. 21, 1964, in the JFK Assassination Records, files of the House of Representatives Special Committee on Assassinations, RG 233, National Archives.

24. Memorandum of Apr. 13, 1964, to the deputy director for plans, RG 233, National Archives.

25. Testimony by Helms to House Special Committee on Assassinations, Sept. 22, 1978, quoted in Mangold, *Cold Warrior*, pp. 174–75.

26. Memo of June 24, 1964, in Allen Dulles Papers, Kennedy Assassination Records, RG 200, National Archives.

27. This meeting is described in a CIA memo to the deputy director for plans, July 8, 1964, declassified Oct. 15, 1993, labeled "Angleton Exhibit #1" in the numbered files (014177) of the House Special Committee on Assassinations, RG 233, National Archives.

28. House Select Committee on Assassinations, *Investigation of the Assassination of President John F. Kennedy*, Sept. 1978, vol. 3, p. 587.

29. Ibid., pp. 614, 647.

30. Ibid., pp. 699–701.

31. Church Committee, *Alleged Assassination Plots*, p. 72.

32. The detailed account of their visit is contained in the report of David W. Belin, a trial lawyer from Iowa on the commission staff. This six-page

document, dated May 15, 1964, declassified Aug. 10, 1993, is in the files of the House Special Committee on Assassinations, RG 233, National Archives.

33. House Select Committee on Assassinations, *Investigation of the Assassination of President John F. Kennedy*, vol. 3, pp. 603–4.
34. AWD Oral History, Kennedy Library, p. 34.
35. "Mississippi Trip" folder, AWD Papers.
36. Interviews with Tom Wicker and Theodore Sorensen.
37. CIA, DCI-2, vol. 1, pp. v, vii.
38. Bancroft, *Autobiography of a Spy*, p. 291; Eleanor Dulles, Oral History.

INDEX

400–401, 487, 489; and Geneva Summit (1955), 413–15; Plans Directorate, 448; effect of Dulles brothers on, 462–63; and U-2, 470–90 *passim;* and Cuba, 492; and Warren Commission, 547; criticism of CIA during, 562

Cominform (Communist Information Bureau), 280, 354; and Italy, 284

Communism, 67, 70–71, 79, 284; Dulles brothers' views of, 267–68; and containment policy, 268–69, 284, 332, 362; and European labor movement, 280–81; and Eastern Europe (1949), 302–3, 312, 321–22, 324, 326, 354–55; as reason for creating CIA, 311; and CIA's collection of accurate data on (1950s), 347–49; and Iran, 363–368; and Guatemala, 368–70, 383–85; and de-Stalinization, 428; Foster's final views on, 460–61, 463; and Cuba, 492–93; and Lumumba, 501

"Como," OSS Italian underground operative, 216–17

Congo, 481, 500, 501–3, 508

Congress, U.S., 123, 322; and World War I, 26, 27; Dulles brothers' influence on (1950s), 339; and McCarthyism, 345–47; and covert actions of 1950s, 385; and Operation MKULTRA, 393; Allen curries favor of, 415–16; calls for procedure for intelligence oversight, 416; and funding of CIA permanent headquarters, 418; and U-2 crisis, 483, 486. *See also* House of Representatives; Senate

Congress for Cultural Freedom, 321

Constantine, king of Greece, 450

Constantinople, Turkey: Allen at embassy in, 76–84; Russian refugees in, 77, 79; social life in, 77–78, 82; Pera Palace Hotel, 77, 79, 491n; and international oil, 87; and Allen's tour of missions, 430. *See also* Istanbul

Containment policy, 268–69, 362, 368; and CIA covert action, 284; and 1952 elections, 332, 437; and brinkmanship, 449

Coolidge, Archibald Cary, 61, 98

Coolidge, Calvin, 86–87, 107, 418, 445

Cooper, Chester, 344–45, 440

Cooper, John Sherman, 542, 554–55

Corcoran, Thomas G., 371, 375

Cornell, Katherine, 119

Correa, Matthias F., 284, 290, 294

Cortesi, Roger, 130

Council on Foreign Relations, 98, 117, 131, 137–39, 146, 175, 249, 270, 279, 319, 336, 347, 364, 480; Allen on board of directors, 122–23; study group on neutrality (1933), 123–25; Eden addresses, 130; Pratt townhouse donated to, 221, 259, 418; Allen becomes president, 259; and Kennan's containment policy, 268; and Dewey election campaign (1948), 290; and Iran, 297; and Eisenhower study group, 297, 305, 307, 330; and Alger Hiss, 297, 298n; and Korean War, 305; Allen resigns presidency, 307; Guatemala study group, 370, 371; study group on communist China, 562; and Allen's death, 565

Counterespionage, 277, 358n, 497; and Popov, 359; and Khrushchev's secret speech, 421, 425; and Israeli Shin Beth, 422; and Angleton, 497, 514–15, 565; Vandenberg's description, 277

Covert action, 32–33, 383, 385, 497; CIA hesitation regarding, 275–78, 281–82; and Italian communists, 284–85; and Dulles-Jackson-Correa report, 286, 291–295; and NSC 10/2, 293–94, 321; Soviet view of Allen's role in, 301; Allen's association with (1950), 306; and Bedell Smith, 307, 310, 335; division under Allen's direction, 320; and Soviet satellites, 322; and absorption into established collection networks, 323–24; OSO and OPC integrated, 325; Psychology Strategy Board, 328; and Donovan, 338n; and CIA role in 1950s, 338; brothers' divergent views on roles, 341; failures in, 354; paramilitary actions, 355–56; and Popov, 357–60; and Guatemala, 371, 375–76, 379, 384; in Latin America, 372–73; Allen's pride in, 384–85; and Operation MKULTRA, 392–96; and Eisenhower, 443–44; Control Committee (5412 Group), 444, 445, 494; Bruce-Lovett report (1956), 445–48, 450, 536; and Helms, 464; and Castro, 494–95, 496, 512; and Congo, 501–4; in briefings of 1960 election candi-

Dollmann, Eugen, 229, 231, 232; opinion of Allen, 231; motives of, 244; prisoner of war, 244; postwar rehabilitation, 253

Donovan, William J. ("Wild Bill"), 21n, 139, 148, 152, 166, 175, 205, 247, 297; recruits Allen into OSS, 141, 142, 492; and analysis of intelligence, 145; skepticism of military intelligence, 179–80; confidence in Allen, 180; and validation of intelligence, 190, 191, 209, 212; and German resistance, 195, 198; and post-Normandy OSS functions, 210–213, 214; and Soviet intelligence, 225; and Operation Sunrise, 236, 239–40, 243, 244; rivalry with Allen, 248; and plan for CIA, 255, 273; and U.S.-Soviet relations, 266; Columbia University confers honorary degree on, 271, 272; maintains social link to OSS veterans, 272; and Truman, 281, 305; Tass reports on, 301; competes with Allen for CIA directorship, 336, 338; final years and death, 338n, 463; and scientific intelligence, 289, 290; Allen's testimonial to, 463, 468

Doolittle, James H., 408–9

Down Town Association, 120, 139, 169

Drain, Richard, 527

Dresel, Ellis, 66, 67, 69, 70, 72, 74–75

Drugs, and CIA, 327, 390, 503; LSD, 390–94; "inviolable control," 392, 396; and Operation MKULTRA, 392–96; secrecy surrounding experimentation, 393–94; Allen's personal interest in, 396; and Lumumba assassination plan, 503

Dryden, Hugh, 479, 483

Dulles, Allen Macy (Allen's father) 5, 25, 34; courtship and marriage, 6–8; family background, 7; Watertown, N.Y., ministry, 8–9; and transmission of family values, 9–10, 14; expectations for his sons, 19–20; death of, 100

Dulles, Allen Macy (Allen's son), 100, 105, 138; and his father, 105, 129, 162, 263–64; at sister's debut, 140; at Phillips Exeter, 206, 263–64; effect of parents' life upon, 263; at Princeton, 264; wounded in Korea, 332–33, 336–37, 338, 375; post-recovery prob-

lems, 396, 457, 498, 536; at his father's funeral, 565

Dulles, Allen Welsh

BIRTH AND EARLY YEARS: 3–6; parents, 9–11, 14, 19–20, 100; education, 10–12, 15, 85–86; introduction to diplomacy, 12–14; childhood views on economic imperialism, 13; interest in languages, 15–16, 25, 28, 151; at Princeton, 16–18, 20; teaches in India (1914), 18–19, 65, 518; chooses diplomatic career, 20, 22, 245

CHARACTER AND PERSONALITY TRAITS: popular image, 14n, 155, 417; affability, 15, 20, 51, 73, 82, 95, 174, 257, 404, 435, 463, 510, 562; pragmatism, 17, 174, 326–27, 484; personality compared to Foster's, 95, 257–58, 337, 340, 341; enjoyment of the wealthy, 129, 430, 450, 452, 491; double standards in personal dealings, 246, 320, 326–27; Anglophilia, 316; flashes of prudery, 320; scruples, 326–27; desire for visibility, 386; security lapses, 416, 432; attains legendary status, 416, 417, 432–33, 463, 464, 488, 531; vanity, 429–30; as story teller, 431, 432, 436–37, 489, 490, 560; intrigued with James Bond, 491–92; personal code of ethics, 501; style of communicating with staff, 517–18; belief in accessibility, 533, 534, 537–38

CIA: Allen advocates national central intelligence service, 272–79, 300; aspires to head agency, 279, 281, 283, 287, 294, 295, 306, 307; Dulles-Jackson-Correa report (1948), 283–84, 285, 287, 290–92, 304, 310, 389, 417; and aggressive covert action against communism, 284, 300, 301, 348–49, 354–57, 359; Bogotazo incident, 286; Darling's history of agency, 291n; Kremlin tracks, 301–3; and Noel Field, 302–3; and Korea, 305; and Bedell Smith, 306–11, 323, 325, 391; offered deputy director post, 307; British intelligence view of Allen, 317–18, 530; distinguishes between

209–10; inability to share his life, 146, 262, 271, 500–501; separated from and then reunited with Clover (1947), 263–64, 271, 280; Clover joins in Iran, 296–97; Clover with on world tour of missions (1956), 429–33; and his grandson, 538–39

FRIENDSHIPS AND PUBLIC PERSON-AGES: missed meeting with Lenin, 26, 27, 48, 416, 467, 559; Walter Lippmann, 44, 387, 562, 563; diplomatic clubmates, see diplomatic club above; bachelor life and friendships, 86, 162, 173, 208; meets Hitler, 112–16, 121, 123, 161, 254; meets Mussolini, 112; and Nelson Rockefeller, 137–38; Donovan, 140, 142, 180, 248, 336, 338, 463, 468; his protégés, 156, 451–52, 472, 493, 514, 524, 535, 561; Truman, 258, 261, 331–32; Kolbe, 270; Forrestal, 281, 283, 285, 291; Kennan, 283, 342, 343; Dewey, 283, 287–90, 305, 330, 416, 506; Alger Hiss, 298, 528; Bedell Smith, 306–11, 323, 325, 391; Gehlen, 312–14; Kim Philby, 316–19; Eisenhower, 330–31, 334, 337, 352, 406, 408–9, 441, 450; Robert Taft, 331; McCarthy, 346; JFK, 412, 510–11, 517, 518, 529–31, 534, 538; Congressional liberals, 415–16; Billington, 429; Bruce Lovett, 445; Lansdale, 451; Kim Roosevelt, 451; Nixon, 454–55, 508–9; Khrushchev, 468, 484; Bissell, 472–73; Ian Fleming, 492; Robert Kennedy, 530; LBJ, 530, 541–43, 552, 556, 558, 561; Golitsyn, 540

GREAT GAME (intelligence): 21, 146, 256, 275, 308, 314, 316, 339, 444; and Kipling's *Kim*, 18, 491; fascination with, 31–33; post–World War I intelligence collection, 36, 37, 39, 41, 51–55, 78–79; as genial spymaster, 155, 156, 162, 170, 387, 413, 454, 464, 488, 490, 496, 499, 562; conflict between military and political intelligence, 210, 213–14; and public persona, 247, 258, 262, 499, 510; advocates national intelligence service, 272–79, 300; distinguishes

between intelligence and espionage, 319–20; on paying for information, 320; on technique of deception, 401

LAW PRACTICE: 245, 295, 300, 391; attends law school, 85–86; joins Sullivan and Cromwell, 88, 90, 92, 95, 97, 100, 119–21; first legal case, 135–36; returns to firm (1945), 257–58, 267; financial incentives of the law, 257

OSS: Allen joins, 141–42, 146–47, 492; constructs network against Nazi Germany, 148; assigned to Bern office, 149–51; code name, 152; Bern living quarters, 152–53; Bern agent network, 153–62, 168–70, 214–20, 250–54; personality changes, 155; reputation for integrity, 155; establishes himself as spymaster, 162; and transmission of information to Washington, 165–66, 232–33; penetration of Gaullist underground, 168; develops contacts, 171–75; penetration of Nazi high command secrets, 175–92; meets Gisevius, 177–79; enemy penetration of his household, 178; Donovan's confidence in, 180; and anti-Nazi Germans, 184–89, 193–200, 204; validation of intelligence reports, 188–92; and Russian Free Germany movement, 202–3; furlough (1945), 204–5, 207; complains about demands in Bern, 209–10; conflict between military and political intelligence, 210, 213–14; Austrian resistance, 214–15; Fritz Molden, 215; and Italian resistance, 216–17; and Ciano's diaries, 218–20; and Clover's arrival in Paris (1945), 221–24; and Yalta, 225–26; Operation Sunrise, 226–32, 234–43; Dollmann's description of, 231; and Nazi redoubt, 240–43; evaluation of Bern operation, 247; lifelong effect of experience, 245–47; Potsdam, 249; Truman abolishes OSS, 255–56; resigns from government (1945), 256

PERSONAL LIFE: health, 9, 35, 288, 435; finances, 82, 85, 93, 95, 119,

emerges as leader in world affairs, 272; and Marshall Plan, 280; and Iranian oil, 295, 296; battles against communism (1949), 300, 301; Kremlin tracks, 301–3; Korean War, 305; influence on policy making, 339–41, 386, 388, 443; and communist threat, 348–49; Vietnam, 561

WRITINGS AND SPEECHES: *The Boer War*, 13–14, 124; *Craft of Intelligence*, 42n, 43, 44–46; lecture circuit (1928), 97; *Can We Be Neutral?*, 124; *Can America Stay Neutral?*, 131; and U.S. entry into World War II (war speech), 136–37; *Secret Surrender*, 187n, 243, 244; "Relations Between Secret Operations and Secret Intelligence," 294; National Association of Manufacturers speech (1947), 361; speech "The Worldwide Battle for Men's Minds" (1954), 380, 381, 393; speech "The Immediate Communist Peril," 459; record of Foster's legacy, 461–463; addresses Young Presidents Organization in Puerto Rico, 526–27; anthology *Great True Spy Stories*, 564; *Great Spy Stories from Fiction*, 564

Dulles, Avery (Foster's son), 133

Dulles, Clover Todd (Mrs. Allen W.), 110, 115, 131; meets and marries Allen, 73–75; her personality, 74, 83, 104–5; a difficult marriage, 75, 82–83, 85, 88, 100 105–6, 111, 205–6; in Constantinople with Allen, 76–78, 82–84; in Washington (1922), 85–86, 445; in New York, 95, 98–99, 103–4; in Paris (1930), 100, 101, 102; and her children, 104–5, 129; aid to German Jews, 121n; and Allen's run for political office, 128, 129; house on Long Island, 129, 130, 299; and Anne Morrow Lindbergh, 130, 134, 136, 270; and British pre–World War II war effort, 134; and Joan's debut, 140; civilian duties during World War II, 140; and Allen's role in OSS, 142, 151, 162, 224; friendship with Mary Bancroft, 167n, 224, 247, 254, 331, 537n; while Allen at war, 205–8, 221; her fiftieth birthday, 206–207; relationship with Foster,

206, 224; with Allen in Europe (1945), 221–24, 226, 235, 239, 248, 254, 256; and her mother's death, 223; and Allen's extramarital relationships, 224; and Operation Sunrise, 237; not allowed to share Allen's work life, 246–47, 262, 271, 500–501; her interest in Jung, 254, 262, 270, 366, 564; separates from Allen, 262, 270; Allen dedicates his book to, 262; and Allen's affair with Wally Castelbarco, 263; reunites with Allen (1947), 270–71, 280, 288; and Allen's hope to return to public service, 281; and election of 1948, 288, 290; joins Allen in Iran, 296–97; urges Allen to accept CIA post, 307; makes permanent move to Washington, 325, 376; and her son's war injury and illness, 333, 337, 536; and Washington social life of 1950s, 340; attends Senator McCarthy's wedding, 346; vacations with Allen: (1953), 366–67, (round-the-world tour), 429, 431–32, (Guatemala), 370–71, 383, (Palm Beach), 493, (Greece, 1960), 510, (retirement travels), 538; sees shah of Iran in Rome, 367; and CIA Langley headquarters, 418; and Foster's final days and death, 457, 458; hopes Allen will retire, 496, 498, 529; social life (1959), 498–99; interest in penal reform, 498–99, 564; and Bay of Pigs, 521, 526; and McCone's appointment, 536; and Allen's final days and death, 560, 564–65; and Allen's funeral, 565; life as a widow, 566

Dulles, Clover Todd (Toddy), daughter, 85, 95, 99, 138, 146, 498; relationship with her mother, 104, 263; and her father, 104–5, 129, 162, 167n, 208, 263; at Bennington, 206; and Allen's affair with Wally Castelbarco, 263; and her father's death, 560

Dulles, Edith Foster (mother), 15, 73, 76; early life, 5–6; courtship and marriage, 6–8; pregnancies and childbirth, 9; family life, 10

Dulles, Eleanor (sister), 9, 10, 11, 15, 45, 263; as economist, 100, 102n, 254; on Eisenhower's inauguration day, 337; State Department desk officer, 339–40, 398; McLean, Va., house, 339–40; and